Indelible Shadows

Indelible Shadows investigates questions raised by films about the Holocaust. How does one make a movie that is both morally just and marketable? Annette Insdorf provides sensitive readings of individual films and analyzes theoretical issues such as the "truth claims" of the cinematic medium. The third edition of *Indelible Shadows* includes five new chapters that cover recent trends, as well as rediscoveries of motion pictures made during and just after World War II. It addresses the treatment of rescuers, as in *Schindler's List*; the controversial use of humor, as in *Life Is Beautiful*; the distorted image of survivors; and the growing genre of documentaries that return to the scene of the crime or rescue. The annotated filmography offers capsule summaries and information about another hundred Holocaust films from around the world, making this edition the most comprehensive and up-to-date discussion of films about the Holocaust, and an invaluable resource for film programmers and educators.

Annette Insdorf is Director of Undergraduate Film Studies at Columbia University, and a professor in the Graduate Film Division of the School of the Arts (of which she was chair from 1990 to 1995). She is the author of books, including *Double Lives, Second Chances: The Cinema of Krzysztof Kieslowski* and *François Truffaut*. Her articles have appeared in numerous newspapers and magazines – especially the *New York Times* – and she is the television host of Cannes Film Festival coverage for BRAVO/IFC. Creator and host of the popular "Reel Pieces" series at Manhattan's 92d Street Y, Dr. Insdorf was a jury member of the Berlin Film Festival, and served as executive producer for prize-winning short films.

Indelible Shadows

Film and the Holocaust

Third Edition

Annette Insdorf

CAMBRIDGE
UNIVERSITY PRESS

PUBLISHED BY THE PRESS SYNDICATE OF THE UNIVERSITY OF CAMBRIDGE
The Pitt Building, Trumpington Street, Cambridge, United Kingdom

CAMBRIDGE UNIVERSITY PRESS
The Edinburgh Building, Cambridge CB2 2RU, UK
40 West 20th Street, New York, NY 10011-4211, USA
477 Williamstown Road, Port Melbourne, VIC 3207, Australia
Ruiz de Alarcón 13, 28014 Madrid, Spain
Dock House, The Waterfront, Cape Town 8001, South Africa

http://www.cambridge.org

First edition published 1983 by Random House
Second edition published 1989 by Cambridge University Press
Reprinted 1990
Third edition first published 2003

Printed in the United States of America

Typefaces Minion 10/12 pt. and Univers67   *System* LaTeX 2_ε [TB]

A catalog record for this book is available from the British Library.

Library of Congress Cataloging in Publication Data

Insdorf, Annette.
Indelible shadows : film and the Holocaust / Annette Insdorf. – 3rd ed.
   p. ; cm.
Includes bibliographical references and index.
ISBN 0-521-81563-0 – ISBN 0-521-01630-4 (pb.)
1. Holocaust, Jewish (1939–1945), in motion pictures.   I. Title.

PN1995.9.H53 I57   2002
791.43′658 – dc21   2002023793

ISBN 0 521 81563 0 hardback
ISBN 0 521 01630 4 paperback

Dedicated to the
Memory of My Father,
Michael Insdorf

and of My Mother-in-Law,
Regina Berman Toporek

Contents

Foreword by Elie Wiesel

A great Hassidic Master, the Rabbi of Kotsk, used to say, "There are truths which can be communicated by the word; there are deeper truths that can be transmitted only by silence; and, on another level, are those which cannot be expressed, not even by silence."

And yet, they must be communicated.

Here is the dilemma that confronts anyone who plunges into the concentration camp universe: How can one recount when – by the scale and weight of its horror – the event defies language? A problem of expression? Of perception, rather. Auschwitz and Treblinka seem to belong to another time; perhaps they are on the other side of time. They can be explained only in their own terms. Only those who lived there know what these names mean. And for a long time these very people refused to speak of it. "In any case," they thought, "no one would understand." An ontological phenomenon, "The Final Solution" is located beyond understanding. Let's be honest: In this sense, the enemy can boast of his triumph. Through the scope of his deadly enterprise, he deprives us of words to describe it.

Having completed his masterpiece "The Blood of Heaven," the late Piotr Rawicz was left with a feeling of defeat. Other survivor-writers could say the same. We know very well that we speak at one remove from the event. We have not said what we wanted to. The essential will remain unsaid, eradicated, buried in the ash that covers this story like no other. Hence, the drama of the witness. He realizes, to paraphrase Wittgenstein, that only what cannot be said deserves to not be silenced. But then, what will happen to his testimony? To his deposition? To his knowledge? If he takes them with him in death, he betrays them. Will he remain faithful in trying to articulate them, even badly, even inadequately? The question inexorably asserts itself: Does there exist another way, another language, to say what is unsayable?

The image perhaps? Can it be more accessible, more malleable, more expressive than the word? More true as well? Can I admit it? I am as wary of one as of the other. Even more of the image. Of the filmed image, of course. One does not imagine the unimaginable. And in particular, one does not show it on screen.

Too purist an attitude, no doubt. After all, by what right would we neglect the mass media? By what right would we deny them the possibility of informing, educating, sensitizing the millions of men and women who would normally say, "Hitler, who's he?" But on the other hand, if we allow total freedom to the mass media, don't we risk seeing them profane and trivialize a sacred subject?

These are the serious and disturbing questions Annette Insdorf analyzes with the deep erudition and striking talent that render this daughter of survivors the best critic in America on Holocaust films.

Certain productions dazzle with their authenticity; others shock with their vulgarity. *Night and Fog* on one side, *Holocaust* on the other. Up against Hollywood superproductions, can poetic memory hold its own? Me, I prefer it. I prefer restraint to excess, the murmur of documentary to the script edited by tear-jerk specialists. To direct the massacre of Babi Yar smells of blasphemy. To make up extras as corpses is obscene. Perhaps I am too severe, too demanding, but the Holocaust as filmed romantic adventure seems to me an outrage to the memory of the dead, and to sensitivity.

Nevertheless, I am wrong to generalize. Certain films resonate with us. *The Garden of the Finzi Continis, The Boat Is Full, The Revolt of Job, Under the World* succeed in moving us without falling into cheap sentimentality. *Les Violons du Bal* and *The Shop on Main Street* are works of art. Unlike certain other films, these don't purport to show or explain everything, the how and why of the Nazi era. They reveal to us, like a secret imprint, human beings undergoing the curse of the gods, and that's all. Their restraint, their humility, I'd almost say their self-effacement, contribute to their strength of conviction.

As for documentaries, they present a different kind of difficulty. For the most part, the images derive from enemy sources. The victim had neither cameras nor film. To amuse themselves, or to bring souvenirs back to their families, or to serve Goebbels's propaganda, the killers filmed sequences in one ghetto or another, in one camp or another: The use of these faked, truncated images makes it difficult to omit the poisonous message that motivated them. These Jewish policemen who strike their unfortunate brothers, these starved individuals fighting for a piece of bread, these "VIPs" who, in the midst of the most naked misery, spend their evenings at the cabaret – will the viewer continue to remember that these films were made by the killers to show the downfall and the baseness of their so-called subhuman victims? Nevertheless, we can't do without these images, which, in their truthful context, assume a primordial importance for the eventual comprehension of the concentration camps' existence.

Annette Insdorf treats these ambiguities with tact and passion. Her criticism is never gratuitous; her enthusiasm, often contagious. While discussing films, she manages to take a step back and evoke – in the name of a nameless suffering – the fear and the hope of a generation for whom everything is still a mystery.

(Translated from the French by Annette Insdorf)

Preface

ver since I was a little girl, I have heard about "the camp," "Auschwitz," "*Lager*," "Belsen" – words mysteriously connected with the number tattooed on my mother's arm. Throughout my adolescence, I never tried to know more: it embarrassed me when my mother got visibly emotional about painful memories of her experiences. When I was a graduate student at Yale, however, I saw the film *Night and Fog*, and, for the first time, I had an inkling of what my parents – among others – had endured. The film provided a shape for, and a handle on, abstract fears. It occurred to me that if I, the only child of Holocaust survivors, needed a film to frame the horror and thus give it meaning, what about others? How great a role are films playing in determining contemporary awareness of the Final Solution?

As my involvement with the cinema grew, I began writing a screenplay in 1979, based on my father's escape from a labor camp, and his hiding in the woods with Polish peasants. The more I struggled to reshape the true stories, the more I realized how difficult it is to make a film about this era. How do you show people being butchered? How much emotion is too much? How will viewers respond to lighthearted moments in the midst of suffering? I was caught between the conflicting demands of historical accuracy and artistic quality. As I sat in Paris movie houses and observed how other filmmakers had yielded to or had overcome such obstacles, I put the screenplay away, and decided to wait until I had more distance from the stories of my father and his heroic cousin – and until I had learned from what others had done on screen.

Perhaps Elie Wiesel's comments about Holocaust literature are applicable to film. In *A Jew Today*, he declares: "There is no such thing as Holocaust literature – there cannot be. Auschwitz negates all literature as it negates all theories and doctrines; to lock it into a philosophy is to restrict it. To substitute words, any words, for it is to distort it. A Holocaust literature? The very term is a contradiction."[1] And to substitute images? Can the camera succeed where the pen falters? These questions gave rise to the following pages, where the reader will find a descriptive voice yielding to a prescriptive one, and film scholarship tinged with moral concerns. I have decided to respect both tones, for the tension between them is inherent in the cinematic experience; surely the goal of the film critic (like that of the filmmaker) is to move as well as observe, to challenge as well as record, and to transform as well as perceive. Moreover, as Terrence Des Pres articulated at a "Teaching Holocaust Literature" session of the 1981 Modern

ion conference, there is a moral imperative implicit in this subject,
ıection between consciousness and conscience.

edge the inspiration and encouragement of Terrence Des Pres, as
ssistance of my agent Georges Borchardt, Robert Bender, Harold
3riski, Karen Cooper, Florence Favre Le Bret, Renee Furst, Claude
Gauteur, Mırıam Hansen, Bernard Henri-Lévy, John Hollander, John Hughes, Michael Insdorf, Stanley Kauffmann, Howard Lamar, Robert Liebman, Arnost Lustig, Peter Morley, Marcel Ophuls, Alan Parker, Alain Resnais, Jeannie Reynolds, Robert Seaver, Charles Silver, François Truffaut, Claude Vajda, Michael Webb, Elie Wiesel, Ken Wlaschin, John Wright, Dan Yakir. For assistance during the preparation of the second edition, I must add the generosity of Arthur Cohn, Axel Corti, Eva Fogelman, Guy Hennebelle, Aviva Kempner, Elizabeth Maguire, and Louis Malle.

I am grateful to the following for helping with photographs: Rick Bannerot, Carlos Clarens, Mary Corliss, Francine Davidoff, Ira Deutchman, Suzanne Fedak, Sally Fischer, Hamilton Fish, Robert Harris, Volker Hinz, Curt Kaufman, Donald Krim, Tom Luddy, Ruth Robbins, Alicia Springer, Elliot Tiber. And I thank my editors at the following publications, where some of the material in *Indelible Shadows* first appeared: *American Film, Cineaste*, the *International Journal of Political Education*, the *Los Angeles Times* (Calendar – Barbara Saltzman), the *New York Times* (Arts and Leisure – Lawrence Van Gelder), the *San Francisco Chronicle* (Datebook – David Kleinberg), *Newsday*, and *Premiere*.

I was able to write the book thanks to a Rockefeller Foundation Fellowship, supplemented by a grant from the A. Whitney Griswold Fund at Yale; the research was facilitated by Yale University's Summer Language Institute, which permitted me to develop and teach two courses on film and the Holocaust. Finally, I owe thanks to my students, and deepest gratitude to those who criticized and strengthened the manuscript – Cecile Insdorf, David Lapin, Edward Baron Turk, my Random House editor Erroll McDonald, and my Cambridge University Press editor Beatrice Rehl.

Introduction

ilmmakers and film critics confronting the Holocaust face a basic task – finding an appropriate language for that which is mute or defies visualization. How do we lead a camera or pen to penetrate history and create art, as opposed to merely recording events? What are the formal as well as moral responsibilities if we are to understand and communicate the complexities of the Holocaust through its filmic representations? Such questions seem increasingly pressing, for the number of post-war films dealing with the Nazi era is steadily growing. I had seen at least sixty such films from around the world by 1980; when I completed the first edition of this book in 1982, another twenty had been produced; and by 1988 there were approximately one hundred new films – forty fiction, sixty documentary – that merited inclusion.

My point of departure is therefore the growing body of cinematic work – primarily fiction – that illuminates, distorts, confronts, or reduces the Holocaust. Rather than prove a thesis, I wish to explore the degree to which these films manifest artistic as well as moral integrity. The focus is on the cinema of the United States, France, Poland, Italy, and Germany,[1] because these countries have released the most significant, accessible, and available films about the Holocaust. This new edition also covers many recent films from Austria and the Netherlands. Throughout Eastern Europe, fine films have treated the effects of World War II, but they are difficult to see in the United States. (Titles are included in the Filmography.)

While it might have been easier to structure the book by chronology or nation, I have chosen a thematic approach because a number of central issues emerged from the films themselves:

1. The development of a suitable cinematic language for a unique and staggering subject. I contrast Hollywood's realism and melodramatic conventions with the tense styles and dialectical montage of many European films, as well as present notable American exceptions. This section includes discussion of the savage satire in black comedies about the Holocaust.
2. Narrative strategies such as the Jew as child; the Jew as wealthy, attractive, and assimilated; characters in hiding whose survival depends on performance; families doomed by legacies of guilt.

The Vilner Troupe, from *Image before My Eyes*, directed by Josh Waletzky. PHOTO COURTESY OF CINEMA 5

3. Responses to Nazi atrocity, from political resistance to individual transformations of identity, and to the guilt-ridden questions posed by contemporary German films.

4. A new form – neither documentary nor fiction – that shapes documentary material through a personal voice. Here, attention is paid to the films made by survivors, their children, and especially to the works of Marcel Ophuls.

A major question throughout *Indelible Shadows* is how certain cinematic devices express or evade the moral issues inherent in the subject. For example, how is Alain Resnais's tracking camera in *Night and Fog* involved in moral investigation? In what ways does editing not only shape but embody the very content of *The Pawnbroker* or *The Memory of Justice*? And to what degree can montage be manipulative? On a national scale, what change in attitude, if any, is implied by the sudden surge in the early seventies of French films dealing with deportation and collaboration? What about the increasing number of German films that are finally turning their lenses onto the Nazi era? Whether the film is a dark comedy like Ernst Lubitsch's *To Be or Not to Be* or an enlightening drama like Andrzej Munk's *Passenger*, these works suggest both the possibilities and limitations of nondocumentary approaches to World War II, especially the ghetto and concentration camp experience.

The term "Holocaust" requires definition, for popular usage has particularized it from a general idea of disaster to the brutal and massive devastation practiced by the Nazis during World War II. I have chosen to use the word in this latter sense, and more precisely to refer to the genocide of European Jewry. For unlike their fellow victims of the Nazis – such as political opponents, Gypsies, and homosexuals – Jews were stripped not only of life and freedom, but of an entire culture that flourished throughout Eastern Europe in the early thirties. As chronicled in Josh Waletzky's superb documentary *Image before My Eyes* (1980), Polish-Jewish civilization was highly developed between the wars and included experimental education (a Montessori school in Vilna), progressive politics (the *Bund*, a Jewish Socialist party), and ripe artistic movements (Yiddish writers' groups like *Di Khalyastre*). The Nazis' avowed intention was not merely to annihilate the Jews, but to wipe their traces from history, and to destroy the very notion that a Jew was a human being. Even within the concentration camps, the Nazis developed a hierarchy among inmates: political prisoners were enemies, but Jews were insects. Hitler declared, "Anti-Semitism is a form of de-lousing . . . a matter of sanitation." Among the female inmates in Auschwitz, for instance, only the Jewish women's heads were shaved.

One of the dangers inherent in my argument, however, is the assumption that the Holocaust "belongs" to – or is the domain of – one set of victims more than another. Does the Holocaust belong to the survivors? To those who were killed during World War II? To those who died in concentration camps or ghettos? To the Jews who were the main targets of the Nazis? To all Jews today? Some individuals claim the Holocaust as a personal tragedy. Many Jews claim it as a religious one. And then there are those who had no direct experience of the Holocaust but feel transformed by learning of its cruelty and mass indifference – as well as of resistance and survival.

And to whom do the dead "belong"? The ending of *Just a Gigolo* (1979), an otherwise negligible British film, presents a chilling image of appropriation: a bumbling young man (David Bowie) with no interest in politics is accidentally killed in a street fight between a Nazi group and its adversaries. The Nazi leader (David Hemmings, who also directed the film) takes the corpse, dresses it in the brown-shirted uniform of the SA, and has the young "hero" displayed and buried as a Nazi. How many of the dead are likewise unable to defend themselves from the post-factum appropriation of groups who claim the Holocaust as theirs?

The Holocaust is often exploited by those who simply have access to the media. The only versions of Nazi persecution that we see in film are the few that have made it to the screen, and often this is less a question of choice, quality, or logic than of chance: the commercial exigencies of film make it a dubious form for communicating the truth of World War II, given box-office dependence on sex, violence, a simple plot, easy laughs, and so on. Nevertheless, it is primarily through motion pictures that the mass audience knows – and will continue to learn – about the Nazi era and its victims. Whenever I show *Night and Fog* in my courses, students are shocked and profoundly moved, for it is generally their first encounter with the palpable images of Auschwitz.

The cinema thus fulfills the function articulated by film theorist Siegfried Kracauer about thirty years ago. In his *Theory of Film: The Redemption of Physical Reality*, the morally vigorous German critic recounted the myth of the Gorgon Medusa,

> whose face, with its huge teeth and protruding tongue, was so horrible that the sheer sight of it turned men and beasts into stone. When Athena instigated Perseus to slay the monster, she therefore warned him never to look at the face itself but only at its mirror reflection in the polished shield she had given him. Following her advice, Perseus cut off Medusa's head with the sickle which Hermes had contributed to his equipment.
>
> The moral of the myth is, of course, that we do not, and cannot, see actual horrors because they paralyze us with blinding fear; and that we shall know what they look like only by watching images of them which reproduce their true appearance . . . the reflection of happenings which would petrify us were we to encounter them in real life. The film screen is Athena's polished shield.[2]

Kracauer's analogy is particularly apt for films that show or reconstruct scenes of ghettos, deportation, and extermination. However, his argument includes the belief that "these images have nothing in common with the artist's imaginative rendering of an unseen dread but are in the nature of mirror reflections." To merely show the savage surfaces of Auschwitz might not lead to much beyond a numbing of response. One of the purposes of this book is to see how filmmakers apply their art in shaping history into a heightened form of communication.

Kracauer understood "that the images on the shield or screen are a means to an end; they are to enable – or by extension, induce – the spectator to behead the horror they mirror." But we are bound to raise the same question as Kracauer: Do such films serve the purpose? His conclusion was that the mirror reflections of horror are an end in themselves, beckoning the spectator "to take them in and thus incorporate into his memory the real face of things too dreadful to be beheld in reality. In experiencing . . . the litter of tortured human bodies in the films made of the Nazi concentration camps, we redeem horror from its invisibility behind the veils of panic and imagination."

In fifty years, the average person will probably not be drawn to source material like archival footage from the camps, or the Warsaw Ghetto diaries of Emanuel Ringelblum or Janusz Korczak. Knowledge of the Holocaust might be filtered through the fictions of the television program *Holocaust* and William Styron's *Sophie's Choice*. This places a special burden on the filmmaker who is trying to illuminate rather than exploit the Holocaust – and on the film critic with a stake in historical truth. As Arthur Schlesinger, Jr., warned, "fiction films do live as much by cumulative dramatic convention as they do by fidelity to fact, and addiction to stereotypes dilutes their value as historical evidence."[3] Does this mean that more first-person accounts by survivors must be filmed before they die? Certainly, but even survivors' accounts can provide only a segment of the truth: many of the most courageous victims perished. Each individual story is a sorely needed (and often dramatically rich) piece of the puzzle. Other pieces might never be found. For example, how many of the six million Jews died not as passive victims but as active opponents of the Third Reich?

Some of these questions require historical and theoretical analysis which falls outside the scope of this book. The issue of anti-Semitism is a case in point: it was not born with the Holocaust. As Bernard Henri-Lévy demonstrates in *The Testament of God*, Jews have always constituted a threat to national authority. Throughout history, they have embodied perpetual resistance to oppression, from ancient Egypt to contemporary Russia. As thinkers ready to transform governments and structures of life, many Jews represent subversion – in the most resilient and constructive sense of the word. It is not hard to understand why some ideologues of the Argentine military dictatorship singled out three Jews in their verbal assault on Jacobo Timerman:

> One of the most elaborate definitions went as follows: "Argentina has three main enemies: Karl Marx, because he tried to destroy the Christian concept of society; Sigmund Freud, because he tried to destroy the Christian concept of the family; and Albert Einstein, because he tried to destroy the Christian concept of time and space."[4]

It is significant that this scene comes not from a German concentration camp but from an Argentine prison in the 1970s.

It might appear facile and cheap to compare the destruction of European Jewry with other attempts at genocide; after all, there is no comparison for the rabid persecution of individuals who were a respected and assimilated part of European life, especially after it became strategically unsound for trains to transport concentration camp inmates rather than the soldiers and ammunition needed for battle. Nevertheless, the impulse behind Nazism – if not the massive scale of its realization – has been shared by other peoples and nations. This can take the form of synagogue bombings in Paris, marches in Skokie, or witch hunts in Argentina.

Consequently, the avowed purpose of this book is not merely an exercise in film criticism, but a grappling with the legacy of the Holocaust. As long as there are people like Professor Faurisson in France who proclaim in print that the gas chambers did not exist, there must be active resistance by those who know they did exist. The luxury of forgetfulness is not possible, because the Holocaust is neither a closed chapter nor an isolated event. As Alain Resnais explained to me about his film *Night and Fog*: "The constant idea was to not make a monument to the dead, turned to the past. If this existed, it could happen again; it exists now in another form." I hope that the following pages result in insight and incitement, reflecting the conviction that films not only commemorate the dead but illuminate the price to be paid for unquestioned obedience to governmental authority. In recognizing our ability to identify with characters, whether Jewish, German, Kapo, or Communist, we move one step closer to guarding against that which permitted the Holocaust to develop – indifference. Perhaps the beam cast by film projectors can pierce the continuing willed blindness.

Part I

Finding an Appropriate Language

The immensity of events calls
for restraint, even dryness,
and this is only fitting where
words do not suffice.

– Czeslaw Milosz
Native Realm

1

The Hollywood Version
of the Holocaust

ew American films have confronted the darker realities of World War II – ghettos, occupation, deportation, concentration camps, collaboration, extermination. The Holocaust has been only touched upon in such Hollywood studio productions as *Exodus, Cabaret, Ship of Fools, Marathon Man, Julia, The Boys from Brazil,* and *Victory,* and brought to the fore in only a handful of postwar films like *Judgment at Nuremberg, The Diary of Anne Frank, Voyage of the Damned,* and – increasingly – movies made for television. When "Judgment at Nuremberg" was first presented as a teleplay on *Playhouse 90* in 1959, however, commerce clearly got in the way of authenticity: the sponsor of the show, the American Gas Association, objected to the use of the word "gas" in reference to the concentration camp death chambers. According to the producer Herbert Brodkin, the sponsor wanted it deleted; he refused; they got their way behind his back: "Although the program was televised live, CBS delayed its transmission for a few seconds, long enough for an engineer to bleep out the word gas each time it was mentioned."[1] The major difference between "telefilms" like *Holocaust* and *Playing for Time* and theatrically distributed features is the commercial interruptions to which the former are subject. In conception, style, and appeal to a mass audience, nevertheless, these *are* "Hollywood" films, simply made for a smaller screen. Moreover, in the cynically realistic appraisal of screenwriter Paddy Chayefsky:

> NBC wanted to do *The War Against the Jews.* That's before they did *Holocaust.* I said the subject was simply too painful for me to write about. But if I had agreed to do it for television, I'd have had to make a soap opera of the whole thing. You'd have to get high emotional moments, regularly, because you have these damn ten-minute intervals all the time. You can never really accumulate the power; you have to capsulize a lot of emotion, and you have to overdramatize things. In fact, the word critics used on *Holocaust* was "trivialize," and in a sense that was an unfair criticism, even though accurate. Trivialization *is* television.[2]

Whether on a small or silver screen, there is perhaps nothing inherently wrong in an entertaining film set against the backdrop of World War II, like *Victory,* for example.

James Woods (Karl) and Meryl Streep (Inga) in *Holocaust.*

But as we move further in time from the realities of Nazism and closer to comforting myths, many people shrug off the complexity of history to embrace the simplifications offered by films. It is consequently a premise of this study that filmmakers confronting the Holocaust must assume a special responsibility, commensurate with its gravity and enormity. Elie Wiesel told an interviewer, "Before I say the words, Auschwitz or Treblinka, there must be a space, a breathing space, a kind of zone of silence."[3] His fear that the Holocaust is becoming "a phenomenon of superficiality" is applicable to films.

The television program *Holocaust* (1978) heightened awareness of both the historical facts and the problems of how to dramatize them on film. This miniseries took Nazi atrocities out of the province of specialized study and made them a "prime-time" phenomenon – with both the benefits of exposure and the drawbacks of distortion. Its case illustrates the rewards and tendencies inherent in films made for mass audiences – from the power of sensitizing, to the danger of romanticizing and trivializing. Indeed, *Holocaust* must be appreciated for its stimulation of concern, both in America and Europe, but questioned for its manner of presentation – including commercials (for example, it packaged devastating gas chamber scenes into neat fifteen-minute segments separated by commercials for an air deodorizer and panty shields).

Holocaust was saddled with the dubious term "docudrama," which coproducer Herbert Brodkin now repudiates: "In my mind, what are called 'docudramas' don't exist. We like to take a real situation, then create a drama out of it."[4] The introductory voice-over says: "It is only a story. But it really happened." *What* really happened? Not

Deborah Norton (Marta) and Michael Moriarty (Erik) in *Holocaust*. PHOTO COURTESY OF LEARNING CORPORATION OF AMERICA

Meryl Streep (Inga) and James Woods (Karl) in *Holocaust.*
PHOTO COURTESY OF LEARNING CORPORATION OF AMERICA

the story of the Weiss family, but the backdrop of events. The second "it" blurs the distinction between fact and fiction, as does the rest of the film. Directed by Marvin Chomsky from a teleplay by Gerald Green, *Holocaust* traces the victimization of the Weiss family – cultured Berlin Jews – by the Nazis, incarnated especially by Erik Dorf (Michael Moriarty). The Weiss family is uprooted, deported, and killed (with the exception of the youngest son, Rudi) in scenes that depict the growth of Nazism, the Warsaw Ghetto Uprising, the "efficiency" of Nazi planning, Auschwitz, the partisans in the forest, the "model" camp Theresienstadt, and the departure of Rudi (Joseph Bottoms) for Palestine.

The ground-breaking telecast sparked a great deal of controversy in the United States; some critics and viewers praised the fine acting of Moriarty, Rosemary Harris, Fritz Weaver, Meryl Streep, James Woods, Tovah Feldshuh, among a uniformly good cast, and the sensitizing effect it could have on mass audiences, while others decried the program for its lack of accuracy (a Jew keeping his suitcase in Auschwitz?!) and melodramatic contrivances. Rabbi Wolfe Kelman, for example, faulted *Holocaust* for distorting the image of the victims: most of those who perished were not cultured Berlin doctors, but ordinary Jews – shopkeepers, housewives, and day laborers as well as Yiddish poets and Talmud scholars – he claimed in an "NBC Reports" program that followed the rebroadcast of *Holocaust* in September 1979. The program came up with some astounding statistics: 220 million people had seen *Holocaust,* and in West Germany alone, 15 million. The broadcast in West Germany on January 22, 23, 25, and 26, 1979, provoked passionate public response. Television station switchboards and newspapers were flooded with reactions attesting to the failure of general education and historians regarding Auschwitz. Many writers credited the program with destroying a taboo and creating a climate favorable to discussing the Holocaust at home, work, and school:

> From now on German has been enriched by a new American word "Holocaust," which simultaneously covers the Jewish genocide, the TV movie and its personalized tragedy, and the emotional and political reactions it provoked. These five days of collective emotion seem to have permitted the younger generation to perceive the Auschwitz trauma and the Jews from a totally new perspective, which could be called "the pedagogy of the Holocaust."[5]

Nevertheless, critics of the telecast presented forceful arguments against its aesthetic – and by implication, ethical – shortcomings. Like Elie Wiesel in the *New York Times,* West German critics denounced the "soap opera" and its "kitschy music," inaccuracies, and sensationalism. As an article in *Der Spiegel* put it, "*Holocaust* as docudrama blurs fact, trivializes events, and neither illuminates nor forces one to think about them."[6] Critics ultimately acknowledged – albeit grudgingly – that drama could have more emotional power than documentary, that trivialized information was better than none, and that the history of the Final Solution could be made accessible only through dramatic presentation: "The death of six million is beyond human comprehension, hence empathy, the death of six is not. . . . Finally, critics maintained that Germans had to experience the Holocaust emotionally, even if it was portrayed in Hollywood terms."[7]

More than ten years later, the effects of the program are less palpable. Although an article in a 1979 issue of *Cahiers du Cinéma* claimed "that the fiction of *Holocaust* has more effect, *today . . .* than all the documentary material ever accumulated on the genocide of the Jews,"[8] time has taken its toll. In the opinion of German filmmaker Peter Lilienthal, "*Holocaust* was like a thriller, and the level of the reaction was on the level of the film: how long did it last?"[9] For the *New York Times* television critic John J. O'Connor, "the event demands intensity and a searing vision. NBC's 'Holocaust' can claim neither."[10]

Intensity does not necessarily mean sweeping drama: given the emotion inherent in the subject matter, perhaps the Holocaust requires restraint and a hushed voice – a whisper rather than a shout – as evidenced by the effective understatement of films like Lilienthal's *David* or Markus Imhoof's *The Boat Is Full.* Simplistic and emotionally manipulative, *Holocaust* is characteristic of American feature films on the subject. For example, *The Diary of Anne Frank* and *Judgment at Nuremberg* – the former originally a hit play and the latter a television drama – depend on a confined theatrical setting, superfluous dialogue, star turns, classical editing (mainly with close-ups), and musical scores whose violins swell at dramatic moments. These studio productions essentially fit the bristling new material of the Holocaust into an old narrative form, thus allowing the viewer to leave the theater feeling complacent instead of concerned or disturbed. The fact that both films are in black and white gives them a stark quality – which is, however, undercut by their lush scores.

The Diary of Anne Frank (1959) was adapted by Frances Goodrich and Albert Hackett from their 1956 Pulitzer Prize–winning play, based on the published diary of a young victim of the death camps, and some brief location footage was shot of the Amsterdam house where she wrote it. Reality also enters by way of documentary footage of camp life. Nevertheless, the authenticity of the tale is compromised by Hollywood conventions of casting and scoring. The thirteen-year-old Anne is played by Millie Perkins, who is clearly much older; when she dresses up, the thin, dark-haired actress bears a striking resemblance to Audrey Hepburn, one of the most popular female stars of the fifties. Peter, the boy on whom she has a crush, is played by Richard Beymer, a teen idol who later played the All-American lead in *West Side Story*. From the very start of the film – a postwar present tense that introduces a long flashback – the soundtrack plays an overly prominent role. Upon returning to his home after the war, Mr. Frank (Joseph Schildkraut) finds and puts on a scarf, and the lush Alfred Newman musical score signals that this is *significant*. (The scarf will subsequently be revealed as a gift from Anne.) The same thing occurs when he is handed Anne's diary; and when Anne and Peter are about to kiss, the music again rises – a redundancy, considering the image. The soundtrack also dominates by means of Anne's voice-over narration, as well as through the punctuation of sirens and Allied bombings that symbolize the continuous danger outside the attic. The only real "cinematic" element added to the play is superimposition, such as the sequence with the sneak thief at the safe on the second floor while at the same time the Jews remain immobile in the attic above. This spatial layering within a fixed frame is an effective device for stressing their claustrophobic life.

Judgment at Nuremberg, directed by Stanley Kramer in 1961, begins with more cinematic élan: an iris shot of a swastika opens up to reveal that the symbol is

Millie Perkins (Anne) in *The Diary of Anne Frank.*
PHOTO COURTESY OF THE MUSEUM OF MODERN ART/FILM STILLS ARCHIVE

on a monument. During the credits, we hear a Nazi marching song; the swastika suddenly blows up; and a hand-held camera leads us through a hazy dissolve into ruins. We read "Nuremberg, Germany, 1948" before meeting the crusty American judge Dan Haywood (Spencer Tracy) who has come out of retirement in Maine to pass judgment on four Nazi war criminals. Most of the film is devoted to the tense trials, which are orchestrated mainly by the raging American prosecutor Colonel Tad Lawson (Richard Widmark) and the equally excitable German defense lawyer Hans Rolfe (Maximilian Schell). Their key witnesses are Rudolf Petersen (Montgomery Clift), a nervous young man who was sterilized by the Nazis for political reasons (Rolfe tries to justify the sterilization on the grounds that Petersen is feeble-minded), and Irene Hoffman (Judy Garland), who must be coaxed to testify about a case of "racial pollution." Finally, the most important defendant – the German scholar and jurist Ernst Janning (Burt Lancaster) – breaks his silence. Respected by Judge Dan Haywood for his earlier writings on jurisprudence, Janning now bitterly explains that in a period of indignity, fear, and hunger, Hitler had returned to Germans their pride. "I am aware!" he yells. "Were we deaf? Blind? If we didn't know, it's because we didn't want to know."

Rolfe's trenchant rejoinder is that if Janning is guilty, as he himself insists, then everyone is guilty: the Vatican, Churchill who indirectly praised Hitler in 1938, American industrialists who helped Hitler rebuild his armaments, and so on. The American judge finally indicts the men in the dock because, even if many more people are guilty, these four individuals *were* responsible for their actions. "If these murderers were monsters, this event would have no more moral significance than an earthquake"; on the contrary, he warns the court, "How easily it can happen." After the four men receive sentences of life imprisonment, Rolfe wagers with Judge Haywood (who refuses to accept the bet) that the sentenced men will be free in five years. The prescient cynic's prediction is fulfilled, for the closing title informs us that not one of the ninety-nine defendants sentenced in Nuremberg is still serving time.

This film raises central issues of responsibility – individual, national, and universal – but almost exclusively through dialogue. The self-conscious opening and frequent visual flourishes do not seem anchored in any conception of a unified cinematic style. Perhaps Stanley Kramer thought he was making the film less theatrical by panning 360 degrees around a speaker like Lawson, or zooming into a tight close-up for emphasis; however, both of these techniques seem gratuitous and manipulative. For example, when Lawson takes the stand as commander of the American troops who liberated the camps, he shows harrowing archival footage of the camps and inmates, of children tattooed for extermination. Rather than letting the images imprint themselves upon us, Lawson (and Kramer) hammer them in: Lawson's voice-over is a harangue, and Kramer intercuts reaction shots which force audience identification with the surrogates in the courtroom rather than a personal response. Here, much of the same footage that is used in *Night and Fog* is material for prosecution rather than illumination. And as in Fritz Lang's *Fury* (1936), projecting a film in the courtroom carries the self-conscious suggestion that film is equivalent to truth.

Judgment at Nuremberg is more successful in the scenes dramatizing personal relations, relying as it does on the casting of recognizable stars. Some are used for their suggestion of integrity (Tracy, Lancaster, Garland), and the relationship between Haywood and Janning resembles that of Rauffenstein and Boeldieu in *Grand*

Maximilian Schell (Rolfe) and Richard Widmark (Lawson) in *Judgment at Nuremberg.*
PHOTO COURTESY OF MUSEUM OF MODERN ART/FILM STILLS ARCHIVE

Illusion, Jean Renoir's classic film about World War I. These men are bound by a code that cuts across national boundaries; their commitment to justice leads to a parallel situation in which the man in charge (Rauffenstein/Haywood) must destroy the other (Boeldieu/Janning), who understands and accepts his fate. On the other hand, Montgomery Clift and Marlene Dietrich connote the dubious psychological or moral states of their own film personas: for example, when the song "Lili Marleen" accompanies Haywood's walk with this German woman, her identity resonates beyond the frame. Dietrich's German accent rings true, whereas Hollywood's traditional neglect of language differences mars other parts of the film. At the beginning of *Judgment at Nuremberg,* there is a realistic quality when Rolfe speaks German and we hear a simultaneous translation. But after a zoom-in to a close-up, he suddenly breaks into English. Subsequently, he and Janning – two Germans – speak English between themselves! It is an accepted convention that an American film should be in English, but a strained one when we initially hear a major character speaking in his native language.

The histrionics of both Rolfe and Lawson are in keeping with their characters.[11] However, a voice of rage is not necessarily the best way to reach an audience; not unlike the violins that enter when Lawson convinces Irene Hoffman to testify, the sentimental tone betrays a fear that the material itself might not be sufficiently compelling. Some might argue that our numbed cinematic and moral senses demand a shout just to shake us out of lethargy. Nevertheless, the danger is that one could get so caught up in the emotion as to be incapable of reflecting on the message.

Otto Preminger's *Exodus* (1960) avoids this danger by presenting Auschwitz through a dispassionate verbal recollection, in the scene where the Irgun (Israeli

Underground) members interrogate Dov Landau (Sal Mineo) before initiating him. The question-and-answer session about the gas chambers and ovens is powerful not because Dov shouts but because he finally remains silent; he cannot reveal "who dug the graves." His questioner (David Opatoshu) divines that Dov – who entered Auschwitz at the age of twelve – learned about dynamite as a *Sonderkommando*, digging mass graves. With these credentials, he is accepted. Auschwitz thus exists as a prelude to the Israeli struggle, and *Exodus* insists on the connection between Nazi and Arab anti-Semitism: the Grand Mufti's urbane emissary tells Taha (John Derek), the Arab friend of Ari (Paul Newman), that they must destroy the Jews. This emissary is a former Nazi, ready to train new storm troopers.

The Boys from Brazil (1978) is an entertaining thriller that raises some important questions of Nazi continuity, but never really explores them. Adapted from Ira Levin's novel, the film is directed by Franklin J. Schaffner for maximum suspense at the expense of verisimilitude. The rather contrived plot revolves around the attempts of Dr. Josef Mengele (Gregory Peck) and his Nazi network in South America to clone Adolf Hitler, and the efforts of Nazi-hunter Ezra Liebermann (Sir Laurence Olivier) to discover their scheme and stop them. Liebermann learns that Mengele managed to create and deposit around the world ninety-four little Adolf Hitlers (we see at least four incarnations, all played by Jeremy Black) through reproduction of the Führer's blood and skin samples. Mengele's group is to assassinate each of the ninety-four fathers, thus replicating Hitler's lack of a father during his adolescence. These two obsessive dreamers – the chief doctor of Auschwitz and the Jewish survivor clearly modeled after Simon Wiesenthal – finally confront each other at the home of one of Mengele's victims. The sinister physician is killed by a pack of black dogs, and Liebermann subsequently destroys the list of thirteen-year-old Hitler clones still at large.

To its credit, *The Boys from Brazil* calls attention to contemporary indifference – an imprisoned Nazi guard (Uta Hagen) yells at Liebermann, "Thirty years: the world has forgotten. Nobody cares!" – and to the relatively untroubled existence led by Nazis in Paraguay and other countries equally hospitable to war criminals. We see the local military leaders bowing and scraping before Mengele at a party dotted with swastikas. The film also conveys a chilling sense of the impersonality of Nazi death dealing: young "Bobby," one of the Hitler clones, sets the dogs on to or off visitors by calling out "Action!" and "Cut!" as if he were directing a film. And when he tells them to kill Mengele, the order is "Print" – appropriate terminology for the clone of a man who murdered by the "remote control" of barked orders.[12] There is also a striking shot that functions as a visual foreshadowing of the plot: when Liebermann visits the home of the first man murdered by Mengele's organization, he is greeted by a surly, dark-haired, blue-eyed boy. A mirror in the hall reflects – and multiplies – the boy's image, endlessly repeating itself into the heart of the frame (like the famous extended mirror image toward the end of *Citizen Kane*). When the plot reveals that there are dozens of little boys with exactly the same appearance, one is reminded of this shot's expressive construction.

Nevertheless, *The Boys from Brazil* is saddled with typical Hollywood conventions, including recognizable stars like James Mason playing Nazis. (And can we really believe that upstanding Gregory Peck with his Lincolnesque gravity is the man responsible for killing two and a half million prisoners in Auschwitz?) Moreover,

Gregory Peck (Mengele), Jeremy Black (Bobby), and Sir Laurence Olivier (Liebermann) in *The Boys from Brazil.* PHOTO COURTESY OF MUSEUM OF MODERN ART/FILM STILLS ARCHIVE

for anyone who saw *Marathon Man,* in which Laurence Olivier portrayed a Nazi dentist on the rampage in New York City, his fine performance here as Liebermann suggests *too* great a versatility. Instead of delving into the suggestive Freudian theme of patricide as a prerequisite for Nazi control (as Visconti's *The Damned* had done), *The Boys from Brazil* opts for a rather evasive explanation: the threat is simply genetic implantation rather than a psychological potential for evil. At the end, Mengele is killed – a historical distortion that allows people to leave the theater with the complacent assumption that justice has been done. The fact remains that Mengele is probably still alive in South America. *The Boys from Brazil* substitutes a hokey plot – the clones are waiting to take over – for the real danger of legally untouchable Nazis. As Pauline Kael warned in her review of the film, "Nazism has become comic-book mythology, a consumer product. Movies like this aren't making the subject more important, they're making it a joke. They're cloning Hitler to death."[13] The menace of Nazism is similarly reduced by the taut action entertainment values of *Victory* (1981). Crisply directed by John Huston, the film takes place in a World War II where Nazis are gentlemen and a POW camp is a soccer training school. With such popular figures as Sylvester Stallone and Brazilian champion Pelé in the leading roles, *Victory* seems closer to "Rocky Plays Ball with the Nazis" than to a realistic assessment of the relationship between the SS and captured Allies. As the film opens, Major Von Steiner (Max Von Sydow) notices that one of the officer prisoners is Colby (Michael Caine), an English athlete of former glory. They strike up a match between Colby's team and the Wehrmacht. Using his influence, the English officer manages to get more food and better clothing for his men and, as the idea snowballs into a propaganda stunt staged by the Nazis, to protect more prisoners. The single note of reality occurs when Colby requests that the best East European players be transferred from labor camps to his barracks. The arrival of these athletes – now skeletal and stony figures – is sobering.

Stallone as Robert Hatch, the quintessential American bad-boy show-off, escapes (thanks to the efforts of the "escape committee" that the Nazis wink knowingly about). But his character, derived from the Bogart hero of the forties ("I ain't sticking my neck out for nobody" finally yielding to noble sacrifice), allows himself to be recaptured in order to help the French Resistance's escape plan for the entire team. Disbelief is truly suspended when the Nazis, instead of shooting Stallone, permit him to play goalkeeper in the big game. With some fancy footwork, the Allies win the match in Paris: the French crowd throbs "La Marseillaise" and storms the field – knocking down armed Nazi guards – to squire the players to safety. With this rosy last image of the mass overcoming (by sheer number and enthusiasm) its oppressors, *Victory* presents an ultimately pernicious illusion about Nazis, their prisoners, and the bravery of the average Frenchman.

Part of the problem is that the large budgets of American studio-made films permit a realistic reconstruction of period décor and costume, whether it be a stadium filled with thousands of people or the proper pleat on love-interest Carole Laure's skirt. Particularly for those who know little about the Holocaust, the apparent reality disguises the fairy-tale aspects of *Victory*. Furthermore, the film's opening image prepares the audience for a gritty reconstruction of suffering, rather than war reduced to a soccer game: a prisoner trying to escape at night through a barbed-wire fence is gunned down by the Nazis. This pre-credit sequence will quickly be forgotten by the film's makers, but only after having served its misleading purpose: to establish the authenticity of wartime imprisonment, German vigilance, omnipresent danger and pain . . . into which a contrived story will be inserted.

Ultimately, the benign Nazi – in a film that contains no contrasting image of a German soldier – is a distortion.[14] After all, this is not World War I, about which *Grand Illusion* presented a comparable situation, the German aristocrat Rauffenstein and the French aristocrat Boeldieu who are gentlemen officers above and beyond national boundaries. In World War II, the Nazi officer was *not* simply defending his country on the battlefield; he was part of a machine that savagely persecuted and executed millions of innocent civilians. The most courageous thing Colby does in *Victory* is to ask Von Steiner for East European players. The German is somewhat embarrassed because the Reich does not recognize their countries; nevertheless, he agrees. One wonders what might have happened had Colby asked for a *Jewish* athlete.

Max Von Sydow plays a similarly virtuous German in *Voyage of the Damned* (1976), which at least presents a range of German behavior. Directed by Stuart Rosenberg, this film is based on a wartime incident illustrating international indifference to the plight of 937 Jews who were permitted to leave Hamburg on May 13, 1939. Representing a broad sampling of class, profession, and situation, they board the S.S. *St. Louis* bound for Havana; Cuban officials refuse to accept the refugees; the good captain (Von Sydow) then assumes the burden of protecting his unwanted passengers. In a last-minute reprieve, the Jewish Agency arranges for Belgium, Holland, France, and England to take in these Jews. This ostensibly happy ending is qualified by end titles that recount the fate of the characters: "Over 600 of the 937 died in Nazi concentration camps."

Above, Soccer star Pelé (Luis); *below,* Sylvester Stallone (Robert) and
Michael Caine (Colby) in *Victory.* PHOTOS COURTESY OF PARAMOUNT PICTURES

Max Von Sydow
(Von Steiner) and
Michael Caine (Colby)
in *Victory*.
PHOTO COURTESY OF
PARAMOUNT PICTURES

Voyage of the Damned contrasts the noble German captain (who does *not* belong to the Nazi party) with the vicious purser (Helmut Griem); it also confronts the reality of concentration camps (from which two of the passengers were released, with shaved heads), corrupt bartering in which Jews were treated as a commodity, and crass blindness to their plight – even by the American government. As a Cuban official (Fernando Rey) puts it, "With elections coming up, Roosevelt will do what is politically expedient." Among the Jews as well, the casting is balanced so that some look more identifiably or aggressively Jewish (Sam Wanamaker, Ben Gazzara) and some less so (Faye Dunaway, Wendy Hiller, Julie Harris). But this very casting is problematic in the sense that *Voyage of the Damned* is primarily an "all-star" movie: everything takes place on the level of star turns and plot twists, rather than through cinematic expressiveness. Because there are so many noted actors playing virtually cameo roles, they emerge as types rather than as fully recognized characters: there is the Whore with the Heart of Gold (Katharine Ross), the Jewish Aristocrat (Oskar Werner), the Slimy Cuban Official (José Ferrer), the Naïve Young Steward (Malcolm McDowell), the Cynical Businessman (Orson Welles), and so on. Thus the film has the same narrative strategy as *Judgment at Nuremberg* and *The Diary of Anne Frank:* a dramatic situation with stars shown in huge close-ups, nonstop dialogue, and a surging musical score. *Voyage of the Damned* is polished and suspenseful but lacks complexity, for while effectively presenting the material, it does little with it.[15]

In this context, a film does not have to be made in or by America to be considered a Hollywood film. Although *Au nom de tous les miens* (*For Those I Loved*) is a French-Canadian production, the fact that it was shot in English, stars Michael York, has melodramatic music by Maurice Jarre, and is a sprawling, big-budget tale, makes it closer to *Holocaust* and *Voyage of the Damned* than to French treatments of the Holocaust. Two versions were shot – a long one for TV and a shorter feature that was released in France in 1983. Directed by Robert Enrico, *Au nom de tous les miens* is adapted from Martin Gray's autobiographical novel and tells the incredible story of this survivor (Jacques Penot), who ultimately becomes a wealthy businessman (Michael York) – and then loses his wife (Brigitte Fossey) and children in a fire. The film begins after the fire, with a ravaged York receiving an anti-Semitic phone call. A tape recording in which his wife admonishes him to tell his story deters him from committing suicide. Instead, he speaks into the machine – "I was born with the war, at fourteen, when the butchers came" – accompanied by flashbacks. *Au nom de tous les miens* moves from Warsaw in the winter of 1939, to the Ghetto in 1940 where he becomes a successful food smuggler, to the graphic brutality of Treblinka, and back to the Ghetto where Martin finds his father (York again) and fights in the Uprising. By 1944, Martin has become a lieutenant in the Red Army, but by 1947, he has moved to New York. (Perhaps the turning point for him was a Russian colonel's line, "the problem with the Jews is that you take the war so personally"!) In 1970, this rich American is in the south of France, where – for the third time in the film – he loses those he loves.

To its credit, *Au nom* has gritty scenes that convey a measure of the horror inflicted upon European Jewry – for example, the brutality of some Ukrainians who search for hidden Jews during a 1942 deportation. And in the death camp of Treblinka, the sight of cadavers (after being gassed) from which gold teeth are extracted before the bodies are buried in a mass pit, is undeniably powerful. Nevertheless, the film is marred by scenes like that of young Martin – after his buddy has been shot for stealing herring – telling a cat that he will be a survivor, or saying to his father (York) in English, "Sorry, Papele." As in *Judgment at Nuremberg,* the inclusion of the authentic language – in this case, Yiddish – renders even more inauthentic the English spoken throughout. Finally, the casting is problematic here, not only because Penot bears little resemblance to York in his dual role, but also because he looks nothing like his mother (Macha Meril); hence, when his New York grandmother tells Martin he resembles his mother, it is ludicrous. The rich story of an actual survivor deserves better treatment.

Melodrama also mars two other European adaptations of best-selling novels – films that feel like Hollywood productions. *The Assault* (1986) is a powerful story weakened by melodramatic music, a voice-over narration *in the present tense* – "and now, Anton does this . . ." – redundant with the images, hokey coincidences, and a lack of character development, especially among the women. Adapted by Gerard Soeteman from Harry Mulisch's celebrated novel, the Dutch film by Fons Rademakers was initially screened at the 1986 Cannes Film Festival in an English-dubbed and shortened version that was very poor. When it was released by Cannon with subtitles in 1987, *The Assault* had improved sufficiently to win the Academy Award for Best Foreign-Language Film.

The two-and-a-half hour version begins in January of 1945 in occupied Holland with the Steenwijk family. When the body of a hated collaborator is found dead in their yard (having been dragged there from a neighboring house), they are killed – with the exception of young Anton. He chooses to be an anesthesiologist (an appropriate profession for someone trying to forget his aborted childhood), and grows into a never-quite-happy adult. *The Assault* ends with Anton and his son at an antinuclear demonstration, where he bumps into a woman who unlocks the past: she tells him that neighbors placed the policeman's body in his family's yard rather than next door because Jews were hidden there.

Derek de Lint (who gives a superlative performance in *Bastille*, discussed in Chapter 10) is excellent as the young and subsequently aging Anton, a man who has repressed his wartime childhood to the extent that he suffers attacks when he is in his fifties. We learn that the central event in Anton's life was meeting a Resistance heroine in the dark of a jail cell the night his family's house was burned in 1945. We see only her mouth – the same mouth that Anton is drawn to on Saskia years later, and for which he presumably marries her. (Monique van de Ven plays both women.) He is marked forever by her blood, just as his identification papers are marked a few scenes later by the blood of a kind German policeman who feeds him.

A momentary but determining encounter provides the narrative thrust of *La Storia* ("History," 1986) as well, but here it is between an Italian woman and a German soldier. Directed by Luigi Comencini from Elsa Morante's sprawling novel of 1974, this Italian drama was first presented as a five-hour miniseries for the RAI, and subsequently cut to a 146-minute theatrical release version. Claudia Cardinale gives a powerful performance as Ida, a Roman schoolteacher through whom we experience the turbulent years from 1941 to 1947. After newsreel footage of Mussolini, we see a young German soldier getting drunk. Because Ida looked too anxiously at a sign about Jews, we assume that the reason she doesn't resist his rape more vigorously is her fear *as* a Jew; this is heightened by an intercut of a woman (probably Ida's mother in flashback) telling her daughter she was baptized so no one will know she is Jewish. The issue of the rape is a son, Useppe, for whose birth Ida runs to a midwife in the Jewish ghetto. This adorable child is loved by Ida and Nino, her older son, who had fought with the Fascists and later joins the partisans. When their home is bombed, Useppe goes with his mother to a shelter for refugees. Carlo (Lambert Wilson) collapses at their door: he is an anarchist – who will turn out to be Jewish – recently escaped from prison. He joins Nino in a partisan group, but this pacifist has a hard time killing a German soldier – until he finds the strength to kick his face with lethal blows.

One of *La Storia*'s most gripping scenes occurs at the train station, as Ida and Useppe are boarding a train to get away. On the next track is a sealed train with Jews crying out for water. Ida tries to stop an older woman seen in the ghetto from boarding, but the latter wants to be with her family in the sealed car. Then Ida's train is requisitioned by the Germans, and she must return to the shelter. After the war, Nino smuggles in an American jeep and is killed by Americans. Useppe has epilepsy, aggravated by a sense of abandonment when Nino doesn't return and Carlo won't respond (having become an alcoholic). Only when Useppe dies of a seizure does Ida admit he was Jewish – meaning that she is too. The bereaved mother goes into a catatonic state, sitting with his body for three days until the police break down the door. Like other Italian films on the Holocaust, Jewish identity is so attenuated as to be nonexistent, except for guilt. Similarly, it shares with numerous films about World War II (such as *Two Women*) the depiction of woman as the embodiment of a nation – occupied, ravaged, and resourceful – in an often harrowing saga of survival and loss.

In *Hanna's War* (1988), however, the heroine is a blazing emblem of the Jewish spirit more than of her country, Hungary. Based on the true story of Hanna Senesh, this Cannon film directed by Menachem Golan does not completely avoid melodramatic excesses, reminiscent of television docudramas (not to mention rock music when freedom fighters prepare to parachute!); nevertheless, Maruschka Detmers's moving performance often compensates for these limitations. In 1938 Hungary, Hanna decides to leave a warm and privileged life with her mother (Ellen Burstyn) for the challenge of Palestine. She writes poems and letters home from Kibbutz Sdot-Yam, and then joins a group of paratroopers in 1943, who will risk their lives in returning to Eastern Europe. Under the crusty British commander (Anthony Andrews), they parachute into Yugoslavia, but Hanna insists on returning to Hungary. She is captured, tortured by Captain Roza (Donald Pleasance), and finally executed by order of Captain Simon (David Warner) – but not before making a passionate and prescient speech about the imminent downfall of the oppressors at her own trial.

The Israeli-born Golan, whose previous directorial credits include *The Delta Force* and *Operation Thunderbolt,* acquired the film rights from Senesh's surviving mother and brother in 1964. He subsequently lost the rights, optioned the memoir of her parachuting comrade Yoel Palgi (*A Great Wind Cometh*), and then reacquired the rights. When asked why he was so adamant about bringing this tale to the screen, he replied:

> How many women can you count who came to prominence in the last two centuries . . . Rosa Luxemburg? Eleanor Roosevelt? Indira Gandhi? Golda Meir? . . . whereas there are numerous men to identify with as humanity's heroes. I grew up in Israel with the stories, songs and diary of Hanna, like every child in Israel. She became part of our education in primary schools. Over the years, for instance, Anne Frank was discovered by the world through a play and then on screen. In Hanna we have a unique young lady who I think represents such fantastic heroic qualities – one of the only ones who physically tried to do something in those dark days – coming from a free place back into terror. There were 33 people recruited voluntarily to do what Hanna did: most were captured, seven were killed. One could say that the operation failed, but the spirit of it is an unbelievable story.[16]

There was a time when Golan did not think it right or possible to make films about the Holocaust. In his words, "Movies are always entertainment, always selling tickets to people who leave their homes and come to a theater. The Holocaust is too horrifying an experience to make a movie from it. Films in a way are romantic, and the Holocaust can't be romantic." But once he defined for himself that *Hanna's War* is not "a Holocaust film, but the dramatic story of a young girl living through a horrifying period," he felt able to present the tale. "You know there's a war, but you don't see it on the screen," he added. "It's a power that exists off-screen. I'm still reluctant to show concentration camp scenes, although I know they should be done."

Auschwitz prisoners in *Playing for Time.*

More successful in this regard is *Playing for Time,* the controversial CBS-TV film starring Vanessa Redgrave as a Jewish musician in the orchestra of Auschwitz; it does not flinch from presenting the demeaning circumstances of concentration camp life. *Playing for Time* was adapted by playwright Arthur Miller from Fania Fenelon's magnificent autobiographical account, and directed by Daniel Mann. By September 30, 1980, when the telefilm was first aired, CBS had learned from NBC's mistakes with *Holocaust:* "Because of the special nature of this presentation," announced a title, "CBS will only interrupt this drama four times." Within its first few minutes, *Playing for Time* re-creates unsavory conditions in the freight cars carrying prisoners to Auschwitz as Fania's young fan, Marianne (Melanie Mayron), relieves herself into a pail, which then falls and causes those around her to cry out for air.

The women's arrival at Auschwitz is a signal for the hair-cutting and scalp-shaving reserved for Jewish prisoners. A finely edited scene conveys the situation with poetic compression: a close-up of Fania being shorn is crosscut with one of Marianne, both silent amid the excessively loud sound of scissors and faraway screams. Numbers are tattooed onto arms in close-up, while a long shot of smoke emerging from a building is explained by the brutal phrase, "They're cooking." The coexistence of debasement and transcendence at Auschwitz is presented through a montage of fire, smoke, and shoveling, accompanied by the voice-over of Fania comforting Marianne with a story about a princess. The authentic source of these scenes is heightened by tinted archival footage that punctuates the film throughout. Fact and fictional reconstruction are yoked when, for example, documentary images of Auschwitz are inserted into a scene of Fania's labor.

As a singer, Fania is taken into the women's orchestra, a relatively privileged domain where the women can hide inside their music. The conductor, Alma Rosé (Jane Alexander), is a complex character because, although Jewish, she is also Gustav Mahler's niece. She feels superior to the players (and closer to the Nazis) because she is "an artist." Indeed, her harsh enforcement of discipline with the musicians – including slapping them – smacks of SS behavior. That Alma is a "special Jew" is evident since her hair has not been shorn. She plays their game and her music submissively, trying to ignore the reality of the camp; "I refuse to see!" she screams once at Fania. Moreover, when Alma is finally poisoned by the jealous Frau Schmidt (Viveca Lindfors), the monstrous Dr. Josef Mengele kisses her violin before placing it in the casket, and salutes her conductor's baton! There is equal complexity in the characterization of Frau Lagerführerin Mandel (Shirley Knight), who is attractive, prone to humane gestures (she puts boots on Fania), and clearly affectionate with a little Polish boy that she takes from a transport (and from his mother). Fania's deepest tears seem to flow when she sings for Mandel after she has sacrificed the boy.

Fania specifies that Frau Mandel is "human" and "that's the problem." A figure of extreme integrity, Fania resists all the ideologies that are represented by various members of the orchestra. Whether the foil be Alma's artistic superiority, the Zionist's hyperbolic patriotism, or the Communist's barely articulated socialism, Fania transcends her fellow prisoners' beliefs. She is a defiant risk taker: a half-Jew, she nevertheless challenges the commandant (after her superb concert) with the statement that her father's name – and therefore her own – is really Goldstein. She refuses to join the orchestra unless they take Marianne too – an act of generosity for which her weak friend will hardly prove grateful when she becomes a Kapo. Fania's integrity is thrown into relief when she spies Marianne obtaining food through giving sexual favors. There is a long pause after Marianne hands her a piece of sausage: will the hungry woman, who has been orchestrating a score all night, be able to swallow such food? The camera remains on Fania's face as she hesitates, smelling and licking the meat, and then slowly begins to chew it, her clouded eyes expressing the price she is paying. (Redgrave here conveys a poignant struggle of physical need and moral repugnance solely through the tension between the lower and upper regions of her face.)

Fania incarnates the spirit that holds the orchestra together, the spirit that Terrence Des Pres describes so accurately in his book, *The Survivor: An Anatomy of Life in the Death Camps:* "The survivor's experience is evidence that the need *to* help is as basic as the need *for* help, a fact which points to the radically social nature of life in extremity and explains an unexpected but very widespread activity among survivors."[17] Fania warns Marianne that she must share at least a little of what she "earns" with the others, so that she won't become an animal. Though refusing to judge anyone, Fania insists on a standard of human dignity that abhors stealing or self-debasement. A similarly generous character is Elzbieta (Marisa Berenson), a Catholic Pole whose first act upon seeing the ravaged Fania is to wipe her filthy face clean with her own saliva. And Fania's "double" on a larger scale, inspiring and binding the inmates together, is the chief interpreter, Mala (Maud Adams), who carries on resistance activities inside Auschwitz. The scene in which she and her lover

Playing for Time production photo. PHOTO COURTESY OF STIGWOOD/YELLEN PRODUCTIONS

Edek are hanged after escaping and being captured is effective in its silence: as the women of Auschwitz pass the pathetically dangling bodies, they remove their scarves in speechless respect.

For the most part, *Playing for Time* succeeds courageously and admirably, with details that are corroborated in Wanda Jakubowska's definitive film about Auschwitz, *The Last Stop* (Poland, 1948). But the real Fania was five feet tall, and fresh out of her teens at the time she was taken to Auschwitz; her stamina and ability to tower over the others were thus even more remarkable when set alongside the sheer physical presence of an exceptionally tall, forty-three-year-old mature actress. One might therefore ask whether CBS was looking for some free publicity through controversy when it insisted on casting an outspoken supporter of the terrorist PLO as a Jewish concentration camp inmate – especially when she was physically a far cry from the real heroine, and when Fenelon publicly opposed the choice:

> Vanessa Redgrave is a very great actress . . . but casting her is for me a moral wrong because she is a fanatic. . . . I wanted Jane Fonda for the role. She has her political views, but she's not a fanatic. Or Liza Minnelli. She's small, she's full of life, she sings. Vanessa doesn't sing and dance, she doesn't have a sense of humor, and that is the one thing that saved me from death in the camp.[18]

Arthur Miller defended the casting by explaining that several actresses had turned down the part because they were unwilling to shave their heads, "yet Miss Redgrave was so dedicated that she lost weight, inflicted needle scars on her scalp and tore at her flesh in the quest for dramatic verisimilitude."[19] Nevertheless, many viewers boycotted the telefilm.

CBS's presentation of John Hersey's *The Wall* on February 16, 1982, was riddled by more frequent commercial interruptions than *Playing for Time*, but *The Wall* (directed by Robert Markowitz) remains a compelling, well-acted, and reasonably accurate piece of TV drama. Like *Holocaust*, it focuses on a few individuals who personalize the extraordinary tale of the Warsaw Ghetto Uprising. Shot primarily in Poland (with the cooperation of Polish television in Warsaw and with a local crew), *The Wall* conveys an authenticity of place – despite the staginess of the freeze frames that end each episode – and also roots the events in history by printing the date as each segment begins.

The Wall opens with crowds of Polish Jews being deported, under the watchful eye of a Nazi film crew. Things are not yet hopeless in the Warsaw of October 1940: a prosperous and accommodating Jew like Mauritzi Apt (Eli Wallach) can still live normally with his family and entertain the prospects of buying their way out of the Ghetto. His daughter Rachel (Lisa Eichhorn) realizes that the time has come to organize the inhabitants when a Nazi soldier abruptly shoots an old Jew in the street. Others in the Ghetto, like the enterprising Berson (Tom Conti), merely try to survive, smuggle, and share their booty on a day-to-day basis. A month later, Apt buys false papers – but only for himself, thus abandoning his children, including Mordechai (Griffin Dunne), who is about to marry his fiancée (Christine Estabrook). By March 1941, "resettlement" of the Jews to the east is announced to the Jüdenrat (the Jewish leadership in the Warsaw Ghetto);[20] as Berson and Rachel learn, the trains being packed with thousands of people daily are bound for Treblinka, the death camp (actually shot on location at Auschwitz). Through a kind of visual shorthand that might not have worked before *Holocaust* and *Playing for Time*, shots of chimneys and smoke are used to suggest the burning of Jewish bodies.

By September 1942, things have worsened: a montage sequence moves briskly from roundup to gunshots, to trains filling with bodies, to arrival at Treblinka, to smoke. As mechanical cinematically as the events it portrays, this sequence acknowledges the impersonal horror in the background of the protagonists' actions. After Berson and Rachel build a new hiding place next to the oven of a bakery for the ever-diminishing group, Berson moves in and out of the Aryan sector to acquire arms. The Polish Underground makes excuses rather than offers of assistance, participating in the revolt only toward the end. The Jews launch their attack on German soldiers, using homemade bombs and the limited ammunition Berson has managed to buy. They succeed in temporarily driving the Nazi tanks out of the Ghetto. *The Wall* crosscuts these action scenes with a shot of a Nazi teletype machine constantly revising the date of the Ghetto's ultimate liquidation. Berson and Rachel finally acknowledge their love, as the group is forced into the sewers where they must hide while waiting for the Underground. Only a few manage to escape to join the partisans in the forest: Mordechai, his wife, Yitzhak (an excitable fighter who had earlier killed the couple's baby when it wouldn't stop crying as they hid in the sewer), and Rachel. In the struggle, Berson has been killed, but *The Wall* asks us to end on a more celebratory note of resistance: "The Uprising began April 19, 1943. A year later there were still Jews fighting."

The three-hour film traces Berson's crucial movement from a "close-up" to "long-shot" perspective: after acting only on an immediate level, he grows to understand the larger struggle and the need for organization. Primarily through this engaging character, we see a spectrum of characterizations: there are "bad" Poles (the hotel concierge who lets Berson escape only for a large sum) and "good" ones (Rachel Roberts as Berson's landlady); "bad" Jews (Apt and Stefan, the Jewish policeman who asks his father to volunteer for deportation to save his own skin) and simply weak ones (Rachel's vain sister and Berson's sickly wife). The larger question that remains inheres in the "docudrama" format itself: the Nazis stage a restaurant scene for their propaganda cameras, forcing a few Jews to look as if they eat well in the Ghetto. A cut to the soup line where each inhabitant receives his meager cup provides a harsh contrast. This leaves us with the illusion that what the Nazis stage is "false," whereas what has been staged for us by director Markowitz is "real." Such reconstructions, however, are more real in terms of melodramatic convention than of historical fact.

John Toland, author of *Adolf Hitler,* called attention to distortions in the film:

> Because the Polish government provided the principal settings, along with thousands of extras and some vintage World War II tanks, the producers of *The Wall* had to make certain compromises with the facts: the number of Nazi casualties in the battle scenes, for instance, is exaggerated, while the fact that few Poles at the time of the Warsaw uprising actively resisted Nazi persecution of the Jews has been conspicuously deleted. What's important, though, is that *The Wall* has managed to retain the surge and spirit of the novel by adhering to its own compellingly drawn approximation of the truth.[21]

That the Americans were careful with Polish interests should come as no surprise: the cautiousness of the American film and television industry is also reflected in the fact that almost all its movies dealing with the Holocaust are adapted from another medium – successful plays (*The Diary of Anne Frank, Cabaret*) or novels (*Exodus, Ship of Fools, Marathon Man, Julia, The Boys from Brazil, Sophie's Choice*). *The Wall* was a celebrated novel by John Hersey before it became a Broadway play by Millard Lampell – who then went on to write the television movie. It seems, therefore, that Hollywood will take a chance on films about the Holocaust only after the material has proven its commercial potential in another medium. And even then, the films merely touch upon the historical horror rather than grasp it. The American cinema often uses Nazi images to evoke instant terror or tears, whereas many European films use the cinematic medium as an instrument to probe responsibility. Perhaps the cinema of a country that has never experienced occupation cannot plumb the depths of the Holocaust experience. Or – more likely – perhaps the commercial imperatives of Hollywood and the networks tend to preempt the possibilities for truthful representation.

Nevertheless, recent American telefilms on the Holocaust have broken new ground. *Escape from Sobibor,* presented by CBS on April 12, 1987, chronicles the only – and relatively unknown – mass escape by Jews from a death camp, in a gripping but restrained manner. Directed by Jack Gold from Reginald Rose's teleplay (based on the book by Richard Rashke), the three-hour "docudrama" filmed in Belgrade recounts the true story of this death camp in eastern Poland. It begins with a voice-over narrator (Howard K. Smith) explaining the stills and map that establish the tale's authenticity. Three men escape, are shot, and displayed. A trainload of Jews disembarks to the strains of "Tales of the Vienna Woods," followed by wrenching separation, selection, and dispersion to the "showers." Only those with a trade will be spared, among them Shlomo (Simon Gregor) and his younger brother Moses, both goldsmiths. One of the most powerful scenes occurs when the latter is ordered to the "Disinfection" site: he sees naked people lined up, screaming as they are forced to the showers, followed by smoke. But the protagonist of *Escape from Sobibor* is really a collective one, including Leon Feldhendler (Alan Arkin), who oversees the escape; Sasha (Rutger Hauer), head of the captured Russian-Jewish soldiers; and Luka (Joanna Pacula), who aids in the revolt mainly by pretending to be Sasha's girlfriend. They engineer a plan whereby sixteen SS officers will be killed, as well as many of the 125 Ukrainian guards.

The taut last part of the film is devoted to the escape: of the six hundred prisoners, approximately three hundred survive the Nazis' guns, barbed wire, and minefield. As they keep running toward the forest, the narrator tells us what happened to these characters – including Leon's murder by anti-Semites in Lublin less than two years after the escape. The end titles present the names of the known Sobibor survivors alive today. Although the score by Georges Delerue is occasionally too intrusive, *Escape from Sobibor* is a commendable dramatization. Arkin exudes a quiet strength, especially in the scene where he visibly controls himself in telling Shlomo that his wife and child were killed. Hauer – despite his entrance only after the film's midpoint – is a towering figure in his defiance. It is important to finally see victimized Jews fighting back – not only thirsting for revenge but caring for their fellows, such as when Leon insists that the escape must be for all six hundred inmates or not at all. This is a chapter of Holocaust history that needed to be told, for the Nazis razed Sobibor immediately after the revolt of October 14, 1943: records were destroyed, and the camp was never liberated by Soviet or Western troops.

Less than two years later, *War and Remembrance* reenacted another crucial episode of "The Final Solution" whose evidence the Nazis tried to hide – Babi Yar. The massacre of approximately thirty thousand Jews outside of Kiev is one of the many Holocaust sections in this thirty-hour miniseries for ABC-TV. Directed by Dan Curtis from a screenplay by Earl Wallace, Curtis, and Herman Wouk (author of the original novel), *War and Remembrance* illustrates both the advantages and the limitations of the television medium. The Babi Yar sequence is proudly narrated by Nazi Colonel Paul Blobel (Kenneth Colley) in the form of a flashback that does not spare details of defenseless Jews stripped, beaten, and machine-gunned into mass graves. In an effort to hide the traces of Babi Yar, his Commando 1005 (made up partly of Auschwitz prisoners) will open these graves and burn the corpses.

War and Remembrance juxtaposes graphic scenes of Nazi atrocities with several World War II stories, especially that of an American family. (It is the sequel to *The Winds of War*, the eighteen-hour miniseries telecast in 1986.) Captain Victor "Pug" Henry (Robert Mitchum) assumes command of a heavy cruiser in the American fleet after the Japanese attack on Pearl Harbor. His son Byron (Hart Bochner) is a torpedo and gunnery officer, while his other son, Warren (Michael Woods), is a fighter pilot. Pug is in love with Pamela Tudsbury (Victoria Tennant), but has remained faithful to his errant wife, Rhoda (Polly Bergen). For narrative purposes, the most important family member is Byron's wife, Natalie (Jane Seymour), a Jew who had the bad luck to be in Italy with her uncle Aaron Jastrow (John Gielgud) – a former Yale professor – when World War II exploded. We meet them on a boat headed for Palestine, led by Avram Rabinovitz (French actor Sami Frey in one of the film's most compelling performances); but they disembark in Italy under the illusion that their special status

Jane Seymour and Sir John Gielgud as Natalie Jastrow and her Uncle Aaron in Herman Wouk's *War and Remembrance.*
PHOTO COURTESY OF JAMES GLOVUS, COURTESY CAPITAL CITIES/ABC, INC.

will keep them safe in Europe. As the war continues, their situation becomes more perilous (and their Jewish identity stronger, as illustrated by a sensitive depiction of a joyous Sabbath dinner in Marseille); they are deported to Theresienstadt, and finally to Auschwitz. The fact that even an American Jew married to a Gentile could become a victim of the Nazis makes the story more accessible to an American audience. Indeed, what sets *War and Remembrance* apart from such pioneering television films as *Holocaust, Playing for Time,* and *The Wall* is not only its scale but also its capacity to reach a much larger audience than these avowedly "Holocaust" dramas. It cleverly "tricks" those who think they are watching a wartime adventure movie into looking at the horrifying reproduction of both Auschwitz and Babi Yar.

Since, for some viewers, *War and Remembrance* is the first encounter with concrete images of Nazi brutality and extermination procedures, the responsibility of the filmmakers is all the more weighty. It would seem that Dan Curtis and his colleagues fulfilled their duty, first through scrupulous research, and second by filming inside Auschwitz. As the producer-director told a *New York Times* interviewer about capturing the "reality" of the Holocaust, "Nobody had ever gone far enough in a film or television program. To put on film the true horror was impossible. Once one false note sneaks in, you're gone. And, in my own eyes, I felt failing would be an absolute crime.... It was enormously important to shoot it where it happened."[22] Although ABC was incorrect in claiming that this was the first time the Polish government permitted a dramatic film to be shot there (Jack Eisner arranged for his autobiographical tale *War and Love* – a Cannon release – to be filmed in Auschwitz in 1984), it *was* the first time that one of the death camp's crematoria was re-created on that site. Having found the original plans and specifications in the files of Auschwitz, the crew built to exact size one of the four crematoria that the Nazis blew up at the end of the war to hide evidence.

Even more significantly, part two presents a "Special Action" (for the audience's benefit as well as for Gestapo Chief Heinrich Himmler's) from beginning to end: a trainload of unwitting Dutch Jews disembarks; they are told there is "plenty of work here for everybody," led to the "disinfection center" where towels and soap are neatly arranged, forced to disrobe, and herded to the showers as panic ensues. To the satisfaction of the SS, the Jews scream while gas fills the crowded chamber, until silence accompanies their deaths. We then see the corpses of men, women, and children being thrown into mass graves as Auschwitz's Commandant Rudolf Hoess complains that "disposal is the problem"; Himmler complies by agreeing to make the construction of crematoria a priority over war labor needs.

Despite the undeniable force of this sequence, Elie Wiesel's contention that Holocaust art is a contradiction in terms bears mention. Melodrama and crematoria are hardly compatible, and the concentration camp experience cannot be accommodated by a square tube associated with diversion. After all, we are invited to be horrified when Hoess insists that the "Special Action" must follow rather than precede lunch: but don't we often get up during the commercials to get a snack or drink, even after scenes of horror? Possibilities for trivialization and distortion remain within the television medium, whatever the scale of the production. For example, the first half of *War and Remembrance* presents daily life in Auschwitz primarily through the male prisoners Berel Jastrow (Chaim Topol) and Sammy Mutterperl (John Rhys-Davies); they are not only strong enough to be useful as labor (and look reasonably well fed) but are part of the political resistance – with access to film evidence that Berel smuggles out. This was the case for only a fraction of the Jews in the death camp; most (and especially women) were too starved, degraded, or isolated to enact resistance or escape. (It is true, however, that in the second half of *War and Remembrance* – telecast in 1989 – Natalie endures Auschwitz.)

The number of films about the Holocaust has grown to such an extent over the past ten years that "reality" often boils down to how a movie compares with previous film treatments. During part two, some viewers might have been struck by how Hoess seemed so "real" – even more than the other characters played by an international cast. Perhaps it was because this was not the first time the actor had incarnated Hoess: Gunther Maria Halmer was indeed the same commandant in Alan Pakula's film version of *Sophie's Choice*. Although he had played his part alongside Meryl Streep in German, and was now speaking accented English, a subliminal link was made for those who had seen *Sophie's Choice*. *War and Remembrance* uses a similar connection in part five, where Hoess proudly shows Colonel Blobel Auschwitz's new gas chambers and crematoria. If the colonel seems even more sinister than the other Nazis in this film, it may be because the actor had already played Adolf Eichmann in *Wallenberg* opposite Richard Chamberlain. Recasting these actors is not merely effective; it raises the issue of whether authenticity and convention can be synonymous. This is not to say that the first eighteen hours of the thirty-hour miniseries are inaccurate: *War and Remembrance* is not only an extraordinarily ambitious and often moving drama, but the most meticulous reconstruction of Auschwitz in a film made for television. For a "Hollywood version" – and at a time when neo-Nazi groups are quite audible in the United States – it is not only commemorative but cautionary; this drama reminds us of the fatal American political indifference to the destruction of European Jewry, while illustrating what can happen when prejudice runs rampant and becomes doctrine.

2
Meaningful Montage

ilms that depict a character's memory of a horrific past – and that character's enslavement by it – can have more consistency and integrity than a movie that purports to show *the* past in an objective way. A fictional reconstruction of a concentration camp is not quite as "truthful" as one person's subjective memory of it, for the latter acknowledges the partiality of the recollection. Most effective are films like *The Pawnbroker,* which move us by alternating the present – marked by indifference to the Holocaust – with the past. This is a cinema of flashbacks: a filmic device that permits the visible, palpable past to surface into the present. Editing in this cinema is not merely continuity, or the smooth linear transition from one shot to the next; the rhythms and juxtapositions of the cutting can create varied effects upon the viewer, from heightened suspense to an awareness of contraries. The montage of such films as *The Pawnbroker, High Street, Sophie's Choice, Night and Fog, Les Violons du Bal,* and *La Passante du Sans Souci* expresses the degree to which the relatively calm present is informed by the turbulent Holocaust.

The Pawnbroker is one of the rare "Hollywood" films (shot entirely in New York!) to take on the Holocaust and its legacy with both thematic and formal vigor. Directed in 1965 by Sidney Lumet, this chiseled black-and-white portrait of a survivor living in New York City is structured through sophisticated editing. Lumet and editor Ralph Rosenblum use montage as a complex visual analogue for mental processes. Although the story takes place in the present, it is punctuated by shots of memory – flash cuts that surface momentarily into the protagonist's thoughts, searing the present with the ineradicable brand of his concentration camp past.

The film begins with a fragment whose meaning will be revealed only midway through the story: in dreamlike slow motion, a young couple, their children, and grandparents relax in a pastoral scene that ends abruptly, yielding to a present tense of vulgar suburban life. The same man, Sol Nazerman (Rod Steiger), now much older, is being pestered by his sister-in-law and her teenage children. He drives back to his

Rod Steiger (Nazerman) in *The Pawnbroker.*

pawnshop on 116th Street, as subjective hand-held shots of lower Harlem identify the camera with his point of view. Nazerman's behavior with various desperate customers – ranging from fatigue to contempt – suggests power, until it becomes clear that Nazerman is as helpless vis-à-vis his black boss, Rodriguez (Brock Peters), as his poor clients are before him.

Nazerman's assistant Jesús (Jaime Sanchez) is the opposite of his employer: an energetic young Hispanic, he wants to move up quickly in the world – as the exhilarating tracking shots of Jesús on ladders or sprinting through crowded streets embody – while Nazerman wants only to be left in peace. When the bitter Jew rejects Jesús' offers of interest and companionship, the offended youth succumbs to his buddies' plans to rob the store. Nazerman also refuses the friendly advances of a social worker, Miss Birchfield (Geraldine Fitzgerald), and spurns Tessie (Marketa Kimbrell), the woman with whom he has been living, especially when her father dies. This cruel indifference is rendered comprehensible only in flashbacks that show Nazerman's earlier brutalization at the hands of the Nazis. Through subliminal flash cuts that gradually lengthen into painful scenes, the linear narrative is thickened with the weight of the past.

The first return to World War II occurs when Nazerman walks away from his shop in the Harlem night. The sound of dogs barking triggers a bleached-out flash cut of dogs chasing a Jewish prisoner who is trying to scale a fence. Like a cinematic poem, the film alternates quick shots of the Harlem scene (a gang of kids beating up a black boy) with the camp locale, creating visual rhymes. With a shaved head and a Star of David on his uniform, Nazerman watches his friend die on the fence; his inability to take action extends into the present. The first flashback thus establishes Nazerman's essential relationship to his surroundings: a spectator who cannot relieve suffering, only observe, register, and perhaps absorb it.

The fact that the "prisoner" in the present is black sets up a second level of oppression in *The Pawnbroker*. While it is admittedly a facile distortion to posit a one-to-one analogy between the Harlem ghetto in 1965 and the camps of the early forties, Nazerman treats his predominantly black customers with the same disdain that characterized the Nazis' attitude toward Jews. He calls them "creatures," "scum," "rejects" – and his job is ultimately one of dispossession. Indeed, the pawnbroker can be seen as a contemporary Kapo, controlling the poor clients who barter with him, but also controlled – and imprisoned – by his superiors. He must remain unmoved by the suffering of these "creatures" in order to survive, even as they relinquish their most personal possessions to him.

Furthermore, the shop with its bars and fences replicates the storerooms of the concentration camp. The second flashback fleshes out this connection as a pregnant young woman tries to pawn her ring. This touches off a close-up of hands against wire that grows into a slow tracking shot of rings being removed by SS men from a long line of trembling hands. Once again, Nazerman is powerless before a victim. This is also the case a few sequences later when a desperate hooker offers the pawnbroker her body along with her jewelry. "Look!" she repeats as she bares her breasts. "Look!" says the Nazi to the same man twenty-five years earlier, pointing to the young female prisoners. As the flash cuts lengthen, we see that one of the women being pointed at is Nazerman's wife Ruth (Linda Geiser), for the film's first pastoral shot suddenly reappears within the flashback. When Nazerman refuses to look, a soldier pushes

Above, Rod Steiger as Sol Nazerman in *The Pawnbroker.* *Below,* lighting externalizes Nazerman's imprisonment.

PHOTOS COURTESY OF THE LANDAU COMPANY

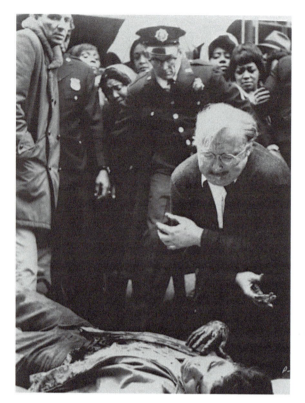

Nazerman mourning over
Jesús' dead body in
The Pawnbroker.
PHOTO COURTESY OF MUSEUM
OF MODERN ART/FILM STILLS
ARCHIVE

his bald head through the glass, forcing him to see. In this film, one pays a price for vision: images are wounds that will not heal.

The violation Nazerman witnesses leads him, not only to refuse the hooker, but then to declare to his boss that he won't accept money if it comes from a whorehouse. Rodriguez counters with the challenge, "Where do you think the money you're living on has been coming from?" Nazerman is verbally beaten into submission when the overbearing boss pushes him to accept his demands. The cinematic technique eloquently expresses Nazerman's fractured state of mind, for flash cuts are once again employed – but within the scene itself. That these men exist in different and unreconcilable worlds is shown by their inability to share the same frame: each taunting "Yes?" of Rodriguez results in a violent cut that assaults our eyes as well as Nazerman's ears. Moreover, the use of the flash cut, already associated with the Nazis, implies that Rodriguez is but a new incarnation of an old demon.

The film's predilection for quick cutting over pans or long takes underlines Nazerman's dissociation from people in general. His inability to touch or even see those around him is then developed in a flashback that begins in a subway car. From Nazerman's point of view, individuals stare at him blankly, until the crowded train becomes transformed into a freight car crammed with Jewish bodies on their way to misery and death. Once again, the memory sneaks up on Nazerman and is then unleashed. This residual image blinds Nazerman to the actual people in the subway train, encapsulating him within a world where he could still feel something, even if only pain. Nazerman is increasingly unhinged by these vivid ghosts, to the point that he vainly challenges Rodriguez to kill him. The next best thing is a return to the past through what is essentially the only *willed* flashback in the film. A pawned butterfly collection engenders the slow-motion scene with which *The Pawnbroker* opened, a flowing recollection of an idyllic moment. This tranquility is shattered by the arrival of three German soldiers – just as, in the film's abrupt return to the present, the daydream is brutally interrupted by the entrance of three thieves. This parallel foreshadows that Nazerman will once again be forced to observe the murder of someone close to him: in this case, Jesús is accidentally shot while trying to save his employer. Numb and impotent, Nazerman can only open his mouth in a scream. No sound emerges.

The mute scream can be seen as the emblem of the Holocaust survivor, the witness of a horror so devastating that it cannot be told. The silent scream might also be the helpless reaction to continued anti-Semitism, as illustrated by the client who calls him a "money-grubbing kike." The intercuts of black neighbors staring indifferently from windows heighten the dissociation between Nazerman and a world that remains ignorant of his tale. Earlier in the film, one of the hooligans had asked him where he got the tattoo on his arm, but the pawnbroker could give no answer. How could he ever explain that this number was carved into his flesh to establish that he was no longer a human being but merely a statistic on its way to extermination? Subsequently, Jesús asks him if the number means he belongs to a secret society, and if so, what does one have to do to join. "Learn to walk on water," Nazerman cryptically replies.

Furthermore, Nazerman's soundless grimace expresses his essential isolation, as if acknowledging that a scream would not reach human ears anyway. *The Pawnbroker* supports this notion by presenting New York City as an urban jungle where people look at one another without seeing. Nazerman is not the only passerby who simply walks past the group of kids beating up a black boy; in the subway car, there is no communication among the passengers; and when he walks through the empty city at dawn, the pawnbroker is dwarfed by large, gray, impersonal structures.

In this dehumanized context, Nazerman's attempt to express his pain ultimately shows his inheritance of a Nazi concept: he wounds himself, rendering flesh a mere object. With his hand slowly descending onto the spike that holds pawn tickets, Nazerman turns his body into a receipt. Religious overtones aside, this excruciating shot conveys how Nazerman's need to feel can be realized only through physical pain. Here, the soundtrack insists on dissociation once more, for instead of a scream, we hear Quincy Jones's jazz score. Nazerman's self-inflicted wound makes concrete one of the film's central themes: survivor guilt. As another survivor points out, he identifies with those who died; when Miss Birchfield asks Nazerman what happened twenty-five years ago, he answers: "I didn't die. Everything I loved was taken away from me and I did not die. There was nothing I could do. Nothing." Nazerman is caught not only between heartless exploiters and oppressed neighbors, but between the dead and the living, between exterminated Jews and manipulative blacks. As a Holocaust survivor, he carries the memory of his murdered family inside him, a living corpse unable to create a new life. By the end of the film, he is a broken pawn.

The narrative structure of *The Pawnbroker* is shared by *High Street* (*Rue Haute*), directed in 1976 by André Ernotte from a screenplay by Ernotte and Elliot Tiber.

This Belgian film takes its tone from the continual utterance of its central character, Mimi (Annie Cordy) – a scream of pain that never really coheres into meaning. Like Nazerman, Mimi is internally disfigured by an ineradicable memory: one night during World War II, her Jewish husband, David (Claude Batelle), was taken away by the Nazis, and when she ran after him to the departing bus, their only child was accidentally killed. This information is conveyed in brief flashbacks that give form to Mimi's involuntary recollections. The camera thus becomes an interpreter of her cry, communicating visually that which she cannot articulate. Unlike Nazerman, however, Mimi is less a "survivor" than a "witness" – a non-Jew who was not personally victimized. Mimi's testimony does not indict Nazi cruelty as much as Belgian indifference.

Unlike the sweetly aggressive Jesús, who is sacrificed at the end of *The Pawnbroker,* the relatively innocent outsider in *High Street* is an arrogant, womanizing, overweight painter whose sole redeeming quality seems to be his compulsion to help Mimi. This American-Jewish expatriate, David Reinhardt, is played by singer-composer Mort Shuman (best known for his performance in *Jacques Brel Is Alive and Well*) with alternating stupor and frenzy. He arrives in contemporary Brussels for a gallery exhibition of his abstract art. When he continually notices Mimi shouting at every bus and verbally assaulting innocent bystanders, he becomes increasingly obsessed with her suffering. He tries to penetrate the solipsistic existence she shares with a protective and sullen man (Burt Struys), but they resist his overtures. Haunted by her enormous eyes that have clearly seen too much, David paints this impenetrable woman until his exhibition consists solely of her image. The gallery opening – with its chic patrons who are simply curious to divine the model's identity – points to a chilling and perhaps self-referential problem: even "honest" art that conveys the horror born of the Holocaust can become merely a titillating diversion for bored, amoral consumers.

Their ultimate indifference to the source of Mimi's searing expression is consistent with responses in other scenes. Mimi tries to stop people from going into a church, screaming, "There's no God in there!" Embarrassed but nonplused, the good Christians enter. Mimi consequently sneaks into the church, climbs to a pulpit, and yells at the assemblage, "They did nothing!" The final flashback reveals that her cry refers to the neighbors – and the priest – who did not lift a hand against the Nazis who rounded up the Jews. Once David understands the root of Mimi's torment, he undergoes a transformation of identity and assumes her burden. Instead of painting on canvas, he finally pounds on glass, shouting obscenities at strangers in a bus. As he smacks the window of the vehicle, the screen becomes this window. It is therefore the audience that is meant to receive his blows on the other side of the glass. David – and the film – ultimately point an accusing finger at all of us, at our capacity for indifference.

Like the relatively sane characters in Ingmar Bergman films such as *Persona* and *Hour of the Wolf,* David succumbs to the "mad" figure: he is overtaken by the stronger personality that has recognized evil. The subjective hand-held shots at the end of *High Street* externalize his skewed perception, inherited from Mimi. Why should this egotistical American artist be subject to her influence? Perhaps the answer – and one of the keys to the film – can be found in her companion's claim that David wants to purge his *own* guilt by helping Mimi. What guilt? we may ask. That of being an affluent, assimilated, arrogant American Jew, spared by

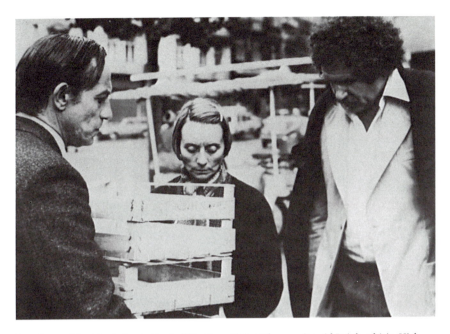

Burt Struys (The Man), Annie Cordy (Mimi), and Mort Shuman (David Reinhardt) in *High Street*. PHOTO COURTESY OF ELLIOT TIBER

the accident of geography? Survival guilt is indeed one of the central (if unstated) themes of *High Street,* beginning with this mysterious companion whom Mimi reviles even as he protects her. The last flashback, accompanied by the man's explanatory voice-over to David, contains numerous close-ups of a young German soldier who watched without expression as Mimi's husband was led away by the armed men in black leather. "I couldn't forget her screams," he says to David – revealing that he is this German who returned after the war to make it up to her. It is clear enough that he has spent the past twenty years paying for his Nazi allegiance; less clear are David's reasons for such frenzied compassion – as well as Mimi's for never mentioning her child. The blocked memory of the boy being knocked down by the butt of a gun while she was blindly pummeling a soldier is revealed only through the companion's tale. The name Mimi cannot utter is the child's, and the pivotal relationship of the film substitutes David the son for David the husband. This also shifts the impulse of the film from victimization to guilt, and from being enslaved by a brutal past to struggling within and against an indifferent present.

Nevertheless, *High Street* is not as successful as *The Pawnbroker* in establishing a troubling actuality. Its secondary characters, such as the marginal types at the local bar, are predominantly benign, and there is little concrete arena for indictment. Whereas the flashbacks in *The Pawnbroker* connect Nazi behavior with its potential manifestations in New York City, Ernotte's montage simply expresses Mimi's inner hell. For her, a group of harmless children barging into the apartment touches off a disproportionately frightening replay of the Nazis in black leather coats bursting into her home thirty years earlier. Each passing bus becomes the vehicle that never

David tries to help Mimi
in *High Street.*

brought her husband back. This is not to say that *High Street* is not effective in moving the viewer with Mimi's harrowing tale; the flashbacks are indeed central to a film in which the heroine incarnates the persistence of memory. But the final image of the film reflects – and elicits – helpless anger, with an abrasive madman on one side, and not-altogether-guilty spectators on the other. Must the viewer extend the closing rhythm with a breast-beating mea culpa? After all, those buying tickets to see *High Street* are probably not the indifferent masses that the film attacks.

If the outsider in *The Pawnbroker* and *High Street* is a secondary character who hovers like a moth around the flame of the traumatized protagonist, in *Sophie's Choice* (1982) he is more centrally the teller of the tale and the eventual lover of the heroine. Neither the film – intelligently scripted and directed by Alan J. Pakula – nor William Styron's already classic novel purport to be about the Holocaust; indeed, the story of Sophie is told – and mediated – by the obtrusive narration of Stingo, an aspiring Southern writer played by Peter MacNicol, with the voice-over of Josef Somer as the older Stingo. As Pakula told *Cahiers du Cinéma* in 1982,

> we must not forget that the book is written in a perfectly classic narrative style, like a 19th-century novel. And I've got that. One of the first lines in the book, "Call me Stingo," is a reference to the first line of *Moby Dick,* "Call me Ishmael." And this fits right into that 19th-century tradition – a young man encountering good and evil, love and death.[1]

Consequently, the play of memory (or subjectivity, to be more precise) exists on two levels: Stingo's voice engenders images of his coming of age in 1947 Brooklyn, while Sophie's voice in 1947 conjures up scenes of her own rites of passage – including Auschwitz. The latter begins one hour and twenty minutes into the film, and lasts only about half an hour. Nevertheless, her gripping flashbacks serve as the heart of *Sophie's Choice*, providing a measure for all its ensuing experiences.

Stingo recounts the love affair between Sophie (Meryl Streep), a Polish-Catholic survivor of Auschwitz, and Nathan (Kevin Kline), a volatile New York Jew obsessed with Nazis. These sequences are shot in vibrant color, and the typically brilliant camera work of Nestor Almendros includes exhilarating shots as the trio cavorts in an amusement park. That Coney Island and Auschwitz are two different worlds is expressed by the difference in visual texture: the harrowing sequences in the ghetto and the concentration camp are in desaturated color, which distances the viewer. The lack of vivid color suggests life drained of vitality – at least for the prisoners: in a particularly memorable shot, as Sophie first enters Commandant Rudolf Hoess's house, where she will work as a secretary, Almendros's camera rises above her monochromatic world to reveal the commandant's lush garden. They coexist within the frame – hinting at the paradoxical nature of this domicile's inhabitants: in a different time and place, they might have been a sympathetic bourgeois family. Not completely insensitive to Sophie's plight, Hoess is shown in the throes of a malaise that overtakes him; Frau Hoess tries to be a good wife and mother, worrying about her husband's being demoted; and in a suspenseful scene, their daughter is on the verge of denouncing Sophie for stealing a radio, but shows off her photo album to the prisoner instead. Nevertheless, this household is a temporary respite, for just outside the commandant's gate – just beyond the garden – Sophie's gray limbo awaits her return.

On an aural level, inside the commandant's house the characters speak German, whereas with other Poles Sophie speaks Polish. Unlike most American films about the Holocaust, *Sophie's Choice* preserves authenticity by subtitling judiciously rather than reducing dialogue to Hollywood English. An advantage of this can be seen when Sophie speaks furtively with a fellow Pole in Hoess's house: despite the elder servant's sternness, their immediate complicity is established by the shared language. The soundtrack is likewise superior to typically melodramatic Hollywood music. Marvin Hamlisch's haunting score is used with subtlety: there is no music during the stark black-and-white opening credits, and the soaring love theme enters only when Nathan comes upon Sophie, picking her up from the library floor where she has fainted. During the World War II sections, we hear a flute-like sound; it is subsequently revealed as originating within the story when we see Sophie's daughter playing a recorder. A gentle flute melody returns in the climactic final scene of Stingo's return to the Brooklyn boarding house where he will say farewell to the lovers: it not only serves as a counterpoint to the dramatic tension of the couple's joint suicide, but links these deaths to that of her daughter.

Alan Pakula had already proved with *All the President's Men* that he was capable of treating potentially sensational material with an unobtrusive style that allowed the story to tell itself. In *Sophie's Choice*, once again, integrity and truthfulness result from his decisions. One of these was to refuse when asked to give *Sophie's Choice* a happy ending.[2] Another was to have each extended flashback preceded and punctuated by an extreme close-up of Sophie's face, tremulous and slightly inebriated, reminding the viewer of whose subjective version of the past is being reenacted. And by working with Almendros for polished but unselfconscious images, he permitted Streep's face to become an exquisitely expressive landscape. Even the casting process – which took almost two years – attests to Pakula's sensitive decision making: he searched for an Eastern European actress who would be physically and linguistically right, and his assistant, Doug Wick, scoured Europe to find potential performers. He eventually came upon a young actress named Magda Vasaryova, but in the meantime, Andrzej Wajda had suggested to Pakula an actress he had directed at the Yale Repertory Theater a few years before: Meryl Streep. Pakula waited for her to complete filming of *The French Lieutenant's Woman* and then waited a few more months as she took Polish lessons. (For the French release, Streep even insisted on doing her own dubbing, studying tapes of Polish-accented French.)

The resulting film has been questioned – by Elie Wiesel, among others[3] – but more because of the moral discomfort inherent in the novel's premise than for the film itself: it universalizes the Holocaust by eliciting sympathy for a survivor in the form of a "lying Polish shiksa" who happened to be beautiful and multilingual enough to live through Auschwitz – as opposed to a heroine who would have been Jewish or in the Resistance. Others have asked whether it is proper to use the Holocaust as a backdrop for Stingo's coming of age (obviously as Styron's mouthpiece). To the degree that people who never had contact with the Holocaust should know about it if they are to grow into civilized and lucid beings, it seems right that *Sophie's Choice* is Stingo's story. The film acknowledges that it is only the survivor who can recount the horrors of Auschwitz, but that it requires an outsider's sympathetic understanding and chronicling ability to give the recollections universal significance and immortality. More than in *The Pawnbroker* or *High Street,* the survivor succeeds in transmitting her tale and – at least temporarily – in overcoming her guilt. Pakula offers us a continually close-up and consequently sympathetic view of Sophie, and despite his distanced style, one senses that he added a personal dimension to the story of Stingo-Styron: As he told the *New York Times,* "My father was a Polish Jew. If he hadn't come to this country, Sophie's story could have been my own."[4]

It is no surprise that one of the films Pakula studied while writing the script for *Sophie's Choice* was *Night and Fog,* still the most powerful film on the concentration-camp experience. Directed by Alain Resnais in 1955, *Night and Fog* is a film whose very shape challenges existing visual language, mainly through an editing style that both reflects and elicits tension. Whether the counterpoint is between image and sound, past and present, stasis and movement, despair and hope, black-and-white and color, or oblivion and memory, Resnais's film addresses the audience's intelligence – and moves beyond a facile stimulation of helpless tears. As François Truffaut pointed out:

> It is almost impossible to speak about this film in the vocabulary of cinematic criticism. It is not a documentary, or an indictment, or a poem, but a meditation on the most important phenomenon of the twentieth century.... The power of this film...is rooted in its tone, the *terrible gentleness....* When we have looked at these strange, seventy-pound slave laborers, we understand that we're not going to "feel better" after seeing *Nuit et Brouillard;* quite the opposite.[5]

Night and Fog begins with a long tracking shot of a peaceful landscape in color. As the camera glides across the grass, the narration, written by survivor Jean Cayrol, introduces the locale – Auschwitz – a façade whose present calm seems to deny its ineradicable ghosts. Simultaneously, the music of Hanns Eisler (a German composer who was himself driven from his country by Hitler's rise to power) laces the scene with a certain delicacy that will become increasingly contrapuntal as the images cut into the horrific past. Our auditory guides carry us into newsreel footage and documentary stills whose black-and-white graininess contrasts with the scenes in color. Moreover, the serene landscape gives way to harsh images of sealed freight cars and barbed wire that signify the arrival of Auschwitz's victims. The camera moving inside the abandoned structures of the concentration camp often stops, acknowledging its own limitations with a cut to a black-and-white still; while confronting and investigating, this fluid camera suggests transience, or the license of smooth mobility that can exist only after the fact. Opposing itself to the rigidity of death captured by the newsreels, Resnais's camera glides past the now empty barracks and crematoria until it can go no further, arrested by haunting photographs.

At these moments, the voice (of actor Michel Bouquet) quietly recalls, probes, offers statistics, and bears witness – all with an admirable lack of emotionalism. (Contrast this with Richard Widmark's histrionic verbal accompaniment to some of the same archival footage in *Judgment at Nuremberg*'s courtroom.) The voice lets the images speak for themselves, illustrating the crucial lesson of restraint that Resnais might have learned from cinema master Jean Renoir: "The more emotional the material, the less emotional the treatment." Likewise, the music invites a more complex response because, according to Resnais, "the more violent the images, the gentler the music." Unlike the pounding dramatic orchestral scores exemplified by Carlo Rustichelli's music for Gillo Pontecorvo's *Kapo* (1960), "Eisler wanted to show that hope always existed in the background," claimed Resnais.

Among other things, the soundtrack enables us to look at unbearable newsreels, such as living skeletons being prepared for hospital experiments. Cayrol's commentary takes into account the audience's predictable difficulty at seeing such horror. For example, it breaks off from its presentation of the gas chamber ceiling clawed by victims' fingernails, insisting, "but you have to know." The stuttering montage is similarly appropriate to sentences that can be completed only with difficulty:

These are the storehouses of the Nazis at war,
nothing but women's hair . . .
At fifteen pennies per kilo . . .
It is used for cloth.

With the bones . . .
fertilizer. At least they try.

With the bodies . . . but no more can be said . . .
With the bodies, they try to make . . .
soap.

As for the skin . . .[6]

The accompanying images render further narration superfluous.

Resnais's revelatory camera is restricted to surfaces, requiring testimony from the past to complete the picture. The vacant images of the ovens are brutally defined by black-and-white photos, and montage activates the silent railroad tracks covered with green grass into sputtering newsreels of transports. The "picture postcard" becomes a stark nightmare, as *Night and Fog* assumes the function of an X-ray: through the spine of documentary footage and Cayrol's calmly vigilant meditation, we are forced to see the deformities hidden from the unaided eye (and camera), and to struggle against the imperturbability of surfaces. "Who is responsible?" asks the narrator, after a wordless presentation of soap and lampshades made from human skin.

The alternation of history and immediacy insists upon responsibility, whether for those during World War II who were responsible *for* the Holocaust, or those today who are responsible *to* it. The quiet landscape of postwar Auschwitz is deceptive, as the narrator insists:

> War slumbers, with one eye always open. . . . Who among us watches over this strange observatory to warn of the new executioners' arrival? Are their faces really different from ours? . . . We look at these ruins as if the old concentration camp monster were dead under the debris . . . we who pretend to believe that all this happened in one time and one place, and who do not think to look around us, or hear the endless cry.

Night and Fog fulfills what the critic and filmmaker Eric Rohmer once said about Resnais – that he is a cubist because he reconstitutes reality after fragmenting it. The effect is not only opposition, but a deeper unity in which past and present blend into each other.

Les Violons du bal (literally "The Violins of the Ball" but released in the United States under its French title) reverses part of the visual premise of *Night and Fog* by shooting present-day scenes in black-and-white, and the past in color. This is a revealing decision on the part of filmmaker Michel Drach, suggesting that his memories are more vibrantly compelling than his contemporary existence. In this 1973 movie, Drach plays himself, a forty-four-year-old French director attempting to make an autobiographical film about his family's struggle for survival during the Occupation. He screen-tests and casts his nine-year-old son David as himself in 1939, and his wife (Marie-José Nat) as his mother. When he tries to sell the idea to a weighty producer, the commercially minded moneyman dismisses the project: "Nobody's interested in the past." The bearded and leather-jacketed Drach obsessively continues seeking actors and locations. For instance, he stops an old woman (Gabrielle Doulcet) emerging from the Metro at the Cirque d'Hiver; a few sequences later, in the film's past tense, this woman will play his grandmother.

The degree to which the director's imagination colors and overtakes the present is shown in the circus itself. As his wife does her spinning act, black-and-white occasionally yields to color, reflecting Drach's subjective vision. The color persists as we then see the little boy Michel in the circus. Similarly, while Drach rides a motorcycle through contemporary Paris, he passes a big old car and stares at it intently: suddenly the car is in a color scene during the war, driven by his wife/mother. The fluidity of his mental shifts in time is expressed by color fading gently in and out as his wife tries on a wig for her role. Drach's enthusiasm, however, does not infect the producer, who continues to shrug at his material and insists, "No stars, no

David Drach (Michel) and
Marie-José Nat (Mother) in *Les
Violons du bal.*
PHOTO COURTESY OF
LEVITT-PICKMAN FILM
CORPORATION

film." A deft piece of editing solves the problem: Drach momentarily bows his head in frustration under his notebook, and the face that reappears is that of Jean-Louis Trintignant, a famous French actor. The transfer of identity between Drach and Trintignant is cleverly literalized when the actor gets on a moving escalator, walking backward on a forward track (like the movement of the film's action). On a parallel escalator, Drach hands Trintignant the key to his apartment. Multiple mirrors give the impression that the two figures converge into one at the center of the screen before Drach gets off the escalator – leaving Trintignant to move forward.

Les Violons du bal proceeds into sustained color sequences set in 1939, in which Michel, his mother, grandmother, brother Jean (Christian Rist), and sister Nathalie (Nathalie Roussel) are uprooted and forced to leave Paris. Lighthearted and affluent, the family changes homes, names, and identities. Jean disappears to join his father in the underground; Nathalie – rejected by her wealthy Gentile fiancé's mother because of her religion – becomes a model in occupied Paris; as the situation grows increasingly dangerous for Jews, Michel is sent off to the country to spend a few months with a farmer's family. His mother and grandmother finally retrieve him, having arranged an escape into Switzerland. The supposedly good-hearted farmer, Monsieur Robert (Paul Le Person), leads them around in circles and takes their money, leaving the three refugees on their own to make a run for the border. Losing all their possessions along the way, they succeed in slipping through the fence just before German bullets can reach them.

This tale of suspense and sentiment is framed and punctuated by the realities of its cinematic fabrication. The effects of intercutting the present are twofold, suggesting a (perhaps forced) analogy between the Nazi era and the turbulent events of May 1968, and acknowledging the indifference of producers to a Holocaust memoir that contains neither sex nor violence. Student demonstrations in black-and-white are juxtaposed with color shots of the Occupation, and when Trintignant takes his car from the garage, a bloodied protester lurks in the shadows. He is the same actor who played Jean earlier, and the crosscutting of this brother in the pastel past with the student in the grainy present implies either of two things: that this boy will play Jean in the film being made; or that the director helps the demonstrator because he reminds him of his brother. The parallel is developed when Monsieur Robert smuggles young Michel to the country while, in the present, Trintignant smuggles the demonstrator to Lyons. Although this equation ultimately cheapens the unique persecution inflicted by the Holocaust, it insists upon the degree to which the director's actions – and social conscience – are rooted in World War II.

More realistic is the reaction of the second producer – an Italian who proclaims proudly, "I promoted Mussolini" – when he sees the rushes midway through: he asks when they will film the sex part, and how many people die. "My characters don't die," says Trintignant with restrained fervor. "A dead Jew might sell," muses the producer, "but a live Jew – impossible." At the end of the film, this producer appraises the rushes with the comment, "It has the makings of a film." Trintignant's response, "But it *is* a film," means not only that *Les Violons du Bal* is completed, but that the film we are watching is not to be confused with reality. His cinematic exclamation point is to clap the clapboard before his face, acknowledging that the subject of the shot – and the film – is the director. This cinematic self-consciousness (or honesty) is appropriate to *Les Violons du Bal,* for it locates the action firmly within Drach's personal recollections. It affirms his mediating presence as image maker (worthy of the cousin of director Jean-Pierre Melville and former assistant to Jean Cocteau). Whereas a straightforward account of the past would have enclosed and sealed it, Drach's intrusive montage extends the Holocaust experience into the present.

Less than ten years later, it became easier for Jacques Rouffio to make a film about a Jew – *La Passante du Sans Souci* (1982) – using at least three of Drach's elements: the crosscutting of past and present, the use of an actress in two roles, and the establishment of a political link between the Holocaust and contemporary forms of fascism. Less formally interesting than *Les Violons du bal,* perhaps the film was facilitated by the fact that it was a vehicle for Romy Schneider (and would turn out to be her last performance before her death), as well as an adaptation of a novel by the noted writer Joseph Kessel. *La Passante du Sans Souci* is a fine tearjerker – a bit excessive in its melodrama but obviously well-intentioned. It begins with Max (Michel Piccoli), a wealthy Swiss Jew who heads Solidarité Internationale. This nonprofit organization is devoted to fighting oppression and aiding political prisoners. When visiting the ambassador from Paraguay (Mathieu Carrière), Max recognizes him as the former Nazi who exploited and destroyed his foster parents during the war. Despite his hatred of political violence, Max kills him and subsequently stands trial in a series of courtroom scenes that include flashbacks to his childhood in Nazi Germany.

Schneider plays his wife, Lina, in the present, and Elsa – the wife of a German resister – in the past. As with Michael York in *Au nom de tous les miens,* there is actually no compelling dramatic reason for using one actress in both roles, beyond the obvious point that Max would fall in love with a woman who resembled his martyred guardian. Schneider is, nevertheless, luminous in both tenses. As Elsa, she saves young Max when the SA beat him and kill his father (in a powerfully graphic scene). She takes him to Paris, where she survives by singing in a sleazy cabaret, and is then killed by the German ambassador (a younger Carrière), who seemed to be in love with her. The present-day tale has a far more upbeat ending: Max is acquitted and reunited with Lina. *La Passante du Sans Souci* thus insists on the continuity between Nazis and contemporary oppressors, as well as on the anti-Nazi struggle, which takes a new form today. Since both men whom Elsa/Lina loves fight governmentally authorized torturers, past and present are linked not only by romance but by the continual struggle that must be waged against fascism.

3
Styles of Tension

M ontage is not the only way for a filmmaker to create tension; the Holocaust experience can be expressed or approached through disorienting camera angles and movement, heightened lighting, distorting visual texture or color, stylized acting, contrapuntal soundtrack or music, and unconventional narrative structure. Films as seemingly disparate as *The Serpent's Egg, Cabaret, Kanal, Ambulance, Passenger, The Boxer and Death, Commissar,* and *Wherever You Are* proceed via dislocation and discomfort, refusing to simplify or prettify painful reality through filters. They suggest that the shocking dimensions of the Holocaust demand stylistic devices of disturbance rather than complacency.

The Serpent's Egg (1977) is not a pleasing film. Ingmar Bergman's English-language study of pre-Nazi Germany is morbid, depressing, and relentless in its tone of paranoia and inescapability. Through the relationship of an unemployed and alcoholic circus acrobat and a cabaret singer, the film presents three ominous aspects of 1923 Berlin: anti-Semitism; a ravaged economy; and scientific curiosity gone wild, severed from moral considerations. The serpent is an ancient animal; likewise, Nazism did not simply hatch: it was nurtured by historical antecedents, both economic and psychological. Beyond the story, however, Bergman weaves into *The Serpent's Egg* a troubled self-consciousness, questioning his own cinematic methods and purposes. By incorporating the films of a mad scientist within *The Serpent's Egg,* the director invites comparison between his images and those recorded by this chilling character.

Abel Rosenberg (David Carradine) is an American Jew – thus doubly an outsider in Berlin – who finds his brother Max dead in their hotel room. He informs Max's ex-wife, Manuela (Liv Ullmann), that Max shot his brains out. The singer, distraught and naïvely generous, takes Abel into her apartment. Abel is questioned by an Inspector Bauer (Gert Frobe), who asks him if he is Jewish. The importance of his religion is developed in the next scene when Abel's former circus boss takes him to an elegant restaurant: he reads from a German newspaper the kind of anti-Semitic propaganda that began appearing regularly in publications like *Der Stürmer* in 1923. Abel doesn't believe "all the political crap," and claims that Jews get into trouble because they "act

Joel Grey (the MC) in *Cabaret.*
PHOTO COURTESY OF MUSEUM OF MODERN ART/FILM STILLS ARCHIVE

stupid" – unlike himself. It doesn't take long for the impoverished alcoholic to "act stupid" indeed, as when he rails at Bauer, "You're holding me because I'm a Jew" before attempting a futile escape. Manuela's cabaret is raided by armed thugs – probably members of the SA, the storm troopers of the early Nazi party, organized in 1921 – who announce that "the sadistic filth" onstage is "part of the Jewish conspiracy." They beat the Jewish director's head to a bloody pulp before setting fire to the cabaret.

Manuela's sole remaining job is in a clinic where Hans (Heinz Bennent), a scientist they have known since childhood, performs suspicious experiments. She gets Abel a job in the archives and they move to an apartment in the clinic, trying to survive the rampant inflation and susceptibility to illness. When Abel finds Manuela dead and realizes that their life in the apartment had been constantly watched and recorded by unseen cameras as part of experiments, he breaks through the walls – behind the façade of the clinic – where Hans calmly awaits him. The elegant doctor projects (both in the present and into the future) for Abel his films of drug-induced human suffering: "In a few years, science will ask for these documents and continue on a gigantic scale," he proclaims. A pre-Mengele figure, Hans predicts the ripening of Nazism: "You can see the future like a serpent's egg. Through the thin membrane, you can clearly discern the already perfect reptile."

The bleak socioeconomic conditions presented by Bergman convey the sense of a hopeless people. German marks are so devalued that their worth is a function of the paper's weight.[1] Meat is so scarce that a dead horse in the street is cut up and sold still dripping blood; Abel wakes up at 4:00 A.M. and observes silent bodies lining up for bread or boarding buses for work. His response, "I wake up from a nightmare and find the real world worse than the dream," is characteristic of the entire film, as each scene grows progressively darker. "Go to hell," he tells a young prostitute who invites his dollars in. "Where do you think we are?" she answers with a jeer. Religion, too, is impotent in this setting, as illustrated by Manuela's visit to a priest (James Whitmore) for solace. As in other Bergman films, from *Through a Glass Darkly* to *Winter Light*, there is no balm for human suffering. The priest begs Manuela's forgiveness for his apathy and indifference, proposing, "We must give each other the forgiveness that a remote God denies us." By the end of the film, however, the combined physical and spiritual poverty has led people to sell themselves as human guinea pigs for Hans's experiments, abandoning all claims to dignity.

The Serpent's Egg's acknowledgment of anti-Semitism and economic devastation grounds Bergman's story in historical antecedents to Nazism, but its resonance comes from a self-conscious style that heightens the material. The film opens with a silent, black-and-white image of a crowd. In slow motion, the people move with desolate faces. A sudden cut to the opening credits is accompanied by upbeat music of the 1920s. When the crowd in slow motion returns a few moments later, there is once again silence. The persistent juxtaposition of the two modes introduces an uneasy relationship between the seen and the heard: the jazzy sound cannot coexist with the black-and-white image. And the self-conscious alternation announces that the film is a mediator rather than recorder of history – not unlike the celebrated opening of Bergman's *Persona*, which calls attention to the celluloid and projector as characters in the ensuing drama.

This exploration of the film's materials and effects is developed in the last part of the film, after Abel finds Manuela dead. A camera takes a picture of his reaction, leading Abel to break all three mirrors – each of which was a one-way window concealing a movie camera. He enters the world the film came from, following the celluloid into the bowels of the clinic. There he finds the master "filmmaker" Hans, whose black-and-white cinematic documents prove far more bloodcurdling

David Carradine (Abel) and Liv Ullmann (Manuela) in *The Serpent's Egg*.
PHOTOS COURTESY OF CARLOS CLARENS

than anything in Bergman's stylized universe. The first film he proudly shows Abel traces the disintegration of a young mother locked in a cell with her infant who (through drugs) never stops crying. After twenty-four hours, maternal sympathy is replaced by anguish and guilt. Ultimately, she kills her child. Another film records a man who, after an injection of thanatoxide, feels as if his flesh is being torn apart – and kills himself. (Hans confesses that Max died in the same manner.) Finally, Hans shows Abel a man and woman under the effects of "Carter Blue" – alternately depressed, hostile, and tender – looking exactly like Abel himself and Manuela in an earlier scene.

Throughout this diabolical display, there are intercuts of the projector and flashing lights that suggest the degree to which it, and its contents, can be instruments of cruel voyeurism. (Indeed, Hans's identity as a voyeur is set up by the way Bergman introduces him: at the cabaret, he watches the show from the side, unseen by the performers.) Hans's last film is the same as *The Serpent's Egg*'s opening – the sad crowd in slow motion. This coinciding of Bergman's image and Hans's record is deliberately ambiguous: do both "directors" force human beings to portray agony in the service of something beyond themselves? or is Bergman contrasting Hans's coldly captured images with his own sensitizing techniques?

This time, Hans provides a soundtrack for the silent group, as his voice-over predicts that, in ten years, there will be a revolution and they will use the hatred inherited from their parents. "Someone will make demands on them. Our world will go down in blood and fire." This is just after Hitler's failed Putsch; the irony is therefore that Hans's prediction will come true, but *not* with a new leader. The "demanding" figure will simply take further Hans's position: "We exterminate what is inferior and develop what is useful." The culmination of Hans's scientific voyeurism

David Carradine (Abel) in *The Serpent's Egg.* PHOTO COURTESY OF CARLOS CLARENS

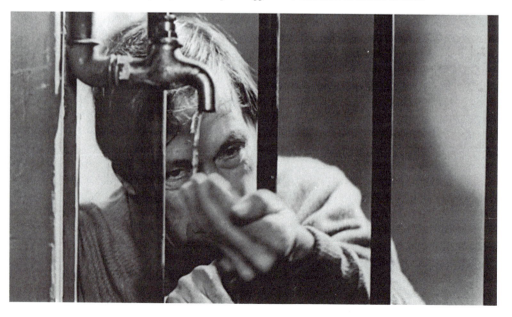

Liv Ullmann (Manuela) and David Carradine (Abel) in *The Serpent's Egg*.
PHOTO COURTESY OF CARLOS CLARENS

occurs when he swallows cyanide and grabs a mirror to watch his own death. His parting statement about seeing the future "like a serpent's egg" takes on another meaning, for the "membrane" can also refer to the celluloid: close-ups of the film stock do allow us to see outlines "of the future." Nevertheless, it is really the past; the result is a dizzying timelessness, which is appropriate to the notion of the serpent – of anti-Semitism – and of cinema.

Why all this cinematic self-consciousness? Perhaps, as in *Persona*, Bergman's aim is to guard against facile identification on the part of the viewer, and emotional manipulation on the part of the filmmaker. Intercuts of projectors and celluloid make us aware of the machines that determine our perception, distancing us from the action even while acknowledging their modus operandi. This seems particularly appropriate to the subject, for Bergman refuses to let the audience do what the Germans did: to get swept up in an emotional surge that ultimately suspends judgment and morality. Making his first film in the land of Bertolt Brecht, Bergman distances us from the horror at the same time that he forces us to look at its methods.

Surprisingly enough, one of the most successful American films in portraying the rise of Nazim is a musical, *Cabaret*. Directed by Bob Fosse in 1972, it is entertaining, engrossing, and ultimately chilling in its stylized tableaux of spreading swastikas. The credits unfold over a dark background which gradually comes into focus (like the film's concerns), a distorted mirror that reflects the cabaret clientele as a grotesque Grosz-like grouping. It is 1931 in Berlin, and into this eerie looking glass pops the painted face of the Master of Ceremonies (Joel Grey) – our depraved guide, our disturbing narrator. His first song, "Willkommen," welcomes the viewer as well as the patrons of the Kit-Kat Club, making us part of the audience in and out of the cabaret. In narrative terms, it welcomes the British student Brian (Michael York) to Berlin, where he takes a room across the hall from Sally Bowles (Liza Minnelli), an outrageous young American who sings at the cabaret. She bowls over the shy English tutor, who finally falls in love with the vulnerable waif that exists under Sally's flamboyantly decadent surface. Concurrently, one of Brian's pupils, Fritz (Fritz Wepper), is entranced by another student, the wealthy Jewess Natalia Landauer (Marisa Berenson). The musical numbers within the Kit-Kat Club reflect, comment upon, and often parody the growing influence of the Nazis.

Sally meets Maximilian von Heune (Helmut Griem), an aristocratic German who showers gifts upon the delighted singer and her less-acquiescent boyfriend, Brian. As Stanley Kauffmann said of *Jules and Jim*, the isosceles triangle becomes equilateral: "Screw Max!" yells Brian. "I do," responds Sally. "Well, so do I" is Brian's topper. Max thinks that the Nazis are "just hooligans" who are serving a purpose by ridding Germany of Communists, but a scene in a beer garden reveals their wide-ranging support as a crowd of ordinary-looking people joins in the singing of a Nazi song. While the situation for Jews worsens, Natalia refuses to marry Fritz – until he confesses that he is Jewish too. Brian asks the pregnant Sally to marry him, but she realizes their life as a couple is doomed and decides to have an abortion instead. The Nazi-hating Englishman leaves Germany for home, and Sally remains at the cabaret. The

Joel Grey (the MC) in *Cabaret.* PHOTO COURTESY OF MUSEUM OF MODERN ART/FILM STILLS ARCHIVE

last image is the misshapen mirror of the first shot, now reflecting a profusion of swastika armbands on Nazi patrons.

The distorted reflection corresponds to *Cabaret*'s musical numbers, which are consistently crosscut with the reality outside. By juxtaposing a production number in which the MC playfully slaps the chorines with the image of Nazis beating up the club's owner, Fosse insists on the cabaret as stylized microcosm rather than escape. Do the numbers neutralize the horror or heighten it? When the MC dabs a bit of mud under his nose like Hitler's mustache, is the character winking at the Führer's supporters or debasing Hitler? In any case, the crosscutting distances us from emotional identification with victimization and invites an intellectual appreciation of both the historical picture and its translation into spectacle. For example, the MC sings, "If You Could See Her through My Eyes" – declaring his love for a woman in a gorilla costume – after Nazis have painted the word "Jew" on the Landauers' doorstep and killed Natalia's dog. The number ends with the MC's conspiratorial whisper, "If you could see her through my eyes – she wouldn't look Jewish at all!"

The only musical sequence that does not take place inside the cabaret, and is not developed by parallel montage, is the seminal number in the beer garden. Fosse begins with a close-up of an angelic-looking boy singing "Tomorrow Belongs to Me." A tilt downward reveals a uniform and a swastika armband. As the camera moves farther back, it includes other young people standing up to join in the song, and then older German citizens, until a long shot presents a throbbing crowd of incipient Nazis. Brian turns to Maximilian and asks, "Do you still think you can stop them?" The most disturbing element in the scene is Fosse's eschewing of distancing devices: he leaves the audience vulnerable to the emotion of the song, and it is only at the end that we pull back, horrified at the ease with which unified voices can become viscerally seductive. This scene affords an insight into the rise of Nazism, for it is the only number that gives the audience a chance to get into the act. These Germans feel important, part of a movement that offers a hopeful tomorrow. Their insidiously wholesome faces serve as a contrast to the comparatively more harmless decadence in the Kit-Kat Club, for the latter at least allows for liberating irony about the Nazis.

A case in point is the eighth musical number, which plays with various displacements. After presenting a row of chorus girls in pink corsets, the camera pauses on the back of a dancer who turns out to be the MC. The host in drag subsequently turns his hat around so that it becomes a helmet, and the chorines shoulder their canes like rifles. They goose-step about the stage, suggesting a perversity that underlies Nazism; indeed, the overt sexual decadence in the Kit-Kat Club consistently de-eroticizes and depersonalizes (mutually dependent processes). The lewd jokes and abstract female flesh suggest that Nazism is predicated upon a denial of love and sex, a display of flesh to be automatized into parade formation. (Fosse's choreography and constant cuts intensify these impressions by fragmenting the dancers' bodies into often faceless patterns.) If, as Sally's last song puts it, "Life is a cabaret, old chum," the corollary is also true: the cabaret *is* life, but life translated into a spectacular reflection. Like the club's patrons, we enter this musical world to forget about reality, only to find that it cannot be kept outside.

The Polish cinema has proven more brutally direct in its representations of World War II destruction. In particular, Andrzej Wajda's *Kanal* (1957) is a relentlessly harrowing reconstruction of the last part of the Warsaw Uprising. Along with *A Generation* (1955) and *Ashes and Diamonds* (1958), it is the centerpiece of what has come to be known as his war trilogy, a three-part exploration of the possibilities for Polish heroism during and immediately after Nazi oppression. *Kanal* is the darkest of the three, a haunting acknowledgment of the doomed Polish Resistance.

A modern analogue of Dante's *Inferno, Kanal* presents a literal and figurative descent: the film begins with aerial documentary footage of Warsaw in rubble, moves to ground level after the credits, and finally curves underground to the sewers, where the last part of the Uprising actually took place. Shot in the sewers of Warsaw, *Kanal*'s realism of detail is often stomach-churning, as we see the characters wading in excrement. Wajda intensifies the claustrophobia through lighting and camera work: the only illumination in the underworld comes from flashlights or matches – bright dots surrounded by blackness. Moreover, the camera (usually positioned at low angle) not only renders the figures heroic, but makes us feel their entrapment, with the ceilings bearing down on them.

As Chapter 9 will develop, Wajda uses close-ups sparingly, preferring group shots that stress relationships and place the characters within a palpable historical space. Thus, when he finally does make an entire landscape of a face, the effect is gripping. It is appropriate that the most memorable close-up is given to the proud musician (Wladyslaw Szeybal) who joins the Resistance at the last moment and is not an experienced soldier like the others. He begins to go mad in the swirling dark – playing an ocarina as he wanders in the dank mist – and a stark close-up serves to isolate him, expressing his self-enclosure.

Kanal commemorates a hopeless situation, a last stand of martyrs who perished in noxious circumstances. There is no way out but death, as two scenes demonstrate: after Commander Zadra (Wienczyslaw Glinski) emerges into daylight and learns that his company has not followed, he returns to the fatal bowels of the sewers. And when the injured hero Korab (Tadeusz Janczar) and his spunky girlfriend, Daisy (Teresa Izewska), glimpse an exit into the sea, a subjective camera from their point of view leads us to the light with them – only to find the exit barred. This caged portal, in the shape of a headstone, is like an epitaph for the Polish men and women who perished there in 1944.

One of Wajda's assistants on *Kanal* was Janusz Morgenstern, who went on to make his own poignant commemoration of Polish martyrs: *Ambulance* (1962) illustrates how a story can be told cinematically using a minimum of means. Without a word of dialogue, the fifteen-minute film dramatizes an incident with symbolic resonance. A tracking shot on a receding road introduces both a backward glance and a subtle feeling of dislocation because one can't see what lies ahead. The sound of Hitler's ranting yields to a military march, immediately establishing the film's context. As an ambulance stops beyond a fence, we hear the exhaust, whose mechanical exhalation seems to blend with the preceding sounds. A group of children are playing next to the ambulance, watched by a grave-looking man. The first child we see is blindfolded in his game, an appropriate image for their ignorance (and ours) as to the purpose of the ambulance. An SS officer calmly and methodically goes about his work – checking the exhaust valve and accelerator, pouring gasoline, and sealing the carbon monoxide fumes inside the van. The children play more and more apprehensively,

Tadeusz Janczar (Korab) and Teresa Izewska (Daisy) in *Kanal.*
PHOTO COURTESY OF KINO INTERNATIONAL CORPORATION

especially when one little girl is pushed aside by the officer and drops her shoe. The snarling dog held by another officer keeps her – and the serious-looking man – from retrieving it. This image of dispossession is juxtaposed with a shot inside the back of the ambulance as it fills up with dark smoke. By placing the audience in the position that the prisoners will occupy, with the doors banging shut in our faces, the film creates a visceral foreboding.

A boy plays with a flying toy whose ejection into the sky causes the dog to suddenly break from its master. The dog runs after the object as the children are herded into the van. The grave-looking man reassures them as he quietly enters alongside. His last look at life – a long take from his point of view of birds flying – provides a poignant opposition between freedom and the earthly hell of fumes awaiting him and his charges. The dog suddenly reappears, offering the child's shoe to its owner; the doors bang shut upon us and we hear the dog's whimper, presumably after being hit. The ambulance goes on its way with its Red Cross – an insignia of salvation – concealing a mobile gas chamber.

Each carefully composed shot of *Ambulance* suggests rather than states a horrific aspect or moral question of the Holocaust. A knowing leap of the imagination turns the exhaust pipes into crematoria chimneys, and the fenced-in yard into a concentration camp. The dog's reversal leads us to question whether a natural creature is inherently evil, good, or simply dependent on the hand that feeds/strikes him. Along with the murder of innocent children and the helplessness before the implacable machinery of death, the film presents the dilemma of resistance: the teacher figure does not revolt physically, but he does defy the Nazi attempt at dehumanization. By comforting the children, he enacts a resistance of the spirit that renders his death a humane choice. It is probable that this character is based on Janusz Korczak, the Polish teacher, social worker, and author whose heroism during World War II created an enduring legend. His progressive orphanage was relocated within the Warsaw Ghetto, where he fed the children both physically and spiritually. In *The Witnesses* ("Le Temps du Ghetto"), Frédéric Rossif's fine documentary of 1962, a survivor chronicles Korczak's refusal of Nazi mentality: an SS officer offered the teacher his freedom if he would round up the children quietly. Knowing they were bound for the death camp of Treblinka, he replied, "No, I will stay with my children." *Ambulance* leads us to provide our own dialogue – necessarily riddled with questions about what we could or should have done in this man's place. If, as George Steiner claims, "the world of Auschwitz lies outside speech as it lies outside reason,"[2] perhaps it can be touched by images.

The complexity of *Ambulance* is shared by another Polish film of the same year, *Passenger* ("Pasażerka"). It is a challenging film of unresolved tensions partly because its director, Andrzej Munk, died in a car accident in 1961 before completing the film. When his colleagues – especially Witold Lesiewicz – pieced the work together, they built this fact into *Passenger*'s opening, thus asking from the outset, how does one make a film about fragments of the Holocaust? The response is a series of images in at least three tenses – the present, the past, and the conditional (what might have happened) – that pit a German woman's self-justifying recollection of Auschwitz against a more likely account. *Passenger* begins with photographs of Munk while a dispassionate male voice-over explains what happened to the filmmaker. These "real" documents are succeeded by stills from the film he was shooting – frozen images animated by camera movement and the verbal narration. Not wanting to speculate on Munk's answers, "we can succeed only in presenting the questions he wanted to pose," acknowledges the voice.

The story begins "today" on a luxury liner, "a floating island in time" that permits its passengers freedom from biography and society. The woman in the stills is Liza (Aleksandra Slaska), returning to her native Germany with a new husband. Her face grows clenched as she spots Marta (Anna Ciepielewska) boarding at Southampton. Liza's shared and troubling past with this young woman is suggested by the sudden whiteout to an eerie nighttime scene depicting naked women trapped inside a circle of dressed women, with dogs barking nearby. Quick shots of a number being tattooed on an arm and heads being shorn establish the concentration camp origin of Liza's memories. The tattoo, followed by a shot of her husband's hand on her arm, prepares us for Liza's version of herself as a victim of sorts. It is noteworthy that the screen suddenly stretches to accommodate her frightening recollections: scenes of the past are in Dyaliscope (wide screen) while shots of the present conform to a more narrow ratio. The alternation between the two formats implies that the present offers a limited frame: only with the informing past can a fuller image be presented.

"I was an overseer. I didn't hurt anyone. If she's alive, it's thanks to me," Liza explains to her husband in a voice-over. This leads into the first version of her time in Auschwitz, where she took charge of the storehouses. "I never dealt with the prisoners, only their things," she claims. "I just did my duty. I always tried to help these women." The images support the self-righteous narration as she selects Marta to be her assistant – even enabling the young political prisoner to see her fiancé, Tadeusz (Marek Walczewski). This first "noble version," in the male narrator's words, ends with Marta being summoned to the death block.

A return to the present shows Liza watching the woman who might be Marta in fragments – stills of shipboard parties – as the male narrator tells what Munk intended to include between the two versions. The second account begins with Liza's confession, "I was stupid enough to feel sorry for her," and proceeds to flesh out the sketchy moments of the preceding one. It becomes increasingly apparent that the storeroom is a privileged space where political prisoners are decently dressed and fed – a contrast to the scene Liza observes beyond the fence: in the camp itself, a group of children wearing Jewish armbands are led into a building. That they are about to be gassed is indicated by shots of a soldier putting on a mask and pouring the Zyklon into the appropriate holes. Furthermore, black smoke is visible from the chimney, casting a dark shadow over the camp.

The extermination of the Jewish children in Auschwitz is subtly confirmed by the next shot of empty baby carriages being rolled into the storehouse. Here, Marta shows her first act of defiance when a baby is heard: she runs to check the sound, brings back a doll that makes crying sounds to appease the Commandant's vicious curiosity, and proceeds to hide a sobbing Jewish child with the help of the other prisoners. She and Tadeusz are not merely lovers, but active resisters engaged in a cat-and-mouse game with Liza. The overseer is jealous of their love but needs Marta; as her superior tells her, they must win the trust of the best prisoners to establish order in the camp. Specifically, she needs the young dissident to give the "right" answers to an international commission visiting the camp. Marta does not answer their questions, but to save her fiancé's skin, she is forced to admit that he visited her in the hospital.

Liza exults in learning that she will be promoted and transferred to Berlin, but Marta sours her last moments in the camp by confessing to subversive activities. The film returns to the present, in which the male narrator says of Liza, "If she always sought to justify herself, it's only human." The hypothetical ending is that the young woman disembarks at the next port and that Liza remains unchanged by the encounter: "It is doubtful that Liza will be challenged with truths that remain buried in the mud of Auschwitz. Nothing can trouble her," for she is among those "who prefer not to remember yesterday's crimes, among people who even today . . ." The narrator breaks off here, forcing the viewer to finish the sentence, and the film. For *Passenger* ends like a stimulant rather than a tonic, insisting that the chapter is not closed. Perhaps the end of the sentence can be found in the last shot – a still of the luxury liner – implying that we remain isolated, unconnected to events, unable to see and touch what is happening around us.

The fact that this film forces us on a formal level to participate in piecing the fragments and versions together ties in with its moral invitation to action. For if Liza's first version presents Marta simply as a lovesick child, the second insists on her being a political resister and a heroic figure. For example, Marta is the only prisoner who yells to a naked and humiliated woman on display to stand tall. When Liza finds a note in the barracks and asks Marta to translate it aloud, she invents a love letter rather than read the names and numbers of SS officers listed. (A subsequent scene clarifies that such notes were smuggled out of the camp to be used by Radio-London on its broadcasts indicting war criminals.) And when Liza threatens that the whole group will be punished if the author of the note does not admit to it, Marta steps forward in an act of solidarity with the covert resistance network operating in the camp. (In the documentary *Genocide* [1975] – part of Great Britain's "World at War" series – we see photographs of the camps that were indeed smuggled out by organized political prisoners during the war.)

A major question raised by *Passenger* is whether postwar justifications by Germans are trustworthy or merely self-serving. The interplay between Liza's self-justifying memory and the political realities of dissenters in Auschwitz uses similar visual material with divergent interpretations. That the first version is Liza's subjective story is evident from the camera work: we do not ever really see Liza, except as a reflection in a mirror or glass window. Rather, we see *through* her eyes in point-of-view shots, such as the long tracking shot of the female prisoners from whom Liza will choose an assistant. Another telling shot is revealed to have been subjective only in the second half: a lengthy pan of the hospital that ends on Marta is repeated later, but this time begins farther back – with *Liza* – before following her glance. The camera movement is also slower the second time, permitting us to see more details.

The only dialogue in the first account is Liza's narration. The second version finally presents direct dialogue, and because this convergence of sound and image is in keeping with cinematic convention, the section seems more subtly "real." It also develops the deadly circle game that flashes into Liza's mind at the opening of the film; with persistent unraveling, it establishes that Liza was responsible for choosing the prisoners who would be caught in the circle. She does indeed save Marta in this scene, but the defiance visible in the prisoner's face suggests that Liza's compassion is a lesser motive than the need for a partner in her own game. Her aim is to break down Marta's integrity by making her a privileged prisoner. Marta's role is akin to that of Antigone in Jean Anouilh's play, who states to the king, "I am here to say no."

Rather than merely substituting this psychological tug of war for a depiction of concentration camp realities, Munk uses the background to show the harshness of existence. Bodies are beaten behind Liza, and *Passenger*'s ultimate condemnation of the overseer is the narrator's assessment, "In the vague, unreal background, there are always people dying anonymously, quietly, over whom she walked unseeing." For those who might feel that the presentation of Auschwitz is too bland, the fact remains that the locale is always mediated by Liza's memory. As the director explained two days before his death, "In the film, Auschwitz is shown from a distance of twenty years and it is seen through the eyes of an S.S. woman. She relates facts coldly while retaining a clear conscience."[3] For Munk, a Jew from Cracow, the point is not an objective reconstruction of camp life but the gradual revelation of a relationship between overseer and privileged prisoner; nevertheless, the psychological and political resonance of *Passenger* extends beyond this relationship – not unlike its frame which widens into Dyaliscope. The viewer is led to ponder this extension by the film's unfinished ending: isn't the situation of a film spectator analogous to that of a ship's passenger? Do we not also enter the theater to be taken on a trip that frees us from history, memory, biography? And don't we have to reconnect with reality when the voyage ends?

Passenger shares at least two elements with *The Boxer and Death*, a superb Slovak drama of 1962. The focus is the complex relationship between a commandant and a privileged prisoner; and the most horrible aspects of concentration camp existence are presented with powerful understatement. In October of 1988, New York's Film Forum unearthed and presented Peter Solan's film, which – except for a screening at the 1963 San Francisco Film Festival – had been virtually unseen in the United States. Based on a novel by the Polish writer Jozef Hen, it tells the story of two former boxers – a German who is now commander of an unidentified concentration camp in Poland, and a Slovak prisoner on the verge of execution for attempted escape. Kraft (Manfred Krug) is bored practicing only with his punching bag, and therefore spares Kominek (Stefan Kvietik) in order to have a sparring partner. The latter is given food to fatten him up, and enough special attention to warrant the suspicion and anger of the other inmates. But Venzlak (Jozef Kondrat) – an older Pole and former trainer – realizes Kominek is telling the truth and gives him pointers. Kominek grows stronger, able to sustain longer matches with Kraft, and finally manages to hold out for the entire ten-round bout staged for a small German audience. Intercut with this victory, however, is the shooting of Venzlak by Kraft's supercilious colleague. The next day, Kominek tempts the commander into one more round, during which he defeats the Nazi officer. The infuriated Kraft sends him to certain death, but relents when his mistress warns that public opinion will be against him *after* the war if he disposes of a man who beat him in the boxing ring. Kraft offers Kominek his freedom.

At this point, the political focus of *The Boxer and Death* becomes sharper: whereas Kominek's survival thus far has been on a purely personal basis, he refuses to be released unless the commander assures him there will be no reprisals. He leaves only after Kraft says the alarm will not be sounded. During his dazzling moments of freedom, he meets Halina, Venzlak's contact who is prepared to hide escapees from the camp. The alarm sounds, prompting Kominek to refuse individual salvation if it is at the price of others being punished. He returns to the camp in an act of both "fair play" and solidarity with the other prisoners. His Polish trainer clearly passed on more than ring maneuvers. We recall, for example, the scene in which Kominek is enraged to find that his bread has been stolen by a Pole in a neighboring bunk: he takes the chunk to Venzlak's barracks and gives it to the trainer – who proceeds to share the bread with the other men. When Kominek says that it was meant only for him, Venzlak ignores the remark. As the film progresses, we realize there is greater resistance in the camp than we might have assumed. Not only does Kominek mention how the first escape failed because the others couldn't keep up with him – suggesting that group survival was already more important to him than his own skin – but he ultimately becomes a symbol of resistance, since he has the right to pummel a Nazi officer. "Playing ball" with the Nazis takes on a new meaning, as Kominek's rules of the game become collective rather than personal.

Despite this focus, *The Boxer and Death* does not shirk from acknowledging realms darker than Kominek's matches. For instance, he passes a group of newly arrived Jewish prisoners, including women and children, still holding suitcases. When he returns to this scene a little later, only the possessions remain – their silence eloquently bearing witness to the Jews' disappearance – and we cut to smoke darkening the sky. Kominek screams as the smoke washes over him, and we do not need to be told what the Jews' fate was. Similarly, a kind of shorthand is established in the film's first scene: when the commander sees six men who tried to escape, he comments to his colleague Holder, "I thought nine were caught." He replies, "Three were Jews." The implication is that whereas the six prisoners (including Kominek) are kept for the commander to decide upon, Jews are killed immediately. Even if the privileged prisoner receives most of the camera's attention – including compelling point-of-view shots and close-ups that lead us to identify with him – long shots of the entire camp standing at attention enlarge the picture: alongside their upright bodies, there is always an occasional figure that has fallen to the ground, inert and ignored. We are also shown the utter uselessness of camp "labor" when the camera whip-pans from one pile of dirt being shoveled to another, and another, until a high-angle long shot reveals that a circle of prisoners is being ordered to simply move the dirt around.

Irony permeates *The Boxer and Death,* especially in the characterization of the commandant. As Jim Hoberman perceptively wrote in the *Village Voice,* "Impatient and self-absorbed, Kraft is a man in whom expediency, personal vanity, and a Nazi sense of fair play are hopelessly entangled."[4] A living paradox, Kraft encourages Kominek to attack him in the ring, even if this means demonstrating that an *Untermensch* can defeat a leader of the master race. A particularly ironic moment occurs when his mistress urges him to spare the prisoner so that Kraft's future reputation will not be sullied: "Do you really think anyone could be so mean as to consider my decision to do away with Kominek unfair?" he asks hotly. Similarly, Kominek must deal with the conflicting impulses of boxer and inmate – to win, versus to survive by prolonging his revelation of skill. (Indeed, Hoberman pungently called Kominek "a beefcake Sheherazade.")

The crisp black-and-white photography, spare, dissonant score, and understated performances are extremely effective. Although the style of *The Boxer and Death* is not as tense as those of other films discussed in the preceding chapter, its complexity derives from the ultimate conceit of the boxing ring as microcosm for the battle of wits between oppressor and victim. In narrative terms, the commandant wins by luring back the prisoner; in political terms, Kominek triumphs by returning in order to organize an escape that is not solitary.

Eastern European filmmakers have also made use of the tension between black-and-white and color, or between moving and still images, when visualizing the horrors of World War II. Aleksander Askoldov's *Commissar* and Krzysztof Zanussi's *Wherever You Are* constitute two gripping examples for – although neither film is about the Holocaust – both use dream sequences that are essentially flash-forwards in time. In *Commissar,* a black-and-white Russian film made in 1967 but shelved until 1988, we find an unusually sympathetic depiction of Jewish characters. Klavdia, a pregnant female commissar in the Red Army, is sent by the government to live with a poor Jewish family that already has six children. Yefim complains, but his wife warms to the commissar and they end up caring for her. After the delivery of her boy – where poetic montage creates one of the most stunning birth sequences ever filmed – Klavdia is summoned back to fight the advancing White Army. Before she decides to leave her baby with the Jewish family and rejoin the struggle, there is an extraordinary episode that turns out to be her glimpse of the future. She is seated in Yefim's dark cellar, the children crying as armies move above them. Yefim

A scene from *Commissar*.
PHOTO COURTESY OF INTERNATIONAL FILM EXCHANGE

begins a Chassidic dance to bring them out of fear. Suddenly, there is a yellow sepia scene of Jews with stars on their clothes being led in the street, as well as Jews in concentration camp uniforms. A return to Klavdia's face in close-up suggests that this was her prescient vision. *Commissar* is not only a superb film in its story and style (effectively utilizing a variety of camera angles, montage, metaphor, and distorted music); for once, an Eastern European film shows Jews hiding someone rather than being hidden (indeed, at great risk when the White Army advances), and demonstrates how they were an integral part of Russian life. Yefim laments that governments change, always for the worse, and whom do they blame whenever there's unhappiness? The Jews – shown here as resilient, generous, and endearing.

Wherever You Are (Great Britain/Germany/Poland, 1988) is an understated but powerful drama in color that touches on the madness of the Holocaust, again through a woman's forceful imagination. Directed in English by the renowned Polish director Zanussi, it tells the story of Julian (Julian Sands), a diplomat who arrives in Poland in 1938 with his wife (Renée Soutendijk), a photographer. Beneath their beautifully civilized appearance, things grow strained, especially after she is thrown from a horse: when she is developing her photos, the image of two girls fades and she sees decapitated heads from what we now recognize as Holocaust archival material. As in *Commissar*, the heroine has an intimation of impending horror. She subsequently observes her husband beating their chauffeur, who chillingly uttered, "Heil Hitler." After a violent lovemaking scene with Julian, she is found hidden in the bathroom, incoherent and savage. He must put her in an institution in Cologne, where he witnesses Nazis burning books and smashing Jewish stores to the cries of "Juden raus!" His wife suddenly seems normal for a while, but then relapses into madness. In her irrational fits, she is like a fragile vessel of violence – a harbinger of the Holocaust – and she is ultimately killed in the asylum by the Nazis. Was her madness a result of the fall from the horse, or Julian's latent animality, or hints of growing Nazism around her? Or wasn't it simply that she knew the images captured by her camera – and/or mind – would become too real to live with?

4
Black Humor

Comic films about the Holocaust raise two major questions: to what extent is humor appropriate when dealing with such devastation? And what illumination can a perspective of humor provide that is not possible in a serious approach? Mel Brooks's *The Producers* is certainly not about the Holocaust, but its protagonists are right on target when they select Nazism as the most outrageous and tasteless subject for comic or musical treatment. The aim of these producers (Zero Mostel and Gene Wilder) is to make a quick buck, but this hardly describes the situation of filmmakers who use comedy as a weapon. The type of humor exemplified by *The Great Dictator, To Be or Not to Be,* and *Seven Beauties* is of course "black" – the kind that leaves a bitter taste after the laugh.

To give Hitler, Mussolini, and other mad megalomaniacs a comic kick, Charles Chaplin wrote and directed *The Great Dictator* (1940). In this satire, he played both the ranting Adenoid Hynkel and the victimized little Jewish barber. There was something curiously appropriate about the little tramp impersonating the dictator, for by 1939, Hitler and Chaplin were perhaps the two most famous men in the world. The tyrant and the tramp reverse roles in *The Great Dictator,* permitting the eternal outsider to address the masses, and the dreaded icon to seem a buffoon. The film opens with a title that sets the rather serious tone of Chaplin's brand of comedy: "This is a story of a period between two World Wars – an interim in which Insanity cut loose, Liberty took a nose dive, and Humanity was kicked around somewhat." This establishment of an absurd universe is developed in the World War I sequence that begins the film's action: the tramp as a soldier (looking very much like his earlier persona in *Shoulder Arms* of 1918) pulls a string to release a bomb. However, the unexploded shell follows the tramp with a mind of its own – an agent of destruction out of control. A Big Bertha cannon that circles till it faces the tramp continues this idea of man-made instruments turning against their creators, as does a plane that whips around and flies upside down with the tramp and Major Schultz (Reginald Gardner) inside. This is an appropriate image for war: a topsy-turvy situation devoid of human guidance. The tramp saves Schultz's life, learns that the war is over, and is taken to a hospital, where amnesia detains him until Hynkel takes power years later.

In the film's present tense, we find that the little soldier is a Jewish barber – and a dead ringer for the dictator of "Tomania." Hynkel's first speech combines

barking, broken German, and English in a verbal assault on the Jews. (This scene should be appreciated in the context of Chaplin's own ambivalence toward sound. If Hitler aped Chaplin's image, the silent comedian gets even by draining the dictator's speech of meaning.) So heated is his discourse that microphones droop, bend, and twirl away from his face. When he leaves the cheering and saluting crowds, even the statues have raised arms: the traditionally armless *Venus de Milo* is in "heil" position, as is Rodin's *The Thinker*. While these are basic sight gags, they contain darker implications: art and culture have been recast in a Nazi image and perverted into propaganda. The sequence ends with Hynkel's adviser Garbitsch (Henry Daniell) suggesting that violence against the Jews will make people forget their empty stomachs.

The action shifts to the ghetto, where storm troopers harry the Jewish inhabitants. The amnesiac barber has just returned from the hospital, unaware that Jews must now accept humiliation and defacement of property. Along with Hannah (Paulette Goddard), a young Jewess who hits the troopers over the head with a frying pan, the tramp resists the hooligans. Major Schultz (now a Nazi) suddenly arrives on the scene and, remembering that our little hero once saved his life, has him released.

Garbitsch and Herring (Billy Gilbert) continue to feed Hynkel's delusions of limitless power; as the ghetto burns, the Jews escape to idyllic "Osterlich," and the dictator decides to invade this neighboring country. His obstacle is Benzini Napaloni's army (from "Bacteria") – already massed at the border. Hynkel invites his flamboyant fellow dictator (Jack Oakie) to a lavish dinner where they try to upstage one another. Both are undone by mouthfuls of hot English mustard, as it becomes clear that they have bitten off more than they can chew. The barber escapes from prison in a Nazi uniform with Schultz, while troopers mistakenly arrest Hynkel as he is out duck shooting. This ultimate reversal leads the barber onto the rally platform, before which a huge assemblage awaits Hynkel's major address. The comic parody of Riefenstahl's insidious *Triumph of the Will* (1935), even to the use of looming shadows and overbrilliant lighting, suddenly shifts gears: the audience is faced with Chaplin the polemicist's straightforward plea for peace, brotherhood, and an end to oppression everywhere.

The undisguised parallels, such as Herring/Göring and the realism in the ghetto sequences, were quite courageous for an American film of 1940. At a time when the swastika was a feared symbol, Chaplin transformed it into a double cross (an all-too-perfect mark for what Hitler was doing to Germany). *The Great Dictator* acknowledges the existence of concentration camps, as when a customer tells the barber that all the men have "gone there." Indeed, the images and conversations of the ghetto display both an ethnic realism ("Jewish" faces and Yiddish speech rhythms) and a historical one (destruction of property and brutal SS pranks). The one element that might strike some viewers as less than realistic is open resistance, which Chaplin presents as a constant possibility and responsibility. Almost every scene in the ghetto contains an illustration of Hannah's line, "We can't fight alone, but we can lick 'em together."

"Springtime for Hitler" in *The Producers.*

Adenoid Hynkel in *The Great Dictator*.
PHOTO COURTESY OF CARLOS CLARENS

This spunky young woman talks back to the SS, smacks them with a skillet, and becomes a symbol of hope by the end of the film. Mr. Jaeckel (Maurice Moscovich), the ironic resident sage of the ghetto, tells the men they have to make a stand. And when Schultz escapes from the camp to this group, he immediately arranges a meeting to organize resisters. These scenes serve to encourage Jewish resistance while parallel scenes undercut Hitler: the underdog seems stronger while the omnipotent ruler looks merely inflated. This image is most cleverly presented in *The Great Dictator*'s famous globe scene: Garbitsch strokes Hynkel's ego by predicting he will rule the world after "wiping out the Jews. Then the brunettes." Hynkel cackles and then picks up a giant globe that turns out to be a balloon. In an exquisitely choreographed dialogueless sequence, accompanied by music from Wagner's *Lohengrin,* he twirls, caresses, and kicks the world around (including the memorable backside kick). But the balloon bursts: Hynkel cannot hold onto his image of the world.

The next scene portrays the barber succeeding where the dictator could not: in a more restrained but equally choreographed number, he shaves a customer to the brisk rhythms of a Brahms gypsy melody (perhaps an allusion to the vitality of the "brunettes" that are second on the Nazis' wipeout list). Unlike his lookalike, the little barber knows just how far to press, and his sharp instrument does not prick what he holds. Moreover, an instrument of potential terror used appropriately acquires aesthetic "rightness." The juxtaposition of these two scenes suggests that the barber's razor will be the agent of Hynkel's deflation – as, indeed, Chaplin's keen humor is

Storm troopers come to the Jewish ghetto in *The Great Dictator.* PHOTO COURTESY OF
CARLOS CLARENS

to Hitler's image in this film. A similar example of creative editing occurs when the
ghetto burns: there is an intercut of Hynkel playing the piano before a shot of smoke
designating the destruction of the Jewish neighborhood. A twentieth-century Nero,
Hynkel is not even a very good musician.

The dictator is most resoundingly mocked when he speaks, for his emphatically
guttural rantings result in nonsense speech. The overemotional speaker gets so carried away with his histrionics that he splashes water into his pants.Hynkel jumbles
German and English until the only recognizable word is *Jüden,* emitted with much
facial contortion. The final speech is consequently a complete reversal of *The Great
Dictator*'s comic tone, methods, and impact. Although it is not the film's first serious declamation – Hannah had earlier addressed the camera with the hope that her
people might be left alone and not forced to go away – the ending disrupts the dark
humor that precedes it.

Mistaken for the Führer, the barber entreats the crowd to refuse the yoke of
oppressors."Greed has poisoned men's souls," he laments, but "the power they took
from the people will return to the people." With increasing passion, he quotes Saint
Luke about the kingdom of God being manifest in men, and closes with a social
democratic vision of the future. "Look up, Hannah," he intones, as sentimental string

music accompanies a close-up of her tearful, hopeful face. While many have attacked the ending's clichéd sentiments, forced optimism, and disruption of tone, it can be seen as Chaplin's acknowledgment that the preceding comedy is inadequate to the gravity of the events depicted. Although *The Great Dictator*'s procedure is comic, its aims are serious – as announced in the opening titles. André Bazin was perceptive when he claimed that Hitler had stolen Chaplin's mustache and *The Great Dictator* was his way of getting even;[1] this film was also an attempt at *liberating* laughter, whereby Chaplin could toy as deftly and maliciously with Hitler's image as Hynkel with his ephemeral globe. The year was only 1940, and war was declared during the film's production. In Chicago, with its large German population, the film was banned.

Public response was less than kind two years later, when Ernst Lubitsch made *To Be or Not to Be*. Black comedy was hardly a familiar experience for film audiences in 1942, which may explain why this film was so misunderstood and savagely criticized. The director of such treasured comedies as *Trouble in Paradise*, *Ninotchka*, and *The Shop Around the Corner* was clearly taking some gargantuan risks: a comedy about the Nazi occupation of Poland? Jack Benny as a Polish actor playing Hamlet? A character who looks exactly like Hitler responding to a chorus of "Heil

Under the sign
of the double cross
in *The Great Dictator*.
PHOTO COURTESY OF
CARLOS CLARENS

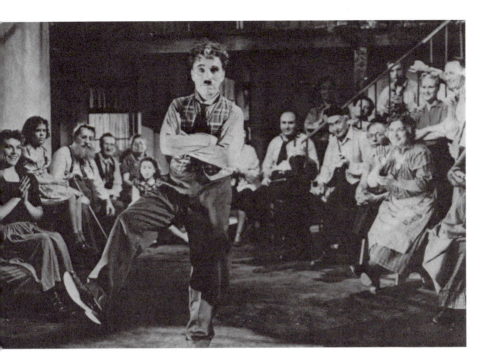

Above, Charles Chaplin as the little barber; and, *below,* the barber's
resistance in *The Great Dictator.* PHOTOS COURTESY OF CARLOS CLARENS

An impassioned Hynkel in *The Great Dictator.* PHOTO COURTESY OF CARLOS CLARENS

Hitler!" with "Heil myself"? And, if the film didn't have enough problems, the sudden death of its female star, Carole Lombard, in a plane crash shortly before the film's premiere, made it that much harder for audiences to roar with laughter.

Now that films like *Dr. Strangelove* have accustomed viewers to savage satire, *To Be or Not to Be* can be better appreciated in its juxtaposition of farce and melodrama. Now that *Hogan's Heroes* has made bumbling Nazis a staple of television culture, Lubitsch's prototypes – especially the saucer-eyed Sig Ruman as "Concentration Camp Ehrhardt" – no longer seem to be in bad taste. Forty years later, we can see how Lubitsch translated painful events into a timeless meditation on ego, vulnerability, role playing, and the need for humor. From a story by Lubitsch and Melchior Lengyel, Edwin Justus Mayer fashioned a pungent screenplay full of provocative Lubitsch touches – innuendo, wry wit, affectionate deflation of characters – and an almost unrecountable plot. The Nazi blitzkrieg of Warsaw provides the backdrop for the exploits of a band of Polish actors that never stops "performing" – whether to the thunder of applause or bombs. Occupying center stage are Jack Benny as the vain, hammy, and jealous Josef Tura, and Carole Lombard as his clever, luminous, and less-than-faithful wife, Maria.

Josef and Maria Tura adopt a series of poses in order to sabotage the Nazi invaders. Maria improvises alluringly with the suave Professor Siletsky (Stanley Ridges), who is a Nazi spy, and then with the buffoonish Colonel Ehrhardt. Josef impersonates Ehrhardt with the real Siletsky, and then Siletsky with the real Ehrhardt. Each encounter builds upon, reflects, or reverses a preceding one. Ehrhardt is informed of

Siletsky's death while Tura is in his office posing as Siletsky. The masquerade leads to a macabre scene in which the impostor is placed in the same room with Siletsky's corpse. The two look identical, but Tura quickly masters the situation with a handy razor. He removes the corpse's beard and then pastes it back on to make it appear that the real Siletsky was a fake. This scene partly accounts for the difficulty audiences of 1942 had in accepting the film. It is predicated on the kind of dark humor that would seem palatable only thirty or more years later, with Hitchcock making macabre fun of rigor mortis in *Frenzy* (1972) or Blake Edwards playing with corpses in *S.O.B.* (1981).

The mixture of genres and tones was equally disconcerting, for *To Be or Not to Be* moves swiftly and unpredictably from comic inventiveness to frightening authentic-looking war footage, and back again. Suddenly there are scurrying bodies illuminated only by bursts of fire against a black sky; the storefronts that introduced us to the film's comic world with a series of Polish names are now shattered. In a letter defending his work, Lubitsch felt it necessary to underscore the gravity of these scenes, despite the satirical tone pervading the film:

> When in *To Be or Not to Be* I have referred to the destruction of Warsaw, I have shown it in all seriousness; the commentation under the shots of the devastated Warsaw speaks for itself and cannot leave any doubt in the spectator's mind what my point of view and attitude are toward those acts of horror. What I have satirized in this picture are the Nazis and their ridiculous ideology. I have also satirized the attitude of actors who always remain actors regardless of how dangerous the situation might be, which I believe is a true observation.[2]

Other disturbing touches include the ultimately uncomfortable humor when a Polish actor impersonating Hitler orders two German pilots to jump from a plane. With no more than a "Heil Hitler!" – and without parachutes – they obediently jump. Funny, but . . . As Theodore Huff wrote in his *Index to the Films of Ernst Lubitsch*, "the Lubitsch burlesque, laid in Nazi-invaded Warsaw, was called callous, a picture of confusing moods, lacking in taste, its subject not suitable for fun making. While others felt that such merciless satire and subtle humor were good anti-Nazi propaganda, the picture was, perhaps, ill-timed."[3] The *Philadelphia Inquirer* called it "a callous, tasteless effort to find fun in the bombing of Warsaw," and the National Board of Review, while favorably disposed to the film, cautioned, "Sensitive people won't like it."[4] The line for which Lubitsch was most vociferously attacked was Ehrhardt's answer to Tura's repeated question, "You've heard of that great, *great* Polish actor, Josef Tura?" The colonel recalls with amusement, "What he did to Shakespeare, we are doing now to Poland." Lubitsch refused to delete the line because he did not believe that he was making a joke at the expense of the victims.

Lubitsch was so distressed by the response to *To Be or Not to Be* that he wrote an open letter to the *Philadelphia Inquirer*:

> Never have I said in a picture anything derogatory about Poland or the Poles. On the contrary, I have portrayed them as a gallant people who do not cry on other people's shoulders in their misery, but even in the darkest day never lost courage and ingenuity or their sense of humor. It can be argued if the tragedy of Poland realistically portrayed as in *To Be or Not to Be* can be merged with satire. I believe it can be.[5]

But the mixture of tones created a pervasive ambiguity. The Nazis are, finally, not easy "villains" at all: that Ehrhardt and Tura display the same childish narcissism ("So they call me Concentration Camp Ehrhardt!"/"You've heard of that great, *great* Polish actor, Josef Tura?") underlines the shared human emotions beneath their national identities. Tura, in his role playing, suggests the universal fallibility and the occasional charm that can be attributed to every character in the film.

Should Lubitsch be praised or blamed for never really damning his characters, whether Nazi pigs or Polish hams? In 1942 it might have seemed a cop-out to show that the Nazis' most powerful motivation was fear of their own superiors. Nevertheless, *To Be or Not to Be* did deflate the image of a national enemy: Hitler is ultimately "just a little man with a mustache," not unlike the buffoon incarnated by Chaplin in *The Great Dictator*. Moreover, the fact that the Gestapo constitutes a source of humor rather than horror becomes fairly horrifying itself, for Lubitsch invites an awareness of our own responses through the juxtaposition of moods. Forty years validate to some extent how Lubitsch's famed art of indirection was appropriate not only for sex but also for politics; he believed not in direct attack but in subtle subversion. *To Be or Not to Be* proposes that the way to undercut tyranny is to play your roles cleverly till you amass the power to direct. As the title implies, the source of these characters' strength is theatrical – whether they perform as thespians or as spies.

The film opens with a voice-over narration establishing a real time and place, 1939 Warsaw, and a real figure, for we witness Adolf Hitler staring at Maslovsky's Delicatessen. How did he come to be there? wonders the narrator. A scene at Gestapo headquarters provides the answer, as Hitler is greeted by the officers and answers (deadpan), "Heil myself." But these seemingly real scenes turn out to be a play in rehearsal, and Hitler is an actor named Bronski (Tom Dugan), who ad-libs because "I thought it would get a laugh." Bronski's arguments with the director – who doesn't think he looks enough like Hitler – lead him to test his costume in the street.

The interplay between theatrical artifice and reality continues as the actors break and listen onstage to a radio broadcast of the real Hitler. This intrusion of reality is extended when government representatives enter to cancel the show because they fear it will offend the Führer. A safe classic is substituted, with Tura playing Hamlet. During the famous soliloquy, a handsome young flier, Lieutenant Sobinski (Robert Stack), gets up from the audience and visits Maria in her dressing room ("To be or not to be" being the prearranged signal for him to come backstage), where she puts on another act that is more compatible with her sweet, fan-magazine image. But all these roles explode in the face of the sudden invasion: the actors now know that "the Nazis are putting on a bigger show than ours," and that "there are no censors to stop them." From this point on, the art of acting will be utilized for the sake of survival.

Theater and life intermingle when Maria puts on for Siletsky's dinner the dress she intended to wear in the play's concentration camp sequence. (The costume is more appropriate for the dinner since it is as sexy, glittering, and playful as its owner.) Her act with Siletsky is a Lubitsch mélange of sex and politics, with unmistakable gestures and inimitable metaphors, as Siletsky tempts her to become a spy for the Nazis – and also to succumb to his charms. "Shall we drink to a blitzkrieg?" asks the professor seductively. "I prefer a slow encirclement," she sighs. As he plies her with champagne during this "affair of state," he insists that "by the end of the evening, I'll have you saying 'Heil Hitler.'" Between kisses, she murmurs the phrase, now comically defused.

The most effective and poignant example of the space shared by stylization and authenticity in the fluid Lubitsch universe is Shylock's speech from *The Merchant of Venice*, which another of the actors, Greenberg (Felix Bressart), delivers three times: the first is backstage, where he is merely an extra in *Hamlet*, indulging in every bit player's wishful dream of stardom; the second is in a rubble-strewn street, where Shakespeare's plea for tolerance in the mouth of a Jewish actor acquires a concrete significance – beyond humor; and the third is at the film's climax, when the lives of all the actors in the troupe are at stake. Greenberg performs Shylock for an unwitting audience of Nazi soldiers and their supposed Führer (who is, in fact, the actor Bronski). Greenberg plays his part on a level where poetic text, staging, and memorizing lines constitute rehearsals for resistance, solidarity, and survival.

It is finally survival that *To Be or Not to Be* is about; it explores with sympathy and irony characters who must act in order to live, or adapt and improvise in order to subvert and overthrow. Lubitsch – a German Jew directing in America in 1942 – may have been taking action in the only way available to him: the film asserts that art can heighten and transform experience to the point of effecting social change. *To Be*

Bronski (played by Tom Dugan) playing Hitler in *To Be or Not to Be*.
PHOTO COURTESY OF MUSEUM OF MODERN ART/FILM STILLS ARCHIVE

Jack Benny (Josef), Carole Lombard (Maria), and the theatrical troupe
in *To Be or Not to Be.* PHOTO COURTESY OF IMAGES FILM ARCHIVE

or Not to Be can be interpreted as an affirmation of its own capacity to delight *and* disturb, or to face horror with the ammunition of sharp humor. It suggests that art (including films) can prepare for life – a stage where the two meanings of "to act" are inextricably linked.

The American remake of *To Be or Not to Be* (1984), directed by Alan Johnson and produced by Mel Brooks, is a pale imitation of Lubitsch's comedy. Starring Brooks as Bronski, Anne Bancroft as his wife, Anna, and Tim Matheson as Sobinski, it is a heavy-handed farce – except for the addition of two elements: Anna's dresser is flamboyantly gay, must wear a pink triangle, and is graphically taken away by the Gestapo; second, Jews wearing stars are hidden in the theater company's basement and are taken with the company to England. In one poignant scene, they are dressed as clowns to escape through the theater's center aisle during a command performance for the Nazis. An old Jewish couple is petrified at the sight of the Nazi officers, so the homosexual clown slaps yellow stars on them, screams "Jüden," and shoots them with a gun that pops out a Swastika. Illustrating (as do the characters in Chapter 6) that people in hiding must know how to improvise, these new characters transform horror into farce – and survive.

The black comedies made during World War II are necessarily more naïve and optimistic than a postwar film that acknowledges the extent of the devastation wrought by Nazism. Lina Wertmüller's *Seven Beauties* ("Pasqualino Settebelezze") (1975) goes further than these American treatments with a controversial study of survival that tests audience thresholds of laughter and horror. The story begins during World War II with the escape of Pasqualino "Seven Beauties" (Giancarlo Giannini) from a train carrying soldiers to the front. He meets a friend, and as they roam the dangerous terrain, he begins to recount his past adventures. Through flashbacks to a colorful, music-filled, prewar Naples that is a far cry from the bleakness of Pasqualino's present, we meet a character seemingly different from the prisoner. Pasqualino enters a Fellini-esque music hall where one of his sisters is performing a hilariously lascivious song and dance: from Pasqualino's gangster suit, mustache, cigarette holder, cocky hat angle (not to mention the red light in which he is bathed), we know immediately that this is a comic-strip "Godfather." He threatens to kill the pimp who has "ruined" his sister now dancing onstage. Pasqualino must maintain the "honor of the family" – seven less-than-beautiful sisters (whence his ironic nickname) and his mother – who work long hours at stuffing mattresses while he struts around. Pasqualino says repeatedly that the most important thing is respect, and finally kills the pimp.

The story of survival unfolds as Pasqualino and his road buddy, Francesco (Piero di Iorio), are thrown into a German concentration camp. This prison is depicted with a poetic but brutal realism that might be grueling to sit through if Wertmüller did not continually flash back to more vibrant past sequences. For example, the introductory shot of dead naked bodies incessantly filling the screen, accompanied by Wagner's "Ride of the Valkyries," is a visual echo of the rows of beef in the slaughterhouse of Wertmüller's earlier *All Screwed Up* (1973). The camp is run by

Giancarlo Giannini (Pasqualino) in *Seven Beauties*. PHOTO COURTESY OF CINEMA 5

a ruthless commandant (Shirley Stoller), whom Pasqualino decides he must seduce if he is to survive. His earlier histrionics over his sister's "whoring" give way to his own attempts to "sell" his body, with erection a prerequisite for respect. The final scenes, during which he becomes a Kapo to stay alive, are not quite as amusing as those in Naples: the notions of honor and respect, which contain comic resonance in the flashback sequences, become both derisive and poignant toward the end. To maintain his "family" – the men under his command in Stalag 23 – Pasqualino must sacrifice six men; along with the seventh who commits an especially grisly suicide, they form bitter counterparts to his seven women. Finally, when he is ordered to shoot Francesco, we are plunged into a moral limbo as gray and nebulous as the air of the camp itself.

The last part of the film is discomfiting in its depiction of not only massacred bodies, but the psychic destruction of a victim-turned-oppressor. Pasqualino knows that if he refuses to shoot his friend, someone else will do it. As he holds the gun above Francesco, who pleads with him to pull the trigger, *Seven Beauties* raises – and forces the viewer to grapple with – questions about acting humanely and the price of survival. By prolonging the moment, Wertmüller seems to ask, "What would *you* have done in Pasqualino's situation?" After he fires, the camera pans around the entire room in a chilling movement that stops at Pasqualino's face before rising into the eerie smoke. This shot gives us time to ponder Pasqualino's choice and its potential effects. A cut to the bright city of Naples (where his mother, sisters, and fiancée are now all prostitutes) brings us back to the "world of the living" with a lurch. Our "hero" returns, but in a manner that suggests the absence of a fully human being: rather

Shirley Stoller
(the Commandant)
in *Seven Beauties.*
PHOTO COURTESY OF CINEMA 5

Pasqualino escaping in *Seven Beauties*. PHOTO COURTESY OF CINEMA 5

than seeing Pasqualino entering the family apartment, we view its contents through his eyes. The insistently subjective camera does not let us see Pasqualino – only to see through him. His face becomes visible *in the mirror*, a reflection that says, "Yes, I'm alive," while his tired eyes seem to ask, "At what price?" The director neither supports nor condemns her protagonist: she simply presents him to us in both his weakness and his endurance.

As in *Swept Away* (1974), Wertmüller alternates between eliciting sympathy and scorn for the protagonist. She balances close-ups and a subjective camera viewpoint, which evoke empathy, with objective long shots that invite detachment. Critics who assumed that the director was endorsing her protagonist simply by having him survive tended to ignore the cinematic means through which Wertmüller was examining her hero. *Seven Beauties* refuses the complacency of a fixed moral structure. It doesn't tell us what to think; it doesn't offer answers. It makes us laugh, and consequently leads us to ask how the hilarious and the horrifying can be so close. There is no question that Wertmüller works in broad strokes. She was, after all, an assistant to the master of the human grotesque, Fellini, and began her career as a puppeteer. There is therefore a tendency in her films to substitute caricature for character, and spectacle for insight. Nevertheless, the style of *Seven Beauties* contrasts Naples's cartoon world of exaggerated acting, makeup, swagger, color and so on, with a world drained of color. And for those who would argue that Wagner's "Ride of the Valkyries" accompanying Pasqualino's arrival at the concentration camp is not exactly subtle, its use is consistent with Wertmüller's dislocating technique.

From *Seven Beauties'* first swquence – newsreel footage of Nazi destruction to the beat of rock music – the film juxtaposes historical fact with a contemporary sensibility. We see Mussolini, Hitler, and bombs flying, while a voice-over intones, "Oh, yeah." A similar counterpoint between image and sound can be found at the end when Pasqualino's face hardens into a still while a kind of derisive music persists. Whereas Pauline Kael's negative review, "Seven Fatties," maintained that "Wertmüller turns suffering into vaudeville not as part of a Brechtian technique, but, rather, as an expression of a roller-coaster temperament. The suffering is reduced to fun-house games,"[6] her soundtrack does serve to distance us from a facile identification with Pasqualino. The film was vociferously attacked by eminent writers like Jerzy Kosinski and Bruno Bettelheim too, but a far more incisive as well as sympathetic analysis was offered by Terrence Des Pres in *Harper's*. For the author of *The Survivor*, the Wertmüller method is "to give us rough slabs of reality stewing in their own exaggeration. Our first response will be . . . a laughter which trails off finally into profound awareness of the deformity of life as it is. . . ."[7]

Wertmüller's strokes are sometimes excessive, but perhaps this is one of the ways a contemporary filmmaker can combat the lulling effects of cinema and television. Kael is right in stating that "Wertmüller keeps her films moving by hurling salamis at the audience," but maybe salamis are necessary to stimulate an audience spoon-fed by formulas. Wertmüller's use of laughter is tantamount to assault. The target? Our own complacency, whether in a movie theater or a wartime situation. Wreaking havoc with genre, expectation, and propriety, *Seven Beauties* illustrates how a grotesque era of history might be illuminated by a "roller-coaster" style. By having the anarchist (Fernando Rey) commit suicide by jumping into a pool of excrement, Wertmüller gives the laughter an exceedingly bad taste to render a potentially comic moment quite horrifying. One is therefore not likely to forget this scene, nor his words before the fatal leap: "Man in disorder is our only hope." Given the degree to which Nazi behavior was characterized by order and efficiency, from robot-like salutes to well-run crematoria, the disorder inherent in black comedy can be a powerful antidote to systematic insanity. In the words of Eugène Ionesco, "Humor makes us conscious with a free lucidity of the tragic or desultory condition of man. . . . Laughter alone does not respect any taboo; the comic alone is capable of giving us the strength to bear the tragedy of existence."[8]

Part II

Narrative
Strategies

5
The Jew as Child

Many films dealing with the Holocaust focus on children or adolescents: among these, *Black Thursday, The Two of Us, Goodbye, Children,* and *Les Violons du Bal* explore the German Occupation of France through its effects on Jewish children, while *The Evacuees* and *David* depict hunted boys in wartime England and Germany. The most salient feature of this narrative strategy is that it highlights the intimacy of family, insisting upon the primacy of blood ties even as it demonstrates that individual survival was predicated on separation. There are also films that do not center on a young Jew – such as *The Damned* and *The Tin Drum* – but yoke childhood and Judaism together to express weakness and victimization. In a perceptive article entitled "The Jew as a Female Figure in Holocaust Film," Judith Doneson has noted that many Holocaust films focus on the Jew "as a weak character, somewhat feminine, being protected by a strong Christian-gentile, the male, in what comes to symbolize a male–female relationship."[1] While this is clearly the case for films like *Black Thursday,* some of the darker visions of the Holocaust depict the Jew as child – whether male or female – both literally and figuratively. In the case of Visconti's *The Damned* (1969), which will be analyzed in Chapter 8, the only Jewish character is indeed a little girl, Lisa. The perverse Martin (Helmut Berger) is attracted to this wide-eyed girl who lives next door to his mistress, and he gently seduces her. When he returns to the room she occupies, Lisa (Irina Wanka) quietly gets out of bed, walks out of the room, and (we learn later) hangs herself. The response of the police is that, because she is Jewish, it was not even a crime for Martin to have led her to her death.

The helplessness of the Jewish victim before the Nazi onslaught is likewise touched upon in *The Tin Drum* (1979), directed by Volker Schlöndorff and based on Günter Grass's novel. Given its focus on Oskar (David Bennent), a German child who decides at the age of three to stop growing, this portrait of the rise of Nazism creates intriguing rhymes among the child, the Jew, and the midget. It is the wise old midget Bebra (Fritz Hakl) who says *"Mazel tov"* to Oskar, and warns him, "The *others* are coming. They will preach our destruction," before a cut to children yelling "Heil Hitler!" Bebra also tells Oskar that they must be onstage in order to avoid being controlled. It seems

Michel Simon (Gramps) and Alain Cohen (Claude) in *The Two of Us.*
PHOTO COURTESY OF MUSEUM OF MODERN ART/FILM STILLS ARCHIVE

Above, David Bennent (Oskar) and Fritz Hakl (Bebra);
and *below,* Charles Aznavour (Markus) and Angela Winkler (Agnes)
in *The Tin Drum.* PHOTOS COURTESY OF CARLOS CLARENS

more than coincidental that the only Jewish character, Sigismund Markus (Charles Aznavour), is diminutive; he has a toy store and deals in objects for small people (it is Markus who gives Oskar his tin drum); and, like Bebra, he adopts a role – by becoming baptized. That the midget might be a double for the Jew is implied by the fact that both Bebra and Markus give Oskar a surface to play on – the drum and the stage – or a means to resist control. In this sense, the notion of the Jew as child is pushed into the stylized and even grotesque image of a little outsider who is unable to assume full human proportions as long as the Nazis run the show.

The country that has produced the most significant number of films dealing with the Jew as child is France – whose wartime behavior was particularly abhorrent: as we learn in *The Sorrow and the Pity*, thousands of Jewish children were arrested by the French police. They were among the 75,000 Jews that France rounded up and deported with a compliance bordering on eagerness. Robert Paxton and Michael Marrus have chronicled, in *Vichy France and the Jews*, how France and Bulgaria were the only countries in Europe that (while retaining sovereignty over part of their territory) *proposed* to the Germans the roundup and delivery of Jews.[2] Under the Pétainist regime, 1941 saw a well-attended anti-Semitic exhibition in Paris: *"Le Juif et la France* au Palais Berlitz sous l'égide des questions juives" included a pamphlet with directives such as "The exhibition shows you the racial characteristics of Jews: you will be enlightened by the text and image on their penetration into our country and the harm they have done here; you will therefore understand why so many Frenchmen are dead."[3] The recent French films on the Holocaust acknowledge and reject the anti-Semitism that claimed so many children as victims during World War II.

Black Thursday (*Les Guichets du Louvre*) follows two adolescents through occupied Paris on July 16, 1942 – the "black" day on which the French police rounded up 14,000 Jews into a winter sports arena for deportation. Against this backdrop of "La Grande Rafle du Vel' d'Hiv," Paul (Christian Rist), a Christian student, tries to save Jews in general and Jeanne (Christine Pascal) in particular. Directed by Michel Mitrani, this 1974 film quietly indicts not only French anti-Semitism but Jewish passivity. *Black Thursday* begins with French policemen sharing food in a bus: these ordinary men are about to commit extraordinarily monstrous acts, rounding up France's "undesirable" citizens. Paul's motto is "Help the hunted, not the hunter," and he tries to persuade various persons – whose Jewish badges are tantamount to death warrants – to follow him to safety. No one listens. An elegant woman (Judith Magre) responds: "I have nothing to fear: I'm French. And my husband is a POW." A few scenes later, she will be glimpsed in the window of a bus headed for the transports. Paul finally convinces Jeanne that Parisian Jews are doomed when she learns that both her mother and sister have been taken. He leads the hesitant young woman to the safety of the Left Bank, but just before they cross the bridge, she decides to return to her people. A closing title taken from the *New York Times* states: "Only thirty adults survived that 'Great Roundup.' Not a single child returned."

Black Thursday does not flinch from presenting the complacent French, whether they be policemen who hardly balk at "cleaning up" the Jewish neighborhoods, or Gentiles who loot apartments only moments after the Jewish tenants have left. One policeman speaks in disbelief of a Jewish woman who threw her children and then herself from a window rather than be taken: "After all, we're not the Germans," he

Christine Pascal (Jeanne) and Christian Rist (Paul)
in *Black Thursday.* PHOTOS COURTESY OF KEN WLASCHIN

Fleeing the French police in *Black Thursday*.
PHOTO COURTESY OF LEVITT-PICKMAN FILM CORPORATION

rationalizes with smug comfort. Nevertheless, the Jews in this film are equally blind to the situation; in a symbolic touch worthy of Marcel Carné, Mitrani even includes a blind man with a cane whom Paul tries vainly to assist: he turns out to be Jewish as well. These characters can all be seen as children who are in need of protection (by a Christian) or who obey authorities. When Paul implores Jeanne to remove the Jewish star sewn onto her coat, she refuses. After learning of her mother's disappearance, she is offered scissors by a kindly woman. Instead of removing the star, Jeanne points the scissors at herself with the implication of suicide – and the woman tears off the badge for her. When Jeanne warns her religious relatives about the roundup, they are horrified that she has removed her star, and the eldest says in Yiddish, "We have to live according to God's will."

The focus of the film is consequently the Christian youth and his futile generosity. Paul, who began his mission because of an abstract desire to do good deeds, gradually falls in love with Jeanne. When he urges her to go away with him to the country, he declares, "I need your eyes to see," suggesting that the Christian needs to assume the Jewish victim's burden for his own redemption. In her article, Judith Doneson claims that *Black Thursday*, along with other films, presents a symbiotic relationship between the Jew and the Gentile:

> For the Jew this means a reliance upon the Christian for his survival, while the Christian depends upon the Jew as both a witness to his own theology and as a humanizing factor which helps bring out the "goodness" incumbent upon noble Christian souls. This

mutual need is represented as a couple, the Jew being the female, the Christian . . . the male.[4]

Jeanne refuses to tell Paul her name until the last scene, and only after she decides to rejoin her people. She thus acquires an identity only by embracing her fate as a victim. Doneson argues that "[Jeanne] takes on the role of a martyr by figuratively choosing to return to the fire and die as a Jew with her people. Thus does she come to resemble an early French martyr and nationalist [Jeanne d'Arc], a hero to her people. . . ." This theological interpretation does not, however, take account of a simple emotional fact: Jeanne has been separated from her mother and, like Edith in *Kapo,* she chooses the transports in order to be with her. It is this identity – the child torn from parents, rather than prospective martyr – that impelled Jews like Jeanne to reject personal safety.

The cameo appearance of Christine Pascal in *Entre Nous* (*Coup de foudre*, 1983) suggests a subtle link between the situation of Jeanne and that of Lena (Isabelle Huppert) in Diane Kurys's internationally acclaimed film. She appears in the opening twenty-minute sequence that takes place in the French detention camp of Rivesaltes in 1942. Here, she befriends Lena, a Belgian Jew (who – significantly – no longer has a mother). They notice that the camp's cook, Michel (Guy Marchand), has been eyeing Lena, who finally receives from him a note proposing escape via marriage. Unlike Jeanne, the waif-like Lena accepts the suitor's offer in order to reach safety; however, once they are married and out of the camp, her realization that he is indeed Jewish – with a more noticeably Semitic name than her own! – makes her rebel. Nevertheless, they escape together, first via train and later on foot over the mountains into Italy. Lena's helplessness and dependence upon a man are juxtaposed with the ecstasy and despair experienced by Madeleine (Miou-Miou), a Christian woman who marries her sweetheart (Robin Renucci). When the French Gestapo comes to their art school to take away the instructor (Patrick Bauchau), who is a Resistance member, her husband is killed in the cross fire. It's only in 1952 that Madeleine and Lena first meet in Lyons, through their children – Madeleine having married a good-for-nothing actor (Jean-Pierre Bacri). Their friendship becomes all-consuming, as they search for self-definition and independence.

Although *Entre Nous* is obviously not a Holocaust film, the behavior of these women is clearly rooted in their wartime experiences. (Lena, in particular, is shown in a continually childlike position vis-à-vis her husband, as she must ask him for money.) Kurys considered World War II as an actual character and claimed that she found the situation

> explosive because Lena and Madeleine are the children of this war which has wounded them, stolen their youth and left them fearful and ready to grab the first comfort offered: a husband, a home, children, finally some peace – to forget the cold, the hunger, the anguish of deportation. They've suffered too much at the hands of history not to take into their own hands the one thing which depends solely on themselves: their personal history.[5]

Since the film is based on the experiences of Kurys's own mother, *Entre Nous* can also be seen as an exploration of the legacy of occupied France by one of the war's "grandchildren."

The price for cutting oneself off from Jewish family is portrayed in *Natalia* (1988), a first feature by Bernard Cohn. The situation is quite similar to that of *Black Thursday,* although the heroine (Philippine Leroy-Beaulieu) is a bit older than Jeanne, and her Gentile protector Paul (Pierre Arditi) more mature than Paul in the previous film. In this French drama, Natalia is a beautiful woman who is trying to be an actress in wartime Paris – a futile effort for a Jew. She asks Paul, a film director, for help; he responds with false papers, a role, and later his love. But she is denounced, arrested, and taken to a camp. We see Natalia only after her return, a shadow of her former self. The price for her survival has been high: in rejecting Judaism, she missed the death of her father, as well as her mother's departure for the Free Zone; she also abandoned her old boyfriend, Tomasz (Michel Voita), who became a Resistance fighter with Roitman (Gerard Blain), a tough commander. After the war, everyone is wracked with guilt: Paul for having been forced to reshoot Natalia's scenes with another actress, Jacqueline; the actress for having taken the role, since she and Natalia were best friends; Roitman for the fact that Tomasz was killed; and mainly Natalia, for having abandoned her family. Paul's continuing devotion and patience are not enough to make her whole again. The film ends with Natalia finding peace by returning to her parents' old apartment.

Claude Berri's 1966 film *The Two of Us* (*Le Vieil Homme et l'enfant*) acknowledges and mocks French anti-Semitism through the touching story of a nine-year-old Jewish boy (Alain Cohen) who is sent to the French countryside when Paris becomes too dangerous. A prefatory title states that this is a true story, and the protagonist's voice-over narration adds to the illusion of history. The boy's overwrought father (Charles Denner) realizes the child will survive more easily under an assumed name – Claude Longuet – and in the care of a Christian couple. He and his wife entrust him to the parents of a friend. Claude's new "Pépé" (Gramps, played by the celebrated French actor Michel Simon) is a determined but lovable anti-Semite. "In 1939," he expounds, "three percent of the French population was Jewish, but eighty-one percent of the government was Jewish." In the course of the film, he trots out other clichés, including "You can always recognize them by the smell" and "They have flat feet to keep them out of the army, but are the fastest to run to the bank." Never suspecting that the child he is growing to love is "one of them," the old grouch spouts Vichy rhetoric and complains that his daughter "loves Jews and Reds." The Liberation finally comes, and Claude's parents take him home.

The old xenophobe never learns that his "adopted grandson" *is* Jewish, and François Truffaut proposed that "Berri had the tact, the intelligence, the sensitivity and the intuition not to clear up the misunderstanding."[6] However, Gramps's lack of illumination further encloses the film within the domain of tranquil recollection. The voice-over establishes that, like *Les Violons du Bal*, the boy's backward glance retains familial warmth rather than the complexities nurtured by the Occupation. The child never really confronts the father figure, and *The Two of Us* is very much a film that accepts patriarchy – in both visual and narrative terms. When Claude's father recounts a story while feeding him dinner, a long-take three-shot maintains the child and mother spatially below him. Likewise, Gramps is the one who runs the home, and Granny's obedience extends into the political realm when she speaks of Maréchal Pétain as a hero.

Nevertheless, the film is charming and effective through Alain Cohen's dark expressive eyes and Simon's characterization of the lovable bigot. Moreover, Charles Denner's grave and pinched features give the early sequences a feeling of authenticity: in his twitching face, we see the vulnerable Jew who must send his beloved son away until the craziness of war subsides. The farewell scene is especially well designed, because the camera is located within the train, behind the child, as the parents try to keep up with its receding movement. At such moments, *The Two of Us* seems worthy of Truffaut's appraisal:

> For twenty years I have been waiting for the *real* film about the *real* France during the *real* Occupation, the film about the majority of Frenchmen, those who were involved neither in the collaboration nor the Resistance, those who did nothing, either good or bad, those who survived like characters in a Beckett play. . . . Now Claude Berri's first film, *The Two of Us*, makes the long wait worth it.

It is a pity that Truffaut did not live to see *Goodbye, Children* (*Au revoir les enfants*, 1987), as he probably would have admired both the wartime memoir and its modest style. For, like *The 400 Blows*, the focus of Louis Malle's prize-winning drama is a young boy who is less lovable than complex. Indeed, the director said in an interview, "children are so easily and quickly cute that you have to be very careful, especially with this subject. From the very beginning, *Au revoir* was meant to be tough . . . it was important to show Julien as arrogant, a little spoiled, with moments of anguish and solitude . . . I don't know about this love affair between the camera and children's smiles"[7] – which is precisely how Truffaut spoke of directing Jean-Pierre Léaud. In both cases, there is a refusal of facile identification: we can sympathize with the portrait of the director as a struggling youth, but the character does not endear himself to the viewer like the grinning children that populate Hollywood films. *Goodbye, Children* begins in 1943 with Julien Quentin (Gaspard Manesse) being sent by his attractive and wealthy mother (Francine Raclette) from Paris to a Catholic boys' school in the less turbulent countryside. There, the privileged twelve-year-old meets a mysterious and intelligent new boy, Jean Bonnet (Raphael Fejto), who keeps to himself. As they become friends, Julien figures out that he is Jewish, and that headmaster Father Jean (Philippe Morier-Genoud) is sheltering two other Jewish boys as well.

At the end, the Gestapo come for the three children denounced by Joseph (François Négret), a young cook (reminiscent of *Lacombe, Lucien*) who bears a grudge for having been fired. Jean Bonnet and the other two boys are taken from the school, as well as Father Jean: after the assembled children in the courtyard yell, "Au revoir, père Jean!" he responds, "Au revoir, les enfants." Malle's own voice-over enters to tell us that Jean Bonnet died at Auschwitz, Father Jean at Mauthausen, adding, "I will remember every second of that January morning until I die" – a personal epigraph that renders the film deeply poignant. This last scene depicts what Malle called "the most important event of my childhood: it really changed my life." Nevertheless, he waited forty years to explore these memories because, in his words, "I was scared to deal with it, unsure it wasn't sacrilegious . . . It's only when I reached the point of really revisiting it the way I *wish* it had happened – with a more complex relationship between the two boys – that I could make the film." He confessed that

A scene from *Goodbye, Children.*
PHOTO COURTESY OF ORION PICTURES CORPORATION

the friendship between Jean and him did not actually exist: "I didn't even know he was Jewish, although I think the older kids did."

Dedicated to his own three children, Malle's story is told with simplicity and subtlety from the point of view of Julien; although it is a limited perspective, it has the ring of truth. As he put it in *Le Monde,* "Compared to other films which plunge into the wartime era through the eyes of a little boy – I'm thinking mainly of Claude Berri's *The Two of Us* – one can say only that mine is from a particular angle, the gaze of a little *goy*."[8] Beginning with the goodbye to his mother and ending symmetrically with his farewell to Jean and the priest, the film presents Julien's rite of passage through a confrontation with "otherness" and with evil. The audience discovers along with Julien that Jean is Jewish when the latter doesn't pray with the other boys; lights candles while everyone is asleep (except Julien); has the name Jean Kippelstein erased from one of his books; and is refused the Mass wafer by Father Jean. Julien's gaze is indeed central to *Goodbye, Children:* a wrenching moment occurs in the final classroom scene as the Gestapo chief tries to identify which of the boys is Jewish. When the German's back is turned, Julien sneaks a look at Jean; his glance does not go unnoticed and leads to the boy's arrest. Malle confessed that, although he "wrote the last classroom scene exactly as it happened . . . I added Julien's look. Unconsciously, I was trying to express something very obvious – my guilt, or at least sense of responsibility." As in *Black Thursday,* the focus is more on Christian duty and (perhaps unmerited) culpability than on the Jewish victim.

The spectrum of behavior in the film encompasses Father Jean's transcendent decency on the one hand, and nonchalant xenophobia on the other: the fat boy Sagard wonders at the end whether the Gestapo will take them too, and says, "*We* haven't done anything" (as if Jean Bonnet had!). As in Malle's earlier *Lacombe, Lucien*, French collaborators are even more to be vilified than the Germans, who are depicted with a lack of venom. For instance, the first German we see is a young soldier who asks Father Jean to hear his confession; youthful Germans fool around at the Public Baths, clearly not doing anything about a man emerging with a Jewish star on his coat – despite the sign stating "No Jews Allowed"; German soldiers drive Julien and Jean back to the school after they get lost in the woods one night: upon hearing, "the Krauts arrested them," the kindly soldier asks, "Can the 'Krauts' have their blanket back?"; and, most significant, the French collaborationist policemen turn out to be worse than the Germans in a fancy restaurant. When members of the Vichy militia try to arrest an elegant, elderly French Jew, a tipsy Wehrmacht officer at a neighboring table – partly to impress Julien's mother – tells the French policeman to leave.

Malle admitted that he deleted the real slapping of a boy by a member of the Gestapo at the end because "it's more frightening if the Germans are so 'correct' . . . this rather ordinary side of fascism is precisely what renders it unbearable."[9] He also added to the actual events a French nun who informs on one of the Jewish boys, and he invented the story of Joseph's denunciation: "In reality, the cook was hiding from the Germans, and was Jewish," he revealed. Changing the cook's identity enriches the education Julien gets from his peers: instead of encountering merely the decent, helpless Jew, our protagonist comes to understand the wasteful hollowness of vengeance. Malle's ongoing concern with adolescents – from *Zazie dans le metro* and *Murmur of the Heart* to *Lacombe, Lucien* and *Pretty Baby* – culminates in this coming-of-age recollection, where Julien learns that the world can be treacherous. In other words, Malle subsequently realized that, as late as 1944, Germans were insanely anxious to find three Jewish children to kill. In explaining that the arrest of Jean Bonnet led to Malle's becoming a filmmaker because it stimulated his skeptical exploration of how humans behave, he recalled,

> In 1942, we would see children my age wearing the yellow star. I would ask, "Why? Why him and not me?" No one had a good answer. From that moment on, I felt that the world of adults was one of injustice, deception, false explanations, hypocrisy and lies. . . . And following that morning in January 1944 when Bonnet left, the feeling became a certitude.[10]

The Evacuees (Great Britain, 1975) is directed by Alan Parker in a far gentler key than his subsequent films, *Midnight Express, Fame*, and *Shoot the Moon*. Made for the BBC, it traces the provisional exile of two Jewish youths from Manchester to Blackpool, by the sea. *The Evacuees*, written by Jack Rosenthal, begins on September 1, 1939, with a teacher named Goldstone reading off the Jewish boys' names in class. It turns out that they will be matched up with temporary foster parents. After bidding their own families good-bye, they follow Goldstone as he asks people to take in these evacuees. Many feign excuses; one housewife asks, "Are they clean?" and then says, "I'll try one"! The Miller brothers are taken in by Mrs. Graham, where their first humorous problem is the pork sausage being served: they try to say a Jewish prayer over the pork, each holding a hand over his head. The effect of their absence upon their own family is beautifully expressed by a shot of the Millers' dinner table: the camera begins and remains on the empty chairs for a long moment before panning to the parents and grandmother, eating silently.

By January of 1940, Mrs. Graham is running the show, pocketing the letters and food that the mother sends the boys. She is sweet on the surface, but steely inside: when Mrs. Miller comes to see them, Mrs. Graham interrupts her embrace. Finally, the brothers write a veiled letter home that reveals what has been happening to their mail and food. Their mother takes them back to Manchester, leaving Mrs. Graham, who claims tearfully to her husband, "I taught them respect for their betters and elders; I call that love." Her self-justifying attitude is contrasted with the love that emanates from the Millers' Chanukah celebration at home. By March 1941, the children in Manchester are cruel to a new evacuee from London – suggesting that it is not simply in Nazi Germany that people must guard against intolerance. *The Evacuees* is a lovely little film, with humor and pain delicately balanced. Nevertheless, the portrayal of these Jewish boys in the early stages of World War II is relatively mild, containing more humorous recollection – such as Mrs. Miller and her mother wearing pots on their heads for air raids – than serious reflection.[11]

Like *The Evacuees,* Peter Lilienthal's *David* (1979) is about adolescence – not only in terms of the protagonist's age, but Nazism itself; like *Les Violons du Bal, The Garden of the Finzi-Continis,* and *Lacombe, Lucien,* its context is the rise of human monstrosity. *David*'s early image of a chained strong man performing in 1933 might represent the brute strength of Nazism that was about to explode in the mid-thirties. Nevertheless, the focus of this German film, which won the Golden Bear Prize at the Berlin Film Festival, is quietly intimate: it succeeds best in its communication of the warmth and solidarity in a rabbi's family. *David* begins in 1933 Liegnitz, where little David Singer (Torsten Henties) is beaten up by three Hitler Youth children screaming, "Jewish pig!" His father (Walter Taub) is the rabbi who, while conducting a synagogue celebration of the holiday of Purim, offers a historical precedent for the oppression and exile of Jews: "Get thee to the mountain that thou shalt not perish." During dinner one evening, a parade passes by outside that is punctuated by the cry "*Juden raus! Juden raus!*" The rabbi thinks they're saying "Youth, come out"(*Jugend raus*), but we learn that the words are actually "Jews, get out!"

A cut to 1938 finds David (Mario Fischel), now a teenager, in a train to Berlin. Having been kicked out of Gymnasium for being a Jew, he and his brother Leo (Dominique Horwitz) go to a trade school, along with other Jews. The title, "November 1938 – Nationwide Pogrom," establishes that the scenes of desecration, looting, and synagogue burning represent the infamous *Kristallnacht.* The rabbi and his congregation are humiliated and forced to watch their house of worship go up in flames. David is then sent to an agricultural training camp to prepare for his eventual emigration to Palestine. A sudden call from his father demanding David's immediate return causes David to be absent during the roundup of the young members of the training camp – who are led into a building from which none ever emerge. When David's parents are later taken as well, he hides out in their ransacked apartment, teaching himself Hebrew. His next hiding place is with a shoemaker whose relationship to David and his sister (Eva Mattes) smacks of greed more than altruism. They know it is time to move on when the shoemaker's grand- son comes back from army service crying, "They gassed them during the day and burned them at night." After a kind factory owner (played by Rudolf Sellner, former director of the Berlin Opera) gives him false papers, David escapes to Vienna and onto a boat, the soundtrack suddenly alive with joyous music. Although the film does not state his destination, Lilienthal explained that David goes to "the only place in the world where, in 1943, a Jew could be greeted by people singing and dancing: Palestine."[12]

The understatement of the ending is in keeping with the tone of the entire film. The Nazis' systematic destruction of Jewish life – dispossession and deportation to concentration camps – is presented with a respectful distancing from the subject. Without actually showing the horror of the concentration camps via reconstruction, Lilienthal suggests the cruel indifference that permitted genocide to take place. As Carlos Clarens wrote:

> In *David* there is none of the *retro* soft-focus of *The Garden of the Finzi-Continis*... there are no predictable melodramatics as in the TV miniseries *Holocaust:* Lilienthal proceeds through accumulation of detail. Nor is *David* a UFA-style fantasy like *Lili Marleen*.... What's left, then, once you take away any sentimentality, melodrama, and comfortable outrage? Just a tale of madness so epidemic that it eventually spread, in the form of hope and self-delusion, to the Jews themselves.[13]

For example, after Rabbi Singer is arrested, he comes home and reveals a swastika branded on his scalp – but the branding took place off-screen. In fact, the director admitted in an interview that he cut one sequence that would have been more

Walter Taub (Rabbi Singer) and Mario Fischel (the grown David) in *David*.
PHOTO COURTESY OF KINO INTERNATIONAL CORPORATION

violent – and thus potentially exploitative:

> There is one scene . . . of the Nazis coming to the Jewish pension in the evening. They take people out in their pajamas and kick them under the tables. I never gave any direction of insult, but suddenly they found the old vocabulary. It would have been the only violent scene in the film, adding nothing new. It was against the spirit of the film, so I took it out. For me, blood is blood even if it's ketchup. That's where direction ends, for me.[14]

A literal depiction might have been less moving for, as one of the characters remarks, "there's nothing people get used to faster than seeing others suffer." Rather, the film moves slowly and tenderly (though never sentimentally) through the events that uproot and disband a family.

David is one of the rare Holocaust films that conveys the joy and pride of being Jewish. Unlike the blue-eyed blondes of *The Garden of the Finzi-Continis* and *Lacombe, Lucien,* the characters in *David* – many of them played by nonprofessional actors – have a palpable authenticity. Lilienthal found some of his performers in the Warsaw Yiddish Theater, and chose a cinematographer who is particularly sensitive to idiosyncratic faces – Al Ruban, known for his work with John Cassavetes. When questioned about the source of the celebratory Jewish tone of the film, Lilienthal confessed, "At first it was a counter-reaction, because many immigrants were not proud of being Jewish. Therefore, I had to be. And when I learned about persecutions, that was another reason to be proud."[15] Indeed, Lilienthal's own biography has profound connections to *David* and accounts for much of the film's integrity. This German Jew left Berlin for Uruguay with his mother in 1939 – at the age of ten – and returned to his homeland in 1956. His formative years in South America gave him a keen perspective on social unrest and solidarity. After making a number of explicitly political films, he adapted Joel König's autobiographical book in two stages: "I wrote the first version with Jurek Becker. The final draft I did alone, to combine David's character with my own, and his experiences with mine." For example, David washes dishes in a Chinese restaurant toward the end of the film, an episode from Lilienthal's past:

> The only restaurants that weren't hostile to Jews in 1939 were Chinese. Other places had signs saying Jews and dogs not allowed. We couldn't buy ice cream, and we sat on special yellow benches. We weren't allowed into swimming pools. But I thought that this made us very special. I considered it a privilege, not a punishment.[16]

König served as an adviser on the film; the result is a poignant backward glance that, like *The Boat Is Full,* resists melodramatic clichés, manipulative music, and simplified behavior by "villains" or "heroes." As with many victims of the Holocaust, David is hidden by a variety of individuals: he is exploited by some, saved by others. He is intelligent but unremarkable, resourceful but not especially "heroic," hopeful but not visibly passionate. As Robert Liebman pointed out:

> His father taught him that when the authorities forbid you to pray, you can outsmart them by praying to yourself. His father also declared that a swastika on one's head is insignificant if one is alive to talk about it: "I'm here, I'm here; that's all that counts." Lilienthal sums up David's familial heritage by simply noting that "he had a strong reason to live – the Jewish religion."[17]

Although the boy progressively loses members of his family, *David* celebrates the spirit that binds him to his rabbi-father, and thus to a rich – if vulnerable – heritage.

Although *Raindrops* (*Regentropfen,* 1981) is not quite as compelling as *David,* this German drama about a young Jewish boy and his family is touching. A directorial debut for two actors, Michael Hoffman and Harry Raymon, this black-and-white film begins in 1933, with Bennie Goldbach (Jack Geula) against a rainy window. That his parents are assimilated can be deduced when his mother asks him, "Are you growing *pajes* . . . Polack?" – illustrating how many German Jews looked down on the more religious Polish Jews. As in *David,* a Passover Seder scene creates a celebratory feeling of being Jewish, but Nazism will soon take its toll. His parents grow increasingly nervous as they are forced to sell the store, leave their small Rhineland town, and wait in Cologne for their quota number in order to come to America. Bennie's games change: the one he and a girlfriend play in a train is "Where are we emigrating today?" His refuge is the movie theater, where the boy runs whenever he sees something unpleasant occurring between his parents. Perhaps because of the relative youth of both the protagonist and the Nazi movement in *Raindrops,* we don't see explicit horror, nor much of the sociopolitical picture. Rather, the focus is on the well-drawn family, as we are made to feel small humiliations – like Bennie suddenly unable to go to his beloved movies because Jews aren't allowed. The authentic flavor of the film can be traced to the fact that it is based on Raymon's past; Hoffman, who grew up in postwar Germany, apparently spurred the conception of the film by

Mario Fischel (the grown David) in *David.*

PHOTO COURTESY OF KINO INTERNATIONAL CORPORATION

Scenes from *The Revolt of Job*. PHOTOS COURTESY OF CINECOM ENTERTAINMENT GROUP

questioning Raymon about the prewar years. Although he obviously did manage to come to America, the end of *Raindrops* is a tense question mark around the family's survival.

An effective cinematic variation on the theme of "The Jew as Child" is *The Revolt of Job* (*Jób Iázadása*), a Hungarian drama of 1983. Here, the child is a Christian orphan, adopted by an elderly Jewish couple in 1943. Job (Ferenc Zenthe) and Roza (Hédl Temessy) – childless because seven births were followed by seven funerals – realize that they have little time left in their small Hungarian farming village. The husband buys Lackó (Gábor Fehér), trading two calves for him at an orphanage. This seven-year-old boy learns about Judaism and love; he observes (through windows) his "mother" lighting Sabbath candles or men studying Torah – as well as servants making love – and warms to the care of his new family. For Job, to have a descendant is to defy death; moreover, to have a Christian son is to defy the Nazis, for he can leave the child all that he has acquired during a lifetime of hard work. As the threat of deportation hovers over the Jewish citizens, Lackó gets beaten up by other children for being a "Jewboy." Finally, to the boy's bewilderment, Job, Roza, and the other Jews are taken away from the village by armed authorities.

Directed by Imre Gyongyossy and Barna Kabay from a script they coauthored with Kátalin Petenyi (Gyongyossy's wife), *The Revolt of Job* confronts with sensitivity and courage subjects that are still provocative in Eastern Europe – anti-Semitism and fascism. Although the filmmakers are not Jewish, the tale is personal: during the war, Gyongyossy was left as a small boy by his parents with an old Jewish couple. As he told the *New York Times*, "There came a day and they disappeared, I didn't know why . . . and until now I am awaiting them, like a child."[18] More than half of Hungary's Jewish population was killed by the Nazis toward the end of World War II, and *The Revolt of Job* acknowledges both Hungarians who collaborated and those who aided the Jews. One can question the film for its portrayal of Jews merely as passive beings, aware of and accepting their impending death; on the other hand, its loving re-creation of Jewish values, rituals, and continuity renders *The Revolt of Job* a haunting tale of a child whose contact with Judaism affirms life in the face of death.

6
In Hiding/Onstage

I n the art of motion pictures, the depiction of claustrophobia is a challenge: what can a filmmaker do with the inherently "theatrical" concept of enclosure in which spatial restrictions and protagonists' paranoia – as in films dealing with the Holocaust – conspire to prevent free movement? What "landscape" is possible when characters are essentially defined by fear, impatience, or passivity, as in *Under the World?* The answers afforded by films like *Samson, Angry Harvest, Forbidden,* and *The Boat Is Full* suggest that the magnification of a face can be as cinematic as the mobility of a camera – especially when the character being hidden is himself hiding an emotion. The limitation of action to a single room might feel like theater, but the close-up (when used judicially and subtly) makes such scenes radically filmic. Moreover, films like *The Condemned of Altona* and *The Last Metro* concern themselves explicitly with theater as an integral component of hiding. By exploring dependence, choice, and occupation within personal relationships, they illuminate these themes on wider political and moral levels as well.

Theater is both the source and narrative center of *The Condemned of Altona* (*I Sequestrati di Altona*). Adapted by Abby Mann and Cesare Zavattini from Jean-Paul Sartre's play, this 1962 Italian-American coproduction directed by Vittorio De Sica masterfully incorporates Brecht's play *The Resistible Rise of Arturo Ui.* Like *Hamlet*'s strategy – "The play's the thing/Wherein I'll catch the conscience of the king" – the interplay of theater and actuality provides much of the drama. The German magnate Gerlach (Fredric March) claims that his son Franz (Maximilian Schell) – a former Nazi officer whose entire company was killed in Smolensk in 1941 – died after being tried in Nuremberg. Actually, he is locked in a hidden part of his father's mansion, seen only by his sister Leni (Françoise Prévost). She reads him newspapers from 1945 as current events to maintain his illusion that Germany is still at war. When Gerlach learns that he is dying of cancer, his other son, Werner (Robert Wagner), returns to the house with his wife, Johanna (Sophia Loren). She discovers Franz's existence and persistently tries to free him from his spatial and psychological prison.

Faithful to the artistic source of the film, De Sica sets his scenes with theatrical devices from the outset: when the doctor tells Gerlach that he has only six months to live, he pulls down a window shade whose shadow descends on the patient like a curtain. Gerlach then speaks through an X-ray machine, which creates the frightening image of a disembodied voice. This image subsequently links Gerlach with Hitler,

whose voice is heard on the radio, and with Franz, who continually tapes and plays back his own harangues. Indeed, all the major characters in *The Condemned of Altona* are agents of voice or exist primarily through their speech, in true theater style: Johanna is a stage actress, Werner is a trial lawyer, Leni reads aloud deceptive newspapers, Gerlach has cancer of the throat, and Franz's self-mystification ("One voice shall remain to cry no, not guilty," he screams) and subsequent disruption of the Brecht play are enacted through declamations.

Franz is introduced via voice: we hear a few words and then a tape rewinding. Only afterward do we see fragments of a face – close-up of mouth and then eyes – with a tape recorder and microphone. Franz's first action is to make Leni "testify that all is rubble." He directs his living scenario before walls painted with horrific faces reminiscent of Munch's "The Scream." These skeletal visages of mute agony (corresponding to the pre-credit sequence in Smolensk that ends with a freeze frame of a soldier's silent scream) externalize Franz's character. And his aggressive action vis-à-vis Johanna is to shine a bright light on her. Johanna and her brother-in-law are linked by two scenes that take place in a theater: after we see Werner accusing four punks in a courtroom of anti-Semitic activity, there is an abrupt cut to a man and a woman listening to Hitler on the radio. It is only later that we learn they are onstage, rehearsing Brecht's play; Johanna reads a letter aloud, her voice vying with that of the Führer. When Franz is finally persuaded to leave the house, he goes to Johanna's theater and wanders zombielike into the performance. Assuming that the actor *is* the Führer, he berates the audience to respect Hitler, yelling "Pigs!": his voice competes with Hitler's on stage, as Johanna's did earlier.

In a larger sense, *The Condemned of Altona* is about overcoming the voice of the father. Gerlach loses his power of speech, and is later definitively silenced by his son in Franz's closing suicide/patricide; Hitler is drowned out by Johanna and then Franz. Both characters enact a denial of the patriarch/dictator through theater – Johanna in a literal sense, and Franz by turning his room into an expressionist stage, replete with grotesque décor, high-contrast lighting, elaborate mise en scène, and his own Nazi "costume."

Expressive camera work heightens Franz's theatricality. He is seen from a high angle when he puts on a blanket and talks like a machine gun, returning to Smolensk in 1941. As he assumes different voices, the camera alternates between this high angle and a low one, giving visual form to his different identities. His performance is a rehearsal rather than a revival, for Franz's stage is a projection into the future – a trial in the year 3059. He is concerned with how the "decapods" (crablike inhabitants of the thirty-first century) will judge twentieth-century man, and tries to remain the voice that cries "not guilty." When he finally does emerge into the night air, his face is reflected in a pool of water. He wipes away the reflection, unable to look at the self-image he created. At this point, Franz goes to the theater whose façade contains pictures of Johanna and of another consummate performer – Adolf Hitler. But Franz cannot accept the fact that the theater is greater than Hitler's image, nor that *Arturo Ui* is performance rather than life. As a theatrical spectator whose disbelief needs no

Catherine Deneuve (Marion) and Laszlo Szabo in *The Last Metro*.

Maximilian Schell (Franz) in *The Condemned of Altona*.
PHOTO COURTESY OF MUSEUM OF MODERN ART/FILM STILLS ARCHIVE

suspending, he hyperbolically supports Johanna's earlier comment, "The theater is the world compressed and with meaning."

Theater liberates Johanna and Franz in different ways, as both insist on discovering the truth. In the Brecht scene, it shatters his illusions, allowing him to stop living in "bad faith" and to start facing a new world. And yet, the film seems to ask, is this world (of 1959) really a new one? A Hamburg where people on the street hardly blink at this man in a Nazi uniform? Where "schoolbooks say Hitler was like Napoleon," according to Johanna? A courtroom in which teenagers are charged with defacing a Jewish cemetery? A brother who is clearly capable of becoming another unscrupulous Gerlach? Johanna's response, the imaginative transformation of theater, is thus a perpetual antidote to what she perceives as a chronic disease: "You are afflicted with a national infirmity – a lack of imagination for the suffering of others."

Franz's situation is quite different from that of the other hidden characters throughout Holocaust films. "If I wanted to escape," he boasts, "I'd have gone to the Argentine long ago." He does not even realize that his hiding is imprisonment, because Leni fuels his delusion that war continues to rage beyond his room. However, his situation is somewhat analogous to that of the character Samson in Andrzej Wajda's 1961 film of the same title, a man who is similarly caught between two women – one who perpetuates his imprisonment (Kazia) and one who represents liberation (the actress Lucyna). Franz and Samson are prisoners without a sense of time; dependent on Leni and Kazia for news of the outside world, they are persuaded that to go outside is dangerous; the women want them to remain within.

Samson opens in a Polish university where the young hero Jakub Gold/Samson (Serge Merlin) is the victim of growing anti-Semitism. When he accidentally throws a brick at the one student who tried to help him, he is sent to jail. This first enclosure is rendered visually compelling through Wajda's typically expressive composition, lighting, and camera work. He meets the heroic professor Pankrat (Tadeusz Bartosik), and one shot balances Pankrat's cell on the left with Samson's on the right: there is light only on each face, a glimmering bond in the pervasive dark. The faces are further linked by a panning camera movement. An explosion gets Samson out of jail, but his next prison is the Warsaw Ghetto. A magnificently layered shot expresses the situation through economical deep focus: the soldiers in the foreground hammer in bars, closing off our view of the midground where the crowd faces us, and in the background more soldiers are visible. Samson survives in the Ghetto by burying the dead inhabitants. When he must carry his own mother (Irena Netto) to burial, he accepts a friend's offer to escape, and heads for the Aryan sector. Here, he takes refuge with Lucyna (Alina Janowska), an actress who tries to keep him from returning to the Ghetto. When she finally confesses that she too is a Jew – "I escape from the Ghetto every day" – we become aware of the fundamental role playing necessary for survival under the Occupation. Lucyna is an actress on stage and off, and she extends her ability to assume a persona into her efforts to protect Samson: she dyes her hair blonde, and then cuts it to change her appearance.

Samson leaves her apartment and her love – a departure foreshadowed by a shot of the couple in bed through the bars of a chair, suggesting imprisonment – and meets a group of street performers who put a mask on him. Wajda shows the solidarity of theater people and their ease in adapting to maleficent conditions when they help him regain the path to the Ghetto. Samson finds the apartment of Malina (Jan Ciecierski), his former cell mate, who lives with his daughter Kazia (Elzbieta Kepinska). That she will destroy his identity is hinted when she washes Samson's sweater – inadvertently removing the Jewish star – and reinforced when she cuts the hero's hair. This "Delilah" falls in love with the hidden boarder, and when the actress comes looking for him, Kazia tells her the only place to find her former lodger is Gestapo headquarters. Lucyna gives herself up to the Nazis while Kazia tries to win Samson's love by assuming the role of protector, not unlike the actress in Wojciech Has's 1963 film *How to Be Loved* (*Jak być Kochana*), who hides the reluctant hero played by Zbigniew Cybulski – and both scripts are by Kazimierz Brandys.

Theatrical lighting once again connects the film's prisons as Samson's rocking chair casts intermittent bars on Kazia's face; when Samson lowers his head, he places them both behind reflected bars. He rocks himself into a lamentable passivity, claiming that he will never leave the cellar, until he is roused by the memory of his mother's admonition: "Our ordeal has gone on for more than five thousand years. You have to be as strong as Samson." After Malina is struck by a German van and carried away, Kazia brings her charge upstairs: the screen goes white as Samson leaves the cellar, a subjective burst of illumination signifying escape from the dark. (This is the case for the audience as well, for we have been seeing only as much of the outside world as the prisoner.)

Samson abandons the clutching Kazia and finds what will become his last hiding place, inside the printing plant of a clandestine newspaper. Now allied with Pankrat and the Communists, he enacts a heroic finale by throwing a grenade at snooping German soldiers. A beam falls on him, killing him, and *Samson* ends with a whiteout; this rhymes visually with the earlier explosion of light, suggesting a final escape – and illumination through heroic action. *Samson's* voice-over narration changes from an objective (if poetic) third-person to the first-person – the hero's inner voice inciting him to act. Thematically, this shift represents a movement from manipulated object to ruler of his own destiny, no longer at the mercy of women. The dark woman in *Samson* cuts his hair, implying the emasculation of the male; the fair woman cuts her own hair, prefiguring her self-destruction. These symbolic actions point to the mutual dependency or psychological occupation experienced by characters under political occupation.

In both *Samson* and *The Condemned of Altona* (shot the same year), the women are curiously polarized into the savior-actress (Lucyna and Johanna) and the possessive protector (Kazia and Leni), but all of them ultimately shield or prod the vulnerable male because of their own frustrated needs. They are, in a sense, director figures, *metteuses-en-scène* who manipulate the lead actor. This reflects how the "hiding" hero of films about the Holocaust must be – or become – a performer, able to assume and play roles, create a set/home, constantly improvise, and be prepared to "take the show on the road." Perhaps the most masterful elaboration of this theme is François Truffaut's 1980 film *The Last Metro* (*Le Dernier Métro*), in which a Jewish theater director and his actress-wife play out an offstage drama in order to elude the Gestapo and the French police.

The Last Metro takes place during the German Occupation of Paris, just as the Free Zone is about to be invaded. Lucas Steiner (Heinz Bennent), a German-Jewish stage director, is forced to go underground amid mounting anti-Semitism in 1942. He entrusts the management of the prestigious Théâtre Montmartre to his wife Marion (Catherine Deneuve). She must surmount the subtle threats of the pro-Nazi drama critic Daxiat (Jean-Louis Richard),* the romantic appeal of her new leading man, Bernard (Gérard Depardieu), and the curfew that requires their curtain to come down in time for the night's last subway service. Thus, the limitations imposed by war define the possibilities of theater. Marion's central preoccupation, however, is her husband: he is not in South America, as everyone believes, but hidden in the cellar of the theater. The play the company puts on is *La Disparue* (The woman who disappeared) but it is really Marion who disappears every night – under the stage.

Like Kazia, Marion cuts Lucas's hair, and like Leni, she prevents the man from going outside – even going so far as to club Lucas over the head when he tries to leave the hiding place. Nevertheless, Marion's actions are unselfish and she is closer to Johanna in *The Condemned of Altona* – strong in her identity as actress. Role playing, improvisation, and a vivid imagination enable both Lucas and Marion to survive as well as mount good plays. The 813 days he spends literally underground are bearable only because Lucas devises a way to participate in the performances above: through a utilities duct in the wall, he can hear the rehearsals, and he prepares notes that

---

* Daxiat is modeled on Alain Laubreaux, a Jew-baiting French drama critic of *Je Suis Partout*, the most virulently collaborationist newspaper during the Occupation.

Above,
François Truffaut
directing Heinz Bennent
and Catherine Deneuve;
below,
Catherine Deneuve
(Marion) and Heinz
Bennent (Lucas) in
The Last Metro.
PHOTOS COURTESY OF
LES FILMS DU CARROSSE

become Marion's suggestions to her director, Jean-Loup (Jean Poiret). While the set is being constructed onstage, Lucas builds his "apartment" below with props. And when the French police arrive to search the cellar, he quickly "strikes the set" so that the Gestapo find no trace of a hidden Jew.

Theater is a cover in *The Last Metro* – literally for Lucas who is really underground and wants to be onstage, and figuratively for Bernard who is onstage but really wants to be in the Resistance. Bernard is the only one in the theater company who refuses to assume a compliant persona vis-à-vis the authorities: after Daxiat pans the show, Bernard beats him up in a restaurant. This is the sort of flamboyant gesture an actor might indulge in (as, indeed, did Jean Marais at the time), but *not* a member of the Resistance. Similarly, *The Last Metro* often translates a political question into a theatrical concern. One way to read the film is in terms of displacement: we constantly see characters being moved around, not only onstage but up and down the stairs: Bernard refuses to take the place of Rosen, the Jewish actor with Aryan papers; and we don't really see anti-Semitism as much as French individuals who want for themselves the desirable situations occupied by Jews – their theaters, their women, their artistic authority. (Lucas reads to Marion that French fascists claim of Jews, "they steal our most beautiful women," and Daxiat tells Jean-Loup that the only way to keep the Théâtre Montmartre is to allow him to be codirector.) The Nazi impulse in Paris is depicted in terms of expulsion – "France is off-limit to Jews," declares Daxiat on the radio – or loss of place. More specifically, it is symbolized by Lucas being forced off his stage into placelessness – a room as self-enclosed as a stage.

We do not see any truly painful images of Nazi behavior in *The Last Metro*, for Truffaut's concern is clearly more with his characters than with the German Occupation. For example, there are very few Germans in the film – a soldier who pats a boy's head, another who paints the Sacré-Coeur in a Paris street, the genteel husband of a French woman who attends the opening night party, and (the most dangerous) a lieutenant at Gestapo headquarters whose admiration of Marion is expressed by his holding her hand too long. Truffaut's premise seems to be that there was as much to fear from the pro-Nazi French as from the Germans. Marion tells Lucas that the number of letters denouncing Jews is up to fifteen hundred a day – an acknowledgment of a French rather than German phenomenon. "That's why there are almost no Germans in the film," Truffaut admitted in an interview.[1] "One of the most monstrous things during the war was the 'Rafle du Vel' d'Hiv,' and it was the French who did it," he elaborated, referring to the roundup of fourteen thousand Jews by the Paris police on July 16, 1942. (This event, which facilitated deportation to concentration camps from Paris's sports arena, the Vélodrome d'Hiver, is also treated in *Black Thursday* and Joseph Losey's *Mr. Klein*.)

Despite *The Last Metro*'s sensitivity to the plight of Jews in wartime France, anti-Semitism is hardly its main theme. While the film calls attention to the fact that actors had to have an Aryan certificate in order to appear on stage or screen, it does not dwell, for example, on the point that Jews had to ride in the last car of trains. Truffaut's contention that "this film is not concerned merely with anti-Semitism but intolerance in general" is evidenced by the fact that *The Last Metro* encompasses a homosexual director (Poiret) and a lesbian designer (Andréa Ferréol) with great ease.[2] Why include these characters whose sexual orientation is not an issue?

In Truffaut's words,

> Suzanne Schiffman [coscreenwriter and assistant director] and I observed that the collaborationist, extreme-right press condemned Jews and homosexuals in the same breath. The French pro-Nazis had a very naïve image of Germany – virile male strength. It's absurd to look only at films like Visconti's *The Damned*: sure, there were lots of homosexuals in the SS. But for the Nazis, the weak were "female" in a pejorative sense. Hence, the phobia against homosexuals. It always pops up in reviews of the collaborationist newspaper *Je Suis Partout* [I am everywhere]: you read, for instance, "a play that reeks of Jewishness and effeminacy."[3]

In *The Last Metro*, this accusation is leveled by Daxiat at the Steiners' productions, and many of the film's lines and details come from actors' memoirs and research. The film has an extremely realistic specificity of background, décor, and costumes (down to the women's dark-toned legs – makeup rather than stockings!); the first shots are archival photographs and footage, accompanied by a male voice-over narration that roots the story in a precise time and place. Nevertheless, *The Last Metro* is closer to Lubitsch's *To Be or Not to Be* than to Marcel Ophuls's *The Sorrow and the Pity*, for Truffaut's affectionate tale puts his actors rather than the Occupation in the foreground. As he explained at the press conference of the 1980 New York Film Festival (where his film was the closing-night selection), "It's an invented story nourished by real details but deliberately outside my reality. The Occupation is the echo chamber for the actors. My intention was to make a dramatic comedy with true or plausible elements."

By the last part of the film, the director's relationship to the audience and material is downright playful. "Our story awaits its epilogue," announces the narrator, and locates us in the summer of 1944. Marion enters a hospital room, approaches a wounded and sullen Bernard, and says, "He's dead now." We assume the reference to be to Lucas, especially when she asks Bernard to make a new start with her. As the scene progresses, the window behind them (showing people moving) is suddenly a painted backdrop; their faces seem more heavily made up; and the eruption of applause reveals that this has been a play. Truffaut suggests how easy it is to confuse "theater" with "reality," and then elicits a sigh of relief when Lucas is spotted. He moves, symbolically enough, from shadow into light to accept the applause, and then joins Marion and Bernard onstage to take a bow.[4] He is back where he belongs, a survivor of claustrophobia, loneliness, and the pernicious if abstract intolerance of the French.

As Peter Pappas wrote in his perceptive review of *The Last Metro*:

> the most extraordinary performance of the film, the one true revelatory appearance, belongs to Heinz Bennent, playing the role of Lucas Steiner. Bennent's performance is evocative in the most Proustian sense of the word; it is the madeleine which pulls us into the obscurely remembered past. Through Bennent's portrayal of Steiner, which is to say, through Steiner's every delicate movement of his body, every aristocratic nuance of his hands, every measured step of his feet, we are swallowed into a Paris that no longer exists: the city of Sacha Guitry, Alain Cuny, the young Jean-Louis Barrault, and, of course, Louis Jouvet.[5]

Although more screen time is devoted to Marion and Bernard, it is Lucas who towers over the other characters – even from the basement. (Bennent's performance is all the more remarkable when we recall his Nazi-linked incarnations in *The Serpent's Egg* and *The Tin Drum*.) Through Lucas's bitter acknowledgment, for example, of a children's crossword puzzle that posits, "You can never trust one" for a four-letter word beginning with *J* ("juif"), Truffaut creates a muted but unflinching depiction of the French anti-Semitism that the Nazis inflamed. *The Last Metro* is certainly idealized and tame in its imagery, but cinematically vital in its juxtaposition of stage and cellar, resister and performer.

The Last Metro shares with *Forbidden* (1986) a brave Christian woman hiding the Jewish man she loves – who goes a bit stir-crazy in his isolation. Directed by Anthony Page, this German-English coproduction made for HBO is based on Leonard Gross's novel, *Last Jews in Berlin*. It tells the true story of the Countess Maria von Maltzan, a German heroine of World War II. In this taut drama, she is called Nina von Halder (Jacqueline Bisset), and she first sees Fritz Friedländer (Jürgen Prochnow) when they both come to the aid of an old grocer attacked by young Nazis for selling to Jews. Her voice-over narration establishes the background of the Nuremberg Laws, which forbade amorous relations between Jews and Gentiles. Despite these laws, she falls in love with Fritz, an assimilated Jewish writer and editor (whose father was the first Jewish judge in Berlin). Simultaneously, the feisty anti-Nazi countess volunteers to help a Swedish pastor hide Jews – activities she cannot even tell Fritz about. When she becomes pregnant, Nina convinces Fritz's elegant mother (Irene Worth) to let him go underground, and hides him in her own apartment. "I feel like your jailer," Nina admits. "You are my connection to life," Fritz acknowledges. The woman seems to be the stronger of the two, but we gradually realize that she needs his love as much as he needs her protection.

 Forbidden tells a story that is about social class as well as religion: Fritz and Nina are able to love each other in a manner that might not have been possible if he were a religious Jew. He confesses that he never learned Yiddish, didn't have a Bar Mitzvah, and rarely attended synagogue (unlike his friend Max, whom Nina temporarily hides as well). When the couple finally have a fight, she claims that maybe he feels less Jewish for loving a German. He counters that perhaps she feels less German for loving a Jew. Miraculously enough, when the Gestapo search the apartment, they fail to find him. Even more amazing is the final sequence of the Russians' arrival in 1945: on the verge of killing Fritz, a soldier hears him chanting in Hebrew and – realizing that this German is a Jew (like himself) – spares his life. Nina's voice-over concludes that they married after the war. Nevertheless, *Forbidden* is not limited to what Nina will do for love. Indeed, the most dramatic moments are generated by her complex feelings about hiding Fritz and saving other Jews. For the countess, acting humanely is the priority – even if it means sacrificing her life or that of the man she loves.

Then again, if the noble act of saving a Jew from the Nazis is inspired by lust, is the action less noble? This question is raised in *Angry Harvest* (1985), a fascinating German drama directed by Agnieszka Holland, a Pole living in Paris. Leon (Armin Mueller-Stahl), a Polish-Catholic farmer, hides a Viennese-Jewish woman (Elizabeth Trissenaer) who has escaped from a transport bound for a concentration camp. Racked by fear of the Nazis, ambivalence about buying things from fleeing or deported

Jews, and guilt over his growing lust for Rosa, Leon finds his faith and his mettle tested. Although she must finally submit to him physically, Rosa remains faithful in spirit to her husband. Despite differences of class as well as religion (Leon used to be a servant), he and his hidden charge become a mutually dependent couple for a short time.

Holland, whose father was Jewish, had tried to make a film set in the Warsaw Ghetto while still living in Poland. "But I got scared," she confessed during an interview in Manhattan when *Angry Harvest* premiered at the New York Film Festival in October of 1985. "You have to be so cruel to show the reality of Poles and Jews during the war. Reconstructing with fake blood and plastic corpses! Formally, I'd have to find something beyond embarrassing sensationalism." Instead, West German producer Artur Brauner (who had also produced Andrzej Wajda's *Love in Germany* from a script by Holland) offered her *Angry Harvest*. "It didn't have the clichés of SS men with rifles, deportations and concentration camps," she recalled. "Rather, it dealt with more universal questions of human beings in extreme situations of danger and dependence – especially between a man and a woman."

The Holocaust backdrop was not quite autobiographical for the two authors of the original novel. Hermann Field, an American Quaker with leftist sympathies, was arrested in 1949 at the Warsaw airport. Accused of being a spy, he was imprisoned for five years – without the benefit of a trial. Sharing his cell was Stanislaw Mierzenski, a Pole who had served in the Resistance during World War II. But he had been in the AK – the nationalist, anti-Communist home army – rather than the organization aligned with the Red Army; during the Stalinist early fifties, this rendered him highly suspect. Neither prisoner spoke the other's language. However, their common German was enough to communicate. As Holland explained, "in order to not go crazy, they decided to write a novel based on their experiences. But they didn't want it to be about their own immediate situation, so they took the nearest historical parallel, the Holocaust. The book was then published simultaneously in Poland and America."

Holland's own cultural dislocation might be one of the reasons *Angry Harvest*'s tensions are explored with such sensitivity. From the clash of religions to that of classes, she illustrates the differences between Leon and Rosa – "the very differences that create wars in the first place," she acknowledged. But there is great subtlety in this portrait, as no character is shown to be completely heroic or villainous: some Poles are ready to hide Jews, others are quick to rob and denounce them. For example, the priest and his sister act with decency – the former arranging another hiding place for Rosa, the latter eagerly assuming responsibility as a Resistance courier – while Cybolowski (played by the great Polish actor Wojtech Pszoniak) is a crass opportunist. The spectrum of possibilities exists within Leon himself, as we see him struggle with the conflicting impulses of strict Catholic education, patriotism, lust, fear, and conscience. He can refuse to give a Jewish man the two thousand dollars he needs for a hiding place (in exchange for a vast orchard), but he offers Rosa all his money. He can try to rape her in the stable, but later ensures a safer hiding place – even if they will no longer be together. Rosa is no less complex a figure, a Jewish victim who manifests a chafing at dependence rather than gratitude. Here, the Jew is not submissive but intransigent about her values, not meek but masterly.

Their relationship can be likened to that of a Swiss man and a German-Jewish woman in *The Boat Is Full* (1981), although this restrained and moving Swiss film by Markus

Imhoof deals with a much larger canvas than Holland's. Indeed, it is closer at moments to *The Last Metro*, as both films lead us to comprehend and identify with an endangered group held together by strong women. Because its focus is on life as theater rather than theater as life, *The Boat Is Full* is ultimately more successful at re-creating the real terms and textures of Jews in hiding. These victims of Nazism are neither wealthy nor famous: when they escape, they take almost nothing with them.

Like Lucas's pipeline in *The Last Metro, The Boat Is Full* is structured by open areas becoming blocked and vice versa, whether spaces or emotions. This tension is announced in the first shot, when the camera tracks forward to a tunnel that workers are filling with bricks. We learn that this is to stop the train from bringing more Jewish refugees into Switzerland from Germany. The camera then positions itself inside the tunnel (a subtle hint that it is on the train's side and will assume its point of view), preparing for the next shot – a cut to night and the refugees being forced to leave the train.

Only a few of these victims escape into Switzerland, thrown together by chance: "Being Jewish isn't enough," declares a Protestant minister – only political refugees are allowed to remain in Switzerland. However, an exception for families with children under the age of six prompts the group to pretend to be a family. Accordingly, Judith (Tina Engel), who is trying to find her non-Jewish husband in a Swiss prison, passes herself off as the wife of Karl (Gerd David), a Nazi deserter. The elderly Ostrowskij (Curt Bois) becomes her father and claims that a French orphan named Maurice is his grandson; because the child speaks no German, they say that he is deaf and dumb. Another young child, Gitty, becomes Maurice's sister, and Judith's brother Olaf (Martin Walz) assumes the uniform of the Nazi deserter. Together, they take refuge in a shed that turns out to belong to a middle-aged Swiss couple. The initial reaction of the wife Anna Flückinger (Renate Steiger) upon discovering these "visitors" is fear and distaste; nevertheless, she gives them food (for which they try to pay with silverware) and gradually begins to feel more responsible for them. Her coarse husband, Franz (Mathias Gnaedinger), was originally even more anxious to get rid of them, but he too comes to realize that if they are on the run, it is not because they are criminals. Flouting Swiss law, which does not permit refugees to remain unless they are political, the Flückingers help them in increasingly more risk-defying ways.

When the district policeman questions them, he is initially pleased to accept the refugees' jewelry in exchange for needed papers. But like the Flückingers – as well as most of the characters in the film – he is unpredictably subject to change. Whereas the couple shifts from an initial reluctance to be implicated to finally sympathetic action, the policeman swerves from a readiness to help to later bureaucratic steeliness. A soldier who watches over Judith's husband (Hans Diehl) in prison abruptly offers him a chance to escape on his bicycle. Some of the people want their town rid of these foreigners. Others shelter them, offer them food, and even accompany them when they are forced back to the border. The film's focus is therefore personal, suggesting that the Swiss persecutors of the Jewish refugees were less "evil" than callously indifferent. Or are these terms synonymous?

Being forced back to the border was the fate of ten thousand Jews who were returned by Swiss authorities to Germany – in other words, to concentration camps. As is true of the Holocaust in general, inhuman policies were implemented at least in part by ordinarily decent people, willingly blind to atrocities. According to Imhoof, the crux of the problem is "the half-heartedness of people who came into contact with the refugees – their complicity."[6] Imhoof's direction is sober, perhaps reflecting his immersion in Brecht's writings (the subject of his dissertation at the University of Zurich). His refusal of facile emotion can be seen in the film's total lack of music and in its understated acting. Rather than manipulating the audience, *The Boat Is Full* reveals the spectrum of human response to persecuted people: like the spectators watching this film, some will accommodate them – whether under their roof or in their sympathy – and some will not. Moreover, the film shifts constantly from danger to relief, from drama to comedy, from brutality to hope, forcing the viewer to be mentally alert and aware that easy expectations – about narrative or human behavior – cannot hold. As Imhoof explained: "Here I tried to accept more emotion, but not soap opera. I want to lead the spectator not only to have feelings like in the circus, but to think. For example, there is no music in the film at all so as not to put 'ketchup' on the scenes."[7]

Imhoof maintains a formal distance from the action, permitting the inherent drama of the situation to assert its quiet power. At the end, for instance, he does not indulge in a violent climax; rather, as Wolfram Knorr's eloquent review in *Die Weltwoche* put it:

> One haze-covered morning, four Jews are driven by Swiss soldiers in a truck to the German border. They have to get out in front of a bridge; their luggage is examined; the deportation order correctly stamped. An officer finds two bars of Swiss chocolate, which he confiscates because rationed Swiss products are not allowed to be exported. But since there are two children among the group, the Swiss display their marked sense

The Jewish refugees in *The Boat Is Full*. PHOTO COURTESY OF QUARTET/FILMS INCORPORATED

of humanity: an officer pushes the already confiscated chocolate into their mouths: "There, eat as much as you can." This bitter, sharp sequence captures the whole paradox of bureaucratic procedure and the wish to be human.[8]

Titles inform us that Judith and Gitty were gassed at Treblinka; Olaf was deported and disappeared; Franz Flückinger received a Swiss prison sentence.

Where the film's first shot tracked into a tunnel being clogged to prevent movement, the movie ends symmetrically with a long shot of a bridge in the rain – another narrow track on which the victims are forced to return to Germany. Like the train that was halted at the beginning, the camera is an immobilized witness. "I didn't want to go into Germany with the camera, so we remained outside," the director admitted simply. The conflicts within *The Boat Is Full* – and perhaps the film's tone – are particularly Swiss. With 8,300 refugees in Switzerland by July 1942, the Parliament considered the maximum level to have been reached and coined the phrase "the boat is full." For Imhoof, this decision, and especially the way many people enforced it, should not be interpreted "as an alibi for the Germans. It's important that the film does not remain only a historical fresco: that's why the focus is on a few people with strangers. I accuse the Swiss people because if Switzerland was really a democracy, it wasn't necessary to let things happen as they did. . . . As always, everything is a little bit restrained in Switzerland, but perhaps that is only our talent for hypocrisy: the creeping anti-Semitism, the almost friendly, argumentative brutality, the selfishness which we idolize."[9]

Imhoof's rationale for making *The Boat Is Full* included a desire to "correct the way things are taught in school – half the children never heard about this Swiss law or World War Two events" – and to question a film that had become a national myth: *The Last Chance* (*Die letzte Chance*), directed by Austrian refugee Leopold Lindtberg in 1945, was a prize-winning story of refugees coming from Italy to the mountains of Switzerland. Lindtberg was Imhoof's first teacher, and he confessed to his student that he had made a mistake in adding a happy ending, but it was the only way at the time to get the film made. "To criticize *The Last Chance* was forbidden," Imhoof explained, and indeed he found himself deprived of a one-hundred-thousand-dollar government subsidy for filmmaking "because they said my film lacks the critical respect for the problems Switzerland had."

Imhoof was obviously thinking of another film about crossing frontiers – Jean Renoir's *Grand Illusion*. It is not simply that this drama about World War I also stops at the Swiss border, but that Renoir's tolerant and complex vision of people also can be felt here. Like the French master's work, *The Boat Is Full* is less concerned with labeling "heroes" or "villains" than with accommodating a spectrum that ranges from Nazi deserters to callow bureaucrats. Some characters act nobly, others act selfishly, and some change in the course of the film – as if asking the audience how we might have acted in their place. Indeed, acting in someone's place ultimately connotes both the role playing forced upon the characters and the sympathetic capabilities of those confronted by their plight. After she begins to care for the refugees, Anna Flückinger complains, "I feel like a fugitive myself," and her husband later states, "I feel locked up in my own house." By the act of caring, they – and we – are paradoxically "taken over" as much as the hidden characters. This empathy is rendered more powerful by the conditions of film viewing, whereby spectators are

Above, Tina Engel (Judith) in *The Boat Is Full;*
and, *below,* Swiss police stop the refugees in the same film.
PHOTOS COURTESY OF QUARTET/FILMS INCORPORATED

immobilized in darkness, forbidden to speak or make a sound, waiting for "The End" as the signal to emerge into the light. Since it is inherently easy to thus induce identification with the characters in hiding, filmmakers must be as careful as Imhoof was in guarding against sentimentality. As Renoir so succinctly put it, "The more emotional the material, the less emotional the treatment."

Renoir's dictum was observed in a superb Argentine drama of 1988, *Under the World* (*Debajo del Mundo*). Directed by Beda Docampo Feijoo and Juan Bautista Stagnaro, the true story of a Polish-Jewish family was re-created in Czechoslovakia (marking the first coproduction between Argentina and an Eastern European country). The film begins in Poland in September of 1942, with a baron sadly informing the group of Jews on his land that the Nazis have demanded their "departure for the Ukraine." The Nachman family does not obey, although the father (Sergio Renan) fears that his family will lose its dignity in hiding from the Nazis; nevertheless, he complies with his sons' attempt to survive under the earth in provisional bunkers. They dig a small tunnel near the baron's land, into which descend Nachman, his wife (Barbara Mugica), three older sons, their young brother, a girlfriend, and her often hysterical sister Rachel. They are helped by a courageous Gentile, Smialek (Victor La Place). But this hiding place beneath the earth is airless; and when they add holes, rain seeps in to create unbearable mud. Rachel runs away, only to return in a wrenching scene (rendered all the more powerful because we hear and see only as much as the buried family): as Nazi soldiers yell in German, she screams down to the Nachmans to come out and save her. They cannot move, for fear of endangering their own lives.

The brothers make other "bunkers," including one right near the Nazi barracks. Life consists of the three elder sons running out for food while their parents and little brother remain in the dark stench. We are not spared the detail of how they must use one bucket for both defecating and drinking water. By 1944, they are in another hiding place, where it turns out they have more to fear from the Polish Nationalists than from the Nazis: one of the brothers recognizes his first schoolteacher in the group of men who surround them. A member of this group later throws a grenade into the bunker, killing the parents. The three sons search for the youngest, who has run into the forest, and finally surrender to the Russians, who set them free. The camera freezes on the three, who do not know what to do with their freedom, and dissolves to an older man in shadow explaining how the story ended. This is one of the three brothers, now living in Argentina, who says in a broken voice that they searched for the youngest until they found his remains. The end titles inform us that the three brothers have lived in Buenos Aires since 1952, and that the men who killed their family were tried for war crimes and executed a year later.

Although the music is at times too intrusive – like the piercing sounds when they are silently trying to dig themselves out of the bunker – *Under the World* is one of the best Holocaust screen dramas in its authentic depiction of both degradation and family unity, both loss and luck, both Polish-Gentile cruelty and generosity. Caryn James's review in the *New York Times* perceptively pointed out that the film

> exists in dangerous artistic territory. . . . This subject comes so loaded with emotional power that one dishonest scene could send the film careening into cheapened sentiment, manipulation or self-righteousness. But the exceptional achievement of

Armin Mueller-Stahl and Elizabeth Trissenaer in *Angry Harvest.* PHOTOS COURTESY
OF EUROPEAN CLASSICS

"Debajo del Mundo" is to display the ugly truth – these hunted people could not take eating or breathing for granted – with a brutal honesty that is enhanced, not evaded, by gracefully composed visual images.

The film . . . is not a philosophical or intellectual examination of evil; . . . it does not try to engage our sympathies easily by singling out one character, as Anne Frank, with whom we are asked to identify. Instead, it focuses on the daily survival of parents and their sons . . . for whom heroism is stealing potatoes under cover of darkness and drama is lighting a fire that could mean discovery.[10]

At the beginning, it is occasionally disconcerting to hear these Polish Jews speaking Spanish – but ultimately no stranger than hearing Poles speaking English in American films. The cultural dislocation was actually an advantage in the making of *Debajo del Mundo:* as the production notes pointed out, the Argentine actors were unaccustomed to the bitter cold and harshly imposing landscape of Eastern Europe. This led them into a deeper identification with the uprooting and physical torment experienced by the characters. Perhaps the film's strength derives not only from the real story on which it is based but also from the fact that it was made by Argentines – a people who, in the 1980s, were all too close to the "disappeared," to hiding, and to the struggle for survival.

7
Beautiful Evasions?

The casting of Dominique Sanda and Helmut Berger as the blond and blue-eyed Jews of *The Garden of the Finzi-Continis* requires an initial suspension of disbelief – particularly if one has just seen Berger as the decadent Nazi in *The Damned* (made the same year). In *Les Violons du Bal* and *Lacombe, Lucien* as well, the Jewish characters are gorgeous, assimilated, and wealthy. These three European films of the seventies are unquestionably beautiful, but there is a sense in which they evade the specifically Jewish identity of the Holocaust victims by defining them primarily in terms of class. While this type of characterization is partly a strategy for attracting a mass audience, and is in fact faithful to a certain segment of Europe's Jewish population, it is questionable because the reason they're being hounded in the first place is qualified or neutralized by their upper-class status. This is also the case with Visconti's *Sandra*, as will be developed in Chapter 8, and with the two Jewish characters of *Cabaret*. Natalia's aristocratic family is described as "stinking rich" and Marisa Berenson's delicate features are the exact opposite of the gorilla with which a cabaret number counterpoints her; and, as far as Fritz is concerned, he has been passing himself off as a Protestant: he confesses that he is Jewish only minutes before the film's end. Once again, Judaism is secondary to status and social acceptability. Apart from potentially reinforcing the cliché that fuels anti-Semitism – that all Jews are rich – this narrative strategy renders the characters' loss painful *not* because they are Jews but because they are dispossessed, stripped of class. Rainer Werner Fassbinder's *Lili Marleen* is a less beautiful variation on the same theme.

The Garden of the Finzi-Continis (*Il Giardino dei Finzi-Contini*) does acknowledge the uniquely anti-Semitic reasons for the characters' deportation. Vittorio De Sica's 1970 film is adapted from Giorgio Bassani's autobiographical novel of the same title. An introductory note informs us that the period is 1938–1943, when Italy is applying "racial laws." All Jews have been expelled from Ferrara's country club; therefore, the beautiful young Micol Finzi-Contini (Sanda) invites her attractive friends to play tennis on the family's massive estate. She and her brother Alberto (Berger) live in an idyllic world of natural expanse and sumptuous architecture, underscored by a lyrical tracking camera that often pans up into the dappled sky. Nevertheless, even this aristocratic family will not find itself exempt from implacable racial laws and ultimate deportation.

The capricious Micol is worshipped by Giorgio (Lino Capolicchio), her friend since childhood days when they would exchange furtive smiles in synagogue. Giorgio's parents are well-to-do, but clearly not in the same league as Micol's blue-blooded ancestors. His father (Romolo Valli) says disparagingly that the Finzi-Continis "don't even seem like Jews," but is quite willing to adapt to the racial laws while considering himself assimilated: "So there aren't any more public schools for Jews, no mixed marriages, no phone listings, no obituaries in the newspaper . . . at least a Jew can still be a citizen," he rationalizes to Giorgio. As the voice of accommodation, he even pretends that Mussolini is better than Hitler, and Fascism better than Nazism – willfully blind to the connection between the two.

The situation worsens as Giorgio is banned from the library where he is writing his thesis. He continues his work in the massive Finzi-Contini library, but soon thereafter, Micol's rejection of him on a personal level mirrors Ferrara's rejection of Jews on the public scale. Visually, De Sica expresses Giorgio's eviction when, in the foreground, he leaves Micol's house on his bicycle: with the sudden approach of the Fascist parade behind him, he is forced outside the frame, which is then filled by the crowd; Giorgio is expelled from an image – and a world – in which there is no room left for individual consideration. His identity as an outsider is most painfully rendered when he sees Micol in bed with her brother's handsome friend Malnate (Fabio Testi). Peering through a window, he is forced to behold what he cannot become, a voyeur yearning to be a participant. The brother Alberto's physical deterioration mirrors Giorgio's spiritual state, and Alberto finally dies of lymphogranuloma. Six months later, the Finzi-Continis are taken from their home by the police and rounded up with all the other Jews at the school where Micol was once a privileged student. Their fate is deftly implied by the soundtrack, a Hebrew prayer for the dead that substitutes the names Auschwitz, Treblinka, and Majdanek for those of departed loved ones.

The wailing cantorial voice accompanying the film's last images underscores how even this aristocratic family must accept its fate as Jews. Their demise is subtly suggested by the last of the still photographs that close the film: from a close-up of desolate ground seen through a fence, the camera moves back to reveal that it is the Finzi-Continis' abandoned tennis court. The initial image, however, links this spot to the barbed wire and barren ground of the concentration camps whose names are cried out by the male voice. Moreover, this is not the first time a camp is mentioned in *The Garden of the Finzi-Continis:* when Giorgio visits his brother who is studying in Grenoble, he encounters a tall blond man with a number tattooed on his arm. He inquires about its origin, and the blond man responds that he got it at Dachau, "a hotel in the woods, 100 chalets, no room with a bath – just a single latrine surrounded by barbed wire – service provided by the SS with the tattoo as a souvenir of their hospitality. The guests at Dachau are Jews, Communists, Socialists like myself . . . what the Nazis call the dregs of the human race." Significantly enough, this is the only major scene that does not exist in the original novel.

The elegance of this response is in keeping with the tone of the film, which neutralizes horror and even strong emotions through high style. For instance, it

Dominique Sanda (Micol) in *The Garden of the Finzi-Continis.* PHOTO COURTESY OF CINEMA 5 is noteworthy that we see Passover celebrations at the homes of both Giorgio and Micol. It is even more noteworthy, or perhaps memorable, that the Finzi-Continis greet the holiday in black tie, embodying a genteel Judaism that contrasts with the unrestrained singing of Giorgio's family. In this sense, their identity as Jews is played down. Whereas the novel tells us that Professor Finzi-Contini "had asked permission to restore, at his own expense, 'for the use of his family and of anyone interested,' the ancient, little Spanish synagogue on Via Mazzini,"[1] the film does not convey this kind of concern. Micol defines herself according to class rather than religion, as in the scene where she tells Malnate she doesn't like him because he's "too industrious, too Communist, and too hairy" – all of which point to the lower-class origins symbolized by his name (badly or lowly born).[2]

When the Finzi-Continis are wrenched from their home, the image is truly aristocratic: they take nothing with them, unlike the other Jews rounded up for deportation. It is this image of dispossession that haunts the viewer, as they are forced to abandon all their beautiful things. Indeed, when a clumsy policeman accidentally knocks over a small statue, the gasp usually heard in the audience at this moment is revealing: the film has led us to identify with a respect for beauty, a care for possessions, an appreciation of objects. The delicacy of the characters is mirrored in De Sica's cinematic style, with its aristocratic love of textures. In the latter part of the film, the camera moves into a close-up of rose petals that have fallen from their stems – a shot that expresses the situation and exquisite sensibility of the Finzi-Continis with a lushness of its own.

Fascist parade in *The Garden of the Finzi-Continis.* PHOTO COURTESY OF CINEMA 5

Ultimately, it is gratuitous and even incorrect to fault *The Garden of the Finzi-Continis* because its central characters hardly seem or act Jewish – for they say as much themselves. Already in Bassani's novel, the narrator admits:

> That we were Jews . . . still counted fairly little in our case. For what on earth did the word "Jew" mean, basically? What meaning could there be, for us, in terms like "community" or "Hebrew university," for they were totally distinct from the existence of that further intimacy – secret, its value calculable only by those who shared it – derived from the fact that our two families, not through choice, but thanks to a tradition older than any possible memory, belonged to the same religious rite, or rather to the same "school"?[3]

De Sica is in a sense as true to his subject here – the crème de la crème of Italian Jewry – as he was to the impoverished Italians whom he depicted in postwar neorealist classics like *The Bicycle Thief* and *Shoeshine*. This is a different kind of realism that records the fragile and vulnerable beauty of a particular world just as it is about to disappear forever.

Michel Drach's *Les Violons du bal*, previously discussed in Chapter 2, is a Proustian exercise, in that everything the director (playing himself) sees in the present serves as a visual "madeleine" to conjure up his childhood in occupied France. We therefore view the past through the child's eyes or, more exactly, through an artist's idealizing memory which selects only that which looks beautiful onscreen. Pauline Kael's review in 1975 focused on this problem:

> *Les Violons du Bal* – the title is Drach's private slang for "The others call the tune" – is a romantic memoir about the efforts of Drach's gracious and beautiful mother to save the family from the Nazis. Drach re-creates the Nazi period as he remembers it – in terms of what his vision was when he was a little boy. And his memory seems to burnish everything: everyone in the family is tender, cultivated, and exquisitely groomed. . . . The smartly tailored hat that Marie-José Nat wears for the flight across the border and the fine gloves with which she parts the strands of barbed wire are the height of refugee chic.[4]

During the final escape through the woods to Switzerland, the mists convey less terror than scenery, and when the mother's hat falls off during her run across a field, it is hardly believable that their accomplice runs back into danger to retrieve it.

Questions of realism aside, *Les Violons du bal*'s definition of Judaism – the ostensible reason for the family's persecution – is sketchy. After one of his schoolmates wonders if Michel is Jewish, Michel asks his mother, "What's a Jew?" Instead of answering, she continues to chop vegetables with a smile. His grandmother tries to explain that it all began with Jesus, "who was good, but then trouble started." The boy inquires why they never told him before. "We never talk about it," says his unperturbed mother. The insubstantiality of their answer is brought home in the next scene for, unaware that being Jewish has become the cause for ostracization, Michel cheerfully tells his friends at school, "I'm a Jew." They hit and taunt him. He runs into an ornate church, where the only person praying turns out to be his grandmother. Michel is surprised to see her there, to which the smiling old lady responds, "So what? I felt like saying a prayer." The casual substitution of houses of worship seems hardly more problematic to this family than learning the new names on their forged papers.

A delightful scene toward the end of the film does little to particularize the identity for which they are being hunted. When Michel is sheltered in the country, the little girl he "romances" gives him a religious medal from her neck. "But I'm Jewish," he blurts out. "So what," says the girl. "My father's a Communist!" A child's equation, an adult's evasion.

It is, of course, beside the point to reproach Drach for not including a religious dimension to which he himself was never exposed. And he does acknowledge stylistically that the film is a personal exorcism rather than a historical document. For example, the first sequence in the past shows the family reading about evacuation procedures. Visually, they are crowded into a narrow area of light in the center of the frame, surrounded by brown wood. Moments later, it turns out that they were being viewed in a thin mirror – which the movers suddenly take away. Drach thus implies that what we are watching is a reflection rather than "the real thing," and that the characters are enclosed within the frame of his own recollections. For a less romanticized chronicle of escape into Switzerland, one must wait eight years until *The Boat Is Full* – a stark drama of what happened to some Jewish refugees *after* they had made it to the border.

Les Violons du bal does not show any nasty Nazis, a decision that seems less like an evasion than a redefinition of the enemy. As in *The Last Metro*, the villains are not German but French, and their cruelty is less physical than verbal or indirect.

Jean-Louis Trintignant as Michel Drach directing *Les Violons du bal.* PHOTO COURTESY OF CARLOS CLARENS

The only German we really see in the film is a kindly soldier seated behind Michel at a fashion show that features his sister. By contrast, the mother of her rich Gentile fiancé tells the pregnant girl that marriage is out of the question because she is "an Israelite"; the French policemen who raid the apartment steal their cash; Monsieur Robert, who seemed to be helping the refugees, deceives them and runs off with all their money. These Parisian Jews live more in the fear of French denunciations and greed than of German bullets.

Lacombe, Lucien also redefines the concept of the enemy – perhaps at the expense of the victim's ethnic identity. Director Louis Malle's focus in this masterful film of 1974 is a French peasant (Pierre Blaise) who joins the fascist collaborationists in 1944, after the Resistance turns him down. The amoral youth meets a Parisian tailor, Albert Horn (Holger Löwenadler), who is now hiding in southwestern France because he is Jewish. With a sense of dignity bordering on snobbery, this former king of Paris haute couture must now accept the venal visitors who exploit him. After Horn makes him a suit, Lucien develops a bizarre relationship with the tailor and his beautiful daughter, France (Aurore Clément): this illiterate, young gun-toting agent for the German police visits them regularly, bringing stolen goods from various fascist raids. Horn grows increasingly exasperated with his situation, and with his daughter's sexual relationship with Lucien. He goes to the fascist enclave to see the boy, and is arrested by a rabidly xenophobic Frenchman. Lucien rescues France and her taciturn grandmother (Thérèse Giehse) from a Nazi roundup; when he tries to drive them to Spain, the car breaks down, leaving them to pass the time in an abandoned house in

Aurore Clément (France) in *Lacombe, Lucien.*
PHOTO COURTESY OF
CARLOS CLARENS COLLECTION

the French countryside. A title informs us that Lucien was arrested, court-martialed, and executed on April 12, 1944.

Lacombe, Lucien's references to Judaism contain no positive resonance. "Monsieur is a rich and stingy Jew" is how the easy-going fascist Jean-Bernard (Stéphane Bouy) introduces Horn to Lucien (while taking money from the tailor). When Lucien asks Horn, "Aren't the Jews the enemies of France?" Horn answers, "No, I'm not" (as opposed to *we're* not). His identity is rooted in having been the best tailor on Paris's chic avenue Pierre-Ier-de-Serbie, an assimilated individual of exquisite taste. Dressed in his dressing gown and ascot, Horn conveys a certain disdain – the haughtiness of having once been high on the social scale. And the blond, blue-eyed France cries, "I'm fed up with being a Jew," before throwing herself tearfully into Lucien's open arms.

Once again, the interest of the film lies elsewhere, for the racial identity of the victims is incidental to the carefully etched portrait of a casual young fascist and his group. There are almost no Germans in the film (a rather pleasant Nazi visits the collaborators at the beginning, and Lucien shoots the one who arrests the Horn family), for it is again the French who are being placed under the microscope. Malle faithfully captures the spirit of obedient collaboration that characterized much of French life. "What they teach French children about the Occupation period is a bunch of lies," he told an audience at Yale University in 1978, referring to the collective amnesia about collaboration, and in *Lacombe, Lucien* he demythologizes the France of "active resisters." The Nazi sympathizer Mlle. Chauvelot says of the Germans: "They're so obliging and punctual. Had we been like them, we'd have won the war." As she reads letters from informers, the coldly efficient woman acknowledges: "We get two hundred a day. One even wrote to denounce himself. It's like a disease." The sickness is presented objectively, with no directorial judgment expressed by self-conscious camera angles or editing. With the exception of the credits and the last scene, the only music we hear comes from within the story (such as France's piano playing) and is never used to manipulate the viewer. *Lacombe, Lucien* portrays the collaborators as creatures of amoral impulse. Lucien's first action in the film is to shoot a bird with a slingshot; later he shoots rabbits, poaches other animals, smacks a hen's head off – wanton killing that may be unpleasant to watch, but that seems natural to the farm boy. But by the time he catches animals in the last sequence – in order to feed France and the grandmother – the hunting is redefined as necessity for survival.

Shot on location in southwestern France, *Lacombe, Lucien* often "feels" like a documentary: its first and last sequences chronicle simple daily existence with little dialogue. Lucien is played by a nonprofessional, a peasant who looks and sounds authentic in his uncomplicated relationship to things and people. His accent is palpably different from that of the displaced Parisians, and his straightforwardness gives the film a unique flavor. (A few years later, Pierre Blaise was killed in an auto accident, without ever having made another film.) Lucien is an uncalculating and spontaneous animal. Everything he is and does is externalized in action: his lack of worldliness is even manifested by the clumsy way he smokes cigarettes. When he sees France standing in a long line for groceries, he pulls her up to the front in order to look important, flashing his "German Police" card. When he shoots the Nazi who comes to collect France for roundup, it seems like an unpremeditated action, sparked by the German's attempt to pocket the gold watch that Lucien originally gave to Horn. Lucien is drawn to the fascists because they accept him and make him feel important, but he is equally drawn

Lucien (played by Pierre Blaise) receives a warning in *Lacombe, Lucien.* PHOTO COURTESY OF CARLOS CLARENS

to Horn's exquisite sensibility and to France's porcelain beauty. As Horn tells him, "I can't bring myself to really hate you," for Lucien seems too naïve to be labeled evil.

Malle's direction allows for deep ambiguity about why certain people become fascists. Some of the individuals in the posh hotel headquarters admittedly have axes to grind: the boss was fired from the police in 1936 as an "undesirable"; the unattractive maid who screams "Dirty Jew!" hysterically at France is jealous of the woman's attractiveness to Lucien; and Lucien himself was told by the Resistance leader that he was not serious or old enough to join their group. In general, these are ordinary people, with recognizable impulses, fears, and needs. *This* is what we're up against, Malle seems to be saying: people who believe what they hear on the radio (the first broadcaster announces, "We hear nothing but Communist lies") or from a bicycle champion (one of Lucien's heroes). Like many shortsighted people in the forties, Lucien does not question the ludicrous fascist position articulated in the scene where the "French Gestapo" group arrest a doctor. "Do you want Bolshevism in France?" they ask him. "But I'm a Gaullist," he responds. "De Gaulle is surrounded by Jews and Communists," they retort.

It seems hardly coincidental that *Lacombe, Lucien, Les Violons du bal, Black Thursday,* and *Mr. Klein* – implicit indictments of the French population – were all made in the mid-seventies. The French philosopher Bernard Henri-Lévy suggests that "until 1969, nobody knew there was something in their history called *pétainisme.* There was a taboo during De Gaulle's era – an image of collective heroism. The people believed fascism came from the *outside*, not that the virus was French. The only country in occupied Europe that didn't try to 'de-fascize' itself was France."[5]

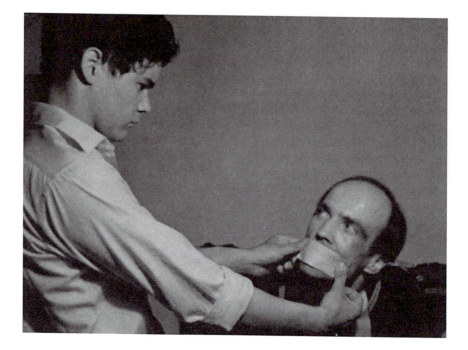

Above, Lucien assumes authority in *Lacombe, Lucien*.
Below, Pierre Blaise (Lucien) and Aurore Clément (France)
in *Lacombe, Lucien*. PHOTOS COURTESY OF CARLOS CLARENS

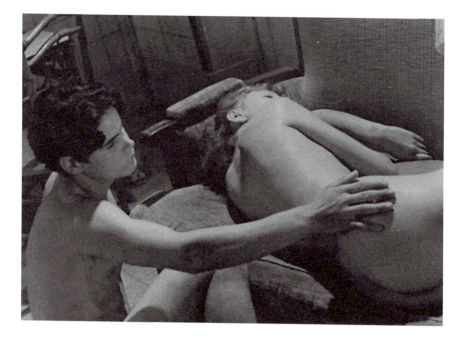

Filmmakers in the seventies – following the stirring example of Marcel Ophuls's *The Sorrow and the Pity* – finally addressed themselves to the fatal indifference and complicity of the French, but only with Jewish characters assimilated (or classy) enough to appeal to an audience still subject to anti-Semitism. This is not to say that the more "authentic" Jewish characters are or should look unattractive; but rather that the predominance of characters who bear neither external nor internal acknowledgment of their Judaism can offer only a fraction of the historical picture. When physical beauty or social class eclipses all other roots of identity, there is a danger that the aesthetic can become an anesthetic; in such cases, the specificity of the Holocaust victim is lost.

Rainer Werner Fassbinder's *Lili Marleen* (1981) is the most insidious of the recent cinematic revisions of the Nazi era, a fairy tale that gives a new twist to Hannah Arendt's term "the banality of evil." Shot primarily in English and then presented on American screens dubbed into German with English subtitles, it is an exercise in displacement: the Nazis are either benign, ineffectual, or secretly good guys; the Jews are wealthy and comparatively safe, while the most deceitfully manipulative character in the film is the Jewish father. "Money, he's got plenty," says his son. Beyond what some viewers construe as the film's obvious irony, it is no wonder that *Lili Marleen* was the number one box-office hit in Germany: it offers a myth about the late thirties that is comforting for those who prefer to avoid guilt and responsibility. "It's not as bad here as some people might think," says a Nazi official to the heroine in Gestapo headquarters.

Lacking a coherent point of view, the film offers a love story between Robert Mendelsson (Giancarlo Giannini, looking and sounding less convincing than in *Seven Beauties*), a rich Swiss-Jewish conductor who helps obtain false passports for endangered Jews, and Willie (Hanna Schygulla), a wide-eyed cabaret singer of dubious talent. Robert's father (Mel Ferrer) suspects the Aryan Willie might foul up their operation, and maneuvers her expulsion from Switzerland. Back in Germany, Willie's career is guided by the influential Nazi Henkel (Karl-Heinz von Hassel), and her recording during the early months of World War II of the tune "Lili Marleen" turns her into a celebrity. Even Hitler wants to meet Willie, and her rendezvous with the Führer is presented as her disappearing through a massive door into a heavenly blast of white. She and her pianist, Taschner (Hark Bohm), are given a sumptuously vulgar apartment, as Willie continues to perform the song so beloved by German soldiers.

Despite her status as a Nazi icon, Willie helps Robert's Jewish resistance organization in its attempt to obtain proof of what is happening in Poland. During a tour of the German front, she smuggles out accusatory film of concentration camps – a fact Mendelsson keeps secret from his son lest Robert return to this *shiksa* rather than marry the nice Jewess that Papa has picked out for him. When Robert is captured, Mendelsson makes a deal with the Gestapo for seventy-eight people plus his son to be returned across a bridge into Switzerland, presumably in exchange for the film. After the war, Willie and a leading Nazi (Erik Schumann), who was really helping the Resistance all along, are on the run, having no witnesses to testify to their good deeds. Willie sneaks into a concert hall where Robert is conducting: seeing his wife and cozy family, she conveniently disappears into the night.

It is significant that *Lili Marleen*'s opening and closing locale is Switzerland, where the Jew is unthreatened if he stays put: Robert's difficulties arise only when

Above, Hanna Schygulla (Willie) in *Lili Marleen.* *Below,* Willie and Henkel (played by Karl-Heinz von Hassel) visiting the Führer in *Lili Marleen.* PHOTOS COURTESY OF UNITED ARTISTS CORPORATION

he is in Germany. And even there, the worst torture inflicted on this Jew is to be locked in a cell plastered with posters of Willie, forced to listen to the same few bars of "Lili Marleen" without end. The Nazis never do anything particularly vicious onscreen, and during the big party sequence, they are more interested in hearing Willie sing than in acknowledging Hitler's birthday. This sequence is quite long and colorful, laced with a kind of nostalgia for the boisterous camaraderie of the "good old thirties." The quintessential German is perhaps Willie, naïve but decent as she claims, "I'm only singing a song," when Robert tells her that cruel things are happening.

It is really the Gemans who are portrayed as victims, for every time Willie performs "Lili Marleen" in a radio broadcast, there are intercuts of sad young German soldiers. (The bomb footage and the faces tend to be identical in every scene, as if Fassbinder had run out of film.) The displacement becomes evident when Henkel informs her that she is heard by six million soldiers. "Six million?" she repeats incredulously. A loaded number indeed. And Fassbinder reserves his sympathy for Taschner, who is dispatched to the Eastern Front when he talks back to the SS. This particular action serves to reinforce the complacency of "But what could we do?" The Jewish resistance organization is likewise depicted as a relatively ineffectual clan: one of its members, Aaron (Gottfried John), abruptly blows up the bridge after Robert is returned to his father. "I don't like that kind of deal" is his feeble explanation.

Fassbinder casts himself as Günther Weisenborn, the head of the resistance organization. (Whether consciously or not, he appropriated the name of a German director who made *Memorial*, a documentary celebrating Gentiles who resisted the Nazis.) With dark glasses, thick beard, and paunch, he becomes a caricature with far more fidelity to forties movies than to wartime realities. Similarly, the music of *Lili Marleen* distances the viewer from potential identification with the Jewish characters: almost every time they are shown, the melodramatic and heavily percussive score roars in. One is reminded of Volker Schlöndorff's remark in an interview: "It's really quite difficult to give credence to the action in a Fassbinder film. The excessive melodrama tries to conceal the failure of imagination."[6]

The only self-consciously masterful touch in *Lili Marleen* is the name given to Willie's Nazi patron: Henkel. For those who have seen *The Great Dictator*, it is difficult to forget the parodic Hynkel and not to view Fassbinder's Nazi as little more than a joke. This is especially the case when Henkel toys with a globe in his office – a visual echo of Chaplin's delirious dance. Apart from the knowing wink this scene might constitute, *Lili Marleeln* is as flat as the globe balloon at the end of Chaplin's ballet.

Finally, since the Mendelssons are the only Jewish protagonists in a film about the Nazi era, Fassbinder would have us believe, once again, that Judaism is tantamount to wealth, lack of solidarity, and clever calculation. *Lili Marleen* allows the viewer to assume that a Jew could always buy his way out of real danger. Ferrer's soulless characterization of the despotic patriarch and the Jewish victim in one is more ruthless than religious (the same kind of Jew that Fassbinder presents in his earlier [1979] film, *In a Year of Thirteen Moons* – a former Bergen-Belsen inmate who becomes a fiercely powerful businessman). When it is difficult to accept responsibility – so you don't have to think about your own role – how convenient to project onto the victims the despicable characteristics of the oppressors.

8
The Condemned and Doomed

mong the Italian films that deal with the postwar legacy of the Holocaust, at least three explore guilt in an upper-class family eroded and ultimately doomed by its accumulated ghosts. The major elaborators of this theme are Luchino Visconti (*Sandra* and *The Damned*) and Vittorio De Sica (*The Condemned of Altona* and *The Garden of the Finzi-Continis*), directors particularly sensitive to history's weight on individuals. For these two filmmakers, who began their careers as neorealists shooting nonprofessional actors in the street, and ended with sumptuous period adaptations (*The Innocent* and *The Voyage*), the past is often a burden that individuals must comprehend and then surrender – lest they become prisoners of history. Liliana Cavani's *The Night Porter* presents a variation on this theme of imprisonment by the past. In Visconti's *Sandra* (*Vaghe Stelle dell'Orsa*), for example, the heroine maintains, "We have no ghosts." The 1965 film itself illustrates the contrary, denying her claim with an abundance of both literal and figurative shadows.

Sandra (Claudia Cardinale), a beautiful young Italian Jewess married to the American Andrew (Michael Craig), returns from a chic modern environment in Geneva to her family home in the crumbling hill town of Volterra for a dedication ceremony: the statue of her father – who died in Auschwitz – is to be unveiled. Her brother Gianni (Jean Sorel) also returns, a troubling and troubled erotic presence vis-à-vis his sister. Sandra believes that her Gentile mother (Marie Bell) and the lawyer Gilardini (Renzo Ricci) denounced her father during the war, and eventually confronts each of these characters. In this tense environment, Sandra searches for her distinct identity in terms of class, sexuality, Judaism, and her American husband, but it is ultimately in terms of her father and his legacy that she defines herself. Whereas Andrew wants her to leave the patrimonial home, claiming that "the past is but a time for choosing the future," Sandra says she will remain, "unable to forget, doing penance."

Sandra's guilt over being alive while her father was murdered in a concentration camp is heightened by her mother's screams, "You have your father's Jewish blood in

Dirk Bogarde (Max) and Charlotte Rampling (Lucia) in *The Night Porter*.

your veins." (Having been spared his suffering, Sandra actually went to Auschwitz after the war to work as an interpreter during survivor investigations.) Visconti's heroine seeks lucidity about her relationship to her family, but the film's stark contrasts between darkness and light and its doubling of figures suggest the difficulty of clear perception. As Bertolucci, heavily influenced by Visconti, would develop through the self-conscious style and obtrusive lighting of *The Conformist*, what one sees depends on how it is illuminated (whether by a lamp or a mentor – or a film). Part of Sandra's home is sealed off, perhaps like an area of her mind that remains in darkness. When she meets Gianni in the water tower where they used to hide as children, leading to a flashback of their mother, the high-contrast lighting turns Sandra's face into a mask. And when the camera pulls back from the siblings to their reflected images in the water, it expresses the split within the characters: a part of them exists in a submerged union. Moreover, Sandra's departure at this moment makes her ascent (up the twisting stairs) look like a simultaneous descent into the water – a contradictory movement in space that represents her confusion in time.

A subsequent scene in which their past appears, bathed in rich firelight, clarifies that Sandra and Gianni are awash in memories. A harsh corollary is provided by their lighting in the present that consists, in the scene that follows, of a naked bulb suspened under a dark chandelier. Beneath this emblem of the upper class that is more ornamental than functional, the simple light bulb is the agent of vision – and

Claudia Cardinale as *Sandra.* PHOTO COURTESY OF CORINTH FILMS

it is Gianni who turns it on. Throughout the film, he moves in and out of light, alternating between hiding and revelation until his definitive merging with darkness at the end of the film: Gianni's suicide is crosscut, significantly enough, with the unveiling of their father's image.

This is not the first occasion of visual rhyming between father and son in *Sandra*. In an early sequence, Gianni covers his face with his sister's white shawl just after we see the statue of the father covered with a white sheet. The reason for this kind of doubling is not merely symmetry, but to suggest that Sandra's ambiguous relationship with her brother derives its meaning from – and is in a sense a substitute for – unresolved feelings about her lost father. Indeed, the behavior of Gianni and Sandra seems less like that of lovers than of children pretending to be concentration camp inmates: they feel persecuted; they leave notes for each other in secret places; and Gianni finally writes to her in fear and despair, "I don't want to die" – before taking his life. Andrew understands that Sandra "went to the concentration camp to relive [her] father's Calvary," but other elements of the film seem to place a disproportionate emphasis on incest rather than on the Holocaust legacy.

The lawyer Gilardini, perhaps like the film itself, evades questions of denunciation, concentration camps, and Jewish identity to focus on the perverse romance of the children. *Sandra* does not really explore the more basic Oedipal (rather than brother–sister) underpinning of the film – namely, that Sandra's fundamental relationship is to her Jewish father killed in Auschwitz. For the unveiling of his statue, she dresses in white, like an expectant bride. Perhaps incest was a more commercially provocative theme than post-Holocaust Jewish identity. Perhaps Visconti was more interested in extending the patterns of betrayal, denunciation, and accusation, moving from the Holocaust to an allusive treatment of the transmission of a family curse. Or perhaps, as in *The Garden of the Finzi-Continis*, the suggestion of incest is a complex metaphor for the "racial bonds" that tie *Sandra* together. In both cases, the death of the brother allows for the image of a new couple created by the Holocaust – a father–daughter union (even though Micol embraces Giorgio's father as a substitute for her own lost one).

In *The Garden of the Finzi-Continis*, it is no coincidence that the book Micol reads when she is sick in bed is *Les Enfants terribles* – "*molto chic*," as she says to Giorgio. Jean Cocteau's novel has deep connections with aspects of this film: through the ambiguous brother–sister relationship; the attraction the siblings hold for the young man (Gérard/Giorgio) enamored of the strong sister; the fourth party who disrupts the situation (Agathe/Malnate); the possible homosexual impulses of the brother; and the enclosure from which the siblings refuse to go out ("the room"/"the garden"). Micol tells Giorgio that the reason she can't love him is that they are too similar, "like two drops of water. It would be like making love with my brother."

Both Paul in Cocteau's work and Alberto in De Sica's are sickly, mothered by the sister, tormented by her absence, and perhaps romantically attached to her. As artists in the former and as Italian aristocrats in the latter, the siblings do not go out and mix with ordinary people. (The hermetic enclosure of the Finzi-Continis against the outside world is particularly visible during Alberto's funeral: as they walk behind the hearse, an air-raid signal is heard. They remain oblivious to the

Micol (Dominique Sanda) comforts her grandmother in
The Garden of the Finzi-Continis. PHOTO COURTESY OF CARLOS CLARENS

sound, quietly following the coffin.) This suggests that the family, by being too close for comfort, is doomed to die out. Such a theme is not unconnected to the Holocaust, for the enforced insularity of the Jewish family can be seen as a response to an increasingly hostile environment. At the end of *The Garden of the Finzi-Continis,* the painful truth is that the family can survive only through separation. At the beginning of *Kapo* and at the end of *Black Thursday,* for instance, the young women jump onto the transports bearing their mothers away. By contrast, De Sica implies that both the aristocratic Finzi-Continis and the middle-class family of Giorgio have to accept dispersal: Giorgio's father has sent his wife and sons far away; Micol silently enters one room during the roundup as her parents are led into another. Only when Micol is separated from her family and Signor Bassani from his, can these divergent characters come together: when they hug in the classroom, class is finally obliterated and only their common bond as Jews from Ferrara remains.

Incest could thus be seen as an extreme symbol for family bonds so tight that they ultimately choke its members. But when the families are German rather than Jewish, they seem to derive their meaning from the "cursed house" motif prevalent in Greek mythology. Both De Sica and Visconti present aristocratic families doomed to extinction, less by an external threat than by the indifference of the patriarch to anything but the family's success. As *The Damned*'s Baron von Essenbeck puts it, his one objective has been "to hold on to the unity and prestige of our firm."

The Condemned of Altona, like *Sandra*, is about a wealthy family that contains itself within a large house that has a hidden part. The shipping magnate Gerlach learns that he has only six months left to live. He wants to leave his empire to his reluctant son Werner, an upstanding lawyer whom we see accusing four thugs in 1959 Hamburg of desecrating a Jewish cemetery (implying a sizable inheritance of anti-Semitism by present-day Germany). He and his actress wife, Johanna, return to the family home, where she discovers one of the Gerlachs' secrets: the elder son, Franz, who was tried in Nuremberg for war crimes, is not dead as reported. He is locked upstairs, seen only by his sister Leni, about whom Werner laments, "It's a relationship I don't like to think about." Johanna penetrates the refuge and tries to unify the family. She learns that Gerlach's empire is the result of his collaboration with the Nazis during the war, including the use of his land for a concentration camp where thirty thousand Jews died. And she realizes that all his children are dominated by his legacy of guilt, from Franz, who yells at his father, "It's because you're an informer that I'm a torturer," to Werner, whose integrity melts at the fiery touch of power. Gerlach's response when Werner says he can't give orders – "Wait until after I die; then you'll think you're me" – functions as a self-fulfilling prophecy.

Like Andrew in *Sandra*, Johanna is an outsider who tries to undo the burden of the past: however, she is no more successful than Andrew in liberating these prisoners of history. Rather, a similar triangle of sexual tension emerges through the initially happy couple and the forbidden brother (in-law), Franz. As it becomes increasingly clear that Werner's motive is personal aggrandizement, while Franz's is blindness stemming from guilt, Johanna beckons Franz into the "real world" – insparable from the world of theater. Unable to come to terms with his past (as a torturer whose entire company was killed in Smolensk in 1941), present (an abrupt end to his conviction that the war is not over), or future (inheriting his father's dynasty), Franz jumps to his death – taking his father with him. Under the high-angle camera, his body assumes the form of a broken swastika.

"Franz has a memory that will doom us all," proclaims Gerlach – a fact borne out by the film's events. Both men die because they are unable to let go of their past actions, the father through pride and the son through guilt. They therefore incarnate vestiges of Nazism that must self-destruct before a new society can flourish. Gerlach can even be seen as a Hitler figure, guilty not of direct killing but of indirect mass murder. He is a veritable patriarch, a despot who demands obedience from his "children." In the Brecht play performed by Johanna's company, the Hitler figure, Arturo Ui, is seen on a pedestal, much like Gerlach when he surveys his empire from above. Symmetrically, then, Gerlach must fall at the end.

De Sica's own appraisal of *The Condemned of Altona* supports the notion that his focus is wider than the film's immediate conflict; as he told the *New York Times*:

> A critic once described me as "the poet of suffering." Certainly the horror, the pain and suffering of the war years brought profound changes into my approach

Françoise Prévost (Leni) and Maximilian Schell (Franz) in *The Condemned of Altona*.
PHOTO COURTESY OF MUSEUM OF MODERN ART/FILM STILLS ARCHIVE

to life and I suppose, therefore, it was natural that when I saw Jean-Paul Sartre's play, "The Condemned of Altona," I was immediately filled with a burning desire to translate this indictment of oppression into cinematic terms. Set in postwar Germany as a study of fanatical Nazism, it remains an accusation against all dictatorships.[1]

Gerlach himself becomes the paradoxical mouthpiece for the awareness of postwar oppression when he reveals to Franz the existence of Joseph McCarthy's red-baiting witch hunts, Russian denial of personal freedom, and torture in Algeria.

The themes of guilt, incest, and the postwar Nazi legacy are given a more perverse treatment in Liliana Cavani's 1974 film *The Night Porter*, shot in English by the Italian director. Here, two "families" are created by the Holocaust: an organization of neo-Nazis who meet periodically in Austria and "eliminate" dangerous witnesses; and a sexual union between Max (Dirk Bogarde), a former SS officer, and his "little girl," Lucia (Charlotte Rampling), whom he knew as a concentration camp inmate. In the Vienna of 1957, Max is a night porter in an elegant hotel. When Lucia enters the lobby with her conductor husband (Marino Mase), there is a tense exchange of looks whose significance is fleshed out in flashbacks: Lucia was one of a group of naked prisoners being filmed by an officer – who is revealed in a subsequent flashback to be Max. These past images punctuate the present narrative with urgent frequency and suggest that Lucia survived by being his plaything.

Amid the growing tension of their mutual anxiety over being alone together, Max "eliminates" a former prisoner who has been his friend. He and Lucia are finally reunited in a scene of violent passion, the more steamy for their accumulated repression. Rather than "file her away," as he is told to do, he locks his willing partner in his apartment where they replay their concentration camp scenes. *The Night Porter* thus depicts not only the political continuity between the Holocaust and 1957 Austria, where Nazism is alive and well, but the psychological grip of a past that locks characters into repetition compulsion. Lucia is not the only former prisoner who seeks to re-create the conditions of intense sensation: there is also the young male dancer who used to perform seminude for the SS, and who now has Max arrange lights in his hotel room so that he can do his number once more.

On one level, the obscene instances of replay constitute a role reversal, for one flashback presents Lucia as a Nazi emblem: in the requisite smoky cabaret scene (of which variations can be found in *The Damned, Cabaret, Just a Gigolo, The Serpent's Egg, Lili Marleen,* and John G. Avildsen's 1980 *The Formula,* where a particularly distasteful nightclub projects concentration camp footage as the background for nude

Charlotte Rampling (Lucia) in *The Night Porter.*

dancers and rock music), Lucia sings in German, wearing only pants, suspenders, and an SS cap. (Redolent of *Salomé*-like decadence, the scene ends with the opening of a gift: inside the package is the head of a prisoner.) In the present tense of *The Night Porter*, Max chains Lucia, and at the end, their obsessive love re-creates a concentration camp situation in which both are victims. They experience paranoia because they are being pursued; they no longer go out; finally, hunger and lack of air make them regress to an animal level. Max and his "little girl" move inexorably toward a consummation in death. One can see this merely as perversion and exploitation of the Holocaust for the sake of sensationalism. Or one can take seriously Max's confession that he works at night because during the day, in the light, he is ashamed. His repressed guilt is perhaps as great as his initially repressed lust, and Max's ultimate action is to turn himself into a physically degraded and emotionally shattered prisoner.

The characters incarnated by Bogarde and Rampling in *The Night Porter* carry associations with the roles they played five years earlier in Visconti's *The Damned* (*La Caduta degli dei*): here he is Friedrich, a German businessman who ruthlessly rises to power – aided, manipulated, and ultimately undone by the Nazis – and she is Elisabeth, daughter of the aristocratic Von Essenbeck family, who dies in Dachau because of her husband's anti-Nazi activities. Bogarde's potential for sleek savagery and Rampling's skeletal beauty are well suited to these demonic films where the only exit is death. Visconti's film is clearly the more rich and complex, exploring a powerful family à la Krupp/Thyssen as a microcosm of German society in the thirties.

At his birthday party, the magnate Baron Joachim von Essenbeck (Albrecht Schönhals) announces his retirement from the steelworks and the transfer of power to one of the family members. He begrudgingly appoints the Nazi Konstantin (René Kolldehoff) because he realizes that the steelworks will become increasingly interdependent with the state. This choice rejects his antifascist son-in-law Herbert (Umberto Orsini) and his depraved grandson Martin (Helmut Berger). Martin's mother Sophie (Ingrid Thulin) is the mistress of an outsider to the family, Friedrich Bruckmann (Bogarde); this businessman is appointed managing director of the firm, largely through the support of Aschenbach (Helmut Griem), an SS officer and cousin of the Von Essenbecks. This manipulative Nazi plays the other characters off against one another – first urging Friedrich to kill Joachim and Konstantin, and then Martin to kill Friedrich and Sophie – until all the power remains with Martin, who can easily be cotrolled by the SS.

Despite *The Damned*'s numerous scenes of murder and sexual perversion (rape, incest, pedophilia, transvestism), it constitutes a historically faithful tapestry of the rise of Nazism. The tensions within the Von Essenbeck family parallel the larger struggles of German society. For example, Konstantin is a member of the SA, the brownshirts who established Hitler's power on the popular level and were then eliminated by the military faction, the black-shirted SS. Konstantin wants the steelworks to provide arms for the SA, but Friedrich – puppet of the SS – refuses. This conflict culminates in the "Night of the Long Knives," with the SS wiping out the unprepared fascists.

Visconti frames the characters' demise with actual incidents such as the Reichstag fire, to which the film's opening refers; the book burning at the universities; and the Night of the Long Knives. Through the mouthpiece of the liberal Herbert, he acknowledges the complicity of German capitalists: "Nazism was born in our factories, nourished by our money." And the director points to class structure and division by introducing Friedrich into the family. As the outsider who wants to get inside – the bourgeois who yearns for the power of the elite – Friedrich is ultimately the agent of disorder. It is not one of the aristocrats but the bourgeois who shoots both the father and his surrogate, Konstantin.

The convoluted plot of this melodrama has mythic, biographical, and aesthetic resonances. As in *Sandra* and *The Condemned of Altona*, the aristocratic family of the thirties is cursed through internal blindness, ambition, lust, and – perhaps most significantly – complicity with an immoral state. That Visconti views this family as doomed is implied in the film's original title – *La Caduta degli Dei* (The fall of the gods). In its German version, *Götterdämmerung*, the title derives from the last part of Wagner's *Ring* cycle, in which the fate of the gods is sealed. The very structure of *The Damned* reinforces an implacable destiny, for the first and last images are identical – the demonic fire of the steelworks. And the Wagnerian strain returns when a drunk Konstantin sings a selection from *Tristan und Isolde* during a boozy SA gathering. It is provocatively placed between a Nazi drag show and the bloody massacre of the brownshirts by the SS.

Visconti's juxtaposition of Wagner's music and transvestism illustrates a problematic aspect of *The Damned*. Visconti often indulges in gratuitous shots of handsome male faces in makeup, or a group of young male bodies frolicking in the nude. Not unlike the character of Von Aschenbach in Visconti's next film, *Death in Venice*, the director is drawn to the beauty of young boys – albeit in a more refined manner than the coarse fumblings in the SA scene. There is a certain ambivalence in his work, not only vis-à-vis the decadence whose very stylization is close to his heart, but with respect to the doomed aristocrats. Visconti himself came from an upper-class family, against which he chafed in his Marxist youth. The love of opulence, however, remained, as evidenced by the glistening surfaces from *Senso* to *The Innocent* (not to mention his numerous opera productions starring Maria Callas at La Scala).

A comment recently made by a French filmmaker seems applicable to Visconti. Pascal Thomas, director of *Heart to Heart*, said in the *New York Times* that "directors say they make a film about a brutal character in order to denounce him, but that's not true. They experience a certain voluptuousness in the character's presence."[2] Given Helmut Berger's striking appearance, it is not such a shock that Martin triumphs: in Visconti's enclosed cinematic universe, there is always an attraction for the rebellious son of aristocrats, drawn to forbidden sexual practices.

Like much of *The Damned*, Martin's introduction elicits a response of perverse fascination. Onstage for Joachim's birthday celebration, he cavorts in Dietrich drag while singing one of her numbers from *The Blue Angel*. The scene functions on at least three levels: it symbolizes Martin's rebellion against the Von Essenbeck clan, his own decadence (subsequently developed in scenes with little girls), and the decadence of

Germany in the 1930s. While Martin sings, shots of a woman watching from the wings are intercut. The deep red filter adds to the ambiguity of her expression: is she smiling? embarrassed? proud? enamored? malicious? She is subsequently revealed as Sophie, Martin's mother. The red tone in which she was bathed will continue to surround her, as discomfiting as it is rich.

Containing few natural outdoor shots. *The Damned* relies heavily upon heightened lighting and carefully worked-over color to express the turbulence of its characters. The morbidly compelling red returns after Joachim's blood-spattered body is found in bed. The central characters convene in the room where the performance took place a few hours earlier, and the red light remains visible on the stage in the background. Konstantin, Sophie, Friedrich, and Martin drink, sweat, and plot, accentuated by theatrical lighting. Under his mother's influence, Martin nominates Friedrich to run the steelworks, thus opposing himself to Konstantin. It is the lighting that tells us who the real manipulators are: shots of Konstantin or Sophie reveal only half their faces. The other half is in darkness, as if the character were showing only half his cards. By bathing them once again in a red glow, Visconti associates these characters with blood and fire.

The flames that recur in *The Damned* suggest the hell on earth that Nazism became. Whereas we hear about the burning of the Reichstag, we actually see the burning of books in the universities. (Among the writers reduced to ashes are Thomas Mann, Helen Keller, Marcel Proust, Jack London, George Bernard Shaw, and Émile Zola. The attitude of a venerable professor who watches the conflagration is neatly summed up in his remark, "I don't want to know anything.") As mentioned before, the film opens and closes with the fire of the steelworks which, by the end, bears a relation to the destructive flames set by the SS. The red glow that surrounds Sophie as well as some of the other "damned" reflects these fires and the red background of the Nazi flag. This family of imagery, combining blood, passion, and flames, pulsates throughout the film.

Another work of art that begins with an image of fire and a premonition of doom had been of great interest to Visconti: *Macbeth*. In 1945 the director had tried unsuccessfully to find a producer for a film version of Shakespeare's play. *Macbeth* can be invoked as an antecedent to *The Damned* if one looks closely at the characterization of Sophie. She gives Friedrich the malevolent strength to kill the patriarch, urging him to prove himself. And Visconti's close-ups of her naked breast, hard and angular as she stretches out upon her bed, are more comprehensible if one recalls Lady Macbeth's "Unsex me here,/And fill me from the crown to the toe top full/Of direct cruelty! . . . Come to my woman's breasts,/And take my milk for gall." Sophie's breast has more of a defiant tautness than a maternal curve as she stokes Friedrich's ambition. By the end of the film, she lies in a drugged daze – fingering incestuous relics of her son's youth – a pale ghost not unlike the Lady who cannot wash the blood clean from her hands. In contrast to earlier scenes filtered with almost lurid color, Sophie's face is now so ashen that it looks no different once she is dead.

Both works are structured by an implacable destiny that destroys the ruthless power seekers. They are initially undone by the return of someone supposedly eliminated: when Friedrich plays the new lord at the dinner table, the reaction shots of shock that precede Herbert's entrance make it seem that they've seen a ghost. Like Banquo, Herbert has returned to haunt his tormentors with guilt. And as with Banquo, his offspring survive – potential adversaries of the murderers of their parents. The sense of fulfilling a legacy, which once again recalls the "cursed house" theme, is convened through Martin and the young Günther (Renaud Verley). In the opening sequence, the Baron pounds on the dinner table three times for everyone's attention. When Friedrich assumes responsibility for the Von Essenbecks, a close-up of his hand pounding twice on the same spot expresses his sense of control. Instead of the third thump, his hand clenches into a fist, unable to fulfill the Baron's pattern; a cut to Martin's hand clenching playfully foreshadows the next stage of succession. Likewise, Konstantin predicts that, in ten years, his son Günther will be in command. The sensitive young man (an ally of Herbert) refuses. But when Martin informs him that Friedrich killed his father, Günther becomes a perfect target for SS manipulation: Aschenbach channels his *hate* and thus draws him into the Nazi mentality. Because his desire for vengeance will be used by those in command, Günther may very well inherit power himself, as his father predicted.

All these characters are ultimately pawns in the hands of the state, as incarnated by the smooth Aschenbach. If Martin seems triumphant at the end, it is because he is the weakest and most easily manipulated. Aschenbach, the literal link between the family and the state, is able to pull all the strings because he believes that "personal morals are dead." In his first conversation with Friedrich, Aschenbach speaks in the first-person plural, and this "we" establishes his symbolic nature. (He is also driving an impressive Mercedes at the time, which – as in *The Conformist* – suggests a control of situations beyond the vehicle.) When the family members verbally assault one another, Aschenbach sits calmly at a distance, eating grapes. His ability to shape the violent impulses of both sons says a good deal about Nazism. Aschenbach allows for two needs that Freud saw as preeminent in civilized man: aggression and obedience. In *Group Psychology and the Analysis of the Ego*, Freud described the group as "an obedient herd, which could never live without a master" and concluded: "The leader of the group is still the dreaded primal father; the group has an extreme passion for authority; in Le Bon's phrase, it has a thirst for obedience."[3] Aschenbach urges the murder of established fathers (Joachim by Friedrich, Friedrich by Martin) and the adoration of a new one (Adolf Hitler). The killing of the patriarchs is pushed to an extreme by Martin, who rapes his mother before forcing her and his stepfather to commit suicide. Upon satisfactorily examining their dead bodies, he raises his arm in the Nazi salute, identifying himself with the new state – and a more demanding father. This last image of Martin is superimposed on the fire of the steelworks, now raging with the accumulated presence of Aschenbach's victims. From the hell of this "heil" comes the ammunition of the Nazis.

The endings of these post-Holocaust films, focusing on the demise or rebirth of the father, go beyond the concept of family. When the father is a Jewish victim, as in *Sandra* and *The Garden of the Finzi-Continis*, he represents a severed link in historical continuity, and the responsibility for reforging the chain falls on the child.

Martin (Helmut Berger) oversees the marriage of Friedrich
(Dirk Bogarde) and Sophie (Ingrid Thulin) in *The Damned*.
PHOTO COURTESY OF MUSEUM OF MODERN ART/FILM STILLS ARCHIVE

But when the head of the family imposes his will and rules with an iron hand, he
can represent the head of state who likewise "protects," frightens, and dominates the
people. Gerlach's motto is "Serve the government in power." Those who inherit this
thirst for obedience – either demanding submission or offering it – are doomed to
repeat the mistakes of the fathers.

Part III

Responses to Nazi Atrocity

In extremity life depends on solidarity. Nothing can be done or kept going without organizing, and inevitably, when the social basis of existence becomes self-conscious and disciplined, it becomes "political" – political in the elementary human sense.

– Terrence Des Pres
The Survivor

9
Political
Resistance

W hy do most of the films that present political resistance to the Nazis during the Holocaust – such as *The Gold of Rome, Jacob, the Liar, The Fiancée, The Last Stop, Kapo, Samson, Landscape after Battle, Kanal, Ashes and Diamonds*, and *Professor Mamlock* – come from Eastern Europe? Is it because most of the organized resistance during World War II came from the left, and its survivors prevailed in Communist countries?[1] Political resistance certainly does not mean only organized activity by the left; however, there have been very few feature films dealing with issues like Zionism, the political role of the Church in Poland, or the ambiguous political resistance of rightists who applauded (silently) the extermination of Jews while fighting against Nazi invaders of their homeland. Part of the problem is that it was precisely a sense of Jewish solidarity that prevented Jews from openly revolting: knowing that any aggressive act against the Nazis would result in retaliation against Jews elsewhere, these martyrs submitted to death. Would it be worth killing one Nazi if that meant an entire Jewish community would be wiped out – as was the case in Lublin? Their sacrifice was political to the extent that they knew it would protect fellow victims and ensure that Judaism would not perish.

As far as organized resistance during World War II is concerned, there are three major obstacles to overcoming ignorance, especially about the Jewish component:

1. Active resisters risked their lives as a matter of course, and few survived. There is consequently a lack of written or photographic records of their work. Moreover, as Terrence Des Pres notes, "Certainly it is not true that they did not revolt; to live was to resist, every day, all the time, and in addition to dramatic events like the burning of Treblinka and Sobibor there were many small revolts in which all perished."[2]
2. Countless Jewish survivors of Auschwitz admit to having had no knowledge of the organized political network that existed in the camp. Indeed, political prisoners enjoyed comparatively more mobility and access to information than Jews, who were programmed for extermination. Accounts of *individual* survival have therefore paid scant attention to group solidarity.

Zbigniew Cybulski (Maciek) in *Ashes and Diamonds*.

3. Almost all the existing photos and newsreels of the ghettos and camps were taken by German cameras. A documentary like Frédéric Rossif's *The Witnesses* (1962) is thus able to trace with poignancy the destruction of the Jews in the Warsaw Ghetto by recutting original Nazi footage, but it cannot show what those cameras would not, or could not, record. How can one reconstruct images or activities that were secret even to the Ghetto inhabitants? Thus, we see thousands of starving and humiliated Jewish faces that elicit sympathy, but few defiant ones to command respect.

Lucy Dawidowicz has called attention to this problem in an article about *The Warsaw Ghetto*, produced in 1968 by BBC Television as a "documentary" film. How faithful could this film be to historical reality when it was assembled from photos and film footage produced by Nazi propaganda teams?

> When the Germans undertook to photograph the Warsaw ghetto in 1941 and 1942, they intended to use the film to justify their anti-Jewish policies and atrocities. From the records left by the Jewish diarists in the Warsaw ghetto (Adam Czerniakow, Emanuel Ringelblum, and Chaim Kaplan) showing how the Nazis staged the scenes to be filmed, the propaganda objectives of the Nazis become quite transparent. The film would graphically illustrate how generous the Germans were in providing the Jews with a place of their own in which to live. The ghetto would then be shown as a place of pleasure and plenty, where the Jews, looking like the hook-nosed monsters of racist stereotypes and the bloated capitalists of Streicher's *Stürmer* caricatures, gorged themselves on food and drink and reveled in vulgar, even depraved, entertainments. Indeed, the faces of the Jews we see during most of the film definitely conform to those racist stereotypes.[3]

Although the British film was clearly intended to condemn German treatment of the Jews, "the images of the Jews which persist in our minds . . . are the very images which the Nazi propagandists originally wished to impress on the minds of *their* viewers."[4] Dawidowicz offers the crucial reminder that "no photographs were made of the schools which the Jews operated for their children, sometimes legally, more often clandestine institutions.[5] . . . The Germans made no films of Jewish cultural activities, of the secret lending libraries, . . . of the political parties and their youth organizations, of the valiant men and women, boys and girls, who conceived, planned, and carried out the ghetto uprising."[6]

A variation on this problem can be found in documentary films that include footage from Leni Riefenstahl's *Triumph of the Will* (1935), such as *Genocide* (1975), also made by the BBC in their "World at War" series. We see crowds that signify the swelling of support for Hitler, but this footage was filmed precisely to buttress that support, grandiosely displaying the numbers already on the Führer's side. The voice-over that explains the development of Hitler's popularity thus turns propaganda into history. Such prevalent distortion must be demystified.

Few motion pictures are as successful as Carlo Lizzani's *The Gold of Rome* (*L'Oro di Roma*) in sympathetically exploring both political and religious self-definition. This Italian production of 1961 is based on real events and was shot in the actual places where they occurred. The Gestapo demands from the Jewish community of Rome one hundred pounds of gold – or two hundred families will be taken hostage.

These primarily poor Jews (the rich have already fled to less menacing locales) try frantically to come up with the gold, while David (Gérard Blain), a young Jewish shoemaker, insists that they must not give in to such demands. He urges them to prepare for armed resistance, but the frightened crowd wants to believe that the Germans will be appeased by the gold.

As the collection grows (including the offerings of non-Jews), the well-meaning president of the Jewish community goes to David for advice. Here, Lizzani judiciously chooses to frame the young dissenter in a manner that expresses solidarity: rather than isolating David in a close-up, he includes in the shot a window that reveals his comrades outside. These comrades, however, abandon David when the one-hundred-pound level is reached. In a shot rendered excruciating by hindsight, Jewish women steal and dump the group's arms in the river, for fear of provoking the Germans. The gold collection proves to have been in vain: Rome's Jews are rounded up and deported. Only David manages to escape, joining the partisans "to be not just a Jew fighting the Germans but an Italian fighting them."

The Goliaths that David must struggle against are not merely the Nazis, but the other Jews who believe they will be saved if they yield their gold. David acknowledges that it is not easy to overcome centuries of indoctrination that Jews should not kill. This pacifist streak, inherent in the faith, has been internalized even by David, so that when he must kill a German for the first time, he can't pull the trigger. A partisan yells "Shoot!" to the paralyzed novice, and only at the last moment does David kill the soldier. To emphasize the moral price David pays for his first murder, the German's death is presented in slow motion, drawing out his agony.

A contrasting image of solidarity is suggested through Giulia (Anna Maria Ferrero), a beautiful Jewess who is protected by Massimo (Jean Sorel), a Christian medical student in love with her. Like her other admirer, David, Giulia ultimately abandons the community and is baptized – but when she realizes that the Germans have arrived to seize the Jews, she decides she must go with them. Despite her love for Massimo and fears for her person, Giulia reassumes the burden of Jewish communal identity in the penultimate scene. Subsequent shots imply the extinction of Rome's Jews, for we see a montage of the now empty ghetto, accompanied by the sound of Massimo's hollow footsteps as he searches vainly for Giulia. Like Nicole in *Kapo* and Jeanne in *Black Thursday,* Giulia chooses to die as a Jew. While *The Gold of Rome* does not condemn her for this decision, the film valorizes David's resistance over Giulia's martyrdom.

A similar paradigm – a romantic triangle composed of a woman, a Jew, and a noble non-Jew against the backdrop of political resistance – can be found in a splendid Dutch drama of 1985, *The Ice Cream Parlor (De IJssalon).* Written and directed by Dimitri Frenkel Frank, it is a film of well-drawn characters and delicate feelings, attesting to the decency manifested by much of Holland's population during World War II. An Amsterdam ice cream parlor in February 1941 is a microcosm of both encroaching Nazism and Dutch resistance. Otto (Gerard Thoolen) is the middle-aged, warm, cultured Jew who has fled Berlin and now owns the shop; as his situation becomes more precarious, he does not believe – or want to know – what is happening to the Jews (not unlike the real individuals presented in the

Dutch documentary, *Shadow of Doubt*). His old buddy Gustav (Bruno Ganz) – now a major in the German Army but *not* a Nazi – tries to protect him. Gustav falls in love with Trudi (Renée Soutendijk), a seemingly cold but ultimately caring woman beloved by Otto. Although she and her brother are not Jewish, he guards the ice cream parlor from Nazi attacks with his antifascist friends. When the Gestapo finally come for Otto and torture him, he does not betray the Resistance; consequently, he grows from an engaging victim wearing blinders into a lucid hero. Trudi undergoes an even greater transformation: although she loves Gustav, she becomes a political – as opposed to merely romantic – heroine when this German officer refuses to risk everything to save his Jewish friend. She lures the Oberstamführer to Otto's place and shoots him, displaying even more courageous strength than the male protagonists.

The Shadow of Victory (1986) is another stirring Dutch film that explores wartime resistance, both Jewish and Gentile. Written and directed by Ate de Jong, this taut action drama begins in 1942 with Jews being rounded up as well as Dutchmen obtaining arms, and maintains a dual focus on both the Dutch Resistance and a Jewish scheme for survival – movements that are not necessarily compatible. (For example, one Jew at the beginning curses the Resistance because of reprisals brought about by its actions.) Peter van Dijk (Jeroen Krabbe) is an ambitious and reckless Resistance leader who still has time for romantic escapades: in addition to his wife, he loves a pregnant girlfriend and another Resistance comrade. Peter and his group can't decide whether David Blumberg (Edwin de Vries) – a young and elegant Jew who supposedly has a list of six hundred Jews to be saved, authorized by a General Von Spiegel – is a collaborator or a compatriot. Whereas Peter opts for violent action vis-à-vis the Nazis, David's means are more quietly subversive: it turns out that he invented this German general with permits for six hundred victims to emigrate to unoccupied Switzerland in order to give the Jews hope, time, and courage. *The Shadow of Victory* raises the question of whether his actions are necessarily less "heroic" than Peter's. Their efforts culminate in a gripping prison break: although almost all the protagonists are killed, there is a shadow of victory, especially because Peter's mistress and baby survive. The last shots of the film are the same as the beginning: nothing outside has changed, except that the Jews have been deported and our heroes are dead. But it is hard to forget Peter's last defiant act with a grenade, taking a German commander with him as he dies.

David Blumberg's attempts to nourish Jewish hope are comparable to those in *Jacob, the Liar* (*Jacob, der Lügner*), a 1978 East German film directed by Frank Beyer from Jurek Becker's script and original novel. In a ghetto, Jacob (Vlastimil Brodsky) maintains everyone's morale with optimistic newscasts from his hidden radio. Through this sole contact with the outside world, the inhabitants are told that the Russians are advancing. Jacob refuses to show his radio to anyone, and when a little girl (Manuela Simon) begs to listen to it, the reason becomes apparent: from behind a wall, it is Jacob's voice that becomes the radio announcer's for this child. The "voice box" does not exist, and the news bulletins are merely Jacob's wishful fabrications. When he finally admits to his friend Kowalski (Erwin Geschonneck) that he never had a radio, Kowalski hangs himself. The film thus raises the question of whether Jacob

Vlastimil Brodsky as *Jacob, the Liar* (*right*).
PHOTO COURTESY OF MUSEUM OF MODERN ART/FILM STILLS ARCHIVE

was not in fact wrong: though well-meaning, he offered illusions that kept the Jews from banding together and fighting. His lies prevented not only suicides (he tells the doctor that no one tried to kill himself since he began reporting the "news") but also the will to organize and resist.

Jacob, the Liar begins with an invitation to question what we believe and to believe what we question. A title states, "The story of Jacob never really happened this way." There is a cut to Jacob. "Really it didn't," continues the written narration. And after another shot of Jacob comes the line "But maybe it did." (Indeed, the film presents a rather benign version of events, for the Nazis are depicted as humane in two instances: a kindly German policeman sends Jacob home after a guard claims it is past curfew, and another soldier passes him two cigarettes.) A flashback reveals that our hero used to be a cook in a restaurant, flipping potato pancakes in the air. His nourishment of the ghetto community, however, is verbal and plentiful: when he says the Russians have advanced three kilometers, his friends' subsequent version to others makes it five kilometers. The truth is that deportation is imminent, and *Jacob, the Liar* ends with the entire ghetto crowded into a transport. Jacob imagines a scene in the snow, hiding from brutal reality in dreams that halt in a freeze frame. The final credits superimposed on stills of the faces in the train suggest, through stopped images, arrested lives.

Jacob, the Liar does not really grapple with the danger of its protagonist's stories. Jacob tells the little girl Lena that things will be better when the Russians come: she won't have to wear an identifying star and will have as much as she wants to eat. When Lena then imagines being a waitress in a café, we see her fantasy. Later in the film, Jacob tells Lena a story about a princess, which a slow-motion dream sequence literalizes. Lena is the princess in a beautiful dress, but the fact that a Jewish badge is still attached to it conveys the poignant subjectivity of the image. On an individual level, the escape into imagination might be a means to survive. For the survival of a group, however, Jacob's lies are pernicious.

Another film from East Germany offers one of the most inspiring visions of solidarity and integrity ever put on film: *The Fiancée* (*Die Verlobte*), codirected by Günter Reisch and Gunther Rücker in 1980, is based on Eva Lippold's three-part autobiographical novel, *The House with the Heavy Doors*. The author – who was in a Nazi prison from 1935 until 1945 – served as adviser on the film, which is set in the thirties. Hella (Jutta Wachowiak), a young Communist, is sentenced to ten years in prison for distributing anti-Nazi propaganda. Two things keep her alive in this debasing environment: love for the man who was her accomplice and commitment to a cause. These spiritual lifelines enable her to be generous with the other women, and to be respected by murderesses and political prisoners alike. Much like Fania Fenelon in *Playing for Time*, she acts with an authority born of innate dignity, refusing to allow the other inmates to fall into self-pity or aimless bickering. Wachowiak plays the courageous heroine with such conviction that the film remains a stinging experience – even for those who do not agree with the political cause for which she is struggling.

Hella is the spiritual sister of the resisters in *The Last Stop* (*Ostatni Etap*), one of the only Holocaust films directed by a woman – Wanda Jakubowska. The 1948 Polish production, from a script by Jakubowska and Gerda Schneider, is also one of the most powerful and historically accurate feature films made about (and in) Auschwitz. *The Last Stop* celebrates female solidarity: as is true of the women in *The Fiancée, Passenger, Kanal* (whose most heroic figure is Daisy), *Playing for Time*, and *The Wall*, their survival is predicated upon this solidarity. Since *The Last Stop*'s first dramatic scene is the birth of a baby followed by its immediate murder, the film suggests that the shared identity of childless mothers was the source for many women's relationships in the concentration camps. Mothers whose children were taken from them (or even women who realized they might remain childless because they had stopped menstruating)[7] channeled their frustrated maternal instincts into caring for their fellow inmates. It is possible that the conditioning of women as nurturers made them better suited to social survival.[8]

The Last Stop has tremendous authenticity because the film was made *where* it happened; by and with people *to whom* it happened; and in the native languages. The Poles speak Polish, the Russians Russian, the Germans German, and the French French. The filmmaker, who was herself imprisoned in Auschwitz, re-created an unrelenting portrait of the brutality of the Nazis (as well as of some Kapos and *blochowas*) on the one hand, and of the saving solidarity of the female prisoners on the other. (Since the only existing print in the United States is at the Museum of Modern Art in New York, the following plot summary will be more exhaustive than that of other films discussed in these pages.)

We are introduced to Auschwitz through shots of hundreds of women standing in the cold, mutely accepting the vicious insults and blows of the *blochowa*, the prisoner responsible for maintaining order in her block. (Such women received special privileges for their usually harsh treatment of others.) Because one Polish woman in labor sinks to the ground, the *blochowa* punishes the entire group, ordering them to continue standing in the cold. Her attempt at divisiveness ("Tell the Russians and French they're suffering for the Pole") does not have its intended effect, since most of the prisoners in *The Last Stop* are united against the Nazis: on an immediate level, each woman around the pregnant one comforts her; on a visual level, a high-angle shot of the group embraces how they weave together, rocking gently in place as one body.

The baby is born, delivered by the Russian doctor Eugenia (Tatiana Gorecka), a figure of dignity and purpose. But the German chief doctor takes the infant away, makes out a report, and proceeds to "inoculate" the baby – presumably murdering it. The mother joins the group of politically active women in the hospital, a privileged locale that retains contact with the outside world.[9] They try to smuggle information out of the camp, and their dreams are crosscut with the realities of German officers who are trying to reduce the time and cost of gassing.(When a man suggests that it would make more economic sense to use the prisoners as labor, a woman officer insists that the priority of the camp is the destruction of "racially nondesirable elements." With cold-blooded calm, they establish a goal of killing fifty thousand per day.)

The realization of their goal is demonstrated in the film's next sequence, as a train pulls into Auschwitz in the night. The camp commandant, speaking only German, and his armed soldiers brutally separate the twenty-five thousand Polish Jews from each other and take their luggage away. He notices that Marta (Barbara Drapinska), a young woman from the transport, is translating his orders into Polish and consequently he makes her his interpreter – thereby sparing her life. The rest of the group is herded off, leaving the space empty except for a child's abandoned doll. In close-up, a German's boot steps on it, symbolizing the fate of its young owner. Each woman is methodically stripped of all her jewels, possessions, clothes, hair, and then is tattooed on the left arm. Like the audience, Marta is a newcomer to this incomprehensible hell, forced to translate not only German into Polish, but apprehension into comprehension, or the act of seeing into an awareness of evil. She asks another prisoner about the emaciated body she sees on the barbed wire and thus learns about "the Moslems" – a nickname for the skeletal inmates "who can't take it any more" and succumb to death. Marta (and the audience) are then informed that the rising smoke she sees comes from the cremated bodies of her entire transport. As with the woman in labor at the beginning, Marta's sudden loss of family will turn her into a defiant member of the resistance, replacing blood ties with those of active solidarity.

Jakubowska shows both the brave opposition to the Nazis and the cowardly acquiescence. A group of elegant women arrive at Auschwitz still in their furs; by the next shot, they are in prison garb. Class tensions arise as the coarse *blochowa* lords it over these socialite Poles – this is her one chance in life to act superior to them. However, as some of these ladies come to realize her power, they connive to become her "friend," bringing her little gifts and thereby enjoying the warmth of her private room. The most pernicious member of this group is Lalunia, a profoundly silly woman who, upon the death of Eugenia, pretends to be a doctor to save her own skin. The wife of a pharmacist, she is appointed by the chief doctor to replace Eugenia – who is tortured and killed for telling the truth to the commission of neutral

Above, the women prisoners in *The Fiancée*; and, *below,*
Jutta Wachowiak (*left*) as Hella in *The Fiancée.* PHOTOS COURTESY OF KEN WLASCHIN

countries formed to investigate Auschwitz. (The Nazis have suddenly improved the look of the hospital, but Eugenia blurts out *in German* to the visitors, "It's all a lie. Innocent people are being killed!") Lalunia steals things from the hospital to give to the *blochowa,* and this group of selfish prisoners side with their oppressors.

These ladies remain ignorant of how the women are being organized through the hospital. In particular, a group of Russian female officers, arrested as prisoners of war, instill more spirit into the Auschwitz community. The resistance arranges for Marta and Tadek, a male prisoner, to escape in order to get to the Allies the Nazi plans to liquidate Auschwitz. They succeed in publicizing the Germans' strategy to hide the traces of their death factory – but are then captured. Marta is to be hanged publicly, although a knife slipped into her hands by one of the prisoners, followed by a shot of a trickle of blood, suggests to the viewer that she takes her own life. She declares that the liberators are coming, and suddenly there are indeed planes flying overhead. Her dying words to a woman who cradles her are "You must not allow Auschwitz to be repeated" – the informing impulse of *The Last Stop,* from its first image to its last.

In the course of this film, most of the major characters die; and yet the central character, which is the Cause, remains – a whole greater than the sum of its parts. From the opening scene, in which prisoners comfort each other, the emphasis is on unifying in the face of the enemy. Those who speak Russian understand Polish and vice versa, whereas a point is always made of translating whatever is said

Nazi guards in *The Fiancée.*
PHOTO COURTESY OF
KEN WLASCHIN

in German. In fact, the precise cause of Eugenia's torture (and death) is that she refuses to divulge who taught her the damning German words she had uttered to the commission. This older Russian woman is the most noble of the prisoners, while her replacement, Lalunia, seems the most despicable. Between the two exists a spectrum ranging from the savage *blochowa* to the self-sacrificing inmates. As in *Samson*, *Passenger*, and countless other Polish films, hope lies in (presumably) Communist resistance.

Stylistically, *The Last Stop* is straightforward, presenting overwhelming events with effective simplicity. The music is less noticeable than in other films on this subject, except when it has narrative significance. From a truckload of French Jews bound for the gas chambers, a woman yells to one who has survived the selection, "You must live to tell everyone what happened to us." Understanding French, the German in charge orders the survivor to board the truck as well. When the young Estelle does so, she begins singing "La Marseillaise," and is soon joined by other voices as the truck approaches the chimney. The use of the French anthem is deeply moving here, for these women (and the audience) know it is the last song they will ever sing. Jakubowska also uses music as ironic counterpoint: when the inmates are being beaten and forced into the gas chambers, the women's orchestra plays Beethoven and Brahms (a historical fact); while Eugenia is being tortured, the German officer puts on a dance record of a Russian song. Contrapuntal music was appropriate to Auschwitz – and therefore, perhaps, to the films about it.

It is unfortunate that Gillo Pontecorvo did not think along these lines when he made *Kapo*. This Italian/French coproduction released in 1960 offers not only an American star, Susan Strasberg (who had originated the role of Anne Frank on Broadway), but a musical score that seems American in its conception: like that of *The Diary of Anne Frank* and *Judgment at Nuremberg*, it is relentless and often maudlin. For example, the heroine screaming at the sight of naked people being marched off to the gas chamber – an already horrifying image – is cheapened by the accompaniment of hysterical music. As well as directing, Pontecorvo also collaborated with Carlo Rustichelli on the score with far less impressive results than in his later masterpiece, *The Battle of Algiers* (where he worked with Ennio Morricone). In *Kapo*, we see the transformation of a delicate Parisian adolescent, Edith (Strasberg), into Nicole, a hardened concentration camp prisoner put in charge of other inmates. She is introduced playing the harpsichord – a musical connection that will be repeated throughout the film: whenever the past is invoked, the sentimental harpsichord theme returns.

During a Nazi roundup, Edith jumps onto a transport bearing her mother away. Once inside the chaotic darkness of Auschwitz, she is spared by a doctor who gives her the clothes of a dead prisoner. She becomes Nicole, number 10099 – a new identity for a new system of being. "You're not a Jew any more," the doctor tells her. She is taken to a labor camp where the kind interpreter Teresa (Emmanuelle Riva) establishes that half the prisoners are political, including many Russians. Nicole's adjustment is difficult for, like Marianne in *Playing for Time*, she is not in control of her physical needs: when she puts her frozen hands on a stove, she not only burns them badly but the Kapo also beats her and gives her fifteen days in solitary. Hunger subsequently leads her to steal Teresa's potato. When another woman is killed, Nicole quickly takes the socks off her feet. And when she realizes that food can be obtained for sexual favors, she complies. By the next scene, Nicole's long hair – which had been shaved off – has grown back and she is playing cards with Carl, the Nazi who killed her friend.

Nicole assumes the mentality of a fierce and isolated survivor: she becomes a Kapo, content to be eating and sleeping well – even if it means beating other women. When a Russian prisoner, Sasha (Laurent Terzieff), accuses her of being like the Nazis, she has him punished. However, when he is forced to stand by a high-tension barbed-wire fence all night (if he moves he dies), Nicole's first glimmer of humanity emerges. They eventually fall in love and plan an escape that, for the politically minded Sasha, must include other prisoners as well. Romance and social commitment conflict when Sasha learns that everyone will get out *except* Nicole, since to arrange the escape she must remain behind the others to turn off the electric power of the fence. They go through with the plan nevertheless, and enjoy only a Pyrrhic victory in which many prisoners are shot. The wounded Nicole asks Carl to remove her Nazi badge, and before dying reassumes her Jewish identity by reciting a Hebrew prayer.

The last shot of Sasha emerging from a mass grave suggests that survival means stepping over dead bodies. *Kapo* thus questions the price of individual safety and celebrates collective spirit as the means to heroism. When Nicole tells Sasha to escape, he worries about friends suffering possible reprisals. And toward the end, everyone but Sasha is willing to sacrifice one person – Nicole – for the sake of many. He admits to Nicole that she will be killed if she turns off the electric power and concludes, "I ask you to do it all the same." Will she choose self-sacrifice over selfishness? Even the Nazi Carl questions the survivor mentality when Nicole declares of camp life, "Now I like it: I eat well, sleep well. . . ." (Carl is indeed linked to Nicole in visual terms, for he has only one hand – a bond with Nicole's burned hands from touching the heater.)

It is Nicole's connection to Teresa that provides the film with its greatest resonance, for the translator mediates between the two sides of Nicole's nature. Like Marta in *The Last Stop* and Marta in *Passenger* (all three characters based on an actual interpreter at Auschwitz), Teresa is a Resistance figure of truly heroic proportions. As in *Passenger,* the translator is put to a test in a public action and, refusing to give information, is punished. In *Kapo,* the high-tension fence is the place that measures integrity: Teresa purposely jumps onto it when she realizes her life has no more dignity – and dies; Sasha is forced to stand beside it an entire night without moving; and Nicole's act of solidarity is to turn off its electric power. As Nicole grows stronger – mirroring her oppressors – Teresa grows weaker. This transfer is made literal by the repetition of food stealing: first Nicole steals Teresa's potato, appropriating her source of nourishment; later, after fifteen days in solitary, Teresa steals another woman's bread. Once Teresa is dead, Nicole begins to reassume that part of herself that Teresa represented.

Kapo traces Nicole's transformation from a frightened, orphaned, and selfish victim into a political heroine who ultimately embraces her heritage and sacrifices herself. She is therefore similar to Samson in Wajda's portrait, who also moves from passivity to meaningful political action. *Samson* focuses on a young man in the process

Above, Prisoners arrive at Auschwitz in *Kapo.*
Below, Susan Strasberg (*left*) as Nicole in *Kapo.*
PHOTOS COURTESY OF MUSEUM OF MODERN ART/FILM STILLS ARCHIVE

of shaping his values through loss, as he is stripped of rights, freedom, family, and the sense of his own manhood. In prison for accidentally killing a fellow student, he meets Malina, a kindly, apolitical humanist, and Pankrat, an inspiring Communist professor. Malina says of Pankrat, "He's a man of steel, but I'm not sure that a man should be made of steel" (thus paving the way for Wajda's 1977 *Man of Marble* and 1981 *Man of Iron*). Because Malina represents individualism and the refusal of political action, he is quickly disposed of by the narrative. Similarly, Samson's sense of Judaism is diminished, while his political identity – fueled by Pankrat – grows. For example, he tells the actress who hides him that he wants to return to his people in the ghetto. Her response to his idea that no individual survival is possible within the concept of Jewish destiny is: "That's false solidarity." The film supports the argument that abstract sentiment for the Jewish ghetto is less tenable than concrete solidarity with the Communist Resistance. Wajda intensifies his thesis by having the camera pan between Samson and Pankrat in prison, unifying them within the frame a number of times. And if Samson's assumed name suggests that his strength derives from his Jewish identity, Kazia (the second woman who hides him) destroys this when she cuts his hair, cuts him off from the world, and removes the Jewish star from his sweater. His strength, Wajda seems to propose, can exist only in terms of a larger political struggle: at the end, the hero's own voice urges him to show his strength by killing the German persecutors. He smiles, throws a grenade, and dies in the rubble.

The inadequacy of individual survival and the denial of positive Jewish identity are also explored in Wajda's *Landscape after Battle* (*Krajobraz Po Bitwie*). Based on

Liberation of camp prisoners in *Landscape after Battle*. PHOTO COURTESY OF NEW YORKER FILMS

the autobiographical stories of Tadeusz Borowski – the Polish writer who survived
Auschwitz, Dachau, and the postwar displaced-persons camps, only to commit suicide in 1951 at the age of twenty-nine – this 1970 film returns to the themes and
stylistic devices of Wajda's masterful World War II trilogy. It begins with the liberation of a men's concentration camp, expressed – without recourse to dialogue – by
a breathlessly mobile camera, jubilant Vivaldi music ("The Four Seasons"), and
the men's physical explosion of energy. The only diffident character is Tadeusz
(Daniel Olbrychski), a bespectacled young writer who is more interested in reading than in taking revenge on a German guard. For all their exhilaration, the men
realize they have nowhere to go: in the film's first dialogue, they are told by the
American officer in command that they must remain in the former SS barracks, now a
DP camp.

These Poles are technically free, but psychologically still at war. A Polish sub-
lieutenant continually insults a Communist; American soldiers make fun of a Polish
priest; and the food-obsessed Tadeusz is punished for cooking on the sly. Before he
is thrown into a hole, however, the former prisoners try to protect Tadeusz from
the authorities – even without knowing what he has done. When some American
women come to see the camp, Tadeusz accosts one and asks her with bitter humor,
"Do you know the crematory tango?" This loner meets another person branded by
the war, Nina (Stanislawa Celinska), a young Jewish woman who was hidden as a
Catholic. After arriving at the DP camp in a truck with other women, Nina tries to
convince Tadeusz to run away with her, but he is even more passive than Samson in
Kazia's cellar. His memories are like the number tattooed on his arm: "You can't kiss
that off," he warns Nina. "It's expert German craftsmanship, indelible." Chained to
these memories, Tadeusz refuses to leave the gutted landscape of postwar Poland. He
insists that he can't erase his Polishness, for "a country isn't just a landscape; it's the
people, the traditions, the language."

Tadeusz's ties to Poland are less nationalist than mythic, for he takes refuge in the
written word rather than seeing the people around him. Nina, on the other hand,
declares, "I'm neither Polish nor Jewish." In her acknowledgment that "Jews disgust
me" and "Israel terrifies me," she is as rootless as Tadeusz. Having first seen each
other when Tadeusz was distributing wafers for the Mass, they seem linked by a false
communion: the wafer passed from the hand of a disbeliever into the mouth of a
Jewess. After roaming outside the camp, they decide to return, but an American
soldier accidentally shoots Nina. Tadeusz takes this in stride, telling the American
in command that "the Germans have been shooting us for six years, and now you.
What's the difference?" After a fight with the priest beside Nina's dead body, Tadeusz
finally leaves the camp, on a train dotted with red flags.

Tadeusz's psychic self-enclosure during the first part of the film is made tangible
by the solitary confinement that he seems to enjoy: he can read in the hole and not
be bothered by the others. Although Wajda elicits sympathy for this tortured loner
through close-ups, he also invites criticism of Tadeusz's disconnected artist's soul.
Tadeusz is thus closely linked to the musician in Kanal, an outsider who joins the
Resistance even though he is less a fighter than an artist. Once in the sewers, he loses
his mind in the labyrinth, quotes Dante, and plays an ocarina while the others search
for an exit. Wajda's entire war trilogy – A Generation (1955), Kanal (1957), Ashes
and Diamonds (1958) – devalues the lone hero in favor of collective consciousness.

The tension in *A Generation* (*Pokolenie*) is between Stach (Tadeusz Lomnicki) and Janek (Tadeusz Janczar) – the committed hero and the agonized martyr. Like the antihero of *Landscape after Battle*, Janek is a victim of Polish history, an indecisive and unconnected young man. Stach, on the other hand, is an embryonic version of the men of marble and iron that would form the center of Wajda's later work: he is a laborer and a resister (perhaps reflecting the fact that Wajda himself joined the Resistance at the age of sixteen). As Boleslaw Sulik's introduction to the war-trilogy screenplays proposes:

> *A Generation* presents a positive hero of working-class descent, and it idealizes his social environment and his own experience. The plot, a story of a boy's growth to maturity through contacts with revolutionary resistance groups, showing the development of political awareness and a gradual assumption of responsibility for his own and others' actions, has been the socialist-realist favourite ever since Maxim Gorky.[10]

In *Kanal*, the solidarity of the Polish Home Army fighters in the sewers is emphasized by a constantly panning and tracking camera that literally binds them together and insists on the flexibility (and subservience) of the camera vis-à-vis the characters. The famous four-minute tracking shot that introduces us to the protagonists acknowledges each one, but only within the visual/political context of the group. *Ashes and Diamonds* (*Popiol i Diament*), on the other hand, synthesizes *A Generation* and *Kanal* by focusing on the dilemma of Maciek (Zbigniew Cybulski), a former Home Army fighter, on the day World War II ends. He is given the assignment to assassinate Szczuka (Waclaw Zastrzezynski), the representative of the new order – the Communist party. (It is important to know here that the Polish Nationalist Home Army had been as forcefully anti-Communist as anti-Nazi.) The central tension of the film is the existential hero versus the cause, the individual who sees no reason to kill a sympathetic old man versus the political dictum that takes little account of private morality. Wajda masterfully expresses this tension through the use of deep-focus photography, which maintains Maciek and Szczuka in a charged proximity. In addition, his frequent use of a low-angle camera perspective results in a feeling of entrapment, as the ceilings seem to continually bear down upon the characters' heads.

Sulik sees Wajda's work as "animated by a true heroic impulse, desperately frustrated . . . made absurd by its context, its nobility corrupted by the modern Polish experience. . . . In *Ashes and Diamonds* this ever-present nostalgia for heroic action found an additional, direct channel in the performance of Zbigniew Cybulski."[11] This actor – like his character – could not sustain the feverish romanticism of his turbulent life, and died while trying to jump onto a moving train in 1967. Maciek, too, dies a useless and drawn-out death – suggesting perhaps that the new Poland has no place for the romantic individualist. It is clear, nevertheless, that Wajda is attracted to this fiery spirit, even as he questions it. What gives his work its complexity is that – despite the hopeful message of political solidarity – his characters have the courage of their confusion. Samson, Tadeusz, Stach, and Maciek all struggle to comprehend politics and are often sacrificed to or comprehended by the struggle.

In Wajda's films, the Jews and the self-centered characters die, paving the way for the Communist order. The paradigm for this treatment can be found in what may

Above, Daniel Olbrychski (Tadeusz) and Stanislawa Celinska (Nina); and, *below,* Tadeusz and his books in *Landscape after Battle.*
PHOTOS COURTESY OF NEW YORKER FILMS

be the first fiction film made about the Holocaust, *Professor Mamlock* (1937), from the Soviet Union. Hailed by New York critics as timely, it was banned in Chicago in November 1938 as "purely Jewish and Communist propaganda against Germany"; Ohio and Rhode Island followed suit; Massachusetts banned it for Sunday showings in March 1939 "because it might incite a riot on the Sabbath." *Professor Mamlock* was the first film to tell Americans that Nazis were killing Jews; however, what must have made the censors really nervous was that it is a political film that places its faith in Communism. The story of *Professor Mamlock* is by Friedrich Wolf, the German playwright and friend of Brecht who was forced to flee his country in 1933. Wolf's play, *Dr. Mamlock's Way Out*, was suppressed in Germany but had a two-year run in Moscow. There, it was seen by Herbert Rappaport, who had fled from Austria after being an assistant to G. W. Pabst. He met with Wolf, suggested the film version, and went to work with him and codirector Adolph Minkin on a screenplay (which was first written in German).

Shot in Leningrad on sets that are redolent of German "atmosphere," *Professor Mamlock* begins on February 27, 1933, as an agent provocateur yells to German workers, "Destroy the Reds and drive the Jews out of the country!" In a hospital, the respected surgeon-scientist Professor Mamlock (S. Mezhinsky) says, "I don't care much for politics." His son Rolf (O. Zhakov) is in love with Mamlock's assistant Inge (N. Shaternikova), who believes in Nazism as a way of "cleansing French and Asiatic elements out of science." The peaceful doctor is against Rolf's political sympathies, and forbids him to return home if he goes to Communist meetings. After the Reichstag fire, Nazi attacks escalate, the slogans always blending "Communists" and "Jews" as if it were an equation: storm troopers barge into apartments; books are burned; men are brutally taken away. Dr. Hellpach (V. Chesnokov), a rival, enlists the aid of storm troopers to expel Mamlock from his operating room, and the professor is paraded through the streets with the word *Jude* scrawled across his white doctor's smock. Hellpach wants to operate on the Nazis' chief of staff – but the officer himself insists on the more experienced Mamlock! True to his Hippocratic oath, Mamlock returns to the clinic and performs the operation. Hellpach's sleazy tactics include forcing patients to sign a petition to rid the clinic of Mamlock, and warning the other doctors that they will lose their jobs if they don't sign as well. As symbolic cross shapes and shadows become more and more noticeable around the Jewish doctor, he suddenly falls (offscreen) after we hear a shot. Later, while Mamlock recovers from what might have been a suicide attempt, all he wants is to see his son.

In the meantime, Rolf has become actively engaged in "the People's Front." When he and a friend are jailed and refuse to give information, they are ordered to a concentration camp. Resistance comrades and Inge help Rolf escape, and the camera points up the spontaneous solidarity of nameless people. Mamlock is killed – but not before declaring to the Nazi soldiers, "You are doomed." The film ends on Rolf and his comrades, expressing a hope for the future. *Professor Mamlock* implies that the doctor dies not simply because he is a Jew, but because he never allowed politics to touch his life. Blinded by his love for abstract science, Mamlock did not realize what the Nazis were plotting, and would not even permit Rolf to consort with the underground. By the end, it has been made clear that science, culture, respect, and integrity are no bulwark against the Nazis, and that the only answer is organized resistance. Unfortunately, the assumption implicit in *Professor Mamlock* and other East European films is that Judaism can inhibit resistance. The message from Communist countries – derived from Marx's own pronouncements on "the Jewish Question" – is that Jewish identity must be subsumed into larger political realities. For compelling examples to the contrary, with Jewish characters standing up for themselves and organizing others *as Jews,* one would have to wait for *Playing for Time* and *The Wall* – both made, ironically enough, for American television. Whether it's Fania in the women's orchestra of Auschwitz, or Berson and Rachel in the Warsaw Ghetto, their generous actions relocate politics from the sphere of factions to the radical domain of daily interchange.

Although organized Jewish resistance has received scant cinematic attention, partly for lack of photographic testimony, *Partisans of Vilna* (1986) is a masterful attempt to fill the void. It is not only a historically crucial document, but a powerful story of solidarity, resistance, and survival. Behind this American documentary are some extraordinary and little-known facts. On New Year's Eve, 1941, a young poet named Abba Kovner read aloud a manifesto, "Let Us Not Be Led Like Sheep to the Slaughter," at a meeting in the Vilna ghetto of Lithuania. This call for resistance to the Nazis led to the formation of the F.P.O. (Fareynikte Partizaner Organizatsie – United Partisans' Organization), which unified differing political parties into one Jewish underground. When the Red Army liberated Vilna in 1944, 600 Jews were left from the original 87,000. Of these 600, 40 survivors are interviewed in *Partisans of Vilna*. The 130-minute film was conceived and produced by Aviva Kempner and directed by Josh Waletzky – whose previous film was *Image before My Eyes,* the loving re-creation of Polish-Jewish life between the wars. Where *Shoah* (1985) ends with the Warsaw Ghetto Uprising, *Partisans of Vilna* is like a complementary continuation, beginning with the armed uprising of the Jews in the Vilna ghetto.

A male voice sings a gentle melody with Yiddish lyrics; it could well be a love song. The subtitles reveal that he is saying, "Do you remember how I taught you to hold a machine gun in your hands?" In these few moments, one can discern the thrust of this documentary, and the romance of politics that inflamed the idealistic Jewish youth of the Vilna ghetto. Speaking Yiddish, Hebrew, or English, the defiant survivors offer a kaleidoscopic picture of idealism, heroism, and ingenuity, as well as dilemma, betrayal, and loss. Their testimony is blended with Yiddish resistance songs, archival footage, and historical background (narrated by the actress Roberta Wallach). The result is a complex story of choice under Nazi occupation. To remain in the ghetto with family members or to go into the woods? To follow the Jewish ghetto leader's demand for accommodation to Nazi orders (in the hope of saving at least some Jews) or to revolt openly (knowing reprisals would follow)? To fight as a Jewish partisan brigade or to be part of the Red Army? And, in one of the film's most revealing sections, to yield the Communist leader Wittenberg upon the Germans' demands, or risk the liquidation of the entire ghetto by refusing to give him up? The decisive episode was resolved when Wittenberg – realizing that the majority of the Vilna ghetto wanted his surrender – gave himself up to the Nazis and a certain death.

Not all the stories are so distressing. The central figure in *Partisans of Vilna* – poet Abba Kovner, who subsequently testified at the Eichmann trial – recounts that the Ghetto resister felt they had to make their presence felt by blowing up a Nazi train. Fine, but who had ammunition, or even knew how to make a bomb?

Clandestinely leafing through manuals in the library, and utilizing whatever bits of explosive material could be found, the young Jews fulfilled their dream. Kovner remains an extraordinary presence in the film, with his calm voice reminiscing in Hebrew, his long white hair framing a still handsome face. He offers an evocative trajectory of wartime experiences, from the monastery where "the Jews in hiding outnumbered the nuns," to the ghetto where priorities were decided upon – "what *must* be done, and then what *can* be done" – to the forests where the Soviet Army was the only one that would accept Jewish partisans, but also disbanded the Jewish unit when its exploits became too successful. His testimony is interwoven with that of the feisty men and women whose eyes gleam when they recollect their gutsy activities. For example, survivor Baruch Goldstein tells, in Yiddish, how he smuggled a machine gun into the ghetto at great risk; crosscut with his tale are episodes recounted by Kovner, in Hebrew, which corroborate and expand an account of personal heroism into collective action.

Partisans of Vilna was conceived in 1981 by Kempner, a lawyer who had done fund raising for documentary films. A founding member of the International Network of Jewish Children of Holocaust Survivors, the producer had a personal stake in this material: "I was the first American war baby born in Berlin," she said in an interview.[12] "My father came to the U.S.A. from Lithuania before the war, and served in the U.S. Army in the Pacific. After the war, he was with the Army in Berlin and met my mother, who had survived by passing as a Polish Catholic in Germany. And because he was in the Army, I was born a U.S. citizen." Waletzky – a New Yorker born in 1948 – accepted her offer to direct *Partisans of Vilna* partly because there had been so few films on Jewish resistance. His assessment of this phenomenon is that

> the public value of the Holocaust in America has always been to stress the tragedy. It's certainly the overriding reality. So it's not surprising that one particular aspect – which was seen as a countervailing one – has been late in coming out. Death and destruction are more important in the overall scheme. Resistance becomes significant only after basic facts are known and assimilated into the culture as a whole. The myths that were politically expedient after the war have already served their purpose and are now ready to be examined.[13]

He fulfilled his avowed aim to take advantage of the living, firsthand memories of survivors. They were spread out geographically, but unified in memory: all had fought as Jewish partisans in the Vilna ghetto or nearby forests. The multiple and therefore corroborating testimony of the men and women interviewed ranges from poignant to comic, nostalgic to bitter.

They establish how the immediate task of the F.P.O. was to recruit members in the ghetto. The first candidates were from the ranks of the youth movements, who were qualified for armed underground activity. Another primary task was to establish a courier system – "primarily female," according to Kempner – "to other ghettos, so that the idea of Jewish resistance to the Nazis could be disseminated. Delegations were sent to Warsaw, Bialystok and Kovno to spread the word and organize a unified resistance like Vilna's F.P.O." After the ghetto was liquidated in September 1943, many of the Jewish underground fighters then joined the partisan forces in the surrounding area. For Waletzky, "Vilna exemplifies how Jews responded *where conditions allowed*: they took to the woods and took up arms. The Jews of the Warsaw ghetto didn't have

A scene from *Partisans of Vilna.*
PHOTO COURTESY OF AVIVA KEMPNER

forests. The impulses toward resistance were widespread, but the conditions varied greatly." Although this chronicle of wartime idealism, loss, and resiliency doesn't shrink from presenting the realities of Nazi extermination – especially in the Ponar area whose pits were filled daily with living Jews one moment and became mass graves the next – it is an inspiring testament to courage and solidarity.

10
The Ambiguity of Identity

eorge Steiner has argued persuasively that the context of the Holocaust goes beyond politics to metaphysics – that the deep anti-Semitic loathing built up in the social subconscious was rooted in Judaism's "claims of the ideal," to use Ibsen's phrase. Given that "some political scientists put at roughly 80 percent the proportion of Jews in the ideological development of messianic socialism and communism," "when it turned on the Jew, Christianity and European civilization turned on the incarnation – albeit an incarnation often wayward and unaware – of its own best hopes. . . . The secular, materialist, warlike community of modern Europe sought to extirpate from itself . . . the carriers of the ideal."[1] Steiner sees the Holocaust not as a political or socioeconomic phenomenon, but as the enactment of a suicidal impulse in Western civilization:

> It was an attempt to level the future – or, more precisely, to make history commensurate with the natural savageries, intellectual torpor, and material instincts of unextended man. Using theological metaphors, and there is no need to apologize for them in an essay on culture, the holocaust may be said to mark a second Fall. We can interpret it as a voluntary exit from the Garden and a programmatic attempt to burn the Garden behind us. Lest its remembrance continue to infect the health of barbarism with debilitating dreams or with remorse.

This suicidal impulse can be seen in films that focus on *individual* responsibility vis-à-vis Nazi domination – such as *The Shop on Main Street, Mr. Klein, General della Rovere,* and *The Man in the Glass Booth.* They depict the breakdown or transfer of identity among bystander, survivor, and victim, and locate the drama within the self, where a Jewish or Nazi identity is gradually assumed.

Mephisto (1981) is a striking cinematic exploration of Nazism as devil's work. István Szabó, the Hungarian director who had already probed the Nazi era through the haunting flashbacks and dreams of *25 Fireman's Street* (1973) and the urgent role playing in *Confidence* (1979), turns here to the story of an intelligent German actor whose accommodation of Nazi rule constitutes a selling of his soul in exchange for success. The prime minister sees "perfect evil in the mask" that the actor wears as Mephistopheles in Goethe's *Faust,* adding with approval, "Mephisto is also a German national hero." The film is adapted from the novel by Klaus Mann (son of Thomas) who fled Germany in 1933, wrote the prophetic book in 1936, and found no one to

publish it because of its obvious parallels between the protagonist Hendrik Höfgen and the German actor Gustaf Gründgens. (Although imprisoned at the end of the war, this personal friend of Göring returned to prominence in postwar Germany, and publishers told Mann that the book would be seen as a defamation.) After a second publisher's refusal in 1948, less than a year later Mann committed suicide.[2]

The German-language film traces the external rise and internal fall of Hendrik, played with flamboyant verve by the Austrian actor Klaus Maria Brandauer. In Hamburg of the thirties, this talented actor desperately wants to move up in the theatrical world, and charms various women to this end. As a stepping-stone to success, he marries the aristocratic Barbara (Krystyna Janda), and is then made a member of the State Theater in Berlin. After playing the role of his dreams, Mephisto, Hendrik accepts a film offer in Budapest – where he learns of the Nazi takeover in Germany. Instead of remaining in exile, he is lured back to Berlin by the promise of favor with the actress Lotte Lindenthal (Christine Harbort), mistress of a powerful Nazi general (Rolf Hoppe). Hendrik plays Mephisto once again, acclaimed not only by the public but also by the diabolical General. Under the Nazi's aegis, Hendrik becomes Germany's most celebrated actor and, finally, director of the State Theater. Stripped of wife, mistress, principles, and self-respect, he ultimately becomes a mouthpiece for the General, acting at every public (and private) occasion. Despite his second marriage to a similarly ambitious and compromising actress (Ildiko Bansagi), at the end he is alone and aware of the price he has paid for his empty success.

Hendrik's first appearance on screen is vivid: as the applause for Dora Martin (Ildiko Kishonti) swells, we see a man backstage screaming, crying, and covering his head with histrionic abandon. This actor is so jealous of Dora's applause that he raves like a spoiled child. That his crazy energy lacks a channel (and is thus potentially dangerous) is implied in the next sequence, where his black mistress, Juliette (Karin Boyd), declares, "You love only yourself, and even then, not enough." This lithe dancer realizes that his face is a mask: Hendrik changes expressions (and positions) with suspicious versatility. Although he and his friend Otto (Peter Andorai) agitate for populist theater and openly despise the troupe's Nazi sympathizer, Miklas (Gyorgy Cserhalmi), Hendrik already manifests a willed blindness: when he sees a group of Nazis yelling, "Jew, out of here" while beating up a man, he merely thinks they're drunk. Increasingly, he retreats into the theater as a shelter from the world's turmoil, especially after coming back to Germany from Hungary.

In the second half of the film, a new relationship takes shape: the General is to Hendrik as Mephisto is to Faust, a parallel that is heightened by the openness of both manipulators. Although the Nazi official insists on calling the actor "Mephisto" offstage, it is really his own name that he utters. The unnamed General (at least partially modeled on Göring, since he declares the famous line, "When I hear the word 'culture,' I reach for my revolver") feeds Hendrik's vanity in order to control him; when the actor fulfills the Nazi design, he rewards Hendrik with the post of director of the State Theater. That this is merely another role for Hendrik to play is expressed by the glasses he suddenly begins wearing – a new prop for a new part. He

Klaus Maria Brandauer as Hendrik Höfgen in *Mephisto*.

Hendrik Höfgen playing the role of his life in *Mephisto*. PHOTO COURTESY OF ANALYSIS FILMS

rationalizes that freedom is not a prerequisite to his art, but soon learns that *Kunst* (art) is not immune from the taint of Nazi doctrine: his own playing of Mephisto grows more diabolical in its precision and control via surprise: the Arno Breker kind of sculpture encouraged by the state is inhumanly immense and perfect; and even the version of *Hamlet* Hendrik directs has been reinterpreted as a saga of "Nordic man" who is "not weak."

Hendrik's transformation is enacted through the inextricable blend of life and theater that characterized the growth of Nazism. This is particularly well expressed by the intercutting of a "political" rehearsal with scenes of Hendrik's performances; Miklas leads a large Hitler Youth Group, teaching them to speak their lines louder and with more vigor. This kind of life *is* theater: Dora Martin puts it well when she says of Germany, "Here, the curtain is gradually descending," before leaving for America. And when the General congratulates Hendrik in his balcony box during the intermission of *Faust,* Szabó masterfully cuts from their meeting to a long shot of the theater, as the crowd below slowly turns to gaze upward at the box. They watch the two men on this new stage, dazzled by the spectacle of Mephisto in makeup alongside the General in uniform. Szabó acknowledged in an interview that "these are two actors in love, speaking about the problems of their craft. The General even tells Hendrik that he learned a lot from him, especially the element of surprise."[3] Appropriately enough, the General's birthday party at the end is held inside the theater, which has been taken over for the lavish ball.

In the final sequence, the General squires Hendrik away to an empty stadium, where he teases him with the idea that it would make a great theater. Bellowing the actor's echoing name and pushing him into the center of the arena, the General directs his little mise en scène with malevolent mirth, and demonstrates how powerless the performer is. Hendrik is caught in the inescapable light, a theatrical device that now blinds him. The stark white light gives his face the cast of the Mephisto mask; we see that even this supposed engineer of evil is trapped by his device, unable to control the lunacy of Nazism. "What do they want of me? I'm only an actor," he whispers to the camera in close-up, his pale face fading into the glare that surrounds him.

As Brandauer pointed out in an interview: "After World War Two, everyone said, 'I was only an artist; I was only a professor; I was only a policeman.' . . . The big question is responsibility. Everyone must be a member of society and take a position vis-à-vis their society."[4] If, as the General declares, "there's a little Mephisto in everyone," it is even more true that there's a little Faust in everyone. Szabó leads us to identify with the latter by using a subjective camera at two key moments: from the point of view of the General and his mistress Lotte as they acknowledge the bowing spectators at the theater; and, near the end, from Hendrik's point of view, greeting the guests at the birthday party. In both cases, the camera identifies itself with power and records how people humble themselves to its gaze. According to the director, "If the spectators find something in the film, in a character, which ties into their personal problems, you have won. Cinema means identification – to live and feel something together – and to meet yourself in a mirror. This actor who works with the Nazis is us during the film."[5] The one who understands this process best is Juliette, for she perceives that Hendrik likes to be a "well-behaved boy," enjoying his rewards for obedience.

Hendrik is hardly an "evil" character; after all, he hides an old Jewish friend in his home even when he is working for the Nazis, and he risks the General's displeasure by pleading for his politically suspect friend Otto. He is, quite simply, weak – and so obsessed with his career that he jumps into the spotlight, even when he knows that he is hiding in the glare. The last image reinforces how the light of spectacle can blind as well as illuminate if the actor and spectator are not aware of who controls the stage, and to what purpose.

The Shop on Main Street (*Obchod na Korze*) traces the wartime transformation of Tono Britko (Josef Kroner) – a simple peasant who enjoys nothing more than soaking his tired feet in a bowl of water – into a number of other identities. In this 1965 Czech film codirected by Jan Kadár and Elmar Klos, it is 1942 in Slovakia, and Tono is designated the Aryan Controller of the button shop owned by the elderly widow Rosalie Lautmann (Ida Kaminska). The half-deaf Jewish woman does not understand that they are living under Nazi occupation, nor that Tono is to "occupy" her little store. This occupation is paradoxical: he should be taking over her shop, but it is she (through goodness) who takes him over. When Tono's brother-in-law (Frantisek Zvarik) gave him this job, Tono lost his true occupation, for he was no longer able to be a carpenter. But Mrs. Lautmann gives him back his occupation, and Tono works behind the store. He arranges with the leaders of the Jewish community to be paid a wage in return for helping Mrs. Lautmann. Like Sol Nazerman in *The Pawnbroker*, Tono gives the illusion of power but has none: both men play with meaningless objects. He thus becomes a "white Jew" – a Christian who helps the victim of anti-Semitism.

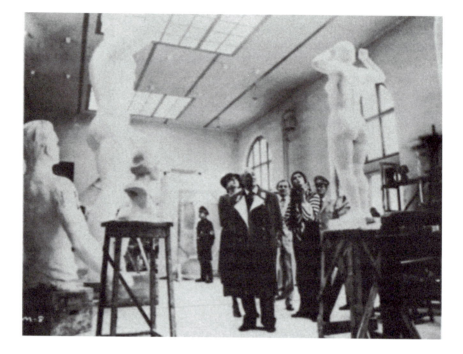

Above, the General (Rolf Hoppe) surveys Nazi art in *Mephisto*;
and, *below*, a Nazi show in *Mephisto*. PHOTOS COURTESY OF ANALYSIS FILMS

Tono is often seen in mirrors or reflected in windows, graphically suggesting his dual personality of Aryan Controller and "white Jew." Moreover, each side is doubled or externalized by another character: his brother-in-law Marcus is the "good fascist" who says to Tono, "We have to become rich; it's our duty, for God and for the Führer." (He also gives Tono a cigarette case with a mirror inside it.) Kuchar (Martin Holly), the old fisherman who helps Mrs. Lautmann, is ostracized for his sympathy: Marcus calls him "worse than a Yid because he helps them," and Kuchar is dumped into the street with a sign, "White Jew." The mirrors in *The Shop on Main Street* imply that Tono is also a reflection of what is happening in this small Slovak city.

When the Jews are rounded up for deportation, Tono wants to protect the Widow Lautmann but is terrified of the consequences. Her deafness is symbolic of the Jewish victims who are either unable or refuse to comprehend what is happening to them. (Mrs. Lautmann even believes the police will protect her.) Tono drinks himself into a stupor and shoves the old widow into the back room. Although he intends to save her, his push accidentally kills her. Tono's remorse and inebriation lead him to hang himself. The last scene is a reprise of a slow-motion dream sequence shown earlier, in which Tono and Mrs. Lautmann stroll together in an idyllic street scene. The sound of a male choir implies a heavenly ascent, and they are dressed in white. Drunken fear overcame his good instincts, but Tono finally achieves transcendence, redeeming himself, as it were, by joining the Jews in death.

Ida Kaminska (Mrs. Lautmann)
and Josef Kroner (Tono) in
The Shop on Main Street.
PHOTO COURTESY OF MUSEUM OF
MODERN ART/FILM STILLS ARCHIVE

A complex variation on the theme of rejecting and then assuming a Jewish identity can be found in *Mr. Klein* (1976). Directed by Joseph Losey from a script by Franco Solinas, this French-Italian coproduction is haunting, difficult, and appropriate to the director's claim, "I don't see why serious films shouldn't be viewed two or three times, just as books are read and reread."[6] Alain Delon, superbly restrained in the role of a wealthy and egotistical French art dealer in Paris during the Occupation, produced as well as starred in *Mr. Klein.* We initially see Robert Klein in his opulent home, bartering with a Jew (Jean Bouise) who must sell his precious possessions before fleeing. It is January 16, 1942, and upon ushering his client out, Klein finds a Jewish newspaper (*Informations Juives*) on his doorstep. Angry at such a "joke," Klein goes to the newspaper bureau to report the mistaken delivery. In an ostensible attempt to clear his name, he also obtain's the other Robert Klein's previous address and visits the man's seedy Pigalle apartment. The concierge (Suzanne Flon) takes him for her absent tenant; while inspecting the apartment, Klein pockets a photostudio envelope – and when he goes to pick up the pictures, the photographer seems to recognize him as the fuzzy person in one of the badly taken snapshots. The art dealer returns home to find the police waiting, as there is now some suspicion that he may be Jewish.

A letter from an unknown woman named Florence invites Klein to a château outside Paris where it is finally acknowledged that he is not the other Robert Klein: the aristocratic Charles-Xavier (Massimo Girotti) asserts that they are not the same person, and Florence (Jeanne Moreau) admits, "He never spoke to me about you." (She likens the other Klein to a serpent, reading in our hero's face that he is more of a vulture.) Nevertheless, he takes the other Klein's place at dinner. We are still uncertain of whom we can trust, as a mysterious man on a motorcycle leads Florence to run out. (The murky snapshot of Klein had also included a motorcycle, a girl, and a dog.) Klein then journeys to Strasbourg to question his father, who affirms, "We've been French and Catholic since Louis XIV!" He returns to the Pigalle apartment, where he continues to seek traces of the absent tenant. He begins a search for his namesake's mistress, while the Paris police make preparations to round up Jews for deportation. A dog attaches itself to him (the other Klein's dog in the picture?) while his own mistress, Janine (Juliet Berto), decides to leave him. A newspaper article leads Klein to a morgue and the bodies of five men who tried to blow up Gestapo headquarters: is the other Klein dead? He telephones Klein's Pigalle apartment, and a man answers, who may or may not be the other Klein. The two agree to meet. But when Klein arrives in front of the Pigalle building, he is just in time to see the police leading out a man by force.

Klein gives himself up, ostensibly to follow his namesake and have a confrontation. He is taken to the Vélodrome d'Hiver, where thousands of Jews are already being segregated in alphabetically designated areas. Klein's lawyer (Michel Lonsdale) tries to save him, showing him a certificate proving that he is not a Jew, but Klein insists on following the man who just raised his hand in response to the voice over a loudspeaker calling out "Robert Klein." He jumps onto the transport – inches away from the Jewish client who sold him the painting at the film's opening – headed for the camps.

The fictitious story of Robert Klein is thus constantly juxtaposed with the real background of French anti-Semitism, and includes a symbolic or metaphysical

Jeanne Moreau (Florence) and Alain Delon (Robert) in *Mr. Klein.*

dimension. Although Pauline Kael dismissed *Mr. Klein* by claiming "the atmosphere is heavily pregnant, with no delivery,"[7] the film's richness can be discovered through close analysis. For example, the credits unfold over a tapestry of a vulture with an arrow through its heart – an image whose meaning will be revealed at an auction a few scenes later, and whose import permeates the film. The auctioneer interprets the canvas as representing indifference, followed by cruelty, arrogance, greed, and finally remorse, and he points out the cabalistic origin of the signs. By invoking Jewish mysticism, the film suggests not only the concrete aesthetic significance of the tapestry, but the symbolic component of these attributes: they describe France – incarnated at the outset by Klein – in its movement from indifference to remorse vis-à-vis the Jews.

On the one hand, Losey situates Klein's quest for his "double" within the historical reality of the Occupation. The introductory titles acknowledge that the central character is fictitious – or a composite of the experiences of several individuals – but the facts "are a matter of history. They took place in France in 1942."[8] The film begins, not with Klein, but with the cold medical examination of a naked, middle-aged Jewish woman: the doctor measures her features to ascertain if they might be "Semitic." Later, the camera pans quickly from Klein leaving a café to the sign "No Jews Allowed." In a cabaret whose wealthy patrons include Germans, a transvestite singer does a German song. Along comes a long-nosed caricature of a Jew who takes her jewelry; a poster from the viciously anti-Semitic film *Le Juif Süss* is visible behind them. The performer removes his mask and says, "I'm going to do what *they* should do – leave before being thrown out!" This distasteful theater scene is followed by a kind of "rehearsal" in which the French police practice for the day when they will round up the Jews. This culminates in the last segment, as massive crowds of Jews are herded into the sports arena. That French citizens did little to prevent the roundup is shown when Klein is in a bus filled with Jews under arrest: he throws a scribbled note out the window, but the people in the street make no protest. As in *The Last Metro*, we see very few Germans, for Losey's indictment is aimed at the French.

At other times, *Mr. Klein* enters a truly Kafkaesque realm, more hallucinatory than historical. It seems no coincidence that the title brings to mind "Mr. K.," for Losey depicts an absurd universe of paranoia where the antagonists remain nameless and faceless. Indeed, the casting – and occasionally the visual construction – specifically evoke Orson Welles's film of Kafka's *The Trial* (1962): Jeanne Moreau's role as Florence amounts to a cameo part and functions partly as an allusion to her role of Miss Burstner, the neighbor of Joseph K. (Anthony Perkins). Moreover, Suzanne Flon as the concierge is the same actress who played Miss Pittl in Welles's film. A shot in the police bureau presents an enormous room with high ceilings, the walls filled with files. In the center is a long table where people consult these dossiers – reminiscent of the inhuman office in *The Trial*. The German Occupation takes on the look of Kafka's dark visions.

As one of Losey's later films, *Don Giovanni* (1979), would illustrate, this director is no stranger to stylization. For all its realism of detail, *Mr. Klein* is also structured through a dense pattern of imagery. In particular, the film implies the bestiality of people during the Occupation through animal symbolism: a long shot of the black-caped police against the white walls of the station makes them look like bats; *Moby-Dick* is a recurring allusion, first when Janine reads from it in bed, and later when Klein finds a copy of it in the Pigalle apartment (could Klein's obsessive pursuit of his nemesis be a variation on Captain Ahab?); Florence speaks of the invisible Klein as a snake who has gone into hibernation, and of the man before her as a vulture. This brings us back to the vulture of the tapestry, to the vulture handle on Klein's lawyer's cane, and to Klein's initial activity of preying on the misfortune of clients.

From the first scene of *Mr. Klein* to the last, we view his gradual transformation from elegant opportunism to an ultimately inexplicable self-sacrifice. Klein is introduced after the humiliating objectification of the Jewish woman by the doctor, and the art dealer then measures the Dutch painting for sale in a clinical manner that seems to rhyme with the preceding scene. Klein's treatment of the unnamed Jewish client is clearly more polite than the doctor's with his chilling feature measurements, but Klein shows no real sympathy for the Jew before him. That he might have another side (or identity) is suggested by the mirrors prevalent in the film: we see him together with his reflection when he first receives the Jewish newspaper; when he phones the newspaper from a café; and when he is paged by an unidentified man in another café. This doubling of Klein's image prepares us for the ambiguity central to the story. At the outset, and especially on first viewing, one might assume that he is indeed *both* Kleins; as the Commissioner (Fred Personne) puts it, after Klein reports the newspaper mistake to the police, "A man comes forward, the better to hide." Isn't his pursuit of the other an example of "the lady doth protest too much"?

Once he becomes the potential victim of racial prejudice, we are led to identify with Klein: for example, Losey draws out the moments when our hero is waiting for the mailman, forcing us to experience the wait with him. And when Klein goes to the château, we enter through his point of view (along with a hand-held camera that conveys uncertainty). We see only as much of the "enemy" as the protagonist, perhaps because the other Klein is a composite figure: he fits into all milieus – those of collaborator, gangster, aristocrat, resister (a piece of music found in his apartment turns out to be "L'Internationale," the Communist anthem). We are never really sure why Klein I sacrifices everything to pursue the other – is Klein II's life simply more interesting than the art dealer's? – but the film suggests that a search for spiritual redemption might be the reason.

When Klein is supposed to leave France with a false passport, he laments to his lawyer that the French have become "too civilized, well-mannered, processed," having perhaps realized that his own life was the epitome of indifferent leisure. But like the dog that follows him – which he initially kicks but finally accepts – Klein's second identity sticks to him, and he finally makes it his own: he gets off the train leading him south to safety and calls his nemesis on the phone. The tapestry remains the key to the film, its pattern offering remorse as the central emotion. When Klein's father decries indifference as "a still, flat sea around a drowning man" and asks his son if he knows what remorse is, Klein responds, "Yes. It's like a vulture pierced by an arrow, but which continues to fly." One could even say that remorse is the key for France, or at least for the producers of this film (which officially represented France at the 1976 Cannes Film Festival), as well as for Klein. The last image reinforces this sentiment as we see the same strip of film – men's faces in the transport – repeated, to the voice-over accompaniment of the film's opening conversation between Klein and the Jewish man. The film slows down and fades out, suggesting not only the slow death in store for these travelers, but the auctioneer's line about remorse: "A vulture, its heart pierced by an arrow, which continues to fly." Among the persecuted Jews, Klein achieves a measure of transcendence by merging his destiny with theirs.[9]

Klein's psychological transformation into the person for whom he is mistaken is comparable to that of Grimaldi (Vittorio De Sica) in Roberto Rossellini's 1959 film, *General della Rovere* (*Il Generale della Rovere*). This shady character in wartime Italy is arrested by the Germans for taking money from families of imprisoned Italians. Müller (Hannes Messemer), the German in command, makes him a proposition: Grimaldi will be spared if he pretends to be General della Rovere, a recently killed partisan leader. Through this impersonation, the Nazis hope to learn the identity of the prison Resistance chief. Grimaldi gradually turns into the noble general for whom he is mistaken, and finally chooses to be executed with other partisans rather than reveal the Resistance chief's name.

The focus of this magnificent black-and-white study of guilt and redemption is the process by which Grimaldi's second self emerges to confront the Nazis. Rossellini, who had already explored wartime Italy in the Rome of films like *Open City*, locates this story in Genoa, where black-shirted Fascists march and sing. He establishes the self-indulgent character of Vittorio Emanuele Bardone, alias Grimaldi, from his first gesture: he takes a piece of sugar from his pocket, unwraps it, throws away the wrapper and eats. His acquiescence (bordering on obsequiousness) toward the Germans is then indicated as he helps Colonel Müller, whose car has a flat tire. When this German asks where he's from, Grimaldi answers, "Naples." But when Müller counters by complaining that the Germans aren't liked in Naples, Grimaldi smiles accommodatingly and says he's "not from there exactly." Grimaldi begins to understand something beyond personal comfort only after he is imprisoned: confronted by the graffiti on the cell wall – scratched by its inhabitants just before they were to be shot – he shivers with a new awareness.

A letter from the general's wife moves Grimaldi to tears, especially when she quotes the real general's words: "When a man doesn't know which course to take, he must choose the more difficult." Müller announces that he must execute ten men as retribution for a Resistance attack in Milan. Grimaldi/della Rovere assumes the burden of his adopted identity and chooses to die with the patriots – even though Müller tries to stop him. He writes his last comforting words to the Countess della Rovere, as her husband, and then addresses the ten victims, as their general. Grimaldi finds a new truth in playing his role: he discovers within himself the resources of courage and sympathy that enable him to die as a real hero.

When one was stripped of possessions, status, and external self-definition by Nazi brutality, the question of "Who am I?" became problematic. And if one lost family or friends, the isolated self was all the more vulnerable to remorse, guilt, internalized aggression, and the assumption of other identities. A remarkable film in this regard is *The Man in the Glass Booth* (1975), adapted from Robert Shaw's play and directed by Arthur Hiller for the American Film Theatre series. Maximilian Schell is even more compelling as the quick-tempered, quicksilver Goldman than in his previous Holocaust-related roles, including *Judgment at Nuremberg* and *The Condemned of Altona*. The film opens in contemporary New York, where Arthur Goldman is a

Vittorio De Sica (Grimaldi) and Hannes Messemer (Müller) in *General della Rovere*. PHOTO COURTESY OF IMAGES FILMS ARCHIVE

wealthy, charismatic, and rather manic Jew who constantly harps on the Holocaust (especially that "the Pope forgave the Jews"). From the telescope of his penthouse, he glimpses a Jewish peddler in the street and (the camera suddenly becoming subjective) Nazi soldiers. The sound of marching feet also locates us within Goldman's distorted perspective, and he utters the crucial but ambiguous words, "*Mea culpa.*"

In this extremely literate script by Edward Anhalt, Goldman then reminisces about his father, who died in a concentration camp, bids farewell to his five mistresses seated around the dinner table, and claims, "A Christian is just a nervous Jew who thinks he bought himself an A-1 insurance policy." The verbal bravado winds down and Goldman begins to disintegrate before our eyes: wearing a yarmulke, he takes photos of tortured victims from a trunk, lights candles, beats his chest, and singes his arm. The soundtrack establishes the origin of this bizarre rite as we again hear marching feet, this time followed by Hitler's voice, sirens, screams, and gunfire. When armed men suddenly break in, it turns out that he was burning off an SS insignia. This man is not Goldman, but Dorf – a former Nazi officer.

The scene shifts to his trial where witnesses offer harrowing testimony about Dorf's savagery during World War II. Berger, who had been a cinematographer in the Polish ghetto, tells about mutilated corpses that were returned to the ghetto where relatives were forced to assemble the parts; Dorf had made him shoot extreme hand-held close-ups of this. Samuel Weinberg, a former concentration camp inmate, testifies how he dreamt of revenge. "Not in the camp," Dorf insists, embarking on his insidious line of defense – attacking Jewish meekness. He boasts that the Jews were sheep who didn't believe what was happening, and the judge (Luther Adler) even asks Weinberg why there was no revolt if there were hundreds of prisoners and only twenty guards. "Our fate was beyond our imagination," responds the witness (without, however, dwelling on the crucial point that Jews in the camps were subject not to mass cowardice but to a loss of the very desire to live – or to resist dying – after witnessing daily atrocity).

Dorf's other line of defense is the insistence on collective rather than personal guilt: "If I'm psychotic, eighty million Germans were psychotic." (His net for guilt trapping is so wide that he calls the My Lai massacre a classic example of Nazi work. The judge snaps, "Irrelevant.") Dorf declares, "You will love me because I have done what you all want to do . . . murder," as Hans-Jürgen Syberberg's Hitler figure would paraphrase five years later. Dorf's demented reasoning insists that all this happened out of love, not hate: "The Führer who rescued us from our fears and made us believe in ourselves . . . that Jews had to be destroyed because he – and we – were afraid of Jews. . . . If we only had someone now to lead us, a father to kill for, and in killing, live." It therefore seems downright silly when Charlie Cohen (Lawrence Pressman), loyal assistant to Dorf's previous self, Goldman, testifies that the man in the glass booth *has* to be a Jew – because of his sense of humor and perfect Yiddish! "No Gentile could be as anti-Semitic as Goldman," he claims in defense of his former employer.

As it turns out, Charlie may not be as naïvely mistaken as he seems. When the doctors are called in to identify Dorf through X-rays, Dr. Alvarez goes back on his previous testimony and confesses, "That is not Dorf" – and that he was paid to replace the X-rays. The camera moves in to a close-up of Goldman/Dorf? as he becomes catatonic. We are once again led to identify with his being overtaken by the past: through subjective camera and sound, the judge appears out of focus, and

Maximilian Schell
(Goldman/Dorf) in *The
Man in the Glass Booth*.
PHOTO COURTESY OF
CARLOS CLARENS

the soundtrack repeats the memories of marching feet, sirens, and screams. "Dorf" removes his shirt and falls amid the imagined sound of gunfire, frozen in a Christlike pose. We are given no explanation, merely a final close-up of his enigmatic face.

Who is the man in the glass booth? The film suggests that he *is* a Jew, and a dramatic emblem of survivor guilt. All stems from the mea culpa we hear at the beginning – guilt over having survived, leading to identification with the enemy ("I killed them"). His testimony also reveals a streak of Jewish self-hatred, especially for the "meekness" of those who died without revolt. In this sense, Goldman/Dorf is related to the protagonists of *Kapo, The Gold of Rome,* and *Mr. Klein,* for all these films posit Jewish identity in the context of the Holocaust as inseparable from going to one's death. The ultimate ambiguity – or distortion – of these films is that to assert yourself as a Jew is also to embrace your own death.

The man in the glass booth is like the pawnbroker of Sidney Lumet's film, encased both literally and figuratively. Goldman (whose flashbacks are aural whereas Nazerman's are visual) is isolated by his memories, branded by what he has seen and been. As in the last shot of *Mephisto*, the protagonist's spatial entrapment signifies guilt, with the self fragmenting into roles. These films support George Steiner's speculation about the Holocaust, for Jews are depicted in them as "carriers of the ideal," or that which the Christian characters need in order to achieve their own redemption. That Hendrik in *Mephisto* hides a Jewish friend in his apartment even while mouthing Nazi rhetoric adds a humanizing – and self-justifying – dimension to his character. That Tono, Klein, and Grimaldi choose death in solidarity with another identity revalorizes them. Finally, Goldman's conscience dramatizes the haunting bond between those who felt compelled to die and those who were condemned to live.

In *Tel Aviv–Berlin* (Israel, 1987), director Tzipi Tropé develops this theme through the tormented character of Benjamin (Shmuel Vilozny), a Berlin Jew who escaped from Auschwitz and ended up in Tel Aviv. He marries Lea (Rivka Noiman) – a rather plain woman who came to Israel from Poland before the war – with whom he has a daughter. But Benjamin's German roots become increasingly palpable in the late 1940s, creating a tension between cultural and religious identity. He becomes obsessed with two people who represent his past: beautiful Gusti (Anat Harpazy) is another Auschwitz survivor from Berlin; and Jacob Miller (Josef Carmon) is a former Auschwitz kapo. Irresistibly drawn to loving the former and killing the latter, Benjamin virtually abandons his wife and child. His ineradicable Berlin identity – a class difference expressed by his wearing a hat and bowtie, or listening to German music – overwhelms his adopted Israeli one. But, at the end, when he confronts Miller with a gun, the ex-kapo begs him to shoot; Benjamin leaves behind the gun and Miller kills himself instead. Tropé implies that this confrontation has liberated Benjamin to some extent from his ghosts, and that he might return to his wife. *Tel Aviv–Berlin* is remarkable for a number of reasons: one of the extremely rare Israeli films to deal with the Holocaust, it is also one of the few Holocaust fiction dramas directed by a woman. (Tropé acknowledged in an interview that the story is loosely based on her own parents.) As its title suggests, this compelling psychological portrait locates within the protagonist the conflict between two cities: they represent not only past and future, but an assimilated cultural identity versus anonymity among other Jews.

Bastille, a fascinating Dutch drama of 1984, elaborates on the theme of post-Holocaust Jewish identity through the story of Paul de Wit (Derek de Lint, playing skillfully against his established glamour-boy image), an assimilated history teacher in contemporary Amsterdam. As the film progresses through flash-forwards, we learn that Paul – who was born in hiding in 1943 – has never come to terms with the death of his parents in Auschwitz, and the simultaneous disappearance of his twin brother, Philip. At the beginning of *Bastille*, directed by Rudolf van den Berg from Leon de Winter's novel, Paul is happily married to a non-Jew and has two lovely daughters. But he is suffering from writer's block on a book he is preparing about the French Revolution: its premise is, what would have happened had the flight to Varennes succeeded? His hypothesis that the course of history is based purely on chance – *what if*, in 1791, Louis XVI and Marie Antoinette had escaped? – is an attempt to rewrite the past; in other words, we can infer, what if the Holocaust had not destroyed most of European Jewry, including his family? The camera literalizes this connection by moving from a stack of books about World War II to his manuscript, entitled "Bastille." As his wife Mieke (Geert de Jong) realizes, the book camouflages Paul's mourning for his parents.

Chance is indeed crucial for this writer: when he goes on a research trip to Paris, he happens upon the office of Mme Friedlander (Dora Doll), a professional tracker of information on Jews last seen before the war's end. Chance also leads Paul to strike up

Above, Derek de Lint and Loudi Nijhoff; and, *below,* Dora Doll and Derek de Lint in *Bastille.*
PHOTOS COURTESY OF EAST – WEST CLASSICS

a relationship with Nadine (Evelyne Dress), a doctoral student who lives her Judaism as fully as Paul has repressed his. And it is chance that leads to the climactic search for his brother: in the background of a photo he has taken of Nadine at the Place de la Bastille, Paul spots a man's face remarkably similar to his own. With echoes of both *Mr. Klein* and *Blow Up*, the film follows his obsessive attempt to magnify the image of the bystander and trace the whereabouts of this "double." *Bastille*'s complex narrative structure brings us to the film's "present tense" (glimpsed since the beginning), namely a nighttime drive on a dangerously wet French road to find Nathan Blum. In the course of *Bastille,* Paul rediscovers his Jewish identity through the search for remnants of a past scarred by the Holocaust.

Despite the emphasis on chance, the film posits a certain determinism: the truth of Paul's Jewish heritage *must* emerge, after having been repressed. Indeed, *Bastille* can be compared to *The Official Story* (1985), an Argentine drama whose focus is also a history teacher who has evaded honest scrutiny of personal history. Both films are about coming to terms, moving from a first scene in a classroom to the teacher's wrenching confrontation with loss. As both Alicia (Norma Aleandro) and Paul learn, a lovely family life is not enough if the character has not faced up to a larger identity; in Alicia's case, it is as an Argentine implicated in the nation's horrific military dictatorship; in Paul's case, it is as a Jew connected to the Holocaust. The main difference, of course, is that the enemy in *The Official Story* is external and explicitly political; the enemy in *Bastille* is internal. Like his mentor Professor Polak, who is shown eating roast suckling pig, Paul is depicted as a totally assimilated Jew who has shrugged off his religion. That there are consequences for this repression is suggested by Paul's becoming ill after eating pork.

The very form of the film suggests something quintessentially Jewish – a questing movement, or rootlessness. Paul is uncomfortable in Amsterdam; later, Paris is filled with unpleasant encounters; and the image of Israel is established in the beginning classroom scene as problematic because of its treatment of Palestinians. The movement through space is paralleled by temporal jumps, as the technique of flash-forwarding is appropriate to *Bastille*'s theme of the play of time. And, paradoxically enough, the flash-forward punctuates a trip into the past – both the French Revolution and the Holocaust. It even ends (rather inconclusively and disappointingly) on a spatial as well as temporal road: in a fantasy scene, Paul's inert body is placed by two men in powdered wigs into the royal carriage en route to Varennes.

Jewish identity – confronting it, accepting it, and absorbing it into one's life – is the central theme of *Bastille*. Many of the film's other Jewish characters – such as Polak and the Paris restaurant owner who plays a record of "My Yiddische Mama" at the same time every day – are clichés because, according to the director (in the film's pressbook), "in order to bring out Paul's *hidden* Jewishness, I had to confront him with the most extreme clichés." The Jewish female characters, on the other hand, offer a potential salvation: in addition to Nadine, Paul's student invites him for Passover. "There's no point," he tells her. She replies, "Does history have a point?" This exchange is reminiscent of a central conversation in Eric Rohmer's *My Night at Maud's,* where a Marxist professor redefines Pascal's "Wager" to a devout Catholic: even if there is only one chance in a thousand that history has a point – or, for Pascal, that God exists – he must take that chance because it is the only one that gives his life meaning. Similarly, Paul needs to renew a historical bond – to Jewish traditions that bind and heal.

11
The New German Guilt

The New German Cinema created a stir in the 1970s comparable to that of the French New Wave a decade earlier: the work of talented young filmmakers like Werner Herzog, Rainer Werner Fassbinder, Wim Wenders, and Volker Schlöndorff impressed itself upon American film-goers, especially for its richness of cinematic expression. The Holocaust was hardly their main theme, but one could argue that it was in the background of such disparate films as Herzog's *Aguirre, the Wrath of God* and Fassbinder's *The Marriage of Maria Braun*. The demented demagogue who leads his soldiers on a death trip is a Spanish conquistador in Peru, but his incarnation by the German-speaking Klaus Kinski suggests an image of Hitler (especially when he says, "We need a *Führer*"). And Fassbinder's resilient heroine (Hanna Schygulla) is a product of her culture, indeed an incarnation of postwar Germany – a survivor of sorts. Even in Wenders's *Wings of Desire* (1987), a major sequence takes place on a movie set where Peter Falk is acting in a period film about Nazis and Jews.

The first German fiction film to deal with the Holocaust was *Only a Day* (*Nur ein Tag*, 1965), directed by Egon Monk – a former assistant to Bertolt Brecht – from the writings of Gunter Lys. This stark but effective black-and-white drama took the form of a report on a German concentration camp, Altendorf, in 1939. Although the protagonists are not sufficiently individuated – the hero is more of a collective protagonist, including Jews, Bolsheviks, and criminals – admirable attention is paid to the details of concentration camp life among male prisoners. For example, an older Jew who realizes he is being called to his death leaves his spoon – a precious commodity – to his son; another Jew, ordered to retrieve his cap from the barbed-wire fence where SS men have thrown it, removes his shoes and tosses them to his comrades before approaching the fatal fence. The last scene is especially powerful in its understatement: over the image of Germans smoking good cigars in a restaurant, we hear the sounds of pain, humiliation, and terror from the camp, where SS men are bullying Jewish prisoners.

It wasn't until the late seventies that a growing number of German films began to confront the Holocaust, revealing and eliciting responses ranging from profound guilt to perverse fascination. Sparked perhaps by the televising of *Holocaust*, many

Ingrid Caven as *Malou*. PHOTO COURTESY OF JEANINE MEERAPFEL

filmmakers made the long-overdue attempt to assess a suppressed past. Among the most notable results were *Auschwitz Street, The Children from Number 67* (both shown in the Museum of Modern Art's New German Cinema series, January 1981), *The Tin Drum, Our Hitler, The Confessions of Winifred Wagner,* and *The White Rose.* By the early eighties, the work of three women directors – Helma Sanders-Brahms (*Germany, Pale Mother*), Margarethe von Trotta (*Sisters* and *Marianne and Juliane*), and Jeanine Meerapfel (*Malou*) – suggested that film was becoming a sharp instrument for dissecting the German past (just as subsequent Austrian motion pictures, including *The Inheritors,* the "Where to and Back" trilogy, and *'38,* would deal with that country's legacy). All three filmmakers explored family relationships in the attempt to pierce the collective amnesia that characterized postwar Germany.

Germany, Pale Mother (*Deutschland, Bleiche Mütter*), released in 1980, is Helma Sanders-Brahms's story of a German couple transformed by the war, told from the point of view of their now grown daughter Anna on the soundtrack. This narration (by Helma Sanders-Brahms herself) permits both the initial nostalgia and the ultimate questioning that constitute the film's backward glance. Anna's parents are not Nazis, but they want Germany to win the war. The father, Hans (Ernst Jacobi), is one of the first soldiers mobilized to Poland precisely because he is not a member of the Party. The mother, Lene (Eva Mattes), gives birth to her daughter in a gripping scene that crosscuts her labor with bombs falling: the child born of war is extremely bloody in close-up, as if marked by the external as well as internal violence. Expulsion will become the norm for both mother and child as their house is reduced to rubble. Lene carries Anna (Anna Sanders) and their meager possessions on her back, seeking shelter in the gutted landscape. By the end of the war, this exhausted survivor is reunited with her husband, whose closest friend, Ulrich (Rainer Friedrichsen), is a Nazi who now – conveniently – denounces the Party. One side of Lene's face swells and stiffens, externalizing an ugly infection and inner hardening that could be interpreted as both personal and national. Although the ostensible source of the disease is removed (all her teeth), the effects remain to torture Lene. Mother Germany – even purged of Nazis – continues to suffer quietly.

Von Trotta's *Marianne and Juliane* (winner of the 1981 Chicago Film Festival's Golden Hugo Award under the title *German Sisters*) contains a scene where the sisters, upon seeing *Night and Fog* for the first time, become ill. Similarly, in her previous film, *Sisters* (1979), there are nightmares and eerie symbols about which the director admitted: "It's always going back to the past, to the suppression of our Nazi past. In the fifties, parents wouldn't talk about the war, the guilt, the burden of awareness."[1] Consequently, a new generation of filmmakers has begun to do "the enlightenment work," in their words.

Meerapfel's *Malou* (1982), for example, is a partly autobiographical account of a young German-Jewish woman trying to learn about her mother, Malou (Ingrid Caven). Like the director, Hannah (Grischa Huber) was born in Argentina after her parents had fled Nazi Germany. Hannah's search for her dead mother's life is really an attempt to shape her own identity, as she grows obsessed with photos, relics, and the Jewish cemetery. "You'll forget everything one day," observes her exasperated husband Martin (Helmut Griem). "But I have to understand it first," she answers – representing, perhaps, an entire generation of Germans vis-à-vis their Nazi past. For Meerapfel, "That's what the film is about. After the war, there was

Jeanine Meerapfel directs Grischa Huber (Hannah) in *Malou.*
PHOTO COURTESY OF JEANINE MEERAPFEL

reconstruction – the German Economic Miracle – but they never really elaborated history. They were ashamed, but this guilt was like a barrier to understanding. It was taboo: children were never able to ask their parents about it. So I had to 'give a hand' to help the dialogue."[2]

The "dialogue" has been aided by German television, for which Meerapfel subsequently made *In the Country of My Parents,* a personal documentary about being a Jew in Germany today. And *Auschwitz Street* (*Lagerstrasse Auschwitz*) was directed in 1979 by Ebbo Demant for a German television series entitled *People and Streets.* This one-hour documentary is structured by the male narrator's insistence on assuming – and sharing with the audience – the burden of Auschwitz's existence. According to the director, who was born in Berlin in 1943, "no place exists that has moved me so much as Auschwitz . . . a place which must be made visible and palpable to every German who acknowledges his history." Consequently, the narrator's continual reminder that this street in Poland is "our street" includes sobering and complex material: by interviewing three former SS "culprits" (as they are called), Demant gives barbarism an all-too-human incarnation. Looking very unlike a chalk-faced Gregory Peck posing as Dr. Mengele in *The Boys from Brazil,* and very much like familiar and tired old men, each of the three convicted murderers – now imprisoned for life – speaks dispassionately about his crimes. Resisting the stereotype of icy Nazi monsters, these avuncular prisoners suggest not only that Auschwitz is "ours," but how easily the Nazi "I was only following orders" could be ours as well.

In only sixty minutes, Demant offers five effective and integrated approaches to the Holocaust: interviews – not only with three "culprits," but also with two victims, and with a number of German teachers visiting Auschwitz today; devastating black-and-white stills from the forties "to which one can say nothing, but which must be shown"; concrete relics of concentration camp life, such as prisoners' drawings, the hospital death book that meticulously records, at five-minute intervals, the names and medical terms of death, and a mountain of luggage taken from the inmates on arrival, "suitcases like gravestones"; a calm and gently didactic voice-over narration that describes and prods, posing questions like "Have you ever lain bone to bone next to someone with tuberculosis or diarrhea?"; and finally, a visual strategy that (like *Night and Fog*) opposes the fluid camera tracking through present-day Auschwitz in color to the stillness in the gray photos of the past. The comparatively objective camera and subjective voice move back, respectively, in time and space; the result is that past and present, as well as space and time, lose their boundaries in the immensity of this concentration camp. As the narrator informs us, "Between the beginning and end of Auschwitz Street are 270 meters, or five years." Ultimately, Auschwitz extends beyond January 27, 1945, and beyond the individuals who died or killed there.

Auschwitz Street acknowledges at the outset the general climate of indifference to the subject. Its first setting is a German school where, in 1978, teachers continue to present "a better version of Hitler," fascist texts, and the possibility that the gas chambers were a lie. To counteract these distortions, Demant's document moves to the actual place and individuals that gave a form to Nazi atrocity. The first "culprit" interviewed in prison is Josef Erber, found guilty in 1966 of joint murder in seventy cases. In a medium close-up, he describes calmly how, at first, gassed people were buried. "But then the blood serum rose up," so the corpses were dug up and sent to the crematories. The unseen interviewer finally asks Erber if he is still haunted by the smell of burning flesh. His response: "Yes, but we couldn't change anything."

The second interview, which follows color footage of the prison bunks' grotesque sardines-in-a-can design, is more horrifying because the director plays a kind of trick on the audience: by having Josef Klehr describe fatal injections *before* he is introduced as one of the culprits, he allows us to assume that this loquacious old guy was a prisoner himself. The former hospital orderly – convicted of 475 cases of joint murder – even jokes (when the interviewer poses tough questions), "You sure are tormenting me here a lot!" With some self-righteousness, Klehr claims that his injections were less cruel than the gas chambers – which he evocatively describes as a beehive: when the victims entered, one heard a sound like bees, slowly growing silent. What made it simpler for Klehr, he admits, is that his prisoners neither cried out nor resisted; when the questioner pushes him on this point, Klehr acknowledges, "They must have thought, 'my suffering is over.' " Once again, the culprit's explanation does not permit the viewer any easy judgment: "What should I have done? It was ordered," he insists, relying upon the common knowledge that those who did not obey were themselves killed.

In contrast to their tormentors, who are interviewed in prison, the two "victims" we meet are both photographed outside on Auschwitz Street. Dr. Stanislav Klodzinski, a prison orderly, offers sentiments surprisingly similar to those voiced by the culprits: manifestations of sympathy were forbidden, requiring orderlies to look dispassion- ately on the other inmates' suffering. The second survivor emerges out of what seems to be an arbitrary selection among an interminable row of camp photos. One man's road to Auschwitz – sending letters and medicine to friends in Cracow – is presented by the narrator, aided by photos: "He had a life" is the understated conclusion. Bearing witness to this life is the task of his son, who is interviewed not far from the spot where he watched his father's murder. Mieczlav Kieta recounts in his native Polish how he was forced to observe the humiliation and the blows; "the worst thing," he says quietly, "is that I couldn't say anything to my father." The narrative spine of this documentary snaps into place when Kieta specifies that the SS man who selected his father for death was Josef Klehr.

The third culprit, Oswald Kaduk – sentenced for joint murder in one thousand cases – seems to feel little remorse that he used to crush prisoners underfoot. As a kind of antidote to this image of heartlessness, Demant then presents a group of Hessian teachers visiting Auschwitz: "For these Germans, this street in Auschwitz is our street." Nevertheless, the group is hardly consistent in its responses. Some express shock, some guilt, some numbness. One young woman refuses the guilt and replies, "For us, it's terribly far away." To bring the experience closer – to the spectator, at least – the film moves to a mountain of prisoners' abandoned luggage with the urgent admonishment, "Look at these suitcases!"

Finally, the camera tracks outside along the gray street, moving slowly but surely to a spot of sunlight in the middle. Having found a literal glimmer of hope amid the darkness, the camera stops there and, one assumes, the film is over. However, after the credits end, the film continues – like a living presence unable to rest in the sunshine. Through the nervous movement of a hand-held camera, we see abandoned files of the Frankfurt trials. The voice prods, "Should the end of our street be like this?" as a high-angle shot reveals the disarray stemming from neglect. *Auschwitz Street* thus ends not only in the strip of illumination embodied by the film, but with an insistence on action that faces up to the past. Its very strategy of catching the audience unawares – recommencing after it is ostensibly finished – reminds the spectator to be vigilant, both inside and outside of the theater. Given the subject, this suggests an important lesson: just when one thinks something is over, it can easily begin again.

The same "double ending" appears in *The Children from Number 67* (*Die Kinder aus N° 67*), directed in 1979 by young German filmmakers Usch Barthelmess-Weller and Werner Meyer. Although the film is a fictional reconstruction of life in 1933 Berlin, it offers a surprise similar to that of *Auschwitz Street:* at the end, the action resumes a few moments after the final credits have ended. The directors' motivation might be comparable, since *The Children from Number 67* – while drawing the viewer into sympathetic identification with its characters – yields a sobering lesson on the rise of fascism and the need for resistance. The film opens with a band of kids who furtively pull down a Nazi flag at night. An angry man yells that they need the firm hand of discipline – the film's first acknowledgment of the connection between rigid patriarchal rule and totalitarianism. This stiff order of father and state is undercut by a liberating laugh when the credits appear with the second part of the title, *Heil Hitler, Give Me Some Horseshit* (*Heil Hitler, ich hätt gern'n paar Pferdeäppel*). The film reveals not only the value of such a debunking rejoinder to the salute, but the economic necessity that assisted the growth of Nazism: the children earn money by literally collecting horseshit, which they sell to farmers for fertilizer.

The Children from Number 67 revolves around the courtyard of No. 67 and, as in Jean Renoir's explorations of a self-enclosed community in the 1930s (such as

René Schaaf (Paul) and Bernd Riedel (Erwin) (*far left*) in *The Children from Number 67.* PHOTO COURTESY OF ROAD MOVIES FILMPRODUKTION

"la cour" in *Le Crime de Monsieur Lange*), the politics emerge from the interaction among its inhabitants. Erwin (Bernd Riedel) and Paul (René Schaaf) are introduced as best friends, whether they are playing hooky or swiping Nazi flags for shoeshine cloth. There is, however, a fundamental difference between them: Paul's hunger leads him to secretly steal rolls, while the more enterprising and ethical Erwin becomes the self-appointed detective for the bakery. The reason for this moral gap can be deduced from the family scenes: Paul's father (Peter Franke) is unemployed and so bitter that he assumes Hitler would have to be better than what he has now. In Erwin's less strict household, they make a virtue of necessity, sharing everything from bath water to ideas. The latter spirit tends to animate the courtyard during the first half of the film, culminating in an ebullient outdoor party. Beyond amusement, this fête illustrates concrete solidarity, because all the proceeds are offered to Paul's impoverished family so that they can remain in the building. The celebration comes to an abrupt halt when Nazis enter, impervious to the warmth of the inhabitants.

Half a year later, April 1933, finds the families in a less joyous mood. More swastikas are visible in the background, and Paul's parents are already saying that Nazi atrocities are none of their business. Erwin's family, however, makes responsibility its business, to such an extent that the father is arrested. Against the backdrop of growing fear – a Nazi boy learns boxing, "so I'll have no one to be afraid of" – Erwin and a few others refuse to follow the fascist flock. The boy's actions may seem slight – he removes the word "Jew" smeared on a sign on a neighbor's door – but they represent the resistance that had to be enacted on the level of daily life. By the end of the film, Paul is sporting a swastika and enjoying the acceptance of his school chums, while Erwin remains alone in his refusal to wear such an armband.

Despite the poor English subtitling (which never explains, for example, that HJ means Hitler Jugend, or Youth Group), *The Children from Number 67* provides profound insights into a prewar Berlin whose high unemployment rate contributed to Nazism. Moreover, it suggests that Hitler was seen as the answer not only to economic problems but to the desire for discipline and the outer trappings of order. At the beginning, the children are morally "correct," using the Nazi flag to wipe their shoes. As they grow up, however, they become subject to fascist parental influence, as illustrated by the Nazi's son who is not allowed to participate in the courtyard party, and therefore bullies the others.

Two kinds of group solidarity are presented, the rigid line of saluting Nazis versus the courtyard of dancing individuals, chaotically spilling out of the camera frame. When Erwin's little girlfriend Miriam (May Buschke) offers Paul costumes and shows him how to "walk like Frankenstein," she moves with the stiff gait of a Nazi soldier – an aggressive rigidity linked to "having no one to be afraid of." Opposed to this is the constructive disorder of dance, with its connotations of partnership as well as freely improvised steps. *The Children from Number 67* thus shows that some succumbed to Nazism through the Hitler Youth because they were ostracized even from sports if they refused to salute. And it calls attention to the "good" Germans

Erwin and his parents in *The Children from Number 67.* PHOTO COURTESY OF ROAD MOVIES FILMPRODUKTION

like Erwin's family and the kind teacher who is dismissed for his lack of zeal in the Nazi cause. The film's focus is both historical and personal, suggesting what it was that might have attracted Germans to Nazism, while celebrating a family that remains resolutely antifascist.

The celebration of resistance on a military rather than a personal level animates *Top Secret – The History of the German Resistance against Hitler* (*Geheime Reichssache*). Jochen Bauer's 1979 documentary concentrates on the trial of those who plotted Hitler's assassination in the abortive July 20, 1944, uprising. The remarkable thing about much of the archival footage is that it was shot on the order of Goebbels by hidden cameras and then captured by the Allies. The very same images of which the Gestapo was so proud thirty-five years before become a damning revelation of their kangaroo court. Bauer animates this material with a voice-over narration, occasionally sentimental string music (for example, behind dissolving stills of men who conspired against Hitler and were killed), and cinematic devices such as masking ovals to emphasize noble victims.

Top Secret begins with the German invasion of Poland on September 1, 1939, moving from the dehumanizing ghettos to early attempts to assassinate Hitler. "This is the beginning of the Holocaust," the verbal accompaniment states, to splotched documentary footage of poverty in the Warsaw Ghetto. We see the conditions that fed not only into the uprising but also into the concerted earlier efforts to remove the Führer: an ordinary carpenter risks his life, as do the "White Rose" students in Munich – and finally the Wehrmacht officers. Rather than lament over the fact that hordes "followed orders," *Top Secret* seeks out the largely forgotten individuals who enacted conscience. The narrator quotes the general who wrote, "I'm ashamed to be a German" – juxtaposed with concentration camp footage. A conspirator standing before Judge Roland Freisler's People's Court refuses to say he's ashamed for calling the Nazis' acts murder – and instructs that, after his death, an iron cross be erected on his property in Prussia with the inscription, "Here lie fourteen Christians and Jews. May God have mercy on their souls, and their murderers." The price for such conviction was not cheap: two hundred conspirators were hanged, their families arrested, their children kidnapped. The dedication at the end of the film reads, "To the brave few who tried to end the system in Germany at the cost of their lives and to the many victims of Nazism everywhere" – recovered heroes for an era of reevaluation.

The high cost of questioning Nazism for a German, in World War II or today, is suggested by *All in Order* (*Ordnung*), Sohrab Shahid Saless's austere study of a contemporary engineer who becomes increasingly alienated from his middle-class life. His "disease" is passive resistance. In the constant gray pallor of this 1980 black-and-white film, the engineer hardly says a word – except on Sunday mornings. Walking up and down a quiet suburban Frankfurt street, he wakes everyone by yelling "*Aufstehen!*" (Get up!). The literal awakening grows figurative, for by the end of the film, the shout is "Auschwitz!" It is the word that stops sleep, the insistent note that pierces equilibrium, the call that unifies a community in discomfort. Although this film by a Persian exile is not explicitly about the Holocaust, its protagonist seems to be a product of the experience: the grief-stricken conscience, perhaps, of his middle-class neighborhood, he personifies the price and the responsibility of waking up to Auschwitz.

The White Rose (1982), directed by Michael Verhoeven, is another quietly told tale of heroism. Although many German directors – including Volker Schlöndorff – tried to make a film about the courageous dissidents of the White Rose Society, only Verhoeven was finally able to secure the approval of the victims' relatives. The filmmaker, born during the war, spent five years doing research and interviews, and then took great care in casting unknown actors who bore a strong resemblance to the White Rose students whose society was formed in Munich in 1942. They printed and disseminated flyers to alert their fellow Germans to the horrors of the Holocaust and the need to resist. For almost a year, the Gestapo was unable to destroy these young, clever, and increasingly numerous enemies, but in 1943, the White Rose Society came to an end. Its founding members were sentenced to death for high treason and guillotined. *The White Rose* follows these events from the arrival of Sophie Scholl (Lena Stolze) in Munich on her twenty-first birthday. She attends the university with her brother Hans (Wulf Kessler), who keeps his subversive activities secret from her. When Sophie discovers that he and three other students are responsible for the anti-Nazi leaflets found in classrooms, she insists on joining the society, despite the obvious risks. She outwits postal clerks to obtain stamps, steals paper from government offices and – when forced to work in a munitions factory – secretly puts dough into detonator caps. The male students are dispatched as medical orderlies to the Eastern Front, where they witness Nazi atrocities. Upon their return, the White Rose Society becomes more defiant, especially when it paints anti-Nazi slogans on campus. The Scholls are caught, and they take full responsibility for all the acts of the society in order to protect their friends. Nevertheless, the other members of the White Rose are tracked down, sentenced, and executed in the spring of 1943.

The White Rose is admirable not only as a moving film but as a political instrument. The German version ended with a six-point declaration charging that the verdicts of the Third Reich against the White Rose have never been declared null and void by the present government. This sparked great controversy and, as a result of the film, the federal Ministry of Justice negated the Nazi verdicts. Nevertheless, the law under which the Scholls were executed has never been reversed in German courts. According to a *New York Times* article, German resisters who were imprisoned during the Nazi era do not know whether the Federal Republic still recognizes their convictions.[3] The fact that *The White Rose* was also a box-office hit in West Germany is heartening, for it grapples with the revelation of shame and the call for courage proclaimed in one of the White Rose flyers of 1942:

> It is certain that today every honest German is ashamed of his government. Who among us has any conception of the dimensions of the shame that will befall us and our children when one day the veil has fallen from our eyes and the most horrible crimes – crimes that infinitely outdistance every human measure – reach the light of day?[4]

Verhoeven's choice of Lena Stolze for the role of Sophie Scholl was so perfect that the young stage actress was subsequently cast as the same character in another German film, *The Last Five Days* (*Fünf Letzte Tage*, 1982). Directed by Percy Adlon – who already displayed in *Celeste* (1981) that he was a master of the long take, the telling detail, and the slow revelation of a woman's personality – this film traces the last five days in Sophie's life, February 18–22, 1943. Adlon's focus is the nurturing friendship that develops between the heroine and her cell mate, Else (Irm Hermann), who has been imprisoned because of a presumably anti-Hitler sentiment found in a letter on her person during a train check. The film is constructed in scenes that truly illustrate "the more emotional the material, the less emotional the treatment," for the [refusal] of melodramatic clichés renders the scenes powerful. There is a simple blackout after each hour or scene, and a female voice-over introduces each day. Apart from the credit sequence, there is no music during charged scenes like the discovery that Sophie and her brother Hans separately confessed, each assuming all the blame to save the other, or Else telling Sophie about how the SA took away her Jewish boss on Kristallnacht. The music enters only approximately halfway through the film in an appropriate manner: during an extremely poignant scene, the women place cookies, chocolate, and apples onto plates – each article presented in loving close-up as they open packages. The two men who work in the prison bring butter and other things, demonstrating how sharing is superior to individual hoarding. As they eat their precious food and drink their tea, the introduction of music expresses that this is a privileged moment. "How rich we are," says one of the women and, despite their incarceration, the line rings true: they have not only physical sustenance, but the spiritual nourishment of lucidity, generosity, and integrity. At the end, the camera moves in to a paper in Else's hand, left by Sophie on the last day: the word *Freiheit* (liberty) dominates the screen in a close-up.

Nothing could be further from the sober starkness of *All in Order* than the stylized symbolism of *The Tin Drum* (*Die Blechtrommel*); nevertheless, both hinge on the protagonist's refusal to assume adulthood in German society. The central character in Volker Schlöndorff's 1979 sumptuous adaptation of Günter Grass's novel is Oskar (David Bennent), who decides at the age of three to stop growing. He is the narrator of his own tale (a point of view dazzlingly reinforced by the use of subjective camera at Oskar's birth, the lens emerging from darkness to unfocused lights and sounds); refusing a more objective frame of reference, the film thus permits a number of interpretations of Oskar's relationship to Nazism.

The boy is born "between faith and disillusion," as he puts it – attitudes that can apply to the Nazi cause as well. On one level, Oskar is the symbol of resistance to fascism, or the debased world of adults. His only activity is playing his drum, aggressively beating his own rhythm. At a Nazi rally, his loud tempo subverts the military band until the scene grows hilarious: the rally becomes a dance, as everyone suddenly waltzes to the "Blue Danube." Here, as in numerous other scenes, Oskar seems to undercut the SS, supporting the wise midget Bebra's claim that you must be onstage in order to avoid being controlled. And the keen perception that the Germans were "a credulous people who believed in Santa Claus but Santa Claus was really the gasman" is Oskar's. Finally, it is significant that Oskar chooses to grow again only after Nazism is destroyed.

On another level, Oskar as stunted growth incarnate can be an image of Germany. His agent is noise, specifically a piercing scream that shatters glass. (When storm troopers subsequently destroy a Jewish store, they break glass too.) How can one avoid seeing Oskar's activity as analogous to *Kristallnacht,* the night the Germans burned nearly two hundred synagogues, smashed eight hundred Jewish stores, and arrested twenty thousand Jews? Early in the film, his scream is followed by a Nazi parade – the juxtaposition suggesting that the shout engenders the march. In a comprehensive *Film Quarterly* interview with Schlöndorff, John Hughes analyzes Oskar's symbolic value: "For Grass, Oskar represented the destructive infantilism of the Nazis as well as the 'scepticism' of the fifties generation. For Schlöndorff, finally coming to terms with the 1959 epic in the late seventies, Oskar also represented the most vitriolic and rage-ridden currents of the post-1968 protest movements."[5] Schlöndorff elaborates on this question by confessing that the infantile nature of Oskar is what first "hooked me into the book."

> I began to see Oskar as a very wide-ranging metaphor. . . . I did identify with this monster in the most intense way. I was aware of the fact that Oskar was anathema to the puritan mind – a dwarflike, immoral, abnormal child. I was convinced that I had to show how very *normal* he is – neither good nor bad, and certainly not more monstrous than the so-called normal people around him. . . . I wanted to show the monstrous things hiding inside "normal" ones.[6]

The Tin Drum is clearly not a "message" film, but a complex poetic picture bordering on fantasy. Despite the realistic setting – even including titles like "September 1939" or "the first battle of World War II" – its hyperbolic images occasionally heighten horrific events to the point of aesthetic delirium. For instance, following an image of Nazis, w see a decapitated horse's head filled with eels. Again, the juxtaposition creates a visual connection by which Nazism feeds into the revolting head. Is the horse Germany, severed from its living limbs and inhabited by slimy creatures? Or is it resistant to the literalizing imagination?

If the image of Nazism is stylized, that of Judaism is toned down and its attendant persecution assumed by two other groups, the Poles and the Kashubians. The SS never mentions Jews, and its target here is the Polish Post Office in German Danzig. Similarly, Oskar's grandmother says at the end that "the Kashubians weren't Polish or German enough" – a line often applied to the Jews. (Oskar's last word in the film, as he leaves on a train, is "*Babka*" – not the German word for grandmother but the Polish/Kashubian one.) The only direct allusion to the genocide of a race enters through the subplot of Sigismund Markus (Charles Aznavour), the Jewish toy-store owner whose first response to persecution is to become baptized. These elements derive from Grass's novel, whose focus never claims to encompass the Holocaust. Rather, as Schlöndorff articulated,

> Grass shows Nazism deriving from the banality of middle-class life aspiring to become something else. For Grass, these people aren't very innocent. They wanted to feel important, to feel like generals in control of history. And this is a very dangerous energy because it has a certain legitimacy. That's what fascism is built on: *making everybody in the street feel important.*[7]

If *The Tin Drum*'s focus on a willful child constitutes flirtation with the demonic, *Our Hitler*'s kaleidoscopic collage of the Third Reich smacks of relentless obsession with it. Stylistically, Hans-Jürgen Syberberg's audacious 1978 seven-hour, four-part extravaganza has little in common with new German documentaries, realistic stories, or even symbol-studded narratives. Nevertheless, its dogged determination to evoke the impulses, development, and aftermath of Nazism suggests a comparable legacy

David Bennent (Oskar) in *The Tin Drum*. PHOTO COURTESY OF CARLOS CLARENS

of German guilt, stemming from a shared, suppressed past. Syberberg's point of departure is a refusal of American cinematic convention as exemplified by *Holocaust*, and a return to German romanticism – which Hitler himself tapped. *Our Hitler, A Film from Germany* (*Hitler, ein Film aus Deutschland*) is consequently an exploration of both history and cinematic form, opposing spectacle to narrative, theater to realism, and bristling questions to smooth answers. In a *New York Times* interview with Lawrence Van Gelder, the forty-five-year-old director said, "You have to find a new style, a new aesthetic . . . to describe the history of these 50 million people dead. It was not only my task to rebuild the history but to go beyond it."[8] In Susan Sontag's incisive opinion, Syberberg succeeds in this aim:

> To simulate atrocities convincingly is to risk making the audience passive, reinforc-
> ing witless stereotypes, confirming distance, and creating meretricious fascination.
> Convinced that there is a morally (and aesthetically) correct way for a film maker to
> confront Nazism, Syberberg can make no use of any of the stylistic conventions of
> fiction known as realism. Neither can he rely on documents to show how it "really"
> was. Like its simulation as fiction, the display of atrocity in the form of photographic
> evidence risks being tacitly pornographic.[9]

When *Our Hitler* premiered in New York in 1980, much of the critical response was passionately positive. *The Village Voice*'s J. Hoberman declared, "part illus-trated lecture, part symphony, part circus sideshow, part fever-dream, *Our Hitler* is a prolix, extravagant, staggering work. It is exhilarating, exhausting, infuriating, and devastating."[10] Syberberg's "Phantasmagoric meditation" juxtaposes the grotesque with the banal, inundating the spectator with actors, puppets, documentary footage, recorded speeches, Richard Wagner's music, and props that represent Hitler. Blown-up photographs become the background in Syberberg's system of rear-screen projection, permitting the performers to move into and through images of the Third Reich. This cinematic device has its psychological counterpart: *Our Hitler* hinges on the act of projection – a continual play of screen and mind – for Syberberg believes that the Germans projected their darkest impulses onto Adolf Hitler. As one of the characters declares, "Never has so much been projected by so many onto one man."

Our Hitler, A Film from Germany begins as a circus whose ringmaster acknowledges: "We aren't showing the reality or the suffering of victims, arrogance and righteous anger. . . . It's about war and genocide, Auschwitz as the battlefield of race war." Different actors incarnate Hitler as Chaplin's "Great Dictator," Hitler as house painter, Hitler as Hamlet meditating on a skull marked "Jew," Hitler as Napoleon with hand tucked in his fly rather than his coat, and finally Hitler as a puppet who declares, "I'm the devil incarnate, but a human being who laughed at Mickey Mouse, just as you do." For *Newsweek*'s Jack Kroll, the puppet image is particularly apt: "Using all the techniques of mass culture, Hitler turned his people into puppets. Syberberg reverses this process and shows Hitler himself in the guise of many different puppets, implying that Hitler was really obeying the secret voice of the people whose dark dreams he brought to life."[11]

In reversing the idea that Hitler pulled the strings, Syberberg insists on the collective complicity of the German people. Hitler draped in a toga (played in this incarnation by Heinz Schubert) emerges from the grave of Richard Wagner and states: "I did what they wanted me to do, but dared not do. . . . Am I not your secret desires? . . . If you reject me, you reject the masses." This chilling pronouncement was rephrased by Syberberg when he told *The Village Voice* that the German people "elected him and he was the poor guy to do their dirty work."[12] Consequently, the director's desire for "people to realize that we are the inheritors of a certain legacy from Hitler" points to venal ventriloquism – whereby dictators bark what the people want to hear. Hitler's reassuring rantings about the superiority of the Aryan race coexist with "loyalty and obedience – still the substance of the German people," in the words of the Heinrich Himmler character.

With Hitler as a symbol rather than merely a deranged man, Syberberg's style is dizzyingly symbolic, fighting the Führer's image with his own ammunition of irrationality. It places the longing for heroic transcendence that Hitler exploited into the collective psyche of German romanticism with titles like "The Grail," "A German Dream," "The End of a Winter's Tale," and "We Children of Hell." The effect is twofold: as *New York* magazine's David Denby pointed out:

> In Syberberg's view, Hitler is the horrifying climax of German romanticism and the fulfillment of German longings (and, by extension, the longings of the whole world). This movie, Wagnerian in length and density, and filled with passages of Wagner's most solemnly exalted music (principally from *Parsifal* and *Götterdämmerung*), is a monstrous catalogue of romantic ecstasies – visions of renewal, paradise, extinction – declaimed in language that is frequently as clotted and jargon-ridden as the libretto of the *Ring Cycle*.[13]

Above, a Hitler-puppet in *Our Hitler;* and, *below,* Harry Baer and puppets in *Our Hitler.*
PHOTOS COURTESY OF ZOETROPE STUDIOS

Secondarily, Syberberg's densely allusive spectacle distances the viewer from any possibility of emotional identification – the very process that permitted Hitler to manipulate the masses. Reveling in its artifice, the film demands a mental response of alertness, discrimination, skepticism, and tolerance. Even when the soundtrack describes how Ukrainians strip and shave their victims before sending them to the gas chamber, the image keeps us at arm's length: Himmler (again played by Heinz Schubert) lies on a bed in the hands of a masseur. As the voice-over offers horrifying accounts and statistics about the liquidation of Russian Jews, the actor is bathed in an eerie gold light, his unreality balancing the authenticity of the soundtrack's contents.

Shot as a TV film on a single sound stage in twenty days, for under a half-million dollars, *Our Hitler* reveals the influence of Bertolt Brecht (the subject of Syberberg's first films). Far from documentary or narrative, it is alternately didactic, original, boring, vertiginous, obfuscating, and revealing. Especially toward the end, Syberberg seems carried away by the very romanticism that fed into the Third Reich: as his black-caped, twelve-year-old daughter wanders through the set, her hair filled with celluloid, one is reminded that the film is dedicated, not to the victims or survivors of the Nazi era, but to Henri Langlois and the Cinémathèque Française of which he was the director. Syberberg's apparent taste for art as salvation leads him to audacious and often forced analogies: in Part I, he lashes out against "enemies of culture," with the suggestion that Erich von Stroheim was a victim of Louis B. Mayer's machinery. The connection between genocide and censorship or mutilation of film is downright silly – almost as cheap a shot as Jean-Luc Godard crosscutting (and thus equating) a picture of Golda Meir with one of Hitler in his film on the Palestinians, *Ici et Ailleurs* (1976). The only time Syberberg's Hitler repents is for aesthetic reasons: he knows he did wrong to ruin UFA – Lang, Lubitsch, Murnau.

At other points, the director's targets seem more justified. In Part II, a porn film-maker (Harry Baer) tells us that Hitler "sells" now; "*felix culpa*" (happy guilt) is good entertainment and good business. Moreover, Syberberg admitted in an interview, "You see, I can feel guilty and be proud, in spite of it. I am full of energy because I am guilty and my work and thoughts are devoted to exorcising that guilt."[14] (And there is the problematic addition of the word "Our" to the film's title by its American distributor, Francis Ford Coppola.) *Our Hitler* suggests that we still have much to be guilty about: a Hitler puppet recognizes his legacy in today's worlds, as he praises Idi Amin Dada, the death penalty, Yasir Arafat, the United Nations where 110 states disregard human rights, and torture in Latin America. Sontag is right to point out the connections "from Hitler to pornography, from Hitler to the soulless consumer society of the Federal Republic, from Hitler to the rude coercions of the DDR."[15]

The wide-ranging (and often far-fetched) spectacle of *Our Hitler, A Film from Germany* should be evaluated alongside another film by Syberberg, which is its antithesis in style: *The Confessions of Winifred Wagner* (*Winifred Wagner und die Geschichte des Hauses Wahnfried 1914–1975*) is indeed a documentary that simply allows the daughter-in-law of Richard Wagner to discourse upon her pleasant friendship with the Führer. Shot entirely in medium close-up, it is nevertheless "cinematic" in capturing the twinkle of her eye or the phlegm of her cough. Perhaps more successfully than *Our Hitler,* this 1975 film presents the paradox of the "decent" people who followed Hitler. Syberberg's presence is palpable not merely as the interviewer, but as an intrusive commentator. Like Godard, he alternates between

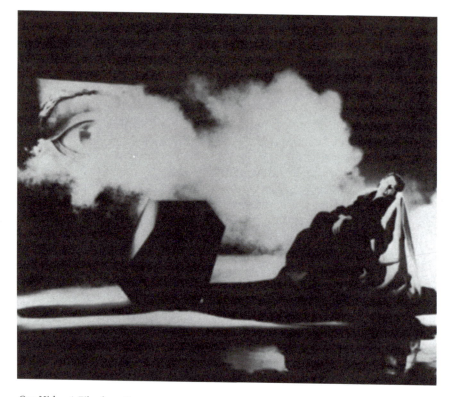

Our Hitler; A Film from Germany. PHOTO COURTESY OF ZOETROPE STUDIOS

a documentary presentation of recorded material and the dialectical inclusion of his voice-over and printed words. For example, after Winifred claims that it wasn't really Hitler who wanted to destroy the Jews, there is a quotation from one of Hitler's brutally anti-Semitic speeches. This crosscutting heightens the tension between the woman's honesty and her willful ignorance vis-à-vis seeing Hitler as anything other than a friend. "The banality of evil or the evil of banality?" asks Syberberg, and subsequently warns against facile condemnation: "It's easy not to be a Nazi when there's no Hitler around."

In the early 1980s, Austrian filmmakers began addressing themselves to the Nazi past and its palpable legacy. *The Inheritors* (*Die Erben,* 1983) is a disturbing but forceful film directed by a young Austrian, Walter Bannert, who infiltrated the resurgent fascist movements in West Germany and Austria. In 1979, he had been in a restaurant frequented by leftists when neo-Nazis swept in and wrecked the place (a scene re-created in the film). Subsequently, he went to mass right-wing demonstrations in Nuremberg and Munich, and entered their world by claiming he was making a documentary about the extreme right as well as the extreme left in Germany. But when *The Inheritors* premiered in Vienna, the neo-Nazis – realizing they'd been duped – came en masse and screamed "Lies!" during the screening. Theaters received telephone threats, police were posted, and many cinema owners canceled engagements.[16] Why all the fuss? Because *The Inheritors* paints a chilling picture of the popularity of the right-wing among youth through the story of Thomas (Nikolas Vogel), a middle-class boy who joins the neo-Nazis. The most potent scene occurs when he visits the home of his comrade's grandfather. The old Nazi proudly displays a lamp made from Jewish skin in Auschwitz. Thomas, who has been hearing at the mass rallies that Nazis never murdered Jews, questions the remark. The old man acknowledges that, among themselves, the truth can be told – and proudly.

One of the film's shortcomings, however, is that *The Inheritors* places all the blame on parents: those of Thomas are concerned only with making money – especially his cold and shrewish mother – while those of his friend Charly are pathetic. At the end, Charly's hard-drinking father rapes his own daughter; this gives the boys a justification for murder. The Party therefore provides the young with an alternative family and sense of purpose – as well as an outlet for their violent instincts. Likewise, the neo-Nazis abuse all the young women in the film, who, either willingly or not, are depicted as pliant sex objects. The problem here is that although *The Inheritors* seems like an anti-Nazi film to enlightened viewers, it could be taken by some right-wingers as justification or provocation. Instead of including at least one alternative or sympathetic antifascist adult who explains what makes sexism and fascism reprehensible, Bannert focuses only upon the Party's appeal to Thomas. In fact, when his classmates call him a fascist and ostracize him, we are led to feel sorry for the outsider.

Perhaps more successful in this context is *Kassbach* (1979), a Viennese film by Peter Patzak. This contemporary portrait of a middle-aged, neo-Nazi grocer and the right-wing organization to which he belongs proposes that the dangers of xenophobic racism have not disappeared. Their present target is foreign workers, but Patzak connects this to the Nazi past in a number of ways: the credits include a still of naked women running in a concentration camp; Kassbach revels in the memory of giving a Nazi speech in July 1943; the thugs – one of whom says, "We need a Hitler" – beat up a "Jewboy." These violent sexists are shrugged off by a TV commentator at the end who labels them "extreme-right . . . on the fringe . . . and of no danger to the general public." Nevertheless, the film insists on the ever-present menace – to everyone – of latent fascism.

The richest Austrian cinematic exploration of the Holocaust and its aftermath is *Where to and Back,* a trilogy directed by Axel Corti from a semiautobiographical screenplay by Georg Stefan Troller. The first two parts, *God Does Not Believe in Us Anymore* and *Santa Fe,* were coproductions of Austrian and German television; *Welcome in Vienna,* winner of the Grand Prize at the 1986 Chicago Film Festival, was made for theatrical release. *God Does Not Believe in Us Anymore* (1981) begins in Vienna in 1938, and takes Ferdinand (Johannes Silberschneider) – a Jewish youth, suddenly orphaned on *Kristallnacht* – through the early years of the war in Czechoslovakia, Paris, and Marseille. His coming-of-age story is intertwined with the tale of "Gandhi" (Armin Mueller-Stahl). This former German officer who joined the Resistance was imprisoned in Dachau and escaped to Austria; his story extends the theme of Nazi victimization from Jews to resisters.

In *Santa Fe* (1985) – winner of both the International Press and Tokyo Prizes at the 1985 Monte Carlo TV Festival – the refugees who arrive in New York harbor believe they are finally safe and free. But for exiles who speak "Emigranto," as one of the more successful new Americans puts it, adjustment is a difficult process. The film's focus is Freddy (Gabriel Barylli), a young Austrian who dreams of making a new life in the mythic American West. But the other characters are even more vivid, from the assimilated photographer Popper, who acknowledges, "Hitler took away everything but our German accent," to Frau Marmorek, who has been rendered mute by concentration camp life. (Her muteness, like that of characters in Jerzy Kosinski's *The Painted Bird* and Elie Wiesel's *The Testament,* as well as the film version of *The Pawnbroker,* can be seen as an extreme version of the frustration of rootless beings who have witnessed too much – and know that their tales of horror won't be believed.) The former writer Treumann (Peter Luhr) is an especially poignant figure, now reduced to running a delicatessen; he says wearily about his former countrymen, "They'll never forgive us for what they did to us" – a phrase that lies at the heart of the trilogy.

Welcome in Vienna (1986) focuses on two uprooted "Americans" – Freddy and Adler (Nicolas Brieger), a Jewish intellectual from Berlin – who return to Austria as victors. Freddy falls in love with Claudia (Claudia Messner), a Viennese actress whose father is welcomed by the CIA – despite his Nazi allegiances. And when Freddy and Adler become occupiers at the war's end, they must deal with Treschensky (Karlheinz Hackl), a clever Austrian opportunist. *Welcome in Vienna* is based on the actual experiences of Troller, a Viennese Jew born in 1921. Like Freddy, he and his family were forced to flee Austria in 1938, but he returned in 1944 as an American soldier. The slightly surreal quality of returning to one's war-ravaged homeland, pockets filled with chewing gum and cigarettes, is one of the emotions that the film explores. When it was presented at the 1986 Cannes Film Festival, Troller recalled that in 1938, "after the Nazis entered Vienna, we knew we had to leave. But it was a wrenching idea: I adored this country that hated me. I didn't want to emigrate."[17]

The Troller family fled, via North Africa, to the United States. Along the way, they learned how isolated refugees could be: after fifteen days on foot, they arrived in France and were placed in a camp for "foreign enemies." According to the screen-writer, "the French didn't know there was a difference between refugees and Nazis" (a – perhaps willed – misundestanding that is beautifully dramatized in the detention camp sequence of *God Does Not Believe in Us Anymore*). This Viennese exile joined the U.S. Army in 1943 and, along with other German-speaking soldiers (many of them Jewish), was subsequently dispatched to Austria in a division that interrogated prisoners of war. The homecoming was often filled with disillusionment; as we see in *Welcome in Vienna*, Freddy discovers that his former home is merely rubble, that love is transient, and that success depends on adapting to those in power.

The best exemplar of this accommodation is Treschensky, whom we first meet as a German soldier. According to Corti, "this Austrian represents the widespread species of the eternal *homo Austriacus*... whose only motivation is opportunism." (If Treschensky occasionally seems reminiscent of the unctuously clever Klaus Maria Brandauer in *Mephisto*, Karlheinz Hackl is indeed a theater actor from the same milieu as Brandauer. And in a small but memorable part, he portrayed the Nazi officer in *Sophie's Choice* who asked Meryl Streep to choose which of her children should go to the gas chamber.) Treschensky – and even the left-leaning Adler, after he is refused by the Communist party – manage to feel at home in the postwar Vienna of cabarets, black-market dealing, and sudden prosperity. But Freddy cannot decide whether to remain in his native city, or return to America. And if the trilogy suggests that the United States was the savior for Austrian Jews, America is hardly blameless in the moral universe of *Welcome in Vienna*. With the Cold War approaching, new allegiances were forming, and as Troller put it, "The Americans got along well with the Germans – whether they were Nazis or not. They were obsessed with the desire to fight the Russians. They thought they had fought the wrong war. We, the refugees, were more and more isolated."

Despite the wrenching events depicted in the trilogy, Corti eschews manipulative melodrama in favor of subtle touches. For example, we know that *God Does Not Believe in Us Anymore* begins with *Kristallnacht,* not because we see Nazis beating Jews and destroying their shops, but because a woman is sweeping the shards off the street the next day. Freddy's definitive departure from Vienna is quietly and effectively expressed when he drops his keys down a grate in the gutter. Similarly, Freddy's decision to embrace an American identity at the end of *Santa Fe* is indicated by his throwing strips of the German-language newspaper *Aufbau* from the top of a New York skyscraper. And if Freddy was reduced earlier in the film to stealing crumbs from pigeons in the park, we feel how things have improved for him in a beautiful moment when he feeds them. The director avoided melodrama by limiting the music to Schubert's late string quintet, used sparingly throughout all three films. And he insisted upon shooting the trilogy in black-and-white rather than color, since we tend to think of the era based on newsreel footage. This permitted him – especially in the first film – to seamlessly intersperse archival material; but unlike most fiction films that incorporate documentary footage, this one admirably has newsreels marked with the date and often the place of origin.

Corti (a non-Jew born in Paris in 1933, now living in Austria) and Troller (who now resides in Paris) had already collaborated on two films for television. When the TV stations of Germany, Austria, and Switzerland then proposed that each country contribute a film about emigration in the twentieth century, the Swiss movie became *The Boat Is Full* while, according to Corti, "the German one was about emigration for political reasons. Georg and I wanted to deal with specifically Jewish emigration, and the result was *God Does Not Believe in Us Anymore*. It was very successful, so they asked us to make another film about the experiences of Jewish immigrants in the U.S."[18] *Santa Fe* followed, but Corti was not content to end the tale in New York. "I thought the *return* of the immigrants would be even more interesting," he explained, "as they were gone from Europe only seven years, 1938–45. They arrive in uniforms, as Americans, as victors, as liberators in their own beloved country. And they see that they are welcome in Vienna only to the extent that they have dollars, chewing gum, chocolate, etc. So we decided to make both films, and that *Welcome in Vienna* would not be only for TV." The third tale was indeed released in Austrian theaters, first in 1986. Corti admitted that this depiction of anti-Semitism, convenient forgetfulness, and opportunism was "hardly a hit. But a year after the Cannes Film Festival presentation, it did work in Vienna because they heard of the success in Paris." Indeed, *Welcome in Vienna* enjoyed extraordinary acclaim in France – both critically and commercially – where its theatrical run lasted eighteen months.

For Corti, a leading director of cinema, theater, television, and radio, the trilogy is partly an attempt to create awareness by confronting anti-Semitism: "After 1945," he recalled, "Austrians said, 'As for us, we've been liberated. The Nazis were the Germans.' They lifted up the carpet and swept all the filth under it. It's still there today; it's just that the lumps are getting bigger here and there . . . and a few of us stumble over them." Having grown up in Italy, Switzerland, England, Germany, and Austria, the versatile director and actor – who is also a fully trained farmer – developed a lucid if compassionate eye that sees through nationalist flags. As critic David Thomson wrote about *Welcome in Vienna* in the catalogue of the 1987 San Francisco Film Festival:

> This story is itself absorbing, as we see Austria carried from the age of Schnitzler, Musil and Freud towards that of Kurt Waldheim. But it is the manner of Axel Corti's work that is most remarkable. He is a realist, but one whose appetite for life, gesture and place is inseparable from his moving camera and his apparent reluctance to repeat camera set-ups. Without hysteria or ostentation, he is always showing us fresh points of view in a human and social panorama in which there is so much ambiguity, caution, compassion and irony that any naive rush to judgment is drained of energy. . . . Axel Corti is the first director of the great line of Viennese filmmakers who actually works in Vienna. He is the true successor to Erich von Stroheim, Fritz Lang, Billy Wilder and Otto Preminger. . . . It is very moving to see how he belongs in a tradition born out of historical disaster, but making artistic glory, in which Austria and America are points of departure and arrival.

If Claudia, the actress in *Welcome in Vienna,* incarnates the opportunism of postwar Vienna, Carola – the actress in *'38: Vienna before the Fall* (1986) – represents a futile decency in prewar Austria. Both characters are attractive Gentile performers whose blond hair and fair skin contrast with their dark Jewish lovers. *'38*, directed by Wolfgang Gluck, begins in Vienna in September of 1937. Carola Hell (Sunnyi Melles) and Martin Hoffmann (Tobias Engel), a playwright of Jewish birth and features, are in love and blithely unaware of the impending danger. But in Berlin the following month, Carola insults the Nazi authorities who flatter her, and is subsequently arrested and detained for twenty-four hours. When she and Martin try to escape together to Prague, he is not allowed across the border. Through his eyes, we see Viennese Jews forced to paint JUDE on their doors, clean the streets, and perform other demeaning tasks. Just when we hope that a sympathetic taxi driver will smuggle him to Prague, Martin is taken away by two members of the Gestapo.

Once again, a spectrum of response to Nazi oppression is visible: Martin's former housekeeper offers to hide him – but her young son is already a Nazi; the playwright's Jewish publisher commits suicide; and it seems that the best-intentioned citizens must abandon their country once it is annexed in the *Anschluss.* Adapted from Friedrich Torberg's novel, *This Too Was Vienna, '38* gains in power toward the end, as we identify with Martin's increasing vulnerability, hope, and aborted escape. Although it lacks the complexity of *Welcome in Vienna,* the fact that *'38* is set in a more "innocent" time places the emphasis on love rather than political accommodation, disillusionment, and guilt.

Part IV

Shaping Reality

"About seven thousand
Germans served in Auschwitz.
They must be around me –
but where? And who?"

– Shadow of Doubt

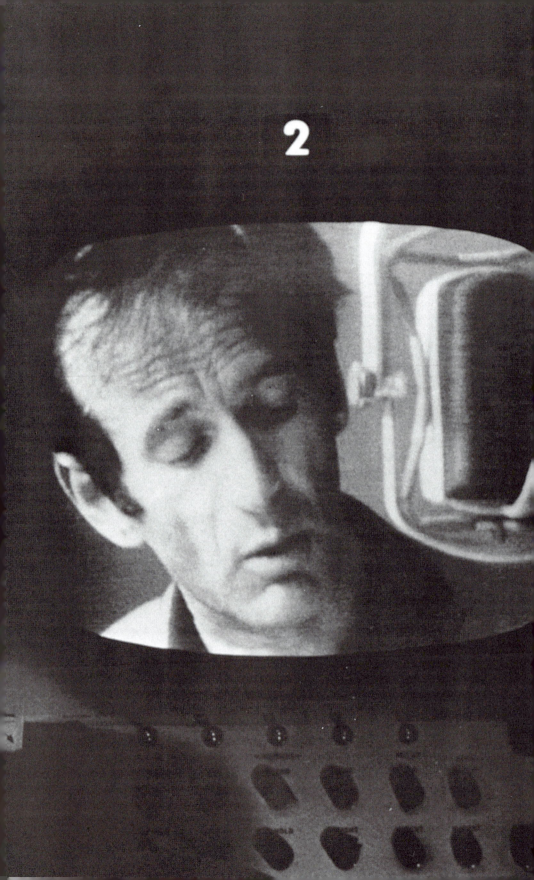

2

12
The Personal Documentary

I t was once assumed that documentary films were impersonal records of real events or people: you set up the camera, shoot the situation, and it might appear on the TV news. Critics like André Bazin nourished this theory by stressing that the lens (called the *objectif* in French) is "impassive" and that "between the originating object and its reproduction there intervenes only the instrumentality of a nonliving agent."[1] The underlying fallacy here – as anyone who has ever taken a photograph can attest – is that framing, camera angle, lighting, and proximity to subject are "objective." The selection of high-angle versus low-angle, for example, results in a different image: the subject might be the same, but the camera placement determines whether it seems insignificant, threatening, or neutral.

The corollary assumption was that a fiction film is an artificial construct, strongly plotted into a linear narrative progression, using actors, sets, visual tricks, and so on. Such oversimplified categories no longer hold, especially after the advent of Italian neorealism. This film movement in postwar Italy eschewed polished scripts, professional actors, makeup, studios, and addressed itself to the daily problems of impoverished Italians. Films like *The Bicycle Thief, Open City,* and *La Terra Trema* ascribed a new dignity to "reality" and to the notion of the cinema as a sensitizing mirror. The closest analogue in American culture is perhaps *Let Us Now Praise Famous Men,* in which Walker Evans's stark photographs of American sharecroppers in the 1930s are animated and deepened by the direct perceptions of James Agee's rich prose. The camera-conscious writer acknowledged that his aim was "to recognize the stature of a portion of unimagined existence, and to contrive techniques proper to its recording, communication, analysis, and defense. More essentially, this is an independent inquiry into certain normal predicaments of human divinity."[2]

Particularly when dealing with the overwhelming and still palpable realities of the Holocaust, certain filmmakers have been able to transform the documentary into a personal genre, closer to the memoir or journal. This is not to denigrate the more "objective documentaries," such as *The 81st Blow,* whose importance cannot be overestimated. (Indeed, one could argue that the most authentic and affecting film on the

Elie Wiesel in *Sighet, Sighet.*

Holocaust is *Memory of the Camps* – or *A Painful Reminder* in its longer, 69-minute version – an incomplete document of Allied footage of the Liberation, found in the archives of London's Imperial War Museum in the mid-1980s and subsequently presented on WNET's "Frontline" [narrated by Trevor Howard]. With Alfred Hitchcock as "Treatment Advisor," this material had been edited after the war, but then deemed too gruesome to show audiences. Despite a missing last reel and intermittent sound, *Memory of the Camps* contains devastating images of Bergen-Belsen, as well as camps including Dachau and Ebensee.) But there is simply not enough space in this study to do justice to the vast amount of fine work done by masters from Erwin Leiser (*Mein Kampf*) and Pare Lorentz (*Nuremberg*) to Irmgard and Bengt von zur Muhlen (*The Liberation of Auschwitz*) and Arthur Cohn (*The Final Solution*). The focus in this chapter is the documentary whose subjectivity is foregrounded, or whose point of departure is the attempt of the filmmaker/child of survivors to grapple cinematically with his or her legacy.

Films like *Night and Fog*, *Sighet, Sighet*, and *Shadow of Doubt* use "documentary" footage such as newsreels and interviews, but are in fact as formally rich as the best of "fiction" films: they contain a narrative spine, poetic sinews, an edited pulse, and a profoundly personal voice. It is a truism that documentaries depend upon the editing stage for the creative shaping of material, but in the case of films that examine the impact of the Holocaust, montage is the very embodiment of the need for multiple perspectives. Editing can shape the "reality" of newsreels and photographs into personal storytelling – or manipulate these elements (and the viewer) through the imposition of soundtrack. Still photographs constitute raw material, and are often animated by the use of an optical printer: as Chris Marker demonstrated in *La Jetée* (1963), movement can be created by panning across or zooming into static images. Moreover, the very stillness of Holocaust photographs represents the death of its subjects, while the movements of the optical printer embody the filmmaker's examination of the past.[3] Given the degree to which these still frames can be manipulated by filmic technique, directors must be wary of overdramatizing and not allowing the testimony to speak for itself.

For instance, much of the same archival footage appears in *The Witnesses* (*Le Temps du Ghetto*), Frédéric Rossif's chilling French "documentary" of 1962, and *Genocide*, produced by the Simon Wiesenthal Foundation in 1981 (and not to be confused with the 1975 BBC film of the same title mentioned in Chapter 9). *The Witnesses* is structured by the survivors themselves quietly recounting their experiences: each is seen in close-up, speaking out of a black void. By shooting a woman first in close-up and then in profile, the camera suggests a "mug shot" parallel: the subject is still a prisoner – of her memories. *Genocide* (directed by Arnold Schwartzman) is narrated by Orson Welles, a paternalistic voice whose very celebrity tames the material into a cohesive structure. While his tone is generally sober, the film is punctuated by the voice-over of Elizabeth Taylor, speaking – or rather acting – the accounts of individual survivors. With little acknowledgment of the source of the material, Taylor's tearful tales are accompanied by overbearing music as well as screams and gunshots. To what extent is this a truthful depiction of the Holocaust experience? What is the difference between a story told dispassionately by the person who lived it, and a written text performed by a star? And is the former ultimately more "objective" than the latter?

Part of the answer lies in dispensing with the terminology and appreciating the film's composition and effects. As we saw in Chapter 2, *Night and Fog* (1955) is a formally intricate film that both reflects and invites tension. Its director, Alain Resnais, had no direct connection to the concentration camps – and therefore refused the project when it was proposed to him by Argos Films and the Comité d'Histoire de la Seconde Guerre Mondiale. "To make a film about the concentration camps, it seemed to me you had to have been an inmate, or deported for political reasons," the director confessed. "I accepted only on the condition that the commentary would be written by Jean Cayrol because he was himself a survivor. I agreed to make the film with Cayrol as the guarantee of the montage and images."[4]

Night and Fog thus contains the dual perspective of the witness – Cayrol/voice – and the visitor – Resnais/image (the identity with which the majority of an audience necessarily identifies) – the survivor and the artist who tries to make sense of survival. Resnais's presence as postfactum investigator rather than participant is expressed by his visual style, especially a tracking camera whose smooth movement actively penetrates the scene. Resnais was well aware that newsreels of crematoria, mountains of women's hair, or rows of headless corpses (the skulls piled in a pail nearby) would challenge audience tolerance. It was partly for this reason that he engaged in "much formalist research," prying *Night and Fog* away from the "documentary" category to what he now calls "something more lyrical – an evocation. The idea that stimulated us in our work was, 'Do we have the right to do formalist research with such a subject?' But maybe with this element, it would have more of an audience. For me, formalism is the only way to communicate." Consequently, Resnais's investigative camera and jarring editing constitute the personal terms by which the concentration camp experience can be perceived and comprehended.

An interesting cinematic variation on the dual perspective of witness and visitor can be found in *Falkenau, the Impossible: Samuel Fuller Bears Witness* (France, 1988). Directed by Emil Weiss – born in Transylvania in 1947 to Jewish parents – the 52-minute documentary explores the Czech concentration camp from at least three vantage points, anchored in the visual and verbal testimony of American film director Sam Fuller. Most significantly, we see Fuller's first "movie," a 21-minute, black-and-white silent film that he shot as a young soldier when his regiment liberated the camp. The now-seventy-six-year-old filmmaker speaks from a director's chair in a dark screening room, his voice accompanying the 1945 images. In addition, Fuller visits the present-day remains of the Falkenau camp (now Sokolov) and shows us a German map of Europe containing a staggering number of dots to identify where the Nazis had camps (more than one thousand, according to Weiss). The third perspective is provided by newsreels from the mid-1940s.

Falkenau begins with clips from Fuller's fictional *Big Red One* (1980), but the most riveting section is his "home movie," which he describes as a drama staged by an American officer: the division commander took leading male VIPs from the neighboring town – who claimed they knew nothing of the Falkenau camp – and forced them to dress and bury the corpses. Despite Fuller's lack of cinematic experience at the time, he knew the value of camera movement for, as he pans from the camp to the town, we see how very close they were. Fuller's extraordinary memory enables him to narrate the footage with authority. However, when he subsequently speaks in the courtroom of the Nuremberg trials, or rambles about whether you can make a film about the Holocaust (his answer to Weiss is, "Nothing is impossible with the camera, my boy!"), he is not as persuasive or compelling. Weiss respectfully poses questions and gives Fuller free rein, but the viewer is left wanting to know more about the young European director's own response to these issues of wartime horror and representation.

One Man's War (*La Guerre d'un seul homme*, France, 1982) goes further than *Falkenau* with the juxtaposition of newsreel footage and a voice recorded at a future time. In this fascinating "documentary," director Edgardo Cozarinsky accompanies French newsreels of World War II – mainly propaganda which suggests that the French were manipulated by scurrilous leaders who tapped into the people's willful ignorance about Nazism and collaboration – with a voice-over from the Paris diaries of Ernst Jünger (read by the French actor Niels Arestrup). Jünger was a German writer and career officer stationed in France during the war. As in *The Sorrow and the Pity*, it is disturbing to see the French masses rallying to the Nazi cause (and the crowds at the end cheering the Resistance consequently feel a bit suspect); however, the only acknowledged horror in the film comes, ironically enough, from the text of this German officer who grows sick of the whole enterprise. Cozarinsky – originally an Argentine Jew, now living in France – has defined his film as a "documentary fiction," for the voice we hear throughout is not the objective narration of a traditional documentary but an intimate memoir. *One Man's War* is a subtle dialogue between the public deception of French newsreels and the private reflection of a German officer. Cozarinsky acknowledged that he used Jünger's monologue as if it were *musical* material – a disenchanted, contrapuntal voice alongside the optimistic, aggressive voice of the newsreels. This self-conscious style creates both an awareness of the complexities of the Occupation and a wariness of ideologies or certitude.

When the survivor himself occupies more of the film's center stage, the style might be less noticeable. *Return to Poland* and *Sighet, Sighet* begin with the same premise – the return of a Jewish survivor to the country from which he was definitively uprooted as a child – but they diverge in style. Marian Marzynski is the director, writer, and constant visual center of the former, a one-hour film made for American public television (WGBH in Boston, aired nationally on November 18, 1981). It could be termed a "reportage" in its fearless examination of contemporary Poland. *Sighet, Sighet* (1964), on the other hand, is a poetic meditation written and narrated by the giant of Holocaust literature, Elie Wiesel. This 27-minute film made by Harold Becker is structured by visual juxtaposition, whereas *Return to Poland* continuously follows its director in time and space. Marzynski's film begins in a train that carries the forty-four-year-old director into Poland – for the first time in twelve years. His voice-over establishes that he was born in Warsaw in 1937: "War was my kindergarten . . . my game was survival," explains the accented voice. Hidden by various Poles after surviving the Warsaw Ghetto, he then left at the age of thirty-two – "a disillusioned immigrant" – following experiences of anti-Semitism. The personal meaning of the train is conveyed when he describes how his father cut a hole in

Marian Marzynski visits a nun who sheltered him
in *Return to Poland.* PHOTO COURTESY OF OREN JACOBY

the floor of the transport bearing him to a concentration camp, and jumped out to join the partisans. And after the war, his mother rode countless trains looking for her son.

When Marzynski arrives in Warsaw, a neighbor tells him that his house is gone. He walks through the empty space, testifying to the camera, "This was my home." The past exists only in still fragments, as he learns in the subsequent sequences. An exhibition of "forbidden photos" informs crowds of the upheavals of 1956, 1968, and 1970 and implies a continuity with present-day difficulties. (One gets a sense throughout *Return to Poland* of the importance of images: Marzynski's friends live in a tiny apartment that lacks conveniences, but they do have a TV that is constantly on. And the negotiations between Solidarity and the government that Marzynski sits in on are a battle over media coverage.) The young faces absorbing brutal images of invasion and repressive retaliation seem hopeful – for politics has become their bread – but the little girls to whom Marzynski speaks reflect a collective amnesia vis-à-vis Jews. They have been assigned to study historical monuments in the area. He asks them what the Warsaw Ghetto was, and what is a Jew. One answers, "Jews are mainly old people." "Do they look different?" "Their eyes are different." The director wonders, "Why were they locked in the Ghetto?" "Um, they did something to Hitler or he did something to them" is the sweetly innocent reply. There are only four thousand Jews left in Warsaw – which had three million before the war – and these children will probably never play with one.

The image Marzynski presents of Catholic Poland is complex. On the one hand, he tells of sixteen Christian families who, one after the other, accepted him as a "moral duty" after he was smuggled out of the Ghetto in 1942. The Christian orphanage that became his home is presented as a comforting refuge, but one whose pastor says matter-of-factly to Marzynski, "Ninety percent of us Poles are practicing Catholics, and we want you back too." A darker picture is offered when he visits his parents' town, where the central square is paved with gravestones from the Jewish cemetery, "so they would be walked on." It is difficult for this survivor to find the past, but the present thrusts itself upon him: in a high school English class, the young women tell him the situation of Solidarity is good, and he witnesses a demonstration of Polish "hippies" that prompts his remark, "Poland enters the kindergarten of political democracy."

Since Marzynski remained in Poland until the age of thirty-two, he *is* a Pole and ends his tale with the hope that "Poland too will survive." This stance is unavailable to Elie Wiesel, whose hometown, Sighet, is no longer even part of the same country. What was once Hungary is now Rumania; what was once the home of ten thousand Jews is, after their deportation to Auschwitz, now a testament to oblivion: "Nothing has changed – only the Jews had disappeared," he repeats quietly. What was once called "Jewish Street" is now "The Street of the Deported" – ignoring the question of who was deported or why. After twenty years, Wiesel returns for one day to the place "where the world lost its innocence and God lost His mask." Sighet is presented through still photographs rather than moving images, perhaps because the present town is dead to him. The image that accompanies Wiesel's arrival "home" is a photo of him as a child with his mother. Home cannot be a place, only a time; and this time could not be documented by a movie camera, only by photographs. The camera of *Sighet, Sighet* moves across and animates these photos of happy faces; a few sequences later, it pans across the remnants of the Jewish cemetery – the only place where Wiesel could feel at home. In hushed slow cadences, Wiesel tells us that he tried to light candles for the dead, but the wind blew them out.

Had *Sighet, Sighet* presented merely this disillusioning return to a Transylvanian town, it would have been a moving meditation. However, its style and concerns extend Wiesel's voyage into an even greater lament and indictment. As the film opens, his voice (and a gentle melody) carry us from the present – expressed by a low-angle tracking camera under skyscrapers – to the past, captured in still photographs. Wiesel finds a town "petrified in its own forgetfulness, and the shame that springs from that forgetfulness." However, as in *Night and Fog*, the images that embody this restrained observation are contrapuntal, both at the film's opening and during the closing reprise. The city looming over the fluid camera is not Sighet but New York, and Wiesel's feeling of isolation exists not merely because of his native village's indifference. For included in this personal documentary are shots of the quiet modern studio in which Wiesel is taping, a slow pan of dials, reels, and two technicians seated beyond the booth, followed by an extremely long take of Wiesel reading his text – a solitary face and voice reaching beyond New York's high-rise buildings. The repetition in the title implies a gap between the city Wiesel remembers and the one he sees: "the town that had once been mine never was." But on another level, Sighet's "double" is quite modern: the film subtly suggests that perhaps New York, too, is petrified in its forgetfulness.

The poetic meditation of *Sighet, Sighet* can be contrasted with the confrontational aesthetic embodied by *Now . . . after All These Years* (*Jetzt . . . nach so viel Jahren*), made for German television by Harald Lüders and Pavel Schnabel in 1981. They too focus on a town that had a thriving Jewish community of over five hundred in 1928. Today, the only Jewish component of Rhina – 150 miles north of Frankfurt – is the cemetery. The one-hour film opens with shots of this graveyard before introducing the Youth Fire Brigade today. On-camera interviews with the townspeople elicit stock responses: "People don't like to talk about the past." "It wasn't me, it was the others." ("Don't ask me, I'm not Hitler," offers one old codger.) And another red-faced citizen defends Nazism because "morally, *they* were a lot better off than people now." The role of the filmmakers grows more investigative as they pore over a book that covers two hundred years of Rhina's history (to the voice-over speech of Alfred Rosenberg, the Nazi party's "intellectual leader," about ridding German towns of Jews). They find that the pages for November 9–10, 1938 (*Kristallnacht,* which included the burning of Rhina's synagogue) are missing. Despite the mayor's claim that all the records were destroyed during the war, Lüders discovers that a teacher had falsified documents.

Now . . . after All These Years continues its investigation in New York City, which is expressed by jazz, neon, and brisk montage. Lüders and Schnabel track down a few survivors from Rhina and show them photos of how the town and its people

Elie Wiesel in *Sighet, Sighet.* PHOTO COURTESY OF MUSEUM OF MODERN ART/FILM STILLS ARCHIVE

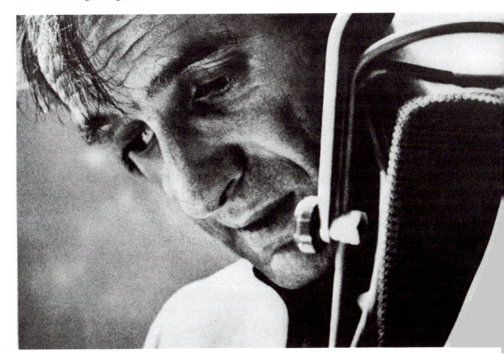

look today. The camera offers a poignant commentary when it remains on an old woman seated in a lawn chair in front of her apartment building. She looks alone in a rather alien world – New York with its big radios blaring and Hispanic kids staring – after having explained how nineteen members of her family were killed by the Nazis. Subsequent shots of the diamond exchange on 47th Street and the Lower East Side demonstrate quietly that the Jews have not disappeared from New York as they have from Rhina.

The most audacious part of the film is the return to Rhina, where the filmmakers assemble its inhabitants in the same room where the Jews were rounded up some forty years before. Here, they play the New York footage, including the interviews with these long-lost neighbors. As might be expected, the Germans are upset to hear an old Jewish woman answer the question, "Did anyone help you?" with the reply, "Help me? What for?" The townspeople become defensive, antagonistic, and visibly troubled by "all this permanent digging – we want to forget that." The teacher admits, "We didn't want to know," and urges, "Just educate the children and be orderly." The raw footage of the film within the film shakes up the Rhina audience, while the editing of *Now... after All These Years* asks us to beware of convenient indifference: a cut to the orderly Youth Fire Brigade we saw at the beginning now confers upon this contemporary group an ominous quality.

When Lüders first came to New York with this film in an attempt to find American distribution, I asked him, "Are you Jewish?" "No," he answered. "Then what led you to make this film?" "I'm German" was the simple reply. The twenty-nine-year-old's confrontation of present with past stemmed from his frustration that the subject was being evaded, that young people know so little about it, and that whenever he asked a German about the Holocaust, the answer was always that someone else had been responsible.

A few years later, Lüders was one of the subjects interviewed in *Dark Lullabies* (Canada, 1985), a one-hour documentary written and codirected (with Abbey Jack Neidik) by Irene Lilienheim Angelico, the daughter of German-Jewish survivors. Angelico narrates and is visible throughout her two journeys, through which she tries to understand her legacy as a member of the "second generation." The first part chronicles her trip to Israel, where she finds strength in her Jewish identity from interviews conducted at the First World Gathering of Jewish Holocaust Survivors. The second voyage is to Germany, where she is helped by Lüders: not only does he articulately express the problem of his generation – "Young Jews, especially children of survivors, can look into the past and feel closer to their people. For Germans, it's exactly the other way around" – but he introduces her to a young woman who recounts an amazing story about suddenly learning that her town had been a camp during World War II. Nevertheless, Angelico's interviews with her German contemporaries do not all share this acknowledgment of Nazi horror: for example, a young neo-Nazi is chillingly ironic in his dismissal of "Holocaust" as Hollywood fabrication, and far from ironic in his assertion that he would obey his superiors without question.

Angelico then visits Dachau, which shocks both filmmaker and audience alike with its loveliness – a town filled with shops and children. She goes through the gates of the former camp, musing that she is the same age as her father was when he got out of Dachau. A splendid shot of Angelico in the background with the barbed

Codirector Harald Lüders visits a survivor in New York in
Now ... after All These Years. PHOTO COURTESY OF ARTHUR CANTOR, INC.

wire dominant in the foreground visually expresses how the Holocaust continues
to overwhelm her. (When the film aired on WNET on December 23, 1987, it
was effectively double-billed with *Pour mémoire,* Edgardo Cozarinsky's excellent
one-hour French documentary about Nazi hunters Serge and Beate Klarsfeld. It
chronicles their attempts to discover, publicize, and record the Nazis living peacefully
today – 95 percent in Germany and Austria, 5 percent primarily in Latin America.
It contains some of the same archival footage incorporated by Angelico.) *Dark
Lullabies* covers a fascinating spectrum of the generation born after the war: while
some Germans try to deal honestly with the past, others avoid, deny, or perpetuate it.

The suggestion that the enemy is not necessarily a monster, or even evil, but perhaps
indifference itself – a willed ignorance that allows genocide to sprout unchecked, like
weeds choking an untended garden – is also a major concern of Rolf Orthel's *Shadow
of Doubt* (*Een schijn van twijfel*). Made in The Netherlands in 1975, its title refers to the
self-protective blindness that permitted Germans and Jews alike to ignore the extent
of the Final Solution. Closer in tone to the lyrical *Night and Fog* and *Sighet, Sighet* than
to the straightforward *Now ... after All These Years,* this 53-minute inquiry blends
interviews of former SS men and survivors with an autobiographical return to the
director's blissfully ignorant childhood in The Hague.

Orthel's film begins where *Night and Fog* leaves off, as the director narrates with
sober control his personal attempt to comprehend the Holocaust. Still photographs
incarnate memories of "suitcases, evacuation, curfew, underground," and he recalls
a girl with a Jewish star: "I was told she was special and forgot about her." In 1944,
the eight-year-old boy did not know what Auschwitz was, but thirty years later, he
hunts for evidence of its existence in the stillness broken only by howling wind.

Mozart's Rondo in A Minor mitigates the painful images snatched from aging stills and newsreels of the camps. In addition to some of the stock footage also visible in *Night and Fog* and *The Witnesses, Shadow of Doubt* contains "forbidden footage," purchased by the director from a man who was persecuted for filming the killings in 1941. Mozart also accompanies Orthel's camera tracking through the now placid Auschwitz and Westerbork. The latter was initially built to house refugee German Jews, but later became the transit point from which they and their Dutch counterparts were deported to the concentration camps.

The place itself can tell him little, so the director collects testimony from a number of witnesses, including a Dutch doctor whom nobody would believe when he told them about Auschwitz, and a French woman who keeps the Holocaust memory alive in her shop: a book on deportation dominates the display window with its frightening photographs. *Shadow of Doubt* intensifies their impact by presenting close-ups of the horrified eyes in the photos. A German with a swastika tattooed on his arm explains that he had the symbol blotted out in 1941 after growing disillusionment with what it represented. A former SS guard, today a doctor, claims his work in the camp was merely "daily routine"; when he is asked, "Did you sleep well?" he responds, "When one is young, one always sleeps well." Another German admits he felt no guilt at the time – "How could one help, alone, among thousands?" – and cautions against facile condemnation: "It's easy nowadays to worry, 'would you help'...but at the time, [we] had no experience of that." The prisoners looked like a gray mass to him, so ill that they were unrecognizable. Occasionally, he gave them a bite of bread, but more would have gotten him into trouble with the SS.

The film's title comes from an interview with Primo Levi, who recalls that in his camp (Monowitz), there was an Italian who refused to understand German and Polish so as to avoid knowing what was happening. Like this prisoner, people gratefully exploited their silence and "the shadow of doubt" – unsure exactly what awaited them. The title can be extended to all those who chose not to grasp and react against the enormity of extermination. The final interview is with the curator of Auschwitz, a former inmate who never really left – an embodiment, perhaps like all survivors, of memory. When the film ends on the dark space between two monuments, Orthel's exemplary quest serves as a reminder to keep one's eyes open rather than hiding in the "shadow."

With its kindred title, *In Dark Places* (1978) is an even more personal document since the director, Gina Blumenfeld, is the child of Holocaust survivors. The subtitle of this one-hour film, "Remembering the Holocaust," underscores the act of vigorous and vigilant recall that informs Blumenfeld's work. In her own words, "As a film-maker and the daughter of Holocaust survivors, my primary goal was to make a film about the memory of this historical tragedy – about how we remember such an experience – and why we might try to forget." Her concern is less to reconstruct the event than to comprehend its legacy, especially for what has come to be known as "the second generation." The first insight is provided by an interview with Armand Volkas, director of the New Artef Players, a theater group. He tells of growing up in an area where he was the only Jew: "I felt I had this burden, this historical inheritance." His mother's concentration camp stories marked him deeply, especially those about the emotional and moral support the women gave each other. And the burden is rendered more specific when he admits about his grandfather, "In a way, I feel I'm living my life for him."

This assumption of a dead relative's identity perhaps provides part of the artistic fuel for Volkas's theatrical productions. In a clip from their theater piece, "Survivors," we see an effective metaphor for concentration camps – a grave game of "Simon says." Blumenfeld intercuts contrapuntal footage from 1934 Nuremberg in which crowds salute Hitler, and she weaves the voices of survivors around the images. Volkas's father attests to constant nightmares, and Nahum Shulman explains that, after seeing everyone die around him in the *shtetl*, he can't look back. The director's own identity is invoked when she asks a subject from voice-off, "Mom, who did you lose in the war?" "Everybody" is the simple reply. Shots of the transports are accompained by both train rumblings and piano music, the harsh sounds of the period combined with the poignant tone of recollection.

Another woman, Genia Schwartz, recounts how her parents and sisters were taken to "selection" in Lodz in 1942. Her sister tried to save her parents as well as her own two children; a nurse told her she had to choose one pair to save. (She took the children and managed to hide her parents with friends.) An intercut of the ghetto suggests the degree to which it continues to exist in Genia Schwartz's mind; after starving there for four and a half years, she wanted to believe the commander who said he'd give them work "in factories." Interspersed shots of cattle cars and barbed wire inform us that these factories turned out to be Auschwitz. An abrupt cut to light music and a photo album offers a different image of remembrance: a young doctor and his family take "A Visit to Mauthausen," as a title puts it. One wonders about the effects of this trip upon his teenage daughter – who said she wanted to see "the gory things." "It was creepy, it was weird!" she remarks after a display of slides of the gas chambers. The reason for placing Susan Sontag's interview at this point becomes clear when the celebrated writer speaks of being twelve years old in 1945 and seeing pictures of Nazi horrors in a book: "I knew I was Jewish but I didn't know it meant what I saw . . . hundreds of bodies stacked like firewood." Sontag was familiar with Hollywood representations of violence and death, and realized that "all those movies I had seen had nothing to do with reality." Her voice returns after the presentation of pictures from the Dachau Memorial Museum, with the crucial phrase that typifies many films about the Holocaust: "Remembering is a moral obligation."

Sontag's participation in the film places Blumenfeld's personal attempt at commemoration into a lucid historical and political perspective. Insisting that history is tantamount to complexity rather than the simplification people desire from it, she perceives, "They want to have their indignation refueled. I think the only thing that's good to learn is how complicated things are." Articulate and low-keyed, Sontag points to the abundance of Nazi symbols today – "the consumerist use of Hitler" – and suggests that the word "Holocaust" is misleading. "The fire image is unearned, a little bit cheap," she explains, for it was neither spontaneous nor natural – just a "directed and controlled political event." Sontag raises the important issue that the concentration camps were a drain on the economy and military effort, "counterproductive from a military point of view." Her incisive interpretation comprehends the long tradition of anti-Semitism in German-speaking countries: "Hitler said, 'Even if we lose the war, at least we will have killed the Jews.'"

A return to Armand Volkas and his actors counteracts the sentiment of this quotation. They call for resistance to the negative stereotypes of Jews that remain a part of our culture (rendered concrete by a display of caricatures), and to the myth of passivity, which they see as false. Another clip from their play, "Survivors," presents a stylized re-creation of victims on a train headed for death. Using only voice, gesture, dramatic lighting, and locomotive sounds, they turn their stage from a dark place to one that pulsates with fearful light. Like the film, their performance is an artful process of testimony and legacy.

An end title tells us that the film is dedicated to "Israel Blumenfeld, Scholar and Warsaw Ghetto Fighter," and it seems appropriate in retrospect that the opening line was Volkas's "I think my father is a hero." *In Dark Places*, if first of all an attempt to validate and commemorate the experiences of parents, is also, however, an effort to shed light on the Holocaust. Like her younger subjects, Blumenfeld has found a way to confront the past, and the film is an act of integration – of history and actuality, intelligence (Sontag) and emotion (Schwartz), newsreel footage and stills, theater and film, survivors and children, a daughter's somewhat perverse fascination in "A Visit to Mauthausen" and Nahum Shulman who "can't look back." As one of the interviewees – clinical social worker Ben Pomerantz – acknowledges: "Involvement with the Holocaust is an attempt to undo the past, the damage done to family and culture. But that's hopeless, mindless." The goal is therefore integration – a coming to terms. The closing epigraphs move from the despair of "dark places" in Isaiah 59:10 to hope, in a quotation from Job. The film thus ends with one possible stance toward the Holocaust – an allusion to being tested and the potential for rebirth.

We Were So Beloved (1986), Manfred Kirchheimer's documentary about the German-Jewish refugee community of New York's Washington Heights, is another cinematic quest for the filmmaker's roots. Through narration, interviews, photos, and appropriate quotations from *Mein Kampf*, this 145-minute film explores his past – both personal and historical – as well as its implications for today's world. Kirchheimer's approach is sympathetic rather than judgmental, whether he is interviewing his father, who admits to cowardice (he would not have hidden Jews had he been a Christian neighbor), refugees who say they forgive the Germans, or those who declare they want vengeance. The director's parents were smart and lucky enough to leave Germany in 1936, with five-year-old Manny, for Washington Heights. This "Frankfurt-on-the-Hudson" was a refuge for his family and their approximately twenty thousand exiled neighbors, but they had to work hard to create a new life. What becomes apparent is that they consider themselves very German, still speak the language, and recall – with a blend of nostalgia and bewilderment – the sentiment vis-à-vis German neighbors that gives the film its title. Kirchheimer probes attitudes that illuminate aspects of the Holocaust: for instance, Mrs. Marcus, a survivor who had been on the S.S. *St. Louis*, confesses, "I wasn't used to having my own opinion," adding that German Jews were taught to obey. (She even claims that had the Jews on the *St. Louis* been Polish rather than German, they would have fought and taken over the ship to go to America.) This regard for authority sets up a discomfiting connection between Nazis and German Jews, which culminates in an incident recounted by Mrs. Lieber, a Washington Heights rabbi's wife: their Orthodox congregation unquestioningly fired her husband in 1959 because they heard he flew in a plane on the Sabbath. The congregation's attitude was "Follow the majority, no questioning," according to Mrs. Lieber, who says Americans are more independent thinkers. The myriad of perspectives in *We Were So Beloved* includes Max Frankel, a Jewish *New York Times* editor, who acknowledges that he "felt deeply deprived at not being allowed to march in German youth parades," and that many Jews would have been obedient followers of Hitler had they been accepted, and MIT professor Louis Kampf who perceptively explains how people find an ideology to justify their fear.

A Generation Apart (1984) is another personal documentary by and about children of survivors coming to terms with their parents and the Holocaust legacy. Directed by Jack Fisher and produced by his brother, Danny Fisher, the one-hour film contains raw moments of familial encounters. It is affecting because the survivors have moving stories, interesting faces, calm delivery, while the second-generation members articulate a spectrum of discomfort. One young man points to the burden of expectation inherited from parents: "I felt that everything was taken from them, so it was up to me to fulfill them." The filmmakers' older brother argues that parents use the Holocaust as an instrument to make children feel guilty, and confronts his younger sibling with the remark, "Do you really want to lay on everybody this Holocaust business? How relevant really is it to your personal life?" And, in a powerfully cathartic scene, a young woman named Shelly is told by her mother, "In the camps, if you loved someone too much, you would lose them. I was afraid if I loved too much I would lose you. So I kept you at a distance. I think I owe all my children an apology."

The personal tone of these films is less palpable in some of the other films made by children of survivors. When *A Generation Apart* was released in New York, the other half of the effective double bill was *The Well* (1984), a Yiddish-language short whose focus is also a young man dealing with the Holocaust. But this half-hour film by David Greenwald (whose parents were interned in Auschwitz) is fictional, telling the story of a boy in 1939 Eastern Europe who dreams of America as filtered through *Life* magazine. When he gets to the Promised Land of New York, the garment business work is hard and demeaning, and he must live with the uncertainty about what happened to his parents in Europe. At the end, he learns about the Holocaust.

Film director and editor Steven Brand presumably could have made a documentary about his own circumstances as a child of Viennese Jews who escaped from Austria in 1939. But he chose to devote his energies over a five-year period to the story of another "2G," Yossi Klein. The result was *Kaddish* (1984), a 90-minute film about this Jewish activist from Boro Park, Brooklyn, and his complex relationship with his father. Zoltan Klein, who died during the filming, survived the extermination of Hungarian Jewry by hiding for six months in a hole in the ground. His son was aware from early childhood of this wartime past; indeed, he recalls bedtime tales that were really horror stories. Among the troubling aspects into which Brand delves is Yossi's obsessive Judaism, inseparable from paranoia. As a child, he imagined being chased by Nazis on the Coney Island boardwalk; he would look for holes in the ground where he could hide. When Yossi grew up, it was in the shadow of his father, although the thrust of his activities became Russian Jewry rather than the Holocaust. In the course of the film, Yossi acquires a stronger sense of his own identity, especially after the year-long Kaddish (mourning) following his father's death.

Breaking the Silence: The Generation after the Holocaust (1984) was written and produced by Eva Fogelman, a psychotherapist who has led many intensive therapy sessions for children of Holocaust survivors. In the press notes from the film, she states, "as a child of survivors... when I discovered that parental silence about the Holocaust was a barrier which prevented young Jews from connecting with their rich heritage that was destroyed by the Nazis, my impulse was to bring them together." Directed by Edward Mason (director of Harvard Medical School's Mental Health Film Program), the one-hour documentary focuses on nine members of a second-generation discussion group who meet regularly to explore their shared legacy. It becomes apparent that many survivors, out of a desire to protect their children, did not speak to them about the Holocaust; likewise, numerous offspring tried to spare their parents pain by not asking about the wartime past.

Breaking the Silence consequently takes its title from one of the aims of the discussion groups – an aim fulfilled in part by the catalyzing process of the filming. Most effective are the scenes in which children talk to their parents, trying to understand and come to terms with them. For example, Rosalie (whose gorgeous voice and stirring song about survival are heard over the end credits) admits she had to leave a restrictive home, while another "2G," Yolanda (whose intriguing paintings we see), is shown close to her mother. The film's most poignant moment occurs when an older survivor breaks down before his grandchild, explaining, "I lost everyone and that's why the baby is so important"; fortunately, the camera moves back into a two-shot to show his daughter comforting him. *Breaking the Silence* also includes interviews with such noted writers as psychologist Robert J. Lifton, Helen Epstein (author of *Children of the Holocaust*), Menachem Rosensaft (founding chairman of the International Network of Children of Jewish Holocaust Survivors), and history professor Moshe Waldoks, who speaks eloquently about the life-affirming qualities of Judaism.

An important addition to the growing body of "second-generation" documentaries was recently made in Israel, a country whose films have been curiously silent about the Holocaust. *Because of That War* (1988), directed by Orna Ben-Dor-Niv – a child of survivors – for the Israeli Film Service, focuses on a popular rock duo whose songs are rooted in their parents' Holocaust experiences. Triggered by a record album, "Ashes and Dust," the film traces how singer-composer Yehuda Poliker and lyricist-producer Yaakov Gil'ad transform Holocaust stories – as well as childhood memories and fears – into art. We first encounter them in the context of rehearsal, and then we meet the real dramatic focus of the film, Poliker's father, Jacko (an Auschwitz survivor from Greece), and Gil'ad's mother, Halina (a Majdanek survivor from Poland). Although it is revealing to hear the two young men discuss the extent to which they were shaped by their parents' experiences, it is even more penetrating to witness Halina lecturing to young students about how she lost her mother, or Jacko talking about being the only survivor from a family of fifty. The film moves toward a double harmony at the end: not only does the duo perform its affecting songs, but we see both sets of parents meeting so that Halina can write Jacko's story. *Because of That War* thus explores both the burden of survivors and the responsibility willingly assumed by their children.

Who Shall Live and Who Shall Die? PHOTO COURTESY OF LAURENCE JARVIK

The burden assumed by Laurence Jarvik, the son of a Dutch Jewess, is more explicitly political in *Who Shall Live and Who Shall Die?* (1981), made when he was twenty-four years old. He was clearly out to make a more "objective" document with little acknowledgment of his own identity, yet the film betrays a profound urgency to investigate the action – or lack of it – taken by America (and its Jews) during the Holocaust. Made over a period of three years for a mere hundred thousand dollars, this black-and-white film looks raw and unsophisticated, but the very poverty of its means allows a devastating political story to recount itself. It is a tale of American shoulder shrugging and eye lowering while millions were dying in Nazi concentration camps. Combining interviews with Jewish leaders, American officials, and survivors, as well as newsreels and previously classified information, Jarvik probes the degree to which the Jews of Europe *could* have been saved, had concerted action been taken by the Allies.

The first layer of the 90-minute film locates the problem in official government reaction, beginning with the refusal of the United States to admit refugees during the thirties. "Keep America out of Europe and Europe out of America," declares a spokesman in a newsreel. (A contrasting piece of archival footage offers a glimpse of a Jewish pageant to mobilize government action to save Jews.) *Who Shall Live and Who Shall Die?* shows that the American government knew about the extermination as it was happening, and that it chose political calculation over humanitarian consideration. We then learn of the efforts that led to a reversal of American policy and the establishment in 1944 of a special governmental agency to rescue the Jews.

And what did the American Jewish leadership contribute? Five hundred rabbis organized and marched on the White House . . . while the majority of American rabbis boycotted them. "Don't rock the boat" seemed to be the reigning attitude – especially for Jews who might have felt unsure of their own safety (and status) in the

United States. In Jarvik's words, "I originally wanted to make a film which would have shown how the Allied governments were criminally negligent towards the Jews. Instead, I unearthed a story which was more shocking and depressing than the one I originally sought."[5] What Jarvik found through research and interviews is that the American Jewish establishment thwarted the efforts of the one group that was actively seeking immediate rescue of European Jewry. This group was the Emergency Committee to Save the Jews of Europe, led by Peter Bergson and Samuel Merlin, two Palestinian Jews. A forceful case is presented by the volatile Bergson, as he insists that it was the American Jews who sabotaged his committee's effort. At this point, the second layer of *Who Shall Live and Who Shall Die?*'s historical unraveling comes sharply into view: it is not simply that the War Department rejected the idea to bomb the railway lines leading to Auschwitz, but that well-to-do American Jews did not make much noise about what was happening to their counterparts in Europe. They might have been generous with financial assistance, but were very reticent about pressuring the government into action.[6]

For Jarvik, "the most disturbing thing I came across in my research was a State Department document in which [American Jewish Congress leader] Stephen Wise advocated that Bergson be deported, saying he was worse than Hitler because he would bring anti-Semitism to the U.S." A searing corroboration can be found in Elie Wiesel's *A Jew Today*, where he points to the "amazing display of detachment . . . shared, in fact, by the leaders of the free Jewish communities. Why not admit it? Their behavior in those times remains inexplicable, to say the least. . . . For the first time secure Jewish communities took no interest in their distressed brothers' plight."[7]

Concentration camp prisoners in *Who Shall Live and Who Shall Die?*
PHOTO COURTESY OF LAURENCE JARVIK

A child who was taken prisoner in *Who Shall Live and Who Shall Die?*
PHOTO COURTESY OF LAURENCE JARVIK

Although Wiesel does not appear in *Who Shall Live and Who Shall Die?* the questions he raises in this "Plea for Survivors" thicken the film's revelations:

> How can one help but wonder what would have happened ... if our brothers had shown more compassion, more initiative, more daring ... if a million Jews had demonstrated in front of the White House ... if the officials of all Jewish institutions had called for a day of fasting – just one – to express their outrage ... if Jewish notables had started a hunger strike, as the ghetto fighters had requested ... if the heads of major schools, if bankers and rabbis, merchants and artists had decided to make a gesture of solidarity, just one.... Who knows, the enemy might have desisted. For he was cautious, the enemy. Calculating, realistic, pragmatic, he took one step at a time, always waiting to measure the intensity of the reaction. When it failed to materialize altogether, he risked another step. And waited. And when the reaction was still not forthcoming, he threw all caution to the wind.[8]

Bergson's aim was to at least reduce the wholesale slaughter: "If we had made it a retail murder, it couldn't have been done." Requests were made to set up a Jewish army, purchase Jews, bomb Auschwitz, construct rescue centers, and organize commando raids into the camps. All were turned down. Josiah DuBois, general counsel for the War Refugee Board, explains how he tried to bring two million Jews to America where they would be treated as prisoners of war: only one thousand were taken to Oswego in upstate New York. Jarvik follows these verbal accounts with chilling footage of Buchenwald and of children showing their tattooed arms. The price for American callousness?

Jarvik's program notes claim that *Who Shall Live and Who Shall Die?* "invites the viewer to form his own judgments, and therefore has no narration. It was produced privately, with no partisan, organizational, or governmental support." Nevertheless – and like most good documentaries – *Who Shall Live and Who Shall Die?* develops a point of view, namely an implicit celebration of Bergson's activism and an indictment of governmental as well as personal indifference. The careful arrangement of interviews and newsreel footage results in a profoundly disturbing document that is certain to offend many viewers. For Jarvik, "We all have the responsibility to ask what was the role of our fathers and our organizations. The film tries to look at patterns of responsibility so that in the future, people will look at these moral dilemmas and do the right thing."[9]

Despite his lack of filmmaking experience, the boyish investigator opted for a movie rather than a book because of a

> belief that people in positions of authority do have personal responsibility: they're not just puppets of history. When you write a book, people see the title, "Assistant Secretary of War," not the three-dimensional person of flesh and blood. I wanted to show the individual people involved in the political situation of the time.
>
> Given that people are mystified by politics, this film was to demystify. You see someone sitting at a desk: if a certain piece of paper comes his way and he puts it in the *in* box rather than the *out* box, this can mean thousands of lives. Just because you work for the government, or a Jewish organization, doesn't let you off the hook.

Jarvik had personal reasons for delving into this particular issue: his mother managed to get out of Holland in time. "You want to explore why your family survived – who did, who didn't," he admitted. "But there's also the fact that my father is American. What's important is that I'm an *American* Jew: what did my government do? What did my people do?" From the personal foundation of Jarvik's ancestry, *Who Shall Live and Who Shall Die?* is a persistent effort to unearth, comprehend, and prevent the acquiescence behind extermination.[10]

As If It Were Yesterday ("Comme si c'était hier"), on the other hand, is an effort to discover, celebrate, and perpetuate the resistance that saved Jewish children in Belgium. This ninety-minute 1980 documentary directed by Myriam Abramowicz and Esther Hoffenberg consists of interviews with some of the Belgians – especially Gentile – whose clandestine efforts saved four thousand children marked for extermination during World War II. Both directors are children of survivors, the former an American photographer, the latter a French artist. Abramowicz began the project after meeting the Belgian woman who had hidden her own parents from the Nazis; Hoffenberg – who narrates the film – felt herself implicated in the stories of survival (her parents were hidden in Poland), and decided to join Abramowicz – despite the fact that neither had ever made a film before: "It seemed obvious to us that all this could not, must not, be lost, and that a book would not suffice. Everything must not only be known, but also seen and heard. And all this was urgent, time was pressing and passing."[11] They shot the interviews in twenty-two days and spent three years shaping and releasing the film.

As If It Were Yesterday begins with stills and interviews that take us back to 1940. Some of the Belgian "saviors" are interviewed in French, some in Flemish, but three major facts come through in all cases: everyone was well-organized; people from all professions and classes contributed to the salvation of Jewish children; and there was always an emotional price to be paid for separating parents from their offspring. We meet an old priest who provided sanctuary for fifty-four children; the woman who hid at least twenty-three persons, including Abramowicz's parents; Maurice Heiber – former head of the Committee for the Defense of the Jews – who tells the touching story of a Jewish child hidden by Gentiles (at Christmas, he stole the tiny Jesus figure from the crèche, with the explanation that "little Jesus was a Jewish child and so he has to be hidden"); Judith van Monfort, who placed endangered youngsters with families or institutions because "we had to take action against Nazism and Fascism – you can't talk with them"; Yvonne Jospa, who states their three priorities during the war were (1) save the children, (2) save the parents, (3) prepare identity cards; and David Ferdman, a businessman who bought letters of denunciation and bribed informers.

In addition, the directors interview the now grown children who were saved by these Belgians. The result is an affecting kaleidoscope of day-to-day heroism, with special attention paid to the efforts of women. A majority of the subjects interviewed are female; in Hoffenberg's words, "Only they could walk on the street holding a child's hand and not attract attention, or hide false identity cards under bunches of leeks in a shopping bag. Their mutual help network was extraordinary." Even the soundtrack is a predominantly female voice – not only the gentle narration, but the music of "Neige," with her high-pitched incantations. Abramowicz elaborated on this point by confessing, "You see women because women made this film. It's the kind of things you don't see in Army films, for example. It was *natural* for us to talk to women as well as men."

The effect of the filmmaking experience on Abramowicz was profound:

> I no longer dream about concentration camps, where I could somehow almost imagine a scene as though I'd been there. The film made me understand that people react because it's *in* them to react against injustice; that Jews were not alone; and that it's important to look for positive things, even in something as horrible as the Holocaust.[12]

Amid the grim testimonies from the Nazi era, *As If It Were Yesterday* suggests the glimmer of hope to be found within horrific circumstances; like *Avenue of the Just* (1978, U.S.A.), a documentary about the "Righteous Gentiles" of World War II, it brings to light the generosity and courage of these modest heroes and heroines – by whose graces the filmmakers are alive today.

Three recent personal documentaries made by or with children of survivors expand the hopeful perspective of *As If It Were Yesterday* by focusing on how certain Gentiles protected and saved Jews during the Holocaust. Pierre Sauvage's *Weapons of the Spirit* (1987) is not only revelatory but inspiring; like Phillip Hallie's fine book, *Lest Innocent Blood Be Shed*, it is about the village of Le Chambon-sur-Lignon in the south of France. This Protestant community hid approximately five thousand Jews during World War II – around the same number as its population. Sauvage, a Jewish filmmaker who was born in Le Chambon and spent his early years there, returns to this peaceful village to chronicle and explore its "conspiracy of goodness." His voice-over narration (in English) and his questions to the villagers (in French) render *Weapons of the Spirit* an autobiographical voyage with universal implications.

In the director's words: "There, the day after France fell to the Nazis, the pacifist pastors of Le Chambon proclaimed the need to resist violence 'through the weapons of the spirit.' There, at the risk of their lives, the peasants and villagers of the area defied the Nazis and the collaborationist Vichy regime, turning their tiny community into occupied Europe's most determined haven of refuge for the Jews."[13] Its resistance was not particularly organized – indeed, a villager says that if they had been organized, they probably would have failed – but was an accumulation of personal decisions to "love thy neighbor as thyself."

These religious individuals were guided by pastor André Trocmé and his wife, Magda (who speaks in the film). The community took in Jews without question – and without the urge to convert them. In fact, their behavior seems all the more remarkable because it is juxtaposed with an opening newsreel sequence of an anti-Semitic exhibition in Paris at the time. While it is true that there *were* reasons for Le Chambon's unique nobility – from geography (remote farms) to a history of persecution as Huguenots – other questions remain unanswerable: for example, how does one explain that the local French prefect, Robert Bach, filed false reports that would protect the Jews?

Sauvage interweaves these elements with vivid interviews: we meet the man who was in charge of making fifty false IDs per week; the woman who placed children; other survivors; and quite a few "saviors" who simply practiced what they preached. They come across as modest relics of a time when decency was enacted by a very precious few. And although it seems curious that Sauvage and his family did not keep in touch with their rescuers after the war ended, his return via the film gives him the stirring opportunity to let viewers share in his renewal of communication with those who saved him.

The Los Angeles–based filmmaker succeeded in his avowed aim: "Most important of all, I had to convey the heroism of my protagonists without betraying the simplicity and seeming casualness that was inherent in that very heroism. Whatever the temptations, I knew I mustn't make these people seem 'larger-than-life.' The point, after all, was precisely the opposite; if somebody hadn't already used the title, I might well have called the film *Ordinary People*."[14]

So Many Miracles (1987) chronicles another cinematic return, that of Israel and Frania Rubinek to their native Poland. Directed by Katherine Smalley and Vic Sarin for Canadian television, this fifty-minute documentary is narrated by the Canadian actor Saul Rubinek, who accompanies his parents. They are to visit the elderly Christian woman who hid them from the Nazis for twenty-eight months, having received a letter about her wish to see them again before she dies. *So Many Miracles* masterfully juxtaposes, not only the Rubineks' preparation and Sophia Branja's anticipation, but the highly emotional tone of the parents, and the understated reflections of their son. For example, Saul Rubinek speaks quietly of having been born in a displaced persons camp after the war, and later of his sister dying at birth on Sophia's farm; his father is much more dramatic and emphatic when recounting how he was the only survivor out of nine children, of how he watched helplessly from a hole in the wall when his grandfather was rounded up with the other Jews and beaten by Nazis.

Before they reach Sophia's farm, the camera captures some powerful moments; for instance, Frania Rubinek is reunited first with an old girlfriend, and then with a teacher – both of whom she has not seen in over forty years. The inherent drama of this reality is interwoven with fictional reenactments that extend the family's subjective reality. A minimal example occurs when Israel Rubinek tells of witnessing a murder: we hear gunshots as the camera zooms madly in and out of the Polish street. This is extended when we learn that Sophia already knew the young couple and offered to hide them: we see young actors re-creating the journey by cart to her farm. (These were actually not professionals, but Polish townspeople who offered to participate in *So Many Miracles*). According to the film's producer and codirector Katherine Smalley:

> We chose the docudrama style because Vic and I share the conviction that film really communicates only emotionally. We had the opportunity to re-create the emotional experience in a way you wouldn't otherwise get from someone simply standing there and telling you the story. It's debatable that . . . if used more minimally [as in the half-hour version broadcast on Canadian TV] it's perhaps more effective, because you aren't testing the limits of credibility. But for us, it's almost as though you're going back in the memory of an individual and trying to reconstruct the imagery.[15]

The most moving part of the film, nevertheless, is the "documentary" record of the Rubineks' reunion with Sophia Branja and her son Manek. They relive the hiding, the fear, and the courage that characterized wartime; for example, Manek (then a child) once saved them when SS men spent a night in the same room: he coughed and made noises all night to cover the sound of Israel Rubinek coughing inside the stove. The title accumulates meaning, as we realize how many times they could have perished: according to the Rubineks, they survived because they stuck together through love. We are also offered hints as to why Sophia would take such risks, from the fact that the young couple had occasionally been generous with her, to Sophia's initially receiving money from Frania's sister, to her belief that if the Jews were exterminated, the same thing could happen to the Poles. Yet none of these explanations account for the degree of her noble actions – especially if we acknowledge what a small percentage of the Polish population rescued rather than harassed Jewish neighbors. Although we cannot fathom why Sophia laid her life on the line while others stood by indifferently, selfishly, or brutally, *So Many Miracles* is a moving tribute to Christian decency.

Saul Rubinek's perspective – the child of survivors who attempts to grasp and make sense of his parents' legacy – informs *Voices from the Attic* (1988). But because this superb one-hour film is directed as well as narrated by Debbie Goodstein, herself a child of Polish-Jewish survivors, it is even more in the "first-person singular." Goodstein's voice-over establishes that her mother was hidden for two years with fifteen other Jews in an attic in Poland during the war. After the entire family decides to return for a visit, her mother and sister decline (on-camera). Consequently, Aunt Sally Frishberg becomes the focus, explaining everything to Debbie and the five cousins who accompany her and Sally's husband to Cracow, Warsaw, Auschwitz, and finally their hometown. If the survivor provides the facts, the members of the second generation offer the necessary questions and connections; for instance, they acknowledge always looking for safety exits, not riding subways (which are reminiscent of death trains), and leaving summer "camp" because the word meant something horrible.

When Sally recognizes neighbors and places, the film grows more complex; although the mood is upbeat, a Polish child says, "Heil Hitler," and later they find a fresh swastika. And yet, her tales of Polish decency sound authentic when she recounts how farmers shared food with them. (As in *Under the World,* her family initially survived by digging holes underground and remaining there for three months.) One farmer, Grocholski, and his wife took them into their attic in exchange for furs and jewelry. It was supposed to be for a few days or weeks. The number in hiding grew to sixteen, and the time period became two years; because thirteen survived, we are told, sixty are alive today. As in *So Many Miracles,* the most poignant moment occurs when Sally embraces the eighty-year-old Maria Grocholska. But this rescuer says it's still a secret that she hid the Jewish family because neighbors might hurt her if they knew. Indeed, the extent of Polish anti-Semitism is illustrated by the fact that when Sally's family returned home after the war, three Poles came to tell them to leave – or be killed.

Voices from the Attic ends with a big party where Sally's daughter thanks Maria. When we then see a photo of Maria, who died in 1988, there is comfort in the knowledge that they arrived in time to thank her personally (and in time to make the film). Two cultures and two generations have come together in the course of this cinematic voyage, commemorating ghostly voices as well as confronting harsh new ones.

13
From Judgment to Illumination

ocumentaries tend to do poorly at the box office, where audiences prefer diverting fiction to stark reality. This is unfortunate, because some of the most powerful and important films about the Holocaust are "nonfiction" but not "nondramatic." Consequently, television has played a significant role in bringing at least two of the following to American audiences: *Kitty: Return to Auschwitz, The Sorrow and the Pity* (both telecast on PBS), and *The Memory of Justice*. All three are compelling personal documents – moving pictures that achieve their greatness through uniquely cinematic means. Brave and often abrasive, they demonstrate that the facts of the Holocaust are richer than the fictions an artist could invent. Particularly in the films of Marcel Ophuls, the montage is the message – namely the juxtaposition of multiple viewpoints which, together, shed light on human response and responsibility.

When *Kitty: Return to Auschwitz* (1980) was aired on American television, on February 4, 1981, the question raised after *Holocaust* – how much truth can be found in a fictional reconstruction of the Nazi era? – was replaced by the acknowledgment of how much drama could inhere in documentary. This ninety-minute film directed by Peter Morley for Yorkshire Television in Great Britain is real "docudrama" – the simple presentation of one survivor's recollection that yields a profoundly moving and often shattering story. Kitty Felix Hart, a fifty-one-year-old radiologist in Birmingham, returned in 1978 to Auschwitz – where she and her mother had been prisoners for two years – with her son David, a Canadian doctor. Morley had been afraid to take responsibility for her first trip back to the concentration camp, and decided to have the son come along; the film would therefore be Kitty telling him about her experiences "for the sake of continuity."[1] They were accompanied by a small crew and, as the director confided, "Nothing was staged. I just followed her, and didn't even know – when the taxi arrived at Auschwitz – whether she'd turn right back and leave." He used no photographs of the camp or newsreel footage: "The word-pictures this lady paints are more horrific than any photo. But," he added, "children *can* see this."

The film begins in Birmingham where we view Kitty at work and then hear her reminisce about her childhood in the Polish town of Bielsko-Biala, her enforced labor at the Farben plant, and her arrival at Auschwitz in April 1943 at the age of sixteen. The camera rises over Auschwitz-Birkenau in color as the white taxi pulls up, and it simply follows mother and son through the vast ghost town of the concentration camp.

Kitty Hart in *Kitty: Return to Auschwitz.* PHOTO COURTESY OF PBS.

Kitty's motivation for returning becomes clear when she explains how people are writing "that it never happened: I owe this to all the people who have died. Everybody's ashes are here." Her desire to bear witness takes methodical and comprehensive form: she recounts gruesome details as if they were engraved in her memory. Kitty is straightforward in her recollection of how prisoners had to lie in their own excrement, wash in their own urine, and cling to their individual bowls that served as both soup plate and toilet pan. A slow and silent tracking shot of the row of holes that constituted the toilet seems endless; the holes begin to look like gaping wounds, or soundless mouths. According to the director, "It was almost unimaginable that twenty thousand women were going to the toilet at once, and we had the problem of giving scale to that ghastly place. We got a dolly at great expense from Warsaw because this was the only way to show how huge it was."

Moving into the barracks, Kitty tells David one of the principles that kept her alive: you had to take things off the dead, but never off the living. She would remove ration cards and clothes from corpses when her work included carrying bodies. Still, Kitty was always cold, and she recalls her public flogging of twenty-five strokes because she had gone to get wood to heat the barracks. More significant to her survival than food or warmth, though, was the presence of her mother, who worked in the hospital block. At times, she saved Kitty by hiding her under sick people. And Kitty would occasionally give her mother bread. It becomes clear that what often kept people

Marshal Pétain in *The Sorrow and the Pity.* PHOTO COURTESY OF CINEMA 5 alive in Auschwitz was having another person to care for. (All this is recounted with a measure of calm, but Kitty breaks down when she remembers how she had to load all her friends' corpses onto a cart.) Finally, she got work in "Canada," the privileged storeroom. This was a focal point for the Resistance, and she explains that when the crematorium was blown up on October 7, 1943, by one of the *Sonderkommando* units (Jewish male inmates forced to clean out the gas chambers), it was with ammunition bought by gold hidden in "Canada." Leading her son slowly to the pits where people were burned alive, Kitty – in a shocking moment – digs for . . . and finds . . . ashes. She also recounts how she was taken from Auschwitz in 1944 on a "death march" where, after seeing her friends shot, "obsession for revenge is what kept me going." A male voice-over narration explains what happened to Kitty and the members of her family after the Liberation, and the film ends with her talking about the effects of this experience on her present life.[2]

Morley observed the physical change in Kitty upon their arrival in Auschwitz: "She ignored me. She became like a creature on the prowl. And there was suddenly more of a Polish accent." There was an effect upon the director as well: "I didn't want to pry, intrude, shoot her from the front upon arrival. I tried to be as discreet as possible. But we, the crew, cried. For about three months, I couldn't put my head on the pillow without thinking of that experience." To see Kitty testifying within the physical context of the now silent death camp results in a uniquely cinematic event, as historically significant as it is emotionally wrenching. The historian John Toland acknowledged, "To my surprise, her oral history turned out to be at least as effective as any written account I've read, if not more so."[3]

If the power of *Kitty* comes from one person's recollection, simply recorded, the impact of *The Sorrow and the Pity* (*Le Chagrin et la pitié*) emerges through kaleidoscopic montage. Marcel Ophuls's four-and-a-half-hour 1970 documentary about French collaboration and resistance during World War II is composed of volatile fragments – interviews, newsreels, photographs, film clips, and recorded speeches – that cohere into a revealing "Chronicle of a French Town under the Occupation," as the subtitle puts it. Like *Night and Fog*, it is the story of a place – Clermont-Ferrand – which, under the filmmakers' scrutiny, yields the story of a time. Clermont-Ferrand is thirty-six miles south of Vichy, capital of France from 1940 to 1944; many of its inhabitants were supporters of Pétain until the area was occupied by the Wehrmacht in November 1942; it was also a pivotal spot for the Resistance, feeding one of the most important underground networks – the Auvergne. The film is wisely rooted in a locale whose resonance is established and extended by the editing. Rather than presenting the interviews as separate segments, Ophuls crosscuts them with one another – for instance, a former German soldier and a former Resistance fighter – and with archival footage. Divided into two parts – "The Collapse" and "The Choice" – *The Sorrow and the Pity* demythologizes France's heroic self-image as a nation of resisters; through interviews with thirty-four witnesses – twenty-four French, five English, five German – it gives voice to a spectrum that ranged from complicity with the Nazis (a majority of the population) to organized resistance.

The montage of editor Claude Vajda yokes the interviews conducted by Ophuls and coproducer André Harris into a dramatic structure. For example, French anti- Semitism is discussed at intervals by people like former premier Pierre

Mendès-France, and then culminates near the end of the film in Dr. Claude Lévy's testimony: he states that Pierre Laval, head of the Vichy government, offered the Germans four thousand Jewish children whose deportation hadn't even been requested. This condemnation of official French policy is judiciously placed after the attempts of Count René de Chambrun, Laval's son-in-law, to whitewash the image of the collaborationist vice-premier: "I am sure today that the French people know that Pierre Laval did everything to defend them," claims his son-in-law. This kind of contrapuntal editing is introduced at the outset of *The Sorrow and the Pity*, with two scenes that precede the credits: a wedding in a small German town in May 1969 and, a month earlier, some remarks by Marcel Verdier (a pharmacist in Clermont-Ferrand) to his children about having been in the Resistance. As the film unfolds, we learn that the bride is the daughter of Helmuth Tausend, former captain in the Wehrmacht, stationed at Clermont-Ferrand from 1942 to 1944. This portly German businessman, cigar in hand, will become one of the central witnesses, discoursing complacently about how the French were "reassured" by their presence: "We didn't loot or rob, so they soon learned that we weren't a wicked enemy." Parts of this interview are juxtaposed with the testimony of Resistance fighters such as Verdier, and newsreels that convey the flavor of the time. As the pharmacist speaks about the devastating lack of food during the war, we see footage of closed markets and signs like "Use saccharin."

The dramatic shaping of this documentary material creates the impression of multiple conversations, or at least complementary appraisals. A record of the eighty-four-year-old Marshal Pétain taking office in 1940 – "giving France the gift of my person" – is accompanied by a montage of the people being interviewed in 1969, like Tausend and Mendès-France. And when Mendès-France recounts the trial where he was convicted of desertion, his lawyer's comments about the anti-Semitism that was rampant at the time are interwoven as a supportive commentary. After the champion cyclist of Clermont-Ferrand, Raphaël Géminiani, says, "We never saw the Germans," the film returns to Verdier, who claims the opposite. A German soldier who was stationed in Clermont-Ferrand tells the interviewer he had a French girlfriend and adds, "a decent girl, mind you." A cut to newsreels of French women whose heads were shaved publicly because they consorted with German men redefines "decency." And the next interview selected within the connective tissue of *The Sorrow and the Pity* is with Madame Solange, a hairdresser who supported Pétain and still doesn't understand why she was tried and imprisoned after the war.

Despite the obvious sympathies of the filmmakers, there is fairness of presentation toward all the subjects. Whether consciously or unconsciously, they reveal themselves to the camera, which maintains the same objective angle for "heroes" and "villains" alike – usually a medium close-up – and presents them in their own environments. (We often see the children of both Verdier and Tausend listening to their fathers. An intercut of the bride when the German speaks of having been ambushed in Clermont-Ferrand underlines that these individuals do not live in a vacuum of either time or space: they have a past and a future, as well as an immediate sphere of influence.) The witnesses are personalized by being in their natural contexts: most of the politicians behind their desks; the Grave brothers (former Resistance fighters) in their Yronde wine cellar; Christian de la Mazière (right-wing volunteer in the Waffen SS) walking through the opulent castle of Sigmaringen. Only in this last sequence is the interviewer obtrusively present (André Harris rather than the retiring Ophuls).

Marcel Ophuls's *The Sorrow and the Pity.* PHOTO COURTESY OF CINEMA 5.

In general, the filmmakers' presence is restricted to subtle visual embroidery like an intercut of Mendès-France's hands, gesticulating expressively, or a pan to Mme. Solange's fingers nervously playing with the hem of her dress. Furthermore, the English-language version relies neither on subtitles nor dubbing, but simultaneous voice-over translation. A different voice is used for each subject, thus permitting us to hear both the actual person and an overlapping translation.

By simply asking probing questions, the interviewers elicit telling answers. Mazière, for instance, admits that he was raised in a family steeped in anti-Semitism; that the military French were impressed by the German army: "The French like rank and always turn to a soldier"; and that he knew Jews were being arrested, but never imagined a destination like Auschwitz. Mendès-France acknowledges that anti-Semitism and Anglophobia are always latent and easy to revive in France. (Indeed, he preceived rising anti-Semitism at the beginning of the war as a link between Germany and collaborationist France.) Similarly, "Colonel Gaspar" (wartime head of the Auvergne Maquis) warns against growing neo-Nazism and claims this is the reason he agreed to be interviewed.

In a sense, the most vivid subjects are Louis and Alexis Grave, farmers who were sent to Buchenwald after an anonymous letter denounced them. Looking as if they had stepped out of a Jean Renoir film like *Toni*, they offer Ophuls some of their wine from the barrel and laughingly tell him they sang "L'Internationale" at the beginning of the Resistance "not because we were Communists, but because Pétain sang 'La Marseillaise.' " When he asks them toward the end if they've tried to avenge themselves for the denunciation, their response is a shrug of "what for?" The numerous peasants who instinctively became resisters have a strong presence in *The Sorrow and the Pity*; one complains, "Why do they always put the old at the head of the government?"

(pointing to the massive documentary that this film's editor, Claude Vajda, would make ten years later – *The Sick Men Who Govern Us*). Their behavior is illuminated by a remark from Denis Rake, a former British secret agent in occupied France: "The French workers were fantastic . . . they'd give you their last cent if you didn't have money. . . . The middle class didn't help much – they had more to lose – but the common people were marvelous." And Emmanuel d'Astier de la Vigerie, former head of the "Liberation" group, celebrates the Resistance as the only experience he ever had of a "classless society."

The Sorrow and the Pity elicits disturbing realizations rather than quick judgment by the inclusion of propaganda films from the Occupation. We can better comprehend how a Nazi might fight the French after seeing a 1940 German newsreel of French prisoners: soldiers from Morocco, Senegal, Algeria, "a shame for the white race . . . *these* are the guardians of civilization!" We might understand the average Parisian who saw a French newsreel teaching people how to recognize Jews ("cross-bred from Mongols, Negroes, and Aryans"). And the clip from *Jew Süss*, a viciously racist German film that was dubbed and presented as a *French film* in France, demonstrates the ways pernicious stereotypes were being fed through the media. The fact that this was one of the most popular films of 1943 is not unrelated to Dr. Lévy's recollection of the French handing groups of victims over in bundles to the Germans: "The Paris police, which carried out the roundup of the Jews with a zeal entirely beyond praise – except from the Germans – arrested the children."

Louis Grave, former Resistance fighter, in
The Sorrow and the Pity. PHOTO COURTESY OF CINEMA 5.

All these fragments point to the need for political awareness in daily life. Elaborating on this theme in *L'Avant-Scène du cinéma*, Ophuls wrote, "the terribly bourgeois attitude which consists of believing that you can separate what is conveniently called 'politics' from other human activities – like a profession, family life, or love – this popular attitude constitutes the worst evasion imaginable of life, and of the responsibilities of life."[4] *The Sorrow and the Pity* demonstrates that the collaborationists were hardly monsters: manipulated by the media and concerned mainly with individual survival and comfort, they took what was often the easy path of unquestioning obedience. Mme. Solange, for instance, reveals her continued blindness when she says: "I was for the Maréchal. I wasn't political, but I was for Pétain." Ophuls asks the collaborationist hairdresser whether it ever occurred to her, when she was held under water by an angry group at the war's end, "that at the time you supported the regime, the same thing was being done to others?"

> *Mme. Solange:* Oh, I don't know. I never thought about it.
> *Ophuls:* You are honest enough to say you were for Pétain. . . . Why?
> *Mme. Solange:* Maybe it was his ideas.
> *Ophuls:* Which?
> *Mme. Solange:* What he wanted to make of France. I thought he was a fine man.
> *Ophuls:* Do you still think so?
> *Mme. Solange:* Yes.

(Curiously enough, this is the only woman interviewed in *The Sorrow and the Pity*, and the omission of female Resistance figures seems a distortion.)

Ophuls's questions occasionally betray the degree to which *The Sorrow and the Pity* is a personal film for him. (Jacques Siclier points out in *La France de Pétain et son cinéma* that "André Harris and Alain de Sédouy were the executive producers. They have often been credited, incorrectly, with the direction of the film, which was solely the work of Marcel Ophuls.")[5] The son of director Max Ophuls (*Lola Montès, Letter from an Unknown Woman, The Earrings of Madame de . . .*), he and his Jewish family were forced to leave Germany when Hitler rose to power. They remained in France till 1941 and then fled to America. The younger Ophuls admitted in *L'Avant-Scène*,

> Maybe it's because I was uprooted several times in my childhood and grew up in the shadow of a political menace that these watertight compartments they want to erect seem to me absurd, that the tenacious desire to maintain them at whatever cost corresponds to a sickly need to flee, to exonerate oneself, and it explains all the aberrations of contemporary history.

Ophuls would learn that some elements of the French media in 1971 were still unprepared to open the dark chapters of French history. The film was originally conceived for French television (ORTF) but became a coproduction of the Norddeutscher Rundfunk (Hamburg), Société Suisse de Radiodiffusion, and Télévision Rencontre (Lausanne). When the film was completed, the ORTF refused to show it – exerting, in Ophuls's words, "a particularly crafty form of censorship, censorship by inertia." It opened theatrically in Paris at the Studio Saint-Séverin, a tiny Left Bank art house that could hardly accommodate the thousands of people who lined up daily. It therefore moved three weeks later to the larger Paramount-Elysées. Finally, in the fall of 1981, *The Sorrow and the Pity* was aired on French television.

Jacques Siclier chronicles the effect of the film in 1971: "The reality of France under the Vichy regime was all there with its ambiguities, shadows, cowardice, moral decomposition, and its authentic part of resistance. The generation that had just made 'May '68' discovered a truth that had been masked by imposed certitudes. *The Sorrow and the Pity*, refused by our television, inaugurated a 'cinema of awakening.' "[6]*

One of the notable films it spawned was *Special Section* (*Section Spéciale*, 1975), a terse indictment of French wartime "justice" directed by Costa-Gavras. Like *Paths of Glory* (Stanley Kubrick, 1958) which dealt with a miscarriage of justice during World War I, *Special Section* shows how easily corruption filtered into the French machinery of Vichy. After a Polish Jew and a Communist are shot by a firing squad in 1941, a group of young French leftists attempt to assassinate German soldiers in retaliation. They succeed in killing a high-ranking German in the subway, whereupon a minister (Michel Lonsdale) insists on quick punishment *before* the Germans intervene. The French go so far as to suggest a death penalty that would be retroactive for acts of treason. The minister of justice refuses to go along with this, but because the Maréchal signs the decree, even he finally signs (rationalizing to his daughter, however, with the exaggeration that his refusal would have meant one hundred hostages killed by the Germans). In order to choose the six "guilty" men they need, the bureaucrats scour the files of Jews, anarchists, and Communists, finally selecting four communists and two Jews – despite the puniness of their "crimes."

We see "men of honor" suspending conscience to follow orders and go along with the crowd – even if it means sacrificing the innocent. Nevertheless, *Special Section* is not a simplistic film of the left, for young Communist party members are shown to be as ready as right-wing ministers to sacrifice individuals and set examples in the name of a cause. As in other French film treatments of World War II, the enemy is hardly German: in fact, the major in charge (Heinz Bennent) is a civilized gentleman who can quote the writings of Montesquieu, and the young French leftists can't bring themselves to assassinate a pleasant German who smiles at them, nor another who holds a camera rather than a gun. The target of Costa-Gavras is not merely within the French nation (in the upper echelons of power) but within the individual who allows politics to overcome conscience. Indeed, the film's opening sets the stage for the film's concerns in an effectively oblique manner: we see close-ups of musicians and hear different sounds of instruments, all leading into a performance of *Boris Godunov* (which contains the crucial phrase, "Country, weep for yourself"). Like *Special Section*, this opening is a gradual revelation of the parts that make the whole – each instrument playing its role in the grand design. Likewise, the film's narrative structure is one of accumulation, as each individual repeats the same suspension of conscience until the inhuman political machine has no impediments.

The Sorrow and the Pity thus revived and revised ideas about France's role in World War II, and Ophuls's personal quest to comprehend this era became a collage of collective memory. Two of the major "messages" implicit in the methodical juxtapositions are the inadequacy of easy moralizing, and the need for political education and constant reflection. Particularly for an American audience, the final statement of Anthony Eden, former British prime minister, is crucial: "If you haven't experienced the horrors of the Occupation, you have no right to judge." And there is a lesson for

---

* "Cinéma d'éveil" also carries the notion of warning.

everyone in the experiences of Mendès-France: "I learned that when certain tendencies or demagogies are nourished and whipped up, they revive, and we must always prepare young people against this propaganda; we have to talk to them about it, maybe more than we did one or two generations ago." Ophuls extends this line of reasoning into *The Memory of Justice* (1976), a four-hour, forty-minute exploration of war crimes within the context of the Nuremberg Trials. Divided into two parts – "Nuremberg and the Germans" and "Nuremberg and Other Places" – this ambitious documentary builds into its very fabric the identity of the filmmaker. It is not simply that we see him interviewing the subjects or feel his presence through intrusive editing; but Ophuls includes personal scenes with his German wife, his film students at Princeton, and even his grappling with cutting and arranging the overwhelming material. *The Memory of Justice* is consequently less a finished product than an active process. The director explained in 1981:

> I try to be autobiographical in *The Memory of Justice* because of my wife's childhood and my childhood – my reaction against what we feel has been misunderstood. I felt a very great misunderstanding concerning *The Sorrow and the Pity* (the movie of my life, like Conan Doyle and *Sherlock Holmes* – I try to get rid of it, but it won't go away): there is no such thing as objectivity! *The Sorrow and the Pity* is a biased film – in the right direction, I'd like to think – as biased as a Western with good guys and bad guys. But I try to show that choosing the good guy is not quite as simple as anti-Nazi movies with Alan Ladd made in 1943.[7]

The intimate tone of this mammoth documentary – which Ophuls prefers to call "nonfiction" – begins at the outset of Part I, where he asks his wife how she feels about it. She admits that although her father was not a Nazi, he was no exception to other people. (Subsequently, she confesses that she was in the Hitler Youth Movement; an older Jewish woman softens the announcement by adding that, as a child, even she had wanted to be in the Hitler Youth Group because of their pretty jackets.) Ophuls's daughter complains that her mother doesn't want her to see films of the concentration camps, and it becomes apparent that this engaging woman is not very happy with her husband's obsessive burrowing into the past. When she says she would prefer him to make "a Lubitsch film or *My Fair Lady*," he inserts a poster of an appropriate film – *The Band Wagon.* The soundtrack complies as we hear "New Sun in the Sky" from this film. The music continues into the next scene – Ophuls's car moving through a snowy landscape – where the songs "That's Entertainment" and finally "I Guess I'll Have to Change My Plan" grow contrapuntal. The place is Schleswig-Holstein, and the director-investigator is searching for Hertha Oberheuser, a former Nazi doctor who was sentenced to twenty years before she began practicing in the region. *The Band Wagon* soundtrack might appease his wife and lighten the film's tone, but Ophuls is clearly bound to his quest – beyond entertainment – for justice.

The truly ambitious or controversial aspect of *The Memory of Justice* is that Ophuls is concerned as much with the present as the past, as much with the recent experiences of Vietnam and Algeria as with the more devastating but more distant horrors of Nazism. The juxtapositions of the pre-credit sequence establish his insistently connective issue: (1) a plea of "Not Guilty" offered in Nuremberg on November 20, 1945; (2) violinist Yehudi Menuhin in Berlin in 1973 saying that every human being is guilty; (3) Vietnam War coverage from NBC News; (4) expressions of remorse by

Above, Mrs. Marcel Ophuls in *The Memory of Justice*. PHOTO COURTESY OF HAMILTON FISH.

Below, Telford Taylor, Chief U.S. Prosecutor, Nuremberg Trials, in *The Memory of Justice*. PHOTO COURTESY OF HAMILTON FISH.

Noel Favrelière, a French paratrooper who deserted in Algeria; (5) Colonel Anthony Hecht, an American decorated for service in Korea, explaining that he respects both those who fought in Vietnam and those who were morally opposed; (6) Eddie Sowder, a Vietnam War deserter (who is also interviewed in Peter Davis's *Hearts and Minds*); (7) Telford Taylor, Chief Prosecution Counsel at the Nuremberg Trials; (8) a German visiting the Dachau Museum in 1973; (9) Marie-Claude Vaillant-Couturier, a French senator and concentration camp survivor; (10) a title of the quotation from Plato – that people are guided by a vague memory and ideal of justice.

These fragments are elaborated in the course of the film as Ophuls proposes that Auschwitz, Dresden, and My Lai belong within the same frame of inquiry. Terrence Des Pres's masterful review of the film in *Harper's* points out:

> It can be argued that the film minimizes the evil of the Hitler years, that it obscures the nihilistic nature of that war and undermines the uniqueness of the Holocaust by comparing these enormities with the lesser atrocities of Algeria, Vietnam, Kent State, and so on.... But as [Ophuls] himself has said, to compare is not to equate. On the contrary, comparison can function to dramatize distinctions.[8]

For example, Dr. Mitscherlich brings up America's slaughter of the Indians, but makes the important distinction that Indians were an alien people while the Jews were neighbors. Similarly, Edgar Faure, former Nuremberg prosecutor and then president of the French National Assembly, warns against lumping Algeria with World War II: he claims that it's completely different for a country to try to keep a colony than to invade neighboring countries. Significantly enough, this is placed after Favrelière's interview and the acknowledgment of torture in Algeria: the paratrooper says he felt like an SS man in his French army uniform and "deserted so as not to kill." He joined the Algerians.

If Ophuls offers a point of view, it is that each view is partial. His technique of the cut often constitutes an undercut, as he tends to counterpoint a statement with testimony or footage to the contrary.[9] Albert Speer says he assumed for economic reasons that conditions in the concentration camps were better than they proved; Ophuls inserts harrowing archival footage of three skeletal prisoners. Hans Kehrl, Speer's planner, complains that Nuremberg was worse than the camps when there were no rations; shots of the concentration camps mock his claim. A young German denies that the Holocaust ever happened and proposes that the Americans built ovens in Dachau; the next scene juxtaposes Joan Baez singing "Where Have All the Flowers Gone?" in German with footage of the transports. German propaganda films coexist with American propaganda (a *March of Time* newsreel that delights in America's capacity to bomb Dresden twice); the mother of Nazi hunter Serge Klarsfeld tells how her husband was arrested by the Nazis and killed at Auschwitz, between shots of Frau Kuenzel (mother of Beate Klarsfeld, Serge's wife) saying that the Germans could not ask the SS what they were doing. As in *The Sorrow and the Pity*, the simultaneous voice-over translations in English are remarkably consistent with the tones of the speakers: a different voice is used for each subject, thereby personalizing his or her address. And as in the previous film, there is a fairness of presentation, since almost all the subjects are treated "objectively" by the camera – the same medium close-up is used for both Nazis and Jews – and each individual is seen in his own expressive home or office décor.

Defendants at the Nuremberg Trials in *The Memory of Justice*. PHOTO COURTESY OF HAMILTON FISH.

For instance, two contrasting attitudes to the Vietnam War are embodied by the homes and family styles of dead war heroes. First there is Barbara Keating,

> a woman whose pride and pleasure in the fact that her husband died a War Hero is evident not only in her crisp words, not only in her expensive dress and finely styled hair, but also in her substantial suburban house, in the special cabinet where she displays her husband's war medals, and finally in the fact that Ophuls, throughout the interview, stands on the stairs with Mrs. Keating at some distance above him on the landing.[10]

Marine music is audible in the background, and Ophuls often cuts to her American flags. The widow is also crosscut with Louise and Robert Ransom, for whom the death of their son was a meaningless sacrifice. They sit with Ophuls around a modest kitchen table, speaking simply and with visible pain about their loss. Just as these people were free to present themselves and their surroundings as they wished, so the viewer is free to make his own conclusions about the viability of either response. Those with prowar sentiments will probably approve of Mrs. Keating; those opposed to the Vietnam War will probably side with the Ransoms. Nevertheless, the totality of *The Memory of Justice* implies a condemnation of the Vietnam War, particularly when Lord Shawcross (prosecutor for the British at Nuremberg) observes that you can't compare Germany with Vietnam, where the government asked for help, even if the methods of napalm bombing were comparable. The inclusion of the compelling Daniel Ellsberg, footage of Kent State University, and articulate army deserters makes it difficult to regard Mrs. Keating's smugness without some discomfort.

It is within the frame of Nuremberg that she – and all the other elements of *The Memory of Justice* – must be considered; this context implies that personal conscience overrides government dictum, and therefore the state and those who represent it can and must be held accountable for moral atrocities. Ophuls's crosscutting refuses to let the matter rest with the conviction of Nazi war criminals; in Des Pres's words, "Ophuls endeavors to change our awareness of Nuremberg, from a piece of history to an internalized image of our struggle for a clarity of moral vision which has not yet risen, and may never rise, to its conclusion." The film's very title suggests that justice is absent from the present, while its format shapes newsreel footage, photographs, and interviews into a quasi-narrative of continuing guilt and continuing responsibility. The problem is not simply Beate Klarsfeld's contention that former Nazis are living in West Germany, or a stage manager's ironic claim that he must have been at Nazi rallies alone because everyone else says they weren't there; it is also in Telford Taylor's observation that *The Diary of Anne Frank* was popular in Germany because Germans never saw themselves as evil in the book. There are countless possibilities for evasion, and Ophuls continues to struggle against them – even if it's with the humorous intercut of a "Do Not Disturb" sign on a Howard Johnson hotel room door: Americans are hardly exempt from the charges of indifference.

The Memory of Justice ends with three crucial images: footage from the Nuremberg Trials in which a young Marie-Claude Vaillant-Couturier gives testimony about Auschwitz (one night she heard screams, and learned subsequently that because of a gas shortage, children were being thrown into the ovens alive). As she leaves the stand, this woman who would become a French senator looks at the defendants in the dock; Ophuls freezes the image, intensifying the confrontation for which she waited

The Nuremberg Trials in *The Memory of Justice.*
PHOTO COURTESY OF HAMILTON FISH.

Serge and Beate Klarsfeld, Nazi hunters, in
The Memory of Justice. PHOTO COURTESY OF HAMILTON FISH.

so long. We then see Yehudi Menuhin playing with the Berlin Philharmonic – a unification of Germans and Jew, and a transcendence through art. The violinist insists, "I'm not the judge. Judgment should ideally come from the one who committed the crime, or suffered by it." Although the last word is given to the artist who refuses to judge, the last image is the famous Warsaw Ghetto photograph that includes a little boy with his hands raised in surrender. The camera moves in to this still image, stopping at the child's lifted arms. The return to this raw material insists upon Nazi persecution as the root of Nuremberg and thus of the entire film: the Holocaust remains an uneasy shadow. Moreover, the movement of the camera constitutes an act of selection and investigation. Like Resnais's active camera in the equally personal documentary, *Night and Fog*, Ophuls's last shot expresses the burden of filmmaker and viewer alike – a refusal to be still in the face of inhumanity.

Twelve years after the release of *The Memory of Justice*, another Ophuls opus was released, demonstrating that time had not diminished the director's quest for justice – nor his vigorously dialectical style. *Hotel Terminus: Klaus Barbie, His Life and Times* is both a superlative historical document and a riveting detective story, illuminating with indignation and irony an entire era. The four-and-a-half-hour film is not simply about Klaus Barbie and his long-awaited trial in Lyons in 1987; spanning three continents and four languages, it explores the Nazi officer's nefarious activities in wartime France; service to American counterintelligence after World War II; and welcome in Bolivia, where – as Klaus Altmann – he was security adviser to

South American dictators. Known as "the Butcher of Lyons," he was extradited to France in 1983, and finally condemned four years later to life imprisonment for crimes against humanity. Nevertheless, Barbie hardly ever appears in *Hotel Terminus*; rather, interviews with individuals along a vast international spectrum provide pieces of a puzzle that ultimately resists completion: as in Orson Welles's *Citizen Kane* or Andrzej Wajda's *Man of Marble*, the protagonist is no longer available to the camera, and the investigation is all. The absence of the central figure (and Barbie was indeed an absence at his trial) suggests the impossibility of ever truly penetrating the psyche of a public figure. As Ophuls acknowledged during an interview in October 1988, just before the film's American premiere at the New York Film Festival: "Going into the film, I had no way of knowing if he would be present or absent from the film. Of course he *is* there, in an extremely effective dramatic manner. Another question is whether we find out anything about him: I can't answer that."[11]

Just as *Man of Marble* ultimately reveals more about the questing filmmaker (Krystyna Janda) than the forgotten worker-hero (Jerzy Radziwilowicz), *Hotel Terminus* is permeated with Ophuls's lacerating wit and moral vigilance more than with Barbie's crimes. It is not simply how he asks questions of everyone from anti-Semites to survivors who describe torture under Barbie (and he is sometimes a prosecutor rather than a mere interviewer, as exemplified by his almost bullying Alvaro De Castro, Barbie's bodyguard in Bolivia). It's the way he says, "Merry Christmas," after an uncooperative German closes the door in his face during the holiday season. Or the way he cuts from a German bookstore owner in Bolivia who threw out Barbie and his wife and whose books were later torched to footage of Nazi book burning. Or his crosscutting filmmaker Bertrand Tavernier interviewing his father – who says *Night and Fog* opened the eyes of Frenchmen – with a woman who was condemned after the war for collaboration and wrote a book exonerating herself (she calls *Night and Fog* a propaganda film). The irony is perhaps most palpable when we hear Fred Astaire singing, "I pick myself up, dust myself off, and start all over again," as we see President Reagan visiting the Bitburg Cemetery. It is hard not to become complicitous with what Ophuls called his "angry flippancy," especially when a former SS officer offers as proof of how great a guy Barbie was that his dogs adored him, "and dogs can always tell good from bad." Indeed, the director's irony is continuous with some of the film's most impressive voices: for instance, when he mentions to Simone Lagrange – a Jewish survivor who was tortured by Barbie as a thirteen-year-old girl – that she's rather short, she replies, "I guess I forgot to grow in Auschwitz." It is no surprise that he called *To Be or Not to Be* "a good and serious film," since Lubitsch's dark comedy (with its roots in Jewish and central European humor) is not unrelated to *Hotel Terminus*. As Ophuls admitted at his New York Film Festival press conference, "one of the ways for a pessimist to avoid becoming a cynic is to try to be funny."

Hotel Terminus originated with a phone call from Victor Navasky, editor of *The Nation*, asking Ophuls if he'd like to cover the Barbie trial for the magazine. "I'd never gone to any trial – much less a Nazi's trial – but having seen *The Paradine Case* and *Witness for the Prosecution*, I thought, 'trials are interesting: I'd like to go.' But *The Nation* doesn't pay much, and there would be 6–8 weeks in a Lyons hotel room, in addition to financing the research. So we got a book contract; but I didn't write it, because the trial didn't come. Time went by, and it was like finding a button on a sidewalk and having a costume made." Finally, he received a phone call from an American named John Friedman who was interested in producing a film that Ophuls would direct. The result was *Hotel Terminus*, a motion picture financed by American sources – perhaps appropriate in that Ophuls is an American citizen who served in the U.S. Army. (The book is to be published by Simon and Schuster, including trial notes, letters, diary excerpts, and the expanded transcripts of the film.) Forty hours of interviews led to 120 hours of rushes, which were edited by Albert Jurgenson and Catherine Zins into a tight four and a half-hours. Ophuls evocatively described the trial-to-montage stage as "hanging around like bees near honey, waiting to see how the film will hang together. When we get to the editing room, scripting and editing are one continuous process." He managed to create a strong structure that is simultaneously linear/chronological, contrapuntal, and cohesive.

A more complex symmetry was suggested by James Markham's perceptive interview in the *New York Times* when he wrote:

> There is, of course, an eerie parallel between the geographic progresses of Klaus Barbie and Marcel Ophuls – though one headed to South America at the war's end and the other to North America at its outset. And a sense of being at home in Germany, France and among the numerous Americans – most of them erstwhile counterintelligence agents who "handled" Barbie – profoundly informs the film, which is multilingual in the fullest sense.[12]

Although Barbie is not quite the whale to Ophuls's Ahab, the latter follows with tenacity the traces of a monstrous enigma. What he finds in the *times* as well as the life of Klaus Barbie is sufficiently troubling to result in a far-from-optimistic vision; he confessed to having "become more pessimistic than I was before. Will the film make a dent in people's lack of attention span? I don't know. We're filmmakers, and what happens once a film is made is out of our hands." If, as he admitted to *Le Film Français* at the Cannes Film Festival in May 1988, *The Sorrow and the Pity* was more of an optimistic "Western with good guys and bad guys . . . full of hope . . . in that the witnesses were vacuuming 'under the rug' for their children," *Hotel Terminus* is closer to his father's film *La Ronde*, whose first half is rather comic, while the second half grows darker. It is also nearer in spirit to a film Ophuls praised at the New York Film Festival press conference, *Welcome in Vienna*.

Part of the problem, as both former Justice Department attorney Allan Ryan and New York District Attorney Elizabeth Holtzman acknowledge in the film, is that Barbie is not an exception: other "useful" Nazi officers were protected by the U.S. government after 1945 in the new war against the Communists, and numerous SS men are alive and well in South America. Moreover, the crimes committed by Barbie are hardly the monopoly of Germans, nor of men in the 1940s. This is not to say that we all contain a Barbie reflex; indeed, Ophuls was adamant in maintaining, "I've tried to resist the idea that there's a Barbie in all of us. I think that's a trendy, dangerous, and poisonous idea. . . ." What *Hotel Terminus* does suggest is the intimate relationship between indifference and cruelty. Although the focus is "the Butcher of Lyons" – with specific attention to his most heinous crime, the deportation of forty-three Jewish children from the town of Izieu – the film closes with Simone Lagrange visiting the house where she lived – and from which she was taken during the war. This survivor gets the last word, speaking to an aged former neighbor who did nothing to save her. The dedication at the end is to a "Madame Bontout – a good neighbor," in Jeanne Moreau's voice. The counterpoint between the two neighbors is what Ophuls called

> the margin of free will. People ask, "why, in this context of a mass-murderer, pin this particular old woman to the wall?" First, she wasn't old at the time. Second, like Marius Klein in *The Sorrow and the Pity*, of course there's a bit of cruelty – like in *Shoah*, the pot-bellied man in the wheatfield in Poland. We're not Englishmen playing cricket: the code of "good behavior" doesn't really apply to our profession. The whole theme of the film is the relationship between shoulder-shrugging and leaving room for the Barbies of this world.

The allusion to *Shoah* is significant, and its director, Claude Lanzmann, appears in *Hotel Terminus* as a witness/cinematic accomplice. Ophuls credited *Shoah* as being "probably the more courageous film – the way into the gas chambers," and resisted the idea that the films could even be compared. "None of the films I've done – and especially not *Hotel Terminus* – is about the Holocaust. The link between cynicism, callousness, indifference, complicity, and crimes against humanity is what the film is about." He added that he nevertheless defined his work in relation to *Shoah*, which had "a great influence on this film: after a few weeks of plain shock and endless admiration [upon seeing *Shoah*], I told myself, 'you're not making a film about the itinerary to the death camp. Your film – since you don't have Barbie – is something else'. *Shoah* encouraged me to go the way of black comedy."

Shoah, Claude Lanzmann's nine-and-a-half-hour documentary of 1985, is unique among films on the Holocaust, not only in its mammoth scale, but in its total absence of archival footage. The truths he is after are not necessarily in the photographs captured by German cameras. Rather, interviews with a myriad of witnesses (from Polish peasants to Jewish survivors and former Nazis) are juxtaposed with the director's return to the scenes of the crime – present-day Auschwitz, Treblinka, and Sobibor. Like Ophuls, he is an intrusive and often aggressive interviewer, so precise that the past becomes almost palpable; for example, when we meet a Polish locomotive engineer in a train approaching Treblinka, we are confronted with exactly how he could transport Jews to this death camp, fortified by the vodka the Germans gave him to induce oblivion. Lanzmann, a Jewish Frenchman who fought in the Resistance – and was a journalist as well as close associate of Jean-Paul Sartre, whose magazine *Les Temps Modernes* he edited – is omnipresent in *Shoah*. He encourages, coaxes, or needles his subjects, revealing his personal stake in the film; as he admitted before *Shoah* opened in New York: "I have a strong sense of urgency to relive all of it, to retrace the steps. In Sobibor, when I ask where the boundary of the camp was, I go across the imaginary line; it becomes real. The zoom in to the sign 'Treblinka' is a violent act. And for the tracking shot into Auschwitz, I pushed the dolly myself. If the film is a resurrection, it's because of how I was compelled to do it."[13]

There are some staggering facts behind *Shoah*, a Hebrew word meaning annihilation. It's not only that Lanzmann spent eleven years on this project, taping 350 hours of interviews in fourteen countries. It's not only that he managed to find former SS officers, including one who offers detailed testimony about the daily operation of Treblinka's death factory. It's also the nature of the revelations throughout *Shoah* that render it a personally overwhelming and historically definitive document. By finding Jewish eyewitnesses who survived because they had been selected for work in extermination camp maintenance, the director accumulated privileged testimony more amazing than fiction. Through the juxtaposition of Jewish "labor commandos" and Nazi officials, the film shows that Jews were forced to participate in – and even finance – their own extermination. In addition to being slave workers in the camps, many actually paid for their train trips to places that would turn out to be their last stop. Lanzmann calls *Shoah* a film of "corroboration": the Poles say the same thing as the Jews, and "this is confirmed by the SS . . . the details are what matters." For example, he quite bluntly cheated to get the testimony of Franz Suchomel, former SS Unterscharführer at Treblinka. Lanzmann used a camera hidden in a shoulder bag and connected to a video-recording van outside. The former Nazi was unaware not only that he was being filmed, but that his interviewer was Jewish. "I had false papers," Lanzmann said rather proudly, "and I showed with arrogance that I lied to these men. And why not? Didn't they lie to Jews when they massacred entire families? They didn't respect the fundamental priority – life – so why should I observe moral rules with them?"[14] Suchomel's details are meticulous, right down to the number of Jews gassed daily – "18,000 is an exaggeration, it was more like 12 to 15,000" – corroborating the remarks of former prisoners. We learn that when things were running smoothly, it took approximately two hours from the arrival of the Jews in boxcars to their incineration in the ovens. This precision renders the Holocaust more concrete, at a time when the word seems both overly abstract and universalizing.

Shoah begins in Chelmno, Poland, a countryside whose pastoral calm hardly intimates that Jews were exterminated by gas there beginning on December 7, 1941. Of the four hundred thousand men, women, and children gassed there by carbon monoxide piped into van interiors, only two survived. One was Simon Skrebnik, then thirteen years old; Lanzmann found him in Tel Aviv and persuaded him to return with him to Chelmno. Skrebnik's reunion at the end of part one with Polish villagers – many of whom now live in the houses of murdered Jews – elicits from his former neighbors a spectrum of response encompassing unanimous acknowledgment of the gassing and continued anti-Semitism. They trot out clichés about the Jews being wealthy, while Skrebnik stands motionless, gently smiling at the camera with a certain complicity. As Ophuls points out in his remarkable essay, "Closely Watched Trains":

> Where else but in those Polish wheat fields, on those station platforms, and in front of those wooden houses is Lanzmann expected to have found nonparticipating witnesses to the arrival of the trains, to the herding of the Jews into the gas chambers, to the smoke rising from the chimneys, people who can testify to the stench invading the countryside? That some of these farmers profess compassion while obviously contemplating every detail of the proceedings with barely concealed relish is not the director's invention. These are real people, not actors.[15]

Among the searing fragments of the first half is a return to Sobibor, and to Auschwitz, into which the camera tracks as if it were a train approaching the camp. Equally riveting is an interview with American historian Raul Hilberg, who shares the director's obsession with detail, and offers a trenchant analysis. According to Hilberg (author of *The Destruction of the European Jews*), the Nazis invented very little – from the portrait of the Jew to propaganda – except for "The Final Solution." He distills quite brilliantly the three stages of Nazi edict vis-à-vis Jews, namely conversion, expulsion, and annihilation: first it was "You may not live among us as Jews"; then "You may not live among us"; and, finally, "You may not live."

Part two combines perspectives including those of Suchomel; Filip Muller (a Czech Jew who was part of the Auschwitz Sonderkommando or Death Squad and survived five liquidations); men from Corfu who tell of those they lost in the crematoria of Birkenau (95 percent of Corfu's Jews were killed during World War II); Walter Stier, in charge of dispatching death trains from the Polish ghettos to the gas chambers; and Jan Karski, former courier for the Polish government in exile, who tried during the war to tell the world of the horrors he had seen in the Warsaw Ghetto. His interview is juxtaposed with that of Dr. Franz Grassler, assistant to the commander in the Warsaw Ghetto. When he has trouble with details, Lanzmann's voice-over prods, "I'll help you remember" – one of the underlying impulses of *Shoah*. As the director explained in an interview, "memories are full of holes. But if you re-create the scene in concrete conditions, you get not just memory but a re-living."

The best example is the sequence in which Abraham Bomba, a Polish-Jewish survivor of Treblinka and currently a barber in Israel, recounts how he was forced to cut the hair of women in the gas chambers just before they were to die. (The Germans processed this hair into ersatz textiles.) "I knew it would be hard to go back," Lanzmann acknowledged, "and that's why I shot it in the barber shop: I wanted to reactivate the scene – and for Bomba to have scissors in hand." At the outset, the barber speaks dispassionately about his wartime shearing as he snips a client's hair. But Lanzmann's questions lead him to a story so "horrible," as Bomba puts it, that he stops and refuses to continue. Lanzmann insists, "I know, I apologize, but go on Abe, you must. We have to do it." With visible difficulty, Bomba recalls how a fellow barber saw his wife and sister in the gas chamber, but was not permitted to speak with them, lest he share their fate. "He did what he could for them – staying with them a second, a minute more, hugging them and kissing them. Because he knew that he would never see them again," Bomba says. Scenes like these exemplify Ophuls's assessment, "I consider *Shoah* to be the greatest documentary about contemporary history ever made, bar none, and by far the greatest film I've ever seen about the Holocaust."[16] And lest one think that Lanzmann's genius lies merely in his capturing moments of gripping truth, there is the overall form of the film, perceptively described by Simone de Beauvoir: "*Shoah*, and its subtle construction, evokes a musical composition, with moments that culminate in horror, serene passages, laments and neutral stretches. And the whole is marked by the almost intolerable din of the trains rolling on towards the camps."[17] The achievement of *Shoah* is that it contains no music, no voice-over narration, no self-conscious camera work, no stock images – just precise questions and answers, evocative places and faces, and horror recollected in tranquility.

In conclusion, *Night and Fog*, *The Memory of Justice*, and *Shoah* tower above other films because of an intimacy with (and commitment to) the cinematic medium as well as the historical facts. They avoid the cheap packaging of "Hollywood" motion pictures – manipulative music, melodramatic clichés, literal violence – in favor of a rich and original structure: cinematic language is pushed and prodded into expressing complex truths, disorienting, stinging, and enlightening the viewer. They preserve the reality of the past while provoking the necessary questions of the present. This is not to say that stories like *Holocaust* should be condemned or even ignored; in these times, *any* film that tackles this subject with visibly good intentions is brave, if not commendable.

Rather, the most noteworthy cinematic attempts have been in the direction of either spareness or stylization. Either the "no-ketchup" *Boat Is Full* or the "salami-hurling" *Seven Beauties* has more value than a nice soap opera about Nazis. In between the sober record and the grotesque tableau, things get diluted, processed, and tamed. Along with the documentaries, films such as *The Pawnbroker, Passenger, Angry Harvest, The Last Stop*, and *Mephisto* succeed best in illuminating the Holocaust: they keep it visible and render it meaningful.

Since 1982, the increase has been not merely in the number of films about the Holocaust, but in the quality. Although these images – captured or created on celluloid – are cast by an event that grows dimmer with the passage of time, there is reason for cautious optimism when we encounter documentaries such as *Shoah* and *Partisans of Vilna*, television dramas like *Escape from Sobibor* and *War and Remembrance*, and fiction films including *Goodbye, Children* and *Under the World*. The growing number of cinematic efforts by children of survivors is heartening, as is the renewed attention of respected American directors. As this book goes to press, Jerry Schatzberg has finished shooting *Reunion* with Jason Robards, an English-language coproduction of France, Germany, and Great Britain, scripted by Harold Pinter from Fred Uhlmann's memoir of the friendship between two teenagers in 1993 Germany; Robert Young is about to film *Triumph* in Auschwitz, produced by Arnold (*Platoon*) Kopelson, and starring Willem Dafoe as a Greek Jew who survives in the camp as a boxer; Irvin Kershner is set to direct *The White Crow*, featuring Robert Duvall as Eichmann and Glenn Close as his interrogator; and Paul Mazursky will soon make his long-awaited film version of Isaac Bashevis Singer's *Enemies: A Love Story* with Ron Silver in the lead. Among upcoming documentaries, one of the most promising is being developed by David Haspel and Sterling Van Wagenen, based on Robert Abzug's monumental study, *Inside the Vicious Heart: Americans and the Liberation of Nazi Concentration Camps*. Despite the danger of oversaturation, there is probably some relevance in a comment like that of Roman Polanski: "It's very strange. I am much more affected by the past now than when I was young. When I recently saw the Frédéric Rossif documentary, *Le Temps du Ghetto* (*The Time of the Ghetto*), it affected me more than when I lived it."[18] Even for those of us who are fortunate enough not to have lived them, images remain indelible shadows.

Part V

Third Edition Update

14
The Holocaust
as Genre

W hen I began exploring how films have grappled with the Holocaust in 1979, there were merely a few dozen titles to warrant attention. As the daughter of Jewish Holocaust survivors, I wanted to bring relatively unknown foreign films to attention, and to assess how American movies had dealt with the legacy of World War II. The word "Holocaust" was just coming into common usage, thanks to the NBC miniseries of 1978. It never occurred to me that, by the year 2001, films about the Nazi era and its Jewish victims would be so numerous as to constitute a veritable genre – including consistent Oscar winners – nor did I foresee how this genre would be part of a wider cultural embracing of the Shoah.

But twenty-two years later, the number of cinematic reconstructions – fictional as well as documentary – is staggering. They both reflect and contribute to the fact that awareness has replaced silence about the Shoah. Immediately following the war, and for decades afterward, survivors rarely spoke about their experiences, partly because they knew the world was not prepared to listen. Now, however, the Shoah Foundation's completed videotaping of more than fifty-one thousand survivors in fifty-seven countries corresponds to two phenomena: younger generations – especially in Germany – want to know more about the Holocaust, and the aging survivors feel the urgency to speak before it's too late.

A brief chronological overview of events might be useful in suggesting how the Shoah has entered mainstream culture, starting with the broadcast of NBC's "Holocaust" in 1978. Survivors began recording testimony at Yale University (an effort spearheaded by a group including Laurel Vlock, Dori Laub, and Geoffrey Hartman), and President Carter appointed the U.S. Holocaust Memorial Council. *Indelible Shadows* was first published a few months before the U.S. Holocaust Museum opened in Washington, D.C., in April 1983. Jewish film festivals sprung up in major cities, and the National Center for Jewish Film was created at Brandeis University. As the Cold War ended, archives were opened in former communist countries, making new materials available for study as well as imaginative treatment.

Schindler's List (1993) was seen by 25 million people in U.S. theaters alone – despite the noncommercial length and use of black-and-white film – while its TV presentation in February 1997 on NBC garnered an estimated 30 million viewers. It led directly to Steven Spielberg's establishment of the Shoah Foundation in 1994, designed to videotape Holocaust survivors around the world. *Life Is Beautiful* a few years later followed in the footsteps of *Schindler's List,* not only with Academy Awards but international popularity. These were merely the most famous of Holocaust-related movies, as documentaries swept the Oscars too. Beginning with *Genocide,* produced by the Simon Wiesenthal Center (another significant institution, and locus of the Museum of Tolerance in California) in 1981, Academy Awards were won by the feature-length *Anne Frank Remembered* (1995), *The Long Way Home* (1997), *The Last Days* (1998), and *Into the Arms of Strangers: Stories of the Kindertransport* (2000), as well as the shorts, *One Survivor Remembers* (1995) and *Visas and Virtue* (1997).

These suggest that Jewish identity in the United States is secure. The Memorial Foundation for Jewish Culture organized a conference in New York entitled "The Jewish People in the 20th Century: Looking Backward and Facing the Future" in January 2001; as one scholar there perceived, the twentieth century saw a change from a Judaism of fate (connected to the Holocaust) to a Judaism of choice. Another described the change as a movement from the emphasis on "descent" to "assent," while a third found that Jews in the U.S.A. (as well as Israel) were increasingly living in neither "exile" nor "redemption," simply perceiving their countries as their homes. We can conclude that, unlike the Jewish studio executives in the 1930s and 1940s who – given rampant anti-Semitism – cautiously shied away from portraying Jewish life on screen, contemporary filmmakers no longer see Judaism as commercially taboo.

Other factors nurtured low-budget documentaries: in addition to cheaper editing equipment and digital cameras, filmmakers benefited from the National Foundation for Jewish Culture's Documentary Fund. Supported in part by Spielberg's Righteous Persons Foundation, the NFJC has awarded completion funds to ten films related to the Holocaust, including *Fighter,* since 1996. With forty Jewish film festivals in the United States alone (and over eighty internationally), an audience clearly exists for all kinds of motion pictures dealing with the Holocaust. From the first major festivals in San Francisco and Philadelphia to fledgling ones like that in Las Vegas, American film-goers have been able to see the best of new documentaries as well as fiction, foreign as well as American. Moreover, the programming of films about the Shoah has swelled in new institutions like the U.S. Holocaust Memorial Museum in Washington and the Museum of Jewish Heritage in Manhattan. Another important outlet is provided by cable television; for example, HBO has presented numerous films, from the Academy Award–winning short, *One Survivor Remembers* to *Conspiracy* (2001), a dramatization of the Wannsee Conference, while Showtime aired *Rescuers* in 1999.

Given the approximately 170 Holocaust-related films I've seen since last updating *Indelible Shadows* in 1989 (not to mention a few that have not yet crossed my path), I could have devoted a whole new book to the recent titles. But this update is intended as a modest supplement to my original work, comprehensive but not exhaustive. And while there are also hundreds of books and articles worth citing, my primary method is close analysis of the films themselves, with notes kept to a bare minimum.

Chiaroscuro lighting heightens the tension between Oskar Schindler (Liam Neeson) on the right and SS commandant Amon Goeth (Ralph Fiennes) in *Schindler's List.* Copyright © 2002 by Universal Studios. PHOTO COURTESY OF UNIVERSAL STUDIOS PUBLISHING RIGHTS, A DIVISION OF UNIVERSAL STUDIOS LICENSING, INC. ALL RIGHTS RESERVED.

As in the first and second editions, my structure is thematic. In the five chapters that follow, I have assembled films that constitute "subgenres." I begin chronologically with the discovery of a few powerful and often prescient films made during or just after World War II. These include *Border Street, Distant Journey, The Last Chance, Long Is the Road, None Shall Escape,* and *Pastor Hall,* most of which posit a belief in interfaith solidarity.

Whereas the first wave of Holocaust films from the 1950s to 1970s focused on Jewish victims and Nazi villains – thereby establishing the basic facts of deportation and extermination – the second wave has concentrated on resistance and rescue. Once the cinema acknowledged that the vast majority of European Jewry was murdered, new movies could ask how the few were saved. In this context, I discuss *Schindler's List* in depth, as well as seminal European motion pictures of the early 1990s like *Good Evening, Mr. Wallenberg, Just This Forest,* and *Korczak.*

Another major trend has been tonal, namely dark comedy. To varying degrees, films such as *Life Is Beautiful* – and secondarily, *Conversation with the Beast, Dr. Petiot, Genghis Cohn, My Mother's Courage, The Nasty Girl,* and *Train of Life* – have been provocative tools in creating film-goers' awareness of the Holocaust. A more problematic tendency is the depiction of the Holocaust survivor as mentally unhinged, from *The Pawnbroker* to *Shine* and *The Summer of Aviya*. Fifth, and perhaps richest, is the group of recent documentaries that return to the scenes of war crimes, including *Bach in Auschwitz, Birthplace, The Children of Chabannes, The Last Days, Loving the Dead, The Optimists,* and *Photographer*.

Finally, to assist in the ever-increasing programming of titles for classrooms as well as Jewish film festivals, my annotated filmography offers brief description/discussion of over one hundred additional movies.

At their best, these films attest to the capacity of the artistic imagination to confront and overcome horror. As the writer Leslie Epstein pointed out in the 1980s, "when the imagination is destroyed, the unimaginable happens."[1] He was referring to Nazi policies which, on the one hand, attacked art, and on the other, appropriated the tools of art for propaganda:

> The books the Germans burned, the paintings they mocked in their Exhibition of Degenerate Art, the music they banned from concert halls, even the humorous sketches they took off the radio, were in the main the work of Jews or representative of what the Germans called "the destructive Jewish spirit." It is of course absurd to say that by exterminating the Jews, the Nazis were attempting to eliminate Jewish art; but it is far from senseless to claim that these oppressors had, by a peculiar twist of thought, come to identify the Jews with some quality of imagination, and that in creating a world without one they were attempting to confirm the possibility of living without the other.

Instead, Epstein suggests, the Nazis offered "blood and kitsch . . . the aesthetics of violence and the exaltation of joy; the frisson of murder together with the idolization of family life, the folk, the state, the leader; the uniting of the saccharine and the grotesque; the joining of the most modern technology to ancient ritual and pagan rhythms."[2]

Like Nazi art, motion pictures have the capacity for escapist entertainment and manipulation: they can distort, evade, and trivialize. But most Holocaust films have engaged instead in creative confrontation, indeed imagining that which is unimaginable in terms of facts and figures. While popular movies like *Schindler's List* and *Life Is Beautiful* proved controversial among critics, they played a considerable role in creating awareness of the Holocaust among mainstream film audiences who had known little about it beforehand.

Some cynics quip that "there's no business like Shoah business," and even I have been tempted to coin a term like "Hollycaust." The Shoah has become a metaphor for suffering, or a template for horror. And films about the Holocaust have provided images – of smoke, of barbed wire, of sealed train cars, of skeletal bodies – that now function as synecdoches, the visual part representing the unimaginable whole. Equally pervasive are museums, memorials, videotaping of survivors for archives, and commemorations of Yom Hashoah every spring. These activities preserve memory, and they also create memory.

As we move further in time from the horrors of World War II, films become increasingly powerful as historical imagination. In an essay entitled "Symmetry and Repetition," Lewis Namier writes: "One would expect people to remember the past and to imagine the future. But in fact, when discoursing or writing about history, they imagine it in terms of their own experience, and when trying to gauge the future they cite supposed analogies from the past; till, by a double process of repetition, they imagine the past and remember the future." Because films often substitute for one's own experience, cinematic memory is a basis for imagining the future.

While there is always the danger of commercialization – horror neatly packaged and leading to numbness or inappropriate happy ends – this seems to me a lesser evil than having the memory of the Shoah disappear from cultural attention. Many decades ago, Siegfried Kracauer suggested that the images on Athena's shield, applicable to the movie screen, "enable – or by extension, induce – the spectator to behead the horror they mirror."[3] But can films really turn us into such metaphorical warriors? To behead horrors . . . unlikely; to behold them, yes, and in beholding, to be held by the power of images – to have one's perception heightened or altered. The beginning of Alain Resnais's *Hiroshima, mon amour* (1959) offers a complex questioning in this regard: a Frenchwoman's voice is telling her Japanese lover that she saw everything in Hiroshima. "You saw nothing," the man's voice responds. "I saw the museums, the reconstructions," she continues. "You saw nothing," he replies. They are both right. She has seen the images that create awareness and sympathy for the victims of the atom bomb. But these have been only representations, not the horrific event itself. Resnais is foregrounding the difference between apprehension and comprehension, between merely seeing (beholding) and being within (held by) something beyond one's control. As the Frenchwoman says later in the film, "the art of seeing has to be learned" – which is as true for the audience as for the characters.

Hiroshima, mon amour, even forty-two years later, helps the viewer to imagine the unimaginable, of innocent bodies devastated by the atom bomb. It can be connected to films about the Holocaust, not only because Resnais's previous film was the groundbreaking *Night and Fog*, but because the best of Holocaust cinema questions how we see and remember at the same time that it tells powerful stories.

15
Rediscoveries

I n the twelve years between the second edition of *Indelible Shadows* and this update, there have been, not only new films worthy of attention, but discoveries of forgotten gems created during and immediately after World War II. *Pastor Hall* (1940, Great Britain) for example, is remarkably prescient in its depiction of both the Nazi menace and resistance to it. Made by the Boulting Brothers, it is based on the 1937 play of German refugee playwright Ernst Toller. Both works were inspired by the life of the Reverend Martin Niemoller, born in 1892 and best known for his cautionary words: "First, they came for the Jews. I was silent. I was not a Jew. Then they came for the Communists. I was silent. I was not a Communist. Then they came for the trade unionists. I was silent. I was not a trade unionist. Then they came for me. There was no one left to speak for me."

Pastor Hall was directed and edited by Roy Boulting, produced by his twin brother John, and scripted by both (plus four additional screenwriters). Set in 1934 "Altdorf," the film depicts how a small and peaceful German village is transformed into a fearful and intolerant place once the storm troopers arrive. Pastor Hall (Wilfrid Lawson) is devoted to his flock, and especially to his daughter Pauline (Nova Pilbeam), soon to be married to the son of his gruff buddy, the General (Seymour Hicks); the General, decorated from World War I, never sets foot in church, however. Fritz (Marius Goring), head of the storm troopers, forces the town to believe in fatherland over faith, and in the state over the individual. Pastor Hall politely but firmly refuses to follow the party line, whether agitating on behalf of a fourteen-year-old neighbor who was raped at a youth camp (there is no redress because the young rapist was the nephew of a high-ranking officer), or secretly burying the ashes of a villager who was labeled "traitor" because he was the bodyguard of (out-of-favor) General Romm.

When Pastor Hall is sent to a concentration camp (presumably representing Dachau, where Niemoller was imprisoned), we are not spared brutal details. A man is shot on the first day as a bogus example to the others. A young Jew is treated even worse than the other prisoners. They sleep on the floor of a large cell, and receive twenty-five lashes if heard praying. Whereas Pastor Hall would be released upon signing a Nazi document, he refuses to do so. When he gets the twenty-five lashes, one of the officers – who used to be a member of his church in Altdorf – cannot bear it and arranges the pastor's escape, only to be shot as Hall flees. Pastor Hall is not interested in simply following his daughter and future husband to America. Although badly beaten, he strides proudly into his old church (whose new pastor makes a hasty exit) to give his last speech, one of resistance to the antihuman regime. The film ends as he walks out of the church into the crowd of armed Nazis waiting to kill him.

This motion picture is brave for its time, acknowledging, in 1940, at least three realities: the existence of Dachau (a mix of Jews, prisoners of conscience, and criminals in the form of Kapos); the need for resistance; and the church's capacity for both accommodation and defiance vis-à-vis the Nazis. It raises the question of whether the Holocaust could have happened as easily if there had been more men like Niemoller. Indeed, the film's opening – a cross and a swastika superimposed during credits – is a provocative juxtaposition: are they in harmony or opposition? It is followed by the printed sentence "To the day the film may be shown in Germany, this film is dedicated." *Pastor Hall* redefines heroism – like Wajda's *Korczak* fifty years later – by celebrating a man who refused personal survival in order to remain with his flock. "Obedience is not the final virtue," Pastor Hall insists, and specifies that "lust for power" as well as "fear" are what he has fought.

The end of the film is more in keeping with Toller's life than Niemoller's. The implication that Pastor Hall has chosen death over accommodation can be likened to the situation of Toller: considered one of the leading German dramatists of his generation, the Jewish writer – born one year after Niemoller – went into exile after his books were burned by the Nazis in May 1933. In the U.S.A., he started an organization that sought international aid for victims of the Spanish Civil War (in which John Boulting fought) but, disheartened, committed suicide in New York in 1939. Niemoller, on the other hand, survived Dachau as well as Sachsenhausen, and became a pacifist who denounced nuclear weapons. A thorny public figure in his advocation of a neutral, disarmed, and reunited Germany, he was elected one of the six presidents of the World Council of Churches – the ecumenical body of the Protestant faiths – in 1961. He died in 1984 at the age of ninety-two.

According to the press kit prepared by the American distributor, Milestone Films, when *Pastor Hall* premiered in London in May 1940, positive reviews coincided with the start of the operation that lifted the British army off the beaches of Dunkirk. But in "pre–Pearl Harbor America, studio heads watched the film and mutually agreed that it would not be distributed due to its controversial nature. Hollywood was not willing – in fact it was afraid – to buck the popular desire of neutrality. The fear of lost revenues in Europe was most likely another part of their thinking. But one man had the will and political clout to release the film. United Artists' James Roosevelt was the son of Franklin and Eleanor Roosevelt . . . James had a brief introduction filmed of the First Lady and added to the US release."

Five minutes of the film were deleted – mostly from the concentration camp sequences – for fear of offending audience sensibilities (not to mention German immigrants). Nevertheless, *Pastor Hall* was still banned in Chicago as well as other American cities, due to protests from German and Italian organizations. From 1947 on, it was unavailable in the United States; but over fifty years later, a new and restored print (including the excised footage) was released by Milestone Films.

For decades, it was almost as difficult in the United States to see *The Last Chance* (*Die Letzte Chance*, Switzerland), directed in 1944 by Leopold Lindtberg from a script and book by Richard Schweizer (writing credits also include Alberto Barberis and

Elizabeth Montagu). This powerful Swiss drama was held for release until eighteen days after the fall of Nazi Germany in 1945; distributed by MGM in the U.S.A., it also shared the top prize at the Cannes Film Festival. *The Last Chance* stars nonprofessional actors as two British soldiers and an American soldier who – somewhat reluctantly at first – lead a group of refugees from occupied Italy into Switzerland. Each character speaks his own language (eight in all), beginning with Johnny (John Joy), the handsome Brit who escapes from a train of Allied prisoners bound for Innsbruck, together with Jim (Ray Reagan), a seemingly shallow American. In autumn of 1943, these young soldiers are trying to get from Italy to Switzerland. They are harbored by a priest (Romano Calo) who is hiding those in danger – including a British officer, Major Telford (Ewart G. Morrison). In a neighboring inn is a group comprised of many nationalities, most of whom appear to be Jewish: Hillel, an old Pole who speaks Yiddish to his little niece, Hanele; a Serb; an Austrian professor; a Frenchwoman; a young couple; and later a heavy-set woman whom our heroes recognize from the opening scene. Played by Therese Giehse (who would be the grandmother in *Lacombe, Lucien* some thirty years later), she had thrown herself on the tracks when her husband was taken away. She is now with her son Bernard.

As in *Pastor Hall*, the priest has great dignity and courage, whether calming the frightened group or speaking frankly with a Fascist informer. He convinces the three Allied soldiers to lead the group to Giuseppe – who carries refugees over the mountains into the relative safety of Switzerland – as the Germans approach. The priest then holds a Mass for the old people who cannot travel: the scene is effective because no music taints the frightening sound of Germans yelling outside. Again like Pastor Hall, the priest proudly exits his church to the waiting soldiers.

The group finds that the Nazis have murdered Giuseppe and other men of the village. They take the children with them up into the mountains. A snowstorm forces them to stay in a shack, culminating in a lovely scene of harmony in which they sing, "Frère Jacques," each in his own language. Bernard sacrifices himself during the suspenseful last leg of the journey across the border, making a diversion so that the Germans on skis follow him while the group escapes. Nevertheless, Hillel and Johnny are shot. Suddenly, men on skis approach the group – only to say that they are in Switzerland! Just as the characters (and audience) breathe a sigh of relief, it turns out to be short-lived. The Swiss officer seems decent, but has to follow orders that allow only political refugees (and families with small children) to remain. Johnny refuses to leave for the surgery he needs unless the group can stay. His ruse works, but Johnny dies. Bernard's mother ends up holding the hand of Hanele – a new family unit. (Markus Imhoof said he made *The Boat Is Full* partly in response to *The Last Chance*, which, in his opinion, erroneously implies that most of the refugees could remain in Switzerland.) At the end, the group of over a dozen refugees trudges through the snow in long shot. As the frame fills with more people, *The Last Chance* suggests all the other stories of those who tried to enter the neutral country – and is visually reminiscent of the penultimate scene of *Schindler's List*, with the survivors walking together across the horizon in Israel. Despite differences including year, nationality, and budget, both films focus on the themes of rescue, resistance, and Gentiles aiding Jews.

The sympathetic priest is also visible in a riveting American film of 1944, *None Shall Escape*. Directed by André De Toth from a script by Lester Cole (who would later be one of the blacklisted "Hollywood Ten") and Alfred Neumann, it was released in the United States by Columbia Pictures. *None Shall Escape* is not only revelatory in its inclusion of the genocide of the Jews, but prescient in its depiction of the postwar trial of an SS leader. The dramatic compositions of cinematographer Lee Garmes (best known for his work with Josef von Sternberg) begin in the first shot of a Nazi flag being lowered. In a courtroom, Wilhelm Grimm (Alexander Knox) is on trial for war crimes and chooses to act as his own lawyer. Three witnesses each engenders a flashback, beginning with the priest (Henry Travers). In 1919 Litzbark, Poland, we see his warm relations with the rabbi, whose synagogue is across from the church. Wilhelm returns from World War I: although he fought alongside the Germans, he is welcomed back to his job as a teacher, and is embraced by his fiancée Marja (Marsha Hunt) – first seen under a cross. Because his leg is wounded, Wilhelm is filled with self-doubt. He reveals a fascist heart, as he has no love for himself or others. Marja leaves for Warsaw, and returns on the day that young Anna (whose father is a nationalist) kills herself, presumably after being raped by Wilhelm. Jan, a youth, throws a rock at Wilhelm, severely injuring his eye. Months later, Wilhelm is free because of inconclusive evidence about the rape of Anna. Amazingly enough, he asks both the priest and the rabbi for money to return to Germany, and they give it to him.

The second witness is his brother Karl (Erik Rolf), whose story picks up Wilhelm's rise to power in Munich with the Nazis. Karl is against the Party, but loves Wilhelm – who sends his own brother to a concentration camp, and takes his nephew Willy under his wing. The third witness is Marja, whose testimony begins in 1939 when she returns to Litzbark as a widow with a beautiful daughter, Janina. Wilhelm has returned too, as a vengeful Nazi leader. For example, he forces the Poles to smile on a food line for a propaganda movie, and then removes the food when the camera stops. We see a spectrum of response to the Nazis: the doctor is too accommodating; the priest is decent, but can't fight Wilhelm head on (at least not until Janina is accidentally killed – her body brought in much like Anna's earlier – and he defies the Nazis by holding a service); Jan is a resister; and Marja is bold and unsubmissive. Willy, who has fallen in love with Janina, is taunted by Marja for his cowardice. When he finally defies Wilhelm by entering the church, Wilhelm shoots him too.

One of the high points of *None Shall Escape* is Marja's subsequent interchange with Wilhelm: "I'm trying to find one spark of pity in your eye," she says. He asks which one. "The left," Marja answers. "That's my glass eye," he adds. "I know," she counters. (Curiously enough, director André De Toth had only one eye as well.) The last part of her testimony is painfully graphic: we see the rabbi trying to stop the burning of the torahs, to no avail, as the synagogue is turned into a stable. When the Jews are rounded up for deportation, he makes a speech, exhorting them to fight back after having submitted too long. The Nazis shoot the Jews. The rabbi is able to get up, with the priest's help, and walks to a sign that creates the shadow of a cross. This is where he stands to say "Kaddish," and the camera shows the pile of Jewish corpses under the cross image made by the sign. Rather than "Christianizing" the Jewish victims, the image suggests the ineluctable coexistence of the two religions.

Eschewing the "happy end" typical of Hollywood movies, *None Shall Escape* has the kind of grit found in European films of the 1940s. (Perhaps this is due to De Toth's background: born in Hungary, he fled to England after World War II began, and then to the U.S.A. in 1942.) In the courtroom, Wilhelm addresses the camera, claiming the Nazis will rise again. We see a montage of international flags – the Russian one visible alongside the American and British – as the film ends. In 1944 America, such anti-Nazi as well as philo-Semitic images should have had a salutary effect.

It is hard to believe that a film as philo-Semitic as *Border Street* (*Ulica Graniczna*) was made in 1948 Poland. Along with *The Last Stop*, it was one of the first fiction features to confront the still searing past; but though Wanda Jakubowska focused on female political prisoners in Auschwitz (with little acknowledgment of Judaism), *Border Street* offers a truly collective protagonist in which Jews are at least as heroic as their Gentile neighbors. Unlike the numerous Eastern European movies that – while sympathetic to their victimized Jewish characters – posited their Communist identity as a greater good than religion, Aleksander Ford's magnificent Holocaust drama renders Jewish life with authenticity and reverence (for example, the last Sabbath meal a family will enjoy together before being taken to the Warsaw Ghetto).

Ford was indeed Jewish. Born in 1908, he began making documentaries – notably, *Legion of the Street* (1932) about Warsaw newsboys. He was one of the organizers of START (Society for the Devotees of Artistic Film) in 1929, and made one of the first fiction films in Palestine in 1934. But his 1936 film about a sanitarium for Jewish children, *The Path of Youth*, was banned as a vehicle for propaganda. During World War II, he left Poland and headed the Film Group of the Polish Army on the Soviet Front. The newsreels and documentaries he made there provided fertile ground for *Border Street*, as did the documentary he shot at the end of 1944 of the Majdanek concentration camp.

After opening credits on photos of Warsaw's bombed buildings, a voice-over narration says this could be any street, introducing the symbolic nature of the story that will follow. On a summer day in 1939, boys play in a courtyard. The camera pulls back to show, behind a basement window, an elderly Jew praying with a boy: little Davidek (Jurek Zlotnicki), visibly separated by a windowpane, clearly wants to play ball with the other kids. Similarly, the camera tracks into a high-floor window to reveal the lovely young Jadzia (Maria Broniewska) practicing piano with her guardian. At first, the camera movement connects the two children from different classes in their desire to be with the others. Later, the camera's equation will prove more profound: Jadzia does not know that, like Davidek, she is Jewish.

Davidek sneaks out to play, but is taunted as a "little Jew," especially by Fredek: he is the son of Kusmarek, a barkeeper whose identity is quickly established when he asks the barber to cut his moustache like Hitler's and shapes his hair like the Führer. Slightly less anti-Semitic is Wladek (D. Ilczenko) – Jadzia's boyfriend – whose father is Wojtan, a Polish officer. Significantly, they live on the middle floor of the building: they are not only middle-class, but occupy a moral middle ground between the Jews and the collaborators like Kusmarek (who lives downstairs).

The only boy who defends Davidek is Bronek (Tadeusz Fijewski), a bit older and – like his father who drives a horse and carriage – unwaveringly decent. This spectrum of behavior from the greedy opportunism of Kusmarek to the noble generosity of Bronek allows for no easy generalization about Polish behavior during World War II. Similarly, among the Jewish characters, there are many gradations: grandfather Liebermann is a religious tailor who speaks Yiddish, while Jadzia's respected father, Dr. Bialek, has been hiding his Jewish background. Liebermann's son-in-law, Natan, is an electrician who turns out to be a brave warrior, inspiring little Davidek to be a resister too.

When the Jews are taken to the Ghetto, the Kusmarek family denounces Dr. Bialek to get his spacious apartment. The unwitting Jadzia is sent to live with her aunt in the country. But our characters will keep reuniting: Davidek smuggles food into the Ghetto, aided by Bronek on the outside. Wladek, who is at first enraged to learn Jadzia has been deceiving him about her religion, ends up helping her – a change of heart about Jews related to that of his father; Wojtan escapes from a POW camp, leaves his army jacket with Liebermann who gives him a new suit, and – although he treats the tailor with a chilly reserve – sees from a hiding place that Liebermann saves his life when the Nazis search the place. Significantly, the gun that he hands his son will then be given by Wladek to Davidek for the Warsaw Ghetto Uprising.

The gun's trajectory relates to a key line spoken by Natan after escaping a POW camp too: Poles and Jews should have fought the Germans together. Indeed, had the Poles not allowed Jewish neighbors to be taken away, the unified groups might have stopped the German invaders. But the separation – of Jews from Gentiles, and perhaps of the nationalist fighting army (Armia Krajowa) from Soviet-aligned units (Armia Ludowa) – weakened Poland.

Whereas the opening of *Border Street* visually suggests social and perhaps moral stratification, the Ghetto is introduced by a tracking camera that equates all Jewish lives. Similarly, when Wladek's father is taken by the Germans and yells, "Long live Poland!" before his mouth is taped, a tracking shot along a line of other men with mouths covered unifies them as well.

Toward the end, *Border Street* depicts the Warsaw Ghetto Uprising with a return to spatial expressiveness. While Davidek and Jadzia descend into the sewers – a palpable image of hell that Andrzej Wajda would develop in *Kanal* (1955) after being Ford's assistant on *The Boys from Barska Street* (1954) – Liebermann prays for the dead and accepts his own impending demise in mid-ground, and Natan ascends to the rooftops with ammunition. Smoke links the three levels, filling Liebermann's room, then the sewers, and surrounding Natan: framed heroically between two flags, he embodies the fighting spirit of the Jewish resisters. Stuart Liebman notes in "L'Holocauste dans le cinéma polonais" that the flag with the Star of David – which the Ghetto fighters raised – remains invisible (p. 213); nevertheless, Stalin condemned *Border Street* because too much emphasis was placed on the Jews rather than the class struggle (p. 215).

Bronek and Wladek manage to find Davidek and Jadzia in the sewers. They are about to lead them out to where Bronek's father waits, but they see men walking toward the Ghetto. "You're going the wrong way," the children point out. "We know where we're going," says a man with a Russian accent, suggesting that the Jews will be joined by Soviet allies. Davidek chooses to follow them, refusing personal safety as a hidden Jew. Armed, he rejoins his grandfather and uncle, even if it means certain death.

Ford's vision is expressed through the image of a dog that has been trained by a Nazi officer to attack Jews. After this dog is injured, Jadzia bandages the paw, causing the animal to be utterly loyal to her. Bronek and Wladek find the Jews in the sewers precisely because the dog leads them to Jadzia's scent. If the dog represents natural instinct, it can be conditioned by Nazi violence, and then reconditioned by tenderness. This fits in with how *Border Street* depicts the younger Polish characters: depending on how their parents shaped their convictions, some betray their Jewish neighbors, and some are rescuers. (Even if Ford was a respected artist and citizen – not to mention the first head of Film Polski, the newly established central organization for film – his own Jewish identity made him a target during the anti-Semitic purges of 1968. He emigrated to Israel, where he directed an English-language drama about Janusz Korczak.)

The spectrum of Polish response to Jewish suffering is also conveyed in *Long Is the Road* (*Lang iz der Veg*, 1948, Germany), a unique motion picture that was virtually impossible to see until the National Center for Jewish Film restored and re-released it in 1996. The protagonist, David (Israel Becker, who wrote the quasi-autobiographical screenplay with Karl Georg Kulb), is denounced by the first farmer he glimpses after escaping from an Auschwitz-bound train, while he is temporarily protected by the second farmer (who also prays for him). *Long Is the Road* was made by and about Jewish DPs (Displaced Persons) just after World War II, directed by Herbert B. Fredersdorf and Marek Goldstein in the American zone of occupied Germany. On the one hand, it tells the story of David: he is deported in the liquidation of the Warsaw Ghetto, escapes from the transport into the countryside, and survives with a band of Jewish partisans. However, as he tries to find his mother in the liberated but ravaged Poland, the collective story of survivors emerges – searching, often in vain, for family members. David meets the orphaned German Jew Dora (Bettina Moissi), and they go together to the DP camp in Landsberg, Germany (whose real inhabitants are in the cast). They marry after a year, and he is finally reunited with his mother. By the end, they are on a kibbutz in Israel, yearning for their own piece of land.

    Long Is the Road is effective as a historical document – authentic in its Yiddish language and actual locations – and as an affecting narrative. Sophisticated in its form, the fictional tale seamlessly interweaves documentary footage. The cinematic shorthand seems decades ahead of its time: Auschwitz is compressed into a synecdoche of barbed wire in close-up; of "Left/Right" barked in German to a row of arriving Jews; and a superimposition of David's father – upon being sent left to his death – chanting the prayer "Shema Yisroel" over a chimney with smoke. After a brief postwar release in the U.S.A., it was deemed too graphic for American audiences, recut, and temporarily forgotten.

The authenticity of locale and language is even more striking in *Distant Journey* (*Daleka cesta*), Alfred Radok's Czech drama of 1948. Shot at the Terezin concentration camp from a script by Mojmir Drvota and Erik Kolar, the film begins with documentary footage before moving into the fictional tale of Dr. Hanna Kaufmann (Blanka Waleska), who is fired because she is Jewish. When her colleague, Dr. Tonik Bures (Otomar Krejca) – a non-Jew – asks her to marry him, the scene is dominated by a menorah and Jewish star in her apartment. This detail becomes an inset on the bottom right of the screen, juxtaposed with documentary footage above and around the square. Throughout the film, other such insets grow into full-frame action. This is an effective and appropriate technique that underscores how the fiction is contextualized by reality, literally taking place against the backdrop of Nazi doctrine, expressed by crowds, marches, and speeches. For instance, after Hanna's parents arrive in Terezin, we see images that had been intercut in the opening documentary sequence (such as a group entering on the right while another carries coffins out).

The desperate Hanna and Tonik decide to follow orders: he goes to a work camp (because he married a Jewess), and she to Terezin. Despite the horrible conditions in the camp, she survives. In the last scene, they walk in the cemetery, moving from Jewish graves to the more numerous Christian ones. Tonik names the concentration camps, extending the focus of the film from Theresienstadt to Auschwitz, and from the plight of the Jews to Christian loss as well.

It is no surprise that Alain Resnais cited *Distant Journey* as an influence on his *Night and Fog*, since its "formalism" (to use Resnais's word) helps to tell the story. Many of the images that would appear in *Night and Fog* accompany scenes in Terezin, with the inset of a young woman whose face is under a Nazi boot in the street. Radok is a master of poetic compression, as when he shows the closet of the Kaufmann family apartment: it is eerily filled with dark coats dotted by "Jude" stars. Later, after Hanna's parents are taken to Theresienstadt, only one coat is left hanging. In another example, her father – who had asked for black dye in order to look younger if taken to the east – leaves on a rainy night transport, black dye dripping down his face. The expressive cinematic storytelling includes a deep-focus, low-angle shot of an older Jewish leader in a big house, just before he jumps from the window. We hear a record player, exaggerated till it sounds like trumpets. In an aurally parallel cut to Tonik's father, a shoemaker, he creates similar sounds on a shoe. The penultimate scene in Theresienstadt of a young woman banging the upside-down remnant of a piano to celebrate liberation is breathtaking: the dissonant gong perfectly encapsulates how much they have lost.

Given their proximity in time and place to the Holocaust, these motion pictures made between 1940 and 1948 have an immediacy that is hard to duplicate. With crosses and Jewish stars literally – or figuratively – sharing the frame, they record, commemorate, and offer a vision of possible Judeo-Christian unity.

16
Rescuers in Fiction Films

n films, perhaps even more than in life, action defines character. Whereas a novel might permit a voice to explain motivation, a motion picture is just that – a moving image, at its best when it shows rather than states. Film externalizes through expression, gesture, and behavior, with dialogue remaining a secondary component in the creation of meaning. This is important to remember when viewing films that treat rescue during the Holocaust (many of which were made in the early 1990s). The facts are not in question: *Just This Forest*, for example, depicts an Aryan Polish woman who tries to save a Jewish child; but why remains uncertain. This is as true of a recent film like *Divided We Fall* as of antecedents such as *Good Evening, Mr. Wallenberg* and *Schindler's List*. They leave it to the audience to ponder why one individual is willing to risk his life to protect a Jew while another remains indifferent or complicit with the murderers.

The relatively recent focus on rescuers is no surprise. After previous Holocaust films that centered on Jewish victims and Nazi perpetrators, there had to be an audience surrogate beyond the oppressed survivor or the criminal – one with whom a viewer would indeed want to identify. Although "righteous Gentiles" comprised a tiny fraction of the European population during World War II, their existence is cause for celebration, on screen and off. Given that motion pictures have always centered on "the hero" who enables "the happy end," stories of Holocaust rescue proliferated in movie theaters and on television in the 1990s. They coincided with Eva Fogelman's inspirational book, *Conscience and Courage: Rescuers of Jews during the Holocaust* (New York: Anchor Books, 1994), which recounts varied and complex stories of wartime decency. As survivors were increasingly encouraged to be interviewed on videotape about their experiences, the number of shorts, documentaries, and fiction features about how they survived – and often with whose assistance – grew.

Chief among them was, of course, *Schindler's List*, whose critical and commercial success made it a cultural phenomenon. Academy Award winner for Best Film of 1993, among other prizes, Steven Spielberg's drama provoked controversy among critics who saw it as safe, reassuring, and misleading in terms of wider Holocaust history. For example, the *Village Voice*'s cover story of March 29, 1994, brought together eight artists and critics (myself included) for a symposium entitled "*Schindler's List*: Myth, Movie, and Memory." Interacting with an articulate group that boasted the *Voice*'s J. Hoberman, Art Spielgelman (creator of "Maus") and the historian

James Young, I was surprised to find that I was the only one defending *Schindler's List*.

A few months later, the film's release in France sparked debate as well. As Antoine Halff wrote in *The Forward* of June 24, 1994, Claude Lanzmann – the director of *Shoah* – charged in *Le Monde* and *Globe Hebdo* that *Schindler's List* " 'commits a transgression by trivializing the Holocaust, thereby denying its unique character.' Mr. Lanzmann's charges, which echoed widely in the French media, brought countercharges from French intellectuals that what he really was defending was the 'unique quality' of his own work, and essentially questioning whether anyone else was suitable to address the topic of the Holocaust." Proud and contentious – "where *Shoah* doesn't have images, he added them!" the filmmaker exclaimed in dismissing Spielberg – Lanzmann argued that any attempt to represent the Holocaust is a betrayal, "an exercise in denial and relativism."

Those of us who teach or write about film professionally did not have high expectations for *Schindler's List*: a Holocaust drama directed by the champion of "feel-good" fantasy? A black-and-white epic from a director whose colorful adventures range from *Jaws* to *Indiana Jones*? Bringing back extinct dinosaurs in *Jurassic Park* is one thing, but re-creating the extermination of the Jews? My own reservations were compounded by a sense of the difficulty of adapting this story to a fictional film. In the mid-1980s, I was contacted by Kurt Luedtke, the Academy Award–winning screenwriter of *Out of Africa*. He was the first to try adapting Thomas Keneally's 1982 book into a film. We discussed the story from a cinematic perspective, and he confessed that the main problem was to seize on motivation: why, at a time when Germans were actively or passively participating in the Final Solution, did Oskar Schindler risk his life to save over 1,100 Jews? Neither of us could find a sufficiently satisfying answer to allow the audience into the psyche of this profiteering bon vivant, Nazi party member-turned-altruist.

The film version of *Schindler's List* invited less skepticism after Spielberg engaged three gifted collaborators. In July 1989, the first draft of a new script was written by Steven Zaillian, who demonstrated his ability to deal with complex dramatic material in adapting *Awakenings*. (He has since made an impressive directorial debut with the film *Searching for Bobby Fischer*, from his own script.) Spielberg then selected as the director of photography Janusz Kaminski, a relatively unknown Polish-born cinematographer, familiar with the physical as well as emotional landscape. And whereas the rumors in 1992 suggested that Spielberg was going to cast a "star" as Schindler – for example, Kevin Costner or Mel Gibson – by January 1993, he had made a daring decision: he cast Liam Neeson, a brilliant actor rather than a star, and a European whose face was not familiar to the public.

Together they created a motion picture that, from the very first shot, tells the story of Oskar Schindler in a heightened visual manner. It is a story of moral polarities – between the demented, omnipotent Nazi commandant Goeth (Ralph Fiennes) and the vulnerable, self-effacing Jewish accountant Stern (Ben Kingsley). In between is Schindler, linked to both by an opportunity he can manipulate, but later by an awareness that both men mirror disparate aspects of his own soul.

A hand lights a Sabbath candle, in color, as we hear the prayer in Hebrew. This image of continuity provides the frame of *Schindler's List* – survival, ritual,

celebration. The candle burns, suggesting the passage of time, and the smoke de-
noting its end becomes the smoke from a train: the film turns into black-and-white.
Color – connected to continuity – is then suppressed until the war is over. It will
recur briefly at three privileged moments of the narrative: Schindler witnesses the
brutal liquidation of the Plaszow forced-labor camp from a hilltop and sees a little
Jewish girl whose red coat is the only dot of color in a black-and-white image. She
manages to hide in an abandoned ghetto apartment. But a few sequences later, her
red coat will be visible atop a pile of corpses. If she represents the glimmer of hope
that might still exist in childhood innocence, it disappears amid the war's horrors.
Toward the end, only after Schindler suggests to a rabbi in his factory that he prepare
for the Sabbath, does color return for a moment in the lighting of candles.

The film's peaceful and timeless religious opening is immediately juxtaposed
with the wartime chaos of the Cracow train station – embodied in hand-held camera
work – where Jews arrive to be herded into the ghetto. Lists of names are being typed.
The triadic introductory structure of *Schindler's List* (which will be "rhymed" by
the triadic concluding structure) moves from a candle, to a list, and – finally – to
a man.

We do not get to see Schindler right away. Spielberg effectively presents details
that suggest a mystery – turning the very problem of point of view that stalled Luedtke
to his advantage. First we see his hands in close-up as he gets dressed, culminating
in the Nazi pin on his lapel. As he enters a nightclub, the hand-held camera behind
his shoulder, we still don't see him fully. When the camera is finally before his face,
his hand hides it partly from our view. Cinematically speaking, the director establishes that his hero reveals little, especially about his motivations. Building on the
premise of Zaillian's script – in which Schindler is treated from an objective distance,
through which we see only the external behavior rather than the rationale – neither
Spielberg's direction nor Neeson's performance attempts to penetrate the protagonist's enigmatic nature. While this might be a drawback – after all, we want to
understand why Schindler changed from an opportunistic employer of slave labor to
a protector – it is perhaps the only authentic approach: no one can really state with
certainty what led this takeover artist to such nobility. The ambiguity of the character
is expressed by the lighting. During the first hour, many shots present Schindler's
face half in light, half in shadow – for example, as he offers Stern a drink for the
third (and unaccepted) time. When he brings his wife, Emilie (Caroline Goodall),
to the nightclub, the darkness makes it hard to "read" his face. After his worker – a
one-armed Jew – is killed by the SS who have forced the Schindlerjuden to shovel
snow, he complains to a Nazi official. To see half his face in shadow – at least until
he makes a decisive choice – externalizes his possibly dual motive of profiteering and
protecting.[1]

Although it is true that the Jews in *Schindler's List* exist as a function of Oskar
Schindler, it is equally true that he exists as a function of the Jews. From the very
beginning of the film, Spielberg crosscuts between their symbiotic trajectories: in
the first sequence, Cracow is the place where the Jews have been gathered, and

Oskar Schindler (Liam Neeson) at a nightclub in the first part of *Schindler's List.* Copyright © 2002
by Universal Studios.

Stern (Ben Kingsley) types for Schindler (Liam Neeson) the list of Jews to be saved. Copyright © 2002 by Universal Studios. PHOTO COURTESY OF UNIVERSAL STUDIOS PUBLISHING RIGHTS, A DIVISION OF UNIVERSAL STUDIOS LICENSING, INC. ALL RIGHTS RESERVED.

where Schindler has arrived to make his fortune. We then see Cracow's Jews being forced out of their homes and into the ghetto – notably the wealthy Nussbaums. Just after their departure from their sumptuous apartment, Schindler takes possession: "Couldn't be better," he says contentedly, testing the firm bed. "Could be worse," Mrs. Nussbaum proposes when they enter the cramped ghetto space; and indeed it is worse, as twelve pious Jews arrive to share the room. The film's intricate structure allows for some irony: the Nussbaums will end up in Schindler's factory, and will be saved by the very German who took their apartment. (A similar irony exists in the subsequent montage sequence of Schindler's generous overtures to the SS men who will order his kitchenware products: each receives a basket filled with cognac and other delicacies, hardly aware that Schindler obtained the black-market goods from Poldek Pfefferberg [Jonathan Sagalle], an enterprising young Jew.)

In response to the allegation that the Jews have no identity in this film (notably that of Frank Rich in the *New York Times* of January 2, 1994), it behooves us to note a number of individuated characters. In addition to Helen Hirsch (Embeth Davidtz), selected by Amon Goeth to be his maid and saved by Schindler via a card-game bet, we get to know Wulkan (Albert Misak), Danka Dresner (Anna Mucha), Chaja Dresner (Miri Fabian), and Adam Levy (Adam Siemion). After a deportation that was to have included Stern, the camera follows the suitcases of the deportees to a storeroom: the image of piles of objects is staggering, especially when it rests on a jeweler who is weighing gold. He stops, stunned, when confronted by a bag of teeth with gold crowns. This is Wulkan, who will be seen again among the Schindlerjuden, and who will play a symmetrically redemptive role in the penultimate sequence: in order to make a gold ring for their savior, the Jewish survivors remove three gold teeth from the mouth of one of their comrades, which Wulkan makes into the ring. An observant viewer will also note such recurring characters as the bespectacled child Danka Dresner – almost taken from her mother at Auschwitz – and the little boy Adam Levy. One of the film's most wrenching moments occurs in the Cracow ghetto when this Jewish youngster, who seems to be working for the Nazis, blows his whistle upon seeing Mrs. Dresner. But after recognizing her, Adam shows her where to hide. (In this scene, *Schindler's List* suggests that the capacity to move from thoughtless cruelty to decency is not limited to Oskar Schindler.) Adam is later seen in Plaszow as part of a group being harassed by the bloodthirsty commandant Goeth: because no one is confessing to having stolen a chicken, Goeth randomly shoots a few men. Adam steps forward tearfully, acknowledging that he knows who the culprit was. "Him," he exclaims, cleverly pointing to a man already shot.

By the next scene, Adam has been relocated into Schindler's factory. Indeed, he is part of another triangle of interrelated characters: Rabbi Levartov (Ezra Dagan), a skilled hinge maker, is taunted by Goeth for not having made enough hinges – but when Goeth shoots him, the gun sticks. Stern takes a gold lighter from the willing Schindler; after it ends up on the desk of the greedy Jewish policeman Goldberg, the hinge maker is in Schindler's care. (The same rabbi will be prompted by Schindler to light Sabbath candles.) The process is repeated for Adam Levy. And a Jewish couple – whose daughter Regina Perlman pleaded with Schindler to save them – arrives at his factory after he has proffered his watch to Stern for Goldberg. From anonymous names typed on paper, these Jewish characters assume faces, especially when they identify themselves for work in Schindler's third factory (Brinnlitz). A graphic embodiment of the film's narrative strategy can be seen as Schindler leaves his workers at war's end: his face, reflected in the car window (this time, fully visible), is superimposed on the Jews bidding farewell. At moments, he is in focus; at others, the workers. The shift of focus within the frame leads us to balance our attention between the two. Moreover, the final scene of *Schindler's List* at the savior's grave in Israel prints the names of the aged survivors accompanying the actors who played them. This constitutes yet another list (perhaps even a controversial one, in that not all the Schindlerjuden were invited to Israel!), one that individuates the Jews even more definitively.

Despite the title, there is, of course, more than one list. In fact, Stern makes the first one for Schindler's debut factory, and his own cleverness matches that of his "boss." For example, in forging a work permit for a fifty-three-year-old man, he crumples and stains it with coffee so the Germans will believe it is not a new piece of paper. We later see a very different list – a Nazi one – that includes Stern's name. With imperious bluster, Schindler manages to locate his accountant and get him off the train. Stern becomes an audience surrogate, a complicitous witness to Schindler's acts who remains wary nonetheless. Like the viewer, he wonders what Schindler is up to – Profit? Altruism? Both? Although he refuses to accept his offer of a drink three times, by the fourth, Schindler has earned Stern's confidence to the extent that the accountant asks for the drink. As Stern types the film's main list – of the Jews Schindler will buy from Goeth – he is not only the witness to, but the instrument of, Schindler's deeds. He makes his mark, his hands implementing Schindler's vision.

Hands are central to the film's theme of polarities, from the very first shot of candle lighting to the closing scene in which the hand of Liam Neeson places a rose on Schindler's grave. This is not merely aesthetic symmetry, but a dramatization of what hands are capable of – from Goeth's, which constantly pull the trigger of his long-range rifle, to Stern's, which ensure survival. In the film's second image, the space occupied by candlesticks is filled by ink bottles in close-up. These containers will be the vessel of a mark to be made – lists for the ghetto. (Later, in a church, Pfefferberg will scold his black-market colleagues about the shoe polish he ordered in metal containers: they turned out to be glass containers, and broke at the front.) During a "selection" in Plaszow, the female inmates try to look healthy by making another kind of mark: a close-up of a finger being pricked leads to shots of women dotting their lips and cheeks with new "rouge"! These close-ups of vital containers can be connected to the scene in which the SS are about to liquidate the hospital of the Cracow ghetto. In extreme close-up, we see small glasses of liquid into which a drop of poison is placed. Two doctors gently administer this potion to the patients; by the time the Germans enter and shoot, these Jews have died a quiet death – and the doctors have performed an act of resistance. Ultimately, these vessels suggest a larger one – the body which contains the spirit – and a perhaps Jewish notion of a dextrous soul.

The film unfolds between hands that light candles and those that place stones on a grave, both in color. The three openings – including a train station and Schindler's toilette – are balanced by three endings (Schindler's departure, the survivors' liberation, and the epilogue in Israel). Exactly midway between these poles is the scene where Schindler – perhaps not unlike William Styron's Sophie – makes a choice. Whereas neither Stern nor the audience has been certain up to this point about Schindler's motives – especially after he throws Regina Perlman out of his office for begging him to save her parents – his order to Stern that the Perlmans be put on his list leaves little doubt. Schindler has shifted from the allegiances suggested by his Nazi pin to more humane and risky ones. The narrative strategy here is closer to that of American films on Vietnam than those devoted to the Holocaust. In *Apocalypse Now* and *Platoon*, respectively, the characters of Martin Sheen and Charlie Sheen are caught between clearly delineated moral poles. Midway through Francis Coppola's version of *Heart of Darkness*, the protagonist shoots a Vietnamese family in a little boat, signifying his crossing over into the realm of Kurtz's violent madness. At the halfway point of Oliver Stone's drama, the hero – who has wavered between two mentors, the peaceful Willem Dafoe and the demented Tom Berenger – places himself on the former's side. Schindler has existed in a moral realm between Goeth and

Stern, the powerful Nazi and the vulnerable Jew. His choice to protect the Perlmans distances him from Goeth, and leads to a magnificent scene in which he tempts the drunken Nazi with "the power of good":

> They don't fear us because we have the power to kill, they fear us because we have the power to kill arbitrarily. A man commits a crime, he should know better. We have him killed, we feel pretty good about it, or we kill him ourselves and we feel even better. That's not power, though, that's justice. . . . Power is when we have every justification to kill, and we don't. That's what the emperors had. A man stole something, he's brought before the emperor, he throws himself down on the floor, he begs for mercy, he knows he's going to die . . . and the emperor pardons him. This worthless man. He lets him go. That's power.[2]

(Goeth tries to be "Amon the Good" for a few hours, but then reverts to his old ways.) Schindler's second choice is no less decisive: rather than leaving Poland with trunks full of cash, he spends it all to save his workers.

It is not simply money that enables Schindler to hoodwink the Nazis. He shares with the protagonists of numerous Holocaust films a crucial talent – improvisation. From Ernst Lubitsch's *To Be or Not to Be* (1942) to François Truffaut's *The Last Metro* almost forty years later, survival is predicated on performance. As Schindler

At war's end, Stern (Ben Kingsley) speaks for the now liberated Jews of Schindler's factory, asking a Soviet cavalryman where they can go. Copyright © 2002 by Universal Studios. PHOTO COURTESY OF UNIVERSAL STUDIOS PUBLISHING RIGHTS, A DIVISION OF UNIVERSAL STUDIOS LICENSING, INC. ALL RIGHTS RESERVED.

explains to Stern, he will bring to the success of their first factory – rooted in the Jews' investment and the accountant's labor – "presentation." Schindler is quite brilliant at presentation, from silk shirts to bravura gestures like hosing down a trainload of hot, thirsty Jews. But one of the film's most effective connections is between Schindler and the Jews who are equally gifted at improvisation – Stern, little Adam, and Pfefferberg (who escapes the ghetto roundup by convincing Goeth he had been detailed to collect strewn suitcases). Although Schindler occasionally appears as too much of a "deus ex machina" – arriving at Auschwitz just as the children of his workers are being separated to be sent to a certain death – his performance is breathtaking: to convince an Auschwitz guard that he needs these children as workers, he thrusts a tiny finger at him and asks, "How else do you expect me to polish the inside of a 45 millimeter shell casing?"

Spielberg hardly needs to show what the Schindlerjuden are spared in Auschwitz. Now that more than two hundred films have been made about the Holocaust, a cinematic shorthand allows for certain tropes. The women who have erroneously been transported to the concentration camp instead of his factory in Czechoslovakia emerge from the showers (which have emitted water rather than gas). Some notice another transport, including many children, entering a building across the way. A pan to the chimney suggests their fate, juxtaposed with that of Schindler's women, who finally arrive at his subcamp at Brinnlitz. (This supposed munitions factory never produces anything of value in seven months – per his instructions – and remains a haven.)

Schindler's List invites us to identify less with the victimized Jews (a given in most Holocaust films) than with an almost inexplicable heroism, as we watch a man risking not only his money but his life. While it could be argued that the documentary about Schindler made by Jon Blair for British television in 1983 is even more moving – the survivors themselves recount their experiences in a fascinating kaleidoscope – the fact of the matter is that film-goers will not pay to see documentaries. Spielberg, the quintessentially accessible filmmaker, was clearly drawn to dramatize the true story because he recognized the cinematic potential of a larger-than-life hero.

In retrospect, there are aspects of Spielberg's earlier work that do indeed prefigure *Schindler's List*. In both *Close Encounters of the Third Kind* and *E.T.* he presents visitors from another world who briefly touch humans in a beneficent way. Like the scientist played by François Truffaut in *Close Encounters*, we too must suspend the rational and accept with awe that some beings defy logic. When we read at the end of *Schindler's List* that fewer than four thousand Jews are left in Poland whereas there are more than six thousand descendants of the Schindler Jews, we realize that Spielberg's film is a mature invocation of mystery and of faith.

It also turned out to be a "pre-text" – both a successful document and an excuse – for the establishment of the Shoah Foundation: Spielberg created an institution that is both commemorative and educational, devoted to the videotaping of Holocaust survivors and the dissemination of these testimonies for study. As of 2001, the foundation had recorded over 51,000 survivors from around the world (including almost 20,000 in the U.S.A.), building on the ground-breaking efforts in this regard by the New Haven–based Revson archive (formerly known as the Fortunoff collection). Moreover, the Shoah Foundation has complemented *Schindler's List* by producing

Schindler (Liam Neeson) welcomes his workers to his new factory at Brinnlitz. Copyright © 2002 by Universal Studios. PHOTO COURTESY OF UNIVERSAL STUDIOS PUBLISHING RIGHTS, A DIVISION OF UNIVERSAL STUDIOS LICENSING, INC. ALL RIGHTS RESERVED.

documentaries centered on Jewish survivors, notably the Oscar-winning *The Last Days* (1999).

Schindler's List shares with *Good Evening, Mr. Wallenberg* an apolitical playboy-turned-savior whose motives are not clear; nevertheless, the Swedish drama of 1990 is far more somber. Rather than celebrating heroism, Kjell Grede's drama focuses on the dark realities and frustrations of Raoul Wallenberg in his effort to save the Jews of Hungary. As played by Stellan Skarsgard, this diplomat-cum-rescuer is more tired and uncomprehending than "heroic": neither an idealist nor a believer, as he puts it, he exhibits less bravura than Neeson's Schindler or Richard Chamberlain's Wallenberg in the NBC miniseries of 1985. Given that Grede's work for European television includes two series on August Strindberg and two plays of Jean-Paul Sartre – *No Exit* and *The Condemned of Altona* – perhaps it is no surprise that his portrait of Wallenberg is as emotionally dark as the visual texture of his gloomy Budapest in December of 1944.

The film opens in 1943 with Wallenberg witnessing through a train window a freight car in central Europe from which Jewish bodies are being ejected. Whereas the curtains are lowered, he keeps raising the shade: the emphasis is on his seeing, not to mention the audience's role as witness. He makes eye contact with a man who jumps out to cradle his child – and is shot – before a dissolve to Stockholm, June 1944. Wallenberg admits to the Swedish rabbi (Erland Josephson) that he is neither an idealist nor a believer. And, given his lack of experience, it is no surprise that the rabbi judges Wallenberg inferior for the mission to rescue Jews as a diplomat – until he says that what he witnessed from the train is the only real thing he's seen in his life.

By December, he is in Budapest, and people already speak of Wallenberg as a hero who has saved thousands. Indeed, we see him providing a group of Jews fearfully awaiting the Germans with Swedish passports that mean immunity. A euphoric scene of his intimidating a German officer and rescuing Jews from a transport is followed by the futility he experiences when a group of Jews is to be deported from a building by a combination of German and Hungarian soldiers. They remain in an unbearable "limbo" situation, forced to stay in an open truck for a few days and nights. Indeed, a Hungarian is in charge, and we see that some of the "locals" act in an even more despicable manner than the Germans. It is the Iron Cross that massacres children, for example (as opposed to the Hungarian police, which later refuse to take part in any more military operations). There is a matter-of-factness to the brutality, as when dozens of armed men face a little Jewish boy. Later, people have no problem watching the roundup of Jews at night, including boys shot at a wall. The Iron Cross ties the hands of Jews together before throwing them into the river. Finally, in a wrenching scene, they shoot children under a milk truck whose bullet holes then ooze milk.

Wallenberg does everything from bribing and bullying to using the Swedish consulate as a refuge for hundreds. He doesn't sleep, his shoes are too small, and he seems closest in spirit to the most extreme of the Jewish characters: Marja (Katharina Thalbach) cannot adjust to the fact that both her daughters were killed. "No one loves a victim," she says. "A victim isn't a real person." He convinces her to live with some hope; by the end, when she sees a Hungarian bullying her neighbor, she picks up a machine gun and kills him.

A few of the twenty Jews who have been kept on the truck do survive, and Wallenberg concludes, "For the first time I feel as if I were no worse a man than any," before being taken to Moscow on January 17, 1945. Given the mystery surrounding his subsequent life and death, perhaps *Good Evening, Mr. Wallenberg* could not have ended in the upbeat manner of *Schindler's List*. Even if, as Stephen Holden pointed out in the *New York Times* of April 23, 1993, Wallenberg "is a master of authoritarian bluff... expert at tweaking bureaucratic paranoia to his advantage" – much like Schindler onscreen a few years later, we might add – he could not save himself after his arrest by the Russians.

Korczak – also made in 1990 – shares with *Good Evening, Mr. Wallenberg* the story of one man trying, vainly, to save "his Jews" in whatever way he can. Both offer a depressing but poignant portrait of a real individual – a veritable martyr – with the difference that Janusz Korczak was Jewish. The masterful direction by Andrzej Wajda makes *Korczak* one of the finest motion pictures about the Holocaust. Although the Polish filmmaker (who received an Honorary Oscar in 2000) was initially tempted to make an English-language bio-pic about the celebrated Polish doctor, writer, and progressive educator, by 1989 he rightfully opted for four crucial elements:

Korczak (Wojciech Pszoniak) leads the children of his orphanage out of the Warsaw Ghetto during the deportation at the end of *Korczak*. PHOTO COURTESY OF NEW YORKER FILMS.

a Polish-language screenplay by Agnieszka Holland; a Polish actor – the brilliant chameleon Wojtek Pszoniak (who played Robespierre in Wajda's *Danton* alongside Gerard Depardieu) – as opposed to the American stars who had been envisioned earlier in the 1980s (including Paul Newman and Richard Dreyfuss); an understated style, including black-and-white cinematography; and, despite the exhortation of producers to attempt a large-scale drama, a focus on the last years of Korczak's life in the Warsaw Ghetto.

Korczak – a coproduction of Poland, Germany, and France – begins with the firing in 1936 of the doctor from his popular radio broadcast, simply because he is Jewish. By 1940, his orphanage has been relocated into the Warsaw Ghetto, and the film traces his indefatigable efforts over the next two years to feed his charges physically, emotionally, and morally. On at least four occasions throughout the film, he is offered the chance to escape, but he consistently refuses personal survival in order to emotionally sustain his two hundred children till the end. With them, he boards the Nazi train bound for Treblinka.

The first shot of the film, a radio broadcast, begins our awareness of transmission. Wajda's film is not simply a moving elegy to Korczak, but a self-conscious reflection on the processes (often flawed) by which history is recorded and disseminated. When Korczak takes a little girl to his medical school class and shows his students an X-ray of her beating, vulnerable heart, a cut to archival footage of a plane at the outset of World War II continues to explore this theme. We then see Warsaw after an aerial attack, with a newsreel camera prominent in the street. Once the film moves – with its central characters – to the Warsaw Ghetto, archival images of corpses and the suffering of the living are crosscut with Wajda's re-creation of Nazi cameramen. The sound of a movie camera accompanies the "authentic" footage, reminding us of the perspective from which the Jews are being presented: given the Nazi agenda, what would the German cameras record in the Ghetto but pathetic, subhuman creatures? Wajda, on the other hand, shows us smart and caring children who happen to be Jewish – and therefore doomed – in an irrational and unacceptable universe.

His choice of black-and-white – crisply and evocatively shot by Robby Muller (*Paris, Texas, Down by Law, Breaking the Waves*) – not only allows for the seamless interweaving of nonfiction and fiction, but fulfills his perception, "Color doesn't correspond to war atrocities. With such a theme, it's better to stand in a cooler corner."[3]

A certain coolness is equally manifested by the soundtrack, which uses very little music. The opening credits are accompanied by Chopin's "Polonaise" (also heard, out of tune, toward the end of Wajda's earlier masterpiece *Ashes and Diamonds*, as a night of carousing ends) on a toy piano, as if played by a child. At the end, when the children are taken from the Warsaw Ghetto to Treblinka, Wojciech Kilar's sad march has great poignancy and dignity. (According to the press book, he conceived it as a sequel to his *Exodus* – composed when Solidarity was created – inspired by the Old Testament.) In between, there is often potent silence, as when Korczak's loyal assistant, Stefa (Ewa Dalkowska), whispers the offer to hide him on the Aryan side while the children sleep.

Korczak's interactions with the film's secondary characters present both anti-Semitism and philo-Semitism. The first Gentile Pole fires him; the second is a woman who refuses to wash the "Jewish shit" of children's underwear in the orphanage; and an alumnus tells the doctor that Poles smash the Jews' windows. But all the other Poles seem devoted – if not to Jews in general – at least to Korczak and his children. We see a man who works in the orphanage pleading to accompany the children into the Ghetto; Maryna (Teresa Budzisz-Krzyanowska), the compassionate head of an orphanage on the Aryan side; and a man in a crowded jail cell making the sign of the cross as Korczak is released. Korczak utters a sadly hollow prophecy in his cell, addressed to a fellow prisoner (who happens to be the boss firing him in 1936): "Never again will a man be persecuted in Poland merely for being a Jew." Given Poland's oppression and virtual expulsion of Jews in 1968, this line is chilling. Moreover, the Jewish father of screenwriter Holland died under mysterious circumstances during the Stalinist era. (As a child, he had participated in Korczak's activities, such as writing for his children's newspaper.) In describing Korczak's personal tragedy, she explained, "he was born into a European family, not knowing Hebrew or Yiddish, and ended up in the Warsaw Ghetto. It's the itinerary not of a man, but of a generation." (Korczak's real name was Henryk Goldszmit, born in 1878.)

Korczak elicited controversy after its premiere at the Cannes Film Festival, which unfortunately coincided with the desecration of Jewish cemeteries in Carpentras, France. In the context of continuing anti-Semitism, a few French-Jewish intellectuals criticized the film for its preponderance of philo-Semitic characters. There was also discomfort with the film's last scene: in dreamlike slow motion, the cattle car of Korczak and the children seems to unhitch from the rest of the Treblinka-bound train, and they jump happily into an open field.

Some critics viewed this as both revisionism and a "Christianizing" of the Jewish victims – despite the fact that after a fade to white, the titles inform us that they were killed in Treblinka. Wajda himself told the *New York Times* of April 14, 1991:

> There would have been nothing easier than showing the death of the children in the gas chamber. It would have been a very moving scene. Everyone would have been crying. But do we have the right, does art have the right to show this? Is art for this? Isn't art for telling it in some different way? Art has to stop short of certain facts, has

Director Andrzej Wajda holds Wojciech Klata, who plays Shlomo in *Korczak*. PHOTO: RENATA PAJCHEL. COURTESY OF NEW YORKER FILMS.

to look for other possibilities. It seems to me that it is beautiful that when we do not agree to the fact that the children were gassed, we create a legend that these children go somewhere, into some better world.

One can add that the pastoral setting suggests the real fate of Korczak's children: the haze into which they run denotes the smoke of the gas chambers, while Treblinka was indeed a forest. Moreover, the Jewish flag being carried by the children is visible. And because the hope of escape is momentarily raised, it is doubly painful to see the title announcing their deaths.

Leading the attack on Wajda was Claude Lanzmann, the director of *Shoah*, who loudly proclaimed that Poland should keep the film to itself. But survivors of the Warsaw Ghetto – including Marek Edelman, the only surviving leader of the 1944 Ghetto Uprising – wrote to newspapers like *Le Monde* in support of Wajda's film, while other Jewish thinkers such as Alain Finkielkraut vigorously defended not only *Korczak* but the right of a non-Jewish filmmaker to treat the Holocaust: "One should not demand of the film more than it could give, or look for what one wants to see. It's true that we'd like for Wajda's film to have treated Polish anti-Semitism during the war. But it is consecrated to one man, Korczak, who carried within him – in a way that irritated both sides – Polish and Jewish destiny," Finkieldraut wrote in *Télérama*. "He considered himself as much a Pole as a Jew."

The most thoughtful and thought-provoking article on *Korczak* came from the respected writer Tzvetan Todorov in *Lettre Internationale*: unlike many of the self-appointed defenders of Holocaust images, he was familiar enough with the details of Korczak's biography to be able to recall how the doctor "was filled with a universal-istic spirit. . . . He shocked numerous friends in Palestine by first taking on the Arab children; he refused to the end to preach hate: the last page of his Ghetto Diary talked about the humanity of the German soldiers positioned under his window. . . ."

Although Wajda was deeply distressed by the French controversy, he felt vindi-cated after *Korczak* was presented in Israel: the film was not only praised, but added by the country's Ministry of Education to the required school curriculum.

The saving of at least one Jewish child is the focus of another Polish film appearing a year later, *Just This Forest*, but, as in *Korczak*, a happy end is not possible. Directed by Jan Lomnicki from a script by Anna Stronska, *Just This Forest* (*Jeszcze Tylko Ten Las*, 1991, also known as *Still Only This Forest* and *Just Beyond the Forest*) is compact, authentic, and affecting. It begins with the visit of the Christian Mrs. Kulgac (Ryszarda Hanin) to the Warsaw Ghetto in 1942; after seeing its misery, she finds Mrs. Stern (Marzena Trybala, who played Korczak's young assistant, Ester, in Wajda's film), her former employer who is entrusting her only daughter, Rutka (Joanna Friedman), to the elderly woman's care. Kulgac is far from happy to be taking the Jewish-looking twelve-year-old, even sneering that it's "typically Jewish" of Mrs. Stern to assume that giving her money makes it worth the risk. After the mother adds clothes, jewelry, and a watch, Rutka leaves with her new protector.

In Kulgac's apartment, her bitchy daughter, Jane (Marta Klubowicz), taunts Rutka, and tries to pocket the money. The next morning, the crudely decent Kulgac takes Rutka to her sister in the country during a train ride that is alternately comic and tense. At first, a peasant, Boleslaw, flirts with the feisty Kulgac. But after Germans force the Poles off the train, he corners them in the forest. Just as Boleslaw is about to extort all her money by threatening to denounce them, another peasant from the train stops him with a raised knife and lets the women go.

There are more twists and turns as they walk toward their destination. After a warm moment during which Kulgac tells Rutka about her old boyfriends, the cry of "Halt, Jew!" causes the child to run away. Although the yell turns out to have been from Kulgac's playful nephews, a real Nazi finds Rutka. Kulgac manages to get her out of a tight spot, unaware that the child kept a family photo with her papers. When the soldier returns her wallet, out flies the revelatory photograph. A slow fade-out on the Nazi following them through the forest suggests their demise. However, because we don't see the women actually being killed, the possibility that they were spared is suggested by Kulgac touching her blouse where bribe money is still hidden.

The strength of *Just This Forest* lies in its understatement, its surprises, and its spectrum of emotion. Many fiction films have depicted Christians rescuing Jews for reasons more affective than altruistic: Gentile men protect Jewish women because of love in *Angry Harvest*, *The Boat Is Full*, *Black Thursday*, and *Holy Week*, for example. Christian women save Jewish men with similar motivation in *Samson*, *Forbidden*, *Martha and I*, and *The Last Metro*. But Kulgac's behavior maintains a poignant mystery.

Of course there are possible explanations. Kulgac prays, and is therefore a religious person; she wants the money; she cares for this particular child and respects her mother; she has political savvy – "They'll kill you, then start on us," she says to Rutka; and perhaps the rescue of Rutka provides Kulgac with her only chance to be superior to her "superiors" in terms of class relations. We can't pin her down, as she constantly oscillates between compassion and innate anti-Semitism, from her first conversation with Mrs. Stern to the last sequence in which she initially says to the officer that she's not with the girl, and then admits that she is. As with many characters in *Just This Forest*, Kulgac's ambiguity feels authentic.

This is equally true in *Divided We Fall* (2000), a Czech drama with so many darkly comic moments that it feels more like verisimilitude than contrivance. Directed by Jan Hrebejk from a script by Petr Jarchovsky – adapted from the latter's novel and based, in turn, on a true story – *Divided We Fall* ended up as one of the five nominees for the Best Foreign-Language Film Oscar. Even though it lost, understandably, to the hugely popular *Crouching Tiger, Hidden Dragon*, the film received excellent reviews when it opened in New York in June 2001.

Toward the end of World War II in a small Czech town occupied by German forces, Josef (Boleslav Polivka) keeps refusing to work with Nazi collaborators, headed by his former employee Horst (Jaroslav Dusek). Whereas the latter is almost farcical in his Germanic gusto, Josef's sympathies are rather with his decent Jewish boss, who – together with his family – has been deported from his beautiful mansion. When he sees the son, David (Csonger Kassai), just escaped from a concentration camp, he decides to hide David in their pantry behind a closet. His wife Marie (Anna Siskova) is supportive, perhaps partly because they are childless and she is able to take care of David.

Josef (Boleslav Poilvka) and his baby amid the postwar rubble in *Divided We Fall*. PHOTO: MARTIN
SPELDA. COURTESY OF SONY PICTURES CLASSICS.

Now that they feel vulnerable, Josef reluctantly agrees to work with Horst, con-
fiscating Jewish property – to the disdain of the neighbors, who know nothing of his
protecting a Jew. Horst's advances to Marie become more blatant, especially when he
barges in one day, and David is hiding in her bed, both under the covers! To prevent
a Nazi clerk from being moved into their apartment, Marie claims to be pregnant.
What wonderful looniness ensues when Josef (who is sterile) insists that David im-
pregnate Marie so that the lie won't be discovered! They succeed, but at the end of
the war, there are more surreal twists. Josef is considered a collaborator, and a Soviet
officer is about to shoot him when David shows his face. The neighbor in charge of
the area is, ironically, the coward who yelled "Jude" to the Gestapo upon first seeing
David. Marie is about to give birth, but – since her doctor has killed himself – Josef
claims that the now imprisoned Horst is their physician and gets him freed to do the
delivery. The final scene of Josef walking with a baby carriage through the rubble is
ambiguous, as he sees characters who died seated calmly around a table. Might Josef
be dead? Or is he simply remembering in a vivid way those who were killed?

The visual style is effective, including scenes of twelve (rather than twenty-four)
frames per second – especially at night – which create tension (as in David's return).
The music is appropriately dissonant, as when David tells Marie that his sister could
have saved herself when offered the chance to be a Kapo (she was given a club and

told to beat her parents to death; they begged her to do so, but presumably she didn't.) There is a fine irony in the names of Josef and Marie, especially when they have a miracle baby (whose biological father is indeed Jewish – the seed of David). Ultimately, Josef is a wonderfully realistic hero – rumpled, weary, and useless until given the redemptive possibility to hide and save a Jew. Like his cinematic ancestor Tono in *The Shop on Main Street*, he is a lazy and reluctant rescuer; unlike Tono, however, Josef rises to the occasion and enables Jewish life to continue.

17
The Ironic Touch

The word "memory" invokes commemoration, a natural result of remembering. But it might be just as necessary in 2001 to dismember as remember – to analyze the details of the World War II past, provoke, and confront the audience with a stimulus to moral as well as historical awareness. A number of recent films have succeeded in creating fertile discomfort through the use of dark humor, from Michael Verhoeven's *The Nasty Girl* and *My Mother's Courage* to such controversial "comedies" as *Genghis Cohn*. Others, such as *Train of Life, Life Is Beautiful*, and *Jakob the Liar*, use humor as a balm and buffer, with comic heroes whose ruses are tantamount to resistance.

The Nasty Girl (*Das Schreckliche Madchen*, 1990) is based on the real experiences of Anja Rosmus, born in 1960 in the Bavarian town of Passau. She won the Scholl Prize, an annual award in honor of Hans and Sophie Scholl – martyrs of the resistance movement about which Verhoeven earlier made *The White Rose* – for her work as a historian unearthing the Nazi past of her hometown. On the night of the awards, she was seated at the same table as Verhoeven; within two years, he had directed a fictionalized version of her story, starring Lena Stolze (who played Sophie Scholl in both *The White Rose* and Percy Adlon's *The Last Five Days!*). *The Nasty Girl* won the prize for Best Director at the Berlin Film Festival – and the New York Film Critics Award for Best Foreign Film – not simply because of the compelling story or the fine acting, but for the ironic style with which Verhoeven chose to tell it. Maybe the distancing devices of Brechtian self-consciousness are necessary, given that the original town of Passau was where Eichmann married, where Himmler grew up, and where Hitler lived for a while as a boy.

Sonja (Stolze) tells her story to a German TV crew, chronicling her evolution from a bright twelve-year-old daughter of two teachers, to a troublemaker in her town of Pfilzig because she wants to write an essay, "My Hometown during the Third Reich." She at first thinks it will be about the resistance of the church, but her research shows the opposite, and alienates her from the hypocritical Bavarian townspeople. In the black-and-white past, she first kisses her teacher Matin (Robert Giggenbach) under a tree. He returns two years later (in color) and they soon marry. Sonja has already won an essay contest, leading to prestige and a trip to Paris, and now wants to write a new essay. But the older people simply don't want to talk to her about the Nazi past. She sues the town to get access to files, but even after she wins, the head of the archives consistently places obstacles in the way of her access. She and her family – loyal parents, husband, and two daughters – are reviled.

Sonja writes the book anyway, and it is a hit. She is finally invited to speak at the local university. There, she reluctantly names the priest who denounced a Jewish merchant during World War II. Because he is now the respected Professor Juckenack, he sues her for defamation. Later, he drops the charges. At the end, Sonja is honored with the offer of a bust of her image in the town hall. She violently refuses, screaming that she won't be coopted, and runs away to hide in a tree (earlier associated with prayer as well as solidity).

The opening of *The Nasty Girl* sets up the film's self-consciousness through an intricate "Chinese boxes" structure: (1) Men drink beer and sing an old German folk song that was appropriated by the Nazis. This fragment turns out to be part of a later scene, and is disturbing in its lack of context. (2) The typical disclaimer of all resemblance to real people or events being "coincidental" adds an ironic touch. (3) A printed quotation from "Die Nibelungen" is equally ironic, given the discrepancy between the opening beer guzzlers and the Norse sagas about warriors. (4) Lena talks directly to the camera next to a statue, high above the street (as she will symmetrically be in the last shot, in her tree). She speaks not from the end point of the experience, but from within; according to Michael Verhoeven, " I wanted to show that this story cannot end somewhere."[1] (5) Graffiti are being washed off a building, but we can still read "Where were you before 1945? Where are you now?" as organ music rises and the credits unfold.

When Sophie addresses the audience and shows slides, they do not work right, interrupting her. We are thus made aware of the presence of technology as a disruptive possibility, which Verhoeven's style often uses. In addition to her voice-over narration at the beginning, she then talks directly to a TV camera, reminding us of the many levels on which storytelling – including both representation and fabrication – is taking place. This is heightened by the shift from black-and-white to pale color, and finally to a bright palette. Moreover, Verhoeven uses back-projection, placing the actors before a previously filmed image. As David Wilson remarked, this "points up the artifice with which the town has camouflaged its forgetting."[2]

In one of the film's most striking scenes, the family seated in their living room seems to be moving horizontally through the bustling but oblivious town, as if the walls had disappeared! (The set was moving on a track over the marketplace.) The director acknowledged that his style was intentionally antirealistic: "I wanted the audience to be reminded that what I'm showing is not 'reality.' " Whereas some viewers might be irritated by the obtrusiveness of these devices, David Denby was right to point out that "such use of the anti-realistic 'alienation effect' forces us to see the material as a parable of German defensiveness and deceit."[3]

Given Verhoeven's training as a medical doctor, one can appreciate the potentially "therapeutic" effects of a film like *The Nasty Girl* – a cinematic antidote to his metaphor likening the danger of not really facing history to the body: "A problem ignored pops up somewhere else." He admitted that he was brought up to be quiet and to behave – "Resistance is very un-German," in his words – while Sonja incarnates a clever and gutsy rejection of Germanic propriety. As Richard Corliss praised in *Time* magazine, "it takes a nasty girl to go after the Nazi boys. . . . Sonja wants to be Joan of Arc, but she's really Nancy Drew, doggedly sleuthing until she cracks a dark mystery."[4]

Anja Rosmus went on to complete a master's degree in sociology, German litera-ture, and art. Her 1993 book, *Wintergreen: Suppressed Murderers*, was a real dismem-berment of the Bavarian past. As the *Washington Post* reported in 1993: "Rosmus wields history like an ax. The storybook town of Passau . . . is chopped to flinders. Behind the town's white-washed facade she reveals a place where evil thrived, where hundreds of foreign children died in labor camps and orphanages,. . . where at least 1,700 prisoners of war were massacred in the closing days of World War II."[5]

Verhoeven continued to give cinematic life to wartime Germany and its legacy in *My Mother's Courage* (1996), the fictional reconstruction of a true story about the deportation of a Hungarian-Jewish woman. Together with *The White Rose* and *The Nasty Girl*, it can be considered the third part of his trilogy confronting wartime guilt as well as postwar amnesia. Based on George Tabori's play, first staged in 1978, the film takes place during one summer day in 1944: Elsa Tabori (Pauline Collins), a cheerful Hungarian-Jewish woman, is suddenly arrested and set on a path to Auschwitz.

Using touches of rather black humor, *My Mother's Courage* fulfills its title when Elsa boldly convinces the supervising SS officer that she has a Red Cross pass. Mirac-ulously, she returns to Budapest in the train compartment of this officer, a vegetarian who sees no irony in telling her he cannot stand the idea of a creature being hacked to death.

With an acutely ironic and distancing gaze, Verhoeven leads the viewer to reflect on how history is represented. The multiple openings of *My Mother's Courage* are as intricate as those of *The Nasty Girl*: on video, a German man denies that he ever took part in the deportation of Hungarian Jews (he will later appear as the SS officer); George Tabori greets the audience with a smile, and his voice-over narration begins; images of Germany's famed Babelsberg Studio are accompanied by another male voice – which turns out to be that of Josef Goebbels in a newsreel; and on the set of the film, Tabori's eightieth birthday is celebrated by cast and crew.

Lest a filmmaker himself feel guilty for reproducing or "using" the Holocaust to make a fiction film, this self-conscious layering provides a frame – and a reminder that what is inside the frame is fabricated. "We have no right to assert that this is reality," said Verhoeven during an interview, "precisely because it is a true story. No, it is only a reflection. The dimensions of this horror, of this truth, are so unimaginable that I could never 'really' reproduce them. This is why I make it clear that it is a film, a 'performance.'"[6]

My Mother's Courage – which won both the Bavarian Film Prize in Germany and a special award from the Jerusalem Film Festival – contains visual allusions to movies from Chaplin's *The Great Dictator* to Claude Lanzmann's *Shoah*. Verhoeven thus acknowledges that his film is part of a now established international genre – "the Holocaust film" – and that there are dangers inherent in a form like the "docudrama," which purports to re-create history. "Cinema can only approximate reality," he insisted.

The more perfectly cinema is able to imitate reality, the more questionable I find it – particularly with this subject. I would rather use drastic changes of style – including slapstick – and homage to films, so we all know, "this is cinema." While I admire the intentions and effect of films such as *Schindler's List*, I have to find my own way – a more European, German way – of depicting these events, which are an important part of the history of my country. This is one of the reasons the film opens and closes in present-day Berlin – to show that this story is being told from a modern German perspective.

Indeed, Verhoeven added to Tabori's story a train filled with characters who resemble figures in paintings by George Grosz or Karl Hubbuch. "I portray the German bourgeois just as the painters banned by the Nazis portrayed and unmasked them. Thus I stand 'degenerate art' on its head," he said proudly. "Think of the 'the black train' as a saloon car brothel sponsored by industry, in which Nazi VIPs took pleasure trips. I didn't want to imply – given the relatively slight German military presence in Budapest, coupled with the forceful initiative of the Hungarian Nazis – that persecution of the Jews in Hungary was simply a Hungarian affair. The black train introduces the powerful presence and appalling participation of German industry and criminal doctors."

Verhoeven makes it clear with a title that Elsa Tabori's story – while true – is atypical: out of 760,000 Jews in Hungary before the German Occupation, 500,000 were killed.

My Mother's Courage was released in New York at the same time as *A Self-Made Hero*, Jacques Audiard's provocative questioning of France as a nation of resisters. They attest not only to the continuing fascination that the war holds for artists as well as audiences, but to a historical reckoning: these films probe degrees of governmental guilt – from the Nazis' Final Solution to French collaboration – with a far from heavy hand. In Audiard's adaptation (with Alain Le Henry) of the novel by Jean-François Deniau, Albert (Mathieu Kassovitz) has missed the chance to be a hero early in World War II. At the end of the war, he appropriates the true stories of others, fabricating a new identity as a member of the French Resistance. He earns the trust of those in power and is promoted to the rank of Lieutenant Colonel.

Audiard offers a wry view of just how easy it was to invent a past in the confusion of 1944–1945. "This was when the great lie that gave birth to my generation was built up, namely France as a war resister," he said at the 1996 Telluride Film Festival. "This is a country that after five years of zealous collaboration tries to reconstruct its identity and its virtue around a great lie." *A Self-Made Hero* is part of a rich cinematic tradition that began with Marcel Ophuls's *The Sorrow and the Pity*: it consists of films from France that explore and ultimately expose how victims of Nazism had more to fear from French denunciation or arrest than from German occupiers.

Claude Berri's 1995 movie, *Lucie Aubrac*, probes even more painfully into the betrayal of French Resistance heroes by one of their own. But *Lucie Aubrac* – based, like *My Mother's Courage*, on the true story of one woman's bravery combined with luck – was questioned by some French critics because of its "melodramatic" or "old-fashioned" form. While World War II is still haunting filmmakers – even after movies ranging from François Truffaut's *Last Metro* to Louis Malle's *Goodbye, Children* – the originality of the European approach in the 1990s seems to lie in its irony.

Audiard maintained that whereas these directors knew the period firsthand, he did not. Consequently, *A Self-Made Hero* is "neither a nostalgic movie nor a reconstruction. The decisive event that made me want to do this film was the Gulf War, and the manipulation of images around it." Like *My Mother's Courage, A Self-Made Hero* includes an eye-winking outer frame that distances the viewer: an older Albert (Jean-Louis Trintignant) recounts the tale to the camera, and we see musicians playing. Subsequent shots of the orchestra self-consciously reveal that they are performing the soundtrack of the movie! Audiard thus fulfills an adage of Jean-Luc Godard, "The only reality in a film is the reality of its own making."

A related – but far more disturbing – cinematic image of French wartime behavior can be found in *Dr. Petiot* (1990), based on one of the most bizarre criminal cases of the twentieth century. Born in 1897, Dr. Marcel Petiot was both a kindly physician and a psychopath, a family man as well as a killer, a member of the Resistance and Gestapo pawn. Despite psychiatric treatment for his extreme behavior, he was elected mayor of his village in 1925. After medical school, he was frequently involved in scandals related to fraud, minor robbery, and patients who died after treatment. He moved to Paris where, in the early 1940s, he helped Jews who were fleeing to more hospitable countries. But, as Christian de Chalonge's re-creation reveals, Petiot (brilliantly played by Michel Serrault) created his own crematorium in his basement furnace. Albeit on a small scale, and with no attempt at ideological justification, he was also killing Jews.

Petiot was arrested by the Gestapo, tortured, and imprisoned for eight months alongside Resistance members. He absorbed the sentiments of the resisters, and upon his release in January 1944, assumed a new identity. He so convincingly became a patriotic leader that he was given the post of Captain of the First Regiment. His mission? To find and interrogate collaborators – including a certain Dr. Petiot. At his trial, Resistance heroes came forward to testify to his courage and dignity. Petiot wrote a book in prison – *Love Conquered* – copies of which he autographed during his trial.

From this material, de Chalonge spent six years developing *Dr. Petiot* with co-screenwriter Dominique Garnier and Serrault (best known for his hilarious performance in *La Cage aux Folles*). They structured the script in three parts – a day and night in 1942, twenty-four hours in 1943, and three days in 1944 – using a heightened poetic style that recalls German Expressionism. The film opens with newsreels of the Paris Exhibition that teaches how to identify Jews. Together with the doctor, we are in a movie theater, and then a German vampire film begins. Petiot stands up so that his shadow on the right balances that of the Dracula figure on the left. By paying homage to *Nosferatu*, Murnau's classic vampire film, de Chalonge achieves two effects: he self-consciously reminds us that we too are watching a film (as will be the case when Petiot is discovered in a movie theater, symmetrically, at the end), and he sets up a parallel between the vampire and Petiot – a man whose darker identity emerges at night. As the director explained to me, "we wanted the whole first part to have an atmosphere of nightmare – black-and-white, with a gradual increase in color, leading up to an explosion of blue, white and red at the liberation of Paris. We're here to amplify fact through poetic transposition. Surreal expressionism reveals more truth than direct recital of fact."

Michel Serrault as Dr. Petiot. PHOTO COURTESY OF ARIES FILMS.

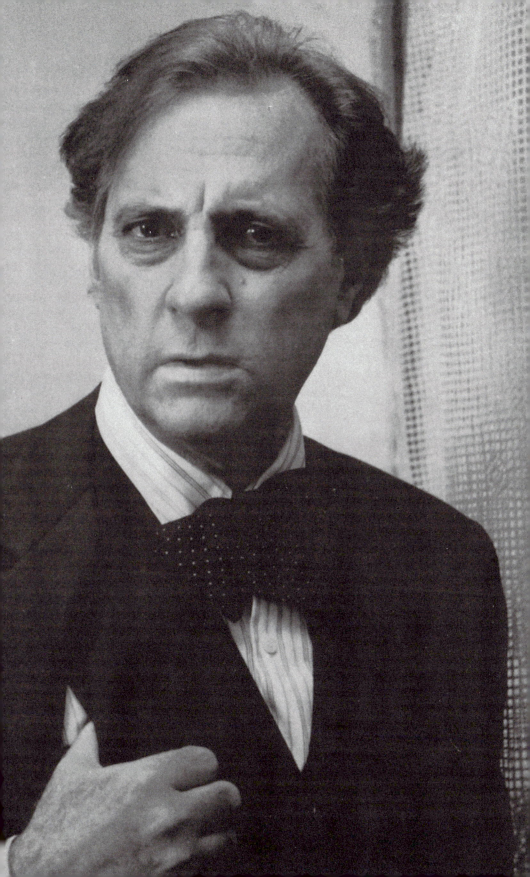

While seemingly loved by his patients, wife, and son, Petiot is a strange and brusque doctor, listening via secret microphones to patients talking in the waiting room, or diagnosing without a full examination. He appears to be a generous, risk-taking Resistance hero who helps Jews to be smuggled across the border. But after he vaccinates his patient Nathan – who thinks he is headed for Argentina – Nathan's trip is merely to the doctor's furnace. (The filmmakers actually met people who knew Petiot: some said, "He saved my life"; others claimed that members of their family were his victims.) Petiot is quite manic, throwing hidden money in the air, driving his bicycle and cart at night – looking like a bat – and working for the French Gestapo. Although clearly not a Nazi, he destroys mainly Jews; at the same time, he is kind to a sick little girl and refuses to take money from her parents.

A fire in his "crematorium" leads police to discover the corpses. Petiot escapes and, by 1944, has adopted the name of Dr. Valery and is working for the Resistance. He writes a letter to the press, which is published in the newspapers, leading to his arrest. End credits tell us that he was guillotined in May 1946. His last words, "I'm a voyager who takes his baggage with him," leaves the mystery of his motivation at the heart of the film – not unlike Iago's refusal to speak at the end of *Othello*. A truly self-made hero, Dr. Petiot remains a disturbing enigma.

The coexistence in one man of demonic power, manic humor, and paradoxical congeniality links Dr. Petiot with the character of Adolf Hitler devised by Armin Mueller-Stahl for his film *Conversation with the Beast* (1996). Directed by the renowned German actor from a script he cowrote with American screenwriter Tom Abrams, this English-language black comedy posits that Hitler did not die in 1945. Rather, as played by Mueller-Stahl in his directorial debut, he lives on: the vain, capricious old codger is now a hundred and three years old but looks seventy (a pact with the devil?). Webster (Bob Balaban), an American Jewish historian, arrives from the U.S.A. to ascertain if this is really Hitler or, more likely, Andreas Kronstaedt, an actor who impersonated him.

He is greeted by Hitler's beautiful wife, Hortense (Katharina Bohm), supposedly in her sixties but looking four decades younger. Hitler tells him that Goebbels had engaged six doubles – one for each day of the week besides Sundays – to impersonate him for purposes of security and public appearances! And he insists that it was Andreas who killed himself in the Führer's place because he was playing him on that day of the week! Flashbacks in black-and-white include an outrageous wedding party after the war: all the doubles are in attendance and get into a childish fight. We also see how Hitler tried to tell others that he was the real thing, but was never taken seriously – not by the West, nor by the East, neither by the Americans nor by the Russians.

Webster believes he has found proof that this is Hitler after tracking down (in Paris) a sixty-eight-year-old deaf-mute who is allegedly Hitler's son. On the tenth day of the interviews, Webster decides to kill Hitler, who seems indeed to be yearning in vain for death. Although Webster has a hard time summoning the nerve, he finally shoots Hitler in the heart. We never see if he really dies. But, as Hitler had said earlier: "if you kill one person, they put you in jail. Kill fifty million, and you are immortal." (At a Washington Jewish Film Festival panel on December 8, 1986, Mueller-Stahl acknowledged that the script began with this sentence.) The film thus raises provocative questions: could Hitler still be alive? or merely his spirit? If this is

Hitler, can one have sympathy for the character? If he were alive, would one have to kill him because justice is too slow?

Like *My Mother's Courage, Conversation with the Beast* quotes Chaplin: there are references to *The Great Dictator*, and to Lubitsch's *To Be or Not to Be* when doubles recite Hamlet's speech at the wedding. In Mueller-Stahl's words:

> If you watch Brecht's *Arturo Ui* or Lubitsch or Chaplin, Hitler is funny. We need our distance to create the character. We have all the other "beasts" on film – Richard III, Napoleon, Frankenstein – but we always try to avoid this beast. I watched his speeches: if you turn off the sound and take away the audience, it's so ridiculously overdone.

Having excelled at playing Jews or men marked by war, Mueller-Stahl seems like the perfect actor-director to essay Hitler. In the former category, he has been memorable in *Avalon, Shine*, and *In the Presence of Mine Enemies*; in the latter capacity, he was the Archduke Ferdinand in *Colonel Redl*, the deserter in Axel Corti's *God Doesn't Believe in Us Anymore*, and the Polish rescuer who lusts after the Jewish woman in his care in *Angry Harvest*. And who can forget his role as Jessica Lange's father in *The Music Box*? It was precisely when he was making Costa-Gavras's drama about the discovery of his character's criminal behavior during World War II that he began writing his directorial debut.

Even before seeing *Conversation with the Beast*, Robert Fulford wrote persuasively in the *Toronto Globe* of August 21, 1996: "Mueller-Stahl embodies on film the calamity of Central Europe in this century. He carries the pain and guilt of the whole German world behind his china-blue eyes, the burden of a monstrous history on his narrow shoulders. The leading German film actor of the past 25 years eloquently represents a culture drenched in guilt and regret."

Mueller-Stahl's approach is as curious as it is thought-provoking, In Washington, he elaborated upon *Conversation with the Beast*:

> Hitler wasn't a human being but a monster. What is Hitler without power? A silly, childish man trying to hurt others. It was Hitler's wish to become either a painter or an actor. Unfortunately, he became a politician. I would have preferred that he be an actor. I was trying to shoot the idea of Hitler, at least – in a desperate attempt to get rid of Hitler. Of course you can't get rid of him. He'll always be there.

Ghostly continuity is also a theme in the wickedly funny *Genghis Cohn*, where Hitler is invoked during the credit sequence as a puppet in the hands of a Jewish comedian. Directed by Elijah Moshinsky (a director of numerous operas) in 1993 for the BBC, the script by Stanley Price is adapted from *The Dance of Genghis Cohn*, a novel by Romain (*Madame Rosa, White Fang*) Gary. Schatz (Robert Lindsay), the police chief of a Bavarian town in 1958, seems to conjure up Genghis Cohn (Antony Sher), the ghost of a cocky Jew whose death he ordered at Dachau. While investigating a series of murders, he can't shake the trenchant comic, who slowly but surely turns Schatz into a Yiddish-speaking, chopped-liver-loving Jew. As his behavior becomes increasingly suspicious, Schatz loses his job, not to mention his identity. By the end, *Genghis Cohn* feels like a "dybbuk" story, as we see how the ghost of Cohn takes over the increasingly receptive Schatz.

Much like Verhoeven in both *The Nasty Girl* and *My Mother's Courage*, Moshinsky juxtaposes five different openings that prepare us for his effectively sardonic treatment of serious themes. As we hear "Bei Mir Bist Du Schoen," Cohn performs on a Berlin stage in 1933: his Hitler puppet with a Yiddish accent not only reduces the Führer to Jewish "shtick" but foreshadows two later scenes of Schatz's deterioration. The themes of spectacle and identity transfer are developed in the second scene, with Cohn's routine as a rabbi on a 1936 Vienna stage. Under his costume is another – that of a Nazi with a swastika. As in the first ventriloquism scene, *Genghis Cohn* seems to ask, who is in control here? With images of both the Jew and Hitler sharing the same comedian's body, the film lays the ground for the introduction of Schatz.

In the third scene, the tone changes: from the upbeat Yiddish tune and brightly lit stages, we move to a dark and silent nightclub. This is 1939 Warsaw, and the camera is behind Cohn onstage as he says, "I finally died in . . ." Cut to the comedian in a concentration camp uniform, getting off a truck. At the Nazi order to shoot, he yells, "Kich mir in tuches!" (Yiddish for "Kiss my ass") before the machine guns kill him. The cut to a very different spectacle – a high-angle shot of a swimming pool in which precision dancers perform – is jarring. We are suddenly in 1958 Bavaria, where police chief Schatz is being lauded for maintaining the lowest crime rate in the state.

The Baroness Frieda (Diana Rigg) invites him to her elegant home, where another spectacle provides uncomfortable humor: when he opens her dead husband's closet, bright lights around an SS uniform express Schatz's awe. As he dons the boots of this Nazi war hero, triumphant trumpets sound. Encouraged by Frieda to try on the uniform – and to ravish her – he is abruptly stopped by . . . Cohn in the mirror! He runs out into the street, still wearing the SS uniform – fly open – and looking like the Hitler dummy of the opening scene.

The second sighting of Cohn is equally ambiguous, as Schatz glimpses him through the glass of his goldfish bowl. And even the third time – Cohn reflected in Schatz's glasses – the visual distortions suggest that the comedian is not "really" there. But when Cohn says, "ever since that day, I've been part of you" – referring to when Schatz ordered his death in Dachau – we know he is onscreen to stay. And Schatz's investigation of a serial killer who attacks during orgasm leads him to tell his men, "People are too scared to shtup" (Yiddish slang for intercourse), without Cohn even being visible.

These scenes might be merely amusing were it not for the exploration of guilt, redemption, and identity transfer that *Genghis Cohn* offers. This is, after all, a Bavarian town like that of *The Nasty Girl*: beneath the bucolic surface are killers – not simply the serial murderer but an ex-Nazi "mass murderer" who escaped prosecution for war crimes. Schatz conjures up Cohn precisely when donning an SS uniform. While the ghost initially frightens him, Schatz grows quite affectionate with his new companion. He becomes so fond of Jewish delicacies that when Frieda visits him, he serves chopped liver, and utters the Yiddish toast, "L'chaim." By the time Cohn takes him to a synagogue to say Kaddish (the prayer for the dead), the Hebrew words seem to emerge from Schatz unprompted. If the words were within him to begin with, has Cohn led him to repentance?

After being glimpsed in the Jewish house of worship, Schatz is deemed unbalanced, and he is forced to be examined by a female psychiatrist. Although she cannot see Cohn, the audience is hilariously aware that he is "pulling the strings," making Schatz into the "Hitler dummy" of the film's opening scene. And by the time Schatz sings "Bei Mir Bist Du Schoen" for her, we know he won't be police chief for long. His house is destroyed – including a Jewish star painted in red on the wall – and Schatz ends up running a kosher food stand. Cohn, on the other hand, appears in a new man's life. Kruger, who shot him in Dachau, is stunned to see the ghost in his home. They go to Schatz's stand: the former police chief seems to sense Cohn's presence, but cannot see him. When Schatz is then beaten up (presumably by neo-Nazis), he says, "Kich mir in tuches," having – in a sense – become the very person he tried to destroy sixteen years earlier.

The epilogue is unsettling as we see Cohn walking on a busy street in the present day. Shot in a cinema verité style, he is still wearing his concentration camp uniform, prompting looks that are more curious than shocked. His voice-over ruminates, "It's not who did it, but why," and then asks, in front of Burberry's fashionable window, "It couldn't happen again, could it?" Without answering these questions, the film works with – and because of – a resilient irony that could be termed Jewish. Given Schatz's earlier dismissal addressed to Cohn, "We've heard enough of your yellow stars, ovens – it's all becoming a cliché" (a line more appropriate to 1993 than to 1958), *Genghis Cohn* presents a new take on the Holocaust, with a psychological revenge that is both sweet and bitter. If *Conversation with the Beast* suggests that the world can never get rid of Hitler, Moshinsky's film demonstrates that the Jewish spirit cannot be killed either.

The very fact that *Genghis Cohn* begins in a self-conscious and stylized manner renders the film a cinematic cartoon in which nothing can be taken at face value. This narrative framing is comparable to two subsequent films of the 1990s that posit Jewish resiliency as an antidote to Nazi dehumanization. To differing degrees, *Train of Life* (*Train de vie*, France, 1998) and *Life Is Beautiful* (*La vita è bella*, Italy, 1997) succeed in using humor as a weapon, both within and beyond the stories. (Roberto Benigni's Oscar-winning international success also opens with distancing devices such as slapstick, which ensure that we do not take scenes as "reality.") But *Train of Life* – directed by Romanian-born Radu Mihaileanu – might indeed have been more effective had it begun with a greater acknowledgment of its "fairy-tale" premise.

Shlomo (Lionel Abelanski) narrates as if his Eastern European shtetl in 1941 were real, thereby begging our suspension of disbelief when incredible things happen. In the face of imminent deportation, ingenious Jewish neighbors take his advice: they build their own train, make costumes for the "Nazi" general (really Mordechai the Woodworker, played by French actor Rufus) as well as the German soldiers they will impersonate. Although they manage to disappear before the real Nazis arrive, they are menaced, not only by the Germans, but by the Resistance members who want to blow up their "enemy" train. Least plausibly, they are stopped by a German roadblock – which turns out to comprised of Gypsies in disguise. The old, wise rabbi (Clement Harari) takes the Gypsies along in the train, and they all reach freedom in Russia. Only in the last shot of the film do we see that Shlomo is narrating from behind barbed wire, in a concentration camp uniform.

Mihaileanu, who was once a member of the Bucharest Yiddish Theatre, said that seeing *Schindler's List* had a great effect on him: "On the one hand, I was very moved by it," the press kit recalls. "At the same time, I began to feel that we can no longer keep telling the story of the Shoah in the same way, solely in the context of tears and horror. . . . My theory was to change the language but not the subject. I wanted to tell the tragedy through the most Jewish language there is – the tradition of bittersweet comedy. It was a desire to go beyond the Shoah – not to deny or forget the dead, but to re-create their lives in a new and vivid way."

The Klezmer-inspired score by Goran Bregovic succeeds in capturing the prewar vitality of shtetl life, and *Train of Life* (which won the Audience Award at the 1999 Sundance Film Festival) is clearly sympathetic to the Jewish characters. It is most effective when Mordechai – having assumed the identity of a Nazi – takes his role as general too seriously. But the film is marred by caricatures like Yossi (Michel Muller), who goes from being the rabbi's assistant (and a "mama's boy") to a pedantic Communist.

The script for *Train of Life* was allegedly sent to Roberto Benigni, who was offered the role of Shlomo. But even if it inspired aspects of *Life Is Beautiful*, the results of the two films are exceedingly different. *Life Is Beautiful* is not, strictly speaking, a movie about the Holocaust. Winner of the Grand Jury Prize at the 1998 Cannes Film Festival, and the Academy Award for Best Foreign Film as well as for Best Actor, Benigni's fable is about love, and the extremes to which a brave and clever fellow will go for *amore*. But because the second half of the film takes place in an unnamed concentration camp during World War II – after a very funny first half – it provoked controversy.

During the first hour, Guido (played by Benigni), an Italian Jew living in 1939, will do anything to be near the beautiful schoolteacher, Dora (Nicoletta Braschi), including taking risks and braving ridicule. Midway through the film – coscripted by Benigni and Vicenzo Cerami – they are happily married, but the Holocaust has reached Tuscany: our comic hero and his son, Giosue (Giorgio Cantarini), are taken to a concentration camp, where Guido will do anything to protect his child. This includes a "fantastical" element: when a German soldier asks for a translator, Guido comes forward (even though he doesn't speak German). As the Nazi barks orders and instills fear, Guido farcically translates the orders into a game so that his son will not be frightened.

Indeed, from the very beginning, Benigni is careful to establish that his film is a fairy tale rather than realism. The voice-over narration introduces a "fable," and the slapstick of the first hour is obviously movie magic. We meet Guido in a car whose brakes fail as he approaches a crowd waiting for Fascist officials: his raised arm to warn them about the brakes is misunderstood, as they respond with the Fascist salute! His clownish personality proceeds to render *Life Is Beautiful* a comedy. Politics are reduced to jokes in the first half, as when Guido asks a man about his political beliefs – then retracts the question upon hearing that the guy named his children Benito and Adolfo. Similarly, he impersonates a Fascist minister at a school: considering the scrawny and buffoonish body Guido reveals as he strips to his underwear, his speech about his "Aryan" body parts is hilarious.

The hints of political danger remain in the background. Being Jewish, Guido's Uncle Eliseo (Giustino Durano) is roughed up by "barbarians," to which he elegantly replies, "Silence is the most powerful cry." At the engagement party of Dora and Guido's wealthy nemesis – where Guido is a waiter – black shirts are visible, and the word "Jewish" is painted on Eliseo's horse. To the horror of Dora's mother (Marisa Paredes), the beautiful young fiancée jumps onto the horse with Guido and rides off. An ellipsis brings us to wartime Italy: Dora and Guido have a son, who is confused by

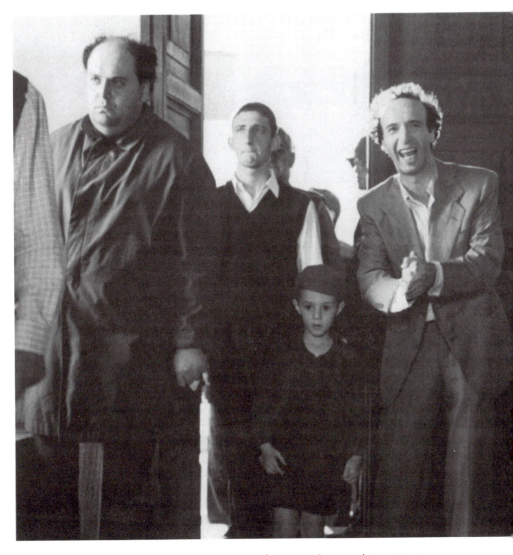

Guido (Roberto Benigni) turns the arrival at an unnamed concentration camp into a game to protect his son (Giorgio Cantarini). PHOTO: SERGIO STRIZZI. COURTESY OF MIRAMAX FILMS. ALL RIGHTS RESERVED.

a sign that states, "No Jews or Dogs allowed." Guido – whose own bookstore has the words "Jewish shop" in front – turns this into a joke to protect Giosue. Throughout the second half of *Life Is Beautiful*, he will continue in this vein, mustering all his comic resources to resist both the physical and psychological destruction of his child.

Once they are deported to the unidentified camp, Benigni makes it obvious that his film is far from documentary. At one point, Guido sneaks into an office and broadcasts on the loudspeaker a personal message for his beloved wife (a non-Jew who has forcibly followed her husband and son to this hell): are we really to believe that he could get away with such a bold microphone takeover? The horror is always muted: for example, while carrying his sleeping boy, Guido approaches an indistinct pile of corpses in the fog. Since the skeletal bodies are clearly painted, the image is blatantly unreal, reminding us that we are watching a stylized representation rather than "reality."

Nevertheless, the character of Lessing (Horst Bucholz), a Nazi physician, seems all too accurate. This dapper doctor is introduced in the Grand Hotel, where Guido is his favorite waiter because they share a passion for riddles. ("Once I say your name, you disappear" turns out to be "Silence.") When he is dispatched to Berlin, he says Guido is the most "ingenious" waiter, and Guido calls him the most "cultured" customer. This will be turned on its head a few years later, when Lessing is assigned as doctor in the very camp where our hero is imprisoned. He gets Guido a position as a waiter for the Nazis. But just as he (and we) think the physician will tell him how to escape, the "cultured" Lessing merely obsesses about a riddle. His inability to see things in balance suggests the myopia that allowed educated Germans to become Nazi doctors.

Guido is finally shot, off-screen, but Giosue has learned well from his father how to hide. When the camp is liberated, he is rescued by an American, rides in a tank (which is what Guido had promised as the prize in their elaborate game), finds Dora, and yells, "We won!" She assumes this refers to the war, but he means the game, culminating in the tank. (For cynics who attacked the film, it also presciently refers to the Oscars that would follow.)

Benigni is not the first filmmaker to juxtapose humor and Holocaust horror, nor the first to elicit controversy. Already in *The Great Dictator* (1940), Lubitsch's *To Be or Not to Be* (1942), and Lina Wertmüller's *Seven Beauties* (1975), black comedy was used as a weapon against Nazism as well as indifference. Chaplin played two parts – the ranting Nazi and the victimized Jewish barber – giving Hitler, Mussolini, and other mad megalomaniacs a comic kick. Benigni told me during an interview in Cannes that *The Great Dictator* was his great inspiration, and that the number on Guido's camp uniform is the same one that Chaplin's barber wore. As in *To Be or Not to Be*, lying – or improvisation – becomes the means to survival. For example, when Giosue accidentally blurts out "*grazie*" (thank you in Italian) among the German children being served in the camp, Guido quickly teaches all the kids to say the word *grazie* out loud. As in *Seven Beauties* – which was shot by the renowned cinematographer of *Life Is Beautiful*, Tonino delli Colli – the Italian protagonist is a clever clown: the very ingenuity that Guido employed to win Dora is what keeps his son alive in the camp.

Life Is Beautiful began as a motion picture and turned into a phenomenon for two main reasons: the aggressive marketing campaign of Miramax, its American distributor; and the criticism it provoked from some intelligent critics. As with *Schindler's List* a few years earlier, commercial success and a string of major awards rendered Benigni's effort suspect among intellectuals. Its multiple Oscar nominations coincided, uncoincidentally, with the nominations accumulated by *Shakespeare in Love*, also a Miramax release. When the latter won Best Film (over *Saving Private Ryan*) – as well as Best Actress for Gwyneth Paltrow – it was clear that Miramax's massive advertising campaign had paid off. To see Paltrow and Benigni (the first actor since Sophia Loren in *Two Women* to win the Oscar in a foreign-language film) "crowned" together indicated marketing muscle.

The phenomenon grew when Miramax decided to create and release a dubbed version of *Life Is Beautiful* in 1999. After becoming the most successful foreign film of all time in the United States (since surpassed by *Crouching Tiger, Hidden Dragon*), *Life Is Beautiful* could be seen in English (extremely well dubbed, particularly by Jonathan Nichols as Guido). Among other things, the dubbing makes the film a fine introduction to the Holocaust for children. (And to hear the characters speaking English removes the film even further from "reality," which is a positive thing.)

Numerous critics chafed at the success of what they saw as a safe and evasive crowd pleaser. Thane Rosenbaum, for example, wrote in *The Forward* of October 23, 1998, "*Life Is Beautiful* may be yet another example of society's obsession with exploiting the images and symbols of the Holocaust, in order to satisfy a popular culture that depends on atrocity for entertainment.... The camps were foremost about death, and, in their aftermath, memory, but on no occasion should they be used as a soundstage for slapstick" (p. 11). Amazed that Benigni's film received the Mayor's Prize at the Jerusalem Film Festival, Rosenbaum countered by quoting Theodor Adorno, "No poetry after Auschwitz," adding emphatically, "other than memoirs from the survivors themselves and documentary footage, art can't be made out of the ashes of Auschwitz, and to attempt otherwise is both sacrilege and sin." His moral outrage was matched by that of Cyril Frey in *Le Nouveau Cinéma* of February 1999: the French article questioned whether maintaining innocence is more important than confronting the truth of danger. (Perhaps the sign "No Jews or Dogs Allowed" should have been a spur to Guido's educating his son – and the audience – about the reality of racial laws and Nazi venom.) And, as Frey points out, the two "survivors" at the end of the film are Dora and Giosue – neither, strictly speaking, Jewish.

J. Hoberman, speaking at "The Holocaust in Cinema: Memory, Politics, Representation" – a conference at the Graduate Center of the City University of New York in March 1999 – called the film "narcissistic" and inappropriately "reassuring, like *Schindler's List*." He faulted *Life Is Beautiful* for protecting the spectator even more than Giosue, and for showing "not only a child surviving Auschwitz, but surviving with innocence intact." Similarly, Frey constantly invokes Auschwitz as Benigni's frame of reference.

Life Is Beautiful, however, is not set in Auschwitz. There is no "Arbeit Macht Frei" sign. The Nazis created a spectrum of camps, from labor, to concentration, to extermination. Benigni's father, for example, was imprisoned in a camp in Germany that was not designed for extermination: as the director told me in Cannes, his (non-Jewish) father was "in Albania when Italy stopped fighting. So when Germans found Italian soldiers, they brought them to Interveleborgen, a camp that had no gas chambers or crematoria." (He added that his father used to tell him and his sisters stories at night of the camp: "We laughed, to avoid the trauma," he recalled.)

Life Is Beautiful was also attacked for implausibility, although Benigni worked with Milan's Center for Contemporary Jewish Documentation to educate himself about this era, when eight thousand Italian Jews were deported. Rosenbaum, for example, wrote about Guido's outmaneuvering of the Nazis, "such quick-footed and quick-witted improvisation is made possible only through a Hollywood lens. The actual camps allowed for no such triumphant moments." But *Life Is Beautiful* turned out to be strikingly similar (if unwittingly) to a real case. In *The Jewish Week* (New York) of March 26, 1999, an article by Stewart Ain reported, "Recently discovered archival records of the American Jewish Joint Distribution Committee document the story of Joseph Schleifstein." Born in 1941, Joseph was sent with his parents to Buchenwald in 1943: "In the general confusion of lining up . . . Joseph's father found a large sack and, with a stern warning to keep absolutely quiet, placed his 2 1/2-year-old child in it. . . . Joseph remained in Buchenwald – hidden from the Nazis with the help of his father and two German anti-fascists – until the camp was liberated by the U.S. Army on April 12, 1945, according to the file." (Joseph was subsequently reunited with his mother, who survived Bergen-Belsen.)

The whereabouts of Joseph Schleifstein were unknown when the article appeared. One month later, the headline on the cover of the April 23, 1999, issue was, "*Life Is Beautiful* Child Breaks 50-Year Silence." Schleifstein had been located for an interview by *The Jewish Week*, and recalled details of Buchenwald more incredible than what Benigni devised. According to the article, he was "initially hidden by his father. But eventually, he said, the Nazi guards learned of his presence and used him to take roll call in the morning. 'I remember saluting them,' he said. 'I became the Germans' mascot and would say, "All prisoners accounted for." . . . I guess they didn't feel a need to kill me.' . . . But when there were formal inspections by visiting Nazi officials, he said he was hidden." After the war, Schleifstein kept his wartime experiences a secret from his two children: " 'The perception of people who went through the Holocaust was that they were damaged stuff,'" he explained. 'I didn't want that stigma.' "

This second article by Stewart Ain also quoted the book *Hitler's Death Camps* by Konnilyn G. Feig, which mentions not only a boys' choir at Buchenwald, but how "in the final weeks of the war, a 4-year-old boy, Stefan Jerzy Zweig, was smuggled into the camp in his father's rucksack. During inspections, the boy was gagged and tucked beneath the floorboards. Zweig later immigrated to Israel and in 1964 was an all-star player on the Israeli national handball team." While stories such as Zweig's and Schleifstein's are obviously rare among the innumerable Jewish children slaughtered by the Nazis, they provide a bit of support for defenders of *Life Is Beautiful.*

The question at the base of the debate is whether humor can coexist with a cinematic representation of the Holocaust. (Theatrical representation was given widespread critical and box-office approval when *The Producers* – a musical comedy based on Mel Brooks's film – opened on Broadway in 2001.) A persuasively affirmative answer was offered by the critic Colin MacCabe in the British periodical *Sight and Sound* of February 1999:

> Comedy is the genre that celebrates the social. Traditionally, comedies end with a marriage, confirming the power of society to reproduce itself. Tragedy is the domain of the individual, traditionally ending with the death of the hero who can't conform to the demands of the community. *Life Is Beautiful* takes for its subject matter the Holocaust – the attempt to build a new social order on the systematic extermination of an entire race. The horror of the camps defies all genres. In a world where murder is an instrument of state policy, all notions of the individual or the social are negated. Benigni's magnificent film attempts the impossible: to make a comedy out of the Holocaust, to find an affirmation of society in the death of all social relations.

To the extent that humor can heighten our understanding of the human condition, its prohibition in art seems senseless. Black comedy, for example, has been an antidote to systematic insanity in great works of literature and film. As Edward Rothstein wrote in the *New York Times* of October 18, 1998 – praising *Life Is Beautiful* – "Humor may be, in its essence, anti-fascistic: It takes what is most self-important, most un-yielding and most unforgiving, and dissolves it into absurdity. Fascism meets its match in farce. . . . For doesn't fascism itself seem like a form of hypnotic enchantment, bind-ing a nation to join in its singular horrors?" (There is indeed something particularly Italian about Benigni's methods, reaching back to the tradition of commedia dell'arte.

Joseph Schleifstein in Buchenwald, where he survived in a manner remarkably similar to the little boy in *Life Is Beautiful*. PHOTO COURTESY OF THE AMERICAN JEWISH JOINT DISTRIBUTION COMMITTEE ARCHIVES.

MacCabe alludes to this in calling the actor-director "the supreme European clown of his generation," while Rothstein reminds us that in the Italian commedia dell'arte, the buffoon often faces death.)

The extraordinary international popularity of *Life Is Beautiful* means that audiences – which might otherwise not have been aware of the Nazi persecution of Italian Jewry – embraced an appealing Jewish hero who inspires respect rather than merely pity. It may have smoothed the way for the release of a Hollywood film in September 1999 (one month after the dubbed version of *Life Is Beautiful*): *Jakob the Liar* invited inevitable – and often unflattering – comparison with Benigni's benignly made fable. In this remake of the East German film of 1974 – both based on the novel by Jurek Becker, who died in 1997 – we once again find the improvisational comic skills of a Jewish protagonist used to both save a child and lighten the movie's tone. The lies of Jakob (Robin Williams, also the executive producer of *Jakob the Liar*) are not just for Lina, the little girl he has found and hidden in his room, but for an entire Polish ghetto in 1944.

This version is directed by Peter Kassovitz, who had been a Jewish child in Nazi-occupied Budapest. He and his parents survived, and emigrated to France during the 1956 Hungarian Revolution. Although Kassovitz is based in Paris, and the film was shot in Poland and Hungary, *Jakob the Liar* has a distinctly "Hollywood" tone. Jakob accidentally hears a broadcast about the Russian advance on a German officer's radio. Then, to stop his friend Kowalski (Bob Balaban) from hanging himself, he claims to have a radio himself (a crime punishable by death). He tells the young boxer Misha (Liev Schreiber) the same thing, to stop him from assaulting a German. Word spreads, and suddenly Jakob is a hero of hope. Only Professor Kirschbaum (Armin Mueller-Stahl, who appeared in the original German film) is on to him; nevertheless, he helps preserve the illusion because the suicide rate in the ghetto has dwindled to zero.

Whereas the original *Jakob, der Lugner* questions the protagonist's lies because they prevent the Jews from organizing and resisting, the American version simplifies by making his lies the impetus for resistance. And whereas the original Jakob is not killed onscreen, Williams's character is more like Benigni's – shot as a resister because he refuses to announce that there was no radio. Most problematic is the ending, reminiscent of the coda in *Korczak*: instead of the freeze-frames on each Jew in the transport found in *Jakob, der Lugner*, the remake literalizes one of Jakob's fantasies – rescue by a Russian tank, accompanied by American swing music. This ending invites a kind of revisionist hope, suggesting that Hollywood is Jakob, preferring illusion to the depiction of gritty reality.

Like all good fairy tales, these films are symbolic rather than literal, allowing our imaginations to confront dark forces as well as love. Ultimately, the lies of Jakob and Guido may be as much for themselves as for the children they are protecting: they too desperately need to escape Nazi dehumanization by putting on a happy face. The audience is led to identify, not only with the desire to protect a child, but with Jakob and Guido's ability to enter and sustain a grand illusion – which is, after all, what a viewer does in a movie theater.

18
Dysfunction as Distortion: The Holocaust Survivor on Screen and Stage

The artistic representation of the dysfunctional survivor is pervasive, long-standing, and lamentable. Like the depiction of the deranged Vietnam War veteran onscreen, the cliché exists even in masterful motion pictures. The survivor's damage has been presented as extreme, from the bloody, speared hand of Sol Nazerman that closes *The Pawnbroker* to the heroine's suicide at the end of *Sophie's Choice*. By the late 1990s, the images were more subtle – and perhaps, therefore, more insidious. In two films released during 1996, *Shine* and *The Substance of Fire*, as well as two plays produced that year in New York – *Old Wicked Songs* and *The Shawl* – the Holocaust survivors are either tyrannical, suicidal, or mentally unhinged.

Shine, the Australian drama that recounts the true story of David Helfgott, and *The Substance of Fire*, adapted from Jon Robin Baitz's acclaimed play, share a father figure who is "damaged goods." Peter Helfgott (Armin Mueller-Stahl) and Isaac Geldhart (Ron Rifkin) create dysfunctional families, and are depicted as dictators unable to really hear what their sons are saying. This image may be dramatically more viable than presenting "normalcy" or adaptation – and is perhaps true to a small segment of the survivor population – but is ultimately a distortion.

Shine, directed by Scott Hicks from an original screenplay by Jan Sardi, is a deeply moving film biography, tracing David Helfgott's life from child prodigy, to institutionalized recluse, to brilliant pianist. It begins in the early 1980s, when David (Geoffrey Rush, who won a well-deserved Academy Award for Best Actor) stumbles into a wine bar on a rainy night. It is apparent from the opening credit sequence, with David's profile on the edge of the black screen, that he has a kind of logorrhea – breathlessly repeated phrases, witty fragments followed by an "oh" that humorously goes down five notes – and doesn't see objective reality very well from behind his thick glasses.

Flashbacks reveal that he is the son of a Polish-Jewish immigrant (Mueller-Stahl) who tyrannizes his silent wife and four children. David wins competitions, but Peter won't allow him to accept offers to study abroad. By his late teens, David (Noah Taylor) defies his father, goes to the Royal College of Music on a scholarship, and is essentially disowned by Peter. In London, our eccentric pianist is trained by Professor Parkes (Sir John Gielgud) and decides to tackle the "Rach 3" – Rachmaninoff's toughest piece. He completes the challenge triumphantly, only to collapse during the applause. After the breakdown, he is institutionalized. Years later, he is the chain-smoking, childlike David (Rush) of the film's opening. He meets Gillian (Lynn Redgrave), a visiting astrologer, who agrees to marry him. Returning to the stage, he plays beautifully for an audience that includes his mother, sister, and first teacher.

While Armin Mueller-Stahl's excellent performance as the overbearing Peter earned him an Academy Award nomination, the representation of the domestic tyrant may be more of a dramatic ploy than realistic reconstruction. *Shine* does not clearly make the point that he is a refugee who emigrated from Poland to Australia before World War II. "He got exterminated, didn't he?" David sputters in the wine bar about "Daddy's daddy" (p. 6 of the published screenplay). Later, he says, "like Daddy and his family before they were concentrated" (p. 19). And in two subsequent scenes, Holocaust imagery is invoked visually: the sight of barbed wire freezes Peter in one (p. 25); in the other, his daughter asks to see his scar – "where the lion scratched you" – and he begins to roll up his sleeve. Whereas the script has him showing a long jagged scar (p. 27), in the film he stops before the arm is revealed, and mutters, "that's what happens when you get too close to the bars."

Thane Rosenbaum's incisive article in the *New York Times* ("Arts and Leisure") of March 2, 1997, also suggests "the legacy of the Holocaust" as one of the possible "suspects" that the film offers for David's descent into madness. The author cites Margaret Helfgott, David's older sister, who wrote to newspapers about the distortion: "In the film, my father seems to roll up his sleeve. Many people who have seen the film interpreted this to mean . . . a number from the concentration camps." She questioned her father's portrayal "as a brutal Holocaust survivor, as if the Holocaust was responsible." Rosenbaum concedes that even if *Shine* is not a Holocaust story, "whether concealed or unintended, the Holocaust images . . . are present."

Mueller-Stahl is best known to American audiences from two disparate roles, the Jewish grandfather in *Avalon* and the father of Jessica Lange – who turns out to be a World War II criminal – in *The Music Box*. He told me that he rooted his characterization of Peter in details that preceded the Holocaust: "We see in Peter how too much love can destroy. As a child Peter had wanted to play the violin but his father wouldn't allow it. So he is trying to be the opposite of his father by pushing his son to be a great pianist. But he's a very strong person and he pushes too hard."

Nonetheless, it is difficult to ignore that the obsession to keep the family together at all costs is connected to the extermination by the Nazis of the family who remained in Poland. Consequently, Scott Hicks might have fallen into the very trap he warned against: "I'm very aware that in making this film, one is dealing with material that has its origins in someone's life story, and it requires great care. It's too easy to be judgmental and . . . to draw pop-psychology conclusions," he said in the production notes prepared by Fine Line Features for the film's U.S. release.

It is even easier to descend into a reductive reading of the father in *The Substance of Fire* – the patriarch as dictator or emotional Nazi with his children. The opening sequence of the film directed by Daniel Sullivan shows a little boy hidden in an attic, watching Nazis burning books in France. The World War II context is developed in the film's present tense, as Isaac (Rifkin) publishes serious books like *The Architecture of Auschwitz*, and is losing money to print a four-volume study of the Nazi medical experiments.

His son Aaron (Tony Goldwyn) tries to convince Isaac to publish an impending best-seller, a novel by his lover, Val (Gil Bellows). When he refuses, Aaron enlists the help of his sister Sarah (Sarah Jessica Parker) – an actress on a children's TV show – and brother Martin (Timothy Hutton), an architecture teacher at Vassar who has Hodgkin's Disease. They agree that their father is running the company into the ground – perhaps due to having been recently widowed – and they take away his control. Isaac refuses to speak to Aaron, becoming more reclusive and mentally unstable. Martin tries to keep an eye on him, but this sensitive son finally dies. After Martin's funeral, there is a possibility of reconciliation as the family sits in Gramercy Park.

The elegantly acerbic, self-made (and self-absorbed) Isaac may initially appear quite different from Peter in *Shine*. Both, however, virtually disown their children. Believing themselves betrayed, these aged orphans prefer self-righteous "mourning" to discussion or compromise; indeed, Peter burns his scrapbook of David's accomplishments, a symbolic death that relates to the book burning in the first scene of *The Substance of Fire*. According to Sullivan (in the press kit prepared by Miramax Films), who also directed the award-winning stage version of *The Substance of Fire*, Isaac's "obsession with his own childhood – the guilt he bears for not being able to share his parents' and grandparents' pain – blinds him to his own children's pain, so that he doesn't see the destruction that's going on right in his own home. His obsession has isolated him."

Critical reaction to the play was enthusiastic; for example, Frank Rich's *New York Times* review declared, "As written with both scrupulous investigative zeal and bottomless sympathy by Mr. Baitz and as acted in a career-transforming performance by Ron Rifkin, Isaac Geldhart is one of the most memorable and troubling characters to appear on-stage this season." Other reviews of the film were also respectful, but the most pungent remark was made by Roger Ebert on the TV broadcast *Siskel and Ebert at the Movies*: "Bringing the Holocaust into this film is a distraction, as it was in *Shine*," he observed on March 30, 1997, "trivializing it as a senseless, aimless plot point."

The plot point is far better integrated in *Old Wicked Songs*, Jon Marans's play directed by Seth Barrish at Manhattan's Promenade Theatre. It begins like a comedy: an uptight young American, Stephen Hoffman (Justin Kirk), arrives in 1986 Vienna to study piano. But instead of the professor he was expecting, he finds Mashkan (Hal Robinson), who is as tolerant of schmaltz or sentiment as Stephen is resistant to it. The former piano prodigy claims to be a WASP, and Mashkan makes anti-Semitic remarks. But by the end of act 1, Stephen confesses that he is Jewish, and it becomes increasingly apparent during act 2 that Mashkan is a Jewish Holocaust survivor. Although he seemed like the stronger one in this two-character play, Mashkan tries to kill himself with sleeping pills, and Stephen realizes this is not the first attempt. Mashkan agrees to tell him his Holocaust story, but – appropriately – it is whispered out of audience earshot, respecting the professor's privacy.

By the end, *Old Wicked Songs* presents a dramatic symbiosis that allows for the revelation of deeper feelings – Mashkan's of solitude, Stephen's of anger. Because their means of expression is music, especially Schumann's "Dichterliebe," the connections to *Shine* become more provocative: music is both subject and metaphor for transcendence, engendering a new father–son relationship. (Indeed, the script of *Shine* ends with a scene that does not appear in the final film: David plays the piano for Professor Parkes, a symbolic substitution for contact with his own father.)

The absence of women – notably mothers – in these works is striking: in *Shine* David's mother is mute and invisible except when cooking in the background, while in *The Substance of Fire*, Isaac's wife is already dead. Would active maternal female characters have diluted their focus on the legacy that wounded, tyrannical males leave to the tormented sons?

An exception was Cynthia Ozick's 1996 play, *The Shawl* – perhaps because the author is female. Directed by Sidney Lumet (more than thirty years after *The Pawnbroker*), it centers on Auschwitz survivor Rosa (Dianne Wiest), who has never accepted the death of her baby daughter, Mogda, born in the camp. She even speaks to Mogda, as if the child were before her. Rosa's niece Stella (Wendy Makkena) is also a survivor, but she has managed to make a modern life for herself. After Rosa smashes the items in her antique shop, she ends up in a Miami Jewish senior citizens' home. The dramatic crux is the arrival of a blandly handsome WASP, the smoothly insidious Gardner (Boyd Gaines). First, he seduces the vulnerable Stella; then he convinces Rosa that Mogda is an illusion and leads her to sign a paper – which turns out to be a statement for Holocaust denial. Rosa and Stella survive this revisionist, but acknowledge that they will never be "normal." Once again, a creative work equates survival with insanity, or at least the inability to move on.

Even an internationally respected Israeli film like *The Summer of Aviya* (1990) falls into a similar trap of stereotyping. The semiautobiographical novel of the Israeli actress Gila Almagor was the basis for her script (cowritten with Haim Bouzaglo and Eli Cohen, the film's director), and she stars as Henya. This moving drama of the tense relationship between a survivor mother and young daughter is told from the perspective of the now grown-up Aviya. She narrates how the summer of 1951, when she was ten, began with the mother (Almagor) attending her boarding-school play. The effect of the presence of Henya, a survivor who has been in mental hospitals since the war's end, is to render Aviya (Kaipo Cohen) suddenly mute. When her mother discovers lice on her, she takes Aviya home and brutally snips off all her hair – making her look like a concentration camp inmate. The bald daughter of the "crazy Partisanka" (as Henya is called) is ostracized. By the end, Henya's mental condition deteriorates, and Aviya must return to boarding school. In the background of this film is the lack of understanding that Holocaust survivors encounter from other Israelis.

By 1995, Eli Cohen directed *Under the Domim Tree* – the sequel to *The Summer of Aviya* – again adapted from Gila Almagor's novel and script. This Israeli drama traces Aviya's coming-of-age in a state-run boarding school. The same actresses play out the continuing tension – Henya is in a psychiatric hospital – but the focus shifts to Aviya's friend Mira: this abused orphan is claimed by a couple as their daughter, but she refuses to have anything to do with them. They go to trial and, just as the judge is about to order Mira to return to them, she remembers her real name and family.

The adjustment is difficult for her as well as the other Polish-Jewish orphans, but the film's central metaphor suggests optimism. Wim, their beloved gardener, has planted tulips under the domin tree, despite the assumption that nothing can grow there. The last scene, of course, shows the flourishing tulips in the hard land – an image of regeneration that is, among other things, an antidote to Henya's hospitalization.

For those of us known as "second-generation," being the children of Jewish Holocaust survivors is a complex process. While the experience of each survivor is too unique and complex for generalization, our parents have transmitted a complicated legacy: we have been made aware both of their devastation in Europe – dispossessed, deported, tortured, and imprisoned during World War II – and of the resilience and hope they created in the postwar years. But would we recognize our parents in the images presented by films as well as plays? Probably not, given that the protagonists consumed by insanity or destructiveness ring false, or at least reductive. Many of our fathers have been gentle, many of our mothers resilient. But popular culture depicts them either as control freaks – who could be seen as identifying with the enemy – or as self-destructive.

The filmmaker Aviva Kempner has been an articulate foe of the ongoing stereotype: "I find it disturbing – as the child of a Holocaust survivor and an avid moviegoer – that survivors are always 'meshugenah' onscreen," the director of *The Life and Times of Hank Greenberg* said to me. "And the females – from Meryl Streep's Sophie to Lena Olin in 'Enemies' – are suicidal. In Israeli cinema, there is an even more egregious stereotyping: although *The Summer of Aviya* is a brilliant film, I was disturbed to learn that Gila Almagor's mother was not in fact a survivor! Can't someone go insane without being a victim of the Holocaust?"

"It's even worse in *The Wooden Gun*," continued the producer of *Partisans of Vilna*.

> In this Israeli film, kids make fun of a survivor who is a ranting madwoman. I find this insidious. Part of the motivating factor in making *Partisans of Vilna* was to offer examples of survivors who clearly went on to make "normal" lives after the war. They talk about that time without going into tears or a catatonic state. The stories of survivors becoming crazy or committing suicide might be the most dramatic; but for me, the greatest drama is in how survivors like my mother and her friends created new lives despite the horror they suffered during the war.

It is no surprise that Israeli films in particular tend to reinforce the cliché. In the new state that was creating a heroic, future-oriented self-image, discussion of the Holocaust was avoided, and survivors were not encouraged to tell their tales. An article entitled "Circle of Pain" in the magazine *inside/out* (2000) tells of a recent study at Hadassah University Hospital in Jerusalem: "Scientists have done it again. They've launched an elaborate ... study to confirm what we've already known for several decades – that the experience of the Holocaust didn't end with its survivors but was handed down to their children like an unwanted heirloom, causing extreme vulnerability to emotional distress," writes Aviva Patz. Published in *The American Journal of Psychiatry*, the study of Israeli second-generation members diagnosed with breast cancer found "that the children of Holocaust survivors scored much higher on tests for depression, anxiety, hostility and negative feelings than patients in the control group." Curiously, the author doesn't make a crucial point that is obvious from one of her examples: "Her parents never talked about their experiences, but somehow Michaela knew they suffered from an inconsolable anguish." If there is trauma for the child of the Holocaust survivor, it is more likely to come from silence than from genealogy – from secrecy rather than awareness.

Simplistic stereotypes are found primarily in fictional plays and films (even when brilliantly acted – like Maximilian Schell's survivor characters in both *The Rose Garden* and *Left Luggage*). But the documentary form is not exempt. *The Long Way Home* (1997), directed by Mark Jonathan Harris for the Simon Wiesenthal Center, is a sympathetic exploration of the postwar period when tens of thousands of European refugees attempted the clandestine voyage to Palestine. "I am certain that 90 percent of those who survived will never really be normal," says a male voice-over, presented without attribution: "They have suffered too much." Harris explained during an interview that these words were spoken by a British chaplain, adding:

> For me, the film is a refutation of that line. Most of all, I wanted to look at how the survivors themselves managed to begin again. For me it is their resilience, their determination, their humanity in the face of the world's indifference, that is most moving and important to convey. The fact that they chose to live again in the world that had betrayed them. That they chose to put their energies into life rather than vengeance – to remarry, to have children, to believe in the future.

Nevertheless, *The Long Way Home* – winner of the Academy Award for Best Documentary – is less convincing on this point than the director's assessment.

One of the few artistic works that move beyond the simplistic stereotyping is *Children of . . .*, a theater piece written and performed by children and grandchildren of survivors. Begun as a workshop under the auspices of the American Jewish Theatre in 1993, the play has been performed throughout schools and religious centers, as well as at the U.S. Holocaust Museum in June 1996. Directed by Gary Resch, *Children of . . .* shares with the works discussed above a father who cannot relate to his son, and the absence of a mother; however, it interweaves fictional scenes with personal monologues by the actors. The summation of their collective experiences is dramatized in the story of the fictional Einsider family. When the father Sol – a survivor of Auschwitz – dies, his grandson Moishe discovers a family secret: during World War II, Sol sent his two-year-old son to France to be saved; after the war, unable to find one another, each thought the other dead.

The grown son, now named Jack Rogers, is a construction worker, a bitter, solitary man with no past. He is unaware that he has a family – that Sol remarried and had a son, Bob. When Moishe finds Jack and tries to arrange a reunion via a Passover seder, Jack throws him out. The reconciliation finally occurs on Passover, after a confrontation between the half-brothers: Jack is jealous because he never had a father, while Bob is resentful because Sol showed him no affection, treating him like a substitute for someone lost to him. Ultimately, each takes a step closer to the other, as well as to understanding their father. It seems that they will try to fulfill the content of the closing song, "Carry On."

According to Mark Ethan Toporek, who plays Jack, *Children of . . .* was meant not only as a therapeutic exercise for the actor-writers, but to sensitize audiences to the particular legacy that Holocaust survivors leave their children: " 'Dysfunctional' is an overused word: all families are probably dysfunctional if you look closely enough," he told me. "It would be unnatural for some of our parents not to have a heightened sense of fear and certain phobias. But many went on to live lives which were that much more precious because of what they had endured." In terms of motion pictures, the reductive depiction of the survivor has indeed become a facile conceit. We are still waiting for artistic representations of Jewish men and women who – although damaged by World War II – are nevertheless capable of regeneration, nurturing, and transcendence.

19
Documentaries
of Return

Although the original intention of my *Indelible Shadows* was to assemble and analyze fiction films about the Holocaust, nonfiction has proven to be not only more appropriate but often more dramatic as an approach to this subject matter. By the second edition in 1989, there was a vigorous body of work which I had termed "personal documentary," characterized by subjectivity: a film would chronicle the return of a survivor to a place that no longer knows him or her, usually a hometown tantamount to loss, or a concentration camp still redolent of terror.

This phenomenon has grown into what could be considered a subgenre of the Holocaust film, especially as children of survivors increasingly journey with a camera into Europe, and into the past. In films of return, the director – frequently a member of the second generation – goes back to the scene of the crime, or of the rescue. Some of these documentaries are investigative, like *Loving the Dead, Birthplace*, and (to a lesser extent) *Shtetl*, in which the subjects attempt to find out how their Polish-Jewish parents were murdered. Some are commemorative, such as *The Last Days* and *Bach in Auschwitz*. Others are celebratory, like *The Children of Chabannes* and *The Optimists*, which chronicle the rescue of Jews in France and Bulgaria. And *Photographer* utilizes the cinematic medium in fresh ways to explore how ultimately untrustworthy – or at least incomplete – images of the Holocaust can be.

The physical return of a survivor to ghostly killing fields was first presented in fairly straightforward documentaries like *Kitty: Return to Auschwitz* (1980) and *Return to Poland* (1981). In 1984, Robert Clary (the actor who played Louis Lebeau in TV's popular series, *Hogan's Heroes*) went back to his former homes of Paris, the Drancy internment camp, and Buchenwald for the film, *Robert Clary 5714: A Memoir of Liberation*. One year later, the actor and teacher Jack Garfein was the focus of *A Journey Back* (Canada, 1985), a documentary made for the CBC in which he returns to Auschwitz as well as his Slovakian hometown (whose synagogue is an abandoned warehouse for ovens). In 1990, Emanuel Rund's documentary *All Jews Out* (*Alle Juden Raus!* Germany) includes on-camera interviews of Inge Auerbacher and her mother returning to their German town as well as their former prison of Theresienstadt.

By the late 1980s, films narrated by second-generation voices also sought out those who hid and saved their parents. For example, *The Righteous Enemy* (Italy and

U.K., 1987), directed by Joseph Rochlitz, begins with the story of his father – who was interned by the Italians – and proceeds to explore Italian resistance (including how Italian officials saved approximately forty thousand Jews from deportation to concentration camps). Melissa Hacker's *My Knees Were Jumping: Remembering the Kindertransports* (U.S.A., 1996) centers on the Holocaust survival of her own mother, famed costume designer Ruth Morley, before expanding to others who were lucky enough to be in the Kindertransports. Interspersed are scenes of their reunion, acknowledging not only their good fortune to be taken in by England between December 1938 and August 1939, but their ruptured childhoods.

When the London-based filmmaker Mira Hamermesh returned to Poland to find the resting places of her parents, the result was twofold: her personal and mournful quest as a daughter expanded into the inspiring discovery of renewed Polish-Jewish life. Made for the BBC in 1991, her fifty-five-minute documentary begins quite subjectively: through Hamermesh's eyes, we see the fictional image of her parents banging on the car window in which she now travels. Her mother died of hunger in the Lodz Ghetto in May 1943, and her father was killed in Auschwitz. Hamermesh includes poignant details: for example, the fragile thermometer her father put in the window survived longer than her parents. She walks on the ground in Auschwitz where he would have spent his last days. In Lodz, she finds her mother's death record.

After feeling haunted by the ghost of her mother, she feels heartened by the young Polish people she meets. Jan Yagelsky is a non-Jewish caretaker of Jewish memory: he too feels the demands of the dead. Alix, a high school student, was told by her grandmother on her deathbed that she is Jewish. She now lights Sabbath candles with young Jews; and when she is in church, the priest delivers a sermon on how Poles must ask forgiveness of their Jewish brothers and sisters. Mateusz, a high school student whose mother is Jewish and his father a tolerant Catholic, has decided to become a religious Jew. In his Warsaw classroom, students and the female teacher speak openly about contemporary anti-Semitism. Yolanta, a non-Jewish actress – part of an amateur theater group in Tykocin, the hometown of Hamermesh's father – puts on a Jewish-themed play, with the whole troupe assuming a "Jewish look." This becomes an eerie touch in the film, as Hamermesh then places these figures in the very landscape of Tykocin – a town whose synagogue is now a museum, a town near a mass grave where Tykocin's three thousand Jews were shot and buried during World War II.

Loving the Dead ends with a juxtaposition of death and life: Hamermesh locates her mother's tombstone in Lodz, and then we see the young Polish Jews singing in Hebrew at a Sabbath dinner. Beyond a Judaism of ashes and memory, Alix – and the director – has found a living religion. This film, which was also shown on Polish television, can be viewed as an antidote to *Shoah*: Hamermesh does not see Poland and Judaism as mutually exclusive.

Birthplace (Poland, 1992) makes an excellent double bill with *Loving the Dead*, as the director Pavel Lozinski follows Henry Greenberg from the United States to Poland. In this powerful fifty-minute documentary, Greenberg – a Polish-born American Jew – returns to his native village to find out what happened to his family during World War II. (He and his mother escaped with false Aryan papers.) He asks peasants – all of whom seem to remember his beautiful mother and decent father – about his little brother and father. Unlike the blatantly anti-Semitic population of *Shoah*, some peasants recall giving his parents food or a night's shelter, trying to justify their small but risky deeds to the son.

He slowly learns that his brother was shot by an SS man, while his father – and this is a more difficult story for him to trace – was murdered by a neighbor with whom he left his cows. Although the neighbor is now dead, Greenberg confronts the man's brother, who is reticent, until the murderer's nephew comes out to threaten him. They finally find the spot where his father was buried. Since Lozinski – a young Polish director whose father, Marcel, is a famous documentary filmmaker – wisely eschews both narration and music, the simple accumulation of details in *Birthplace* is devastating: we see the peasants digging until they find the bottle his father always carried for milk. Finally, Greenberg digs up his father's skull. As in Jedbawne or Kielce, the chilling reality is that the killers were Poles rather than Nazis.

Birthplace provides a spectrum of Polish behavior, from fatal opportunism to qualified decency. It is therefore close in spirit to *Shtetl* (1996), Marian Marzynski's probing three-hour documentary that aired on PBS, with a companion book by the great writer Eva Hoffman. Although it evolves from his *Return to Poland*, he is no longer the central figure, nor is his own biography the point of departure. There are no Jews left in Bransk, a Polish town whose population before World War II was 60 percent Jewish. Marzynski's friend Nathan Kaplan wants to go to Bransk, not only because his parents lived there, but because of his two-year correspondence with Zbyszek, a Gentile devoted to research of Jewish history in Bransk. They journey from Chicago to Poland, where Zbyszek has invited them to stay in his home. (In a bold display of hospitality, his parents sleep in a tent outside.) Nathan and Zbyszek nourish each other.

Relics of Jewish life are presented with vivid and often disturbing details. For example, when they visit an abandoned cemetery in Orla, near the Russian border, it is surreal to see sheep run out. From a convent, they dig up Jewish gravestones that the Nazis took for paving roads: the inscriptions can be read only after Nathan sprays them with shaving cream to bring out the letters. In a climactic scene, they replace the stones in the area that was the Jewish cemetery.

The next two sections of *Shtetl* chronicle subsequent journeys. In the first, Zbyszek comes to America to meet Bransk survivors. After Nathan dies, Marzynski takes Zbyszek everywhere, translating for him in Atlanta or Baltimore. Zbyszek later goes back to Poland with another Bransk survivor, Jack Rubin, once a popular teenager in charge of thousands of geese! As in the first return, they try to find and confront those who either killed or denounced Jews, but this turns out to be futile. Each person they approach is either senile or in denial – until Jack is reunited with an old man who was good to him during the war.

The last section of *Shtetl* is riveting, as our "hero" Zbyszek seems to cave in to cowardice. He is now vice-mayor of Bransk, and has received threats because of his philo-Semitism. He is preparing a ceremony for the five hundredth anniversary of Bransk. Marzynski urges him to include mention of the Jews on the plaque they have erected, as well as in his speech. Zbyszek feels he cannot, claiming that the schism between his public and private self must be maintained. To generalize about individuals or about Bransk becomes impossible.

Because Mira Hamermesh and Marian Marzynski are themselves "child survivors," their point of departure is necessarily more personal than those of objective documentaries like *The Last Days* (U.S.A., 1999) and *Bach in Auschwitz* (*La Chaconne d'Auschwitz*, The Netherlands, 1999). The survivors interviewed in both films of 1999 are linked by a place: Hungary was the country of origin for the collective protagonist of *The Last Days*, while Auschwitz was to be the final destination for the female musicians of the Dutch film. Directed by James Moll for the Shoah Foundation, *The Last Days* won the Academy Award for Best Documentary. It consists not simply of talking heads bearing witness, but newly discovered color footage of the concentration camps, scenes of the survivors' return to Hungary, and a fascinating interview with a former Nazi doctor. With the exception of the Greek Sonderkommando Gabbai, all the survivors are Hungarians who were rounded up late in the war, and their testimony is filed with memorable detail. They include the articulate and engaging U.S. congressman Tom Lantos (who was saved by Raoul Wallenberg); Renee Firestone, who recalls her inability to part with a bathing suit her father had given her when she was a happy teenager; Irene Zisblatt, who kept swallowing the tiny diamonds her mother had given her to buy bread, and kept retrieving them from her feces in Auschwitz; Alice Lok Cahana, who returns with her kind husband, children, and grandchildren to Bergen-Belsen to say Kaddish for her sister; and Bill Basch, who had to betray his friends in order to survive Buchenwald.

Dr. Hans Munch calls Auschwitz "a thankful workplace" because he was able to do medical experiments there. But the aged former Nazi physician says he was acquitted precisely because he conducted "harmless" experiments in order to keep the women from being gassed. It is unnerving to see him in the same shot with Renee: she asks him about her sister Klara, who died there after medical experiments; he matter-of-factly says that six months was the "normal period" for life expectancy in Auschwitz. His recollections, as well as those of three American veterans – one white, one African American, one Japanese American – who liberated Dachau, give the film an effective and affecting contrapuntal structure.

Bach in Auschwitz, directed by Michael Daeron and presented on HBO/CINEMAX, is about the women's orchestra, including interviews with twelve of the concentration camp survivors in nine countries. It begins with the feisty seventy-three-year-old French singer Violette, moves to Anita in England, Helene in Belgium, Flora in Holland, three friends in Israel, Eva in Germany, Margotte in the Czech Republic, and Yvette in the United States. The most moving interviews are saved for the end: Zosia and Helena, both Polish, literally go back to Auschwitz. There, surrounded by silence, Zosia describes how terrible it was to play during selections, deceiving the prisoners with reassuring music. They also mark the place where French Jews sang "La Marseillaise" on their way to the gas chamber.

All the women speak of the conductor Alma Rose, the film's invisible heroine who died in Auschwitz. *Bach in Auschwitz* is not the first reuniting frame for them: we learn that Margotte traveled to Germany to meet with Eva for the first time in fifty years, and Violette paid a surprise visit to Yvette in America. One can only imagine

One of the twelve survivors of the Auschwitz women's orchestra returns to the camp in *Bach in Auschwitz*. PHOTO COPYRIGHT MICHEL DAERON, FROM HIS FILM *LA CHACONNE D'AUSCHWITZ*.

the film's impact had they all been brought together as a group, playing music again! And while the film's structure could have been more dramatic via crosscutting, *Bach in Auschwitz* effectively counterpoints these women's recollections of survival.

Whereas the musicians of this Dutch documentary were spared because of talent, the children chronicled in *The Children of Chabannes* (U.S.A., 2000) survived through a combination of geographical luck and collective rescue. Directed, produced, and edited by Lisa Gossels and Dean Wetherell, this uplifting documentary – shown on HBO and released theatrically – returns to Chabannes, a small village in the Creuse region of central France. During World War II, its population of approximately three hundred managed to save nearly four hundred Jewish children – mainly refugees from Germany and Austria – including Gossels's father and uncle. They are part of a group photograph of youngsters which magically dissolves into the image of the now adult survivors in identical poses before the same château. Indeed, the 1996 reunion of the rescued children and their saviors inspired Gossels to begin making the film. She not only narrates, but interviews her father in the space of the shelter he was granted more than fifty years earlier.

Unlike Le Chambon – the French town celebrated in Pierre Sauvage's *Weapons of the Spirit* – Chabannes's inhabitants were neither Protestant nor particularly

Felix Chevrier and the children of Chabannes in 1942, from the film *The Children of Chabannes*.

religious, and they did not know Jews from before the war. Nevertheless, the OSE (Oeuvre de Secours aux Enfants, a Jewish rescue organization) entrusted the children to the château of Chabannes. Felix Chevrier, a Freemason who administered their sanctuary, was joined by a vast network of courageous villagers similarly outraged by Nazi policies. (The locals did not read the anti-Semitic, right-wing Parisian newspapers.) Chevrier integrated the refugees with local children, and made sure their minds were nourished while they were kept from deportation. Among the heroines are the schoolteachers Reine and Renee Paillassou: now interviewed in their eighties, they recall an exceptional haven from which only six were deported (and they still feel a bitter loss vis-à-vis the four who died).

The Paillassou sisters are among those who recount how – once the Germans had moved into southern France – the children were sent to Switzerland through an underground railroad. And they read aloud a letter that attests to how much luckier the Chabannes child survivors were than those who endured concentration camps. This contextualizes the singular aspect of Chabannes's collective decency. As A. O. Scott wrote in his *New York Times* review of June 9, 2000:

> The survival of a few hundred children hardly mitigates the horror of the Holocaust, and this comparatively happy tale can be understood only with reference to the horrors of its context. There have been documentaries in epochal, large-scale films like *Shoah* and *The Sorrow and the Pity*. But the cinematic fulfillment of the imperative

to remember has more recently been taken up in smaller, more individuated acts of commemoration.%vspace*6pt

Another inspiring filmic commemoration is *The Optimists: The Story of the Rescue of the Bulgarian Jews from the Holocaust* (2001), directed by Jacky and Lisa Comforty. Like *The Children of Chabannes*, it moves from the personal – Jacky's family photo shows his father and two wives! – to the universal, namely how ordinary people acted with atypical decency toward their Jewish neighbors. Jacky Comforty returns to Bulgaria, blending his own narration with compelling interviews. Given the silence he grew up with in Israel vis-à-vis the Holocaust – "each generation tried to protect the other from memories of the past" – his return is both investigative and celebratory. The story he tells is quite amazing: because Bulgaria was officially Germany's ally, it enjoyed more leeway to protect Jews than did an occupied country. We see the tension between policy and polis, between secret deportation orders to ship out all the Jews and the refusal of the population to comply. Bulgaria became Germany's ally because of the political promise of occupying three neighboring territories – Macedonia, Yugoslavia, and Thrace. Despite the sorrowful fact that more than eleven thousand "Aegean Jews" were indeed deported and killed, approximately fifty thousand Bulgarian Jews slated for extermination were ultimately saved.

In March 1943, the deportation orders were foiled by two groups: four Christian men went to see the decent vice president of the Bulgarian parliament, Peshev, who was appalled enough by the news that he began a petition to halt the deportation,

From *The Optimists*, Rachamim Comforty and his two wives: he married Rachelle (*right*) after his first wife Rosa (*left*) died. Photo taken in Bulgaria, 1920. PHOTO COURTESY OF JACKY AND LISA COMFORTY. ALL RIGHTS RESERVED.

From *The Optimists*, Jewish laborers in a Bulgarian forced-labor camp near the Greek border in 1942. Jacky Comforty's father is first on the right. PHOTO COURTESY OF JACKY AND LISA COMFORTY.

supported by one-third of the parliament. (He was forced out of office afterward.) Simultaneously, Bishop Kharaalampiev (now a gently formidable ninety-two-year-old interviewee) called upon Bishop Kiril to save the Jews; Kiril announced that if they were deported, he would go with them.

Why did the Bulgarians refuse to hand over their neighbors? Why was there not even a ghetto there? *The Optimists* suggests that it was partly because Bulgaria had been oppressed by the Turks for five hundred years. And, as a rabbi says, Bulgarian Jews always invited Christians to synagogue, while they went to church on Easter. Anti-Semitism simply was not part of their lives (even if it existed in the ancestral memory of this Sephardic population, who originally escaped from the Spanish Inquisition).

Comforty seeks out the simple daily resistance of the population. For example, a teacher allowed four Jewish girls – including his mother – to become kindergarten teachers even though Jews were not permitted in the classroom; in a moving moment, we see both now aged women reunited. And, ironically enough, where did a baker hide a few Jews? In his oven. Jewish men did go to a forced labor camp, but the details they recall (heightened by evocative photographs) are filled with paradoxes. One tells of having had a phonograph with new American records as we hear "Indian Summer."

Niko, a musician, recalls putting on an opera – Offenbach's *La Belle Hélène* – in the labor camp! Niko is connected to the film's title, as The Optimists was the name of his jazz band. The title might also refer to how the audience feels after watching such a moving testament to human decency.

Comforty's previous film, *In the Shadow of Memory: Legacies of Lidice* (1999), can also be considered a documentary of return, with two crucial differences. Unlike Bulgaria's comparatively uplifting Holocaust story, the Czech town of Lidice was the site of extreme Nazi barbarism. In retaliation for the assassination of Reinhard Heydrich in 1942 – and to deter further acts of resistance in Czechoslovakia – the Nazis killed the Catholic village's 192 men, sent the 203 women to Ravensbruck concentration camp, murdered 82 children – giving up 16 for adoption by German families through the Lebensborn program – and destroyed the landscape of Lidice. When I asked the director why this town was singled out for annihilation, he replied, "two Czech pilots who escaped to London came from Lidice. Heydrich's assassins were paratroopers who came from London. At first Hitler wanted to kill thirty thousand people in retaliation, but he was warned of the effects on the Czech industrial production. So they did a 'smaller' act of revenge."

The other major difference in this documentary is that Jerri Zbiral, the "second-generation" center of the film who goes back to Lidice, is a non-Jewish sister to the children of Holocaust survivors in other documentaries. About her mother's wartime experience, we hear the familiar words, "she wants to forget about it; I have a real need to know." Her Jewish husband, Alan, accompanies her on the return voyage.

As in *The Optimists*, Comforty moves from the personal to the collective, inter-twining Jerri's commemorative/investigative journey with stories of Lidice's other survivors. These include the now elderly Marie, who tearfully recalls how her husband was taken from her, and then her daughter. Jerri joins in the annual memorial at the gym, the place where the Nazis wrenched children from their mothers. She also speaks frankly of the hatred she felt for Germans during her youth – to members of the Bremen Peace Initiative. Like the German professor and students Comforty interviews when visiting the Lidice Museum, these representatives of an anti-Nazi German culture try to convince Jerri that they are as eager to confront – and transcend – the past as she is.

One of the central themes throughout *In the Shadow of Memory* is the relation of parent and child. For Marie, it is simply loss, as the last scene makes clear: when she returned from the concentration camp, she fixed up a room for her daughter – white, clean, and still empty. For Jerri as daughter, it is more complex, as her mother told her enough about the war to make Jerri resentful of Germans. However, Jerri is also the mother of an eight-year-old boy who excels at a computer game. When she is horrified to see that he is "destroying a city," he counters, "but it's Hamburg!" The end credits are accompanied by his sensitive rendition of a melody on hammered dulcimer: since it's "Für Elise," a rapprochement with German culture is at least suggested as a possibility.

The recent emphasis on rescue and resistance, especially in films of return, offers a painfully partial picture, however. Bulgaria and Chabannes were the exceptions, while Europe's pervasive ghettos and concentration camps – from which a tiny fraction survived – were the rule. It is much more difficult to tell the stories of the millions who perished, those who left no trace, and not simply because of the lack of records: who can watch the reconstruction of torture and murder? But a few films have risen to the challenge of using facts and figures in a creatively illuminating way. One of the best recent examples is *Photographer* (*Fotoamator*, Poland, 1998), directed by Dariusz Jablonski, who was Krzysztof Kieslowski's second assistant director on *The Decalogue* ten years earlier. This kaleidoscope in Polish, German, and Yiddish yokes diverse visual and aural elements into a haunting exploration of at least three subjects: the Lodz Ghetto during World War II; photography; and how we bear witness.

Photographer builds on the strengths of a previous Polish documentary, *Chronicle of the Warsaw Ghetto Uprising according to Marek Edelman* (1993). Where Jablonski's points of departure were slides of the Lodz Ghetto – together with the testimony of survivor Arnold Mostowicz – Jolanta Dylewska begins with archival footage of the Warsaw Ghetto, followed by an interview with Edelman. This former leader of the Jewish resistance is filmed in close-up in partial light: with half of his face in the dark, the film suggests that not everything can be revealed to the camera. The first seventeen minutes of *Chronicle* make us see the Warsaw Ghetto fresh, even if the images are familiar: they are slowed down – suggesting stilled lives – and seem ghostly because they are silent. The music of Jan Kanty Pawluskiewicz, like the footage, stops and starts. This counterpoint of movement and stasis, of sound and silence, makes us aware of the mediation not only of Nazi cameras, but of Dylewska's manipulation of the results. Even if the intention of the German occupiers was to chronicle their subjugation of what they considered subhumans, that is not the effect of the Ghetto's Jewish faces today. For example, shots of children accompanied by a female voice-over singing "Raisins and Almonds" in Yiddish are poignant. There is a commemorative aspect throughout *Chronicle* that culminates in two endings: in the first, the camera moves in on grainy photos of the resistance fighters, each identified by name; in the second ending, the groups carrying their small bags during the Warsaw Ghetto deportation – to the death camp of Treblinka – remain nameless.

Whereas most films about the Holocaust show the present in color and the past in black-and-white, *Photographer* reverses the strategy: the most vivid part is the past in color slides that were discovered in a Viennese bookstore in 1987. These four hundred images – among the first ever made with color stock – were taken by Walter Genewein, the Lodz Ghetto's chief accountant. He was an Austrian national appointed by the Nazis to ensure maximum productivity in this prison. From 1939 to 1944, the Lodz Ghetto was the largest work camp established by the Nazis for Poland's Jews. As many as three hundred thousand – slave laborers for the Nazi war effort – were imprisoned there at its peak.

For the duration of the seventy-six-minute film, Jablonski works in a poetically investigative style. Present-day Lodz in black-and-white looks ghostly, as does the Jewish survivor Dr. Arnold Mostowicz, whose interview punctuates the film. Shadows play on his face – part of him is always in the dark, like a reminder of what we cannot see – as he quietly recalls horrific stories that counterpoint the placid photos and dry official reports in German voice-over.

We also hear in Yiddish the reconstructed voice of Chaim Rumkowski, head of the "Judenrat" (Jewish organization) in the Lodz Ghetto. He offers the terrifying rationalization of handing over to the Nazis twenty thousand Jewish children – a compromise for the twenty-four thousand demanded – to save the rest of the Ghetto. While one can question such accommodation to Nazi orders, Mostowicz acknowledges that Lodz's longer endurance than other ghettos was thanks to Rumkowski's compromises. (This Jewish leader was nevertheless murdered in Auschwitz before war's end.)

The liquidation of the Ghetto is expressed by the camera's fluid movement through contemporary Lodz, which is eerily empty (except for a man who seems to be hiding). A flashlight effect heightens the sense of searching for those who might be hidden. Jablonski even superimposes images – perhaps "ghosts" from the slides – onto present-day Lodz. And after Mostowicz's recollection of a scene from Auschwitz – an accountant realizing that his wife and two children had been cremated – two children in the present run out of a door. Then, another kind of photography presents stilled lives: black-and-white passport shots of Jews are illuminated by a moving flashlight beam, an iris effect that brings them out of darkness (and, perhaps, out of oblivion).

These visual strategies are appropriate to commemoration (of the approximately three hundred thousand Jews who lived in prewar Lodz, fewer than nine hundred were left by January 1945) and to questioning indifference. Genewein was blind to everything but productivity and obtaining good shots with his camera (confiscated from an inmate). Jablonski, on the other hand, cares about both the aesthetic and the moral – as we might expect from someone who worked with Kieslowski. In fact, one of the ironies in *Photographer* is Genewein's correspondence with Agfa, in which he complains that his slides have a reddish hue. Might it be the metaphorical presence of Jewish blood? Perhaps, considering the letter is juxtaposed with the image of corpses being carried away.

Jablonski, who graduated from the Lodz Film School in 1990, shows himself to be not simply a documentarian but a stylist, selecting and counterpointing details for maximum dramatic effect and questioning. His camera is never still, whether moving through the streets of present-day Lodz, or before Mostowicz's face, or in the form of the optical printer cutting into and around the slides. The pictures may contain stilled lives, but Jablonski's mobile camera signifies renewed vitality. He also uses sound to animate the stills – children's voices, drumbeats, music – whereas the present has no diegetic sound and therefore feels ghostly. What he seems to be moving toward is a questioning of reality versus truth. Mostowicz says at the beginning that the discovery of the slides shocked him: "They were real but did not show the truth." The slides are authentic, but they evade the deeper reality of Jews treated as subhuman. *Photographer* balances the objective and the subjective – facts from German reports along with Genewein's bloodless diaries and Mostowicz's testimony. The last slide, the Jewish bathhouse in the Lodz Ghetto, therefore has a double meaning: the reality of the showers signifies the truth of Auschwitz and its gas chambers.

Photos and slides are incomplete, a function of the person taking them, just as motion pictures are incomplete. But Genewein's indifference is complemented by Jablonski's concern. If this filmmaker invokes the Holocaust at the end of the twentieth century, it is in the service not simply of memory, but of a contemporary

Jewish children in the Lodz Ghetto, from *Photographer*. PHOTO COURTESY OF SEVENTH ART RELEASING.

From *Photographer*, Himmler (in car) visits the Lodz Ghetto: to his left is Chaim Rumkowski, head of the Judenrat. PHOTO COURTESY OF SEVENTH ART RELEASING.

awareness. Films like *Photographer* are not only investigative documentary, not merely poignant memoir, but also cautionary tale, intended to remind viewers of the price to be paid for indifference – whether more than fifty years ago, or today. Its skillful montage is both method and meaning, suggesting the need for multiple perspectives whose whole is greater than the sum of its parts. It juxtaposes fact, artifact,

ressor, subjective, objective, the hidden and the revealed, so that the au-
are of the fragmentary nature of our perception. At the end, we want to
about what was left out of the four hundred slides . . . but that's another

Annotated Filmography
(Third Edition)

The majority of the films listed below were made since the last update of *Indelible Shadows* in 1989. Those which are not discussed in the new chapters are annotated, with an asterisk (*) appearing before the films that most impressed me (D = director; S = screenwriter; R = rental source). Many are available from the National Center for Jewish Film, as noted by R: NCJF. The address is NCJF, Brandeis University, Lown 102 MS 053, Waltham, Mass. 02454-9110; www.jewishfilm.org; phone 781-899-7044; FAX 781-736-2070; e-mail ncjf@brandeis.edu.

The approximately 170 titles below are arranged alphabetically within sections: following Nonfiction (the largest group) are Fiction: Germany, France, Other European, English-Language, and "Holocaust in Background" (films in which the subject is touched upon rather than foregrounded). While the Filmography is meant to be comprehensive, certain films that I was not able to see are absent. Among them are the five "Broken Silence" documentaries of 2001 made for the Shoah Foundation: *Eyes of the Holocaust* (directed by Janos Szasz, Hungary), *I Remember* (Andrzej Wajda, Poland), *Some Who Lived* (Luiz Puenzo, Argentina), *Children from the Abyss* (Pavel Chukhraj, Russia), and *Hell on Earth* (Vojtech Jasny, Czech Republic). The address is: Survivors of the Shoah Visual History Foundation, P.O. Box 3168, Los Angeles, Calif. 90078-3168; phone 818-777-7802; FAX 818-866-0312; www.vhf.org.

Additional nonfiction films are available from Ergo Media: www.jewishvideo.com. The address is Ergo Media Inc., 668 American Legion Drive, P.O. Box 2037, Teaneck, N.J. 07666-1437. E-mail: ergo@jewishvideo.com. Phone 201-692-0404; FAX 201-692-0663. Another good source for Holocaust-related motion pictures is Atara Releasing, a service of the San Francisco Jewish Film Festival: www.sfjff.org. The address is Atara Releasing, 346 Ninth St., San Francisco, Calif. 94103, E-mail: jewishfilm@sfjff.org. Phone 415-621-0556; FAX 415-621-0568.

Nonfiction:

*Anne Frank Remembered. England, 1995. D: Jon Blair. R: NCJF. A superb 122-minute documentary by the director of *Schindler.* The comprehensive account of Anne Frank's entire life is narrated by Kenneth Branagh, with diary excerpts read by Glenn Close. Blair was allowed to reconstruct the hiding place – where Anne and seven others lived – as it was during World War II. The most poignant part of the film is the director's bringing together of Miep Gies, the risk-taking protector, with Peter, the son of the dentist she hid. He cries, thanks her, and the voice-over tells us that he died of cancer two months later. After all the still photographs and words that have defined Anne Frank for decades, Blair presents filmed footage of the girl at her window on the day of a wedding in her building. It is also fascinating to learn that – sensing she would be published – Anne rewrote her diary to make it better! In telling this unique tale with so many details, Blair succeeds in

illuminating larger Holocaust issues, from victimization by the Nazis, to resistance by people like Miep. Academy Award winner for Best Documentary.

Architecture of Doom, The. Sweden, 1991. D: Peter Cohen. Narrated (in German) by Bruno Ganz, this is a fascinating two-hour documentary about how aesthetics – including Hitler as a frustrated artist – fed into Nazism, and how a cult of beauty led to the gas chambers. It begins with the fact that Hitler was refused admission by the Vienna Academy of Art – while we see some of his (not terrible) watercolors – and also dabbled in architecture. He personally designed the Nazi flag, insignia, and so on, and then personally curated Berlin's annual art show. In general, art was a fertile source of his politics: Hitler said, "Whoever wants to understand Nazism must understand Wagner." Archival footage and the narration present frightening information: 45 percent of German physicians belonged to the Nazi party; films about "delousing" fed the anti-Semitism that led to the gas chambers (getting rid of Jews was a question of hygiene, with Germany as a body politic and the Jews likened to rats); part of the Nazi aesthetic was "beauty through violence" – not only giant sculptures of muscled men and "soft" nude women, but (toward the end of the war) perverse celebrations of defeat, embracing doom. Hitler comes across as a demented artist-turned-critic who recast the world in his own aesthetic image, destroying whatever offended his kitschy taste.

Art of Remembrance, The. U.S.A., 1994. D: Johanna Heer and Werner Schmiedl. R:A strong documentary about Simon Wiesenthal, tracing his trajectory from a Galician-born architect, through the concentration camps, to postwar acts of bearing witness (literally identifying SS guards and locations to the Americans). Even before Spielberg's *Schindler's List*, Amon Goeth was already on Wiesenthal's list in 1945! Using interview material from a variety of places (including Sweden), mainly in German and English, the film conveys not only one man's obsessive need to remember, but his massive contribution to a much needed postwar search for justice. Among the subjects of Wiesenthal's compelling stories are the policemen who arrested Anne Frank – but were never seriously prosecuted – and his own experience of being saved during the war.

Assignment: Rescue – The Story of Varian Fry and the Emergency Rescue Committee. U.S.A., 1997. D: Richard Kaplan. This fine 26-minute documentary narrated by Meryl Streep tells the important tale of the American who helped rescue several thousand refugees in the early part of World War II. Like Schindler, he worked from a list provided by the Emergency Rescue Committee, but soon had to go beyond these names. He arranged American visas especially for artists and intellectuals on the run from the Third Reich, working in Marseille amid mounting intimidation. Effective cinematic touches include the song "Over the Rainbow" as we see refugees in Marseille. The film acknowledges grim aspects of U.S. policy in the newsreel of Martin Dies saying, "Keep America out of Europe, and Europe out of America."

At the Crossroads: Jews in Eastern Europe Today. U.S.A., 1990. D: Oren Rudavsky and Yale Strom. The one-hour documentary is both poignant and hopeful vis-à-vis this complex subject. The point of departure is Klezmer musician Strom's visit to Eastern Europe with his violin, speaking Yiddish to elderly Jews in Hungary, Czechoslovakia, and Poland. (He also speaks English to young Jews trying to shape a new identity.) We see a fascinating counterpoint in Budapest between sad Eli Mermelstein – who lives alone, can't get totally Jewish bread, and sings in Yiddish, "Where are my seven good years?" – and lovely, young, half-Jewish Julie Vajda, who cheerfully plans to go to Israel. Jewish clubs in Warsaw, Krakow, and Wroclaw suggest that it is now "fashionable" to become Jewish, as well as important for young people who yearn for a return to their roots. A conductor and an elderly Yiddish translator are both eloquent on how Jewish culture cannot die in Poland – specifically, Hasidic melodies and Yiddish poetry – where it was born. A concert by Rabbi Shlomo Carlebach is an occasion for celebration, as is a performance by Strom.

Bach in Auschwitz (La Chaconne d'Auschwitz). The Netherlands, 1998. D: Michael Daeron.

Back to Gombin. U.S.A., 2001. D: Minna Packer. A one-hour documentary in which survivors, their children, and grandchildren return to to a Polish town that was once filled with Jewish life. Among them is the director, occasionally narrating or interviewing her own father. Most effective is the juxtaposition of a silent home movie shot in 1937 by a visitor – a ghostly reminder of what has since disappeared. The visitors find old abandoned Jewish tombstones and place them back in the cemetery, during a moving dedication ceremony to which the local population is invited.

Birthplace. Poland, 1992. D: Pavel Lozinski.

Blood Money. U.S.A., 1997. D: Stephen Crisman. Cowritten and produced by Gaylen Ross, this "Investigative Report on Swiss Gold" aired on A&E. It is a hard-hitting two-hour inquiry of how the Swiss dealt with gold during World War II – pretty shoddily, not asking questions about taking looted gold from Germany – and now, the answer is: execrably, refusing to give Holocaust survivors their accounts without a death certificate. The interview with survivor Estelle Sapir is particularly touching, and it is rewarding to see a female Swiss Parliament member who will not let her government rest on this issue.

Can Memories Be Dissolved in Evian Water? France, 1997. D: Charles Najman. An uneven portrait of the director's mother, Solange, a feisty, Paris-based survivor of Auschwitz and Bergen-Belsen. Outgoing, full of bravado, she goes once every two years to Evian for a spa cure paid for by German reparations (with a handsome man whose identity is never clarified). The film is strongest when she sings in Polish, or tells of her harrowing experiences, or when she and her three female friends celebrate their survival on April 15, 1995 (the fiftieth anniversary of their liberation). But the inclusion of an actor in the Evian sequence is irritating: the fictional ornamentation undermines the authenticity of other scenes.

*Carousel. Poland, 1999. D: Michal Nekanda-Trepka for Polish television. The point of departure for this understated 35-minute documentary is Czeslaw Milosz's poem "Campo dei Fiori": it describes smoke from the Warsaw Ghetto palpable at the carousel whirling just over the Ghetto wall on the Aryan side. The subjects interviewed are compelling, from Uprising leader Marek Edelman, to other survivors who were children in the Ghetto, to a Polish woman who realizes she committed a "sin of omission" by not giving a Jewish child a piece of bread. The stories are gripping, such as a woman telling of escape through the sewers: her parents stopped, unable to continue, but she and her brother proceeded with a lantern till he was taken by a rush of water . . . and then miraculously surfaced. The contrast is indeed unbelievable: how could a Nazi-erected carousel keep spinning so close to the Ghetto, covered with ash from the burning prison?

Chantons sous l'occupation (Singing in the Occupation). France, 1976. D: André Halimi. Following the structure of *The Sorrow and the Pity,* interviews and archival footage reveal the collaborationist spirit of show business figures during the German occupation of France. The interviews are set up so that the subject reveals that s/he had fun with nightlife while others were dying. But, as a female writer puts it, would it have stopped the torture if she hadn't gone dancing at the age of eighteen? Best is the line from Arletty – the star of *Children of Paradise* – when interrogated about sleeping with a German: "My heart is French, but my ass is international."

Charlotte. Switzerland, 1992. D: Richard Dindo. An intriguing one-hour documentary about the artist Charlotte Salomon, killed at the age of twenty-six in Auschwitz. Although framed by a brief male voice-over, most of the film is told in Charlotte's own words, narrated by Ann-Gisel Glass in the English version. Charlotte's gouaches – "Life or Theater" – and the text recount life from before her birth: her mother Franciska met her father, a surgeon, grew depressed and suicidal when Charlotte was a bit grown, and then died; her father married the singer Paulinka; Doberlin became enamored of Paulinka, and then Charlotte of Doberlin. Her parents send her from Berlin to Villefranche in 1939 because of the Nazi threat, and there she paints this "spielteater."

Children of Chabannes, The. U.S.A., 2000. D: Lisa Gossels and Dean Wetherell.

Children of the Night. 1999. D: Jolanta Dylewska. S: Marion Wiesel. Produced by the legendary Swiss producer Arthur Cohn, this 18-minute short aired on HBO, and is filled with poignant footage of Jewish children killed in the Holocaust. The very quality of the photographs and archival footage seems as fragile as the lives within them. At the end, photos of individual children – including name and place of birth – are accompanied by the voice-over (of Marion Wiesel) telling us where they died and at what age. The understated cello of YoYo Ma in the background is very effective.

Chronicle of the Warsaw Ghetto Uprising according to Marek Edelman. Poland, 1993. D: Jolanta Dylewska. R: NFJF.

A Conversation with Elie Wiesel: In the Shadow of the Flames. U.S.A., 1989. D: Erwin Leiser. Aired on PBS in November 1989, this one-hour documentary is moving and stimulating in its simplicity. Apart from occasional intercuts of paintings that depict the Jewish experience of World War II, it consists of Wiesel speaking quietly. He begins by stating that indifference is the enemy – the opposite of good, of peace, and of art – and stresses the importance of memory. The film offers a fine portrait of his origins and development, from "living within four walls, living within book covers" in his native Sighet; to praying in Auschwitz; to postwar silence (self-imposed for ten years until he blurted out his story to François Mauriac, who encouraged him to write); to American citizenship because of an accident that broke all his bones, preventing him from returning to France to renew his visa. We see the clip of his accepting the Congressional Medal of Honor and courageously asking President Reagan not to go to Bitburg.

Cross Inscribed in the Star of David, The. Poland, 1997. D: Grzegorz Linkowski. This compelling 27-minute story of a priest who learned late in life that he was born Jewish was shown at the 2001 San Francisco Jewish Film Festival. Father Romuald Jakub Weksler-Waszkinel speaks naturally to the camera while, in the background, we see blurred snapshots of the past. He recalls being surprised that his father opposed his decision to become a priest. While in the seminary, he received a visit from his father, who cried, and then died a few days later. He therefore felt guilty . . . until he got his mother to admit that his biological mother had indeed begged her – in the ghetto that she visited with food – to take the baby. Apparently, the real motther added, "Please, you'll see, he'll become a priest." After his Polish mother died, he took the name Weksler-Waksinel, acknowledging both. The film provocatively dissolves back and forth between him in a synagogue (wearing a yarmulke) and in a church: his cross is inscribed within a Jewish star, literalizing his phrase, "I am a Jew of Jesus Christ." On the one hand, it is a rescue story; on the other, it explores the ambiguity of identity: "Once a Jew, always a Jew?" or "Like Jesus, a Jew who became a Christian?"

Daring to Resist. U.S.A., 2001. D: Martha Lubell and Barbara Attie. Powerful 1-hour video about three brave Jewish women who were willing and able to resist during World War II, enhanced by their photos and home movies.

Diamonds in the Snow. U.S.A., 1994. D: Mina Reym Binford. R: NCJF. A moving video that interweaves the recollection of three Jewish women, each of whom survived the Holocaust as a child from Bendzin, Poland. At the center is writer-director Mira, who was hidden by a kind woman, Maria; after her sudden death, the child's protector became Maria's strict husband, who was himself hiding from the Nazis because he had been a leader in the Silesian uprising a decade earlier! From Israel we meet Shulamith Levin – an orphan who was saved by a kind Gentile family – and Ada Raviv, who spent one year hidden with her grandmother in a hole under a Pole's house. The women acknowledge ambivalent feelings, such as Shulamith's sense of abandonment, and then her refusal to go with her aunt and uncle after the war. There is a wonderful sense of detail throughout, like Ada recalling a roundup as "boots," because that was all she saw. Polish Gentiles offer corroborating testimony, as with Mira's memory of searchlights when she and her parents crawled out of their hole in the ground and tried – in vain – to escape. One of the film's revelations is that there was a local "Schindler," Alfred Rossner, a German whose uniform factory was initially a haven for Jews. He saved about twelve thousand but, as we learn toward the end, died in a Nazi prison.

Eichmann Trial, The. U.S.A., 1997. D: Dan Pollin and Ken Mandell. Made by ABC News, this strong documentary crosscuts between footage of the trial in 1961 (the first televised trial) and recent interviews with those who played a role in them. We get a sense of the tactical importance of the trial – which was not simply about Eichmann, but raising consciousness of the Holocaust in Israel and abroad. The defendant minimizes his power but is condemned to death on the basis of overwhelming evidence, including an interview he gave a Dutch journalist while he was hiding in Argentina. Most upsetting is the point when a witness collapses while testifying, and the voice-over says he suffered a paralytic stroke. A longer version aired on PBS.

Exile Shanghai. Germany, 1997. D: Ulrike Ottinger. R: Atara. A four-and-a-half-hour exploration of the Jewish community in Shanghai that began in 1845, ended by 1950, and was largest during World War II. Why? Shanghai was the only port that required neither a visa nor proof of income/support. Therefore, twenty thousand European Jewish refugees made their way to a country that was initially quite welcoming. But the Japanese occupation in 1943 forced them into the Hongkew Ghetto. First, Rena Krasno articulately explains the history of the Jews in Shanghai, from the Sephardic population (led by Sassoon) to the Ashkenazi exodus after pogroms in Russia. The second hour is devoted to Gertrude and Rabbi Theodore Alexander, who tell wonderful stories that intertwine. She came as a young girl via the *Kindertransport* to London; after three months in a ship, she was reunited in Shanghai with her parents, who had been coming expectantly to meet the boats every day. In the ghetto, she met her future husband. The only problem with the film is that so much time is spent on contemporary Shanghai, with no voice-over. This is effective in the opening juxtaposition of a waltz heard while we see contemporary Shanghai traffic, but grows tedious.

Exiles, The. U.S.A., 1989. D: Richard Kaplan. The focus is on the Jews, especially German, who escaped Hitler's Europe to the U.S.A. The well-chosen archival footage includes interviews with Billy Wilder and Lotte Lenya.

Eye of Vichy, The (L'Oeil de Vichy). France, 1993. D: Claude Chabrol. S: Jean-Pierre Azema and Robert Paxton. Newsreels from the French Occupation provide a perspective of total collaboration, an "official story" that celebrates the Germans while depicting the Anglo-American side as monsters. (The voice-over is spoken by actor Michel Bouquet, who was also the voice of *Night and Fog* almost forty years earlier.) We see the mass French worship of Petain, fueled by images of propaganda that were presented and perceived as truth. At the end, the footage of the liberation of Paris by De Gaulle suggests that the leaders and sides may change, but the camera continues.

Fighter. U.S.A., 2000. D: Amir Bar-Lev. R: First Run Features, 212-243-0600. (www.fighterfilm.com). An upbeat road movie about two friends who survived not only the Holocaust but the Communist regime in Czechoslovakia. Their return to retrace boxer Jan Wiener's wartime trajectory makes for drama and comedy: the famous writer and teacher Arnost Lustig is the chronicler, and Jan (seventy-seven years old and still boxing) the subject. Because Lustig plans to write a story about his buddy, he – rather than the filmmakers – asks the questions and, often, bickers with Jan. "Wiener is not a victim," he announces at the outset, and we do indeed meet a World War II hero: he escaped from Prague into Italy (at one point under a moving train for eighteen hours), ended up as an

RAF flyer, and was then imprisoned from 1950 to 1955 in a forced labor camp because the Czech Communists feared his "Western infiltration." Lustig, who survived Terezin, was a Communist, but realized this was synonymous with being a Nazi and left for the U.S.A. They revisit key places of Jan's past with a certain sense of triumph, like singing on the road to Terezin. Jan was imprisoned in Genoa for nine months, and returns with Arnost to Cosenza, where the inhabitants' elaborate hand gestures are subtitled! Although he finds the now old children of the man who gave him food after he escaped from a POW camp, they don't remember him. Our old codgers fight bitterly, to the extent that filming stops for three days! But they manage to achieve a rapprochement by playing chess on a beach.

Good Morning, Mr. Hitler. The Netherlands, 1996. D: Luke Holland. It is surprising and intriguing to see recently rediscovered color footage of Hitler. However, watching these images from Germany's national cultural festival in 1939 (six weeks before World War II began) should elicit more of a shudder. There is no stench of madness, especially because we see an audience within the film: they watch the footage and seem to be having too good a time. Less sophisticated viewers might get the sense that Hitler was a nice, popular guy, as we don't see the carnage to which his policies led. The film includes an amazing detail, that both Hitler and Charlie Chaplin were born on April 20, 1899.

*Gruninger's Fall. Switzerland, 1997. D: Richard Dindo, from the book by Stefan Keller. This fine feature-length Swiss film about another rescuer is structured by the return of survivors – not to a concentration camp, but a courtroom. This is where Paul Gruniger stood trial in 1940 for disobeying the Swiss order to bar Austrian Jewish refugees from entering the country. A female voice-over (in English) says that they invited the refugees and Gruniger's daughter to the very place where the testimony of the Jews he saved had not been invited before. Approximately two dozen aging Jews – from New York, Buenos Aires, and so on – are shown a newsreel of Hitler's joyous annexation of Austria to the Reich, and then speak about how good Gruniger was to them. One of the townspeople comes and admits that he helped refugees for the money. We learn that many were sent to Diepoldsau, a camp for Jews that was more like a home than a prison. We also go with the survivors to the border where crossing was a matter of life or death. Sadly, the Jews he saved could not help Gruniger once he was suspended and then dismissed, mainly because of their own precarious situation. The film ends with footage of Gruniger from a Swiss TV documentary of 1971, one year before he died at the age of eighty. He says that he saved about three thousand refugees and – even though he was suddenly jobless and homeless – would do the same again. Only years after his death was his reputation rehabilitated.

Hidden Children. Canada/U.K., 1995. D: John Walker. A moving 50-minute documentary about Jewish children hidden during the Holocaust, and their ongoing crises of identity as adults today. Most powerful is the first, a Polish woman who was forgotten by Jewish brigades at war's end when she was a fourteen-year-old orphan: at sixteen, she married the Pole who saved her, spent her life having many babies, going to church, and yearning secretly for contact with her Jewish family. This aim is fulfilled when she is finally reunited with her aunt's relatives in Israel. The second Polish woman, although Jewish, was brought up as an anti-Semitic child; Andre Stein from Budapest speaks of his sadness after years of "identity management" – hidden only psychologically; Miriam Rakowski from Belgium is still dealing with her demons in New York, regretting that the most stable love she had was with Catholic protectors; and Frieda Stieglitz says that no one claimed her after the war. We also meet Jacob, a Jewish Pole who became a priest. He speaks of "dual personality" when visiting Orthodox Jewish relatives – careful not to put on his yarmulke in church, and not to cross himself in synagogue!

*Hitler's Holocaust. Germany, 2000 (shown on ZDF TV). D: Maurice Philip Remy. Partly due to newly released archival footage from former Communist countries, this six-hour documentary is riveting, wide-ranging, and consistently illuminating. Shown on the History

Channel in June 2001, it contains interviews with a vast number of subjects including Jewish survivors, SS men, concentration camp guards, members of the Polish resistance, Western diplomats, and Hitler's bodyguard. It begins with the invasion of the Soviet Union on June 22, 1941. We learn that Germans found corpses in Lvov of people who had been murdered by the Soviet secret police, but said that the Jews did it: "The propaganda worked," as thousands of Jews were killed in the streets by the Russians – which we see in frightening footage. (A German sailor secretly filmed the killing of Jews in Latvia.) It is amazing to hear Hitler's voice from a June 1942 tape because its source is a conversation rather than a speech. Part 2, "Decision," goes back in time and we see how exterminations began with euthanasia of the physically and mentally disabled in 1939, and hear the chilling statistics of the Wannsee Conference: five million Jews from the Soviet Union were targeted for destruction, and a total of eleven million from Europe. In part 3, Warsaw Ghetto survivor Marek Edelman cautions that Nazi films of the Ghetto are deceptive, while the son of Hans Frank – who was known as "the Butcher of Poland" – says that his father was both well-educated and a wretched criminal. We meet Arnold Mostowicz (the central presence in the brilliant film *Photographer*), who recalls being proud to wear the Jewish star in Poland, as well as Israel Gutman: he speaks about the Warsaw Ghetto where one-third of the Jews were rich, one-third merely survived, and one-third were on the verge of starvation. *Hitler's Holocaust* continues with dozens of personal testimonies that place the Final Solution in the context of Hitler's military objectives and racial politics.

House of the World. U.S.A., 1998. D: Esther Polenski. Made by a daughter of survivors, this excellent 54-minute documentary is about Jewish cemeteries in Poland, and about memory. She returns with survivors to Poddebbice, where the cemeteries were destroyed. They rededicate a monument, which she effectively crosscuts with photos and home movies of the 1930s and 1940s. In Lodz, she interviews Laib, the Jewish caretaker of the cemetery, who laments that in ten years Poland will be "Juden-rein" indeed, and that no one will come to visit these graves. This is a poignant record, both personal (she interviews her uncle Adam) and collective. As in *Night and Fog*, there is a hovering question: if nature "forgets" by covering ashes with grass and flowers, how can human memory preserve? This film could be double-billed with either *Loving the Dead* or *A Letter without Words*.

In Our Own Hands. Canada, 1997. C: Chuck Olin. Celebrates the only all-Jewish fighting unit in World War II, young volunteers from Palestine who are finally allowed by the British to enter combat under their own flag (the same Jewish star that is seen as a mark of shame on European coats) in 1944. Interviews with the now old heroes, accompanied by newsreel footage, are heartwarming: like *Partisans of Vilna*, the film recounts an unknown story of Jewish heroism that flourished despite limited circumstances. At first, the British fear trouble from the Arabs, so the volunteers receive neither proper ammunition nor training. But Churchill relents, and they fight in northern Italy. After the war, they remain in Europe, again thorny for the British: not only do they take revenge on fleeing Nazis, but they smuggle weapons to Palestine for the upcoming struggle. Before being sent back, they first find "doubles" among the survivors to take their place in clandestine operations. In Israel, they are the military sophisticates for the war.

In the Shadow of Memory: Legacies of Lidice. U.S.A., 1998. D: Jacky Comforty.

Into the Arms of Strangers: Stories of the Kindertransport. U.S.A., 2000. D: Mark Jonathan Harris. Academy Award winner for Best Documentary Feature, this compelling film documents the rescue of over ten thousand children (90 percent of them Jewish) from Germany, Austria, and Czechoslovakia by the English during the nine months before the outbreak of World War II. Interviews with the now adult *Kinder* reveal how wrenching the experience was, especially for the parents sending their children to a safe haven when they could not leave themselves. Indeed, many of the children – like the writer Lore Segal, also interviewed in the previous (and very fine) documentary *My Knees Were Jumping: Children of the*

Kindertransport – bore the responsibility for trying later to get their parents to safety. The film's kaleidoscope includes Norbert Wollheim, a *Kindertransport* coordinator in Berlin who could not save his own wife and child from death in Auschwitz, and Alexander Gordon, who was interned as an "enemy alien" in England because he fled Germany; he was then deported to Australia on the S.S. *Dunera*, and later returned as a soldier for the British army. We see how difficult it was for the children to be reunited after the war with parents they no longer knew. But they were the lucky ones, as most of the surviving children learned that their parents had died. Narrated by Judi Dench, it was produced by Deborah Oppenheimer, whose mother was part of the *Kindertransport*.

Journey Back, A. Canada, 1985. D: Bryan McKenna. This one-hour documentary made for the CBC returns to Europe with the actor, director, and teacher Jack Garfein. It begins with him at Auschwitz, where he was interned, before cutting to him on Broadway in his current life. Accompanied to the concentration camp by Eric Malling (the Ted Koppel of Canada, according to Garfein), he tells a powerful story of his mother pushing him away from her in Auschwitz: he thought it was because she preferred his sister, and therefore hated his mother throughout the war. Only later did he learn that she had saved him in this way. Another formidable story concerns an old man who protected him by telling Dr. Mengele that they were both renowned Mosaic artists. Garfein returns to his Slovakian hometown and has a reunion with his father's former employee: he had hidden a trunk of their possessions for them, but the only thing left is an embroidery on the wall. Garfein recognizes it from his mother's bedroom, but we learn from the voice-over narration that the man's daughter refused to give back what she considered a wedding present. Even more sadly, the synagogue in this Slovakian town is an abandoned warehouse for ovens. The film then grows more investigative about a leading Nazi sympathizer, Reichstater, now living peacefully in Canada. When Garfein meets him on camera, the old man says that the state was responsible for the deportations of the Jews, not the people. At the end, in Auschwitz, Garfein finds pieces of bone in the snow, lets out a primal scream, and then cries. This film could be paired with *So Many Miracles*, but is marred by an overly cheerful voice-over narration.

Journey into Life: Aftermath of a Childhood in Auschwitz. Germany, 1996. D: Thomas Mitscherlich. R: NCJF. This 130-minute documentary focuses on three survivors, using interviews and powerful archival footage from the liberation of the concentration camps by the Allies. At the beginning, one could almost believe it is a fiction film, because the male voice-over in German speaks of an American officer, Mayflower, who happened to have color film in his camera in 1945. The journey of the film's exploration is expressed by shots from inside a car – roads in Germany, The Netherlands, Israel, and California – and by a dissonant saxophone score. First we hear from Gerhard Durlacher, then Yehuda Bacon, and finally Ruth Kluger: all three were children when taken to Theresienstadt and then to Auschwitz. Kluger is especially fascinating in her tough-mindedness: she already felt liberated even before the Allies arrived because she had decided she was! Together with her mother and foster-sister, Kluger escaped during the death march and joined German refugees, pretending to be non-Jews. She says that after the war, and even now, people want her to remove her tattooed number because they cannot deal with living evidence. A good deal of attention is paid to the aftermath of the war, including the D.P. camps (again with a sense of imprisonment) and the difficulty of emigrating.

Karussell. Germany, 1999. D: Ilona Ziok. The focus is Kurt Gerron, a popular singer, actor (he played the magician in *The Blue Angel*), and cabaret star. But the German-Jewish Gerron ended up in Theresienstadt, where he founded a cabaret; he was also forced to direct the propaganda film, *The Führer Gives the Jews a City*. Excerpts from this film are strong, as are cabaret performances interspersed throughout *Karussell* by contemporary singers like Ute Lemper and Ben Becker (one of the stars of *The Comedian Harmonists*).

The Katyn Forest. Poland/France, 1990. D: Marcel Lozinski. Produced by Andrzej Wajda, this 55-minute film probes the massacre of almost fifteen thousand Polish officers during World War II. For a long time, this atrocity was attributed to the Nazis, but it was really the work of the Red Army. (A title states that the film was made before the truth was publicly acknowledged.) There are three parts: in (1) "Voyage," children of the victims travel to the place, mainly the camp of Kozielsk, which a survivor of Katyn describes: forty-five hundred were interned there, then led to the forest, shot, and put in a mass grave. In (2) "Politique," after seeing archival footage of corpses, we learn that Churchill allegedly asked the head of the Polish government in exile to say the perpetrators were German, not Soviet. Almost as bad is the fact that the U.S. Secret Service destroyed (on Roosevelt's orders) papers that the Poles had sent him about the real murderers – even before he read them. In (3) "Witnesses," we meet Wanda, the daughter of a murdered Polish officer. She tries to get people who live near the forest to talk, but they are still frightened. However, another woman cajoles (in Russian) her old father to tell the truth. He admits that he was forced to sign the opposite of what happened at Katyn. The film reveals that the Stalinists were just as capable as the Nazis of cold-blooded carnage – even of their own allies.

The Last Days. U.S.A., 1998. D: James Moll.

The Last Klezmer. U.S.A., 1994. D: Yale Strom. An affecting documentary about Leopold Kozlowski, the last of the great "Jewish soul" musicians, now based in Krakow. And what a feisty, engaging guy he is! Aged seventy when Strom went to Eastern Europe to interview him approximately ten years earlier, he has a charismatic warmth as well as a superb memory. We see him conducting *Fiddler on the Roof* in Wroclaw, teaching Yiddish songs to eager, non-Jewish Polish women, and then accepting Strom's invitation to return to his home town of Przemysl, Ukraine. He calls an old partisan buddy, Shimon, that he hasn't seen in fifty years. Together, they reminisce, returning to the spots where Leopold will commemorate his dead family. For all his joie de vivre, dark holes are revealed: his father was rounded up and shot with 360 other Jewish men; his mother was killed after Leopold hid her in an attic; his younger brother – an even more talented musician – was killed by Ukraine bandits a week or two before Liberation, when they were in the woods with partisans. He and Shimon light candles, say Kaddish, and then toast the miracle of their survival. The film is most engaging when Leopold demonsrates the soul of Klezmer music, which he sees as natural, simple, and understood only by Jews. But he acknowledges that even if there are almost no Jews left in Poland, the Poles have a great interest in Jewish culture.

Letter without Words, A. U.S.A., 1998. D: Lisa Lewenz. An intimate 62-minute exploration, narrated by the filmmaker. She has discovered the films made by her grandmother Ella, who died nine months before her birth. In remarkably good shape, they provide a rich history, both personal (home movies) and social (very red swastika flags in the streets of Berlin). This German-Jewish aristocrat gave birth to six children, whose stories are filled with ironies. Lisa's father converted to Christianity to protect his children from anti-Semitism (the filmmaker learned he was Jewish at the age of thirteen). The son who was sent to Peru for safety died of yellow fever. (His letter to his sister Dorothy begs her to remain Jewish.) Ella's old bedroom is now City Hall. Ella's father donated a pool to Dresden, and then Jews were forbidden to enter it! When Lisa's aunt escaped to America, a landlord wouldn't accept Jews in Westchester. After we hear Lisa's voice-over with the grandmother's footage – accompanied by a wonderful Argentine tango on bandoneon – Ella's diary is found: a second voice enters (the English voice-over is spoken by Ingrid Scheib-Rothbart). Ella continued filming, whether a Macy's parade in color or annual visits to a devastated postwar Germany. As in *We Were So Beloved*, a nephew acknowledges that had he been accepted into military service, he would have been a brutal German soldier because the German mentality they absorbed was to obey, not think. She integrates not only Ella's film and interviews in the present, but an audiotape of her father in 1969: he hopes his children don't make the same mistakes he did (presumably hiding religious identity). As Lisa's voice says, "The essential challenge is how to let go, but not forget."

*Liberators: Fighting on Two Fronts during World War II. U.S.A., 1992. D: William Miles and Nina Rosenblum. Tells the little-known and profoundly important story of the bonds that have existed – and can exist – between Jews and African Americans, both victims of racism. The first half focuses on the plight of black enlisted men who had to fight for the right to fight, encountering segregation in the army just as they had experienced it in white American society. As one of the black soldiers, Dr. Leon Bass, explains to a Jewish congregation in the present, he was fighting abroad to protect rights that he was denied in his own country. The second half concentrates more on the 761st Tank Battalion and the Jews, presenting black soldiers as part of the group who liberated Buchenwald. The film is indeed framed by the return to the camp by Benjamin Bender, a child survivor, and two of the black liberators. As he tells them during a poignant moment of gratitude, "My grandchild owes you." Liberators encountered controversy after its airing on PBS, as some historians and veterans questioned whether the facts were indeed correct. Written accounts of liberation clashed with oral histories, and a few liberties taken by the filmmakers led to a "throwing out of the baby with the bathwater." In spite of some historical inaccuracies, the film succeeds in conveying – through photographs, documentary footage, and interviews – how racism equated blacks and Jews, as in a German poster of a black jazz musician with a Jewish star on his lapel. Most moving is the reunion in Belgium of black soldiers (accompanied by their families) with the white Belgians who housed them during the war. They gave, and continue to give, the African-American men the fellowship missing from whites in the United States. The fine narration (spoken by Denzel Washington) often understates ironically. We see how these soldiers wanted to fight but, as in the Civil War, had to prove themselves twice as much as white soldiers. They are the true heroes of this particular chapter of Holocaust history, and a spur to warmer relationships between two groups who share traditions of oppression.

*Light in the Dark. England, 1991. D: Robert Marshall, based on his book In the Sewers of Lvov. This 60-minute documentary narrated by Susannah York recounts an inspiring fragment of the Holocaust. In May 1943, twenty-two Jews from the Lvov Ghetto went into hiding in the sewers, where they lived for fourteen months. Four of the survivors are interviewed: Kristine Chiger, who was a child at the time; her mother; Margulies – who often emerged from the sewers to the Ghetto, where he tried (in vain) to rescue his sister-in-law – and his wife. Their only lifeline was Leopold Socha, a foreman in the Lvov sewer department. Initially, it was with the Jews' money that he bought bread and other bits of food for them; but even when the money ran out, he continued to nourish them, and finally brought them into the light. The details recounted are evocative, as when Kristine tells of the little piece of meat he would bring her from his own lunch, and how she tried to make it last.

Lodz Ghetto. U.S.A., 1989. D: Alan Adelson and Kathryn Taverna. Archival images of the period are very powerful – including color stills – but their authenticity is undermined by the "docudrama" format, including "acted" voice-overs, as well as color footage shot in present-day Lodz. Among actors performing bits from letters and diaries are Jerzy Kozinski, whose bullying chatter represents Chaim Rumkowski.

Long Way Home, The. U.S.A., 1997. D: Mark Jonathan Harris.

Loving the Dead. England, 1991. D: Mira Hamermesch.

*Matrilineal. U.S.A., 2001. D: Caterina Klusenmann. Although made as a thesis film for Columbia University's graduate program, this personal documentary is powerful and illuminating. The filmmaker/narrator uses her camera to investigate her origins. Her perseverance in confronting three generations of evasive women helps to heal all three: her tough grandmother, her mother (who suffers from depression), and her sister, who seems content to know nothing about the family's past. At first, when Caterina asks the grandmother in her Lucca, Italy, home if they are Jewish, the answer is no. And when she asks her mother the name of her biological father, she says, "Jose." When pressed, she amends the name to "Yuzek." As Caterina suspected, her matrilineal side is indeed Jewish, and from Poland. Where, at the outset, the grandmother responds to Caterina's questions with irritation (shutting the door, vacuuming loudly, etc.), toward the end she finally admits how the Nazis came to their home, forcing them out with nothing, and how she hid her little daughter with a family. It is fascinating that she suddenly speaks in German, whereas they have spoken Spanish before. The grandmother acknowledges that she kept changing papers and identities, to the extent that being "incognito" means safety, even now. The filmmaker goes to the Ukraine to search for records and then people who might have known her grandfather. After this energizing voyage, the last sequence is wonderfully cathartic for the whole family.

Memoria. Italy, 1996. D: Ruggero Gabbai. Interviews with a spectrum of Jewish men and women who were deported from Italy to Auschwitz – mostly in 1944 – are very moving. In the first part, they are interviewed in Rome or Venice; in part two, they return to Auschwitz and, individually, tell wrenching stories within the very space that tormented them (both during the war and later in memory). One man who survived the Sonderkommando tells of seeing his cousin about to be killed there. He could do nothing except give him a good meal first, and later say Kaddish. A woman walks among the planks where they slept and recalls being jealous of a girl who had her mother there to hold her – till the mother died. The occasional voice-over of Giancarlo Giannini provides historical material.

More Than Broken Glass: Memories of Kristallnacht. U.S.A., 1989. D: Chris Pelzer, shown on WNYC-TV. Survivors recall what it was like to be German-Jewish before and during November 1938, crosscut with archival footage. Among them are Dr. Ruth Westheimer, Ernest Michel, and a German who admits he was in the Hitler Youth.

My Knees Were Jumping: Children of the Kindertransport. U.S.A., 1995. D: Melissa Hacker. As in *Diamonds in the Snow,* the focus is female survivors who transcended a ruptured childhood. These were the children from Germany and Austria who were taken in by England from December 1938 to August 1939. Hacker concentrates on her mother, the costume designer Ruth Morley (who died of breast cancer during the making of the film), as well as the writer Lore Segal with her own mother. Erika, a third survivor, is sad when interviewed alone, but the mood shifts when her children and grandchildren are present. Interspersed are the reunion of *Kindertransport* survivors, and the discussion group of their children, who realize they are not exactly "second generation" because their parents were not in the camps, but were traumatized nonetheless. Although the majority of subjects are female, one of the film's most poignant moments occurs when a man speaks at the reunion: although he was fed and clothed between the ages of eight and sixteen, he never received a hug.

One Survivor Remembers. U.S.A., 1995. D: Kary Antholis. Winner of the Academy Award for Best Documentary Short, presented on HBO, this is a 39-minute portrait of Gerda Weissman, who was fifteen when World War II began in her native Bielsko, Poland. She is a compelling, nonhistrionic presence, calmly but movingly recalling precise details. For example, her mother didn't make her brother's bed after he was taken – to keep the imprint of his head on the pillow. Her father forced her to wear ski boots when they left – which saved her life. She was one of 150 young female survivors of the approximately 2,000 that embarked on the death march in the snow. The German-born American soldier who liberated her became her husband. Antholis discovered Weissman in U.S. Holocaust Museum testimonies, then selected her after reading her autobiography.

Optimists, The. U.S.A., 2000. D: Jacky and Lisa Comforty.

Photographer. Poland, 1988. D: Dariusz Jablonski. R: Seventh Art Releasing, 323-845-1455.

Port of Last Resort, The. Austria/U.S.A., 1998. D: Joan Grossman and Paul Rosdy. R: NCJF. The migration of German and Austrian Jewish refugees to Shanghai just before World War II provides a dramatic subject. Mesmerizing archival footage is combined with interviews to create a portrait of survival more uplifting, of course, than stories confined to Nazi-occupied Europe. Some letters (spoken by the actress Barbara Sukowa, for example) express the darker aspects of poverty, dysentery, and so on. Others tell how they managed to create cafés, shops, and new lives. Because only Shanghai required no entry visa, eighteen thousand central European Jews made the trip. Most of them settled in Hongkew, and some in the French quarter, but their lively community was undercut when the Japanese seized control and placed them in a ghetto. The end title informs us that the majority of the refugees went to the U.S.A., Canada, and Australia before the Communists took over. Music by John Zorn.

Premier Convoi, Le (The first convoy). France, 1992. D: Pierre Oscar Levy. A fine documentary that traces the return of twelve Jewish men who had been deported from France to Auschwitz. Each one tells of being arrested (most of them in Paris) by the French police. Even if two speak Polish and one Yiddish, it is significant that these are not all foreign Jews: many were French Jews with army papers. The first stop is the transit camp of Drancy (or Compiegne) before arriving in Auschwitz, where each relives his experience. There are moving stories, like that of a man whose son died in a corner of the barrack: he seemed to be crying more over his son's stolen bread ration than his death. There is a respectful absence of music, allowing each man to tell his tale and contribute to a whole greater than the sum of its parts.

Punch Me in the Stomach. New Zealand, 1996. D: Francine Zuckerman, based on the stage play by Alison Summers and Deb Filler. R: NCJF. A thrilling one-woman show starring the daughter of Polish-Jewish Holocaust survivors who ended up in New Zealand. Filler is both funny and poignant, assuming the identities of numerous family members. She becomes her wacky relatives with a mere gesture, prop (like reading glasses), or shift in accent. Most effective is how she turns into – even physically – her father, including a white moustache. Known as the "celebrity survivor," s/he recounts how, as a baker, he was spared from death. Filler occasionally narrates to the camera from a dressing room, her face painted à la Joel Grey in *Cabaret*, but with curlers! These fragments suggest both the pain (especially when she re-creates a trip with her father to the concentration camps) and the resilience that enables her to take an ironic standpoint. The title comes from something her uncle says to prove how well he's doing. Filler's primary relationship seems to be with her father; what a delightful moment at the end when the real father is left in the theater audience with her!

Restless Conscience, The. U.S.A., 1993. D: Hava Kohav Beller. An important blend of interviews and archival footage that bring to light those in the military and elsewhere (especially in England) who risked their lives to eliminate the Führer. As in *Top Secret*, it begins with the 170 Germans brought to trial in 1944 after the last German plot against Hitler, including footage of the kangaroo court. The most fascinating revelation is about the British: although Kleist tried to convince them to support the military coup against Hitler if Czechoslovakia was invaded, they rejected him as a traitor. Even though the White Rose movement provided evidence of German resistance, it was ignored by the British. It is also amazing to learn how Canaris, the head of the Abwehr (military intelligence), actually enabled Jews to leave the country.

Righteous Enemy, The. Italy/U.K., 1987. D: Joseph Rochlitz. R: NCJF. This one-hour personal documentary begins with the survival of the director's father, and extends into the larger story of the 3,500 Jews saved by the Italian Army in occupied Croatia – not to mention the 25–30,000 Jews saved throughout Europe by the Italians. Rochlitz's voice-over introduces the island of Rab, where his father was interned after escaping from Vienna in 1938 to

Zagreb, Croatia. He survived the Jasenovac death camp there; then, despite orders from Mussolini to hand over 4,000 Jews to the Croatians (who would give them to the Germans), the Italian Army refused and placed them in the relative safety of a civil internment camp. Serge Klarsfeld talks about the Italians' protection of approximately 15,000 Jews in France as well. And since the Italians controlled most of Greece too, we learn about the rescue efforts of at least a few Greek Jews through marriage to women of Italian descent. Nahmias and his wife recall how – although from Salonika – they were spared by the Italian connection, as her parents were from Trieste. The film wisely includes interviews with the now aged (and still modest) Italians who at the time were diplomats and officers engaged in the rescue operations. Rochlitz also composed the music, and is an on-screen interviewer. *The Righteous Enemy* could be double-billed with *The Optimists*, as both the Bulgarians and the Italians chose not to follow orders, and thus protected thousands of Jews.

Schindler. England, 1991. D: Jon Blair, for Thames Television. Narrated by Dirk Bogarde. Long before Spielberg's dramatization, this powerful combination of interviews and archival footage recounts the extraordinary story of Oskar Schindler. Only thirty-one years old at the beginning of World War II, he was a Nazi spy, a playboy (his wife, Emilie, cheerfully acknowledges on-camera that you can't fight when a husband loves all women!), a black marketeer, a bon vivant, and – as the Jewish survivors attest – a saviour, an angel, and their unlikely protector. Irena Scheck, Murray Pantirer, Lutek Feigen, Leopold Pfefferberg, and Ryszard Horowitz are among those who talk about his protection; for example, Feigen says that when they proved inept in making tools, Schindler bought tools on the black market and gave them to the Germans as if they were from his factory. The narration of Amon Goeth's cruelty is juxtaposed with his former mistress Ruth – denying that Goeth hated Jews – as well as the testimony of the Jewish maid Helen: she recalls Goeth's brutality as well as Schindler's kind encouragement. Emilie explains that, whenever her husband was arrested, the Abwehr (military intelligence) and German armament authorities would get him out. We see the horror from Plaszow to Auschwitz, in view of which Schindler's rescue operations in Emalia and later Brinnlitz are all the more remarkable. At war's end, the survivors smuggle him out: he goes to Argentina with his wife, mistress, and some of the Jews he saved. But he ends up alone in Frankfurt, where he was interviewed by German TV in 1964. His voice-over explains that when he saw the horror emerging around 1941, he felt he had to save Jews. We learn that he died in 1974 at the age of sixty-six: his funeral in Israel brought Jews into a church for the first time.

The Second Front. U.S.A., 2000. D: Deborah Freemon. Narrated by Ed Asner, a fine one-hour documentary on the Partisans: we learn that 25–50,000 Jews joined the Partisans, forming 10–15 percent of their organization. Strongest is the archival footage of the Partisans. Only at the end are we told that Russian cameramen (some Jewish) shot this footage. One wants to know more about it: if the Partisans lacked enough food or weapons, how did they have the means to record their clandestine activities? As in *Partisans of Vilna*, survivors (mostly from Lithuania) recall conflicts like the fear of fleeing the ghetto because of reprisals that would be taken against their remaining families.

17 rue Saint-Fiacre. France, 1999. D: Daniel Meyers. R: NCJF. A moving, straightforward chronicle of how two Jewish children were saved by a French Catholic family in Compiegne, occupied by the Nazis during World War II. It begins in August 1995, with the male voice-over explaining that Rachel and Leon have come from the U.S.A. for the ninetieth birthday of their "adopted" mother Suzanne. A cut to wartime Compiegne with black-and-white photos brings us back to the deportation of Jews, which included the Malmed parents. Suzanne says it was not possible to let the children go to their death: she took in her neighbors' son and daughter and raised them with her own two boys. Though risking death, she even moved them to a house in the country when the final deportation began in January 1944. Rachel tells how their little cousin Charles, hidden elsewhere, was deported to Auschwitz – with 206 other children. (None survived.) In the last part, Rachel and Leon tearfully go through the old Compiegne apartment from which their parents were taken, and we see a home movie of Yad Vashem, where Suzanne and her husband (now dead) were honored. (Leon filmed the tree planting.) End titles inform us that "Rachel and Leon were the only Jews remaining in Compiegne at the end of the war." We see how the ordinary decency – which was extraordinary during World War II – of Suzanne and her son Marcel saved lives.

Shtetl. U.S.A., 1996. D: Marian Marzynski.

Sisters in Retirement. France, 2000. D: Maia Wechsler. The focus for one hour is upon four remarkable women – neither Jewish nor Communist – who resisted during World War II and survived Ravensbruck. Still friends, the now aged ladies recall the indignation that led them to take action after Germany's attack on France in May 1940. Portly Germaine claims that women began the Resistance, which, for her, included giving her family's papers to the Levy family; publishing leaflets and newspapers to counter German disinformation; coordinating with London; and helping prisoners to escape. Genevieve – the niece of De Gaulle – bonded with tall, thin Jacqueline. Anise, who gathered military information for London, tells a great story of how neither she nor her father told the other that they were working for the same Resistance group. Each of these women was arrested, interrogated, and deported. (Germaine says the worst moment was seeing her own mother in the same prison.) They ended up in Ravensbruck, a slave labor camp with 150,000 women and children. Genevieve says the reason for their survival was solidarity among prisoners. All four continued to work for human rights. The archival footage is powerful, but one would like to know more about who shot it, particularly the scenes of the people who served as "mailboxes" for the Resistance. The film is inspirational particularly because these heroines' resistance was spontaneous, without a political agenda.

Sobibor, October 14, 1943, 4 p.m. France, 2001. D: Claude Lanzmann. In this powerful story of resistance, the sole successful revolt by Jewish prisoners of a concentration camp is recounted by Yehuda Lerner, a survivor whom the director of *Shoah* interviewed in 1979. Lanzmann's opening voice-over contextualizes Sobibor as the site of a "reappropriation of power and violence by the Jews," exploding two myths – that Jews were led unwitting to a comfortable death, and that they put up no resistance to their executioners. The opening also introduces how the planning and organization of the uprising were the work of Soviet-Jewish officer Alexander Petchersky. Before meeting Lerner, we hear Lanzmann's troubling statement: "But museums and monuments institute oblivion as much as remembrance. Let us now listen to Yehuda Lerner's living words." These words come from the riveting 1979 interview – to which the director adds new footage of Poland and Sobibor – of a survivor. However, hearing Lerner in Hebrew plus the translation into French – followed by Lanzmann's off-screen questions translated into Hebrew – slows the film down. Despite the undeniable power of *Sobibor*, one can also question the film's lengthy ending: we read a printed list of all the Polish towns from which deportations to Sobibor took place in 1942–1943, while hearing Lanzmann's voice-over repeating it. One wonders, in reading the unsubtitled Polish words for January or February, why they are not in French with subtitles. Yes, we see the cumulative effect of dozens of deportations – a total of 250,000 Jews were taken – that ended with the revolt in October, but the effect is numbing. The strongest part of the film is Lerner's account of how he killed a German officer: it was thanks to German punctuality that the revolt took place at exactly 4 p.m., and the widespread resistance went to 5 p.m.

Survivors of the Holocaust. U.S.A., 1995. D: Allan Holzman. Produced by the Shoah Foundation, this 55-minute documentary is a powerful educational tool composed mainly of survivor testimonies, with archival footage and drawings that corroborate the verbal presentation. Arranged chronologically from 1933 through the postwar Nuremberg Trials, it juxtaposes numerous witnesses to Kristallnacht, transports, Auschwitz, liberation, and Palestine.

Steven Spielberg speaks to the camera at the end. Among the particularly moving tales is that of Dr. Alfred Pasternack, who recounts how his father bought in Auschwitz a smuggled prayer book, managing to organize a seder in 1945.

Terezin Diary. U.S.A., 1989. D: Dan Weissman. S: Zuzana Justman. Narrated by Eli Wallach, the film concentrates on Helga Kinsky, who was a child in the Terezin camp and then Auschwitz. Her recollections are intercut with footage from the Nazi propaganda film *Hitler Gives the Jews a Town* and interviews with Hana Greenfield, a Maine-based artist who discusses cultural resistance in Terezin. The riveting stories include how the first Terezin transport to Auschwitz had five thousand Jews who seemed privileged at first, but were eventually gassed (only thirty-seven survived). We hear about Lederer, a Jew who escaped from Auschwitz in 1944 in an SS uniform (with the help of an SS guard), and returned to Terezin to warn the prisoners to organize; however, he was not believed because – before being gassed in Auschwitz – the first group of prisoners had been forced to send postdated postcards back to those still in Terezin. The pre-credit sequence of archival footage effectively introduces this "model ghetto," a way station meant to mask Auschwitz. A 1986 reunion provides the context of Terezin, through which 140,000 prisoners passed, including 15,000 children.

*Terrorists in Retirement. France, 1984. D: Mosco Boucault. A fascinating celebration of a group of surviving old codgers who remain unrecognized heroes of the French Resistance, as well as witnesses to the possible selling-out of immigrant Jews by the Communist high command during World War II. Narrated by Simone Signoret and Gerard Desarthe, it begins with French newsreels of November 1943 that single out foreign Jews as responsible for terrorist attacks in France. By 1944, twenty-three men arrested by the Gestapo and French authorities have been tried and executed. Most are Polish Jews, under the leadership of the Armenian poet Missek Manouchian. At the heart of the film are seven survivors – five Polish, two Rumanian, all Jews working as tailors in Paris – whom we get to know through interviews and reenactments (by the now elderly heroes) of their wartime bomb placing or shooting, like the subway assassination of a German officer. We meet Boris Holban, who trained young immigrants for terrorist activities: they had little to lose – their families had been killed by the Nazis – and most were Communist. In a juicy scene, one of them shows how he made a bomb in his kitchen, and another shows how he carried it in his pants! Jean was tortured by the French before they handed him over to the Germans, who sent him to Struthof as a Jew, a Communist, and a resister. Even though he ended up in Auschwitz, ironically he was better off than his comrades: according to Manouchian's widow, the high command of the Resistance sent her husband's group to death. (A French policeman warned the Resistance that the arrested Davidovich had named names, and the Communists knew that Manouchian and others were being followed. Nevertheless – and unlike other groups – they were ordered to remain in Paris.) A historian says the French couldn't stand the idea that, at liberation, an army out of the shadows, with foreign names, would emerge. Did the Communist party turn the immigrants over? At the end, Weissberg (the explosives man) is seen walking in a cemetery past a tombstone marked "dirty Jew" and a swastika painted on another, as we hear that he never got French nationality. Ironically enough, had the Gestapo not put up a red poster in 1944 with the names and pictures of the twenty-three executed men on it, they might have been forgotten. But Louis Aragon wrote a poem, "The Red Flag," which was set to music by Leo Ferre: we hear the song over the film's opening. Like that of *The Sorrow and the Pity*, the story revealed here undercuts the image of French wartime heroism, and was therefore also shelved from TV broadcast in 1985 (although it aired a month later).

To Speak the Unspeakable: The Message of Elie Wiesel. France/Hungary, 1996. D: Judit Elek. Wiesel returns with five friends to his home town of Sighet, Transylvania, retracing his journey of fifty years before. He delivers a lovely speech at the ceremony during which he receives honorary citizenship in Sighet: "French is my working language, English my teaching language, and Yiddish my dreaming language." The film's problematic structure includes layers that are not sufficiently clear: for example, the voice of William Hurt (the French version uses the actor Jean-Hugues Anglade) recites parts of Wiesel's writings, but we don't know which. Because the archival footage is not identified, the image of a boy buying books could be from a fiction film as well as a newsreel. Strongest are the human encounters, like Wiesel with a ninety-one-year-old Sighet Jew whose brother was the Wiesels' doctor: he gives him the dead brother's medical diploma, as well as the last letter written by a family member. Previously recorded material is effective, like Wiesel's speech at the inauguration of the U.S. Holocaust Museum at the beginning, and his speech upon receiving the Nobel Prize in 1986 at the end.

Visitor from the Living, A. France, 1999. D: Claude Lanzmann. This is less a motion picture than a taped interview between the director of *Shoah* and Maurice Rossel in 1979. Since it did not fit into *Shoah*, Lanzmann turned it into a free-standing 65-minute video twenty years later. Rossel, sixty-three, remembers in French his stint as a Swiss official of the Red Cross. Bored with being a border guard, at first he became the Red Cross representative in Berlin. He arrived unannounced at Auschwitz. Although Lanzmann prods him, he recalls no stench, no smoke, no skeletal bodies, only the elegant camp commandant who served him coffee. Moreover, he headed the Red Cross delegation to Theresienstadt in June 1944, and wrote a report that confirmed the Nazi hoax of it being a model ghetto, a happy village. It is irksome that he keeps using the term "Israelites" instead of "Juifs" (Jews), as if they belonged in Israel. Lanzmann tries to get him to acknowledge his complicity in the Nazi hoodwinking, but he genially refuses to express guilt. When Lanzmann asked permission of Rossel twenty years later to release the film, he agreed, asking only "not to make me look ridiculous." "It was not my intention to do so," is Lanzmann's ironic last line of the crawl before the film ends abruptly.

Voices of the Children. U.S.A., 1999. D: Zuzana Justman. Three people who were imprisoned as children in the Terezin concentration camp are the focus of this 80-minute documentary. Justman (who spent two years in Terezin herself) uses their drawings and diaries to trace the survivors' war experiences. Interviews with each of the three – one in the U.S.A., one in Austria, and one in the Czech Republic – include their families, thereby raising questions about the effect of the Holocaust on all their lives. The film incorporates the survivors attending a performance of the children's opera *Brundibar* in Prague; given that the Nazis permitted the Terezin inmates to stage *Brundibar* for propaganda purposes during the war, their return to this opera is resonant.

Voyage of the St. Louis. Canada/France, 1994. D: Maziar Bahari. R: NCJF. The German luxury liner that was to take 917 Jewish refugees from Hamburg to Cuba is the basis for a cautionary tale of indifference. Officials in Cuba had been paid $500 per person, but the refugees were inexplicably refused entry (presumably stemming from the tension between President Bau and Batista, head of the Armed Forces, and from U.S. State Department cables to the effect that they should not accept the Jews). We begin with Herbert Karliner, whose observations return to the summer of 1939, then is joined by other survivors. They (and the narration) convey how Captain Schroeder was very decent, how the ship then tried to land off Florida (the U.S. Coast Guard refused to admit them), and how four European countries finally agreed to take them in – Belgium, Holland, France, and England. But once World War II began and the countries were occupied, three-fourths of the passengers were nevertheless deported and killed.

Will My Mother Go Back to Berlin? U.S.A., 1994. D: Micha Peled. A wonderfully personal 53-minute video documentary about the relationship between the filmmaker – an Israeli based in San Francisco – and his mother, Nora, who escaped from Berlin to Palestine in 1937. It begins with him in Berlin, retracing her steps, meeting her old girlfriend Luisa in a classroom (where the camera includes "Nazis raus" – Nazis Out – scrawled on a wall), and plotting to get Nora to return there with him. He arrives in Israel with an invitation from the mayor of Berlin, but doesn't know how to give it to his feisty eighty-year-old mother, who doesn't want to hear of Germany. They talk – seemingly unconcerned about the camera – of intimate details. For example, Peled asks about being the illegitimate child from an affair she had with a married man. The poignant voice-over conveys that they both deprived each other of the thing they most wanted – he a father, and she grandchildren. They visit an Arab to whom she has rented a room – her way of creating peace. He finally shows her the invitation, which she of course refuses. But at the end, Peled returns to Berlin anyway, and the camera leaves him in long shot on a telephone in the station. Although not exactly a Holocaust film – Nora got out of Germany in time – this is still a portrait of Jewish-German identity in the shadow of the Holocaust.

Witness: Voices from the Holocaust. U.S.A., 1998. D: Joshua M. Greene and Shiva Kumar. This film is composed of very strong interviews conducted at Yale University's archive. We meet not only Holocaust survivors but a man who was in the Hitler Youth, an American POW, and a liberator. The archival footage and photos are well integrated. Most moving are Renee Hartman (in 1979), who recalls how she and her sister went to the police after their parents were taken, saying they wanted to go with them; the "Hitlerjugen" who was proud at age ten to be "caught up in the display of might"; and Joseph (there are no last names in the captions, which do include age and year of interview) explaining how the Nazis posted the names of men who would be killed if anything happened to the Germans. Sometimes the camera angle is too tight, cropping a head, as with a woman talking about the end of the Warsaw Ghetto. The film is arranged chronologically and is culled from ten thousand hours of video testimonies.

The Wonderful, Horrible Life of Leni Riefenstahl. Germany, 1993. D: Ray Muller. Three fascinating hours are devoted to this complex, feisty filmmaker (not to mention, at various times, dancer, mountain climber, actress, photographer, and deep-sea diver). Brilliant but apolitical, aesthetically sophisticated but socially prone to tunnel vision, the ninety-year-old Riefenstahl is still tough, attractive, and unrepentant for having made *Triumph of the Will.* As she says in her own defense, she never joined the Nazi party, never said anything anti-Semitic, didn't know about the concentration camps in the mid-1930s, and was not aware of where her own film might lead. It's interesting to see the trajectory of her career, from scaling wintry mountains barefoot in her youth, to photographing underwater life: both are far from the madding crowd of her two acknowledged masterpieces, *Triumph of the Will* and *Olympiad.* We see her among the Nuba tribe – befriending them and capturing their beautiful bodies on film – but when Muller asks her about a "fascist aesthetic" in her work, she dismisses Susan Sontag's analysis. It is hard to believe Riefenstahl when she says that her association with the Third Reich is now such a source of pain that she thinks death would be a welcome release: she is obviously too much in love with life to mean it. The film wisely intersperses footage from the concentration camps, a sense of destroyed bodies in juxtaposition to the Aryan physical ideals she photographed. Although her films were used in the service of evil, her talent and perfectionism make condemning Riefenstahl ultimately too easy. R: KINO.

Zahor. France, 1996. D: Fabienne Rousso-Lenoir. This 22-minute film uses still photos and footage – accompanied by a soundtrack consisting of text and songs (some written by the individuals depicted) – to celebrate the lives of the Holocaust's victims.

Fiction
Germany
Abraham's Gold. 1990. D: Jorg Grasser. Tensions abound in this German drama. An old Nazi is raising his granddaughter because her mother (Hanna Schygulla) is never around. He returns to Auschwitz where he buried the gold teeth of victims, taking along a young buddy (Gunther Maria Hallmer, who played the vicious officer in *Sophie's Choice*). The

younger man thinks nothing of it, but when his old mother figures out the origin of the teeth – and he remains indifferent – she gives him letters and photos that attest to his real origins: he was a Jewish baby whom she saved and brought up as her own.

Aimee and Jaguar. 1998. D: Max Farberbock, and screenplay with Rona Munro, based on the book by Erica Fischer. A not quite persuasive true story of an unlikely love in 1943–1944 Berlin. Felice (Maria Schrader) is elegant, smart, lesbian, and Jewish, working for a Nazi newspaper so she can get things to the underground. She falls for Lilly (Juliane Kohler), a philandering Nazi housewife and mother of four boys, whose husband is in the army. It is hard to grasp what brings these women so desperately together, especially because Felice knows Lilly is a far-from-bright anti-Semite. And why would Lilly toss her whole life away for Felice? While the sex looks great, it is hard to believe that Lilly would allow Felice to move in to her home, and to entertain her Jewish-looking friends there. When Felice finally confesses to Lilly that she is Jewish, Lilly embraces her. But the Gestapo take Felice. At the end, the film tells us only that Felice died. What really happened is far more interesting: Lilly's son converted to Judaism and lives in Israel; Lilly, now eighty-five and living in Berlin, sheltered three other Jewish women at the end of the war.

Bronstein's Children. 1991. D: Jerzy Kavalerowicz, and S with Jurek Becker from the latter's novel. This engrossing post-Holocaust drama, set in 1973 East Berlin, begins with the funeral of a Jewish man. The voice-over of his ninteen-year-old son, Hans (Matthias Paul), now an orphan, leads to flashbacks that reveal the tense relationship he had with his father, Aron (Armin Mueller-Stahl). He learns that Aron and some of his Jewish buddies are holding captive a former SS guard (Rolf Hoppe). When Hans doesn't understand why they simply don't hand him over to the police, Aron explains that they are Holocaust survivors and – although they never personally knew this guard from Neuengamme – don't want to give him to an "inferior" court of "inferior" people. Interwoven is Hans's relationship to two young women: his girlfriend, Marthe (Katharina Abt), is a cheerful actress whose parents take Hans in after the funeral; and his sister Elle (Angela Winkler) lives in a mental hospital, damaged after years of being hidden with strangers during World War II. In the last scene of the flashback, Hans tries to free the prisoner, but finds his father next to the prisoner's bed, apparently dead of a heart attack. Aron calls Jewish identity an invention so intelligently widespread that the Jews have come to believe it themselves! Indeed, how much Jewish identity could there be in 1973 East Berlin, apart from Holocaust memories?

*Europa, Europa. 1991. D: Agnieszka Holland. Mainly in German and Russian, this French-German coproduction tells the powerful and true (if often unbelievable) story of Solomon Perel (seen briefly singing at the end of the film). On the eve of his Bar-Mitzvah, Nazis attack his home in Germany and kill his sister. Since he ran naked from his bath, a girl gives him a Nazi coat – the first signal of his assumption of costumes and identities. His father takes the family back to his native Lodz in Poland. From there, the handsome Sol (Marco Hofschneider) is sent by his father to the east, with his brother Isaac. They are separated at the river, where some opt to go with the Bolsheviks, others with the Germans. Sol is taken to a Communist orphanage in Grodno where he learns Russian and obedience to Stalin. Captured by German soldiers, Sol claims to be Josef Peters, an Aryan from Grodno; because he translates Russian for them, the German soldiers good-naturedly adopt him, especially Kellerman (Andre Wilms). When this cultured German learns Sol's secret, he does not betray him, perhaps because he has a crush on Sol. After he and the rest of the company are killed, Sol tries to rejoin the Bolsheviks, but ironically leads to their defeat. He is sent to an elite Hitler Youth school! Once again, his identity must be transformed, as he swears allegiance to Hitler. He and Leni (Julie Delpy) are attracted to each other, but – because she is a rabid Nazi – he cannot let her discover his circumcision. Together, they see a mass of Jewish headstones, poignantly presented in a slow tracking shot as they are removed from the earth. She turns against him, but Leni's mother figures

out that he is Jewish and is surprisingly loving to him. Sol tries to get into the Lodz Ghetto, but can go only in a sealed train. Powerful glimpses of horror are presented from his point of view. In a battle with the Russians, Sol deserts and surrenders to them; he is not believed, taken to a concentration camp, and about to be killed. Amazingly enough, Sol is recognized by and reunited with his brother Isaac. At the end, we see the aged Sol in Israel forty-five years later.

From Hell to Hell. 1996. D: Dmitri Astrakhan. S: Oleg Danilov and Art Bernd. A wrenching Russian drama with German financing from producer Artur (*Europa, Europa*) Brauner, based on a horrifying fact of postwar history: on July 4, 1946, forty-one Jews were murdered by Poles in Kielce. The fictional tale begins in a concentration camp where the Jewish heroine, Helena, has a flashback to her wedding day in Kielce, which was shared by a Gentile couple. She and Anna Sikorsky share a clinic room to give birth: she and her husband, Hendrik, are blessed with a beautiful girl, but Anna's baby dies and she cannot have more. When the Jews are deported, the desperate Goldes pass the Sikorskys and heed the latter's plea to give them their baby Fela for hiding. Of course they raise the Jewish baby as their own happy Christian daughter, while the Poles move in to the homes left by the Jews. After the war, Hendrik returns as a Red Army hero and helps the Kielce survivors back to life. But this sets the stage for jealousy and rage, both personally between the two mothers (the fathers are more understanding of the claims of the other) and, communally, between the returning Jews and the appropriating Poles. On a night when Hendrik and his men are away, the community attacks the Jewish home with axes and pitchforks, cheered on by other Poles at windows and in the street. Fela has overheard the Sikorskys and protects her real mother from Anna's violence. When the few surviving Jews leave town, Anna tries to stop Fela – not wanting her to suffer from being a Jew – but Fela calls her a murderer. The film ends with the burial of the coffins in a mass grave and the printed names of the real forty-one victims. If the greatest anti-Semitic horrors historically have indeed been German-Russian "coproductions" in the 1940s, it is fascinating that these two countries teamed up to make a film condemning Polish anti-Semitism.

Harmonists, The. 1998. D: Joseph Vilsmaier. S: Klaus Richter. The true story of a famous German singing group during the rise of Nazi Germany is entertaining and moving. The five singers and a pianist struggle at the beginning, then become a huge success in Germany and abroad, but disband after being banned. Why? Three are Jewish (not to mention two of the wives), so they are not permitted to perform after their final 1934 Munich concert. The Comedian Harmonists is the brainchild of Harry (Ulrich Noethan), who puts an ad in the paper. Robert (Ben Becker) barges in for an audition and becomes the cofounder, bringing in Roman (Heino Ferch), Erich (Heinrich Schafmeister) – adorned with a monocle and cigarette holder – Ari (Max Tichof) who loves the ladies, and pianist Erwin (Kai Wiesinger). Ironically enough, their inspiration is the American a cappella group the Revellers, and they do German elaborations of barbershop quintet in black tie and tails. Beyond their romantic stories, the most frightening scene occurs when their unlikely fan – the Gauleiter Julius Streicher (Rolf Hoppe, playing a character similar to his role in *Mephisto*!) – invites them home to perform. Harry gets sick doing a German song, and Bob explains that they can't continue. "A pity," says the Nazi leader, and we think they are going to suffer. But the Harmonists go on tour to America. By the end, the three Jewish members leave on a train for Vienna/Budapest, and we read that both groups formed new versions – with little success. Details like Roman becoming the oldest cantor in the U.S.A. are better elaborated in the three-hour documentary by Eberhard Fechner, with interviews of the four surviving members in 1976.

Leni. 1994. D and S: Leo Hiemer. This very moving German drama could be double-billed with *The Revolt of Job*. In 1937, a young Jewish woman gives birth to a girl in a convent; the elderly nun Jadwiga has agreed to take the infant to an elderly farm couple to raise.

At first, Aibele (Hannes Thanheiser) is not thrilled about having a baby on the farm, and Alwina (Christa Bernal) does most of the rearing. But as Leni grows into a girl (Johanna Thanheiser), it is the "father" who is even closer to her. He is always taking photos of her with the camera that her biological mother gave him when she visited the baby. Things get tense because the mayor is a fervent Nazi and knows that Leni's heritage is "fishy." He forces Aibele to let Leni go back to the convent by making him choose between her and his retarded younger brother, Severin (Martin Abram). The local teacher accompanies the distraught Aibele to Munich to find Leni, but they are not permitted to see her (except through a keyhole). All the children are deported, and Jadwiga chooses to go with them. *Leni* indicts the Catholic Church for complicity with the Nazis and, in an understated way, reveals the insanity of a system that could relentlessly go after a little girl who was already brought up as a good Christian. Like *Korczak*, the film's power lies in basic questions of how such beautiful little children could be considered the enemy.

Life for Life – Maximilian Kolbe. Germany/France/Poland, 1991. D: Krzysztof Zanussi, and S with Jan Jozef Szczepanski. An understated Holocaust drama from a Christian perspective, recounting the martyrdom of the Franciscan priest Kolbe who gave his life in exchange for that of another prisoner in Auschwitz. The film uses a *Citizen Kane*–like structure of flashbacks, and begins with a beautiful credit sequence that has no dialogue: a dog fetches a stick for a soldier . . . and will later search for a prisoner. Hanys (Christopher Walz) escapes from the camp. Poles help him: an old stationmaster gives him clothes, and peasants on a train feed him. But the Nazis arbitrarily select ten men who will starve to death because of his escape. In the first flashback, we see but don't hear Kolbe (Edward Zentara) step forward to change places with a young, screaming man. In the second flashback (from a priest's point of view), we see Kolbe – a figure of strength and integrity – arrested at a monastery. The third is an older carpenter recalling how Kolbe cleverly got land from a prince for the monastery. The fourth shows Kolbe saying that, for love to exist among people, there must be total and instant forgiveness. We learn that his life expectancy was short, as he had only one lung: maybe he therefore saw life as a gift. When a priest tries to get Kolbe canonized, an Italian priest (Jerzy Stuhr) is opposed because Kolbe's sacrifice was for a person rather than religion. We see Hanys as an older man in America: he has clearly wasted his life, unable to rise to the responsibility of having escaped. He watches on television as Kolbe is finally "beatified" – the film continuing its dialectic between the saint and the wastrel.

Martha and I. Germany/France, 1992. D and S: Jiri Weiss. Hardly seeming like a Holocaust drama at first, this film is narrated by the adult Emil: he recalls how, at fourteen in 1934, he was sent by his parents from Prague to the countryside to live with his uncle, Ernst Fuchs (Michel Piccoli). Known as "the doctor with golden hands," he is a cultured, piano-playing Jewish gynecologist, married to a younger and beautiful Hungarian woman. When he finds a man in her bed one night, he divorces her and decides to marry his faithful, dumpy maid, Martha (Marianne Sagebrecht). Both families are opposed: Emil's female Jewish relatives are snobs, and Martha's Sudeten-German brothers are anti-Semitic. With Emil as a surrogate son, they are nevertheless happy – until 1938, when Jews start being persecuted in Czechoslovakia. Ernst convinces Emil to leave the country; Martha desperately and secretly writes to every Fuchs in the New York telephone book to find him a sponsor; Ernst tries to persuade Martha to divorce him so she won't be in danger. When she refuses, Ernst asks her brothers to come when he is away. Although it is unclear if he meant for them to take her away, this is indeed what happens. After Ernst is deported, Emil returns at war's end as part of the Czech army. He learns that the despairing Martha threw herself under a train. This moving love story suggests that if death was to be the couple's fate, they should have stayed together, at least comforting one another until the end.

My Mother's Courage. Germany, 1996. D: Michael Verhoeven. R: NCJF.

Nasty Girl, The. Germany, 1990. D: Michael Verhoeven.

Pedestrian, The. Germany/Switzerland, 1973. D: Maximilian Schell. Intriguing drama about a German industrialist, Geise (Gustav Rudolf Sellner), who has two layers of skeletons metaphorically rattling in his private closet. One level is introduced by a parasitic newspaper editor: Geise drove through a red light – killing his elder son (Schell) – and is now a pedestrian because his license was suspended. Second, the newspaper's research suggests that Geise might have been involved in atrocities during World War II in Greece. Flashbacks reveal brutal scenes of civilians being executed – women and children are shot in a church – presided over by a bespectacled man who might be Geise. A female survivor brought in to follow and identify him is not sure. The newspaper runs the story anyway. The closing sequence is enigmatic: we see out-of-focus fossils in a museum, accompanied by Schell's voice recounting a dream – that people were looking up at a satellite but it was really death. There is a sense of history as both fossils and fetuses in glass jars, or arrested development.

Seven Minutes. Germany, 1990. D: Klaus Maria Brandauer. S: Stephen Sheppard. Although the first half is slow and a bit vague, the second half is taut and involving once we know what the protagonist is up to. Georg Elser (Brandauer) is introduced in 1938 Munich locked in a beer hall, calling for someone to let him out. We learn later that he is there every night, secretly busting a neat square area in a hidden wall. Why? The Führer is slated to speak there, and Elser will place a bomb. But this information comes gradually, and is complicated by the fact that Georg seems drawn to the beer hall for the waitress Anneliese (Rebecca Miller) as well. He works in a quarry, from which he steals explosives. He and his buddy are later brought to the SS because they have materials needed for the war effort; before being released, they are glimpsed by Wagner (Brian Dennehy), an important German official. Georg completes the bomb, installs it, and manages to get his now pregnant fiancée Anneliese out on time – even though she was the one who was supposed to serve water to the Führer. They manage to be on a train to Zurich when the bomb explodes, and it looks like she gets to safety. But he is caught at the border, where Wagner tells him he missed Hitler by seven minutes. The end titles inform us that Elser was put in various concentration camps awaiting a show trial, and was finally executed shortly before the end of the war. One wants to know more about what made Georg tick: why did he resist? Why didn't he simply respond "Heil Hitler" to an officer in the latrine instead of being beaten and pissed upon? Was he part of the resistance?

Sterne (Stars). East Germany/Bulgaria, 1958. D: Konrad Wolf. This black-and-white drama feels both authentic and poetic. Jews board a train that is sealed, and the film becomes a flashback centered on Walter, a good, handsome German corporal stationed in Bulgaria. He would rather draw than deal with politics, but the arrival of Jews from Salonika forces him to a new awareness. Walter is drawn to the strong Ruth, a teacher who seems to know that their destination, Auschwitz, is no farm. Although it is a love story, Ruth quietly pulls back from Walter's attempted kiss, acknowledging the gulf between them. When Walter learns from his crass lieutenant, Kurt, that it is a death camp, he tries to hide Ruth, with the help of Petko, who seems to represent the Communist resistance. But Kurt lies to Walter about when the Jews are leaving: after arranging a hiding place with local Jews, Walter sees the departing train in the rainy night. It is too late for Ruth and the other Jews, but Walter will link up with Petko and help the Communists get arms. There are fine visual touches, like a superimposition of Ruth's face: the image of her is imprinted even though the woman will be destroyed. *Stars* begins and ends with more Jewish detail than other Holocaust films from Communist countries: we hear the Yiddish song of lament, "Es Brennt," and, at the end, the words are printed. Each character speaks his own language, including the Greeks who speak Ladino.

Three Days in April. Germany, 1995. D and S: Oliver Storz. R: NCJF. Based on a true story that took place at the end of World War II. In a small Swabian village, Anna seems to be the bravest soul despite her young age: she is head of the Nazi Youth group, but instinctively comforts a shell-shocked soldier and tries to hide him from the SS. He is shot. Far more knowing is a female singer (resembling a cross between Lauren Bacall and Marlene Dietrich), who hooks up with the local sergeant of the depot. Their lives are all put to the test when a transport of concentration camp inmates shows up on their tracks, and is stopped there. First Anna and then others (mostly women) defy orders and bring food. But when the train doors are opened for ten minutes (because the singer bribed an officer with cognac), the townspeople are too numbed by the sight of the dehumanized prisoners to even move. The situation deteriorates because no one assumes responsibility: the pastor, well-meaning but too weak, and the men finally decide to push the transport back on the tracks so that it will no longer be their problem. As in *The Boat Is Full*, these provincial folk are divided in their feelings, but give in to a cowardice that will prove fatal. Instead of opening the doors of the trains – as Anna begins to do, but stops – they are too afraid, and prefer to leave them to another town. Although Anna is presumably scarred by this incident, the present-day frame shows her as an older woman who kept this secret. Curiously enough, *Three Days in April* is a first feature for Storz, a sixty-seven-year-old screenwriter and theater critic.

France

Années Sandwich, Les (The Sandwich Years). France, 1988. D: Pierre Boutron. A very moving coming-of-age story set in July 1947, introduced by a flashback from contemporary Paris, characterized by anti-Semitic vandalism. Victor (Thomas Langmann) – who lost his parents in the war (we see a black-and-white flashback of a roundup from his point of view) and was hidden with a Christian family – has escaped to Paris. He finally finds work, and much more, thanks to Max (Wojtek Pszoniak), who yells a lot but is a basically tender Jew. We later see his tattoo and learn that his wife and children were killed in the Holocaust. Victor also becomes friends with the rich Felix, sharing movies and books. But Felix isn't allowed to see Victor because he is Jewish. When Max sees that Victor's tears are not just for the loss of his parents but the sense of abandonment by his friend, he pulls him out of it. The title comes from Max telling the boy that these years are like the thin slice of veal between thick gobs of bread: all must be eaten, even if the mustard makes your eyes water. A bit sentimental, but effective.

Dr. Petiot. 1990. D: Christian de Chalonge.

Ivan and Abraham (Moi Ivan, Toi Abraham). France, 1993. D: Yolande Zauberman. A fascinating Yiddish-language drama (also including Russian, Polish, and a Gypsy dialect) set in Poland in the 1930s. Ivan (Sacha Yakovlev) is a Christian boy living with the family of his Jewish friend Abraham (Roma Alexandrovitch). Abraham incurs the wrath of his grandfather, Nachman (Rolan Bykov), because he doesn't like to pray, but has a warm relationship with his father, Mardoche (Alexander Kaliagin), and mother, Reyzele (Helene Lapiower). His sister Rachel (Maira Lipkina) is in love with Aaron (Vladimir Mashkov), a Communist who has just escaped from prison and resists romantic entanglement. But when Ivan and Abraham run away, Rachel and Aaron go to look for them. The boys hide with the horse lover Stepan (Daniel Olbrychski), who promises Abraham a little horse if he can cure the suffering animal – which the boy manages to do. Rachel convinces Aaron to take her to France with him. When the boys return to the shtetl, they find the home burned and the parents killed. This pre-Holocaust scene of anti-Semitic destruction is particularly searing after the lovely sensuality that characterizes the rest of the film.

Je suis vivante et je vous aime (I'm alive and I love you). France, 1998. D: Roger Kahane. A touching wartime drama in which a French peasant becomes a resister. Railroad worker

Julien (Jerome Deschamps) is a quiet guy who lives with his mother, ignoring how much his friend (Agnes Soral) loves him. Under a cargo of deported Jews, he takes a note that was slipped through by a certain "Sarah" and brings its message – the film's title – to an old Hungarian-Jewish couple. They assume that Julien has seen their brave daughter and he plays along, especially after seeing the adorable little boys from whom Sarah was taken. His first act of resistance is to get them false papers. But by the time he brings them the identity cards, they have all been taken – with the exception of Thibault, who was hiding. Julien tries to place the boy with a neighbor, who not only refuses but denounces them to the local police. Julien decides to hide the child in his own home (surprisingly enough, his mother agrees). Reading Sarah's diary, Julien falls in love with the image of her. Amid the cheers when the Allies land in Normandy, he foolishly tries to do something with a Nazi train, is chased, and must leave. He sends the child with a nun and other kids to the woods. After the war, it seems a bit too easy for him to get Thibault back and to find Sarah, who has indeed survived. It ends with her finally meeting Julien and handing him the same note that she had slid out of the train. As in *Life Is Beautiful*, protecting a child is the consummate act.

Lisa. France, 2000. D: Pierre Grimblat. Although well-intentioned and occasionally enhanced by attractive visuals, the feeling of this film is one of contrived melodrama, with Gabriel Yared's score imposing too intrusively. Jeanne Moreau's unmistakably husky voice introduces herself as Lisa, whose younger self (Marion Cotillard) surges in memory. Sam, a young filmmaker, has discovered a can of prewar film with a handsome actor who disappeared, Sylvain. *Lisa* keeps moving back and forth jerkily between Sam in the present, coming to terms with his Jewish parents – who won't talk about the war, and raised him without religion – and Lisa falling in love with Sylvain in the past. (Since she lives in a TB sanatorium as an orphan, it is unclear whether or not she is Jewish.) Her roommate, Henriette, is the girlfriend of a Nazi-loving French soldier and spouts anti-Semitic rhetoric. When the area is occupied, the doctor who heads the clinic hides Jews in a nearby movie-house cellar, and makes Lisa the go-between. Sylvain escapes from a POW camp, which we learn in a typically contrived fashion, milked beyond plausibility: at night, Lisa climbs to the little tower where they once kissed, and where she later screamed (begging our disbelief, considering her weak lungs, amid swelling music), but we see the back of Sylvain's head as he waits way too long for her to see him. He hides with the Jews and, in a presumably parallel tale to Sam's, reacquires Jewish identity. Henriette finds the Jews and denounces everyone. In the most egregious scene, as the Jews and the doctor are taken away or killed, Sylvain is finally allowed to stay with Lisa. But, inexplicably and melodramatically, he kisses her goodbye to join the Jews who are sure to be murdered.

*Lucie Aubrac. France, 1997. D: Claude Berri, based on Aubrac's book. An exciting true story of love and politics set in 1943 Lyons amid the French Resistance. Raymond Aubrac (Daniel Auteuil) is first seen setting a bomb – with his buddies – that blows up a Nazi train. He is also the loved and loving husband of Lucie (Carole Bouquet) with whom he has a son. No one ever questions whether he is right to risk his life for the Resistance: he simply acts, as does Lucie. At first, he is arrested for black-market activities – suspected of terrorism – but his wife's brave ploy works: she warns the prosecutor that he will be killed if Raymond is not released. After they move and assume different names, Raymond is set up, along with "Max" – the alias of Jean Moulin (Patrice Chereau) – and other buddies. Since Hardy (Pascal Greggory) is the only one who escapes, and was not supposed to be at the meeting, he is probably the villain. While Raymond is imprisoned and tortured, Lucie (now pregnant) does not give up. She manages to convince a Nazi officer (Andrzej Seweryn) that his prisoner must marry her so that her unborn child will have a father. She and Raymond are indeed "married," leading to an escape when the truck bringing him back to prison is ambushed. Judaism amounts to a footnote in the film: Raymond's

parents are named "Samuel," and Lucie begs them to change their name. They refuse, and we learn that they have been deported. Raymond and Lucie fly to safety in London.

Pétain. France, 1993. D: Jean Marboeuf. A historical drama that re-creates French guilt in the collaborationist years. Beginning in 1940, we see how Pétain (Jacques Dufilho), Pierre Laval (Jean Yanne), and their ministers accommodate and endorse Nazism in France. Even if their initial reasons are comprehensible – a desire to end bloodshed with an armistice – they become villainous, especially in their anti-Semitism. As they place in motion the Rafle du Vel d'Hiv (the roundup of Jews to Paris's sports stadium, the Velodrome d'Hiver), and letters of denunciation pour in, the Resistance takes hold. When it looks like the Germans are losing, Pétain shows his cowardice in preparing a defense that he was always anti-Nazi. (Laval is right in telling him that he went all the way, whereas Pétain lacked courage.) At the end, we learn that Laval was tried and killed, while Petain lived, imprisoned, another six years.

Voyages. France, 1999. D: Emmanuel Finkiel. This postwar drama by Kieslowski's former assistant – set in Poland, France, and Israel – shows a deep sensitivity to older Jewish people marked by the Holocaust. In the first of three tales, a tourist bus between Warsaw and Auschwitz breaks down on a cold winter day. The mostly Yiddish-speaking passengers are understandably irritable, especially Rivka (Shulamit Adar), who is angry at her husband for having left her at the cemetery when she wandered off on her own. There is a gentle irony throughout this section: Rivka chooses the moment of a bus breakdown to tell her husband she no longer loves him and wants to leave him; moreover, when they finally reach Auschwitz, she sleeps on the bus and doesn't even go in (although the trip was her idea). A particularly chilling moment occurs when the son of a Holocaust survivor urinates in the snow and notices, underneath the train, tracks that led to the concentration camp. In part 2, Regine (Liliane Rovere) receives a phone call in her Paris apartment from Graneck, an elderly gentleman claiming to be her long-lost father. When he (Nathan Cogan) comes to stay with her, it becomes increasingly clear that this is a case of mistaken (if wished-for) identity. Although he packs his bags at the end of the segment, Regine urges him to stay so they can look for his real daughter. The third story centers on Vera (Esther Gorintin), who – in her eighties – has emigrated from Moscow to Tel Aviv. Sweet-faced, stooped, moving slowly, she has accompanied her young neighbors from Russia. Searching for a long-lost cousin in a sun-baked and chaotic city where no one seems to speak Yiddish, she finally finds her in a rest home. Back on a bus, she is overcome by the Israeli heat; by chance, Rivka (from part 1) is on the same bus and helps Vera, inviting her home for a cold drink. When Vera leaves, Rivka receives a phone call from Paris similar to Regine's in part 2, implying that they are sisters: the old man asks her whether she spells her last name Graneck. As in Kieslowski's *Three Colors* trilogy, the triadic structure ends in a connection among all three stories. Finkiel's first feature deftly blends nonprofessional actors with accomplished thespians, and conveys a nostalgia for a disappearing world of Yiddish-speaking characters.

Other European Countries

*All My Loved Ones. Czech Republic, Slovakia, Poland, 2000. D: Matej Minac. S: Jiri Hubac. A moving, Czech-language drama set in 1938. The opening and closing frame contains documentary footage of the real Nicholas Winton, a British stockbroker who saved 669 Jewish children via the *Kindertransports*. Within it is the fictional tale of the Silbersteins, a loving, loyal, cultured, and wealthy Czech-Jewish family. Only little David will survive because he leaves before September 1939 (his adult voice-over narration is heard periodically). His uncle, Sam (Jiri Bartoska), is a famous violinist who wants to marry a lovely young Gentile woman (Agnieszka Wagner), but her father won't permit her to wed a Jew. After he raises the money for emigration to Paris by selling all his possessions, his agent steals it

all, and Sam kills himself. His brother, Jakub (Josef Abraham), is a doctor and an idealist who doesn't believe it's time to flee. The most frightening character is the gardener Spitzer (Marian Labuda), who teaches the children a Nazi marching song, and later becomes the representative of the Gestapo in the area. As in *The Garden of the Finzi-Continis*, the family is dispossessed of their lovely things; but unlike the Italian classic, the existence of Winton (Rupert Graves) – who saves children – counteracts the horror. In a Chekhovian way, the film re-creates a world that is about to fall apart.

Border Street. Poland, 1947. D: Aleksander Ford.

*Burial of Potatoes. Poland, 1991. D: Jan Jakub Kolski. A searing and poetic portrait of postwar anti-Semitism among Polish peasants. The return of Mateusz (Franciszek Pieczka) is met with hostility in a rural community where land is parceled out. The cause seems to be revealed when neighbors return leather and tools to this saddler, and one woman spits out "Jew." Mateusz has indeed returned from a concentration camp; his wife is apparently dead, and his young son, Jurek, has died under mysterious circumstances. After someone tries to burn down his home, Mateusz appears before the neighbors in his concentration camp uniform: it does not have a Jewish star but a *P* inside a triangle, and he drops his pants to show that he is not Jewish. "And," he adds, "I regret not being Jewish. It would be less painful: I'd be dead." It turns out that his son was killed by the complicity of the village because no one sent for a doctor after he was wounded (probably attacked by one of the villagers). Mateusz's revenge is to take the three guiltiest men and make them pull a wagon to unearth his son and give him a proper burial. At the end, he meets a little boy who is Jewish, and whose family was deported. He says he belongs to no one, and Mateusz insists that he is rooted in the land.

Distant Journey. Czechoslovakia, 1948. D: Alfred Radok.

Divided We Fall. Czech Republic, 2001. D: Jan Hrebejk. S: Petr Jarchovsky.

Easter Week (Wielki Tydzien, a.k.a. Holy Week). Poland/Germany, 1995. D: Andrzej Wajda. Based on Jerzy Andrzejewski's novel, a troubling dramatic portrait of the first seven days of the Warsaw Ghetto Uprising in 1943 as seen from outside the Ghetto. Irena (Beata Fudalej), a Jewess, buys her freedom from Gestapo men with a gold coin. She bumps into her former lover Jan (Wojciech Malajkat) during an air raid, and he invites her to his home. In the suburbs, she takes shelter with him and his saintly wife, Anna (Magdalena Warzecha) – who, with her long blond hair, is often photographed like a divine vision. Although pregnant, she never questions her husband about the danger of hiding a Jewish woman. Equally self-sacrificing is Jan's younger brother, who seems to be organizing young boys to fight the Germans (although it is not clear if they are actually going to the Ghetto). Irena is not particularly sympathetic: although she is supposed to stay out of sight, she stretches out on the balcony, her nipples visible beneath her nightgown to us and to the husband of her caretaker. This gives the nasty caretaker an additional reason to denounce her. When forced to leave, Irena yells, "I hope you all burn in hell," before walking into the fiery Ghetto. The film is effective when presenting haunting images like the eerie flames of the Ghetto seen from a roof at night; or its ashes dotting the white sheets hanging in the suburbs; or the Ghetto smoke visible at the carousel that children ride on the Aryan side. The lack of sympathy created for the heroine is a drawback: we almost want her to leave in order to save her protectors! Although we see Polish people willing to risk their lives for a Jew, the nagging question is whether she is worth the risk.

*Gloomy Sunday (Ein Lied von Liebe und Tod), also known as *The Piano Player.* Germany/Hungary, 1999. D: Rolf Schubel. Based on Nick Barkow's novel, *Das Lied von Traurigen Sonntag,* this powerful German romantic drama is set in Budapest during the rise of Nazism. In 1930, Laszlo (Joachim Krol), a delightful and decent Jew, opens a restaurant. He is enamored of the beautiful Ilona (Erika Marozsan). Andras (Stefano Dionisi) becomes their pianist. Ilona is honest about her attraction to him as well, which the open

Laszlo allows. He composes a melancholy and haunting song, "Gloomy Sunday," which leads people to suicide in record numbers. Also in love with Ilona is the German Hans (Ben Becker). When she refuses his marriage proposal, he jumps in the Danube and is rescued by Laszlo. A few years later, Hans is a member of the Nazi party. Although he protects Laszlo from another German officer who kicks him after eating in his restaurant, Hans turns out to be a profiteering bad guy. Yes, he issues exit permits for Jews who can pay a thousand dollars; but when Laszlo is taken and Ilona begs him to help, he forces her to sleep with him . . . and then rescues only an aged Jewish professor from the same transport. By this time, Andras has killed himself with Hans's gun after hearing Ilona sing his lyrics to "Gloomy Sunday." As we leave the wartime story, she is pregnant. In the present tense that frames the film, a clever denouement awaits in the restaurant kitchen: we recognize the now elderly Ilona from her hair comb, and as she washes traces of poison out of a meal just served, we realize that she has exacted revenge on Hans decades later (aided by her son, a waiter). As in *Jules and Jim*, the romantic triangle is persuasive and not judged: each of the characters seems generous, especially Laszlo – the film's real hero – who helps Andras get a record contract and negotiates good terms for him. (Although *Gloomy Sunday* is best known in the U.S.A. via Billie Holliday's rendition, the melody is also heard at the beginning of *Schindler's List*, adding an authentic touch when Oskar enters a nightclub.)

Good Evening, Mr. Wallenberg. Sweden, 1990. D: Kjell Grede.

Jonah Who Lived in the Whale. Italy, 1993. D: Roberto Faenza. A well-intentioned and touching English-language memoir based on Jona Oberski's novel, *Childhood*, but the concentration camps are seen through rose-colored glasses. The film's perspective is that of a child, beginning in 1942 Amsterdam and moving through World War II. The first part lovingly establishes the warmth of Max (French actor Jean-Hugues Anglade) and his wife (Juliet Aubrey) with their little son Jonah. From a shopkeeper who will no longer sell them fruit, to a roundup, their world disintegrates. The first stop is the Westerbork camp, still a rather humane place with a school for the Jewish children . . . until the teacher is taken away. They think they are going to Palestine, but the next shot of barracks establishes their concentration camp destination. Because everything is filtered through a child's eyes, the danger and desperation are muted even here. For example, a doctor allows Jonah's parents to meet in his office for ten minutes in exchange for cigars. The children run around together, play in the mortuary, and eat the remains of the officers' soup from large vats opened by a kindly cook. They are finally liberated by the Russians while playing in an abandoned train. Now orphaned, Jonah is taken in by a kindly Jewish couple who helped his father in 1942; at first he is sullen, but then begins to respond. The director admitted in an interview that he was less concerned with the authenticity of historical reconstruction than the poetic nature of a universal story of childhood amid violence.

Just This Forest. Poland, 1991. D: Jan Lomnicki. S: Anna Stronska.

Korczak. Poland, 1991. D: Andrzej Wajda. S: Agnieszka Holland.

Last Chance, The. Switzerland, 1944. D: Leopold Lindtberg. S: Richard Schweizer.

Left Luggage. The Netherlands/U.K./Belgium, 1998. D: Jeroen Krabbe. S: Edwin de Vries, from Carl Friedman's novel, *The Shovel and the Loom* (1993). A moving story and strong performances compensate for occasionally heavy-handed direction of this first feature (in English) by the great Dutch actor. In this post-Holocaust drama set in 1972 Antwerp, Chaya (Laura Fraser) – the daughter of dysfunctional survivors (Maximilian Schell and Marianne Sagerbrecht) – takes a job as a nanny for a Hasidic family. She is a self-hating Jew whose best friend doesn't even know Chaya's religious identity. Contact with the Kalman family transforms her into a loving Jewish woman, as she cares for the five-and-a-half-year-old child Simcha (Adam Mont), who can neither speak nor control his bladder. The stern but decent mother (Isabella Rossellini) has five children and a taciturn husband, Leibl

(Krabbe), who is too hard on Simcha. When the child finally does speak – thanks to Chaya – and can recite the four questions for the seder, his father corrects him. Chaya confronts Leibl, and learns that he too is a survivor whose brother was killed in a concentration camp. (Photos of the brother reveal that Simcha is his lookalike.) Chaya may be right that Leibl is afraid to love him; and Leibl may be right to feel fear: when altercations with the crazy anti-Semitic concierge lead to Chaya's taking a week off, Simcha dies in the duck pond. Grief unites them, and, by the end, Chaya is kinder to her own father, who is obsessed with finding two suitcases he buried during the Holocaust. The best scene is Schell's understated delivery of how John F. Kennedy's famous "I am a Berliner" line really meant "I am a doughnut."

Life Is Beautiful. Italy, 1997. D: Roberto Benigni.

Long Is the Road. Germany, 1948. D: Herbert B. Fredersdorf and Marek Goldstein. R: NCJF.

Mendel. Norway, 1997. D: Alexander Rosler. Fine coming-of-age story about Mendel, a nine-year-old who arrives with Holocaust survivor parents from Germany in Norway in 1954. Both comic and poignant, this autobiographical tale shows how Mendel is justifiably frustrated by his family's secrets. His mother won't reveal who appears in a hidden photo (it turns out to be her first husband, and the father of Mendel's brother David). His own chain-smoking and coughing father won't let him look at a book of Holocaust photos, so Mendel sneaks a peek. The father claims they are nonbelievers but, as Mendel points out, he is always talking to God; he won't celebrate Jewish holidays, but then won't let them acknowledge Christian ones either. No wonder Mendel is so confused that when he prays, it's to "God, Buddha, Allah, and Jesus," covering his spiritual bases! The Norwegians who first housed them later try (in vain) to convert them to Jesus. Mendel's nightmares are gripping, juxtaposing what he imagines from the Holocaust – like his father's shoes stolen in a concentration camp – with present details like firemen in gas masks rescuing them from a fire in the building. Because he has just seen the famous Warsaw Ghetto photo of a little boy with raised hands, he responds to a fireman's appearance by raising his own arms.

One Day Crossing. U.S.A./Hungary, 2000. D: Joan Stein. S: Christina Lazaridi. Powerful Hungarian-language drama, nominated for Academy Award for Best Live-Action Short. Teresa (Erika Marozsan), a Jewish woman who is passing as Aryan in Budapest, protects her son Peter while her husband leads Resistance efforts against the Iron Cross. He brings home Benjamin, a Jewish child saved from a roundup, and the two boys become friendly. A radio broadcast announcing the end of the war leads the boys to run outside. But war's end is still far away, and the vulnerable boys are missing when Teresa returns home. She runs to the river where Hungarian guards have gathered Jewish victims, and tries to save her son with a certificate attesting to his Aryan identity. Calling for Peter, she finds only Benjamin, now huddled with his own mother. The women's eyes attest to a desperation that leads Teresa to take Benjamin and save him as her own. When she returns home, she finds her son Peter as well, and packs to take both of them to safety. Although made as a thesis film for Columbia University's Graduate Film Program, *One Day Crossing* is gripping, authentic (shot in Hungary), and beautifully filmed.

Our Children (Unsere Kinder). Poland, 1948. D: Natan Gross and Shaul Goskind. The last Yiddish-language film made in Poland, blending three professional actors with Jewish children from an orphanage, all survivors of the Holocaust. Restored by the National Center for Jewish Film, this poignant 68-minute film begins with children attending a show in which two comedians perform "ghetto" numbers. One kid whistles because it's not realistic. The children apologize backstage, under the supervision of their director (Nyusia Gold), and invite the performers to their orphanage. There, the comedians learn more from the children than they bargained for. They overhear a little girl telling others at night how she was on a truck that stopped in a village for repairs. The German officer taunted peasants to buy "a filthy Jewish child"; one guy pulled out money, so the officer threw her off the truck to him. A boy tells of his mother urging him to run away during a roundup: he did, but she was killed, not knowing if he lived or died. And the director has her own story: it is intimated that her child died under awful circumstances. But the next day, the kids seem well and happy. As the orphanage director observes, it's better that they enact their past during the day than leave it for nightmares.

Rose Garden, The. Austria/U.S.A./West Germany, 1989. D: Fons Rademakers. S: Paul Hengge, based on a story by Art Bernd. An uneven post-Holocaust drama in English that begins with strength and subtlety, but ends in a weakly strident fashion and includes the stereotype of the survivor as damaged goods. Liv Ullmann is superb as Gabriele, a Frankfurt attorney. At an airport, she and her little daughter witness a strange man attacking an older one: Aaron (Maximilian Schell) is a Jewish Holocaust survivor obsessed with Krenn, who was an SS overseer of a brutal death camp, and ordered the hanging of about twenty Jewish children on April 20, 1945. At first, Gabriele – now divorced from Herbert (a woefully miscast Peter Fonda with an unconvincing German accent), a selfish lawyer – doesn't want to take the case. But Aaron's mute state leads to her own investigation, which brings us back to the film's enigmatic opening in Hamburg. Aaron was staring at a school which, we later learn, was where he believes his sisters were killed. If Gabriele can demonstrate that Krenn is a war criminal, then Aaron was engaged in a premeditated assault – which would land him in jail. But once he speaks to her in broken languages, it's clear that he cares more for Krenn's trial than his own liberty. With the help of a Hamburg journalist (Jan Niklaus) who is sympathetic to Aaron, she finds the memorial to the murdered children – including his sister Rachel – but we don't know what happened to sister Ruth. A surprise witness at the trial is indeed Ruth (Gila Almagor), who has a tearful reunion with Aaron. Her eyewitness testimony of the murder of the children is presented in graphic flashbacks. These could be considered "pornographic": why should we be shown reenactments of naked children hung? The savvy prosecutor (Hanns Zischler) already has a document saying that Krenn cannot stand trial. The end titles tell us that "the killing of the children at Bullenhuser Road actually took place. The commanding officer . . . was declared permanently unfit to stand trial by a Hamburg court in 1985. . . . Except for the termination of their lives, no further harm was done to them."

Tears of Stone. Iceland, 1995. D: Hilmar Oddsson. Based on a true story, this well-made World War II drama focuses on Annie Riethof (Ruth Olafsdotir), a successful concert pianist married to composer Jon Leifs. But she is the daughter of a German-Jewish industrialist (Heinz Bennent), while he is Icelandic and not able to have his music performed in Germany. They have two daughters, and Jon is enraged when the Nazis allow (or lead to) a situation in which little Lif's violin is bashed and she hides in a radio building. He decides to go to Iceland to conduct his own music. By the time he returns to Germany, Annie is no longer allowed to play, and the girls cannot attend school. Realizing the danger – especially after her parents are taken to Dachau and killed – he goes for help to the influential Nazi who seems to adore Annie. In exchange for his making propaganda broadcasts to Iceland, Jon receives exit visas. But on the boat it turns out they don't include him! The price for their freedom in Sweden is that he must remain in Germany as a Nazi puppet. The stunning exterior shots of Iceland are by Slawomir Idziak, best known as the cinematographer of Kieslowski's *Blue* and *The Double Life of Veronique.*

Train of Life. France, 1998. D: Radu Mihaileanu.

Truce, The (La tregua). Italy, 1997. D: Francesco Rosi. S: Stefano Rulli, Sandro Petraglia, and Tonino Guerra from Primo Levi's book, *La Tregua* (1963). A noble re-creation of the nine months between Primo Levi's liberation from Auschwitz and his return to Turin. John Turturro is superbly restrained as Levi (and well-dubbed in the Italian version), including a calm voice-over narration. But Levi is primarily an observer here, with too few scenes to render him the hero of his own tale. Numerous secondary characters make their way through numerous locations in Russia, contributing to an episodic structure that finally culminates in Levi's homecoming. Rather, the far more vital (if intermittent) character is "the Greek" (Rade Serbedzija), who takes him under his wing, leaves the resettlement camp in Katowice, and is found again with lovely young prostitutes working for him. Although Luis Bacalov's score is beautiful and stirring, it is occasionally too intrusive and epic-sounding for this intimate story of a group of survivors. Levi emerges from passivity to a climactic scene of engagement: he takes on the defense of a young woman from his angry buddy, Daniele (Stefano Dionisi): she too is a survivor, forced into prostitution in Auschwitz. There is food for thought in this film, as when Levi says, "If Auschwitz exists, God cannot." And in defending the woman, he laments that Auschwitz took away the prisoners' compassion – which is even worse than physical destruction.

Warszawa. Poland, 1992. D: Janusz Kijowski. The full title, *Warszawa, Year 5703*, establishes that this is the Jewish calendar, and that the film is a Holocaust tale. Alek (Lambert Wilson) and Fryda (Julie Delpy), both Jews, escape from the Warsaw Ghetto in 1943 through the sewers. Alek is carrying photo negatives of Nazi brutality. In the Aryan sector, he comes upon Stephania (Hanna Schygulla), who both hides him and sleeps with him. He says he has to bring his sister, finds Fryda in a church, and takes her to this rather nice refuge. But it becomes increasingly apparent that Fryda is too jealous of Stephania to remain the "little sister." She is Alek's wife, and when he doesn't tell Stephania the truth, Fryda becomes a destructive creature. Although Delpy's performance cannot be faulted, how troubling that a Jewish character in a Holocaust film inspires such hatred on the part of the audience! Who needs Nazis? Fryda destroys them from within. Stephania contracts typhus, and while Fryda exults, Alek nurses her. It becomes clear that her goodness will triumph over Fryda's childish cruelty. But Fryda leaves for the Ghetto, thereby forcing Alek to follow. As if it were not enough that she leads them to their (presumed) death, Fryda has left a note to incriminate Stephania with the German police.

Why Wasn't He There? Hungary, 1993. D: Andras Jeles. An interesting but uneven Holocaust drama seen from the point of view of thirteen-year-old Eva (Cora Fisher), based on a diary (which the director claimed was forged by Eva's mother!). Her voice-over is unfortunately redundant with the images, as we see World War II changing her world. From a happy twelfth birthday that suddenly turns ugly when the parents of her cousin are taken away, we move to her thirteenth birthday. She lives with her nervous grandmother – her own mother flits in and out – and her father lives elsewhere. When he is arrested, Eva brings him soup daily. They are moved from their beautiful house to the ghetto. Interspersed are scenes from the book she is reading, *David Copperfield*, imagined by Eva as she confides in little David. Perhaps the most resonant line is her musing about whether one will turn out to be the hero of one's own life – a question appropriate to the early 1940s in Eastern Europe.

English-language Films

Anne Frank. U.S.A., 2001. D: Robert Dornhelm. S: Kirk Ellis, based on Melissa Miller's *Anne Frank: The Biography*. Superlative docudrama, from the buoyant life in Amsterdam of young Anne (the excellent Hannah Taylor-Gordon), to her death in Bergen-Belsen. Ben Kingsley is superb as Otto Frank.

Attic, The: The Hiding of Anne Frank. U.S.A., 1998. D: John Erman. S: William Hanley (teleplay) based on Miep Gies's *Anne Frank Remembered*. The focus of this television drama is not the group in the attic, but the bravery of Miep, her husband Jan, and the others who saved Jews. At the beginning, we see that Miep (Mary Steenburgen) works for Otto Frank (Paul Scofield) and Van Damm – Germans who left in 1933. (At a party, they toast "the Germany that was.") As things get worse, Miep and other Dutch citizens show their mettle as rescuers. But when the Gestapo takes the families away, the camera stays on Miep and her helpless suffering. After the war, Otto returns, thinking his daughters might be alive. The scene where he learns from a letter that they are dead is effective in its understatement.

Bent. U.K., 1997. D: Sean Mathias. S: Martin Sherman, from his play. A not entirely successful adaptation of the ground-breaking play about gay prisoners in 1934 Dachau. The earliest scenes are strongest, as we see the decadence of Berlin, with gay orgies, the transvestite Greta (Mick Jagger) singing, and brownshirts carousing with the pretty boys. But this is the "Night of the Long Knives," so Max (Clive Owen) and his lover become targets just from associating with one of the young leaders. The rest of the film never loses the essentially theatrical quality of two men on a stage – also because the guards are watching them – and the end seems pointless. Up until this moment, we believe that Max wants to survive at all costs. For Horst (Lothaire Bluteau), another prisoner, morality is less flexible: he wears his pink triangle proudly, whereas the Jewish Max has bartered for a yellow star (assuming that being gay is considered even lower). Their work consists of moving rocks from one pile to another until it is full, and then back again, an activity designed to drive them crazy. It seems to work, because after Horst is killed by the SS, Max essentially kills himself by going to the barbed wire for electrocution. We are supposed to feel the ennoblement of his donning Horst's pink triangle, but it feels like a hollow victory.

Conspiracy. U.S.A., 2001. D: Frank Pierson. S: Loring Mandel. Made for HBO Films, it is – like the German film *The Wannsee Conference* – an important dramatic reconstruction of the 90-minute meeting that definitively established the Final Solution. On January 20, 1942, fifteen men arrive at a villa outside Berlin for a secret meeting overseen by Eichmann (Stanley Tucci). Last to arrive is Reinhard Heydrich (Kenneth Branagh, in an Emmy Award–winning performance), director of the Reich Security main office: he has been appointed by Göring to map out the final solution to Germany's "Jewish problem." To the general agreement of the group, he speaks of the "storage problem" of Jews, but there are two exceptions: Dr. Stuckart (Colin Firth) – the lawyer who devised the Nuremberg Laws of 1935 proclaiming the legality of a Jew-free society and economy – is in favor of mass sterilization of "mixed Jews," but not evacuation (Heydrich's euphemism for extermination). And Dr. Kritzinger (David Threlfall), ministerial director of the Reich Chancellery, insists that the Führer personally denied the possibility of annihilating all the Jews of Europe. Heydrich, with chilling charm, agrees – making it clear that the Führer will deny but support their acts. Their goal is sixty thousand Jews per day up in smoke, an extension of the currently used mobile gas trucks. With everyone forced into agreement, the meeting ends, and Eichmann puts on Schubert's quintet (also beautifully used in Axel Corti's *Where To and Back* trilogy) about which Heydrich had said, "tears your heart out." Eichmann calls it sentimental Viennese shit. End titles tell us what happened to the men as we see servants cleaning up after the feast. One would like more information about two footnotes: Eichmann says this mansion was once owned by a Jew (a ghostly presence somewhere?), and they gossip that Heydrich's father was Jewish.

Conversation with the Beast. Germany, 1996. D: Armin Mueller-Stahl. S: Tom Abrams and Mueller-Stahl.

The Empty Mirror, The. U.S.A., 1996. D: Barry Hershey. An actor (with a British accent) is impersonating the Führer in his bunker, dictating to an assistant, preening at a mirror, and watching footage of himself projected. Joel Grey plays Goebbels! With intriguing connections to Syberberg's *Our Hitler*, this American film is an oddity.

*Forced March. U.S.A./Hungary, 1989. D: Rick King. S: Dick Atkins and Charles K. Bardosh. An intriguing drama that approaches the Holocaust from the effective perspective of making a film about the subject. The focus is an American actor, Ben Kline (Chris Sarandon), whose popularity comes from a silly TV series. His Hungarian-Jewish father (Josef Sommer) never talks about the war. Ben agrees to act in a movie in Hungary about the poet Miklos Radnoti. Precisely because – as Ben's costar and eventual lover Mayra (Renee Soutendijk)

puts it – "people believe what they're shown; movies become the truth," this film questions its conventions even as it involves us in Radnoti's moving story. Ben has his own demons: for example, his mother died soon after his birth, and he learns that she was not Jewish. As filming progresses, the actor plunges further into Radnoti's psyche, especially because the tough director, Walter (John Seitz), doesn't believe Ben has it in him. He sleeps in the labor camp set rather than at the Hyatt, hardly eats, and recites the poems. The characters articulate what some critics might say, such as the director's line to five men who are not conveying fear: "No matter how close we come, we're not close enough." After Ben's father shows up in Hungary, he claims, "No one can show how it really was," followed by "Who wants to see it?" Ben tries to make Radnoti more of a resister, but the director warns against imposing his emotions on the past. The last part of the film-within-the-film is particularly powerful, and persuasive despite the distancing. Radnoti and the other Jewish labor camp prisoners are ordered to leave the barracks – which are burned – and march back from Yugoslavia to Hungary. We know from the opening that Radnoti did not survive, so the question is not if he will die, but how. Ben finally has his character die meekly, exhausted. The closing scene of the actor floating in his swimming pool, back in Beverly Hills, shows a changed man, now isolated. *Forced March* literalizes what films like *The Pawnbroker* and *Sophie's Choice* suggest: the Holocaust is most authentically depicted when it's bracketed, or separated from the present-tense narrative of characters trying to come to terms with the past.

Genghis Cohn. U.K., 1993. D: Elijah Moshinsky. S: Stanley Price, from Romain Gary's novel.

Haven. Canada/U.S.A., 2001. D: John Gray. S: Suzette Couture. Based on the inspirational autobiographical book by Ruth Gruber, this four-hour miniseries aired in February 2001 on CBS. Natasha Richardson is excellent as the indomitable Gruber, who was responsible for saving almost one thousand Jewish refugees by bringing them from Europe to New York. (Like her husband, Liam Neeson, playing the rescuer in *Schindler's List*, Richardson's character is upset to be saving only 982 Jews when so many more are desperate.) The Jewish, Brooklyn-accented heroine convinces the American government to let in the refugees in 1944. A general herself, she moves like an elegant princess through crowds in Europe, dealing with anti-Semitism even among American soldiers (some of whom resent the fact that their wounded were left behind "so FDR could bring in 1,000 Jews"). Despite melodramatic contrivances and occasionally intrusive music, the miniseries tells a powerful story. (Best is Colm Feore doing an anti-Hitler song and dance to deflect the tension between Jews and Americans on the boat.) When they get to Oswego, New York, the refugees are confronted by soldiers with guns; their fear only grows when they get to their living quarters, which resemble a concentration camp. Initially quarantined, they eventually are enabled by Ruth to work, go to school, and become productive U.S. citizens.

Hidden in Silence. U.S.A., 1996. D: Richard Colla, made for Lifetime Television. An affecting, well-intentioned, well-acted, but sanitized, simplified, and misleading drama. In the true story of Stefania Podgovska Burzminska, called Fusia (Kellie Martin) – who sheltered thirteen Jews during the Holocaust in Przemysl, Poland – the sixteen-year-old instinctively protects as many of the Diamant family as possible when they are taken to a ghetto. They have given her their apartment, where she lives with her little sister Helena. First, she takes in the destroyed Max, who witnessed his parents' deportation. After hiding a few more Jews – in a bigger house, with an attic – she gets a factory job by bribing a German with a brooch. Her supervisor (Joss Ackland) seems imposing at first, but later confesses that he recognizes she is doing the same thing he is. (This is a bit hard to believe.) The Poles are mostly decent: no one notices or denounces the perceptible sounds and bodies in the house. They all survive, and end titles mention that Fusia and Max are celebrating their fifty-first wedding anniversary. What they leave out (according to scholar Eva Fogelman) is that Fusia forced Max to convert to Christianity, thereby alienating his family.

In the Presence of Mine Enemies. Canada/U.S.A., 1996. D: Joan Micklin Silver. S: Rod Serling. A respectful and moving remake of Serling's 1950s teleplay. Set in the Warsaw Ghetto, the drama focuses on Rabbi Heller (Armin Mueller-Stahl), his lovely daughter Rachel (Irina Lowensohn), and his son Paul (Don McKellar), who suddenly returns after escaping from a labor camp. Whereas father and daughter have European accents, Paul sounds too North American, looks too Method-actor angry, and is thoroughly unsympathetic. We are not told or shown enough of what made him so much more bitter than the other Jews who have suffered. Moreover, since the German officer (Charles Dance) and young sergeant (Chad Lowe) have appropriate German accents, Paul sounds like he comes from a different world. As their neighbors keep being taken away in November of 1942, the rabbi tries to keep his dignity: but he too falls apart after the officer sends the sergeant to bring him Rachel. She is raped and becomes ill. The sergeant feels guilty, returns, and offers her escape – while repenting to the rabbi, who agrees that his daughter should flee. But the bullying Paul cannot accept this, and confronts them in the sewer with a gun. At this point, the German sergeant seems more worthy of being saved than Paul, so the rabbi kills his own son in order to let Rachel escape. The wonderful score is by Dead Can Dance.

Island on Bird Street, The. Denmark/U.K./Germany, 1997. D: Soren Kragh Jacobsen. S: John Goldsmith and Tony Grisoni from Uri Orlev's book. This European story, in English, of a child survivor is often gripping. Although based on a true story, it lacks the specificity of a year and location. In a Jewish ghetto of a Polish city, the Aryan population is still relatively free. Alex (Jordan Kiziuk), eleven, lives with his father (Patrick Bergin) and Uncle Baruch (Jack Warden). He is an expert at hiding, whether under rocks, in rubble, or in the cupboard. He reads *Robinson Crusoe*, which ends up being not only a parallel to his own experience, but a tool for survival. When the ghetto is rounded up for deportation, Alex escapes. For weeks, he seems to be the only person there, but a few adults are indeed hidden in an underground bunker. They are betrayed by an apprehended Jew who thinks this will save him. Alex is ingenious, making a ladder that enables him to hide high up where there is water. Although still a child, he becomes a hero: when he notices two men about to be shot by a German, he shoots the soldier. Then, he nurses the wounded Resistance man, even sneaking out to the Aryan side for a doctor. Amazingly enough, his father does return for him, although we have no idea where he has been or how he escaped. The music by Kieslowski's composer, Zbigniew Preisner, is beautiful and used sparingly to underline the boy's loneliness, especially when he sees through a window a lovely little girl on the Aryan side. Although the Polish location, Danish director, and mishmash of accents are not completely unified, this engaging story can be seen by children, especially because Alex is spared the war's horrors.

Jakob the Liar. France/Hungary/Germany, 1999. D: Peter Kassovitz. S: Didier Decoin.

Master Race, The. U.S.A., 1944. D: Herbert Biberman (who would be blacklisted a few years later). This RKO drama is of great historical interest because – like the superior *None Shall Escape* – it was made before the war's end, foreshadowing fleeing Nazis and uneasy alliances in Europe with the Allies. It makes no mention of the Jews, preferring a political identity and a church as the central rallying points. The film begins with Von Beck (George Coulouris) exhorting fellow Nazi officers – who are going into hiding – to turn fear into impatience, impatience into despair, despair into anguish, anguish into hate . . . to preserve the master race. He shoots himself in the leg, and pretends to be a resister in Kolar, Belgium. Here, the collective protagonist offers a spectrum of accents and ideologies. Frank (Lloyd Bridges) returns to his sister Helena – who has a little girl after presumably being raped by a Nazi – and father (Morris Carnovsky). Frank's girlfriend, Nina, is the daughter of a collaborator, so he shuns her. The Russian doctor Andre (with a German accent) is the most heroic character, working with American occupying forces. The prison includes a repentant German officer (with a Hungarian accent). The end of the war is announced when they are in a church, and the prison explodes. Von Beck is unmasked after murdering the collaborationist's widow. His speech at the end, before he is shot, stresses how the disunity of the Allies will lead to their falling apart.

Max and Helen. U.K., 1989. D: Philip Saville. S: Corey Bleckman teleplay from the novel by Simon Wiesenthal. In 1962, the Nazi hunter (Martin Landau) learns that the head of a large Polish factory was once Schultze, the commandant of a camp during World War II. He finds in Paris a potential witness, Max Rosenberg (Treat Williams), a traumatized doctor who wants nothing to do with the past. He nevertheless comes to Wiesenthal's hotel and reluctantly tells his tale in sporadic flashbacks and voice-over. (The constant returns to the present frame are gratuitous, suitable only for commercials.) In 1939 Poland, Max is engaged to the beautiful Helen (Alice Krige), and after the deportation of the parents, they go to the labor camp to build a road. At first, it's a humane labor camp, but the arrival of Werner Schultze (Jonathan Philips) makes it hellish. After Helen begs him to escape, Max ends up in Russia, and is sent to Siberia for ten years after criticizing someone for an anti-Semitic remark. Upon his release, and having learned that Helen is alive in West Germany, he makes his way there. But the man who opens the door (Philips) is the spitting image of Schultze. It turns out to be her son Marek, a sweet Jewish boy who thinks his father died fighting the Nazis. She tells Max she was raped (we are treated to a gratuitous flashback within a flashback) and he leaves, despite her protestations and pleas to stay with her. Helen refuses to testify for Wiesenthal for fear of destroying her son. In an implausibly happy ending one year later, Max returns to her. Although the story is often compelling, it doesn't feel fresh. The accents don't mix at all, and the male actors seem to be trying too hard to play tormented Jews.

Murderers among Us: The Simon Wiesenthal Story. Canada/U.S.A., 1989. D: Brian Gibson. S: Abby Mann, Robin Vote, and Ron Hutchinson. Presented on HBO. Although it doesn't go much further than any of the previous docudramas, the strong story is anchored in a moving performance by Ben Kingsley as the Nazi hunter from the 1940s to the early 1960s. The three-and-a-half-hour telefilm begins with his liberation in May 1945 from Mauthausen, Austria, by U.S. soldiers. Major Harcourt (Craig T. Nelson) is stunned by the skeletal prisoners, and by Simon's drawings of atrocities. A former architect, Simon goes to work for a War Crimes unit, as flashbacks establish how he got false papers for his wife, Cyla (Renee Soutendijk); witnessed the departure of a sealed transport containing his mother; tried to kill himself when captured by Nazis; and – thanks to his painting skill – was miraculously spared from a line of naked men being shot into a pit. In a rather hokey scene that will prove to be the source of his nightmares, Simon is summoned to the deathbed of a young Nazi with a bandaged head who needs to confess to – and be forgiven by – a Jew for his monstrous acts. Via an excessive flashback within a flashback, Simon tells another inmate about it, concluding "God is on leave." He is reunited with Cyla, who wants a quiet life. But Simon is increasingly obsessed with justice, especially because they lost all eighty-nine members of their families. Part 1 ends with Simon taking all the files when Harcourt leaves and the unit disbands. Part 2 begins in 1959 Vienna when he is approached by a half-German, half-Jewish man who wants to work for him, and finds proof that a certain man is Eichmann. Simon helps him track Eichmann to Buenos Aires. At home, Cyla is angry that Simon gave their daughter Anne Frank's diary to read, especially when her classmates deny the Holocaust occurred and she tries to use it as proof to the contrary. Despite threats, and a bomb placed in his home, Simon continues in his quest to bring Nazi criminals to justice.

Music Box, The. U.S.A., 1989. D: Costa-Gavras. S: Joe Eszterhas. A compelling and provocative contemporary drama set in the U.S.A. Ann (Jessica Lange) is a successful lawyer, a good mother to Mikey (Lukas Haas), and a devoted daughter to her father, Michael Laszlo (Armin Mueller-Stahl) – a steel worker who came from Hungary after World War II.

Since Ann is divorced, he is an important male figure for Mikey. When Michael receives a letter from the Justice Department claiming that he is a war criminal who lied to get into the United States, he urges Ann to defend him, which she agrees to do after meeting the prosecutor, Jack (Frederic Forrest). Initially, it does seem like a mistake, as she discredits witnesses at the trial. But their testimony mentioning the particular torture of "Mishka" – push-ups over bayonets in the ground – is uncomfortably reminiscent of Michael's exhorting Mikey to do push-ups. She is summoned to hear a Hungarian's testimony in Budapest, which adds to doubts about her father. But after a stranger gives her some papers, there is enough evidence to have the case dismissed. Ann nevertheless visits the sister of a certain Tibor, who might have been blackmailing her father. There, she sees an incriminating photo of Tibor with the very scar that witnesses described on the partner of "Mishka." Tibor's sister gives Ann a pawn ticket, with which she retrieves a Hungarian music box: in addition to tinkling sounds, it yields photos proving that her father was indeed a torturer and murderer. What's a daughter to do? When she confronts him, he denies it. But at the end, she mails the photos to the prosecutor, thus ensuring her father's demise. This taut and beautifully acted drama is reminiscent of Costa-Gavras's previous film, *Betrayed*, in which the heroine is similarly torn between love and the horrid truth she learns about the man she trusted.

Nazi Hunter: The Beate Klarsfeld Story. U.S.A., 1986. D: Michael Lindsay-Hogg. S: Frederic Hunter. Made for ABC, this docudrama of an extraordinary couple begins in 1960 Paris, where the German Beate (Farrah Fawcett) meets Serge (nicely underplayed by Tom Conti). He sensitizes her to what the Germans have done during the war, with photos, personal tales (his father in Auschwitz), and historical data, until she begins to see through his eyes. They marry, have a son, and she bravely identifies former Nazis who are enjoying new lives. First, she calls Chancellor Kiesinger a Nazi in public, and later slaps him. Then she suggests kidnapping Kurt Lischka, former head of the Gestapo in France: even though he gets away, she uses the publicity well. She persuades the German prosecutor to reopen the Klaus Barbie case, and then deduces that Barbie is in Bolivia. In a strong scene, Simone Lagrange (Catherine Allegret, sounding a lot like her mother, Simone Signoret) recalls Barbie's torture. Once in Bolivia – with her friend (Geraldine Page) who lost her husband and three children to Barbie – Beate brings public attention to bear on Klaus Altmann so that France asks for his extradition. Although she loses the three-month-old fetus she is carrying, Beate is the one who thus gets Barbie to the stage of awaiting trial.

None Shall Escape. U.S.A., 1944. D: Andre de Toth.

Nuremberg. U.S.A., 2000. D: Yves Simoneau. S: David Rintels. This three-hour miniseries for TNT is often strong but ultimately close to Hollywood conventions. It begins with black-and-white newsreel footage and Hitler's voice before the gradual entry of color on May 12, 1945. Supreme Court Justice Robert Jackson (a very fine Alec Baldwin) is asked to be the chief prosecutor for the Nuremberg Trials. It's exciting to see how he and his crew essentially stage another spectacle in the very city where Hitler (and Leni Riefenstahl) staged his own pageant. They rebuild the Palace of Justice and mount a media event that Jackson hopes will be the triumph of moral superiority. If (as Hitchcock suggested) a movie is as good as its villain, *Nuremberg* soars through Hermann Goering (a magnificent Brian Cox), whose "bonhommie" transcends his monstrous acts as Hitler's number two man. He tries to befriend the "jailers" to whom he has surrendered and succeeds in turning a young American soldier, Tex, into his adoring slave. He refuses to acknowledge the court's indictments, seeing them as victors who therefore have the ability to lord it over the losers. Also fascinating is Captain Gilbert (Matt Craven), a Jewish psychiatrist who is to help the prosecution by talking with the Nazi defendants. Of the twenty-one, most are unrepentant; but Albert Speer (Herbert Knaup, who has the most convincing accent) does assume his guilt, and tries to sway the others to do the same. On the stand, he even admits that he tried to assassinate Hitler. A bit distracting is the attraction between Jackson and his trusty assistant, Elsie (Jill Hennessey). Strongest is the courtroom scene of documentary footage of the camps – shown in complete silence, except for sniffling among the spectators. (Indeed, Baldwin's effectively understated speech delivery at the beginning provides a contrast with Richard Widmark's hectoring in the analogous *Judgment at Nuremberg*.) Elsie asks, "How can civilized human beings do that to other civilized human beings?" Jackson replies, "Maybe civilization is overrated." Later, Gilbert proposes that evil is the lack of empathy. But all of this merely scratches the surface of evil.

Promise, The (also called *Never Forget*). U.S.A.,1991. D: Joseph Sargent. S: Ronald Rubin. Made for TNT, this docudrama's strength derives from content rather than style. It begins in 1944 Hungary before quickly moving to southern California in 1980. Mel Mermelstein (Leonard Nimoy) is explaining deportation photos to high school students. A survivor of Auschwitz whose entire family was killed, he makes artworks out of Holocaust artifacts. After the publication of his letter attacking revisionists, he receives a letter from the Institute for Historical Review (IHR) challenging him to prove that the Holocaust existed. Although Jewish organizations including the Anti-Defamation League and the Simon Wiesenthal Center urge him to ignore this baiting for a $50,000 prize, Mermelstein refuses to let the challenge lie. He enlists the support of an Irish-Catholic lawyer, Bill (Dabney Coleman), who predicts that the IHR will not accept Mel's offer of proof. If they don't respond in thirty days, Mel can take the IHR to court for breach of contract, thereby fighting on legal turf rather than the IHR's staged one. This is precisely what transpires, including harassment for his wife, Jane (Blythe Danner) – a rather saintly Southern Baptist – and four children. The eldest, Bernie, moves from resentment toward his father's Holocaust obsession to support. Once in court, the judge acknowledges (for the first time in U.S. law) that gas chambers are a matter of fact. The secondary characters may be too simplistically drawn (Bill is too good to be true), but this film is appropriate for students to see.

Rescuers: Two Women. U.S.A., 1997. D: Peter Bogdanovich. S: Susan Nanus, based on *Rescuers: Portraits of Moral Courage in the Holocaust* by Gay Block and Malka Drucker. Made for Showtime Television, the well-intentioned and uplifting story is nevertheless oversimplified, sentimental, and melodramatic. Elizabeth Perkins plays the noble Warsaw Catholic housekeeper who not only becomes the "Mamoosha" of little Mickey after his rich Jewish mother dies, but smuggles food into the Vilna Ghetto. She is portrayed as a saint with no needs of her own. It is hard to believe that when Mickey is sick, she gets a Jewish doctor out of the ghetto at night, and he later manages to return. When she tells the kind priest about her secret, he cheerfully makes Mickey an altar boy. The voice-over of the grown Mickey establishes that she kept her word to the dying mother by bringing him to Palestine and raising him as a Jew.

Reunion. France/West Germany/U.K., 1989. D: Jerry Schatzberg. S: Harold Pinter, from Fred Uhlman's novel. A slow, sensitive evocation of the growing anti-Semitism in Stuttgart in the 1930s, told in flashbacks from the perspective of Henry Strauss (Jason Robards). This American businessman returns to Germany after fifty-five years for business, but is more interested in finding his old friend Konrad, a Gentile aristocrat. A flashback shows the tense friendship between the boys Hans and Konrad; the latter genuinely admires Hans but can't introduce a Jewish friend to his parents. (Unfortunately, Konrad sort of admires Hitler too.) Hans's father – a doctor who fought for Germany in World War I – and mother send the boy to the United States before committing suicide. Strauss learns at the end from a plaque in school that Konrad was executed as part of a group who tried to assassinate Hitler. (This explains the opening black-and-white scene of a man being hanged.) Because the audience waits for a reunion that never occurs, there is lack of emotional payoff.

The Search. U.S.A., 1948. D: Fred Zinneman. S: Richard Schweizer. Shot in the rubble of the American-occupied zone of Germany, it's the first Hollywood film to deal with the effect of the Holocaust on children. An American GI (Montgomery Clift) cares for a child (Ivan Jandl) who – although not Jewish – is a survivor of Auschwitz. His Czech mother is also searching for the boy through Europe's DP camps. Even if the film's focus is a sympathetic Gentile-American soldier rather than Jewish Holocaust victims, the blend of nonprofessional children, real locations, and a moving story makes it a landmark movie.

Silence. U.S.A., 1998. D: Sylvie Bringas and Orly Yaddin. D: Seventh Art Releasing (323-845-1455). A child's point of view is vividly conveyed in this ten-minute short – blending animation and archival footage of the Holocaust – which provides a fine introduction of the subject for young viewers. Tana Ross narrates her own story, which begins like a documentary until an animated child flies over the city. After the train ride to Terezin, the Jews turn into insects and then back into people. At the end of the war, archival footage is followed by color animation: when the train to Sweden then suddenly shifts to black-and-white, it suggests Tana's stream of consciousness. The same effect transpires when a train conductor abruptly becomes a black-and-white Nazi. In Sweden, Tana lives with her great-uncle and great-aunt, who tell her to keep silent about her experiences.

Swing Kids. U.S.A., 1993. D: Thomas Carter. S: Jonathan Marc Feldman. An entertaining, well-intentioned, but occasionally "Disney" version of the Holocaust. With music used as resistance, the focus is the developing conscience of Peter, a young German: in 1939 Hamburg, Peter (Robert Sean Leonard) and Thomas (Christian Bale) have refused to join the HJ (Hitler Jugend) and – like their buddy Arvid (Frank Whaley) – are devoted to American swing, jazz, and dancing. But Nazism is on the rise, and there is a growing tension between their wild embracing of "Nigger-kike-music" and the discipline of uniforms. Peter's mother (Barbara Hershey) is trying to make ends meet via accommodation, especially because her husband was an anti-Nazi violinist destroyed by the Nazis six years earlier. She is courted by Herr Knoff (an uncredited Kenneth Branagh), a witty, civilized SS officer who both tries to protect her family and use Peter to get information. Peter is forced into the HJ after trying to steal back a radio confiscated by the Nazi block leader; Thomas then joins, ostensibly to be with his friend. But Thomas turns into an authentic Nazi, even denouncing his own father. Peter is confused and increasingly revolted by the Nazi mentality. His main support turns out to be Frau Linge (Julia Stemberger), a Resistance figure. At the end, Peter sees more clearly his need for defiant resistance, even if he will cause pain to his mother and little brother. When Thomas's troops violently enter a dance hall, the former friends fight, and Thomas almost kills Peter. But he stops and, in an implausible moment as Peter is boarding a truck to the work camp, yells their old greeting, "Swing Heil," with a salute. This sentimentalizes an ending that should have been tougher. Nevertheless, the film effectively delineates a milieu of anti-Semitic films and posters in which HJ boys beat up Jewish kids.

*Triumph of the Spirit. U.S.A., 1989. D: Robert Young. S: Andrzej Krakowski and Laurence Heath. A powerful drama based on the true story of Salamo Arouch, a Greek Jew who survived Auschwitz mainly as a performance piece for officers. He had been the 1928 middleweight boxing champ of the Balkans, and was then pitted against other prisoners for the Nazis' amusement. He lived not only to tell his tale but to be a consultant on the set where his tale was cinematically re-created. Whereas the similarly themed *Boxer and Death* stressed the political resistance of the boxer, here the story is more Jewish and personal. The sense of a world gone awry is conveyed when Salamo (Willem Dafoe) asks, "How many rounds?" "No rounds," the officer replies. "You fight till one falls and can't get up." Winning bread, which he shares with his father (Robert Loggia), Salamo is victorious in over two hundred bouts. The film includes the female experience in Auschwitz, as his fiancée, Allegra (Wendy Gazelle, of Palestinian descent), and her sister are deported too. Moreover, a Gypsy Kapo (Edward James Olmos) plays an increasingly large role: an

apparent extension of the Nazis at first, he is somewhat humanized when his own survival proves to be as tenuous as Salamo's. Shot in Auschwitz itself, the film has striking moments: for example, the arrival of the train into the concentration camp has a gritty authenticity. Using a hand-held camera, Young captures the chaos of Jewish victims trying to stay with their families as Nazi orders are barked almost indiscriminately. Everyone speaks in the appropriate language (although English is accepted as the common denominator) plus translation. Salamo's victories are often guilt-inducing, and even when he brings the bread he won back to the barracks for his father, he must deal with other prisoners pleading for a bite. Salamo ends up in the Sonderkommando detail on the day of their uprising, but miraculously survives torture and the murder of his fellow inmates. The casting of Willem Dafoe provided *Triumph of the Spirit* with additional resonance, as his previous role was the lead in *The Last Temptation of Christ*: in both films he plays a victim – with the difference that Salamo does not turn the other cheek. This harrowing drama ends – much like *Seven Beauties* and *Sophie's Choice* – with camp survival as a testament to endurance rather than nobility.

Uprising. U.S.A., 2001. D: Jon Avnet. S: Paul Brickman and Avnet. Broadcast on NBC in November, this three-hour dramatization of the Warsaw Ghetto Uprising (four hours including commercials) sympathetically portrays Jewish resistance. It pales compared to the similar stories told in *Border Street* and *Korczak*, but grows increasingly suspenseful in the second half. Despite the mix of accents among Americans playing Poles, the acting is very good. Mordechai Anielewicz (Hank Azaria) is introduced conducting to a record album in 1939 Warsaw. But he will grow into a different kind of conductor, leading a group of men and women to fight the Nazi destroyers. After 350,000 Jews are forced into the ghetto, Adam Czerniakow (Donald Sutherland), head of the Judenrat, is confronted with an outrageous ransom demand for hostages. Even after meeting it, he learns that the men were shot before the deadline. Mordechai is betrayed by a guide, arrested and tortured, but escapes back to the ghetto. Kazik (Stephen Moyer), a charming rogue, is his best ally, while Yitzik (David Schwimmer) is more cautious. After a concert in Dr. Korczak's orphanage is broken up by the Nazis, a German officer taunts and kills an old Jewish violinist in the street. Mordechai and Kazik kill the German, thereby initiating the ghetto's resistance. When Czerniakow receives the deportation order for Korczak's orphanage, he kills himself. Korczak leads his children to the train (a scene that lacks the richness of Wajda's version), and after the doors are sealed comes the first moment of cinematic grandeur in *Uprising*: with potent silence, we see stylized quick images and a surreal landscape. Once the resistance spreads, women are as brave and active as the men, notably Tosia (Leelee Sobieski), whose Aryan looks enable her to move outside the ghetto walls. To destroy the ghetto, the Nazis send Stroop (Jon Voight): he is introduced ironically, appreciating Jewish wine (Rothschild) with Hippler (Cary Elwes), a smooth German propagandist with a movie camera. (He later tells Stroop, "It all depends on where you put the camera and who is telling the story.") The Jews fight even the tanks that Stroop brings on April 19, 1943, forcing the Germans to withdraw. On Easter Sunday, Tosia enters a church on the Aryan side: dark smoke pours in from the ghetto, and the windows are closed (no one acknowledges that Jews are being killed). Kazik, in German uniform, takes the survivors to the Mila 18 bunker, but Nazis pour gas in. Then he takes them to the sewers, but the Germans flood them before pouring in gas. Nevertheless, Kazik oversees a brazen daylight rescue of the Jews into a truck on the Aryan side. Twenty-one years after NBC's *Holocaust*, a miniseries focuses on resistance rather than victimization, and gives women equal credit as fighters.

Visas and Virtue. U.S.A., 1998. D: Chris Tashima. S: Tom Donaldson, based on his play. Academy Award winner for Best Live-Action Short. Although the direction of this 26-minute black-and-white film is a bit heavy-handedly melodramatic, the story is powerful, namely that of the Japanese consul general Chiune "Sempo" Sugihara (now known as the Japanese

Schindler). Stationed in Lithuania in 1940, he wrote visas for Jewish refugees beyond his authority. The film begins with the voice-over of his wife in the 1980s, as we see color footage of the aged couple. She will turn out to be as worthy of praise and honor as her husband. When he is too exhausted and frightened to write more visas, she prods him to do so, and then trains each refugee about what to say before going in. The film's focus is a young Jewish couple who have lost their infant son. Because Mrs. Sugihara cannot breast-feed her baby, the Jewish woman offers her own breast. While this feels contrived, it is nonetheless moving as she hums a Yiddish song while nursing the Japanese infant. The end titles tell us that Sugihara issued two thousand visas, but did not know if his Jews survived. Because he returned to Japan in disgrace, they didn't find him until 1968. Before he died in 1986, Yad Vashem honored Sugihara.

Holocaust in the Background

Adam's Circus. Israel, 1994. D: Lihi Hanoch. Video feature recording of the Gesher Theater's production of *Adam Resurrected* in Israel. It's a fragmentary, provocative mixture of Holocaust imagery and circus, with backstage interviews of the actors. They seem to be Russian immigrants, dealing with new identities – as well as language, since the performance is in German and Hebrew.

Alan and Naomi. U.S.A., 1991. D: Sterling VanWagenen. S: Jordan Horowitz. Alan (Lukas Haas), a happy fourteen-year-old Jewish boy in 1944 Brooklyn, is forced by his well-meaning parents (Amy Aguino and Michael Gross) to befriend the new neighbor Naomi (Vanessa Zaoui), a young French girl. Traumatized by the sight of Nazis killing her father, a French Resistance fighter, she does nothing but tear paper all the time. He reluctantly tries to get close to her (while regretting that he can't play stickball with his friend), and breaks through her wall using her doll and his dummy. She makes progress, and is even able to go to school. But when a bully taunts them with anti-Semitic remarks, Alan fights him, touching off Naomi's hysteria. She disappears, and is finally found amid coal in a furnace room. The film ends at a sanitarium, where she has once again withdrawn. There is good attention to period details, lovingly re-created, but the score by Dick Hyman is overdone (especially a song over the end credits).

All That Really Matters. Poland, 1992. D: Robert Glinski. A gritty and moving drama based on the lives of Aleksander Wat, his wife Ola, and their son Andrzej. During World War II, the Jewish-Communist Wat family is warm and loving with each other. They are moved from Nazi-occupied Warsaw to the east, but the Stalinists seem just as mindlessly or absurdly cruel as the Germans, and Alex is arrested at a friend's dinner party. Ola and Andrzej are deported to Kazakhstan, where they are treated horribly – even by the other deportees because they are the only Jews. Ola's ordeal is harrowing, from prison to an announcement that her husband is dead. Fortunately, this turns out to be a lie, and she is briefly reunited with Aleksander. Instead of a happy ending, the more realistic denouement shows how they are told they cannot board the departing train together. But, as we learn from the end titles, they moved to Paris.

American History X. U.S.A., 1998. D: Tony Kaye. S: David McKenna. An uneven, often powerful drama about a neo-Nazi youth leader in Venice, California, Derek Vinyard (Edward Norton in a superb performance), and his younger brother Danny (Edward Furlong). The film's good intentions are clumsily executed, such as the schmaltzy music when they remove Nazi souvenirs from their wall (as opposed to our hearing the music they would really be listening to). The disjointed narrative turns out to be the perspective of a paper Danny is writing for school. Derek is released from three years in prison, and has clearly changed: he distances himself from the skinheads – especially their mentor, Cameron (Stacy Keach) – and his adoring peers turn against him. It is hard to believe that Derek manages to convince the *Mein Kampf*-loving Danny in just one conversation to abandon the cause. How and why did he change in prison? We do see telegraphed moments (the other white supremacists rape Derek in the shower), but not a transformation. Yes, his former teacher Sweeney brings him books in jail – but which books? What do they reveal? Does he even know what the swastika tattooed on his heart referred to? Derek is very concerned about protecting the children in his family, but one yearns for a scene in which he learns what the Nazis did to children. We also don't see enough of what made such a smart kid turn racist in the first place. At the end, the vicious cycle begins again, now more of a race war than a religion-based or Holocaust-inspired one. What remains with the viewer, however, is not the blandly reformed Derek, but the black-and-white image of him after being arrested: seen from a low angle, his naked torso imposing, he smiles in slow motion. Even though handcuffed, this skinhead is totally in control.

Apt Pupil. U.S.A., 1998. D: Bryan Singer. S: Brandon Boyce, from Stephen King's novella. A chilling contemporary drama about Todd (Brad Renfro), a smart adolescent who is fascinated by the Nazi era, and is therefore drawn to Kurt Dussander (Ian McKellen), a reclusive man who might be a former Nazi. Todd forces him to talk about the concentration camps. His grades decline; he hallucinates in the shower; he wakes up in a sweat, but he clings to their meetings. Much of the attraction is power: first, he has the ex-Nazi under his control because he can to go the FBI with proof. But when Kurt feels his own grip on the boy loosening, he tells him he has put into a safe-deposit box the story of their meetings – thereby implicating him as an accessory to a criminal. (This is compounded by his pretending to be the boy's grandfather with the guidance counselor [David Schwimmer].) Todd is being turned into a vulnerable monster, especially when a bum (Elias Koteas) – who suspects a pedophilic relationship after observing them – comes to his house, gets drunk, and is stabbed by Kurt. When Todd arrives, Kurt locks him in the cellar with the body – still alive! – so he finishes the murder. Most disturbing is the end: after an Israeli agent (Jan Triska) and FBI operative (Joe Morton) have arrested him, Kurt is hospitalized. But Todd has obviously internalized the Nazi impulse to control by destruction: when the guidance counselor comes to see his parents about "grandpa" – whose photo as a Nazi is in the newspapers – Todd threatens to claim that the decent counselor was out to molest him. The style is heavy-handed, as when the patient in the neighboring hospital bed turns out to be a Jewish concentration camp survivor who recognizes Kurt's voice and quietly freaks out.

Awakening. Hungary, 1995. D: Judit Elek. A sensitive drama about Kati, a teenager in 1952 Hungary whose mother has just died. Because her father works far away, she is initially placed with her aunt and uncle. But she awakens to freedom, staying out at movies and ignoring school. Her primary relationship continues to be with her mother, whose image she constantly sees. They even talk to each other, the mother trying to protect and encourage Kati. Though literally on-screen, the mother is a projection of Kati, who sees brief images of the past: these include her childhood as a Jew during World War II (she wears the required star) and her parents lovingly touching each other. Kati moves back into her old flat, and falls in love with an older man. The mother's ghost urges Kati to wait, but the independent youngster tells her to drop dead. In the ambiguous ending, she and the man finally make love after her graduation; she asks if that's all there is, he says yes and cries, and she tells her mother that she will always love her.

*Enemies, A Love Story. U.S.A., 1989. D: Paul Mazursky. S: Mazursky and Roger Simon, from the story by Isaac Bashevis Singer. A dark comedy about a weak Polish-Jewish Holocaust survivor who ends up with three wives in postwar America. Herman (Ron Silver in a nicely understated performance) is first seen hidden in a barn which Nazi soldiers search. This turns out be his nightmare in Coney Island, where he lives with his wife Jadwiga (Margaret Sophie Stein): this Polish peasant saved his life, and is the former maid of Herman and his first wife (believed dead). But he is also in love with his mistress, Masha (Lena Olin), a

Russian-Jewish concentration camp survivor who lives with her mother (Judith Malina) in the Bronx. As if his life weren't complicated enough, an ad in the newspaper addressed to him leads Herman to the Lower East Side, where he discovers that his first wife did not die: Tamara (Anjelica Huston) may be brittle, but she's alive and well. Herman does little more than shuttle among these women, a reluctant bigamist. When Masha announces that she is pregnant and Herman must marry her, he does so – thereby becoming a polygamist. Then it turns out that Masha wasn't pregnant . . . but Jadwiga is! By the end, Masha has committed suicide, Herman disappears, leaving Jadwiga and Tamara playing with the baby (named Masha). The Holocaust background is mainly a basis for establishing character: why there is such a voracious carnality when Herman is with Masha; why Herman feels so spineless; why Jadwiga is trying to become a good Jew; and why Tamara is resigned to being a "ghost."

For My Baby (a.k.a. *Goodnight Vienna*). The Netherlands, 1998. D: Rudolf van den Berg, and S, with Michael O'Loughlin. An intriguing but not quite successful surreal psychological drama in English. Alan Cumming is excellent as Daniel, a stand-up comedian in Vienna whose parents are Holocaust survivors. When he is doing abrasive shtick onstage with a Viennese accent, it feels like a continuation of his role as MC in *Cabaret*. And the sight of him wearing a wig and dress when he visits his sick mother in the hospital recalls the cross-dressing aspect of *Cabaret* as well. It turns out through flashbacks that, seven years before his birth, his little sister Hanna was killed in a concentration camp. His mother hardly noticed him as a little boy, but when he donned Hanna's dress, she hugged him as a long-lost daughter. So he kept up this charade while remaining haunted by his dead sister. Most effective are his caustic routines, like "Knock, knock." "Who's there?" "Gestapo." "Gestapo who?" "WE ask the questions." And there is a possibly redemptive love story with Lillian (Juliet Aubrey), an American singer who arrives in Vienna on scholarship. Less successful are melodramatic contrivances like her learning that her sponsor Vitfogel (Frank Finlay) is really her father (whom she thought dead since childhood) – the very man whom Daniel's father was tracking as a former Nazi. So Daniel must deal with the fact that their baby has a Nazi grandfather as well as a survivor grandfather. The film is curiously evasive about Daniel's Jewish identity: first his father is cremated, then his mother, and the word "Jewish" is never mentioned. If there is a distorted depiction of dysfunctional survivors in numerous films, *For My Baby* takes the image a generation further: it suggests that children of survivors are likely to have more than chips on their shoulders, needing – if not an exorcism – at least a good therapist.

Get Thee Out. Russia, 1991. D: Dimitri Astrakan. A compelling, if uneven, first feature by a Jewish director from Leningrad, filled with images of pre-Holocaust anti-Semitism. Around 1912, Motl – a wealthy, upstanding Jew – applies for and receives the right to be a trader outside the shtetl. But Motl's personal quest for assimilation will be lost in the onslaught of a larger issue: as intercut black-and-white images suggest, a pogrom is fast approaching. When he goes to a local inn to buy vodka, there is a chilling introduction of outside agitators who have been brought in to massacre the Jews. They sharpen their axes while drinking and menace Motl. The personal and the political continue to intersect as his daughter runs off with Petya, the son of Motl's non-Jewish friend, to get married in a church. They return and announce the wedding, inducing shock and finally acceptance. But horror ensues when they see that the city's shtetl has been destroyed, and that the villages are next. Everyone tries to convince Motl to run away with his family, but at the end, he picks up an axe and marches toward the killers. He is joined by Petya's father and the local policeman, ending on a freeze-frame of his biblical face before a fade into white. The most troubling character is Motl's non-Jewish buddy Alyosha, for whom he does a great deal, and who is generally drunk. When he hears of the pogrom, he declares that maybe it's right, because the Jews got all the brains, and they provide the vodka that ruins men like him! The anti-Semitism thus comes, not only from the government, but from jealous countrymen.

Mr. Death: The Rise and Fall of Fred A. Leuchter, Jr. U.S.A., 1998. D: Errol Morris. A provocative documentary which – like all of Morris's films – displays his fascination with quirky individuals who are obsessed with their idiosyncratic work. Here, the stakes are higher: although the first half-hour chronicles how Leuchter became a proud execution technologist, the rest covers his having been a defense witness in Holocaust denier Ernst Zundel's 1987 trial in Canada. Fred matter-of-factly recounts his "humane" efforts for executions that reduced pain, shame, and the degrading urinating/defecating of the person executed. He makes a distinction between the capital punishment that he defends and capital torture, which he opposes. (It's fascinating to learn that he drinks forty cups of coffee and smokes six packs of cigarettes daily, even if we never see him smoking.) Morris uses documentary footage of Zundel, and a videotape made in Auschwitz, as Leuchter amasses material that will be tested in Massachusetts. He is to determine whether the gas chambers there really existed. Morris's critique emerges when he repeats footage: the second time, it is accompanied by the voice-over of the architectural historian Van Pelt, who mapped where Leuchter excavated secretly. He says that over half a million people were killed in the camp, and that more human remains are found every year. The lab – not having been told where the samples came from – concluded that the fragments did not contain the hydrogen cyanide that would constitute proof of gas chambers. But a man from the lab now says the test wasn't right for this kind of analysis. Fred contends that Auschwitz was a slave-labor camp for the simple reason that it doesn't make sense to execute so many people! He believes that Zundel's trial was about freedom of speech rather than Holocaust denial. But he has been wearing metaphorical blinders and, like a Greek tragic hero, endures a downfall caused by hubris. Prosecuted and reviled in the United States, he is accepted only by the Institute for Historical Review.

New Land. Israel, 1994. D: Orna Ben-Dor Niv. S: Kobi Niv. A very moving drama about children who come from Poland after the Holocaust to an Israeli refugee camp. Anna (Ania Bukstein), who is eight, and her fourteen-year-old brother, Jan (Michael Phelman), are looking for their lost mother, now that their father has died. Jan, who speaks Hebrew, becomes part of the new land and joins a kibbutz. Anna, however, fiercely sticks both to her smelly teddy bear and to her past identity, wanting only to find her mother. Their story is intertwined with that of other refugees, most poignantly that of the Polish Marisha: this beautiful young blonde hid and then married her former professor, an old Jew named Pinchas. We learn that she even slept with a Nazi to spare Pinchas's life. Now that he is dying of tuberculosis and needs medicine, she is pressured by a black marketeer for sex in exchange for the medicine. He finally gives it to the crying Marisha without sex; she gets it to her husband, who quickly feels better. But assuming that she slept with the man for the medicine, he hangs himself before she wakes up. Less tragic is the fate of the Greek Jews sharing their "house": the woman lost her daughter and husband in the Holocaust, and the man she is with lost his wife and son. She is now pregnant, and they seem to be such a comfort to each other. After hearing a doctor say that the Greek women survived by acting as whores for the Nazis, she tries to remove her tattooed number with an iron; but this horror yields to the birth and happy departure of the new family.

Set Me Free. Canada, 1999. D: Lea Pool, and S with Nancy Huston and Monique Messier. A strong coming-of-age drama set in 1963 Montreal. Hanna (Karine Vanasse) is forging an identity amid conflicting impulses. Her overworked mother (Pascale Bussieres) is Catholic, and her emotional father (Miki Manojlovic) is a Polish-Jewish survivor, a poet who is unable to maintain a steady job. His violent temper keeps Hanna and her brother Paul at a distance, and closer to their suicidal mother. Hanna sees Godard's film *Vivre sa vie* and completely absorbs the prostitute character played by Anna Karina: she even goes so far as to play at being a prostitute one night, with almost disastrous consequences when she tells the "john" she changed her mind. Hanna is trying a variety of sexual roles, including a lesbian relationship. She also seems to have a crush on her Catholic schoolteacher (Nancy Huston), who looks like Anna Karina and treats her tenderly. Hanna runs away after her mother is hospitalized for an overdose. When she finally returns to her agonized father, his response is beautifully Jewish: "I made you an Osso Buco, full of all the things your body needs," even listing the vegetables and their vitamins. At the end, she is reunited with her mother, and now has an eight millimeter camera loaned by her teacher – suggesting the partly autobiographical quality of the film for Lea Pool (who identified herself as "second-generation" at a New York Film Festival press conference).

Shine. Australia, 1996. D: Scott Hicks. S: Jan Sardi.

Shining Through. U.S.A., 1992. D: David Seltzer, and S from the novel by Susan Isaacs. After an auspicious beginning, it becomes a hokey, conventional, clichéd Hollywood melodrama, with unrelievedly schmaltzy music and an unbelievable happy end. The drama is narrated by Lisa (Melanie Griffith, quite good) as an old woman telling the BBC about her World War II experiences, which we then see in flashbacks. Half-Jewish and half-Irish, she gets a Manhattan job as a bilingual secretary for Ed (Michael Douglas), a powerful, humorless, and secretive man. She figures out that he is a spy and, nourished by war films, Lisa wants to contribute to the war cause too. After they fall in love, she convinces him to let her try to infiltrate a Nazi home for information. Once the film moves to Germany, it loses all credibility: whereas Lisa spoke German in the New York scenes, suddenly they are all speaking English with a German accent! To make things worse, during this English-language sequence of her serving a meal to Germans, the boss yells at her in German. She is fired, but General Dietrich (Liam Neeson) takes pity on her and, assuming she has been cleared by security, engages her as a nanny for his two children. Unfortunately, Neeson is so sympathetic that one almost hopes Lisa will fall in love with him and raise his children. He finally realizes that she is not who she says, but assumes she has been sent by the Gestapo to check on his unwavering loyalty. After a number of espionage shenanigans, she is discovered by Ed, who tries to get her over the Swiss border. He is shot just as they cross. Implausibly, he survives, and shows up as an old man to take a bow on the BBC broadcast.

The Substance of Fire. U.S.A., 1997. D: Daniel Sullivan. S: Jon Robin Baitz.

The Summer of Aviya. Israel, 1990. D: Eli Cohen. S: Gila Almagor.

The Third Miracle. U.S.A., 1999. D: Agnieszka Holland. S: John Romano and Richard Vetere, from Vetere's novel. This drama about faith and the mechanism for making saints in contemporary Catholicism begins with a haunting flashback to 1944. In grainy images of a Slovakian town about to be bombed, a little girl prays on church steps, and the bombs miraculously don't come down. This is observed by a wounded German soldier. We cut to 1979 Chicago, where Frank (Ed Harris), a priest, is a kind of church-appointed "spiritual detective" who investigates supposed miracles to determine if someone should be recommended for sainthood. A flashback reveals that he destroyed a community's faith the last time by revealing that Father Falcone was highly flawed. Now he is investigating whether Helen (Barbara Sukowa) – a laywoman who died, and whose favorite statue sheds blood – might be a saint. What complicates matters is that Frank is drawn to her hip, nonbeliever daughter, Roxanna (Anne Heche), and vice versa. He decides that Helen is worthy, and must now convince the hierarchy, including the tough archbishop Werner (Armin Mueller-Stahl). At the tribunal, Werner is not only condescending and dismissive, but questions Frank's faith. After a number of plot turns, Frank reveals the Gypsy village where the child Helen stopped bombs, and Werner looks ill: we know that he was the wounded German soldier in 1944. How did he become an archbishop?

Under the Domim Tree. Israel, 1995. D: Eli Cohen. S: Gila Almagor.

Writing on the Wall, The. U.S.A., 1994. D: David J. Eagle. S: Carol Starr Schneider. A fine one-hour CBS Schoolbreak Special, based on a true story. Three white teenagers from affluent California families deface a synagogue and write anti-Semitic slogans on a rabbi's garage door as well as an older Jew's car. The kind Rabbi Markowitz (Hal Linden) places education and trust over revenge, and offers in court to teach them during probation (instead of having them incarcerated for two years). All three gain a totally different perspective after seeing the Wiesenthal Foundation's documentary *Genocide* and learning about the Holocaust by following the trajectories of three teenage boys in the 1940s. The rabbi has them watch *Schindler's List* and takes them to the Museum of Tolerance, leading to a rehabilitation. (There is a special resonance in the casting: his wife is played by Millie Perkins, who was Anne Frank in the original film version.)

Zentropa (originally titled *Europa*). Denmark/France/Germany/Sweden, 1991. D: Lars Von Trier. A fascinating and complex drama, moving from black-and-white to color, and from Max Von Sydow's ponderous voice-over hypnotizing the viewer, to richly self-conscious visuals. Mostly in English, it begins with the arrival in postwar Germany of Leopold Kessler (Jean-Marc Barre), a young American whose father fled Germany and whose uncle (Ernst-Hugo Jaregard) works on the railroad. Leo wishes to do his part to unify the two nations (and the two parts within himself). His strict Teutonic uncle prepares him to be a sleeping-car conductor. In this dark world, Leo meets Katharina (Barbara Sukowa), the wealthy daughter of the railroad company Zentropa. She flirts with him; he is invited to their home, a dark place where she wears furs because there is no heat. He is told to watch out for the "Werewolf" group – Nazi partisans still carrying out attacks against those cooperating with the Allies. Leo unwittingly allows two little boys onto the train, not knowing they are assassins. It turns out that Zentropa's trains were used to transport Jews to concentration camps. By the end, the doomed Leo has become a pawn in an absurd game. The film's use of front and back projections – layering the image with different textures – is appropriately unsettling, making us question what we see.

Filmography (Second Edition)

This list is by no means complete, but the following films deal – either directly or indirectly – with the Holocaust. Titles are all in English, with the original foreign-language title following whenever it is significantly different. As one quickly learns when researching a film in various reference books, release dates are not always to be relied on, although every effort has been made to be correct. Each film is listed with the name of the director (D) and, whenever possible, its screenwriter (S) as well. For those wishing to rent prints of films listed, a rental source (R) is given whenever available in the United States. Addresses of rental sources (generally 16-mm prints, occasionally videocassettes) are provided at the end of the 1989 Filmography.

Fiction Features

Aguirre, the Wrath of God. West Germany, 1973. D and S: Werner Herzog. R: NYF.

All in Order (*Ordnung*). West Germany, 1980. D: Sohrab Shahid Saless.

Ambulance. Poland, 1962. D: Janusz Morgenstern. S: Tadeusz Lomnicki. R: A-DL.

And Now, My Love (*Toute une vie*). France, 1974. D and S: Claude Lelouch. Videocassette: Embassy Home Entertainment.

Angry Harvest. West Germany, 1985. D and S: Agnieszka Holland.

Army of Shadows. France, 1969. D and S: Jean-Pierre Melville, from novel by Joseph Kessel.

Ashes and Diamonds. Poland, 1958. D: Andrzej Wajda. S: Jerzy Andrzejewski and Wajda, from novel by Andrzejewski. R: FI.

The Assault. Holland, 1986. D: Fons Rademakers. R: Cannon.

The Attic: The Hiding of Anne Frank. U.S.A. (TV), 1988. D: John Erman. Teleplay: William Hanley, from Miep Gies's *Anne Frank Remembered.*

A Bag of Marbles. France, 1975. D: Jacques Doillon. S: Doillon and Denis Ferraris, from novel by Joseph Joffo.

Bastille. Holland, 1985. D: Rudolf van den Berg.

The Big Red One. U.S.A., 1980. D and S: Samuel Fuller. R: SWANK.

Birth Certificate. Poland, 1961. D: Stanislaw Rozewicz.

Black Thursday (*Les Guichets du Louvre*). France, 1974. D: Michel Mitrani. S: Albert Cossery and Mitrani from the book by Roger Boussinot. R: FI.

The Blum Affair. East Germany, 1948. D: Erich Engel. S: Robert Stemmle. R: FI.

The Boat Is Full. Switzerland/West Germany/Austria, 1981. D and S: Markus Imhoof. R: FI.

Border Street. Poland, 1948. D and S: Aleksander Ford. R: FI.

The Boxer and Death. Czechoslovakia, 1962. D: Peter Solan. P: Studio Hranych Filmov, Brastislava.

The Boys From Brazil. U.S.A., 1978. D: Franklin J. Schaffner. S: Heywood Gould, based on novel by Ira Levin. R: FI.

Brussels-Transit. Belgium, 1980. D and S: Samy Szlingerbaum. R: Atara.

Cabaret. U.S.A., 1972. D: Bob Fosse. S: Jay Presson Allen. R: HUR.

Charlotte. Holland/West Germany, 1981. D: Franz Weisz. S: Judith Herzberg. R: Atara.

Child of Our Time. U.S.A. CBS-TV (CBS Playhouse), 1950. D: George Roy Hill.

The Children from Number 67. West Germany, 1979. D and S: Usch Barthelmess-Weller and Werner Meyer. R: Atara.

Collective Scene with the Saint. Poland, 1974. D: Mariusz Walter, with Andrzej Wajda playing a director trying to reconstruct an incident at Auschwitz.

Commissar. Soviet Union, 1988. D: Aleksander Askoldov.

The Condemned of Altona. U.S.A./Italy, 1962. D: Vittorio De Sica. S: Abby Mann and Cesare Zavattini from the play by Jean-Paul Sartre. R: FI.

Confidence. Hungary, 1980. D and S: István Szabó. R: NYF.

The Confrontation. Switzerland, 1975. D: Rolf Lyssy. S: Georg Janett and Lyssy. R: NYF.

Conspiracy of Hearts. Great Britain, 1960. D: Ralph Thomas. S: Robert Presnell, Jr. R: FI. (Also a USA TV drama, 1956: Alcoa/Goodyear Theater, directed by Robert Mulligan.)

The Damned (La caduta degli dei). Italy, 1969. D: Luchino Visconti. S: Nicola Badalucco, Enrico Medioli, and Visconti. R: FI.

David. West Germany, 1979. D: Peter Lilienthal. S: Lilienthal, Jurek Becker, and Ulla Zieman, from the autobiographical novel by Joel Konig. R: KINO.

Death Is Called Engelchen. Czechoslovakia, 1963. D: Jan Kadar and Elmar Klos.

Death Is My Trade (Aus Einem Deutschen Leben). West Germany, 1976. D and S: Theodor Kotulla, based on the novel by Robert Merle.

Diamonds of the Night. Czechoslovakia, 1964. D: Jan Nemec. S: Arnost Lusting and Nemec from Lustig's novel. R: Icarus Films.

The Diary of Anne Frank. U.S.A., 1959. D: George Stevens. S: Frances Goodrich and Albert Hackett, from their play. R: FI.

The Distant Journey (Ghetto Terrezin). Czechoslovakia, 1949. D and S: Alfred Radok.

The Enclosure. France/Yugoslavia, 1962. D: Armand Gatti. S: Gatti and Pierre Joffroy.

The End of the World. Poland, 1964. D: Wanda Jakubowska. (Sequel to *The Last Stop*).

Entre Nous (Coup de foudre). France, 1983. D and S: Diane Kurys. R: FI.

Eroica. Poland, 1957. D: Andrzej Munk. S: Jerzy S. Stawinski from his novels.

Escape from Sobibor. U.S.A. (CBS-TV), 1987. D: Jack Gold. Teleplay: Reginald Rose, from book by Richard Rashke.

Escape Route from Marseille. West Germany, 1977. D: Ingemo Engstrom and Gerhard Theuring.

The Evacuees. Great Britain. BBC-TV, 1975. D: Alan Parker. S: Jack Rosenthal.

The Execution. U.S.A. (NBC-TV), 1985. D: Paul Wendkos. Teleplay: William Wood and Judith Parker, from the novel by Wood.

Exodus. U.S.A., 1960. D: Otto Preminger. S: Dalton Trumbo from the novel by Leon Uris. R: UA.

Falsch. Belgium, 1988. D: Jean-Pierre and Luc Dardenne. R: MD Wax/Courier Films, New York.

Fear Not, Jacob! West Germany, 1981. D: Radu Gabrea. S: Meir Dohnal, Frieder Schuller, and Gabrea.

The Fiancée. East Germany, 1980. D: Günter Reisch and Gunther Rücker. S: Rücker, from three autobiographical novels by Eva Lippold.

The Fifth Horseman Is Fear. Czechoslovakia, 1964. D and S: Zbynek Brynuch, based on a story by Jana Belehradska. R: FI.

Five Minutes of Paradise. Yugoslavia, 1959. D: lgor Pretnar.

Following the Führer. West Germany, 1985. D: Erwin Leiser, dramatic sequences directed by Eberhard Itzenplitz, written by Oliver Storz.

For Those I Loved. France, 1983. D: Robert Enrico. S: Enrico and Tony Sheer, from book by Martin Gray and Max Gallo.

Forbidden. U.S.A./Great Britain, (HBO), 1986. D: Anthony Page. Teleplay: Leonard Gross, from his novel *Last Jews in Berlin.*

A Friendship in Vienna. U.S.A. (Disney Channel-TV), 1988. D: Arthur Allan Seidelman.

The Garden of the Finzi-Continis. Italy, 1970. D: Vittorio De Sica. S: Cesare Zavattini, Vittorio Bonicelli, and Ugo Pirro, based the novel by Giorgio Bassani.

Gare de la Douleur (Pain Station). France, 1984. D: Henri Jouf. (Short.)

General della Rovere. Italy, 1959. D: Roberto Rossellini. S: Sergio Amidei, Diego Fabbri, Indro Montanelli, and Rossellini. R: IMAGES and NYF.

A Generation. Poland, 1955. D: Andrzej Wajda. S: Bohdan Czeszko. R: FI.

Germany, Pale Mother. West Germany, 1980. D: Helma Sanders-Brahms. R: NYF.

God Does Not Believe in Us Anymore. Austria, 1981. D: Axel Corti. S: Georg Stefan Troller and Corti. R: Roxie Releasing.

The Gold of Rome. Italy, 1961. D: Carlo Lizzani. S: Lucio Battistrada, Giuliani de Negri, Alberto Lecco, and Lizzani. R: FI.

Goodbye Children. France, 1987. D and S: Louis Malle.

Grand Illusion. France, 1937. D: Jean Renoir. S: Charles Spaak and Renoir. R: IMAGES.

The Great Dictator. U.S.A., 1940. D and S: Charles Chaplin. R: FI.

Hanna's War. U.S.A., 1988. D: Menachem Golan. S: Golan and Stanley Mann. R: Cannon.

High Street. Belgium, 1976. D: Andre Ernotte. S: Elliot Tiber and Ernotte.

History. Italy, 1986. D: Luigi Comencini. S: Suso Cecchi d'Amico and Cristina Comencini, from the novel by Elsa Morante.

Hitler's SS: Portrait in Evil. U.S.A. (NBC-TV), 1985. D: Jim Goddard. S: Lukas Keller.

Holocaust. U.S.A. (NBC-TV), 1978. D: Marvin Chomsky. S: Gerald Green. R: LCA.

How to Be Loved. Poland, 1963. D: Wojciech Has. S: Kazimierz Brandys.

I Survived Certain Death. Czechoslovakia, 1960. D: Vojtech Jasny.

I Was a Kapo. Poland, 1964. D: Tadeusz Jaworski.

The Ice Cream Parlor. Holland, 1985. D: Dimitri Frenkel Frank.

In the Presence of Mine Enemies. U.S.A. (CBS-TV, Playhouse 90), 1960. D: Fielder Cook. S: Rod Serling. With Charles Laughton and Robert Redford.

The Inheritors. Austria, 1983. D: Walter Bannert. S: Erich Richter and Bannert.

Inside the Third Reich. Austria, (ABC-TV), 1986. D: Marvin J. Chomsky. S: E. Jack Neuman.

It Was Night in Rome. Italy, 1960. D: Roberto Rossellini. S: Sergio Amidei, Diego Fabbri, Brunello Rondi, and Rossellini. R: FI.

Jacob, the Liar. East Germany, 1978. D: Frank Beyer. S: Jurek Becker, from his novel. R: FI.

Jud Süss. Germany, 1940. D: Veit Harlan.

Judgment at Nuremberg. U.S.A., 1961. D: Stanley Kramer. S: Abby Mann. R: UA. (Also done in 1959 on CBS-TV, Playhouse 90, directed by George Roy Hill, with Claude Rains in the Spencer Tracy film role and Maximilian Schell playing the same role in both versions.)

Julia. U.S.A., 1977. D: Fred Zinnemann. S: Alvin Sargent, based on Lillian Hellman's *Pentimento.* R: FI.

Just a Gigolo. Great Britain, 1979. D: David Hemmings. S: Joshua Sinclair.

Kanal. Poland, 1957. D: Andrzej Wajda. S: Jerzy S. Stawinski. R: FI.

Kassbach. Austria, 1979. D: Peter Patzak.

Kristallnacht. U.S.A. (short), 1979. D: Chick Strand. R: Canyon Cinema, 2325 3d St., San Francisco, CA 94107.

Lacombe, Lucien. France, 1974. D: Louis Malle. S: Patrick Modiano and Malle. R: FI.

Landscape after Battle. Poland, 1970. D: Andrzej Wajda. S: Andrzej Brzozowski and Wajda, based on stories by Tadeusz Borowski. R: NYF.

The Last Five Days. West Germany, 1982. D. and S: Percy Adlon.

The Last Metro. France, 1980. D: François Truffaut. S: Suzanne Schiffman, Jean-Claude Grumberg, and Truffaut.

The Last Stop. Poland, 1948. D: Wanda Jakubowska. S: Gerda Schneider and Jakubowska. (There is one print in the Museum of Modern Art in New York.)

Lena. U.S.A. (TV), 1987. D: Ed Sherin. Teleplay: Jonathan Rintel and Yabo Yablonsky.

Lili Marleen. West Germany, 1981. D: Rainer Werner Fassbinder. S: Manfred Purzer and Joshua Sinclair from Lale Andersen's autobiography.

Lissy. East Germany, 1957. D: Konrad Wolf. S: Alex Wedding and Wolf, from a novel by F. C. Weiskopf. R: FI.

Lucky Star. Canada, 1980. D: Max Fisher.

Malou. West Germany, 1982. D and S: Jeanine Meerapfel.

The Man in the Glass Booth. U.S.A. (American Film Theater), 1975. D: Arthur Hiller. S: Edward Anhalt, from the play by Robert Shaw. R: PAR.

The Marathon Man. U.S.A., 1976. D: John Schlesinger. S: William Goldman, from his novel. R: FI, PAR.

Marianne and Juliane (Die Bleierne Zeit). West Germany, 1981. D: Margarethe von Trotta, based on the book by Christiane Ensslin. R: NYF.

The Marriage of Maria Braun. West Germany, 1978. D: Rainer Werner Fassbinder. S: Peter Märthesheimer and Pia Fröhlich. R: NYF.

The Martyr. Israel, 1976. D: Aleksander Ford.

Mephisto. Hungary, 1981. D: István Szabó. S: Peter Dobai and Szabó, based on the novel by Klaus Mann. R: KINO, C5.

The Mortal Storm. U.S.A., 1940. D: Frank Borzage. S: Claudine West, George Froeschel, and Andersen Ellis, based on the novel by Phyllis Bottome. R: FI.

Mr. Klein. 1976, France. D: Joseph Losey.: Franco Solinas.

Murderers among Us: The Simon Wiesenthal Story. U.S.A. (HBO), 1989. D: Brian Gibson. S: Abby Mann, Lane Slate, Ron Hutchinson.

Murderers Are among Us. East Germany, 1946. D and S: Wolfgang Staudte. R: FI.

My Name Is Ivan (Ivanovo Detstvo). USSR, 1962. D: Andrei Tarkovsky. R: FI.

Natalia. France, 1988. D: Bernard Cohn.

Nazi Hunter: The Beate Klarsfeld Story. U.S.A. (ABC-TV), 1986. D: Michael Lindsay-Hogg. S: Frederic Hunter.

The Night Porter. Italy, 1974. D: Liliana Cavani. S: Italo Moscati and Cavani.

The Ninth Circle. Yugoslavia, 1960. D: France Stiglic.

Once upon a Honeymoon. U.S.A., 1942. D: Leo McCarey, S: Sheridan Gibney and McCarey. R: FI.

One Man's War. France, 1981. D and S: Edgardo Cozarinsky, based on Ernst Jünger's Parisian diaries. R: NYF.

Only a Day. West Germany, 1965. D: Egon Monk.

The Only Way. Denmark, 1967. D: Bent Christiansen. R: JWB Lecture Bureau.

Open City. Italy, 1945. D: Roberto Rossellini. S: Sergio Amidei, Federico Fellini and Rossellini. R: IMAGES.

The Oppermanns. West Germany/Great Britain (TV), 1983. D: Egon Monk, from Leon Feuchtwanger's novel.

Ordinary Fascism. USSR, 1967. D and S: Mikhail Romm.

Our Hitler, a Film from Germany. West Germany, 1978. D: Hans-Jürgen Syberberg. Released in U.S. by Zoetrope Studios, San Francisco.

La Passante. France, 1982. D: Jacques Rouffio. S: Rouffio and Jacques Kirsner, from novel by Joseph Kessel.

Passenger. Poland, 1962. D: Andrzej Munk (completed by Witold Lesiewicz). S: Zofia Posmysz and Munk, based on the novel by Posmysz. R: FI.

The Pawnbroker. U.S.A., 1965. D: Sidney Lumet. S: Morton Fine and David Friedkin, from the novel by Edward Lewis Wallant. R: FI.

Pebbles. Austria, 1982. D: Lukas Stepanik. R: Atara.

Playing for Time. U.S.A. (CBS-TV), 1980. D: Daniel Mann. S: Arthur Miller, from Fania Fenelon's autobiography.

Postcard from a Journey. Poland, 1983. D: Waldemar Dziki.

The Producers. U.S.A., 1967. D and S: Mel Brooks, R: IMAGES.

Professor Mamlock. USSR, 1937, D: Adolph Minkin and Herbert Rappaport. S: Friedrich Wolf, from his play.

Raindrops. West Germany, 1982. D and S: Michael Hoffmann and Harry Raymon.

The Raven. France, 1943. D: Henri-Georges Clouzot. S: Louis Chavance. R: FI, BUD.

Return from the Ashes. Great Britain, 1965. D: J. Lee Thompson. S: Julius J. Epstein, from the novel by Hubert Monteilhet. R: UA.

The Revolt of Job. Hungary, 1983. D: Imre Gyongyossi and Barna Kabay. S: Katalin Peteny, Gongyossi and Kabay. R: Cinecom.

Roads in the Night. West Germany, 1980. D and S: Krzysztof Zanussi.

Samson. Poland, 1961. D: Andrzej Wajda. S: Kazimierz Brandys and Wajda. R: FI.

Sandra (Vaghe Stelle dell'Orsa). Italy, 1965. D: Luchino Visconti. S: Suso Cecchi d'Amico, Enrico Medioli, and Visconti.

Santa Fe. Austria, 1985. D: Axel Corti. S: Georg Stefan Troller and Corti, R: Roxie Releasing.

The Serpent's Egg. U.S.A./West Germany, 1977. D and S: Ingmar Bergman. R: PAR.

Seven Beauties (Pasqualino Settebelezze). Italy, 1975. D and S: Lina Wertmuller.

The Shadow of Victory. Holland, 1986. D and S: Ate de Jong.

Ship of Fools. U.S.A., 1965. D: Stanley Kramer. S: Abby Mann, based on the novel by Katherine Anne Porter. R: FI.

The Shop on Main Street. Czechoslovakia, 1965. D: Jan Kadar and Elmar Klos. S: Ladislav Grosman. R: FI.

Skokie. U.S.A. (CBS-TV), 1981. D: Herbert Wise. S: Ernest Kinoy.

Somewhere in Europe. Hungary, 1947. D: Geza von Radvanyi.

Sophie's Choice. U.S.A., 1982. D and S: Alan Pakula, from the novel by William Styron. R: SWANK.

Special Section. France, 1975. D: Costa-Gavras. S: Jorge Semprun and Costa-Gavras, based on the book by Hervé Villeré. R: UNIV.

Stars. East Germany, 1958. D: Konrad Wolf and Rangel Vulchanov. S: Anzhel Vagenstein and Christa Wernicke. R: FI.

Sweet Light in a Dark Room (Romeo, Julie a Tma). Czechoslovakia, 1959. D: Jiri Weiss. S: Jan Otcenasek. R: FI.

A Tear in the Ocean. France, 1971. D and S: Henri Glaeser, based on the novel by Manes Sperber.

Tel Aviv – Berlin. Israel, 1987. D and S: Tzipi Tropé (212-473-4209).

Temporary Paradise. Hungary, 1981. D and S: Andras Kovacs.

'38: Vienna before the Fall. Austria, 1986. D: Wolfgang Gluck, from Friedrich Torberg's novel *This Too Was Vienna.*

The Tin Drum. West Germany, 1979. D: Volker Schlöndorff. S: Jean-Claude Carrière, Franz Seitz, and Schlöndorff, from the novel by Günter Grass. R: KINO.

To Be or Not to Be. U.S.A., 1942. D: Ernst Lubitsch. S: Edwin Justus Mayer. R: IMAGES.

To Be or Not to Be. U.S.A., 1983. D: Alan Johnson. S: Thomas Meehan. Prod.: Mel Brooks. R: FI.

'aradise. Czechoslovakia, 1962. D and S: Zbynek Brynych, based on the book
    ustig. R: ICARUS.
?ath. Bulgaria, 1984. D: Borislav Punchev. S: Chaim Oliver.
reet. Hungary, 1973. D: István Szabó. R: FI.
    J.S.A. (NBC-TV), 1989. D: Ian Sharp. S: William Bast and Paul Huson, from
    Fish's *Pursuit.*

The Two of Us (Le Vieil Homme et l'enfant). France, 1966. D and S: Claude Berri.
Under the World. Argentina, 1988. D and S: Beda Docampo Feijoo and Juan Bautista Stagnaro.
    R: New World Pictures, 1440 So. Sepulveda Blvd., Los Angeles, CA 90025.
Victory. U.S.A., 1981. D: John Huston. S: Evan Jones and Yabo Yablonsky. R: PAR.
Les Violons du Bal. France, 1973. D and S: Michel Drach. R: FI.
Voyage of the Damned. Great Britain, 1976. D: Stuart Rosenberg. S: Steve Shagan and David
    Butler. R: FI.
The Wall. U.S.A. (CBS-TV), 1982. D: Robert Markowitz. S: Millard Lampell, from the novel
    by John Hersey.
Wallenberg: A Hero's Story. U.S.A. (NBC-TV), 1985. D: Lamont Johnson. Teleplay: Gerald
    Green.
The Wannsee Conference. West Germany, 1984. D: Heinz Schirk. R: Prism Entertainment
    (video), 1988 Century Park East, Los Angeles, CA 90067.
War and Love. U.S.A., 1985. D: Moshe Mizrahi. S: Abby Mann, from Jack Eisner's novel
    The Survivor. R: Cannon.
War and Remembrance. U.S.A. (ABC-TV), 1988. D: Dan Curtis. S: Earl Wallace, Dan Curtis,
    Herman Wouk, from the novel by Wouk.
The Wave. U.S.A. (ABC-TV), 1981. D: Alex Grasshoff. S: Johnny Dawkins, from autobiograph-
    ical story by Ron Jones.
Welcome in Vienna. Austria, 1986. D: Axel Corti. S: Georg Stefan Troller and Corti, R: Roxie
    Releasing.
Welcome to Germany. West Germany, 1988. D and S: Thomas Brasch.
The Well. U.S.A. (short), 1983. D: David Greenwald. R: The Well Productions, 108 W. 15
    St., New York, NY 10011.
Wherever You Are. Poland/West Germany/Great Britain, 1988. D and S: Krzysztof Zanussi.
The White Rose. West Germany, 1982. D: Michael Verhoeven.

Documentaries
The Alien's Place. Holland, 1979. D: Rudolph van den Berg. R: Icarus Films.
As If It Were Yesterday. Belgium, 1980. D: Myriam Abramowicz and Esther Hoffenberg.
Auschwitz and the Allies. Great Britain, 1983. D: Rex Bloomstein, from book by Martin Gilbert.
    R: FI.
Auschwitz Street. West Germany, 1979. D and S: Ebbo Demant.
The Avenue of the Just. U.S.A., 1978. D: Samuel Elfert. S: Arnold Forster. R: A-DL.
Because of That War. Israel, 1988. D: Orna Ben-Dor-Niv.
Before Hindsight. Great Britain, 1977. D: Jonathan Lewis. R: MOMA Circulating Film Library,
    11 W. 53 St., New York, NY 10019.
Breaking the Silence. U.S.A., 1983. D: Edward Mason. Prod.: Eva Fogelman. R: Cinema Guild.
California Reich. U.S.A., 1975. R: RBC Films, 933 N. La Brea Ave., Los Angeles, CA 90038.
A Campaign to Remember (with Ted Koppel). U.S.A. (short), 1988. D: Gregory Stone. S and
    Prod.: David K. Haspel. R: U.S. Holocaust Memorial Council, Washington, D.C.
Chaim Rumkowski and the Jews of Lodz. Sweden, 1982. D: Peter Cohen. S: Bo Kuritzen.
    R: Cinema Guild.
Children in the Holocaust. U.S.A. (ABC-TV), 1981. D: Joseph S. Kutrzeba. Narrated by
    Liv Ullmann.

The Confessions of Winifred Wagner. West Germany, 1975. D: Hans-Jürgen Syberberg.

A Conversation with Elie Wiesel. U.S.A. (PBS-TV), 1988. D: Erwin Leiser.

Cooperation of Parts. U.S.A., 1988. D: Dan Eisenberg.

The Courage to Care. U.S.A. (short), 1985. D: Richard Gardner, dist: A-DL.

Dark Lullabies. Canada, 1986. D: Irene Angelico and Abbey Neidik for DLI and National Film Board of Canada. R: Phoenix Films.

The Eighty-first Blow. Israel, 1975. D: Haim Gouri, David Bergman, Jacquo Erlich. R: National Center for Jewish Film.

Falkenau: Samuel Fuller Bears Witness. France, 1988. D: Emil Weiss.

Fighters of the Ghetto. Israel, 1968. D: Mira Hamermesh.

The Final Solution. 1984. An Arthur Cohn production based on the work of Bengt von zur Muhlen and Gerhard Schoenberger.

Flames in the Ashes. Israel, 1986. D: Haim Gouri. R: National Center for Jewish Film.

Forever Yesterday. U.S.A. (WNEW-TV), 1980. Holocaust Survivors Film Project.

The Gathering. Great Britain (BBC-TV), 1981. Prod.: Rex Bloomstein.

A Generation Apart. U.S.A., 1984. D: Jack and Danny Fisher. R: City Lights Productions, 505 8th Ave., New York, NY 10018.

Genocide. Great Britain (Thames-TV for *World at War* series), 1975. D: Michael Darlow. S: Charles Bloomberg. Narrated by Sir Laurence Olivier. R: A-DL.

Genocide. U.S.A., 1981. D: Arnold Schwartzman. S: Martin Gilbert and Rabbi Marvin Hier. R: Simon Wiesenthal Center, 9760 West Pico Blvd., Los Angeles, CA 90035.

George Stevens: A Filmmaker's Journey. U.S.A., 1985. D: George Stevens, Jr. R: Castle Hill, 1414 Ave. of the Americas, New York, NY 10019. (Contains powerful color footage of the liberation of Dachau.)

Holocaust – The Survivors Gather: A Look Back. U.S.A., 1981. D: Joel Levitch. R: PBS.

Hotel Terminus. U.S.A., 1988. D: Marcel Ophuls. R: Samuel Goldwyn Co., 10203 Santa Monica Blvd., Los Angeles, CA 90067.

Image before My Eyes. U.S.A., 1981. D: Josh Waletzky. S: Jerome Badanes.

In Dark Places. U.S.A., 1978, D: Gina Blumenfeld. R: PHOENIX.

In Search of Jewish Amsterdam. Holland, 1975. D: Philo Bregstein.

In the Country of My Parents. West Germany, 1982. D: Jeanine Meerapfel.

In the Name of the Führer. Belgium, 1977. D: Lydia Chagoll.

Irreconcilable Memories. West Germany, 1979. D: Klaus Volkenborn, Karl Siebig, Johann Feindt.

A Journey Back (with Jack Garfein). Canada, 1985. D: Bryan McKenna. R: CBC.

Kaddish. U.S.A., 1984. D: Steven Brand. R: First-Run.

Kitty: Return to Auschwitz. Great Britain (Yorkshire Television), 1980. D: Peter Morley. R: PBS.

Kristallnacht: The Journey from 1938 to 1988, U.S.A. (PBS-TV), 1988. D: Peter Chafer. R: PBS.

The Last Sea. Israel, 1980. D: Haim Gouri, David Bergman, Jacquo Erlich. R: Natl. Center for Jewish Film.

L'Chaim – To Life! U.S.A., 1973. D: Marold Mayer. R: Harold Mayer Productions, 50 Ferriss Estate, New Milford, CT 06776.

The Legacy: Children of Holocaust Survivors. U.S.A., 1980. D: Miriam Strilky Rosenbush. R: Viewfinders, P.O. Box 1665, Evanston, IL 60204.

Let Ye Inherit. Hungary, 1986. D: Imre Gyongyossi and Barna Kabay. R: Cinecom.

The Liberation of Auschwitz. West Germany, 1986. D: Irmgard and Bengt von zur Muhlen. R: National Center for Jewish Film.

A Light in the Dark. 1984. D: Naum Medavoy.

Lodz Ghetto. U.S.A., 1988. D: Alan Adelson and Kathryn Taverna. R: The Jewish Heritage Project (212-925-9067).

Mein Kampf. Sweden, 1960. D: Erwin Leiser.

a, 1965. D: Donald Brittain and John Spotten. R: A-DL.

. U.S.A., 1976. D: Marcel Ophuls. R: FI.

ps. Great Britain, 1985. Exec. Prod.: Sidney Bernstein. Prod.: Sergei
olin Wills. Treatment Adviser: Alfred Hitchcock. (Longer, 69-minute
Painful Reminder.)

ass: Memories of Kristallnacht. U.S.A. (WNYC-TV), 1988. D: Chris Pelzer.

.S.A. (CBS-TV), 1978. *60 Minutes* "On Fania Fenelon." R: A-DL.

Night and Fog. France, 1955. D: Alain Resnais. S: Jean Cayrol. R: IMAGES.

Now . . . After All These Years. West Germany, 1981. D: Harald Lüders and Pavel Schnabel.
R: Arthur Cantor, Inc., 33 West 60 St., New York, NY 10023.

Nuremberg. U.S.A., 1946. Compiled by Pare Lorentz and Stuart Schulberg. R: IMAGES.

Obedience. U.S.A., 1962. Milgram experiments at Yale University. R: NYU Film Library, 156
Washington Square, New York, NY 10003.

Of Judges and Other Sympathizers. West Germany, 1981. D: Axel Engstfield.

Of Pure Blood. France, 1975. D: Clarissa Henry and Marc Hillel.

The Other Face of Terror. Great Britain/Netherlands, 1985. D: Ludi Boeken.

Our Time in the Garden. U.S.A., 1981. D: Ron Blau. R: National Center for Jewish Film.

Out of the Ashes. U.S.A. (PBS-TV), 1984.

The Package Tour. Hungary, 1986. D: Gyula Gazdag. R: NYF.

Paper Bridge. Austria, 1987. D: Ruth Beckermann.

Partisans of Vilna. U.S.A., 1986. D: Josh Waletzky. Prod.: Aviva Kempner. R: European Classics.

The Past That Lives. Holland, 1970. D: Philo Bregstein.

Pour Memoire. France, 1987. D: Edgardo Cozarinsky.

The Precious Legacy. U.S.A. (short), 1984. D: Dan Weissman. R: Modern Talking Pictures,
45 Rockefeller Plaza, New York, NY 10010.

Return to Poland. U.S.A. (PBS), 1981. D: Marian Marzynski. R: WGHB, 125 Western Ave.,
Boston, MA 02134.

Reunion. U.S.A., 1946. D: Henri Cartier-Bresson, for the United States Information Service,
(USIS).

The Righteous Enemy. U.S.A., 1987. D: Joseph Rochlitz.

Say I'm a Jew. U.S.A., 1985. D: Piers Marton.

Shadow of Doubt. Holland, 1975. D: Rolf Orthel. R: NYF.

Shoah. France, 1986. D: Claude Lanzmann. R: NYF.

The Sick Men Who Govern Us. France, 1980. D and S: Claude Vajda, based on the book by
Piere Accoce and Pierre Rentchnick.

Sighet, Sighet. U.S.A., 1964. D: Harold Becker. S: Elie Wiesel. R: IMAGES.

So Many Miracles. Canada, 1987. D: Katherine Smalley and Vic Sarin. R: CBC.

The Sorrow and the Pity. France (produced for Switzerland's Lausanne Télévision Rencontre),
1970. D: Marcel Ophuls.

Spark among the Ashes. U.S.A., 1986. D: Oren Rudavsky. R: Filmmakers Library, 133 E. 58 St.,
New York, NY 10022.

The Spies Who Never Were. Canada, 1981. D: Harry Rasky. R: CBC.

Terezin Diary. U.S.A., 1989. D: Dan Weissman. R: The Terezin Foundation, 262 Central Park
West, New York, NY 10024.

The Ties That Bind. U.S.A., 1984. D: Su Friedrich.

To Mend the World. Canada. 1987. D: Harry Rasky. R: CBC.

Top Secret – The History of the German Resistance against Hitler. West Germany, 1979. D: Jochen
Bauer. S: Karl-Heinz Janszen.

A Tree Still Stands: The Jews of Eastern Europe. U.S.A., 1989. D: Oren Rudavsky.

The Trial. West Germany, 1984. D: Eberhard Fechner.

Triumph of the Will. Germany, 1935. D: Leni Riefenstahl. R: IMAGES.

Villa Air Bel: Varian Fry in Marseille. West Germany, 1987. D: Jorg Bundschuh.

Voices from the Attic. U.S.A., 1988. D: Debbie Goodstein. R: Direct Cinema.

The Warsaw Ghetto. Great Britain (BBC-TV), 1968. R: IMAGES.

We Were German Jews. 1981. U.S.A./West Germany. D: Michael Blackwood. R: Blackwood Productions, New York.

We Were So Beloved. U.S.A., 1986, D: Manfred Kirchheimer. R: First Run.

Weapons of the Spirit. U.S.A., 1987. D: Pierre Sauvage. R: 7860 Wonderland Ave., Los Angeles, CA 90046.

What Is a Jew to You?. U.S.A./Australia, 1986. D: Aviva Ziegler.

Who Shall Live and Who Shall Die?. U.S.A., 1981. D: Laurence Jarvik. R: KINO.

Witness to the Holocaust. 1984. U.S.A. R: National Jewish Resource Center, 250 W. 57 St., New York, N.Y. 10019.

The Witnesses (*Le Temps du Ghetto*). France, 1962. D: Frederic Rossif.R: FI.

You Are Free. 1983, U.S.A. (short). D: Ilene Landis. R: Direct Cinema.

Rental Sources

A-DL: Anti-Defamation League of B'nai B'rith, 823 UN Plaza, New York, NY 10017

Atara Releasing, Jewish Film Festival, 2600 10th St., Berkeley, CA 94710

BUD: Budget Films, 4590 Santa Monica Blvd., Los Angeles, CA 90029

CBC: Canadian Broadcasting Corporation, 245 Park Ave., New York, NY 10167

Cinema Guild, 1697 Broadway, New York, NY 10019

Direct Cinema, POB 69589, Los Angeles, CA 90069

FI: Films, Incorporated, 5547 N. Ravenswood Ave., Chicago, IL 60640

First-Run Features, 200 Park Avenue South, New York, NY 10003

HUR: Hurlock Cine-World, 13 Arcadia Rd., Old Greenwich, CT 06870

Icarus Films, 200 Park Ave. South, New York, NY 10003

IMAGES: Images Film Archive, 300 Phillips Park Rd., Mamaroneck, NY 10543

JWB: Jewish Welfare Board/Jewish Media Service, 15 E. 26 St., New York, NY 10010

KINO: Kino International, 333 W. 39 St., New York, NY 10018

LCA: Learning Corporation of America, 1350 Ave. of the Americas, New York, NY 10019

National Center for Jewish Film, Lown Building/102, Brandeis University, Waltham, MA 02254

NYF: New Yorker Films, 16 W. 61 St., New York, NY 10023

PAR: Paramount Non-Theatrical, 5451 Marathon St., Hollywood, CA 90038

Phoenix Films, 470 Park Ave. South, New York, NY 10016

Roxie Releasing, 3117 16th St., San Francisco, CA 94103

SWANK: 350 Vanderbilt Motor Pkwy., Hauppague, NY 11787

UA: FI

UNIV: Universal 16, 445 Park Ave., New York, NY 10022

NOTE: Many videocassettes (including *The 81st Blow, The Last Sea,* and *Flames in the Ashes*) are available for purchase from Ergo Media, POB 2037, Teaneck, NJ 07666.

Notes

Preface

1. Elie Wiesel, *A Jew Today*, trans. Marion Wiesel (New York: Random House, Vintage Books, 1978), p. 234.

Introduction

1. The omission of Czech films such as *Transport from Paradise, The Fifth Horseman Is Fear*, and *Diamonds of the Night* is due not to disrespect but to limitations of space, language, and print accessibility. See Dan Isaac, "Film and the Holocaust," in *Centerpoint* 1 (Fall 1980), special issue on "The Holocaust" for more on the Czech contribution.
2. This and the quotes that follow are from Siegfried Kracauer, *Theory of Film: The Redemption of Physical Reality* (New York: Oxford University Press, 1960), p. 305.
3. Arthur Schlesinger, Jr., "Filmed in New York," *American Heritage* 33, 1 (December 1981).
4. Jacobo Timerman, *Prisoner without a Name, Cell without a Number*, trans. Toby Talbot (New York: Knopf, 1981), p. 130.

1 The Hollywood Version of the Holocaust

1. Alex Ward, "A Producer of the Provocative: Herbert Brodkin," *New York Times* (Arts and Leisure), November 15, 1981, p. 44.
2. "An Interview with Paddy Chayefsky," *American Film* 7, 3 (December 1981): 63. Excerpted from John Brady, *The Craft of the Screenwriter* (New York: Simon & Schuster, 1981).
3. Ellen Fine, "Dialogue with Elie Wiesel," *Centerpoint* 4, 1, issue 13, "The Holocaust" (Fall 1980): 19.
4. Ward, p. 39.
5. Jean-Paul Bier, "The Holocaust and West Germany: Strategies of Oblivion 1947–1979," *New German Critique* 19, Special Issue, "Germans and Jews" (Winter 1980): 29.
6. Andrei S. Markovits and Rebecca S. Hayden, "*Holocaust* before and after the Event: Reactions in West Germany and Austria," *New German Critique*, p. 58.
7. Ibid., p. 60.
8. Sylvie Pierre, "Le Four Banal," *Cahiers du Cinéma* 301 (June 1979). According to "NBC Reports," a poll conducted in West Germany after the telecast showed that 30 percent found Nazism to be "a basically good idea" that was carried out wrongly.
9. Author's interview with Peter Lilienthal, New York, July–August 1981. This view is corroborated by Dieter Prokop's research, "*Holocaust* and the Effects of Violence on Television," *International Journal of Political Education* 4, 1/2 (May 1981): 59.

10. John J. O'Connor, "Diverse Views of Nazi Germany," *New York Times* (Arts and Leisure), September 9, 1979, p. 41.

11. One does not have to look far for the source of Lawson's indignant speeches: when I heard Abby Mann, the screenwriter of *Judgment at Nuremberg*, speak at a meeting of the Holocaust Survivors Memorial Foundation in 1980, his half-shouted, half-cried address was vividly reminiscent of Lawson's pitch.

12. This is also in line with Hans-Jürgen Syberberg's view of the Führer, as presented in *Our Hitler*. In the director's words, "Hitler was the greatest filmmaker of all times. He made the Second World War, like Nuremberg for Leni Riefenstahl, in order to view the rushes privately every evening for himself.... It is very interesting that the only objects that remain of the Third Reich are fragments of celluloid," Quoted by Steve Wasserman, "Filmmaker as Pariah," *Village Voice*, January 14, 1980, p. 29.

13. Pauline Kael, *When the Lights Go Down* (New York: Holt, Rinehart & Winston, 1980), p. 454.

14. See Dan Yakir, "Bad Guys Never Looked So Good," *New York Post*, August 6, 1981, p. 31, on the "honorable" Nazis of *Victory, Lili Marleen, Raiders of the Lost Ark*, and *Eye of the Needle*.

15. Peter Demetz's point, made in hosting a series of German films on public television, is applicable to these Hollywood products: "Melodrama does not advance our understanding of history.... The question is how the fictions of the cinema illuminate the realities of war, slavery and resistance." Quoted in O'Connor, "Diverse Views of Nazi Germany," p. 41.

16. Author's interview with Menachem Golan, New York, October 29, 1988.

17. Terrence Des Pres, *The Survivor: An Anatomy of Life in the Death Camps* (New York: Pocket Books, 1977), p. 160.

18. Jack Kroll, "The Activist Actress," *Newsweek*, September 29, 1980. See also Howard Rosenberg, " 'Playing for Time' Unveiled by CBS," *Los Angeles Times*, September 8, 1980, for an informative interview with executive producer Linda Yellen.

19. James Atlas, "The Creative Journey of Arthur Miller," *New York Times* (Arts and Leisure), September 28, 1980.

20. In *The War against the Jews*, historian Lucy Dawidowicz explains that the functions "assigned to the Jewish councils, though few, were onerous beyond the capacity of any nongovernmental agency: they were charged with the responsibility for carrying out the evacuation of the Jews from the countryside, for providing food supplies en route and housing in the cities of concentration..." (New York: Holt, Rinehart & Winston, 1975, p. 117).

21. John Toland, "Can TV Dramas Convey the Horrors of the Holocaust?" *TV Guide*, February 13, 1982, p. 10.

22. Aljean Harmetz, "Waging Wouk's 'War and Remembrance,' " *New York Times* (Arts and Leisure), November 6, 1988, p. 31.

2   Meaningful Montage

1. Jonathan Rosenbaum, "Les Choix de Pakula," *Cahiers du Cinéma* 23 (April 1982): ix (my translation).

2. Janet Maslin, "Bringing 'Sophie's Choice' to the Screen," *New York Times* (Arts and Leisure), May 9, 1982, pp. 1, 15.

3. Elie Wiesel, "Does the Holocaust Lie beyond the Reach of Art?" *New York Times* (Arts and Leisure), April 17, 1983, pp. 1, 12.

4. Aljean Harmetz, "Miss Streep and Kline Cast in Movie 'Sophie,' " *New York Times*, July 22, 1981, p. C21.

5. François Truffaut, *The Films in My Life*, trans. Leonard Mayhew (New York: Simon & Schuster, 1978), p. 303.

6. This and the following quotation from *Nuit et brouillard* are taken from the complete text to be found in *L'Avant-Scéne* 1 (February 15, 1961): 51–54.

3 Styles of Tension

1. The scene brings to mind George Steiner's *In Bluebeard's Castle*, where he discusses Elias Canetti's "intriguing suggestion that the ease of the holocaust relates to the collapse of currency in the 1920s. Large numbers lost all but a vaguely sinister, unreal meaning. Having seen a hundred thousand, then a million, then a billion Mark needed to buy bread or pay for bus tickets, ordinary men lost all perception of concrete enormity. The same large numbers tainted with unreality the disappearance and liquidation of peoples." George Steiner, "A Season in Hell," in *In Bluebeard's Castle: Some Notes Towards the Redefinition of Culture* (New Haven: Yale University Press, 1971), p. 51.
2. George Steiner, *Language and Silence* (New York: Atheneum, 1966), p. 123. Corroboration for the existence of these mobile gas chambers can be found in the Belgian documentary, *As If It Were Yesterday*, where a priest recalls "the Nazi vans."
3. From a conversation with Stefania Beylin, September 18, 1961, published in *Film* 41/61 and reprinted in the press book for the 1964 Cannes Film Festival.
4. J. Hoberman, "Out of the Past," *Village Voice* (October 25, 1988).

4 Black Humor

1. André Bazin and Eric Rohmer, *Charlie Chaplin* (Paris: Les Editions du Cerf, 1972), pp. 28–32.
2. Herman G. Weinberg, *The Lubitsch Touch* (New York: Dover Publications, 1977), p. 247.
3. Ibid., p. 175.
4. James Shelley Hamilton in *The National Board of Review* magazine, March 1942.
5. Weinberg, p. 247.
6. Kael, *When the Lights Go Down*, p. 139.
7. Terrence Des Pres, "Black Comedies," *Harper's* (June 1976), pp. 26–27. Bettelheim vilified Des Pres's book as well as *Seven Beauties* (both of which did not conform to his own experience of the Holocaust and were therefore suspect); in *Surviving and Other Essays* (New York: Knopf, 1979), he inveighs against *The Survivor* by using images from the film. Bettelheim's claim that Pasqualino is "made to stand for the archetypal survivor, the image of us all" (p. 275) stimulated Des Pres into responding with an impeccably documented critique in *Social Research*, "The Bettelheim Problem" (Winter 1979). Here he perceives how Bettelheim "plainly puts no stock in the idea of art as *criticism of life*, but rather clings to the Romantic notion that the protagonist, simply by virtue of occupying center stage, carries the endorsement of the artist and audience..." (p. 636). Des Pres points instead to "Wertmüller's use of parody and displacement" as keys to understanding *Seven Beauties*.
8. Quoted in Martin Esslin, *The Theatre of the Absurd* (New York: Anchor Books, 1961), p. 133.

5 The Jew as Child

1. Judith Doneson, "The Jew as a Female Figure in Holocaust Film," *Shoah* 1, no. 1, p. 11.
2. Robert Paxton and Michael Marrus, *Vichy France and the Jews* (New York: Basic Books, 1981). See "Quand Vichy déportait les juifs," *Le Nouvel Observateur*, June 1, 1981, pp. 112–128.
3. See, for example, the pernicious reportage by Robert de Beauplan in *L'Illustration*, September 30, 1941, pp. 59–60. It was also pointed out to me by the French critic Claude Gauteur that the most popular film in 1943 France was the viciously anti-Semitic *Jew Süss*.
4. Doneson, pp. 12–13.

5. Annette Insdorf, "Childhood Memories Shape Diane Kurys's 'Entre Nous,'" *New York Times* (Arts and Leisure), January 24, 1984, pp. 13, 20.
6. This and other Truffaut quotations are from François Truffaut, *The Films in My Life* (New York: Simon & Schuster, 1978), pp. 331–333.
7. Author's interview with Louis Malle, New York, November 1, 1987. Subsequent quotations are from this interview.
8. Danièle Heymann, "La Blessure d'une amitié perdue," *Le Monde*, 5 October 1987, p. 1 (translations are my own).
9. Olivier Péretié, "Un petit 'détail,'" *Le Nouvel Observateur*, 2–8 October 1987, p. 106 (translations are my own).
10. Heymann, p. 9.
11. *A Bag of Marbles* (*Un sac de billes*, 1975), on the other hand, is the story of two Jewish children who must move from Paris to southern France. Directed by Jacques Doillon, it is really the story of Joseph (Richard Constantini), tracing his development from incapacitating fear to first love and courageous action. His brother Maurice is more visibly heroic, insisting on helping other Jews cross the border once he is safely over himself. As in Doillon's subsequent film with children, *La Drôlesse* (1979), the use of nonprofessional actors is effective. For instance, the father – who dies in Auschwitz – is played by Joseph Goldenberg, owner of a famous restaurant in Paris's Jewish district. Unfortunately, this film never received American distribution.
12. Annette Insdorf, "A Passion for Social Justice," *Cineaste* 11, 4 (Winter 1982): 37.
13. Carlos Clarens, "The Dark Ages," *Soho Weekly News*, January 19, 1982, p. 39.
14. Annette Insdorf, "*David:* A German-Jewish Film about the Holocaust," *Martyrdom and Resistance* 8, 2 (March–April 1982): 4.
15. Insdorf, "A Passion for Social Justice," p. 37.
16. Robert Liebman, "Two Survivors: Lilienthal and His Film *David*," *Long Island Jewish World*, October 30–November 5, 1981, p. 21.
17. Ibid., p. 20.
18. Seth Mydans, "Hungary's Wartime Anguish Is Relived through 'The Revolt of Job,'" *New York Times* (Arts and Leisure), May 27, 1984, pp. 15, 20.

6   In Hiding/Onstage

1. Annette Insdorf, "How Truffaut's 'Last Metro' Reflects Occupied Paris," *New York Times* (Arts and Leisure), February 8, 1981, p. 21.
2. See Stuart Byron, "Truffaut and Gays," *Village Voice*, October 29–November 4, 1980, p. 64, which applauds the director's "unworried acceptance of homosexuals" as "evidence of the supreme humanism of François Truffaut."
3. Insdorf, "How Truffaut's 'Last Metro' Reflects Occupied Paris," p. 21.
4. Throughout the film, Lucas is rarely in the light. "There is no sunshine in the film," Truffaut added. "Visually, Nestor Almendros [the cinematographer] and I made a great effort not to have day scenes until fifty minutes into the film. You feel more in the period when it's nocturnal." Interview with the author, New York, October 1980.
5. Peter Pappas, "The Last Metro," *Cineaste* 10, 4 (Fall 1980): 11.
6. Annette Insdorf, "A Swiss Film Bares Another Chapter of the Holocaust," *New York Times* (Arts and Leisure), October 18, 1981, p. 1.
7. Ibid., p. 15.
8. Excerpted in program notes, Museum of Modern Art, New York, April 25, 1981.
9. Insdorf, "A Swiss Film," p. 1.
10. Caryn James, "From Argentina, How 6 Polish Jews Hid from the Nazis," *New York Times*, October 5, 1988, p. C19.

7   Beautiful Evasions?

1. Giorgio Bassani, *The Garden of the Finzi-Continis*, trans. William Weaver (New York: Harcourt Brace Jovanovich, 1977), p. 16.
2. When I interviewed Dominique Sanda in 1981 and asked how she felt about playing the Jewess, the actress confessed: "I was eighteen and rather carefree. The gravity of the film and subject probably didn't touch me as deeply as it should have. I threw myself into it without asking too many questions or analyzing too much. I was proud to be that character and De Sica was exquisite."
3. Bassani, p. 22.
4. Pauline Kael, *Reeling* (Boston: Little, Brown, 1976), p. 421.
5. Author's interview with Bernard Henri-Lévy, Paris, June 3, 1981.
6. John Hughes, "*The Tin Drum:* Volker Schlöndorff's 'Dream of Childhood,' " *Film Quarterly* (Spring 1981), p. 6.

8   The Condemned and Doomed

1. *New York Times*, October 27, 1963.
2. Annette Insdorf, "Making Comedies of Character," *New York Times* (Arts and Leisure), July 14, 1981, p. 13.
3. Sigmund Freud, *Group Psychology and the Analysis of the Ego*, trans. James Strachey (New York: Bantam Books, 1971), pp. 17, 76.

9   Political Resistance

1. It is certain that the predominance of Polish films about World War II is a reflection of the devastation undergone by this country. As François Chevassu wrote in his analysis of Polish cinema: "Six million dead, the Warsaw Ghetto (200 survivors out of 500,000 persons), the Warsaw Rising (300,000 dead), and the total destruction of the capital with its one million inhabitants. It is therefore understandable that the war is the major theme of Polish cinema, and one needs no ideological references to explain it. Finally, one has to add that two forces direct this country: the Communist Party and the Catholic Church." "Naissance du cinéma polonais," *L'Avant-Scène* 47 (Spécial Polonais, April 1, 1965), p. 6.
2. Terrence Des Pres, *The Survivor: An Anatomy of Life in the Death Camps* (New York: Pocket Books, 1977), p. 181.
3. Lucy Dawidowicz, "Visualizing the Warsaw Ghetto: Nazi Images of the Jews Refiltered by the BBC," *Shoah* 1, no. 1, p. 5.
4. Ibid., p. 6.
5. Exceptions can be found in *L'Chaim – To Life!* (Harold Mayer, 1973), a documentary that contains archival material about Jewish schools in the Ghetto.
6. Dawidowicz, p. 6.
7. A doctor imprisoned in Buchenwald reported that "one hundred percent of the female prisoners ceased to menstruate at the very beginning of their term of captivity; the function did not reappear until months after their liberation" (Eugene Weinstock, *Beyond the Last Path*, trans. Clara Ryan [New York: Boni & Gaer, 1947], p. 235); and female survivors of Auschwitz claim that the Nazis put something in the soup to stop their periods.
8. Significant research has been undertaken in this regard by Joan Ringelheim at the Institute for Research in History: "Women and the Holocaust" includes a projected television documentary.
9. Eugen Kogon provides corroboration in *The Theory and Practice of Hell*: "In every concentration camp where the political prisoners attained any degree of ascendancy, they turned the prisoner hospital, scene of fearful SS horrors that it was, into a rescue station for countless prisoners. Not only were patients actually cured wherever possible; healthy prisoners, in danger of being killed or shipped to a death camp, were smuggled on the sick

list to put them beyond the clutches of the SS" (trans. Heinz Norden [New York: Farrar, Straus, 1953], p. 141).

10. *The Wajda Trilogy* (London: Lorrimer, 1973), p. 9.

11. Ibid., p. 24.

12. Annette Insdorf, "A Saga of Jews Who Fought Back against Nazi Oppression," *New York Times* (Arts and Leisure), September 14, 1986, pp. 17, 32. Further quotations are from this article.

13. Ibid.

10   The Ambiguity of Identity

1. This and the following quotation are from George Steiner, *In Bluebeard's Castle: Some Notes towards the Redefinition of Culture* (New Haven: Yale University Press, 1971), pp. 45–46.

2. Following Gründgens's death (a possible suicide) in 1963, another attempt was made to publish *Mephisto*. This time, distribution was obstructed by Peter Gorski, Gründgens's adopted son, on the grounds that the book dishonored the memory of his father. The German courts complied with Gorski's request, and although published, *Mephisto* was banned again in 1971. The courts stated that the German reading public was not interested in a "false picture" of theatrical life after 1933 "from the perspective of an expatriate." Today the book is available in Germany; and, thanks to the film, has even become a best-seller.

3. Author's interview with István Szabó, New York, March 1982.

4. Annette Insdorf, "Oscar Treatment of Art in the Nazi State," *Newsday* (Sunday, April 4, 1982), pp. 7–8.

5. Ibid., p. 8.

6. Robert Chazal, "Un classique de demain," *L'Avant-Scène* 175 (November 1, 1976), p. 5.

7. Pauline Kael, *When the Lights Go Down* (New York: Holt, Rinehart & Winston, 1980), p. 396.

8. Dr. Claude Lévy, one of the key people interviewed in *The Sorrow and the Pity*, served as adviser on "historical documentation" for *Mr. Klein*. Nevertheless, we learn from a note that accompanied the published script of the film that Losey had no pretensions to historical accuracy: "The entire film is indeed centered on the ambiguity of Klein's personality. This is one of the reasons why the narrative unfolds in winter (while the roundup of Vel' d'Hiv took place in July), that Klein gets from Paris to Strasbourg easily.... The historical consultant was really supposed to indicate more precisely the spirit, the mentality, and not to remove the eventual anachronisms . . . which mattered little to the director." (Jacques-G. Perret, *L'Avant-Scène* 175, p. 8.)

9. Losey's notes about the characters specify that Janine too undergoes a transformation: "A simple object of pleasure at the outset, she becomes completely different by the end. . . . Her compassion for the victims of the roundup brings out our own compassion. She achieves a degree of maturity that permits her to observe Klein with a critical eye, while still loving him." (*L'Avant-Scène* 175, p. 7.)

11   The New German Guilt

1. Annette Insdorf, "Von Trotta: By Sisters Obsessed," *New York Times* (Arts and Leisure), January 31, 1982, p. 22.

2. Author's interview with Jeanine Meerapfel, April 1982.

3. Annette Eberly Dumbach and Jud Newborn, "Again, Wartime Events Stir Germany," *New York Times* (Arts and Leisure), May 1, 1983.

4. Annette Insdorf, "In Germany, A Blitz of Conscience," *Los Angeles Times* (Calendar, Sunday), July 24, 1983.

5. John Hughes, *Film Quarterly* (Spring 1981), p. 2. (See Chapter 7, note 6.)

6. Ibid., p. 5.

7. Ibid.
8. Lawrence Van Gelder, "A German Filmmaker Looks at Adolf Hitler," *New York Times* (Arts and Leisure), January 13, 1980, p. 1.
9. Susan Sontag, "Eye of the Storm," *New York Review of Books* 27, 2 (February 21, 1980).
10. J. Hoberman, "The Führer Furor," *Village Voice*, January 14, 1980, p. 28.
11. Jack Kroll, "The Hitler within Us," *Newsweek*, January 28, 1980.
12. Steve Wasserman, "Filmmaker as Pariah," *Village Voice*, January 14, 1980, p. 29.
13. David Denby, "'Whoever Controls Film Controls History,'" *New York*, January 28, 1980.
14. Wasserman, p. 31.
15. Sontag, "Eye of the Storm."
16. Gerald Peary, "A Film of Rage," *Los Angeles Times* (Calendar, Sunday), March 18, 1984.
17. Annette Insdorf, "'Welcome in Vienna' – Ironies of Prejudice," *Los Angeles Times* (Calendar), February 23, 1988, pp. 1, 8. Following quotations are from this article.
18. Annette Insdorf, "Axel Corti's Films Explore World War II's Impact," *New York Times* (Arts and Leisure), August 16, 1988, pp. 18, 22. Subsequent quotations are from this article.

12 The Personal Documentary

1. André Bazin, *What Is Cinema?* vol. 1, trans. Hugh Gray (Berkeley: University of California Press, 1967), p. 13.
2. James Agee, *Let Us Now Praise Famous Men* (New York: Ballantine Books, 1972), p. xiv.
3. The importance of the optical printer was suggested by one of my Yale students, Jeremy Epstein.
4. This and other quotations are from the author's interview with Alain Resnais, Paris, May 1980.
5. Author's interview with Laurence Jarvik, New York, December 1981.
6. It should be mentioned that the case of American Jewish response to the Holocaust is not as clear-cut as the film suggests. Historian Lucy Dawidowicz undercuts Jarvik's findings with a minutely chronicled account of attempts in the U.S.A. to save European Jews ("American Jews and the Holocaust," *New York Times Magazine*, Sunday, April 18, 1982). Her conclusions are that "the European Jews were not rescued, not because American Jews were passive but because American Jews lacked the resources to rescue them" (p. 48), that Bergson had come to the U.S.A. "to raise money for the Irguan Zvai Leumi, a terrorist military organization in Palestine" (p. 48), and that there had been "deliberate obstruction and suppression of the continuing flow of information about the murder of the European Jews.... A handful of men in the State Department had managed to sabotage even the limited possibilities of rescue available" (p. 112). She locates the blame firmly within the State Department, especially with Assistant Secretary of State Breckinridge Long.
7. Elie Wiesel, *A Jew Today*, trans. Marion Wiese (New York: Random House, Vintage Books, 1978), pp. 225–226.
8. Ibid., p. 227.
9. This and other Jarvik quotations are from Annette Insdorf, "'Who Will Live?' Explodes Myths of Holocaust," *Los Angeles Times* (Calendar), January 14, 1982, p. 7.
10. The questions raised by Jarvik's film have been treated in a number of books, including Arthur Morse's *While Six Million Died*, Walter Laqueur's *The Terrible Secret*, and Yehuda Bauer's *American Jewry and the Holocaust*. In September 1981, a commission of leading American Jews was formed to inquire formally into the role of the U.S. government and the American Jewish community during the Holocaust (see *New York Times* [Sunday, September 27, 1981], pp. 1, 40).
11. This and following quotations are from Annette Insdorf, "Heroism amid the Holocaust," *Newsday*, May 18, 1982, p. 21.

373

)vice directors are even more gratified that audiences are sensing connections
.e film and contemporary problems. "Among people who have seen *As If It Were*
at festivals," Abramowicz recalled, "there was one woman from Buenos Aires,
.ple. She said, 'This is what is happening with us now in Argentina. We have to
r friends, to organize, to falsify documents.' We hope the film shows reactions
_ .man level, using the Holocaust as a backdrop. Jews died because they were Jews,
because of what they represented in society. But ultimately, people are beckoned every
day, everywhere, for whatever reason, to combat persecution."

13. Pierre Sauvage, "*Weapons of the Spirit:* A Journey Home," *The Hollywood Reporter*, March 17, 1987, Section S, p. 20.
14. Ibid., p. 21.
15. Author's interview with Katherine Smalley, Jewish Museum, New York, November 13, 1988.

13 From Judgment to Illumination

1. This and other quotations are from author's interview with Peter Morley, London, November 1980.
2. Curiously, it is never mentioned in the film that Kitty is Jewish. When I asked the director why, he replied: "Kitty doesn't particularly identify herself as being Jewish. I didn't want to nail it to the bannerhead at the very beginning. I felt this film should be a new way of perceiving Auschwitz, and there were more non-Jews than Jews killed. I didn't want this to be another thing about Jews and the Holocaust, but about people who were incarcerated and incinerated there."
3. John Toland, "Can TV Dramas Convey the Horrors of the Holocaust?" *TV Guide*, February 13, 1982.
4. This and other Ophuls quotations, as well as quotations from Mme. Solange, Anthony Eden, and Pierre Mendès-France, are from *L'Avant-Scène du Cinéma* 127/128 (July–September, 1972): 10, 14, 65.
5. Jacques Siclier, *La France de Pétain et son cinéma* (Paris: Henri Veyrier, 1981), p. 251.
6. Ibid.
7. Author's interview with Marcel Ophuls, Paris, June 1981.
8. Terrence Des Pres, "War Crimes," *Harper's*, January 1977, p. 88.
9. Ophuls was nevertheless adamant when I suggested that the film is more illuminating than judgmental: "There has to be judgment. There's nothing more shitty than the term 'non-judgmental.' What would be the use of trying to communicate the difficulty of reaching judgment, if the working hypothesis is that there is no necessity for it?"
10. This and later quotations are from Des Pres, "War Crimes," p. 89.
11. Author's interview with Marcel Ophuls, New York, October 2, 1988. All subsequent quotations are taken from either this meeting, a phone interview in Paris on June 11, 1988, or the New York Film Festival press conference held on October 3, 1988.
12. James M. Markham, "Marcel Ophuls on Barbie: Reopening Wounds of War," *New York Times* (Arts and Leisure), October 2, 1988, pp. 21, 27.
13. Annette Insdorf, "*Shoah:* Testimony More Amazing Than Fiction," *Los Angeles Times*, December 31, 1985, pp. 7, 9. Subsequent quotations are from this interview.
14. Ophuls's rousing assessment of Lanzmann's "deceit" is worth quoting: "I can hardly find the words to express how much I approve of this procedure, how much I sympathize with it. This is not a matter of means and ends, this is a matter of moral priorities." From Marcel Ophuls, "Closely Watched Trains," *American Film*, November 1985, p. 22.
15. Ibid., p. 20.
16. Ibid., p. 18.
17. Simone de Beauvoir, "The Memory of Horror," *L'Express*, April 28–29, 1985.

18. Joan Dupont, "Roman Polanski and 'Frantic,'" *New York Times* (Arts and Leisure), March 27, 1988, p. 36. (*Le Temps du Ghetto* is distributed in the U.S.A. under the title *The Witnesses.*)

14 The Holocaust as Genre
1. Leslie Epstein, "Atrocity and Imagination," *Harper's Magazine*, August 1985, p. 16.
2. Ibid., p. 14.
3. Siegfried Kracauer, *Theory of Film: The Redimption of Physical Reality* (New York: Oxford University Press, 1966, p. 305.

16 Rescuers in Fiction Films
1. "I wanted grey tones, but never on the keylight side. We used silhouettes, and sometimes we let half a face go black." In "Janusz Kaminski talks about . . . *Schindler's List*," *In Camera*, Summer 1994, p. 22.
2. *Schindler's List*, screenplay by Steven Zaillian, July 1989, p. 61.
3. Annette Insdorf, "Save the Child: 'Korczak,'" *Boston Phoenix*, November 15, 1991. Subsequent quotations are from this article.

17 The Ironic Touch
1. My unpublished interview with Michael Verhoeven, New York, October 8, 1990.
2. David Wilson, *Monthly Film Bulletin*, January 1991, p. 24.
3. David Denby, *New York Magazine*, November 5, 1990, p. 97.
4. Richard Corliss, *Time Magazine*, October 29, 1990, p. 15.
5. Rick Atkinson, "Bavaria's 'Nasty Girl,' Clawing at the Nazi Past," *Washington Post*, 1993.
6. Annette Insdorf, "The Moral Minefield That Won't Go Away," *New York Times* (Arts and Leisure), August 31, 1997.

Bibliography (Second Edition)

Books

Abzug, Robert. *Inside the Vicious Heart: Americans and the Liberation of Nazi Concentration Camps.* New York: Oxford University Press, 1985.

Agee, James. *Let Us Now Praise Famous Men.* New York: Ballantine Books, 1972.

Ainsztein, Reuben. *Jewish Resistance in Nazi-Occupied Eastern Europe.* New York: Barnes & Noble, 1975.

The Warsaw Ghetto Revolt. New York: The Holocaust Library, 1978.

Alexander, Edward. *The Resonance of Dust: Essays on Holocaust Literature and Jewish Fate.* Columbus: Ohio State University Press, 1979.

Arendt, Hannah. *The Origins of Totalitarianism.* New York: Harcourt, Brace, 1951.

The Auschwitz Album, text by Peter Hellman. New York: Random House, 1981.

Avisar, Ilan. *Screening the Holocaust.* Bloomington: Indiana University Press, 1989.

Barnouw, Erik. *Documentary: A History of the Non-Fiction Film.* New York: Oxford University Press, 1974.

Bassani, Giorgio. *The Garden of the Finzi-Continis.* Trans. William Weaver. New York: Harcourt Brace Jovanovich, 1977.

Bauer, Yehuda. *American Jewry and the Holocaust.* Detroit: Wayne State University Press, 1981.

Bazin, André. *What Is Cinema?* Vol. 1. Trans. Hugh Gray. Berkeley: University of California Press, 1967.

Bazin, André, and Eric Rohmer. *Charlie Chaplin.* Paris: Les. Editions du Cerf, 1972.

Bettelheim, Bruno. *The Informed Heart.* London: Thames & Hudson, 1961.

Surviving and Other Essays. New York: Knopf, 1979.

Borowski, Tadeusz. *This Way to the Gas, Ladies and Gentlemen.* New York: Viking, 1976.

Brady, John. *The Craft of the Screenwriter.* New York: Simon & Schuster, 1981.

Dawidowicz, Lucy. *The Jewish Presence: Essays on Identity and History.* New York: Holt, Rinehart & Winston, 1977.

The War against the Jews, 1933–1945. New York: Holt, Rinehart & Winston, 1975.

Demetz, Hana. *The House on Prague Street.* New York: St. Martin's Press, 1980.

Des Pres, Terrence. *The Survivor: An Anatomy of Life in the Death Camps.* New York. Pocket Books, 1977.

Donat, Alexander. *The Holocaust Kingdom.* New York: Schocken Books, 1978.

ed., *The Death Camp Treblinka.* New York: Schocken Books, 1979.

Doneson, Judith. *The Holocaust in American Film.* Philadelphia: The Jewish Publication Society, 1987.

Eisner, Jack. *The Survivor.* New York: William Morrow, 1980.

Epstein, Helen. *Children of the Holocaust.* New York: Putnam, 1979.

Epstein, Leslie. *King of the Jews.* New York: Avon Books, 1980.

Erens, Patricia. *The Jew in American Cinema.* Bloomington: Indiana University Press, 1984.

Esslin, Martin. *The Theatre of the Absurd.* New York: Anchor Books, 1961.

Ezrahi, Sidra DeKoven. *By Words Alone: The Holocaust in Literature.* Chicago: University of Chicago Press, 1980.

Feingold, Henry. *The Politics of Rescue.* New York: The Holocaust Library, 1980.

Fenelon, Fania, with Marcelle Routier. *The Musicians of Auschwitz.* Trans. Judith Landry. London: Joseph, 1977.

Fine, Ellen. *Legacies of Night: The Literary Universe of Elie Wiesel.* New York: State University of New York Press, 1982.

Frank, Anne. *The Diary of a Young Girl.* New York: Pocket Books, 1952.

Freud, Sigmund. *Group Psychology and the Analysis of the Ego.* Trans. James Strachey. New York: Bantam Books, 1971.

Friedlander, Albert, ed. *Out of the Whirlwind: A Reader of Holocaust Literature.* New York: Doubleday, 1968.

Friedländer, Saul. *Reflections of Nazism: An Essay on Kitsch and Death.* Trans. Thomas Weyr. New York: Harper & Row, 1984.

When Memory Comes. Trans. Helen R. Lane. New York: Farrar, Straus, Giroux, 1979.

Friedman, Lester. *Hollywood's Image of the Jew.* New York: Frederick Ungar, 1982.

Friedman, Philip. *Their Brothers' Keepers.* New York: The Holocaust Library, 1978.

Garlinski, Jozef. *Fighting Auschwitz.* New York: Fawcett Crest, 1975.

Gordon, Thomas, and Max Morgan Witts. *Voyage of the Damned.* New York. Stein & Day, 1974.

Green, Gerald. *Holocaust.* New York: Bantam Books, 1978.

Gross, Leonard. *The Last Jews in Berlin.* New York: Simon & Schuster, 1982.

Grossman, Mendel. *With a Camera in the Ghetto.* Israel: Ghetto Fighters' House, 1972.

Hallie, Philip P. *Lest Innocent Blood Be Shed.* New York: Harper & Row, 1979.

Hart, Kitty. *I Am Alive.* London and New York: Abelard-Schuman, 1962.

Hellman, Peter. *Avenue of the Righteous.* New York: Atheneum, 1980.

Henri-Lévy, Bernard. *Le Testament de Dieu.* Paris: Grasset, 1979.

Hersey, John. *The Wall.* New York: Knopf, 1950.

Hilberg, Raul. *The Destruction of the European Jews.* New York: Holmes & Meier, 1985.

The Holocaust. Compiled from material originally published in the *Encyclopedia Judaica.* Jerusalem: Keter Books, 1974.

Hull, David Stewart. *Film in the Third Reich.* New York: Simon & Schuster, 1973.

Kael, Pauline. *Reeling.* Boston: Little, Brown, 1976.

When the Lights Go Down. New York: Holt, Rinchart & Winston, 1980.

Kaplan, Chaim A. *The Warsaw Diary of Chaim Kaplan.* Trans. Abraham Katoh. New York: Collier, 1973.

Kogon, Eugen. *The Theory and Practice of Hell.* Trans. Heinz Norden. New York: Farrar, Straus, 1953.

Korczak, Janusz. *Ghetto Diary.* New York: Schocken Books, 1978.

Kracauer, Siegfried. *From Caligari to Hitler: A Psychological History of the German Film.* Princeton, N. J.: Princeton University Press, 1974.

Theory of Film: The Redemption of Physical Reality. New York: Oxford University Press, 1960.

Kraus, Ota, and Erich Kulka. *The Death Factory: Document on Auschwitz.* Trans. Stephen Jolly. Oxford: Pergamon, 1966.

Kurzman, Dan. *The Bravest Battle: The Twenty-Eight Days of the Warsaw Ghetto Uprising.* New York: Putnam's, 1976.

Langer, Lawrence. *The Holocaust and the Literary Imagination.* New Haven, Conn.: Yale University Press, 1975.

　Versions of Survival: The Holocaust and the Human Spirit. New York: State University of New York Press, 1982.

Lanzmann, Claude. *The Bird Has No Wings.* New York: St. Martin's Press, 1976.

　Shoah. New York: Pantheon, 1985.

Laqueur, Walter. *The Terrible Secret: The Suppression of Information about Hitler's Final Solution.* Boston: Little, Brown, 1981.

Leitner, Isabella. *Fragments of Isabella.* New York: Crowell, 1978.

Levi, Primo. *Survival in Auschwitz.* Trans. Stuart Woolf. New York: Collier, 1969.

Levy, Claude. *La Grande Rafle du Vel' d' Hiv.* Paris: Laffont, 1967.

Lusting, Arnost. *Night and Hope.* Trans. George Theiner. Iowa City: University of Iowa Press, 1972.

　A Prayer for Katerina Horovitzova. Trans. Jeanne Nemcova: New York: Harper & Row, 1973.

　Darkness Casts No Shadow. Trans. Jeanne Nemcova. Washington, D.C.: Inscape, 1976. (Basis for *Diamonds of the Night.*)

Marrus, Michael, and Robert Paxton. *Vichy France and the Jews.* New York: Basic Books, 1981.

Michalek, Boleslaw. *The Cinema of Andrzej Wajda.* Trans. Edward Rothert. London: The Tantivy Press, 1973.

Milosz, Czeslaw. *Native Realm.* Trans. Catherine S. Leach. New York: Doubleday, 1981.

Monaco, James. *How to Read a Film.* New York: Oxford University Press, 1981.

Morse, Arthur. *While Six Million Died: A Chronicle of American Apathy.* New York: Random House, 1968.

Niezabitowska, Malgorzata. *Remnants: The Last Jews of Poland.* New York: Friendly Press, 1986.

Novich, Miriam. *Sobibor: Martyrdom and Revolt.* New York: The Holocaust Library, 1980.

Ophuls, Marcel. *The Sorrow and the Pity.* Trans. Mireille Johnston. New York: Outerbridge & Lazard, 1972. (Distributed by E. P. Dutton and Co.)

Pisar, Samuel. *Of Blood and Hope.* Boston: Little, Brown, 1980.

Poliakov, Léon. *Harvest of Hate.* New York: The Holocaust Library, 1978.

Rabinach, Anson, and Jack Zipes, eds. *Germans and Jews since the Holocaust: The Changing Situation in West Germany.* New York: Holmes & Meier, 1986.

Rabinowitz, Dorothy. *New Lives: Survivors of the Holocaust Living in America.* New York: Knopf, 1976.

Ringelblum, Emmanuel. *Notes from the Warsaw Ghetto.* Trans. Jacob Sloan. New York: McGraw-Hill, 1958.

Rosenblum, Ralph, and Robert Karen. *When the Shooting Stops... the Cutting Begins.* New York: Da Capo Press, 1979.

Rosenfeld, Alvin H. *A Double Dying: Reflection on Holocaust Literature.* Bloomington: University of Indiana Press, 1980.

　Imagining Hitler. Bloomington: Indiana University Press, 1985.

Rosenfeld, Alvin H., and Irving Greenberg. *Confronting the Holocaust: The Impact of Elie Wiesel.* Bloomington: University of Indiana Press, 1978.

Semprun, Jorge. *The Long Voyage.* Trans. Richard Seaver. New York: Grove, 1964.

Shirer, William. *The Rise and Fall of the Third Reich.* New York: Simon & Schuster, 1960.

Siclier, Jacques. *La France de Pétain et son cinéma.* Paris: Henri Veyrier, 1981.

Skloot, Robert. *The Darkness We Carry: The Drama of the Holocaust.* Madison: University of Wisconsin Press, 1988.

Sontag, Susan. *Under the Sign of Saturn.* New York: Vintage Books, 1981.

Steiner, George. *In Bluebeard's Castle: Some Notes towards the Redefinition of Culture.* New Haven, Conn.: Yale University Press, 1971.

Steiner, George. *Language and Silence.* New York: Atheneum, 1966.

Styron, William. *Sophie's Choice.* New York: Random House, 1979.

Suhl, Yuri. *They Fought Back: The Story of the Jewish Resistance in Nazi Europe.* New York: Schocken Books, 1975.

Sypher, Wylie, ed. *Comedy.* New York: Doubleday, 1956.

Timerman, Jacobo. *Prisoner without a Name, Cell without a Number.* Trans. Toby Talbot. New York: Knopf, 1981.

Truffaut, François. *The Films in My Life.* Trans. Leonard Mayhew. New York: Simon & Schuster, 1978.

Vogel, Amos. *Film as a Subversive Art.* New York: Random House, 1974.

The Wajda Trilogy. London: Lorrimer Publishing, 1973.

Wallant, Edward Lewis. *The Pawnbroker.* New York: Harcourt Brace & World, 1961.

Weinberg, Herman G. *The Lubitsch Touch.* New York: Dover Publications, 1977.

Weinstock, Eugene. *Beyond the Last Path.* Trans. Clara Ryan. New York: Boni & Gaer, 1947.

Wiesel, Elie. *Night.* Trans. Stella Rodway. New York: Avon Books, 1969.

  A Jew Today. Trans. Marion Wiesel. New York: Random House, Vintage Books, 1978.

Young, James. *Writing and Rewriting the Holocaust.* Bloomington: Indiana University Press, 1988.

Zuccotti, Susan. *The Italians and the Holocaust.* New York: Basic Books, 1987.

Articles

Alter, Robert. "Deformations of the Holocaust." *Commentary*, February 1981.

Atlas, James. "The Creative Journey of Arthur Miller." *New York Times* (Arts and Leisure), September 28, 1980.

Byron, Stuart. "Truffaut and Gays." *The Village Voice*, October 29–November 4, 1980.

Chase, Chris. "A Village That Saved Its Jews." *New York Times*, July 19, 1982.

Clarens, Carlos. "The Dark Ages." *The Soho Weekly News*, January, 19, 1982.

Dawidowicz, Lucy. "American Jews and the Holocaust." *New York Times* (Magazine), April 18, 1982.

Dawidowicz, Lucy. "Visualizing the Warsaw Ghetto: Nazi Images of the Jews Refiltered by the BBC." *Shoah* 1, no. 1 (1981?).

Denby, David. " 'Whoever Controls Film Contorls History.' " *New York*, January 28, 1980.

Des Pres, Terrence. "Black Comedies." *Harper's*, June 1976.

  "War Crimes." *Harper's*, January 1977.

  "The Bettelheim Problem." *Social Research*, Winter 1979.

Doneson, Judith. "The Jew as a Female Figure in Holocaust Film." *Shoah* 1, 1.

Dumbach, Annette Eberly, and Jud Newborn. "Again, Wartime Events Stir Germany." *New York Times* (Arts and Leisure), May 1, 1983.

Dupont, Joan. "Roman Polanski and 'Frantic.' " *New York Times* (Arts and Leisure), March 27, 1988.

Fine, Ellen. "Dialogue with Elie Wiesel." *Centerpoint* 4, 1, issue 13 "The Holocaust" (Fall 1980).

Goldstein, Richard. "Whose Holocaust?" *The Village Voice*, December 10, 1979.

Harmetz, Aljean. "Miss Streep and Kline Cast in Movie 'Sophie.' " *New York Times*, Section C, July 22, 1981.

Harmetz, Aljean. "Waging Wouk's 'War and Remembrance.' " *New York Times* (Arts and Leisure), November 6, 1988.

Hoberman, J. "The Führer Furor." *The Village Voice*, January 14, 1980.

  "Out of the Past." *The Village Voice*, October 25, 1988.

Hughes, John. "*The Tin Drum*: Volker Schlöndorff's 'Dream of Childhood.' " *Film Quarterly*, Spring 1981.

Insdorf, Annette. "How Truffaut's 'Last Metro' Reflects Occupied Paris." *New York Times* (Arts and Leisure), February 8, 1981.

"A Swiss Film Bares Another Chapter of the Holocaust." *New York Times* (Arts and Leisure), October 18, 1981.

" 'Who Will Live?' Explodes Myths of Holocaust." *Los Angeles Times* (Calendar), January 14, 1982.

"Von Trotta: By Sisters Obsessed." *New York Times* (Arts and Leisure), January 31, 1982.

"*David:* A German-Jewish Film about the Holocaust." *Martyrdom and Resistance* 8, 2 (March–April 1982).

"Oscar Treatment of Art in the Nazi State." *Newsday*, April 4, 1982.

"Heroism amid the Holocaust." *Newsday*, May 18, 1982.

"A Passion for Social Justice." *Cineaste* 11, 4 (Winter 1982).

"In Germany, A Blitz of Conscience." *Los Angeles Times*, July 24, 1983.

"Childhood Memories Shape Diane Kurys's 'Entre Nous.' " *New York Times* (Arts and Leisure), January 24, 1984.

"A Saga of Jews Who Fought Back against Nazi Oppression," *New York Times* (Arts and Leisure), September 14, 1986.

" 'Welcome in Vienna' – Ironies of Prejudice," *Los Angeles Times* (Calendar), February 23, 1988.

"A Conspiracy of Goodness: An Overview of Recent Films." *Dimensions* 3, 3 (Spring 1988).

"Axel Corti's Films Explore World War II's Impact." *New York Times* (Arts and Leisure), August 16, 1988.

" 'War and Remembrance' Painfully Authentic." *Los Angeles Times* (Calendar), November 23, 1988.

Isaac, Dan. "Film and the Holocaust." *Centerpoint* 4, 1, issue 13 (Fall 1980).

James, Caryn. "From Argentina, How 6 Polish Jews Hid From the Nazis," *New York Times*, Section C, October 5, 1988.

"4 Films at Once on Holocaust Offer a Dialogue." *New York Times*, Section C, November 1, 1988.

Kakutani, Michiko. "Forty Years After, Artists Still Struggle with the Holocaust." *New York Times* (Arts and Leisure), December 5, 1982.

Kamm, Henry. "Simon Wiesenthal Shepherds His Life's Story." *New York Times* (Arts and Leisure), June 26, 1988.

Kroll, Jack. "The Hitler within Us." *Newsweek*, January 28, 1980.

"The Activist Actress." *Newsweek*, September 29, 1980.

Liebman, Robert L. "Two Survivors: Lilienthal and His Film *David.*" *Long Island Jewish World*, October 30–November 5, 1981.

Markham, James. "Marcel Ophuls on Barbie: Reopening Wounds of War." *New York Times* (Arts and Leisure), October 2, 1988.

Maslin, Janet. "Bringing 'Sophie's Choice' to the Screen." *New York Times* (Arts and Leisure), May 9, 1982.

Middleton, Drew. "Why TV Is Fascinated with the Hitler Era." *New York Times* (Arts and Leisure), November 16, 1980.

Miller, Judith. "Erasing the Past: Europe's Amnesia about the Holocaust." *New York Times* (Magazine), November 16, 1986.

Molotsky, Irvin. "Film Tells How Nazi Ally Saved Its 50,000 Jews." *New York Times*, April 17, 1986.

Mydans, Seth. "Hungary's Wartime Anguish is Relived through 'The Revolt of Job.' " *New York Times* (Arts and Leisure), May 27, 1984.

O'Connor, John J. "Diverse Views of Nazi Germany." *New York Times* (Arts and Leisure), September 9, 1979.

Pappas, Peter. "*The Last Metro.*" *Cineaste* 10, 4 (Fall 1980).

Peary, Gerald. "A Film of Rage." *Los Angeles Times* (Calendar), March 18, 1984.

Ryan, Desmond. "Remembrances: Three Movies on the Holocaust." *The Philadelphia Inquirer*, April 18, 1982. (On *David, Transport from Paradise*, and *Now . . . after All These Years*.)

Sauvage, Pierre. "*Weapons of the Spirit:* A Journey Home." *The Hollywood Reporter*, Section S, March 17, 1987.

Schiff, Ellen. "Plays about the Holocaust – Ashes into Art." *New York Times* (Arts and Leisure), December 2, 1979.

Schlesinger, Arthur, Jr. "Filmed in New York." *American Heritage* 33, 1 (December 1981).

Sontag, Susan. "Eye of the Storm." *The New York Review of Books*, 27, 2, February 21, 1980. Reprinted in *Under the Sign of Saturn*.

Toland, John. "Can TV Dramas Convey the Horrors of the Holocaust?" *TV Guide 30*, 7, February 13, 1982.

Van Gelder, Lawrence. "A German Filmmaker Looks at Adolf Hitler." *New York Times* (Arts and Leisure), January 13, 1980.

Ward, Alex. "A Producer of the Provocative: Herbert Brodkin." *New York Times* (Arts and Leisure), November 15, 1981.

Wasserman, Steve. "Filmmaker as Pariah." *The Village Voice*, January 14, 1980.

Wiesel, Elie. "Does the Holocaust Lie beyond the Reach of Art?" *New York Times* (Arts and Leisure), April 17, 1983.

Yakir, Dan. "Bad Guys Never Looked So Good." *New York Post*, August 6, 1981.

Foreign and Other Periodicals

L'Avant-Scène du Cinéma 1, février 1961: screenplay of *Night and Fog*. English version in *Film: Book 2, Films of Peace and War*, ed. Robert Hughes (New York: Grove Press, 1962), pp. 234–255.

L'Avant-Scène du Cinéma 47, avril 1965: "Spécial Polonais," including the screenplays of *Passenger* and *Ashes and Diamonds*.

L'Avant-Scène du Cinéma 127/128, juillet–septembre 1972: screenplay and assorted documents concerning *The Sorrow and the Pity*.

L'Avant-Scène du Cinéma 175, novembre 1976: screenplay of *Mr. Klein*.

Cahiers du Cinéma 23, avril 1982: interview with Alan Pakula on *Sophie's Choice* by Jonathan Rosenbaum.

Cahiers du Cinéma 301, juin 1979: article on *Holocaust*, "Le Four Banal," by Sylvie Pierre.

Centerpoint 4, 1, issue 13 (Fall 1980). Entire issue devoted to "The Holocaust" with various articles cited in Notes.

L'Illustration, 30 septembre 1941: reportage by Robert de Beauplan.

Impact: Revue du Cinéma Direct 10/11, 1979 (France).

International Journal of Political Education (Netherlands) 4, nos. 1/2 (May 1987): Dieter Prokop's research, "*Holocaust* and the Effects of Violence on Television."

Le Monde, 5 octobre 1987: interview with Louis Malle on *Goodbye, Children by Danièle Heymann.

New German Critique 19 (Winter 1980): special issue, "Germans and Jews."

Le Nouvel Observateur, 1 juin 1981: article, "Quand Vichy déportait ses juifs."

Le Nouvel Observateur, 2–8 octobre 1987: interview with Louis Malle by Olivier Péretrié.

Bibliography (Third Edition)

Books

van Alphen, Ernst. *Caught by History: Holocaust Effects in Contemporary Art, Literature and Theory.* Stanford, Calif.: Stanford University Press, 1997.

Amishai-Maises, Ziva. *Depiction and Interpretation: The Influence of the Holocaust on the Visual Arts.* New York: Pergamon Press, 1993.

Bartov, Omer. *Murder in Our Midst: The Holocaust, Industrial Killing and Representation.* New York: Oxford University Press, 1996.

 Mirrors of Destruction: War, Genocide and Modern Identity. New York: Oxford University Press, 2000.

Cheyette, Bryan, and Laura Marcus. *Modernity, Culture and "The Jew."* Stanford, Calif.: Stanford University Press, 1998.

Clendinnen, Inga. *Reading the Holocaust.* New York: Cambridge University Press, 1999.

Colombat, Andre. *The Holocaust in French Film.* Metuchen, N.J.: Scarecrow Press, 1993.

Davies, Fred. *Film, History and the Holocaust.* Portland, Ore.: Vallentine-Mitchell Publishers, 2000.

Elkes, Joel. *Doctor Elkhanan Elkes of Kovno Ghetto: A Son's Holocaust Memoir.* Orleans, Mass.: Paraclete Press, 1999.

Epstein, Julia, and Lori Hope Lefkovitz. *Shaping Losses: Cultural Memory and the Holocaust.* Urbana: University of Illinois Press, 2001.

Finkelstein, Norman. *The Holocaust Industry: Reflections on the Exploitation of Jewish Suffering.* New York: Verso, 2000.

Fogelman, Eva. *Conscience and Courage: Rescuers of Jews during the Holocaust.* New York: Anchor Books, 1994.

Fridman, Lea Wernick. *Words and Witness: Narrative and Aesthetic Strategies in the Representation of the Holocaust.* Albany: State University of New York Press, 2000.

Friedländer, Saul, ed. *Probing the Limits of Representation: Nazism and the "Final Solution."* Cambridge, Mass.: Harvard University Press, 1992.

Fuchs, Esther. *Women and the Holocaust: Narrative and Representation.* Lanham, Md.: University Press of America, 1999.

Goldhagen, Daniel Jonah. *Hitler's Willing Executioners: Ordinary Germans and the Holocaust.* New York: Knopf, 1996.

Hartman, Geoffrey H., ed. *Holocaust Remembrance: The Shapes of Memory.* Oxford: Blackwell, 1994.

Hilberg, Raul. *The Politics of Memory: The Journey of a Holocaust Historian.* Chicago: Ivan R. Dee Publisher, 1996.

Hoffman, Eva. *Shtetl: The Life and Death of a Small Town and the World of Polish Jews.* Boston: Houghton Mifflin, 1997.

Horowitz, Sara R. *Voicing the Void: Muteness and Memory in Holocaust Fiction.* Albany: State University of New York Press, 1997.

Isser, Edward R. *Stages of Annihilation: Theatrical Representation of the Holocaust.* Madison, N.J.: Fairleigh Dickinson University Press, 1997.

Kremer, S. Lillian. *Women's Holocaust Writing: Memory and Imagination.* Lincoln: University of Nebraska Press, 1999.

Kritzman, Lawrence D., ed. *Auschwitz and After: Race, Culture, and "the Jewish Question" in France.* New York: Routledge, 1995.

LaCapra, Dominick. *Representing the Holocaust: History, Theory, Trauma.* Ithaca, N. Y.: Cornell University Press, 1994.

Lang, Berel. *Act and Idea of the Nazi Genocide.* Chicago: University of Chicago Press, 1990.
    Holocaust Representation: Art within the Limits of History and Ethics. Baltimore: Johns Hopkins Press, 2000.

Langer, Lawrence. *Admitting the Holocaust: Collected Essays.* New York: Oxford University Press, 1995.
    Preempting the Holocaust. New Haven, Conn.: Yale University Press, 1998.
    Ed. *Art from the Ashes: A Holocaust Anthology.* New York: Oxford University Press, 1995.

Leak, Andrew, and George Paizis, eds. *The Holocaust and the Text: Speaking the Unspeakable.* New York: St. Martin's Press, 2000.

Lewis, Stephen. *Art Out of Agony: The Holocaust Theme in Literature, Sculpture and Film.* Montreal: CBC Enterprises, 1984.

Liss, Andrea. *Trespassing through Shadows: Memory, Photography, and the Holocaust.* Minneapolis: University of Minnesota Press, 1998.

Loshitzky, Yosefa, ed. *Spielberg's Holocaust: Critical Perspectives on* Schindler's List. Bloomington: Indiana University Press, 1997.

Milchman, Alan, and Alan Rosenberg, eds. *Postmodernism and the Holocaust.* Atlanta, Ga.: Rodopi, 1998.

Miller, Judith. *One by One, by One: Facing the Holocaust.* New York: Simon & Schuster, 1990.

Mintz, Alan. *Popular Culture and the Shaping of Holocaust Memory in America.* Seattle: University of Washington Press, 2001.

Morris, Marla. *Curriculum and the Holocaust: Competing Sites of Memory and Representation.* Mahwah, N.J.: Lawrence Erlbaum Associates, 2001.

Murray, Bruce A., and Christopher J. Wickham, eds. *Framing the Past: The Historiography of German Cinema and Television.* Carbondale: Southern Illinois University Press, 1992.

Patterson, David. *Sun Turned to Darkness: Memory and Recovery in the Holocaust Memoir.* Syracuse, N.Y.: Syracuse University Press, 1998.

Platt, David, ed. *Celluloid Power: Social Film Criticism from 'The Birth of a Nation' to 'Judgment at Nuremberg.'* Metuchen, N.J.: Scarecrow Press, 1992.

Ravetto, Kriss. *The Unmaking of Fascist Aesthetics.* Minneapolis: University of Minnesota Press, 2001.

Rosenberg, Alan, James R. Watson, and Detlef Linke, eds. *Contemporary Portrayals of Auschwitz: Philosophical Challenges.* Amherst, N.Y.: Humanity Books, 2000.

Rosenfeld, Alvin H., ed. *Thinking about the Holocaust: After Half a Century.* Bloomington: Indiana University Press, 1997.

Rosenthal, Alan, ed. *Why Docudrama? : Fact-fiction on Film and TV.* Carbondale: Southern Illinois University Press, 1999.

Rotem, Simha S. *Memoirs of a Warsaw Ghetto Fighter.* New Haven, Conn.: Yale University Press, 2001.

Rothberg, Michael. *Traumatic Realism: The Demands of Holocaust Representation.* Minneapolis: University of Minnesota Press, 2001.

Santner, Eric L. *Stranded Objects: Mourning, Memory, and Film in Postwar Germany.* Ithaca, N.Y.: Cornell University Press, 1994.

Schuster, Ekkehardt, and Reinhold Boschert-Kimmig. *Hope against Hope: Johann Baptiste Metz and Elie Wiesel Speak Out on the Holocaust.* Mahwah, N.J.: Paulist Press, 1999.

Schwartz, Daniel. *Imagining the Holocaust.* New York: St. Martin's Press, 1999.

Scrase, David, and Wolfgang Mieder, eds. *The Holocaust: Introductory Essays.* Burlington: The Center for Holocaust Studies at the University of Vermont, 1996.

Shandler, Jeffrey. *While America Watches: Televising the Holocaust.* New York: Oxford University Press, 1999.

Sicher, Efraim, ed. *Breaking Crystal: Writing and Memory after Auschwitz.* Urbana: University of Illinois Press, 1998.

Skirball, Sheba F. *Films of the Holocaust: An Annotated Filmography of Collections in Israel.* New York: Garland Publishers, 1990.

Sobchack, Vivian, ed. *The Persistence of History: Cinema, Television, and the Modern Event.* New York: Routledge, 1996.

Toll, Nelly. *When Memory Speaks: The Holocaust in Art.* Westport, Conn.: Praeger, 1998.

Turim, Maureen Cheryn. *Flashbacks in Film: Memory and History.* New York: Routledge, 1989.

Vice, Sue. *Holocaust Fiction.* London: Routledge, 2000.

Warren, Charles, ed. *Beyond Document: Essays on Non-Fiction Film.* Hanover N.H.: Wesleyan University Press, 1996.

Werner, Harold. *Fighting Back: A Memoir of Jewish Resistance in World War II.* New York: Columbia University Press, 1994.

Wiedmer, Caroline. *The Claims of Memory: Representations of the Holocaust in Contemporary France and Germany.* Ithaca, N.Y.: Cornell University Press, 1999.

Wiesel, Elie. *All the Rivers Run to the Sea: Memoirs.* Trans. John Rothschild. New York: Knopf, 1995.

Wood, Nancy. *Vectors of Memory.* New York: Berg Publishers, 1999.

Young, James E. *At Memory's Edge: After-images of the Holocaust in Contemporary Art and Architecture.* New Haven, Conn.: Yale University Press, 2000.

Zelizer, Barbie. *Remembering to Forget: Holocaust Memory through the Camera's Eye.* New Brunswick, N.J.: Rutgers University Press, 2000.

Ed. *Visual Culture and the Holocaust.* New Brunswick, N.J.: Rutgers University Press, 2001.

Articles

Ain, Stewart. "A Real-Life 'Life Is Beautiful,'" *The Jewish Week,* March 28, 1999.

"'Life Is Beautiful' Child Breaks 50-Year Silence," *The Jewish Week,* April 23, 1999.

Avisar, Ilan. "Christian Ideology and Jewish Genocide in American Holocaust Movies." *Literature, the Arts, and the Holocaust. Holocaust Studies Annual* 3 (1985): 21–42.

Barta, Tony: "Consuming the Holocaust: Memory Production and Popular Film." *Contention: Debates in Society, Culture, and Science* 5, 2 (Winter 1996): 161–175.

Davis, Harry. "Narrated and Narrating in 'Il giardino dei Finzi-Contini,'" *Italian Studies* 43 (1988): 117–129.

Doerr, Karin. Memories Of History: Women and the Holocaust in Autobiographical and Fictional Memoirs. *Shofar* 18, 3 (Spring 2000): 49–63.

Doneson, Judith E. "History and Television, 1978–1988: A Survey of Dramatizations of the Holocaust." *Dimensions* 4, 3 (1989): 23–27.

Epstein, Leslie. "Atrocity and Imagination." *Harper's Magazine,* August 1985.

"Blue Skies: Reflections on Hollywood and the Holocaust." *Tikkun* 4, 5 (September–October 1989): 11.

Erhart, Julia. "From Nazi Whore to Good German Mother: Revisiting Resistance in the Holocaust Film." *Screen* 41, 4 (Winter 2000): 388–403.

Felman, Shoshana. "In an Era of Testimony: Claude Lanzmann's 'Shoah,' " *Yale French Studies* 79 (January 1991): 39.

Finkelstein, Norman G. "Daniel Jonah Goldhagen's 'Crazy' Thesis: A Critique of *Hitler's Willing Executioners.*" *New Left Review* 224 (1997): 39–87.

Fuchs, Esther. "Images of Women in Holocaust Films." *Shofar* 17, 2 (Winter 1999): 49–56.

Geuens, Jean-Pierre. "Pornography and the Holocaust: The Last Transgression." *Film Criticism* 20, 1–2 (Fall 1995–Winter 1996): 114–130.

Halff, Antoine. "Battle Erupts among Holocaust Movie Moguls." *The Forward*, June 24, 1994.

Hoberman, J., et al. " 'Schindler's List': Myth, Movie and Memory." *The Village Voice*, March 29, 1994.

Housden, Martyn. "The Mourning After: Memoir, Analysis and the Holocaust." *European History Quarterly* 28, 2 (1998): 265–272.

Insdorf, Annette. "Save the Child: 'Korczak.' " *The Boston Phoenix*, November 15, 1991.

"The Moral Minefield That Won't Go Away." *New York Times* (Arts and Leisure), August 31, 1997.

James, Caryn. "Bringing Home the Horrors of the Holocaust." *New York Times*, February 23, 1997.

Kauffmann, Stanley. "A Predicament." *New Republic* 213, 24, December 11, 1995, pp. 24–27.

Kellman, Steven G. "Cinema of/as Atrocity: Shoah's Guilty Conscience." *The Gettysburg Review* 1, 1 (Winter 1988): 22–30.

Kohler, Eric D. "Hollywood and Holocaust: A Discourse on the Politics of Rescue." *Holocaust Studies Annual* 3 (1984): 79–93.

Konigsberg, Ira. "Our Children and the Limits of Cinema." *Film Quarterly*, Fall 1998, p. 7.

LaCapra, Dominick. "Equivocations of Autonomous Art." *Critical Inquiry* 24, 3 (Spring 1998): 833–836.

Lanzmann, Claude. "From the Holocaust to 'Holocaust.'" *Dissent* 28, 2 (1981): 188–194.

"Why Spielberg Has Distorted the Truth." *Le Monde*, reprinted in *Guardian Weekly*, April 3, 1994, p. 14.

"The Obscenity of Understanding: An Evening with Claude Lanzmann." In *Trauma: Explorations in Memory*, ed. Cathy Caruth, pp. 200–220. Baltimore: Johns Hopkins University Press, 1995.

Leff, Leonard J. "Hollywood and the Holocaust: Remembering 'The Pawnbroker.' " *American Jewish History* 84, 4 (1996): 353–376.

Liebman, Stuart. "L'Holocauste dans le cinéma polonais." In *Cinéma et Histoire*, ed. Antoine de Baeque and Christian Delaye. Brussels: Editions Complexes, 1997.

Liebman, Stuart, and Leonard Quart. "Homevideo: Czech Films of the Holocaust." *Cineaste* 22, 1 (Winter 1996): 49–52.

Linville, Susan E. "Agnieszka Holland's *Europa*: Deconstructive Humor in a Holocaust Film." *Film Criticism* 19, 3 (Spring 1995): 44–53.

Manchel, Frank. "A Reel Witness: Steven Spielberg's Representation of the Holocaust in *Schindler's List.*" *Journal of Modern History* 67, 1 (1995): 83–100.

"Mishegoss: *Schindler's List*, Holocaust Representation and Film History." *Historical Journal of Film, Radio and Television* (Great Britain) 18, 3 (1998): 431–436.

Mazierska, Ewa. "Non-Jewish Jews, Good Poles and Historical Truth in the Films of Andrzej Wajda." *Historical Journal of Film, Radio and Television* 20, 2 (June 2000): 213.

Olin, Margaret. "Lanzmann's *Shoah* and the Topography of the Holocaust Film." *Representations* 57 (Winter 1997): 1–23.

Ozick, Cynthia. "The Rights of History and the Rights of Imagination." *Commentary* 107, 3 (March 1999): 22.

Patterson, David. "The Twilight of Memory: Reflections on Holocaust Memoirs, Past, Present and Future." *Dimensions* 13, 1 (1999): 19–24.

Rabinowitz, Paula. "Wreckage upon Wreckage: History, Documentary, and the Ruins of Memory." In *They Must Be Represented: The Politics of Documentary*, ed. Paula Rabinowitz. London: Verso, 1994.

Rich, Frank. "Extras in the Shadows." *New York Times*, January 2, 1994.

Richmond, Thomas. "The Perpetrators' Testimonies in 'Shoah.'" *Journal of Holocaust Education* 5, 1 (1996): 61–83.

Rosenbaum, Thane. "Questions in Shadows of 'Shine.'" *New York Times*, March 2, 1997.

"With the Shoah, Can Tragedy Become a Farce?," *The Forward*, October 23, 1998.

"At Century's End, a Holocaust Backlash," *The Jewish Week*, December 31, 1999.

Rosenfeld, Alvin H. "The Americanization of the Holocaust." *Commentary* 99, 6 (June 1995): 35–40.

Shapiro, Ann-Louise, ed. "Producing the Past: Making Histories Inside and Outside the Academy" (theme issue of a journal). *History and Theory: Studies in the Philosophy of History* 36 (December 1997).

Sicher, Efraim. "The Future of the Past: Countermemory and Postmemory in Contemporary American Post-Holocaust Narratives." *History and Memory* 12, 2 (Fall–Winter 2000).

Viano, Maurizio. "*Life Is Beautiful*: Reception Allegory and Holocaust Laughter." *Film Quarterly* 53, 1 (Fall 1999): 26–34.

Williams, Linda. "Mirrors without Memories: Truth, History, and the New Documentary." *Film Quarterly* 46, 3 (Spring 1993): 9–21.

Zizek, Slavoj. "Camp Comedy." *Sight and Sound* 10, 4 (April 2000): 26–29.

Relevant Websites

www.annefrank.com – Anne Frank resources on-line

www.auschwitz.dk/ – Stories of Auschwitz and biographies of the major names of the time

www.brandeis.edu/jewishfilm/ – Jewish film archive at Brandeis

www.igc.org/ddickerson/holocaust.html – Annotated links and original material on the Holocaust

www.jer.cine.org.il/holocaustfilm.htm – A listing of the Joan Sourasky-Constantiner Holocaust Multimedia Research Center of the Israel Film Archive – Jerusalem Cinematheque

www.jewishfilm.com – Jewish film archive on-line

www.library.yale.edu/testimonies/homepage.html – Fortunoff Video Archive for Holocaust Testimonies at Yale University

www.nara.gov/research/assets/ – Holocaust-era assets: Records and research at the National Archives and Records Administration

www.nizkor.org/ – The Nizkor Holocaust Educational Resource

www1.oup.co.uk/holgen – Holocaust and Genocide Studies, published by Oxford University Press

www.remember.org/ – A cybrary of the Holocaust

www.ushmm.org/ – United States Holocaust Memorial Museum

www.vhf.org/ – Steven Spielberg's survivors of the Shoah visual history: interviews with Holocaust survivors

www.wiesenthal.com/ – Simon Wiesenthal Center

www.yad-vashem.org.il/ – Israel's Holocaust museum and memorial

www.yivoinstitute.org – YIVO Institute for Jewish Research

Index